BISMARCK

THE STORY OF A FIGHTER

By

EMIL LUDWIG

Translated from the German by
EDEN *and* CEDAR PAUL

Skyhorse Publishing
A Heman Graf Book

TO

GERHART HAUPTMANN·

IN VENERATION AND FRIENDSHIP

Moscia, Summer 1926

Skyhorse Publishing books may be purchased in bulk at special discounts for sales promotion, corporate gifts, fund-raising, or educational purposes. Special editions can also be created to specifications. For details, contact the Special Sales Department, Skyhorse Publishing, 307 West 36th Street, 11th Floor, New York, NY 10018 or info@skyhorsepublishing.com.

Skyhorse® and Skyhorse Publishing® are registered trademarks of Skyhorse Publishing, Inc.®, a Delaware corporation.

Visit our website at www.skyhorsepublishing.com.

10 9 8 7 6 5 4 3 2 1

Library of Congress Cataloging-in-Publication Data is available on file.
ISBN: 978-1-62087-176-8

Printed in the United States of America

That which is imposing here on earth . . . is always akin to the fallen angel; who is beautiful, but lacks peace; is great in his plans and efforts, but never succeeds; is proud, and melancholy.

— BISMARCK

BISMARCK IN 1871

From a photograph by Loescher and Petsch, Berlin

Foreword

A chiaroscuro form, fully equipped, shines forth from the twilight. Bismarck resembles the faces painted by Rembrandt, and must be so depicted. For the last eighty years, partisan hatred has flashed its lightnings round him. In his lifetime he was little loved, because he loved little; after his death he was condemned to figure as a statue, because his inner man remained hard to penetrate. Thus among the Germans he became a Roland carved out of stone.

The aim of this book is to limn the portrait of a victorious and errant warrior. Here Bismarck is depicted as a character filled with pride, courage, and hatred — the basic elements from which his actions resulted. To-day, when part of our nation admires him with partiality while another part condemns him, we must make a profound study of the history of his spirit. Since Bismarck, as a personality, played the part of destiny to the Germans, the German nation must learn to understand the character of this man, to understand him as he really was, and not as distorted by worship and by hatred.

The historical man is always more organic than his system, and more complicated than his monument. Instead of following the academic method, and burdening the portrayal with notes, we think it proper in our day to make public characters plastic, as an example and a warning to every one. The man and the politician are inseparable; feelings and actions determine one another mutually; private life and public life run concurrently. The task of the artist is to construct a whole out of the data furnished by the investigator.

By the beginning of the thirties, Bismarck's inner development was practically finished. During a decade and a half prior to that time he had had to endure the most violent agitations. All that followed, throughout his career, was no more than a deepening of the elementary lines already traced. That is why his youth, which most of the biographers dismiss in a few pages, must be dealt with at considerable length—his youth, the time before his political activities began. The only writer who has succeeded in producing a psychography of Bismarck is the misunderstood Klein-Hattingen, who had to work with the documents that were available in his day. In the year 1911 I myself tried, in what I called a "psychological attempt", to counteract the legend of the Iron Chancellor by the depiction of an enigmatic nature. Ten years later I wrote a trilogy wherein I hoped to present Bismarck dramatically on the German stage.

This new likeness is entirely different from my earlier attempt, which was non-political. Nothing that I wrote in that first book is reproduced here, where the figure is presented in a new light. The only common element in the two works is the fundamental concept of an enigmatic character. Besides, various circumstances have rendered a new and more critical depiction necessary; the post-war epoch has brought with it a fuller knowledge of what was involved in Bismarck's career; a number of memoirs and other relevant documents have been published; and the personal development of the author has contributed to the need for a fresh presentation.

By the new lights, the chiaroscuro surroundings of Bismarck's figure have become even more striking. One who is not trying to carve a monument but to trace the career of a fighter, stands amazed before this life, which was perpetual struggle, occasional victory, unceasing passion, never satisfaction, for the most part sagacity, at times error, but invariably characterised by genius even when mistaken.

Table of Contents

List of Illustrations

Chronological Table

BOOK ONE: 1815–1851

1771. Ferdinand von Bismarck, Otto's father, born.

1790. Wilhelmine Mencken, Otto's mother, born.

1810. Bernhard von Bismarck, Otto's brother, born.

1815. Otto von Bismarck born, April 1st, at 1 P.M.

1816. The Bismarck family removes to Kniephof.

1822. Bismarck goes to the Plamann Institute in Berlin.

1827. Malwine von Bismarck, Otto's sister, born.

1832–1833. Bismarck a student at Göttingen.

1833. Becomes acquainted with Roon.

1835. Barrister at the Municipal Court in Berlin.

1836. Referendary in Aix-la-Chapelle.

1836–1837. Two engagements to marry.

1837. Referendary in Potsdam.

1839. Mother dies.
Takes possession of Kniephof.

1842. Third engagement to marry.

1844. Friendship with Thadden and Blanckenburg.
Plans for an Asiatic tour.
Malwine marries Arnim-Kröchlendorf.

1845. Father dies.
Removes to Schönhausen.

1846. Becomes dike-reeve.
Death of Marie von Blanckenburg.

1847. Betrothal to Johanna von Puttkamer (born 1824).
Deputy in United Landtag.
First speech.
Marriage.

1848. Marie von Bismarck born.

BOOK FOUR: 1872–1888

1872. Kulturkampf.
Three Emperors' League.
Motley's last visit.
Second tender of resignation.

1873. May laws against the Roman Catholics.
Conservative campaign of calumny.
Roon's premiership and retirement.

1874. Attempt to assassinate Bismarck in Kissingen.

1875. Third tender of resignation.

1877. Fourth tender of resignation.

1878. Two attempts to assassinate William I.
Anti-socialist law.
Congress of Berlin.

1879. Change in foreign policy; alliance with Austria.

1880. Illness. Fifth tender of resignation.
Becomes minister for commerce.

1881. Herbert's unhappy love affair.

1883. Triple Alliance.
Dr. Schweninger's successful regimen.

1887. Reinsurance treaty.

1888. Death of William I.

BOOK FIVE: 1888–1898

1888. Reign and death of Frederick III.

1889. Last speech in the Reichstag.

1890. Sixth tender of resignation.
Dismissal. Created duke of Lauenburg.
Non-renewal of the Russian treaty.

1892. Boycotted in Vienna.
Triumphal progress through Germany.

1893. Death of Bernhard von Bismarck.
Serious illness.

1894. " Reconciliation " with William II.
Death of Johanna.
1895. Eightieth birthday.
1896. Revelations concerning the Russian treaty.
1897. Last warning to the emperor.
1898. Otto von Bismarck dies, July 30th, at 10 P.M.

BOOK ONE: 1815–1851

THE WANDERER

Bismarck was by temperament one whom life consumed, but one whom rest killed

—A. KEYSERLIÑG

BISMARCK

I

It is summertime; beneath the ancient oaks of the park, a boy is playing. He is fair-haired, thickset, with dark, fiery eyes. He is four years old; but when we watch him driving his spade into the earth, loading his barrow with clods, and dumping the contents of the barrow beside the pond where he is building a fortress out of earth and stone, we should take him for a lad of six, so vigorously does he pursue his task. When the gardener comes from the house to fetch him because it is time for dinner, he is rebellious, and grows angry.

A simple country house, looking more like the house of a well-to-do farmer than a private gentleman's mansion. It is built of wood, quite unadorned, one-storeyed except for the central part, where there is a second storey five windows wide. When the boy looks out of his window in the first storey, his gaze extends over a flat country where the corn is yellowing. A quiet prospect. When the wind blows athwart Pomerania, the heavy ears catch the breeze, and waves and furrows pass over the fields. "That is all ours," says his father, when he takes the little boy with him to the village. He had recently inherited nearly two thousand acres in Kniephof. That is why he had left Schönhausen in Saxony, and had come to Farther Pomerania when the little boy was one year old.

"That is all ours," thinks the child; for the village and the farm are one. There are no peasants, only agricultural labourers who belong to the estate, who live in thatched huts, and whose position is much more that of serfs than they and the gentry are willing to admit. There is the lime-kiln; and there, the smithy. When the lad goes into the byre, and crawls about among the cows, Brand, the old cowherd, who is nearly ninety years of age, says: "Take care, Herr Junker! The cow may put her hoof on your eye. She won't notice anything, and will go on quietly chewing her cud; but your eye will have gone to smash!" The ancient calls the little boy "Herr Junker"; he speaks Low German. Seventy years later, Bismarck will remember this primitive realist, who had told him stories about King Frederick William I. The herd had with his own eyes seen the king at Küstrin, long before the days of the Great Frederick.

His father, too, has something to tell the little boy when, on feast days, they enter the great hall with its three windows. A number of ancestors, looking forth with stiff dignity from under their helmets, gaze at him from their pictures on the walls; pictures of armed men; pictures in dusty frames. Most of them held sway on the Elbe, more than five hundred years back. Now, when young Bismarck is nine years of age and can understand better, his father has more to tell him. What does the youngster hear? That father's forefathers were all knights. As he sees them there in the pictures, they had for centuries lived in castles and mansions, keeping serfs who tilled their lands; they had been lords of the manor with right of judicature; from immemorial days they had sat on Sundays in their oaken pews at church, set apart from the rabble — as they still are here and there even to-day.

Maybe Herr Ferdinand von Bismarck told his son that they had all been masterful men, these men of the Old March; not supple courtiers, but disgruntled for the most part. Had not an elector compelled the Bismarcks, long ago, to cede their finest forests, and accept Schönhausen as a bad exchange? A hundred years earlier, Ferdinand's great grandfather had carried to the king the refusal of the knights of the Old March when the king had converted their fiefs into a money tax, and they had protested against such a "degradation of the free chivalry into a contributable and miserable estate." Before he died, this king, giving his son, young Frederick, a list of the four refractory families, had included the Bismarcks as "the most distinguished and the worst."

The boy's grandfather had been a heavy drinker and a mighty hunter. In one year, this Bismarck had shot one hundred and fifty-four red deer. Our Bismarck resembles that ancestor in appearance more than any of the others. His father was no longer a knight. Indeed, the grandfather had already been excluded from the order, and, when his young wife died — it was just before the days of Werther — he had published a touching elegy, describing his marriage and his wife in extravagant terms. This pupil of Rousseau, whose only wish was to make his sons "four honourable men", who called them his friends, and was delighted to receive their well-written letters, had a whole library of learned works. From him, Ferdinand (our Bismarck's father) and his brothers had inherited a lack of ambition. True, they all went to war; but they would not go to court; they were content with domestic life.

No wonder, therefore, that Ferdinand, who was now educating his two boys at Kniephof, had retired from active service after his first campaign at the age of three-and-twenty. The king had been so angry, that he had deprived Ferdinand of his rank as cavalry captain and his uniform, which were not restored to him until much later. Even in the worst days, Bismarck's father did not reenter the army. He had married in the summer of 1806, when Emperor Francis had laid aside the German imperial crown. Neither for Jena nor for the War of Liberation had he left his rural retreat to draw the sword, although he was in good health and only forty years of age.

This unwarlike father of our Bismarck, a huge fellow, and quick-tempered like his son, strong and full of deep feeling, had in his boyhood been spoken to by Frederick the Great. This was his only Prussian anecdote. His father, an apostle of the French enlightenment, had brought him up as a nobleman, though as one who was to be free from prejudices of caste. Thanks to this education, he had been able to preserve an inward equanimity throughout life, master in his own house, making few demands, speaking formally to his sons even when they were quite young. Pleasure-loving, gentle by disposition, he lived a carefree life on his estate (where the work of farming was superintended by some bailiff or other) and spent most of his time hunting, or over his wine — for all the Bismarcks had been hard drinkers for centuries. Here are some noteworthy extracts from his letters: "To-day is Otto's birthday. To-day one of our best rams kicked the bucket. What abominable weather. . . . It seems to me that Médoc and Rhenish no longer have enough effect, so I have taken to port and sherry, and hope that there will be an improvement. Nor shall I do without strong coffee." Then come some remarks about oysters, foie gras, etc. "But notwithstanding all these fine remedies, I 've got lumbago — it 's a poor business when one grows old."

The young woman of seventeen, whom he had married when himself thirty-five, was good-looking, but her nose was too long, her eye too shrewd. The sharpness of her features, her knowing look, might have shown the wooer that there were elements in her nature which would be uncongenial to him. Dispassionate reason and ardent ambition were two of the most notable elements in her composition. Her forefathers, the Menckens, who for a century had been professors of law or of history, had handed down these traits to her father, the offspring of this race of humanists. Under Frederick, Mencken had been privy councillor, then the president of the Privy Chancellery, and then, having fallen out of favour, had been dismissed. This had been in the year 1792, the same year in which the king had been so angry with Bismarck's father. Not until 1800 did Mencken enter the service of his third royal master. Then he had censured the dictatorship of Frederick the Great, had demanded from the monarch a self-limitation of power, and had insisted on the need for ministerial responsibility. In fact, he had in all respects shown himself as keen a reformer as Baron von Stein, who had extolled Mencken as a good liberal. The daughter, our Bismarck's mother, had inherited her intelligence and her general outlook from this father. In her, everything was rational; she loved town life, display, the

BISMARCK IN 1826

From a painting by Franz Krüger

court; and she was in all respects the exact opposite of her husband. He only wanted to live and be let alone; she wanted to make a great show in the world.

From her, Otto von Bismarck got his reasoning powers, his piercing and dispassionate intelligence; from her, likewise, came his restless longing for power, which no Bismarck before him had had; but in temperament and character generally, he was his father's son. Thus by his paternal inheritance as well as his maternal he confirmed Schopenhauer's theory.

II

When the mother, five years after the birth of her eldest son, brought Otto von Bismarck into the world, Emperor Napoleon had just come back from Elba, the Congress of Vienna had broken up, and Prussia had entered into its new alliance with Europe. On April 2, 1815, the Emperor, in Paris, issued a manifesto against the alliance; on the same morning in the "Vossische Zeitung", Berliners could read of the birth of a son to Herr von Bismarck at Kniephof. Very early in life, the little boy felt his mother to be an adversary; he was estranged from her already in childhood. Notwithstanding his strong family feeling, he admitted as much to strangers in later years. In hundreds of conversations, he never had a good word to say for his mother. Right on into his old age he would describe her as a bluestocking, who had had no interest in his upbringing. Indeed, he used "extremely bitter" language about her, saying that she had "very little of what the Berliners term 'kindly feeling'." He would add: "Often it seemed to me that she was hard and cold towards me." Two special reasons for animosity dated from early childhood. When, in winter, his mother received guests in Berlin, his father, since the house offered but scanty accommodation, had to give up his own bed; the boy could never forget this. The other grievance was, that when, on one occasion, he had spoken with pride about the picture of one of his paternal ancestors, his middle-class mother had had the picture put away, wishing to break her son's pride of birth. These were terrible moments for the child, and had the gravest consequences!

His earliest memories of boyhood betray the pride which was the moving force of his character. Once he ran away when his brother had treated him badly, and was found wandering down Unter den Linden. Another time, when there was company in the house, he had stowed himself away in a corner, and heard several gentlemen say dubiously: "C'est peut-être un fils de la maison ou une fille." Thereupon, says Bismarck, "I answered quite boldly: 'C'est un fils, Monsieur'—which surprised them not a little."

His education at school was no better. When an old man he still looked back with hostility towards the years he spent at the Plamann Institute in Berlin from the age of eight to that of thirteen. "In early childhood I was sent away from home, and never again did it seem like home to me. From the outset my education was carried on from the viewpoint that everything else was to be subordinated to the development of my understanding and to the early acquisition of positive knowledge." Since he regarded his mother as the ruling influence in the house, he held her responsible for all the severities he had to endure at the boarding school. He never ceased to complain of the stale bread he had had to eat there; of the Spartan character of the education; of the inadequate clothing in winter; of the "unnaturally harsh discipline." When he was eighty he used to tell how "at school they waked us with a rapier thrust."

German nationalism and the liberal extravagancies of Jahn's disciples, together with hostility towards the nobility (as a sprig of which he had to bear the onslaughts of his teachers), served in the lad of ten to increase his inborn sense that he was a member of the knightly order, so that his spirit in this respect became defiant, and he was filled with a hatred for the liberal ideas which he had already learned to dislike in his mother. "I never had enough to satisfy my appetite. . . . The meat was always tough. We had to get up at half past five in the morning, and were quilldriving already from six to seven. We were worse treated than recruits are treated by non-commissioned officers. When we were fencing, we would often be given a violent blow on the arm with one of the foils, so that the weal would last for days." The youngster longed to get back to Kniephof. It was so dull in the Wilhelmstrasse. If the school had been in the part of the town where the great public buildings stood, and where the king sometimes drove by, it would not have been so bad! But away here in the outskirts, everything was tedious and lonely. "When, looking out of the window, I sometimes saw a team of oxen ploughing, the tears would come to my eyes, I was so homesick for Kniephof." Thus he spent the whole year looking forward to the holidays, when he had been promised a visit home.

What a shock the lad had to endure when his mother wrote saying that in July she would have to visit a watering place, so the boys must stay in Berlin! This happened summer after summer. For years the youngsters had no chance of seeing the house and the park, the farm, the barns and the stables, the smithy and the village, once again. In later days, he said that the life at school was that of a penitentiary. Everything that came from his mother, all she wanted and all she taught, seemed evil to the boy.

As he grew older, too, he came to see that his mother's activities and ambitions imperilled the welfare of the household. At Kniephof, year after year, she introduced new machinery and new methods of farming, for she wanted to modernise everything that her husband's conservatism and easy-going ways were allowing to go to rack and ruin. Then, in winter, she made Ferdinand come to Berlin. There the Bismarcks lived in the Opernplatz, which to Frau von Bismarck did not seem a sufficiently fashionable quarter. Otto never forgot the image of his mother, much made up, when she drove off with his father to a ministerial soirée. "I remember as if it had been to-day how she wore long gloves, a high-waisted dress, her hair in bunched curls on either side, and a huge ostrich feather on the top of her head." It was from his mother that he first heard the catchwords of the liberal opposition. When still only a half-grown lad, he had to fetch the Paris newspapers with accounts of the July revolution — and,

were it only because of his mother's tastes, he learned to despise
these things. He wrote in later years: "When, on her birthday,
a manservant fetched me from school, I found my mother's room
decked out with lily-of-the-valley, of which she was especially
fond; and with dresses that had come as birthday presents, with
books, and various gewgaws. Then there would be a dinner party,
attended by a number of young officers, . . . and by gluttonous
old gentlemen wearing stars and ribbons. One of the maids
would bring me a little caviare she had put aside, or some other
delicacy of the sort — enough to ruin my digestion. And what a
lot these servants used to steal! . . . I was not properly brought
up. . . . My mother was fond of society and troubled herself
very little about us. . . . Usually two generations take it in
turns, a whipped and an unwhipped; at any rate, it was so in
my family. I belonged to the whipped generation."

From the age of twelve to seventeen, when he was at the
Graue Kloster high school, he saw the hatred against the nobility
steadily growing in the establishment to which cultured bourgeois
were wont to send their sons. The natural result was that his
pride of birth increased. He was now living in his parents' Berlinese home, exposed during the winter to his mother's hasty ways,
which his father backed up in easy-going fashion. In summer,
Otto was alone with his brother, five years older than himself, a
student now, who "devoted himself to the physical side of life."
Besides the brother, his only associates were a tutor and a maidservant. Thus he had no guidance for his inner life, and during
these decisive years had to fall back upon his own resources.
From the age of seven to that of seventeen, Otto von Bismarck
saw no one whom he would have cared to imitate, had no associate
whom he could love, save only his father. Can we be surprised that
he became cynical so early?

Besides, his father, so the son tells us, was "not a Christian."
His mother was a sort of theosophist. Neither parent ever went
to church. Their sons received religious instruction from Schlei-
ermacher, who regarded prayer critically as a transitional stage
to magic, and only recommended it for the sake of its refining

influence. His mother showed an enthusiasm (which, as Otto remarks, "was in strange contrast with the cold clarity of her understanding in other respects") for Swedenborg, the seeress of Prevorst, and the theories of Mesmer. She believed herself clairvoyant. The only person she could not impose upon in this matter was her husband, although she looked down upon him because his grammar was not faultless. Ferdinand humorously complained to a friend, saying: "With all her clairvoyance, she was not shrewd enough to foresee that towards the close of the market the price of wool would be lower than it had been at the beginning."

Of course the father was invariably pleased with his sons, whilst the mother was never satisfied. The father: "I am always proud of your reports. Yesterday the Bülows were here; I showed them your reports, and was delighted to hear how well they spoke of you." The mother: "Look around you, listen to the world's judgment concerning solid culture, and you will realise how much you will have to do before you can claim the title of cultured man." Once when, at the age of fourteen, the boy had been thrown from his horse, she said: "Your father thinks, my dear Otto, that your horse cannot have been so very unruly, but that you must have been very easily thrown, for you have no better seat than a bundle of old clothes." That is the tone by which parents and teachers make themselves ridiculous, or detested.

Such crosses, in conjunction with a native pride, could not fail to make of him an unequable and refractory youth. The only subject in which he excelled was German. He did not even shine in history. When he was in the first class, from the age of fifteen to eighteeen, his reports were unfavourable at times, saying that he was "censurable for pretentious arrogance. . . . It seems, too, that he has no thought of proper respect for his teachers." He always wanted to sleep on in the morning, and did not grow cheerful until late in the day; this peculiarity, characteristic of neurotic persons, persisted throughout life; Bismarck was not at his best until evening.

His only pleasurable relief in this gloomy youth came from

Malwinchen, his late-born sister, twelve years younger than himself. She was her parents' darling, her brothers' plaything. "Malwinchen now looks quite a character," he writes when he is fourteen. "She speaks German or French as the fancy takes her." From the age of fifteen onwards, he was able to spend his holidays at home. We learn that already at this early age, at a farm, he "amused himself for a few hours with the farmer's pretty wife." At the age of sixteen, in a post-chaise, he had an adventure with a "pretty governess", who became ill and faint, and fell into his arms. Furthermore, he told his brother to send a "love token" on his behalf anonymously to a lady neighbour. Letters from the country show how an all-pervading scepticism was making headway in the mind of the lad of fifteen: "On Friday, three young hopefuls, an incendiary, a highwayman, and a thief, . . . escaped from prison. In the evening, the Kniephof army, consisting of twenty-five men of the Landsturm, set forth against the three terrors. . . . Our soldiers were greatly alarmed when two sections encountered one another; they shouted to one another, but both were in such a fright that neither dared to answer."

Out of such moods it was natural that when he was seventeen or eighteen a complete nihilism in belief and thought should develop. His first political creed, a very short one, was the outcome of his general scepticism. When he left school at the age of seventeen (it was at the time of Goethe's death), he was, "if not a republican, at least convinced that a republic is the most reasonable form of State. . . . These views remained on the theoretical plane, and were not strong enough to overcome my inborn Prussian monarchical sentiments. My historical sympathies were still on the side of authority." He regarded Harmodius and Brutus as criminals and rebels. Every German prince who resisted the emperor incurred his anger.

As far as he could remember, these vague thoughts about the State only led on two occasions to the definite espousal of a party cause. Both of these instances were the expression of his character, and throw light on that character. In his school days, he was already opposed to the old style of parliamentary speeches, saying that he felt " repelled by the reading of the clownish and abusive orations . . . with which the Homeric heroes were accustomed to regale themselves before a fight." Just as he was opposed to political phrasemaking, so, even in those days, he regarded unemotional action with repugnance, and considered that action should be instinct with passionate feeling. He condemned Tell, saying: "In my view it would have been more natural and nobler if Tell, instead of loosing his arrow towards the boy, whom the best bowman in the world might have hit instead of the apple, he had promptly shot the Austrian governor. This would have been the expression of just anger at a cruel order. Concealment and ambush do not please me."

His attitude of opposition to religious belief was adopted in perfect clarity of mind. At the time of his confirmation, when he was about sixteen, he tells us: "Not out of indifference, but as the outcome of mature conviction, I abandoned the practice to which I had been accustomed since early childhood, and gave up saying my prayers, for prayer seemed to me to conflict with my view as to the nature of God. I said to myself that either God ordained everything in virtue of his omnipresence, that is to say, independently of my thought and will; . . . or else, that if my will be independent of God, it would be arrogant . . . to believe that God could be influenced by human petitions."

The only remarkable thing here is his train of reasoning. That he had been brought up sceptically, and that he was much too sceptical by nature to become a believer on his own initiative — these things depended upon himself and upon his parents. But his train of reasoning showed that at this early age he was already a proud realist, who would only concede to a superior power just so much as circumstances made necessary. The youth establishes his nihilism firmly, while avoiding any offence to God by open denial. In diplomatic fashion he throws on God the responsibility for his own failure to go on saying his prayers; he shows a semblance of loyalty beneath which scorn is hidden; and he forces on God an alternative to which the deity can hardly have been accustomed. The conventional genuflexion does not really temper his self-esteem.

That is the spirit in which Bismarck stands for the first time in face of a king.

III

With affected solemnity, a young man is striding across the market-place. His extreme leanness would alone suffice to attract attention. He is wearing a gay dressing-gown and a strangely shaped cap. He twirls his cane, has a long pipe in his mouth, and when he calls "Ariel", a great yellow hound presses up against his knee. Thus equipped he draws nearer to the University of Göttingen, where he is to appear before the magistrate who has summoned the students on account of their unseemly behaviour and dress. A number of fellow-students who pass him wearing ordinary dress and the distinctive caps of their corps, begin to laugh. Promptly the freshman challenges them; their senior has to deal with the matter; the vigour he displays during this first term makes an impression; he is invited to join a corps; and after his first students' duel he plays an active part in the body.

We have a lively description of him at this date in the novel which John Lothrop Motley, his fellow-student, published a few years later. In this novel, Bismarck appears as "Otto von Rabenmark." Motley says: "He was very young . . . not quite seventeen; but in precocity of character . . . he went immeasurably beyond any person I have ever known. . . . I have seldom seen a more unprepossessing person . . . though on better acquaintance . . . I began to think him rather well looking. He had coarse scrubby hair, of a mixed colour, something between red and a whity-brown. His face was peppered all over with freckles, and his eyes were colourless in the centre, and looked as if edged with red tape. An enormous scar, the relic of a recent duel . . . extended from the tip of his nose to the edge of his right ear, and had been sewed up with fourteen stitches. . . . He had recently shaved off one of his eyebrows, his face certainly might lay claim to a bizarre and very unique character. His figure was slender, and not yet mature, but already of a tolerable height. . . . He wore a chaotic coat, without collar or buttons, and as destitute of colour as of shape; enormous wide trousers, and boots with iron heels and portentous spurs. His shirt collar, unconscious of cravat, was doubled over his shoulders, and his hair hung down about his ears and neck. A faint attempt at moustachios, of an indefinite colour, completed the equipment of his face, and a huge sabre, strapped round his waist, that of his habiliments."

Motley likewise tells us that "Rabenmark" plays the piano and the violin, and speaks four languages. Only when the two are alone together does he speak sensibly. Compare what young Bismarck says of himself: "By this sort of behaviour, by offering insults, and so on, I wish to force my way into the best corps. But this is child's play. I have plenty of time before me. I want to lead my comrades here, just as I shall lead other folk in later life." He says that he cannot possibly die before he is nineteen years and nine months old. If he gets beyond that point, he will have twelve years more before him. "There is the substance of a hero running to seed here," says the young novelist, writing about his friend immediately after this first term, a decade before the archetypal figure will come out of the cavern.

Everything in this freshman makes him conspicuous in contrast with the ordinary students: his courage and arrogance, his debauchery and elegance, the mingling of violence and kindliness. "Kindskopf", "Kassube", and "Achilles", are his nicknames at a students' carouse; the eccentric, the eastern, and the invulnerable, are one and all conspicuous in him. When, in an apple-green frock coat with exceptionally long skirts, or in a velvet coat with mother-of-pearl buttons, he displays "an extraordinarily well-furnished wardrobe", instead of going about in ordinary plaid and cap as was then the fashion among students; when, after drinking a great deal of Rhenish and Madeira, he leaves the tavern and wanders down to the river in order to take a nocturnal swim; when he is again and again reproved for unauthorised

smoking and brawling; when he despises the college authorities
even more than his comrades do; when at night he sleeps naked
because linen irritates his skin — his fellow-students hesitate to
make fun of him, for he always challenges them when they do so,
and is always victorious. He fought twenty-five duels in his first
three terms, and was only once wounded; this made a great impression on his seniors, and in this way he speedily attained his
end. He was feared.

At the place where he prefers to dine, five languages are
spoken, and this Pomeranian Junker associates almost exclusively with foreigners. Here he makes two friends, who remain
fast friends for life — for between him and them politics could not
intrude to sow estrangement, as they could between him and the
few others who were his close associates in youth. These two
friends were: Motley, the American, a cheerful man of refined
temperament, free from prejudices; and Count Keyserling, the
Courlander, a man of mature mind and ascetic disposition. On
into old age they remained Bismarck's only intimate friends.
Motley, who was an imaginative writer in his youth, subsequently
became an historian and a diplomatist. Keyserling, a natural philosopher, made no more than casual incursions into public life.
Both these men were older than Bismarck, more self-controlled,
more concentrated in aim. Bismarck found in them a self-
sufficiency which he himself lacked, and a love of liberty which
was lacking to the Germans of his acquaintance. Neither of them
played an active part in the students' corps.

He was supposed to be studying law, with an eye to a diplomatic career. His mother's ambitious longing was that her
father's power and position should be reborn in her son. This was
a middle-class notion, appropriate to the Menckens, but it was
new in the Bismarck family; never before had any one of them
served his king except with the sword. Moreover, in this matter
the mother had no need to repress any of her son's inclinations.
He had no wish to become an army officer; and in these dull and
wasted years from seventeen to twenty, his will could have been
moulded in any direction, for he had no aim of his own.

In politics, likewise, he was too indifferent to follow his first promptings. He had no love for the Burschenschafts, the students' associations, which drank to Kaiser and Reich, and sang patriotic songs. After a brief experience of their ways, he avoided them, "because they condemned students' duels and much beer drinking", and because their members were ill-bred. Thus temperament, and his own ideas of what was good behaviour, led him to eschew the circles at the university where in those days the idea of a German Empire was alone cultivated. But when, at table, any one made fun of the Prussians, few of whom came to study in Hanover, Bismarck was prompt with his challenges. In defence of his own co-nationals he had no fewer than six duels on his hands at one and the same time. He defended Blücher's action at Waterloo with so much zeal that some one said: "This freshman talks as if we were still in the days of Old Fritz!" He seemed to have no interest in the national problem, and would not even go to hear the most celebrated professor lecture on this topic. It was more to his taste to join his American friends on Independence Day, and drink himself under the table in honour of liberty; but when one of them spoke of German disunion, Bismarck bet twenty-five bottles of champagne that Germany would be unified within twenty-five years. The loser was to cross the sea, and they would drink the champagne together. —— He was only thirteen years out in his reckoning.

All the same, he was careful to observe the forms. "Veil your thoughts when you write home," he said to his brother, now a lieutenant. "The Kniephof court is more accessible to diplomatic cunning and to lies than to swashbuckling." His way of life, his dress, and the like, cost a great deal of money; and after he had been a year at the university there were "very disagreeable scenes between myself and the old man, who refuses to pay my debts. . . . Not that it matters very much, for I have plenty of credit, so that I can live a thoroughly dissolute life. The result is that I look pale and ill, and my old man, when I come home at Christmas, will naturally ascribe this to a lack of victuals. Then I shall take a strong line, saying that I would rather be a

Mohammedan than go on suffering hunger, and then I shall get my way."

Is not the student who writes this a born diplomatist? The management of men, the weighing of motives, making the best use of the temporary situation, the repudiation of responsibility for himself, and the art of making his adversary responsible. These are all elements of statecraft; and his mother, who is much mortified by his conduct, fails to realise that her ambition for Otto is guided by a trustworthy instinct.

When the young man of eighteen, sickly, blasé, and lacking energy, like young Goethe, had come home, had restored his health with country diet and tranquillity, and wished to continue his studies — this time in Berlin — his mother seemed already to have half given him up. "I think my mother would like me to don the blue uniform and defend the country in front of the Halle Gate. She said to me to-day, when I got up late, that I seemed to her to have no wish to study." He certainly had no wish to study, but he had still less desire to don the blue uniform. He spent a good deal of his time with one of his cousins, Blanckenburg, and with young Roon, both of whom he was to encounter subsequently in decisive hours. But his favourite companions were Keyserling and Motley. He roomed with the American; and when Motley, wearing a Byronic collar, and having very little command of German, was translating *Faust*, or sitting with his legs cocked up out of the window, so that the people passing below could see his red slippers, Bismarck was in the best of humours. Our Otto only lost his temper when, after the pair had spent half the night in philosophic discussion, his friend, undismayed, would return to the point from which they had started and enquire once more: "whether Byron was to be compared with Goethe." Bismarck said later that what charmed him in Motley were the American's good looks, his large eyes, his wit, and his amiability. It was the same in Keyserling's case. What attracted him to the count was not so much the Courlander's intelligence, as his handsomeness, his man-of-the-world air, and his talent for piano-playing — for Keyserling could play Beethoven hour after hour, and Beethoven was the only composer who could now move our world-weary student.

It seemed as if Bismarck were at the end of his tether. Nothing escaped his mockery, himself least of all. "En attendant," he writes to a comrade, "I live here like a gentleman, grow accustomed to a foppish way of life, speak a good deal of French, devote most of my time to my toilet, and what is left over I spend in visits, and in the company of my old crony, the bottle. In the evenings, I sit in the first row at the opera, behaving myself as impudently as I can; . . . thus I bore myself in a reasonably respectable way. . . . Slothful old Sch., from Göttingen is still here, . . . Also that long, thin sprig of the aristocracy, who lacks everything requisite to make up a man and nothing requisite to make up a chamberlain except a padlock in front of his jaws! He lives here in happy companionship with thirty of his own ilk, who give him no cause for complaint. . . . They don't eat; they don't drink — what do you think they do? They count their ancestors."

Can misanthropy go further? Class and social intercourse, idleness and affectation, he despises alike in himself and in his neighbour. He is disinclined to make any change for the better, and yet at bottom he deplores his own weaknesses. What, then, remains? The clash of swords and marriage! He writes from his father's estate: "I think I shall refuse the portfolio of foreign affairs, amuse myself for a few years with licking recruits into shape, then take a wife, bring up children, till the land, and undermine the morals of my peasants by distilling vast quantities of brandy. If, in ten years or so, you visit this part of the world, . . . you will find a corpulent Landwehr officer, a fellow with a big moustache who curses and swears immoderately, detests the French, and flogs his hounds and his servants brutally, though all the while tyrannised over by his wife. I shall wear leather breeches, let people make fun of me at the wool market in Stettin, and if they address me as 'Herr Baron', I shall stroke my moustache good-naturedly and sell my wool two talers cheaper in consequence. On the King's birthday I shall get drunk and shout

'Vivat.' Indeed, I shall get drunk pretty often, and shall be always talking about crops and horses." From this future he was protected, above all, by a certain dread of marriage; and the dread was not overcome, but strengthened, by several engagements which were broken off. Although, as Motley tells us, " in love he followed the natural impulse with very little scruple ", he was at the same time "always falling violently in love." He himself tells us, in these days, that he will probably ere long experiment in marriage, " or would do so if any of my passionate inclinations were to last long enough. The joke of the matter is that I pass for a cold-blooded misogynist. Thus do people deceive themselves."

At the age of twenty, having been prepared by a crammer, he succeeded in passing his examination for the bar, and had experience of the practice of law for a little while at the Municipal Court in Berlin. His distaste for such imbecilities grew ever stronger, and he only kept on at this job in order to avoid having to become a soldier, for, he said: "I have victoriously resisted the rather urgent wishes of my parents in that direction." He had an invincible dislike to military drill, although he was unrivalled as a swimmer and a fencer; but as regards going to court, he gave way. "I have no great inclination, but my parents want me to go, and no doubt they are right, for it may help my career." At the court ball, the prince of Prussia (at this time nearly double Otto's age) speaks to him, is astonished at the guardsman's proportions of this young lawyer, and asks: " Why aren't you a soldier?"

"I had no prospect of advancement in the army, Your Royal Highness."

"I doubt if you have any better prospects at the bar!"

In this very first dialogue between William of Prussia and Bismarck, amid the distractions of a ballroom conversation we see the difference between the two natures. William is all soldier, Otto anything but a soldier; and when the prince is astonished that Bismarck does not turn his inches to account in the finest profession in the world, the Junker gets out of the difficulty by pretending that his reason is the lack of any chance of promotion. Similarly, in years to some, Otto will often hide his real reasons from William, wishing to spare the other's Prussian military susceptibilities.

All the same, Berlin and official work, the sight of competing lawyers, the glimpse of court life, and thoughts of a career, sometimes entice the young official out of his negation. He sees what heights can be attained. Certainly at this period some of his friends begin to discern traces of the ambition that lurked behind the cloak of cynicism. Twenty years later, Keyserling remembered a conversation he had had with Bismarck in those days, when Bismarck said: "A constitution is unavoidable; this is the way to outward tokens of honour; but inwardly one must be pious." With a smile he added: "I wanted to visit the bestarred excellencies as a wise pilgrim."

Did not this young man of twenty thus early foresee the means without which in modern Prussia nothing can be attained? A constitution, which in his secret heart he detests; and a piety which he certainly lacks! How unmistakable is the inner truth of these memories. He already describes himself to Keyserling as the wise pilgrim he was to become; shows his secret ambition, if not for orders of distinction, at any rate for the attainment of the power which brings such distinctions. Oh, well, but one would have to be pious within. One would have to be, and since one is not, this is "all nonsense." So let us fill up our glasses!

If we want to understand what it was in Bismarck's heart that was already hostile to his ambition, if we wish to see at work the inflexible pride with which he fought against this ambition, we need only watch him in epistolary conversation with a third friend of Göttingen days, Scharlach, to whom he wrote seldom, but very frankly. In a letter written to Scharlach when Otto was a fledgling barrister, we read the confession "that my ambition, which used to be less powerful and to take another direction, is constraining me to an industry such as I have never known before, is making me grasp at any means which seem likely to bring advancement. I don't know whether you will still be inclined, over a good glass of Scharlachberg wine, to smile compassionately at my folly. That would be a mood which I cannot but describe as a happy one, although I do not actually wish to share it. Indeed, I am now so blinded by my passion for work that I have come to regard a pure pleasure which has no utility as a waste of time."

Yet immediately afterwards all this appears to him ridiculous, for he goes on: "My life really seems rather a pitiful affair when I look at it in a strong light. I spend the day in studies which do not interest me. In the evening, when I frequent the court or official society, I affect a pleasure which I am not sufficiently like Sch. either to feel or to desire. I find it difficult to believe that the complete attainment of the ends for which I am working, the longest title and the most resplendent order in Germany, the most amazing distinction, could compensate me for the bodily and mental restrictions which would result from such a life. Often I feel that I should like to exchange the pen for the plough, and the portfolio for the hunting bag. But after all, I can do that whenever I like."

Thus does his inborn pride, a heritage from his father, strive against ambition, a heritage from his mother. Pride chases ambition into a corner; and since his sense of self-satisfaction makes it impossible for him to doubt the success of an undertaking he has once entered upon, he is content at the very outset to proclaim the valuelessness of such success.

Nevertheless he seeks success, reckons up where it can be most speedily secured, reports himself on the Rhine, for the first time in his life remains at home in summer for month after month in order to write the answers to two examination papers which have to be dealt with as a preliminary to his promotion at the bar. He does this almost without thought of self, and yet he does it with a will; and it all happens because he has left the town, and has at length begun to find himself in tranquillity.

Look at him, this Junker of twenty-one at Schönhausen whither his father has now returned, " a place with about thirty rooms, two of which are furnished, lovely oriental carpets, so ragged that one can barely make out the original colour, rats without number, chimneys in which the wind howls — in a word, the castle of my ancestors, where everything tends to nourish melancholy, . . . cared for by a wizened housekeeper, the play-mate of my father, now sixty-five years of age. I am preparing for my examination, listen to the nightingales, do target prac-tice, read Voltaire and Spinoza's *Ethics.* . . . Our old cook tells me that the peasants say: 'Poor young master, what on earth will he be doing?' All the same, I have never been so well content as I am here. I sleep only six hours, and I take delight in my studies — two things which I have long regarded as impossible. I believe that the reason, or, to put it better, the cause, of all this is the fact that last winter I was violently in love. . . . It is fatal that I should have departed so far from my philosophical tran-quillity and irony. . . . 'Aha!' you will say, 'unhappy love, solitude, melancholy, etc.' — the connexion is a possible one, but I am again carefree, and analyse in accordance with Spinoza's principles of causes of love, in order that I may henceforward remain cold-blooded."

Beneath the great limes or the ancient oaks, under the loving eyes of his good father, cared for by a sensible peasant woman, working hard, Bismarck's restless heart was able for a few weeks, and for the first time, to realise a measure of collectedness. His mood was no longer cynical; he had become serene. Spinoza gave his blessing to it all, and taught this born analyst the proper forms of analysis.

With the best possible reports and the most excellent recom-mendations, our Junker set forth for Aix-la-Chapelle. The place was his prudent mother's choice, for the president of this new Prussian colony was of the Arnim family from the Old March. Another two years, she thinks, and the grandson will be treading in the footsteps of his grandfather, Mencken.

IV

The famous spa where three countries meet, filled with foreign-ers squandering time and money, such was Aix in those days.

How was a "mad Junker" of twenty-one to be expected to stick to the practice of law in a governmental building there? Count Arnim, a very distinguished-looking person with English manners, had received his fellow provincial as an hereditary prince. After dinner, he had given Otto a sort of private lecture, drawing up a plan in accordance with which the young lawyer would soon be able to pass through the stages on the way to an assessorship. Then the diplomatist was to begin his career, " and it would be a matter of no importance whether I should go first to St. Petersburg or to Rio de Janeiro."

But the arrogant Junker, for whom his parents had with much labour and pains secured this chance, despises the stirrup offered him to mount by. He prefers to go riding with young English ladies, is thrown from his horse, has a bad fall, and is once more sick of life during his tedious recovery; while he must keep his bed, he reads Cicero's *De Officiis*, and his beloved Spinoza, also *King Richard III.*, and *Hamlet*. At length he is well enough to get up. Now the government may go to the devil! He throws himself into the pleasures of the fashionable world, amazes the company at table by eating one hundred and fifty oysters, and gives a demonstration of the best way to grill them. "My company at table now consists of seventeen English folk, two French, and my own unworthy self. We sit at the aristocratic end: the duke and duchess of Cl(eveland) and their niece, Miss Russell, who is amiable and attractive." Young, pretty, and well-dressed, an Englishwoman of ducal family, Laura is much to his taste. When she leaves Aix, she and Otto are secretly engaged.

How can he earn money enough to be able to marry her? At the gaming table? Here, as in the novels, he only multiplies his debts. At the same time he hears things about the family which startle him. Shortly afterwards he has a love affair with a lady who must be well on in the thirties; then a new fit of diligence. Interspersed come homesickness, grumbles from his parents, cynicism, debts, hunting parties, new good resolutions: "I have learned that I must keep watch over myself; there is still too much romance in me." This sentence, the only one from his own hand relating to these days, gives us a glimpse into the turbulence of his unchained feelings.[1] The engagement to Miss Russell comes to an end of itself.

Next summer he is attracted by another Englishwoman, Isabelle Loraine, not so distinguished as Laura, but even better-looking, a clergyman's daughter, fair-haired and slender. Getting two weeks' leave, and ignoring his extensive debts in Aix, he follows the lady to Wiesbaden; but there he encounters Laura once more, for she is a friend of Isabelle. He finds the situation "extremely piquant", becomes the lover of the second lady, and writes to his friend: "I should tell you in passing that I am engaged, and that I have it in mind, like you, to enter the holy state of matrimony. My intended is a young Englishwoman, a blonde, extraordinarily beautiful, and, as yet, she does not know a word of German. I am going to accompany her family to Switzerland, and shall say good-bye to them in Milan, . . . for I must hasten to see my parents from whom I have been separated for nearly two years. . . . You must come with me to England, to my wedding, which will take place next spring."

With the arrogance of his tribe and inclined to look down upon officials, our adventurer does not make up his mind until two months have elapsed to send a word of excuse for his absence to his chief in Aix-la-Chapelle. "Urgent private affairs," he says, have kept him away from his post. He asks formally for leave, and says he is going to send in his resignation officially ere long. His people at home are more and more estranged from him. His father refuses to send him any more money; his mother, who is ill, is greatly incensed. When at length, having no funds left, he has to come home, he does so as a guest in the carriage of a stranger whom he detests. What had happened?

"I had excellent prospects of what is called a brilliant career;

---

[1] Bismarck's letters of that period to his brother could still be read by Erich Marcks in 1909, for Herbert Bismarck had preserved them. Subsequently, however, his widow thought fit to destroy them. Her prudery is responsible for the loss of documents of national value.

and perhaps ambition, which was then my pilot, might have guided me long or for always, had not a beautiful Englishwoman attracted me out of my course, and led me (without leave) to spend six months sailing in her wake on foreign seas. At length I made her heave to, and she struck her flag; but two months after the capture my prize was snatched from me by a one-armed colonel, fifty years old, with four horses and an income of fifteen thousand talers. With light purse, and sore at heart, I went back to Pomerania, . . . towed by a cumbersome and disagreeable galleon."

Out of health, as at his last return; with his nerves so much disordered that he frequently makes mistakes in his letters; quite off the rails — thus does the son come home to his mortified parents. His ailing mother, greatly disturbed by the decline in the family fortunes, devotes the remnant of her energies to finding a fresh opening for her son, and manages to get a post for him in the Potsdam administration, after Arnim, writing sarcastically from Aix-la-Chapelle, has told her that the young baron had "vainly endeavoured to work hard, but the attractions of Aix society proved too much for him." The official report was less amiably worded. Potsdam was informed that at the lodgings where Otto had stayed for months, and elsewhere, the Herr Baron had left debts amounting to several hundred talers, and these debts had driven him away from Aix.

The accused haughtily replied: "I do not propose to discuss my personal affairs with the royal administration at Aix, and I shall lodge a complaint regarding this impertinent invasion of my private rights." His father, likewise, when an application is made to him for the payment of the debts, grows angry, and refuses in the end to continue the correspondence with the authorities. Thus independent are these Junkers, thanks to a tradition centuries old, in their attitude towards officials whom they wave aside with lordly gestures, and to whom they address themselves once more when it suits their purposes. However, young Bismarck, when strings have been pulled in his behalf, is admitted to the post at Potsdam — upon the written understanding that he is to work regularly and diligently.

Our self-opinionated youth does not get on much better than he did at Aix. It is a one-horse place; the ordinary is beneath contempt; his official superiors are pedants; he is expected to be punctual. After three months our Junker departs without leave. At home, ruin looms ever nearer. His mother is really ill, but no one takes the matter seriously, for she has always been self-centred. His father, now an old man, cannot suddenly learn how to manage his estate. Let the farm on lease, says he. Start a sugar refinery, advises the mother. The doctor diagnoses cancer. She stays in Berlin for treatment. Her son is often with her. Long after she is dead, he grumbles because she made him sit by her bedside reading mystical books aloud to her.

If only he could be free from the liability to military service! Now twenty-three years old, he writes to his father: " A last attempt in Berlin to secure exemption has failed. . . . Still, I have been given hopes of getting off with a brief term, on the ground of a muscular weakness which, as I have told them, I feel when I raise my right arm — the sequel of a wound there, though unfortunately not deep enough. . . . No matter whether I join a fortnight or three months beforehand, I must get through my training before the manœuvres. I shall therefore join as late as possible, some time in March." Thus vigorously does Bismarck, a young and healthy man, try to avoid becoming a soldier; he complains of an imaginary muscular weakness. His reluctance to enter military service is due to his hatred for any sort of compulsion, for he is a master in the arts of riding, fencing, and shooting, and will throughout life again and again give proofs of personal courage. His pride cannot bend. When, at length, he has to join the Yager Guards, he is promptly at odds with his superior officers. " I shall never be able to get on with my superiors!"

Affairs at home are going rapidly from bad to worse. The mistress of the house is ill and pampered; the sons earn nothing and need money; the father cannot provide what they want, and they have to pay twelve per cent. and more for loans. A crisis is imminent. Then came an idea. Where from, who can say? Was

it from the dying mother, the anxious father, the more efficient
of the two brothers (who was still at his studies), or from the
idler who had no taste for any occupation? Anyhow, in their
perplexity they hit upon the simple thought that the sons must
come back to the countryside in order to save the family from
bankruptcy. There is no doubt that Bismarck's desperate nihilism
brought matters to a head. He went to his mother and said that
something must be done. "Otto is so sick of his work in the
administration," writes the father to the elder son, "that he is
weary of life. If he were to give most of his years to it, he might
perhaps in the end become a president with an income of two
thousand talers; but there is nothing to hope from luck. He has
implored his mother to find him something else to do. . . . His
idea is that we should start a sugar refinery, that he should go
to Magdeburg to learn the business, and then come and manage
affairs in Kniephof. Since I am very much distressed that he
should be so unhappy, and since at Kniephof I have seen how
much you are interested in agriculture, and as I recognise that
if I stay in Berlin we shall all go down together, I have made up
my mind that you two shall have Kniephof for your own, and that
I shall content myself with the income from Schönhausen." In any
case the brothers must pass their examinations.

To the easy-going father, who was now nearly seventy years
of age, this decision may not have been a difficult one. That the
young men's mother should have approved it must have depended
upon the imminence of ruin, and perhaps upon her poor state of
health. For her end was near, and we now have to say farewell
to this ambitious woman, who died a few months after the foregoing decision had been taken. She was then only fifty, a mother
whose hopes for her sons had been shattered, a woman who had
expected to be compensated in her boys' success for her disappointment in their father. Nevertheless, a generation later, her
expectations were to be amazingly fulfilled.

More distant relatives, who were by no means willing to help,
felt entitled to complain. This accounts for a warning letter
from one of the cousins, a letter to which we have Bismarck's

answer. In its breadth and frankness, this document presents us with the keenest self-analysis of his life. A year or two before he had been in love with her, and that is why he decided to justify himself to her. He kept the rough copy of the letter, and ten years later sent it to his betrothed as one of his biographical records:

"Affairs and official service are utterly uncongenial to me; I should not think myself fortunate to become an official or even a minister of State; I deem it quite as respectable to grow corn as to write despatches, and in certain circumstances as more useful. I have more inclination to command than to obey. These are facts for which I can give no reason beyond my own tastes. . . . A Prussian official is like a player in an orchestra. No matter whether he be the first violin or the triangle, . . . he has to play his instrument as the needs of the concerted piece dictate. . . . But for my part, I want to play music such as I regard as good — or else not play at all.

"For a few renowned statesmen, especially in countries with an absolute constitution, patriotism has been the motive driving them into the public service; much more often, the mainspring has been ambition, the wish to command, to be admired, to be famous. I must admit that I myself am not free from this passion. Many distinctions, such as those which accrue to a soldier in wartime, or to a statesman under a free constitution, such men as Peel, O'Connell, Mirabeau, etc. — men who had their part to play in energetic political movements — would exert on me an attractive force which would override every consideration, would lure me as a flame allures a moth.

"I am less attracted by successes which I might secure along trodden roads, by examinations, influence, the study of documents, seniority, the favour of my superiors. Still, there are moments when I cannot think without regret of all the gratifications to vanity which awaited me in the public service; the satisfaction of having my value officially recognised by swift promotion; . . . the pleasing sensation of being regarded as a capable and useful person; the glamour which would surround me and my family — all these considerations dazzle me when I have drunk a bottle of wine. I need careful and sober reflection to convince me that they are but cobwebs spun by foolish vanity, and are on the same footing as a dandy's pride in the cut of his coat and a banker's delight in his money; that it is unwise and useless for us to seek our happiness in the opinions of others, and that a reasonable man must live his own life in accordance with what he himself recognises to be right and true, and must not be guided by the impression he makes on others or by the thought of what people will say about him before and after his death.

"In a word, I am not free from ambition, though I regard it as just as bad as any of the other passions, and even more foolish, because ambition, if I give myself up to it, demands the sacrifice of all my energy and independence without guaranteeing me, even in the most fortunate event, any permanent satisfaction. . . . An income sufficient for my needs and enabling me to set up house in town would not be mine, even if I were eminently successful, until I was about forty years old and had been raised to a presidency. By that time I should have become a dryasdust, should have grown hypochondriacal, should have had my health undermined by a sedentary life, and should only need a wife as a sick nurse.

"These moderate advantages, the tickling of my vanity by hearing myself addressed as 'Herr Präsident', the consciousness of rarely helping the country as much as I cost it, and of occasionally working it hindrance and doing it harm — do not allure me. I have therefore made up my mind to preserve my independence, and not to sacrifice my vital energies as long as there still remain thousands of persons (some of them highly distinguished) to whose taste such prizes seem precious, so that they are delighted to fill the place that I leave vacant for them."

This first document of the Bismarckian spirit discloses the pride, the perspicacity, and the contemptuousness which (in addition to courage) formed the leading elements of his character, were the determinants of his success, the cause of his lack of happiness, the background of the tragical conflict of his spiritual life in later years. We see in it his contempt for mediocrity, as displayed in his sarcastic sketch of the pushful man who, at any cost to body and mind, wishes at long last to be addressed as "Herr Präsident." He shows us that there can be no happiness for an official, who always has superiors and never knows freedom. What psychological mastery in this young man of twenty-three, who distinguishes bedazzlement from passion, vanity from fame, concerted playing from a solo, possession from power! At the same time he shows his reader that such nervous titillation as the supposed goods of life may inspire, is due to the suggestive influence of alcohol! We are shown the countryman who steels his body, who prizes health more than a career, who loves the forest and sport more than desks and offices.

Above all, we see a youth filled with incredible pride, who will not render obedience to whomsoever it may be, and who feels the shallowness of any gratification which may demand the sacrifice of his freedom. With how sovereign a gesture does he thrust aside the motive of patriotism and shake off care for problems of State, in order, with sure aim, to shoot to the very heart of passion! If, indeed, he were to be given the vast powers of a dictator, then, like a moth into the flame, he would hurl himself forward, not in order to realise an idea, but in order to command and to win renown. Nowadays that is only possible in free States; in England where, at the very time he is writing, Peel, who had been premier but yesterday, is trying in the Lower House to force free trade on his own party, while at the same time O'Connell is fighting for the liberty of Ireland: two revolutionists, who have only to heed their own energy and insight, and are not forced to consider the wishes of a king! Both of them bring about revolutions. Even Mirabeau wanted to limit the powers of monarchy. But in Prussia, here in this German land without a constitution, without an Upper and a Lower House, these remain no more than the dreams of a fantastical baron who is vainly sweeping the horizon in search of a political movement.

There we have a picture of Bismarck, the born dictator aware of his own powers, uninfluenced by loyalty to a king or by the fear of God, unmoved by love of the homeland or by a sense of

responsibility towards the masses; the great soloist, the misan-
thrope, the fighter, the revolutionist restlessly awaiting change;
the adventurer who despises that which exists because of its
stagnancy; the man whose nervous energy makes him wish, not to
administer but to transform, who desires to command as his own
insight may dictate, and cannot tolerate a superior.

V

Here are the thatched cottages of the labourers at Kniephof.
A dozen or so, in each of which there are four families. They are
extremely poor. A man can barely earn a taler a month, and for
many days in the year he must work for nothing. In return, they
have free quarters, firewood, three acres apiece, pasturage, hay,
and an allowance of grain. When the harvest is bad, the lord of
the soil will give them a helping hand if he be in a good humour.
Since Kniephof is a manor, their lord has judicial authority, is
their ecclesiastical patron, sits on the Kreistag, and can become
Landrat. Thus he is able to help or to hurt whomsoever he pleases.
In 1840 these peasants had neither rights nor securities. They
were slaves, with the loyalty of slaves; for their ancestors had
served the ancestors of their gracious lord.

Bismarck is on friendly terms with them, while always keeping
up his station. "Surely you are Otto the Amiable," writes a friend
to him. " . . . You are the lord who has a warm heart for his
people. . . . I should be only too happy if my people had such
nice things to say of me . . ." But when, on one occasion, a
peasant will not give him the crown of the causeway, there is a
terrible collision. The peasant's cart is stronger built, and the
lord's carriage is smashed up; the consequences may be left to
the imagination. From the first he has explained how he proposes
to lead this new kind of life; has written to his friend saying that
henceforward he intends to be "master and not servant; and no
longer to copy despatches."

Though he was fond of his brother, the two were not able to

work together for long. Bismarck could not live side by side with any one possessing equal rights with himself. Soon they divided their heritage in twain. He took the matter resolutely in hand, writing: " I am about to go halves with my brother. With the aid of a purchaser who has made a very high offer, I have brought him to the point." Thereafter, each of them set to work, slowly and laboriously trying to clear off the load of debt.

As a preliminary, Bismarck spent a few months studying agriculture at the University of Greifswald, and chemistry at the academy of Eldena; had works on botany sent to him by Keyserling; and came across a doctor who could help him in his chemical studies. There were also some more duels, and conflicts with the police. No longer a student, and not as yet a fully fledged country gentleman, he sat at ordinary among the landowners who came to market. " I listen to them with a thoughtful mien, ponder what I hear, and dream o' nights about threshing, manure, and stubble-fields."

True that he retains his mocking tone, but once he has settled on his estate he tries " with the complete ignorance of a bookish townsman " to do all that he can to make the best of his farming. He sends for a number of books from the agricultural society of the country town, keeps his own accounts with care — and in these we read a great deal about loans, borrowed or repaid. He is often, not to say always, short of money; yet when he travels he does so comfortably and expensively. He still gambles from time to time, though he no longer plays high. All his private expenses, his winnings and losings at the gaming table included, are recorded in the estate accounts. He rides round the place, either alone or accompanied by his steward; learns, examines, issues orders; certainly enjoys his rides on Caleb's back. In these rides, he becomes closely acquainted with the lower classes, with peasants and dealers; gets to know the realities of the land; grows weatherwise; notably improves a memory which was already good; enriches his speech with a hundred agricultural metaphors. In this practical life, his appreciation of facts and his contempt for opinions grow. When he gets home at night he sits down to read, over a supply of his favourite mixed tipple, champagne and porter.

During the nine years which follow, about three-fourths of them spent in the countryside, Bismarck read a great deal. He tells us: "Such general knowledge as I possess, dates from the period when I had nothing to do; when, on my estate in the country, I had a library covering all fields of thought and action, and when I literally devoured my books." A great deal of history, especially English history; many sociological works, including the writings of Louis Blanc; much in foreign tongues, especially Shakespeare. His favourite authors were Byron, Lenau, and Bulwer. In this solitude he formed his mind; or, rather, solitude formed him. For a while he was quite content. No one disturbed him, and he wrote: "I must either live in a metropolis or in the country."

For two years, this man in the middle twenties found delight in his rural occupation, "because of its independence." His illusions passed soon enough. We read: "Experience has taught me to recognise the folly of talking about the Arcadian happiness of a life devoted to farming, with bookkeeping by double entry and chemical studies." To vary the monotony, therefore, he rides and goes hunting; or drives to visit his neighbours, and growls afterwards, saying: "If only these people would buy my farm stock of me, instead of asking me to stay to dinner! They didn't even look at my wethers, and in Berlin prices are falling day by day." Sometimes he would go duck-shooting in a punt, his bottle of wine always ready to his hand; between whiles he would read Byron. As a man of knightly birth, he has little in common with the other gentleman farmers; little in common even with those who are noble, for he has travelled widely, has been to court, can tell a good story, is a hard rider, is reputed to be a bold fellow with the ladies, and has plenty of reasons to make fun of these country squires. "If I ask one of them how he is, he answers: 'Very well, thanks, but unfortunately this winter I have suffered a great deal from the scab'."

Gradually his reputation becomes tarnished, for the greater his boredom the more outrageous the sallies in which he seeks distraction and tries to amaze those among whom he is living. He even finds relief in military life. As a sub-lieutenant he joins the Uhlans and goes through his drill. When his little sister is staying with him, he jumps into the carriage and drives at full gallop, having harnessed two saddle-horses to the pole. Coming home late at night from a carouse, he has several falls, and only returns to his senses after a period of oblivion. He swims a great deal, though he has to force himself into the water because of his sensitiveness to the cold. He finds mistresses in all classes, but makes fun of the men of his own station who live openly with their lady friends. Once when some acquaintances fail to turn up at the appointed hour in the morning, and when, to tease him they have barricaded their door with a chest of drawers, he shoots through the open window at the ceiling so that the plaster showers down on them. After dinner, he will sit on the sofa and thence shoot at a target; and it troubles him little when a stray shot hits the joiner's workshop; yet when his groom tumbles into the water, he saves the man at the risk of his own life.

When any one comes to see him, the guest is supplied with an abundance of wine and porter, and told to help himself. After one such drinking bout, he set off on an hour's walk by muddy roads to a neighbouring squire's farmstead, where he greatly shocked a gaily dressed company by his disgraceful appearance. In this way he acquired the name of the Mad Junker, although he was not really mad. The nickname was mainly derived from his insatiable appetite for food and drink, and from his faculty for enduring all things. A guest at the Cuirassiers', he was invited to take the inaugural sip from a tankard which held a whole bottle. Thereupon, to the astonishment of the company, he drained it at a draught. Though he had not been feeling very well at the time, he tells us: "For the next four weeks my digestion was better than it had ever been before." Sometimes he would talk of the progress of political affairs in the capital; always disrespectfully! The young countesses found it most interesting to be taken in to dinner by Herr von Bismarck, though their mothers were rather uneasy.

Once only, during this time, did he make, or rather attempt, a public utterance. In one of the liberal newspapers published on the Baltic coast, a complaint had appeared concerning the damage the Pomeranian nobles inflicted on the fields when out hunting with their English horses and hounds. The farmers' only resource, said the writer, was self-protection. Bismarck's answer was not inserted, but a very carefully corrected draft has come down to us. The writer endeavoured to prove that such winter rides did no harm to the seed, but were good for the breed of horses; moreover, the horses were German, and only the whips English. He could mention many worse malefactors who imported from England, not whips only, but shaving-soap, vests, and even Cheshire cheese. Then he declares that the writer of the original complaint had had personal rather than material reasons. His own name, and of course his pistols, are at this writer's disposal. Then he goes on to social and political questions.

"I can understand perfectly well that when men in red coats, on horseback, with hounds, are chasing a hare, and, thus engaged, look extremely pleased with themselves and their occupation — the spectacle must be very distasteful, not only to the hare, but also to any one who is satisfied neither with himself nor with the world, is clad in black, has no horses, no hounds, no chance of hunting, and indeed no taste for the sport." He admits that he was "born in the caste of the ci-devant nobles, . . . whose overwhelming privilege it is to prefix a 'von' to their names, like a mist-wraith that has outlived gloomier days, and is able to veil from mourning Germany the sunrise of bourgeois and social equality." At the close, he demands that "to Farther Pomerania shall be left its dues and its personal liberties, to this extent, that it shall be entitled to spend its own money upon its own amusements in whatever fashion it may prefer."

This is Bismarck's first political utterance, penned when he is twenty-eight years old. It concerns hares and stubble-fields, but is instinct with the bitterness of the Junker towards classes that wish to challenge his privileges. In this first public appearance, he defends his own class, the upper class, and makes mock of

BISMARCK IN 1834

From a miniature by an unknown painter

underlings who are not able to hunt, maliciously implying that they have no taste for sport. He goes so far as to compare the burgher or the peasant who dislikes seeing the cavalcade of hunters gallop by, with the hare which is the hunters' quarry. If any one were to come to him asking reasonable compensation, he would pay it readily enough. But an open attack upon his privileges, when a champion of the new principles takes the offensive, leads him forthwith to don his ancestors' harness. Bismarck's first political words are those of a protagonist of the class war.

Shortly before this date, boredom had driven him into his third engagement. This time his affianced was a girl of the neighbourhood, Ottilie von Puttkamer; but her mother was opposed to the match, " and a fortnight afterwards I was embroiled with the mother of my betrothed, a lady who, to do her justice, is one of the most ill-natured women I know, and who does not think herself too old to be made love to." Frau von Puttkamer, in view of Otto von Bismarck's unsavoury reputation, wanted to keep the young people apart for a year. Ferdinand von Bismarck tried to mediate — at least it was the father's pen, for Otto had obviously dictated this diplomatic letter to the old man. We cannot help laughing when we read his description of himself as " reasonable and lively, if you will forgive the arrogance." But the lady whom he would fain make his mother-in-law stands firm. She makes her daughter write a letter at her dictation (the other way about from Kniephof!), a spiteful and unjust letter in which the lover is given his congé.

Bismarck is crestfallen; not so much at the loss of the girl, for he has already grown weary of her; but at the affront. He decides, however, that it would be unworthy of his dignity " to show how greatly I have been mortified, and to seek solace in a few pistol shots." After a journey, taken " to rid myself of my spleen, if possible, in foreign climes ", he declares himself " cooled off to such an extent, that I cannot but regard as the greatest good fortune that which a while back made me curse my fate." Yet the wound to his honour still rankled, for four years later, when the young lady's mother sought a reconciliation, and would

gladly have consented to the marriage, he drew back, saying to
a friend: "The feeling on which I have brooded for years, the
feeling that my innermost and truest sentiments were frivolously
maltreated, the betrayal of my confidence, the mortification of my
pride — these have left a residue of bitterness which I cannot
adequately suppress. . . . With the best will in the world, I find
it difficult to forget, even partly, any affront that has made a
deep impression." At this time he makes a general statement to
the effect that he "cannot love." Thus do pride and hatred thrive
in a heart which for the time being knows nothing of love and
sacrifice.

On the journey just mentioned, when he is twenty-seven years
old, he goes first to England. On landing in Hull, he is reproved
for whistling on Sunday, so he returns on board the ship, and sails
to Scotland. Later, in London, outside the House of Peers, he
sees the peers' saddle-horses waiting for them, saddle-horses "instead of carriages", and is greatly impressed. The same when
he sees fashionable folk riding at full gallop. He takes note of
everything that belongs to his own world. He writes to his father:
"The ration of the re-mounts for the York Hussars, horses not
yet doing any work, is a bushel of oats and twelve pounds of
hay. . . . " He goes on to commend "the extraordinary civility
and obligingness of the English, which is quite contrary to my
expectations. Even the common people are well bred, very modest
and intelligent when one speaks to them." Another thing which
strikes him, besides the native civility, is the native appetite:
"This is the country of great eaters. . . . Your food is not
served out to you in helpings. Huge joints, bigger than can be
imagined, stand before you on the table, at breakfast too, and
you cut and eat as much as you please, without its making any
difference to the bill." These remarks to his father about good
food and plenty of it cannot be understood in their full significance until they are compared with countless other passages in
Bismarck's letters in which he, even on into old age, talks with
the utmost seriousness of the pleasures of the table.

The folk at home seem to have been less edified by the masterful tone in which the traveller, when he reached Switzerland, asked his father and his brother to see to it that certain taxes falling due at home should be duly paid. They are to send to this person or that for money, "or make a bargain with some one for grain or spirit. I hope you will regard this affair as of urgent importance, just as if it were your own."

As soon as he returns home, he is disgruntled once more. Pomerania is too small; Germany is a dull place. Abroad, people are more lively. He sits by the fireside, reads Byron, copies out the English poet's most defiant verses. Then he thinks he will follow Byron's example, claps the volume of poetry to, and the account book as well; plans to travel with Arnim, his old schoolfellow. He "will go to Egypt, Syria, . . . perhaps farther afield; if certain arrangements which I have it in mind to make on my estate, can be successfully carried through. I shall play the Asiatic for a few years, in order to make a little change in the staging of my comedy, and so that I can smoke my cigars on the Ganges instead of on the Rega." But his friend renounces this scheme of travel, having fallen in love with Bismarck's fascinating sister, the seventeen-year-old Malwine. India must be given the go-by, for old Ferdinand writes "a letter moistened with tears, speaking of his solitary old age [he is seventy-three, a widower, and deaf], of imminent death and the need to see his son once more." Now, when a friend asks him why he does not go to India, he quizzically rejoins: "I wanted to take service in India under the English flag. . . . Then I thought, after all, what harm have the Indians done to me?" Thus this plan of Byronic world-travel ends in the Farther Pomeranian manner.

This is the romanticism of a country gentleman in search of distraction, who will, if the worst comes to the worst, turn a State to his purposes: "For the last five years," he writes at the age of thirty, "I have been living alone in the country, can no longer endure a squire's life, and am debating whether I shall enter State service or go for a long journey. . . . I am ready to hang myself from sheer boredom when I am alone here; . . . and it seems to me that every well-bred young man must suffer in the same way if he lives alone in the country unmarried." At about this date he writes in his notebook: "Accounts the whole day. . . . Riding and walking all day in the sunshine. . . . Life is like a magic-lantern show." Another time, wishing to pretend to himself that he is in the great world, he enters into his account book the wages of his night watchman and his foreman distiller whom he calls "gardenuit" and "valet-destillateur."

Now the nihilism of the student becomes intensified into the melancholy of the lonely knight in his castle: "Since then I have been rooted here, . . . fairly insensitive, doing my work punctually, but without any special interest, trying to make my underlings comfortable after their own fashion, and free from irritation when I see how, in return, they cheat me. In the mornings I am out of humour, but after dinner I am accessible to kindlier feelings. My associates are dogs, horses, and country squires. Among the latter I enjoy a certain prestige, because I can read easily, always dress like a human being, can carve game with the accuracy of a butcher, ride easily and boldly, smoke very strong cigars, and am able to drink all my guests under the table — for, unfortunately, I can no longer get drunk, although my memory tells me that this condition used to be an extremely happy one. I therefore vegetate, very like a clock, without any special wishes or fears; an extremely harmonious and very tedious condition."

Sometimes he plunges into the great world. Coming back from such a journey to the North Sea, which he now speaks of as his mistress, he has lost so much money at the gaming table that he is glad "by my unsuspicious demeanour to escape having to pay for a passport on the frontier."

Now that his sister is married, he becomes gloomier than ever. He was really in love with her, and remains in love with her all through life. As long as she is still young, he regards her as the prototype of brightness and elegance. He spends many months at a time with his father, reading and smoking, eating lampreys, and sometimes "playing a comedy with him which he likes to dignify by the name of fox-hunting." He describes to his sister how, on a cold and rainy day, the hounds and the huntsmen had surrounded a clump of trees, where, as every one knew, there could be nothing more than a few old women gathering sticks; how the chief huntsman made strange noises in his throat in order to drive out the imaginary fox, until his father "asks me if I have seen nothing, and I, simulating the most natural surprise, say, 'No, nothing at all.' . . . Thus we go on for three or four hours. . . . Then, twice a day, we visit the orange-house, and once a day the sheepfold; every hour we compare the four thermometers in the parlour, tap the weather-glass and note that the weather is fair, and make the clocks keep time so well that only the one in the library is one beat behind when the others have struck the hour." In the same sort of bitter humour, he tells his sister she must write to their father about all her little doings. "Tell him about the horses, how the servants behave, whether the doors rattle and whether the windows let in the draught—in a word, give him plenty of facts. He cannot bear being called 'Papa'; he hates the word."

Thus boredom and kindliness, complaisance and a sense of confinement within narrow horizons, are at war within his heart, and we cannot wonder that at the age of thirty he makes a third venture into State service, "in order to free myself from a sense of weariness with all my surroundings, a tedium which almost makes me sick of life." Loftily, the young man of family writes to the lord lieutenant of Brandenburg: "My circumstances no longer make it necessary for me to live in the country, and it is now possible for me to follow my bent towards State service." Does it not sound as if he were assuming that they had only been waiting for him to offer himself?

This third attempt lasts only for a couple of weeks. Clashes with his chief begin at once, and the angry lord-lieutenant writes: "I have had many strange experiences, but never before have I known a junior barrister to have sixty-three arrears of work." The usual reasons give him his excuse for abandoning his post. When he is not promptly received by his chief, he says to the servingman: "Tell the lord-lieutenant that I am going away, and shall not come back." When, that same evening in Berlin, he meets the chief at a dinner party, and some one asks: "Do you two gentlemen know one another?" Bismarck replies: "I have not the honour", and introduces himself, with huge delight. He has hardly reached home before he delivers his feelings, in letters, saying that he had made the attempt "as a sort of mental wood-cutting, in order to restore my mind to health, since it was lax for want of occupation, and needed uniform and regular activity. But the parochial arrogance and ludicrous condescension of my official superiors was more intolerable than ever, now that I am no longer used to it." Even when he has to act for his brother as Landrat, he is soon sick of the occupation, "and so is my horse." He speedily gives up this work, too.

"Thus do I drift on the stream of life with nothing to steer by except the inclination of the moment, and I am fairly indifferent as to where the waters may cast me up on the shore."

VI

For a long time now, pietism has been in fashion among the country gentlemen of Pomerania. Old Herr von Thadden at Trieglaff; his brother-in-law, Ludwig von Gerlach; and the latter's brother, the general, who was a favourite of the king; old Puttkamer at Reinfeld; Herr Senfft von Pilsach—all of them brought up in the Cadet School, and subsequently officers during the War of Liberation — had been "converted" in Berlin, had brought the sectarian creed home to Pomerania, and had renounced the liberal church. Now they imported pastors of their own way of thinking, preached at home and in the villages, converted their agricultural labourers, did penance, held conferences, and were glad to hear themselves mentioned in the district with anger or curiosity.

Marie von Thadden was a pretty, rather buxom girl, impassioned, musical, and endowed with a sensuality glossed over with piety. She read Jean Paul and the Brentanos, played Mendelssohn, and, as the betrothed of young Moritz von Blanckenburg, had made the acquaintance of the latter's friend, Herr von Bis-

marck, then full of his plans for a journey in Asia. Naturally she
fell in love with him, though she would not admit it to herself, and
pretended to be glad that he honoured her as his friend's betrothed. "His fine carriage, his brilliancy, both internal and
external, attract me more and more; but when I am with him I
always feel as if I were skating on thin ice and might go through
at any moment." To this Gretchen he seems to be a genius, perhaps the very devil; and from her confession we may infer the
existence of a dozen girlish letters from Pomerania which have
not come down to us. The one from which I have just quoted is the
only one that remains, and gives us the impressions formed by a
passionate girl of good family on meeting Otto von Bismarck at
thirty — this man who in Pomerania ranked as a notable man of
the world, and who exercised on the young woman the lure of
a Mephistopheles.

Being a pietist's daughter, she tries to behave like a sister to
him. After he has had a long conversation with her and her
mother at Trieglaff, she writes to her fiancé:

"Never before have I heard any one expound his unbelief, or
rather his pantheism, so frankly and clearly. . . . Of course you
know Otto's unhappy views, with which he himself is greatly dissatisfied. He is certainly straightforward, and that is a promising
disposition of mind. Furthermore he is rather afraid of the vapor-
ous image of God he has created for himself. . . . He can remember perfectly well the night when he last said his prayers,
and how he deliberately gave up the practice. . . . The arrogant
claim of the pious that their views are the only right ones; the
greatness of his God, who could never trouble himself about such
a grain of dust as a mortal; his utter lack of faith; his vague
longing to believe; his indifference to joy and pain; his unfathom-
able boredom and sense of vacancy. 'How can I believe,' he asks,
'seeing that I have no faith? God must either take possession of
me himself, or must instil faith in me without my contributing
thereto, and without wish on my part!' He was greatly moved,
flushing dark-red several times, but could not make up his mind
to leave. Although he had an engagement to dine in the neigh-

bourhood, he stayed here, arguing vigorously. . . . Manifestly Otto was pleasurably touched; love made its way into his soul; . . . you know him well enough, how kindly he can be, and he became so now. . . . A thousand times it was on the tip of my tongue to say: ' Oh, Otto, Otto, begin a new life, give up your disorderly ways!' "

We see that our friend has been catechised. He is armed with the same rationalism as he had been when a boy of sixteen; but he also exhibits all the pride of a passionate nature, and that of one who (just as in his experiments at an official career) refuses to take any trouble, to do anything which may ensure promotion. He thinks it is God's business to take him to himself; just as in his secret heart he thinks that it is the king's business to summon him; then, all of a sudden, he grows kindly. When he comes back, two days later, he is, we are told, quiet and thoughtful, earnest, and sometimes even anxious.

He has himself taken sides with this pretty and much moved girl. For her sake he finds pleasure in some letters from her betrothed, Blanckenburg, who had also been converted, they are letters, of which their author says that they were " written in the youthful Christian zeal of a friend, raining down thick as hailstones upon your sick heart, with the most honest intentions in the world." Three times Blanckenburg writes to Bismarck without getting an answer. Otto must have the will to believe, must read the Bible, must make a clean breast of it. Marie is always there in the background, for it tickles the girl's fancy to have " this friendship with the Farther Pomeranian phœnix who is supposed to be a perfect example of wildness and arrogance, but can be so attractive." When she sends her Moritz a " deep-blue flower, which he wears with rejoicing ", at the same time she sends his friend Otto a dark-red flower, well knowing why.

At Whitsuntide, in the arbour, the engaged couple set to work on him together. The unbeliever is shown a letter from a friend, a consumptive girl who loves Bismarck, and cannot die until he is converted. Extremely exalted letters from Blanckenburg follow, full of asseverations. The consumptive girl dies, though not until

she has "received inner assurance that your soul will not be
lost. . . . Oh, if you only knew how the deceased had prayed
for you!" Bismarck's answers have not come down to us, for
Blanckenburg subsequently destroyed them in a fit of political
spleen; but in his rejoinder we read: "Why did you shed tears?
Why were my own eyes full of tears when I was reading your
letter? Oh, Otto, Otto, every word you write is true." At a later
date, Bismarck confesses that these incidents had a powerful
effect on him. He soon breaks off the correspondence, however,
for his pride makes it impossible for him to endure being sym-
pathised with; moreover he feels that he is being classified and
pigeonholed; in short, he will not hear another word of the
matter.

The rain, falling on stony ground, was speedily sucked up.
There is nothing to surprise us that he should have wept at the
news of the death of a girl who secretly loved him. He was cynical, but extremely sentimental, this man with the frame of a
giant. His tears came readily, as was shown later, more than once,
at moments of great political decisions. He was not the man to
let such incidents pass without showing emotion. His nature was
under a strange spell. In him, the road to faith lay through superstition. All his life, he was superstitious; and when anything exceptionally fortunate happened to him, he was inclined to regard
it as the work of providence. With reference to his last engagement he wrote at this time: "If I had ever doubted that there is
a providence, and that I am an especial favourite of providence,
the breaking off of the engagement entered into with such uncon-
trolled passion would have convinced me of it."

None the less, his scepticism is still active. After a storm at
sea, he writes to his father: "Some of the ladies fainted, others
wept, and in the men's cabin the only sound to be heard was the
loud praying of a Bremen merchant, who before this had seemed
to me more interested in his waistcoat than in his God. . . . All
the same, the fellow's prayer seems to have saved our lives!"
During the festivities in connexion with Marie von Thadden's
wedding, the rockets that were let off set fire to the village, and

the whole place was burned down. Bismarck, when some of the
pious declared that it was more important to pray than to throw
water on the flames, quoted Cromwell: "Put your trust in God,
my boys, and keep your powder dry!" Then he rode to the scene
of action and fought the fire all night. Next day, when there was a
dispute whether insurance was permissible, seeing that it deprived
God of a means of edification, he said: "That is pure blasphemy,
for God can certainly catch us one way or another!"

Ere long, gossip was afoot in Farther Pomerania to the effect
that Bismarck was young Frau von Blanckenburg's lover. Really
there was nothing amiss. They were much together, and talked in
a romantic vein. He was an enthusiast for Byron; she for Jean
Paul, whom Otto did not admire. Soon she became a mother. "Let
me tell you, since you can no longer visit our little circle often,
that Fräulein S., a very vulgar young woman, was there; . . .
and that the day after to-morrow I am going to an æsthetic tea
at Cardemin [Blanckenburg's estate] where there will be read-
ings, prayers, and hock flavoured with pineapple." Thus lightly
does he pay his footing in this society, for he is at ease there, finds
what he is in search of: intelligence and good form, "a family life,
where I am one of the family; almost a home."

True that even in this circle his nerves are on edge. When out
walking, he will suddenly be overwhelmed with melancholy. The
most trifling words will bring on a fit of sadness. "As you know,"
writes Marie, "this readily happens when he feels the influence of
a friend's hand." When Marie teases him, and makes two glasses
that can give a mournful note "sing", he begs her to stop, saying: "That is too sad. It makes me think of Hoffmann's tale
about the soul that was prisoned in a violin."

At the Blanckenburg's house, one day, he meets Johanna von
Puttkamer. She has none of Marie's charm; she is small, dark,
and slight; Italian in type. She has a cordial expression; the
ardour of her heart shines forth from her grey eyes, and radiates
from her enthusiastic personality. What distinguishes her from
Marie is her grace, her naturalness, and also the violence of her
feelings. She cannot think twice, but is easily carried away by

the passion that animates her frail and delicate body. She is one of those girls who cling to any decision that has once been taken. She would devote herself unreservedly to the man to whom she gave her love, asking nothing from him, happy in her self-sacrifice. What she needs is a man who will guide her; what she offers is a port well sheltered from the wind.

The much courted monster seems to her the guide she wants, and she is regardless of his lack of faith. Later perhaps she may have had a temporary misgiving, for Marie writes to her: "Your contradiction certainly did not offend him, for he loves frankness; and as for your prophecy that he will change his views — at bottom he already thinks so himself. But in such a nature, the struggle towards the light goes neither quickly nor easily, and for a long time is hidden from human eyes."

With these words, Marie strikes home in her description. She pictures him as a frozen stream, in which the thaw can only come slowly and by force; she has recognised how enigmatical is his nature. Symbolically, this is what drives him to take office on the dikes. He wants to listen to the Elbe in its spring shudderings; to watch the huge stream as it breaks its way through; to guide its waters, just as he will guide political movements, and just as he will guide himself.

Bismarck's removal from Pomerania to the Elbe was something more than a mere change of residence. Old Ferdinand had died at length, despite sherry and port; and thereupon the younger son, now thirty, took over the estate of Schönhausen in the Elbe valley. He let Kniephof on lease. This was the place where he had grown up, where for centuries none but Bismarcks had held sway; and he was therefore sad at heart about the matter. "The whole neighbourhood of meadows, water, and bare oak-trees, seemed in a mood of gentle melancholy when, after a lot of troublesome business had been got through, towards sunset I paid farewell visits to various places that were dear to me, and where I had often passed the time in sad reveries. At the spot where I had designed to build a new house, a horse's skeleton was lying on the ground, and from the mere shape of the bones I was able to

recognise the remains of my faithful Caleb, who for seven long
years, spiritedly or dispiritedly, swiftly or sluggishly, had borne
me on his back across mile after mile of country. I thought of the
heaths and the fields, the lakes, the houses and the human beings
therein, past which we had trotted together; my life was unrolled
before me in retrospect, right back to the days when as a child
I had played here.

"The rain was rustling upon the undergrowth, and I stared
for a long time towards the dull red sunset, my heart overflowing
with sadness and regret for the sluggish indifference and the blind
search for pleasure in which I had squandered the abundant gifts
of youth, intelligence, property, and health — had squandered
them purposelessly and fruitlessly. . . . I was extremely depressed when I got back to the house. Every tree I had planted,
every oak under whose whispering foliage I had lain in the grass,
seemed to reproach me for handing it over to a stranger; even
more plainly did all the labouring folk reproach me, assembled
now in front of the door to express their sorrow at their present
distress and their anxiety concerning their future under the
tenant farmer. . . . They told me how long they had served my
father; the older men among them were actually weeping, and I
myself was not far from tears."

When we read these heartfelt phrases, some of which, poetically
worded as they are, remind us of Goethe's farewell to his summer-
house, we cannot but ask ourselves why Bismarck was leaving
Kniephof; whether shortness of money had driven him away, or
whether the wish for a better habitation had prompted this surprising change of residence. Nothing of the kind! His motive was
ambition.

For at the time of his father's death, when he came into close
contact with the circle of which an account was given in the last
few pages, when he reached the age of thirty and felt that the time
of his adventurous youth was over, there arose in him a new, we
may say the first, wish to exercise a wider influence; and this wish,
with trifling vacillations, was to dominate him for half a century
to come. As circumstances would have it, the impulse directed

itself towards public life, first of all towards the sphere in which he was to reign in virtue of his heritage. His plans could be realised more quickly in Saxony; there work in the office of the dike-board offered an opening. This fact awakened a slumbering sense of kinship with the fate of the river whose crises he was to describe so eloquently — a sense he was deliberately to transform into deeds. From a dike on the Elbe it was not far to the Landtag; and the circle of the pietists was closely interconnected with Potsdam. When one of the pietists, at about this time, wished to facilitate his reentry into State service, as royal commissary in East Prussia, Bismarck, writing to his brother from Schönhausen, said he was disinclined to accept.

" No doubt I could get promotion in the East Prussian service; but it is my misfortune that every post I might obtain seems desirable to me until I occupy it, and that then I find it burdensome and a bore. That is what would happen were I to accept this offer. If I go to East Prussia, I shall have to refuse the office of dike-reeve here, which the government has already promised me. . . . But the dike service, in conjunction with work in the Landtag, to which I can almost certainly secure election, will give me plenty to do without cutting me off from the administration of my estates. . . . My fixed idea is to pay off some of the debts first of all." At the same time he emphasises his prospects of becoming Landrat. The present occupant of the post, whose health is obviously failing, is not likely to last more than three or four years longer; he says he has medical opinion about this. "On Saturday there is to be a ball in Rathenow. I don't think I shall go, because I have no gloves suitable for a man in mourning."

Thus he has calculated the chances, has got a promise of the reversion of the post of dike-reeve, is sure of election to the Landtag, is informed as to how long the present Landrat is likely to survive. Having made his preparations, he manages to get the extant dike-reeve dismissed for being absent without leave! Simultaneously with sending in his application for the post, he tries to ensure that the contribution from his own estate to the river conservancy board shall be reduced, digs up an old regulation to the effect that the dike-reeve shall be some one whose landed possessions give him a direct interest in the post, and discovers that, centuries before, an exchange of estates relevant to this subject had been forced upon his ancestors. These things are done to strengthen his own claims to the position. All is perfectly legal; all will redound to the advantage of his neighbours, whom he will help by taking the office out of incapable hands. At the same time it is all done in order to protect his own property, to reduce his own expenses, to make his own name widely and favourably known throughout the circle. His ultimate object, of course, is to become Landrat and deputy.

Energy, capacity, realism, and will-to-power — these are the characteristic qualities which Bismarck displays in his first political activity, thereby wresting speedy and infallible success, which success in its turn becomes a motive for new and ever new activities.

VII

A massive and dignified building is the ancestral mansion of Schönhausen, standing among stately limes and oaks. It is not a castle, but is a considerable edifice; and one who looks out of its windows feels himself well born. Writing an impressionist sketch to a friend, Bismarck says: "When I look out of the window through the smoke rising from the cigar in my left hand, look due north, to the right and the left I see, first of all, old lime trees, then an old-fashioned garden with trimmed hedges, gods carved out of sandstone, box-trees, dwarf fruit trees; behind these, a great extent of wheat-fields (unfortunately they are not mine); then, a league or so away, on the high bank of the Elbe, the little town of Arneburg. . . . From the windows in the southern gable, I should see the towers of Tangermünde; and westward, in the mist, the cathedral of Stendal. Within doors, I see a large three-storeyed house, with ancient walls, very thick; hangings of leather and linen with oriental designs and landscapes; rococo furniture covered with faded silk; and, speaking generally, an equipment which suggests considerably more wealth than the present owner of the place has inherited from his forefathers."

The first thing the new master wants in the old house is a wife. During the last years of his father's life, this must have been a perpetual theme of discussion at Kniephof; for thence, and from Otto on his travels, sceptical reports came again and again to the father. "I have made the acquaintance of Louise C. Occasionally she looks perfectly beautiful, but she will soon lose her complexion and grow red in the face. I was really in love with her for four-and-twenty hours; and I should be glad enough if she were to marry Meier and come to live at Selow." When he is in Norderney, he ticks the ladies off: Countess Reventlow, "who has fine teeth and a coppery colour, and will some day become a stately canoness"; Frau von Reitzenstein, "whose well-grown daughter is considered the belle of the place, and would make a splendid wife to go long walks with; she is tall and slender, with good 'understandings' — a girl from the Mosel, no common vintage, neither cold nor sour."

Every adjective shows the connoisseur of woman. We see him sizing them up like horses trotted out before a prospective buyer; he is much more interested in their birth than their wealth, for Bismarck never wanted to marry for money. Now, in Schönhausen, the problem grows more acute. He writes to his sister: "The devil take me, I really must marry; this becomes perfectly clear to me. I feel very lonely now that father has gone; and in muggy weather I grow melancholy, and more ready to fall in love. There is no help for it, I shall have in the end to marry H. E. Every one here wants me to. . . . True, she leaves me cold, but then so do all the others. . . . I must confess that I have still some vestiges of fondness for the wheelwright's wife (unfaithful huzzy!) — a weakness on whose account I am beginning to respect myself. It is a good thing when one cannot change one's loves as often as one's shirt, even though one does the latter very seldom!"

At the date of these plainly worded admissions (which are quite in the Junker's style), and at the very time of the love affair here alluded to, he has been spending a year or more in

the society of the pietists. Indeed, he had made the acquaintance
of Johanna von Puttkamer a year before his father's death. It
would seem, then, that he is very little disposed to let these inner
conflicts exert any influence upon his mode of life; but the
Blanckenburgs had not ceased to think of the couple who, at their
wedding feast, had been placed together by design; so they invited Bismarck and Johanna to join them on a summer excursion
in the Harz Mountains. No doubt they were not free from
thoughts of saving Otto's soul by marrying him to the pious girl,
and of seeing her well placed in a union with the impious nobleman. Blanckenburg, indeed, had commended the young woman to
his friend before the two had met. "She is very clever, extremely
musical, . . . exceptionally lovable; an able, more than able,
student, most original, with a serious and pious mind; . . . she
plays waltzes with the most sublime and childlike simplicity, better
than any one else I have heard. Come and make her acquaintance.
If you do not want her, I shall take her as second wife."

This description is shrewdly designed to influence Bismarck,
for it is free from the overstrained enthusiasm in which the writer
is apt to indulge. Marie's description is more exalted, and full
of secret pride: "A piquant flower, and one which no blight has
ever touched. . . . There is nothing more beautiful about her
aspect than her eyes and her long black hair; she looks quite
grown up, talks freely, is witty and cheerful with every one, man
or woman, and does not make the distinction we do between interesting and uninteresting. . . . A girl to the depths of her
being; . . . pure, limpid, clear — like blue sea-water."

What distinguishes Johanna from her pious friends is a certain
piquant acerbity, which bridges the transition to irony; across
this bridge, the confirmed sceptic draws near to her. Had she not
been original and musical, had she not been able to play waltzes
and to talk without restraint, had she not been on an easy footing
with every one, her purity alone would not have influenced him.
What ultimately made him decide to marry Johanna was neither
her religious faith nor her intelligence, it was the serene but still
unminted gold of a human heart possessing all the powers of self-

sacrifice that were lacking to himself; it was her power of passionate absorption in anything she had once undertaken. She would not be a mere daughter to him, although nine years younger in age and a hundred years younger in experience. She would be a companion: one who would leave his leadership undisputed; would accept his outlook; would always be ready to share his sorrows and troubles, to join him in his mockery and his contempt; would be less proud than he, but hardly less defiant; gentle at home, unyielding in a struggle, tuneful but demure; like himself, full of passion against an enemy, and, none the less, harmonious as he had never been.

On this excursion in the Harz Mountains, they drew rapidly together, "each of them full of wonder in the growing knowledge of the other." Meanwhile, Bismarck was having quiet conversations with Marie, a maturer woman than Johanna, abler and more sensuous. There are echoes of these conversations in her diary: " A lifelong solitary, searching for peace, trying all things, vainly." This is the complete resignation of a man who knows that his choice may lead to happiness, and yet must betoken renunciation. Such are the feelings with which Bismarck enters upon marriage.

For the rest, there were moonshine and cheerfulness; owls hooting in the Wolfschlucht; he often presses champagne on his companions, pays for everything, organises everything. After the return home, influenced by further letters from Blanckenburg, he begins to read the Bible, speaks reservedly about God, and writes in a letter concerning Johanna that he is not yet sure of himself. This letter, which was destroyed with the others, was written in Latin, in case through indiscretion it should fall into the lady's hands.

Suddenly influenza breaks out in Pomerania, and kills Marie's brother. Next the mother falls sick. Marie acts as nurse. During the nocturnal vigils, she writes in intimate terms to Bismarck. She begs him to come quickly; the mother dies; he comes; there are long conversations, and evening prayers; he will not kneel with the others, but is in a melting mood. Then Marie herself

takes the infection, has fainting fits, sends for him, tells him that
now it is time for his conversion, more than time. Here is a second
woman who is praying for him on her deathbed. His spirit is
already touched, and will not this finally decide his course? His
obstinacy yields. He prays for the first time in fifteen years,
"without pondering about the reasonableness of the prayer",
prays that his friend's life may be spared.

With amazement he learns how serene are the dying woman
and her husband, who regard the death as nothing more than a
premature setting out on a journey, and are confident that they
will meet again. Marie dies. It is a blow for the friend who had
loved her. His pain is purely egoistic. "My first sorrow was a
passionate and selfish realisation of the loss I had suffered. . . .
This is really the first time I have lost any one through death;
any one whose departure left an unexpected vacancy in my life.
The loss of one's parents is on a different footing. . . . The relationship between child and parent is not usually so intimate. . . .
Such a sense of vacancy, the idea that I should never again see
one so dear to me, one who had become necessary to me, one of
whom I had seen far too little — this was so new to me that I
found it very difficult to believe in the reality of what had happened, and the whole incident seemed incredible." The next time
he sees his widowed friend, he utters momentous words, saying:
"This is the first person I have lost whose heart, I am confident,
beat warmly for me. . . . Now I believe in eternal life — or, if
there is no such thing, the world was not made by God."

In the most natural way in the world, his anguish has moved
him to prayer, as it may move any one, believer or not. He had
actually prayed "in the train", as Blanckenburg quaintly remarks. In the most natural way in the world, amid these scenes
of deep feeling and of mourning, influenced by the dying woman's
request and by the friendship of the survivors, did Bismarck turn
to God. Even now, he makes a typical Bismarckian reservation.
The sceptic leaves a way of retreat open. The cold clarity with
which at the age of sixteen he had justified his relinquishment of
prayer, has not wholly disappeared in these thoughtful moods of

the grown man; and in what he says to his friend he raises a doubt as to whether, after all, God made the world—which, Spinoza notwithstanding, seems to him extremely doubtful.

The evening before his departure, while still in his friend's house, Bismarck writes a letter in which he is supposed to have summarised what had happened, and stated how deep an impression these events had made on his mind. Thereupon Blanckenburg, with embraces and tears, is said to have exclaimed: "To-day you make me incredibly happy!" These declarations, which to Bismarck come naturally enough (seeing that he is impressionable by disposition) in view of the moods prevailing in the house and the experiences of the last few weeks, betray in the background a longing for the conquest of the maiden whose excessively pious father is not merely a pietist but a quietist. Thus his avowal of belief in God is not a deception, or is at most self-deception. Bismarck had nothing material to gain by this marriage, nor was he driven by passion to possess the girl. He wanted her as member of a particular circle, one which had become to him a second home. Her faith had been strange to him, and had become acceptable under certain conditions. Although in his inner man the prayer of a beloved woman was still echoing, a woman he had loved and never possessed, his feelings now turned towards another woman, whom he looked upon as likely to make a good companion, and therefore wished to marry.

A few weeks later, he met her once more in the Blanckenburgs' house, made his declaration, and was immediately accepted. On the way home, in an inn at Stettin, he wrote to Johanna's father asking her hand in marriage.

With the art of the born diplomatist, the letter is written to suit the pious mood of the recipient. Never in his life did Bismarck call so often on the name of God as in this epistle, and in the second one he wrote to Herr von Puttkamer; he even introduced ecclesiastical phraseology quite foreign to his ordinary style. He knew that he must make open admission of his errors and of his previous unbelief, if his present faith were to find credence; and although all he said may have been true, it was none the less shrewdly fashioned to promote the success of his design. In this respect, it was like the complaint he sent in against his predecessor as dike-reeve. While he was speaking of God, his tone was humble: "At that time God did not hear my prayer, and yet he did not reject me, for never since then have I lost the capacity of praying to him, and I feel, if not peace of mind, at least confidence and courage such as I had long ceased to know. . . . I am convinced that, thanks to my invincible frankness and my loyalty to that which I have disclosed to none but yourself, God will vouchsafe success to the righteous man."

When he comes to speak of himself, he assumes a prouder tone: "I shall not dwell upon my feelings and designs in regard to your daughter, for the step that I am now taking speaks more loudly and more eloquently than words. Nor shall I further my cause with you by promises, for you know better than I do the untrustworthiness of the human heart, and my only guarantee for the welfare of your daughter is to be found in my prayer for the blessing of the Lord."

The pious father is extremely reluctant to give his daughter to a man "of whom he has heard much evil and very little good." Upon receipt of his non-committal answer, Bismarck assumes the offensive, suddenly turns up at Reinfeld, finds "an inclination to drag out the negotiations indefinitely, . . . so that who knows which direction they might have taken, had I not turned to my betrothed at the very first sight of her, and, by a resolute embrace, to the speechless amazement of her parents, promptly put matters on a different footing, so that within five minutes everything was satisfactorily settled." Here is the real Bismarck. By promptitude and personal courage he quickly carries through what has long been prearranged in his mind. Surprise attack was always the technique of this statesman.

Now he throws all his amiability into the scale, instantly makes a conquest of the household, drinks champagne and hock with the old gentleman, waltzes with his betrothed while Herr von Puttkamer plays the piano. Even the mother, a difficult woman, highly cultured, soon "took the bearded heretic to her excellent heart"—

for just now he had grown a beard. It is true that he has long conversations with his betrothed about religious matters, but thanks to her natural simplicity he is free from the sense of oppression which harassed him at the Blanckenburgs', and he is delighted when she says to him with a smile: "I should have given you your congé had not God shown his grace to you, or at least given you a peep of it through the keyhole!" This metaphor of a peep through the keyhole was truer than she would have liked. She did not know what Otto had written to his brother:

"In matters of faith, we differ somewhat, more to her distress than to mine. Still, the difference is not so great as you might imagine, for many external and internal happenings have wrought changes in me of late, so that now (a new thing in me, as you know) I feel justified in numbering myself among those who believe in the Christian religion. Although in respect of some of the doctrines, perhaps those which Christians as a rule consider the most important, I am — so far as I am clear concerning my own views — by no means fully reconciled with the Christian outlook, nevertheless, tacitly as it were, a sort of Treaty of Passau has been signed between myself and Johanna. Besides, I like pietism in women, and detest members of the female sex who make a parade of enlightenment." Need he speak more plainly? We see in his utterances, the tastes of a connoisseur of woman, echoes of his experiences with the female heart, and also his old animus against his mother. If he has reached the other side of Jordan, it is on a rather fragile bridge. He himself describes the whole history of his "conversion" as a Treaty of Passau, that is to say as a mutual tolerance established between religious disputants. Pietism in women is to his taste, and therefore he is glad that his own wife is of that persuasion.

His general attitude towards his engagement is that of a man of the world. His letters to his brother and his sister have little to say about God, but a great deal about a knight-errant who is about to settle down at the domestic fireside: "For the rest, I think I am very fortunate, far more than I had hoped to be, for, to put the matter unemotionally, I am going to marry a woman of exceptional intelligence and rare nobility of spirit, who is at the same time extremely amiable and facile à vivre, more than any other woman I have ever known. . . . In a word, I am exceedingly well content; and I hope you, too, will be pleased." As regards money, she will bring him little, so he must see to the financial side. " Other details, such as the immeasurable astonishment of the natives, and the annoyance of the old ladies, . . . I will tell you by word of mouth. For the nonce I will merely ask you and Oscar to have a kindly feeling towards my future wife. Reinfeld is close to the Polish frontier; one hears the wolves and the natives howling all night; and in this and the six neighbouring circles, people are thick on the ground, eight hundred to the square league; Polish spoken here. A pleasant countryside." His own estate is only a few leagues away.

He is very much tickled at the amazement of the innumerable girl cousins, all of whom are somewhat affronted that they knew nothing of what was going on. Since he has been to court once or twice and is a travelled man, they agree in saying: "Well, we would rather have had some one else; still, he is a very distinguished person." His own friends are alarmed at the prospect of his becoming "pious", though he himself is not disturbed by this. During these first weeks (when, inspired by the will-to-believe but always influenced by his native scepticism, he zealously studies the Bible), he tells Blanckenburg, the converted converter, that he does not know whether Christ was the son of God or only a divine man; that he is dubious about the doctrine of the Fall; that a great many of the contradictions in the Bible are too much for him; that he is not yet settled in his mind. In one of his letters, he makes an obviously admiring comment on the devil, writing in such a way that Johanna is horrified.

VIII

The period of the engagement is used by him for the education of the woman of his choice. Never among Germans has a man of the world or a poet written more charmingly and brilliantly to any woman; and never did Bismarck write like this again. The letters show him at the climax of his humour and his knowledge, his fancy and his imagination, his finesse and his delicacy. With an unerring hand he gently guides her on to his own road; and, while he continues to provide fresh nutriment for her piety, while he allows her to congratulate herself on having tamed the savage, he himself slowly tames the country girl, who is really much wilder than he is, and much younger. This transformation is so remarkable that on one occasion she writes to the Mad Junker: "You are so fond of the formal, whereas I am so glad to disregard convention, if it can possibly be done."

At first she is a little afraid of boring him, and writes: " Do not look at me so sarcastically. . . . Very little is needed to make me shed floods of tears, and you must not do that. . . . Have patience with me, and await the coming of the spring and the results of your tilling." Then she suddenly remembers what a terrible man he is said to have been: " I expect you to show me all the fidelity of your heart. What if I deceive myself? What will happen then? Mistrust is the most dreadful thing in the world. . . . Your handwriting seems to me to have become more wilful than that of the old letters you have shown me. Is it so with your heart likewise, Otto? " Then she answers her own question in feminine fashion: " Never mind if it be so; I shall myself be all the more acquiescent, Beloved, and shall try to bend what I cannot break. But if, after all, you will not go my way, I shall quietly go yours." Thus in four months, with gentle force, he has brought her to complete surrender. When she wants him to read Jean Paul, or to wear a velvet coat (which he detests quite as much) she good-naturedly puts up with his No.

He is grateful to her for this self-surrender, and thanks her with all the cordiality of a man who has long been a solitary. Although before his engagement he had found in himself the elements requisite for an active and orderly life, although the turning-point in his career had come a year earlier, he lays all the credit for these changes to her account, and increases her self-satisfaction by his victories.

The first time he returns home after they are engaged he writes: "When I drove into the village, I felt (as never before) how delightful it is to have a home. . . . You can hardly conceive, Darling, with what hopeless lack of feeling I used to enter the house when I came back from a journey. . . . Never was the vacancy of my existence more evident to me than at such moments, until I became absorbed in a book (none of which could be gloomy enough for my mood); or mechanically went about my daily work. . . . Now, how differently do I look at everything; not only the things that concern you, the things which may or may not suit you (though for a couple of days I have been racking my brains to find the best place for your writing-table); my whole outlook on life is a new one, and I am keenly interested in my work as dike-reeve and other administrative details." Nevertheless, before he realises what he is doing, he has copied out for her two of Byron's gloomy poems, poems that cannot be gloomy enough for him, lengthy outpourings of melancholy. He writes beneath them: "All nonsense!" He sends them to her none the less.

In his second letter he is already, imperceptibly, beginning her education. She must work hard at her French, for otherwise she will be at a loss in good society. This is put most delicately and most charmingly, but he says it. Soon afterwards he tells her she must learn to ride. A few weeks later: "I am no longer interested in those utterly miserable English poems. . . . Now I watch a black cat playing with them in the sunshine, rolling them over and over like a ball, and I am glad to see this." All the same, he sends her some more transcripts from Byron; and in the next letter some French poems expressive of world weariness. With amazing self-deception, he adds: "You need not mind my reading them now; they no longer do me any harm."

Once, after quoting a poem, he gives free rein to the spirit of his earlier days: "Most congenial to me is the wish to become, in such a night, a sharer in the delight, a portion of the tempest of night; mounted on a runaway horse, to gallop down the rocks into the thunder of the Rhinefall." Hardly has the girl, not without alarm, grasped the meaning of these words from her fiancé, these reminiscences of his wild youth, when suddenly she finds that—an accomplished horseman—he has reined in his steed at the top of the rocky descent, has laughed the whole mood out of window amid the smoke of his cigar, ironically writing: " A pleasure of this sort can only be indulged once in a lifetime."

Thus full of contradictions is the heart of Otto von Bismarck.

When he describes his actual doings, he is more cheerful. For days he writes in the mood of a midwife who is always awaiting the birth; writes of the movement of the Elbe, of the provisions that have been made to master the ice when it breaks up. When he stands in the water half the night, in command of these under-takings, he is enjoying himself. Bismarck always enjoys himself when he is dealing with the great forces of nature. "Good-bye! The clashing fragments of ice are calling me, playing the Pappen-heimer March, and the chorus of mounted peasants is singing. Why don't the fragments of ice really sing? How lovely that would be, and how poetical! It is like new life to me that this weary season of waiting is over, and the real work has begun. . . . Je t'embrasse, your slave, Bismarck." What a tempo, what joy in life! Then comes a postscript: " Send me the envelope of the letter which took five days to reach you. I will lodge a complaint about the matter in Berlin." Next he tells her about the great night when the ice had broken up. " The floes were clashing against one another, riding on one another, heaping themselves up as high as a house, and from time to time jamming into a dam across the Elbe. The waters were pent up for a time, until at length they swept everything madly before them. Now all the giants have been broken to pieces in the struggle, and the water is thickly covered with small masses of floating ice, which still clash to-gether angrily as the river carries them down like broken chains towards the open sea."

In such cataclysms of nature, which are in truth reflections of his own soul, we hear the revolutionist in Bismarck sounding a battle-cry, and we realise that his lineage alone is responsible for making him a legitimist.

Vigorous and full of life as he is in these hours of battle, when the elements are threatening, and when he imposes his will on them — indoors, he is only much moved when, with wise statesmanship, he is able to accommodate a dispute. Enthusiastically he reports:

"This morning I was extraordinarily pleased when I was able to settle a dispute among forty-one quarrelsome peasants, each of whom was infuriated with the other forty, and each of whom would gladly have paid thirty talers if thereby he could have inflicted ten talers loss on any of the others. My predecessor as dike-reeve had been dealing with the matter for four years, and had probably found it a lucrative source of income. . . . After four hours, I had persuaded them to come to terms; and the moment when, with the signed document in my pocket, I got back into my carriage, was one of the few joyful ones I have as yet had as the outcome of my official position. . . . This incident has shown me once more that true pleasure in an official position can only be expected when one works in a circle where one comes into personal contact with the people whom one rules. As president or minister of State, one never comes into contact with human beings, but only with ink and paper.

"When I consider how little even the greatest and mightiest statesman is able, in his official capacity, to promote happiness and lessen misery; when I become convinced that neither a minister nor a king can close his eyes in the conviction (unless, of course, he be a self-deluded fool) that in the long run he has spared any of those under his care a sorrow, or brought any one of them a joy the more — then I cannot but think of Lenau's melancholy poem, *Der Indifferentist*. . . . Our mortal life can only be fruitful for our own souls. . . . Whether we can help others than ourselves to earthly well-being, is, after all, a matter of indifference in comparison with this existence of our own at whose end stands eternity. After thirty years, all has turned to dust, which is blown about through the millenniums that follow; and to those who are now dead, what does it matter whether, in life, they were joyful or sorrowful?"

Look at him sitting there in his carriage, with his signed agreement. He is thirty-two years old, and perhaps thoroughly content with himself and the world for the first time in his life. He is thinking about the forty-one peasants, of what had made them quarrel with one another and hate one another, and how he had come and looked into their souls, how he had thought for them, and had in the end managed to bring them to terms with one another. Then, in place of these peasants, States and nations flit before his eyes, and he wonders what a statesman may feel, a minister or a king, who has done on the large scale what he to-day has been able to do on the small. Once more he glimpses the detested by-ways of bureaucracy, the sight of which distorts the vision of every one in Prussia; and he feels afraid of his own devilish will-to-power, forces his gaze back to narrow horizons, whistles the happiness of his fellows down the wind, and, indifferent once more, drives up to the ancestral door.

At home, he has plenty of time on his hands. He spends it in writing sheet after sheet to Johanna, laying before her his opinions, his feelings, and his doubts; delving into his earlier life to find anything that can suitably be recounted to her. He tells her of the correspondence with her namesake and predecessor in his love, and she trembles as she wonders whether a man can love so ardently twice. He tells her of the long letter he had written to his cousin when he resigned State service, and adds, after this interval of a decade: "In the main, I still subscribe to the views I then expressed regarding the futility of our State service. . . . Sometimes, even now, when one of my former fellow-students has quickly made a success of his career, I am mortified at the thought that I might have done the same thing. But I always console myself with the reflection that man seeks happiness vainly when he seeks it outside himself." While writing this with perfect sincerity, he is vigorously promoting his candidature to the Landtag, and pulling strings to secure the appointment as Landrat.

In a sovereign and gently parental fashion, he deals with her doubts and her sentiments: "Why should you weep so bitterly, my angel? . . . Tell me why? (I am a man of the Old March, one of those who want to know the reasons for things. I was brought up in Pomerania from the age of two to the age of seventeen, and therefore am sometimes slow to understand a joke.) Tell me why you should weep?" When, after his visit, she writes to him a letter full of yearning, he replies: "You must learn to be thankful for the joys you have had, and not, like a little child, to cry for more directly one of them comes to an end!" Thus does he, who has never been satisfied in his life, preach content to this ardent girl. If she is surprised at the number of her wooers, this surprise affronts him, mortifies his pride. He says that she should rather look contemptuously at any one who does not recognise her value, and should say to such a person: "'Monsieur! Le fait est, que Mr. de B. m'aime, ce qui prouve, que tout individu mâle, qui ne m'adore pas, est un butor sans jugement'. . . . You should not be so modest, now that I, after wandering for ten years among the rose gardens of North Germany, have, at long last, plucked a buttercup." The inborn pride of the Junker, who as yet has done nothing to prove his worth, leads him to consider that the woman of his choice is by that very choice given precedence over all women in the world.

He now reads the Bible often, and is fond of quoting it. His attitude towards marriage is thoroughly Lutheran. He is always saying: "We must be one heart and one flesh; must suffer together, and express our thoughts in unison. Do not hide anything from me. You will not always have joyful experiences in contact with my long thorns. . . . We must be content to scratch our hands on them together, even till the blood comes."

He gives her vivid descriptions of the old families of servants and handicraftsmen on his estate, and tells her how their ancestors served his. "I find it very difficult to dismiss any one who has once served me. . . . I cannot deny that I am proud of such a persistence of the conservative principle here at home, where my forefathers lived for centuries in the same rooms, where they were born and where they died; where the pictures on the walls of the mansion and of the church show them in their clanking armour; the long-haired cavaliers of the days of the Thirty

BISMARCK IN 1847

From a lithograph by Mittag, after a sketch by Bürde

Years War, with their pointed beards; men in full-bottomed wigs, with red-heeled shoes, trampling noisily over the boards; the pig-tailed cavalrymen who fought for Frederick the Great; at last the effeminate sprig of the same line who now prostrates himself at the feet of a black-haired maiden."

Another time, the Junker is struck with the seamy side of his conversion. The new-made Christian decides that he must pay more heed than of yore to the poor on his estate. "When I think how a taler can help such a hungry family to better fare for weeks, it almost seems to me like robbing the poor who are a-hungered and a-cold that I should spend thirty talers in coming to visit you. Of course I could devote that sum to the poor, and still make the journey. But that would leave matters as they were; double the amount, tenfold the sum, would still serve merely to allay a fraction of the suffering. . . . As a sophist, therefore, I must appease myself by saying that my journey is not an extravagance undertaken for my own pleasure; it is a duty I owe my betrothed. . . . The amount the journey costs me must certainly be given to the poor! This is a very ticklish problem. How far am I justified in devoting to my own pleasure what God has entrusted to my administration, while there are still, in my immediate neighbourhood, persons who are ailing from cold and hunger, persons who have pawned their bedding and their clothing, so that they cannot go out to work? 'Sell that thou hast, and give to the poor, and follow me!' But how far may not that lead us? The poor are more numerous than all the treasures of the king would suffice to feed. Well, we shall see what will come of it."

On this occasion, when his young faith is put to a practical test, Bismarck for the first (and, with so much Christian sentiment, for the last) time impinges upon a problem against which, in days to come, he will be shipwrecked because of his failure to understand it. True, his sophism is a jest, one which does not convince his own intelligence. Still, that he should talk of his personal expenditure as a robbery of the hungry poor; that, were it only for five minutes, he should hesitate to indulge in the

pleasures proper to his station (pleasures which he is only in a
position to enjoy because those forefathers of his, pictured on
the walls, were robber knights) — is all new in Bismarck, is
foreign to his disposition; and, because foreign, it is transient.
Certainly this lord of the soil is willing enough to care for the
underlings who dwell thereon. But never can the Junker understand or tolerate that such people should fight for their own hand,
or should deem themselves entitled to a charter guaranteeing them
the right to a better life. For the very reason that, in reality, he
never became the true Christian he is reputed to have become
owing to his " conversion ", Bismarck was never, in his subsequent
life, able to understand or accept the social mission of his epoch.

Since he wrestles with his betrothed more than with himself on
behalf of the Bible and the faith, pathetically to-day, banteringly
to-morrow, we are always moved by what he writes on these
matters, for here he is always sincere. He has just been discussing Biblical criticism, and then suddenly breaks out: " Who the
devil is Pauline, another cousin I have never heard of before?
Apropos of the devil, I cannot find in the Bible any passage where
we are forbidden to take the name of the devil in vain. If you
know of one, please give me chapter and verse." There, in very
truth, we see the Knight, Death, and the Devil, riding on their
way together. His forefathers, he writes, were not true Christians. " Nor did my mother accept the faith. Did you ever hear
the story of the Frisian chief who was about to be baptised? He
asked where his unbelieving forefathers were. When told that
they were all damned, he refused to be baptised, saying: ' Where
my forefathers are, there would I fain be also.' " After this remarkable lapse into paganism, he goes on bravely: " I only introduced that as an historical instance, and I lay no stress on it."

The superstition that is native to the man moves him more than
religious faith. In all the phases of his life, right on into the
closing years, Bismarck used to calculate the age at which he
must die, and then, quoting a figure, would, like a statesman,
put his alternatives before God. " If I do not die after x years,
I must do this or that after y years." Or he writes to his be-

trothed: "You will hardly believe how superstitious I am. Just when I had opened your letter, the great clock suddenly stopped at three minutes past six — an old English pendulum clock which my grandfather had had from youth upwards, and which has been standing on the same spot for seventy years. . . . Please write to me quickly to tell me that you are perfectly well and cheerful."

The springs of his being murmur most plainly when he writes lengthy monologues in diary form, giving no thought to the recipient of his letter, absorbed in the contemplation of his own melancholy moods. In these passages he uses the stately metaphors of his virile speech. "It is doubtless profoundly characteristic of human nature. . . . One who lays stress upon the futility, the nullity, the pain, which dominate our life here below, will command more attention than one who touches upon the less mighty elements which are transiently aroused in us by the easily fading flowers of untroubled serenity. . . . That which is imposing here on earth . . . is always akin to the fallen angel; who is beautiful, but lacks peace; is great in his plans and efforts, but never succeeds; is proud, and melancholy."

Here are mirrored the great reflexions of his ego. On such evenings, when in the lofty room he sits alone writing his letters, there rises from the depths of his soul some such phrase as the one just quoted, modelled in the grand style, like a poet's confession. When morning comes, and the day calls him, when the world and its battles summon, the hereditary knight awakens. Now he speaks of Byron's verses on grief, which are full of such nocturnal moods, as "a cowardly poem, to which I contrapose the verse of the rider's song:

'Unless your life you set at stake,
Your life you cannot hope to win.'

"I interpret this couplet as follows: 'With sublime trust in God, set spurs to your horse, and let the wild courses of life gallop with you across country, risking your neck, but fearless; since you have, one day or another, to part from everything dear to you on earth, though not for ever. . . . ' Meanwhile, I will have nothing to do with Mr. Grief."

IX

Like a blood-horse in the stable, which hears the sound of galloping without and longs to join in the hunt, does Bismarck feel when he learns that the king of Prussia intends to form a united Landtag out of the eight provincial Landtags; that this united Landtag is to be summoned to Berlin in order, at length, to discuss the terms of the constitution which the present king's father had solemnly promised the people after the War of Liberation. This was the first true parliament in German history. The thoughts of the proud Junker in his youth seemed about to be fulfilled. The signs indicated that Prussia was to become that State with " a free constitution ", the lack of which, when Otto von Bismarck was twenty-three, had induced him to withdraw from public life. Now, when the great moment had come, he was not to participate! If he were to have a seat in the united Landtag in Berlin he must have a seat and voice in Magdeburg. That was the prospect, more than all else, which had lured him from Pomerania, had induced him to undertake energetic work in the assembly of the Ritterschaft. But his peers had only appointed this youngest of the Saxon Junkers as a substitute deputy to the Landtag, should a vacancy occur there.

Now he sits at home in Schönhausen, reading how the representatives of Prussia had, as the centre of public attention, met for the first time in a sort of family diet. In heart and brain, he feels the stirring to action, on one side or the other; there in Berlin are his seniors, all unfortunately in perfect health, who cut him off from his place in the sun. Well, he must make it his business to unseat one of them. Bismarck contends that a certain baron who has just become a lord lieutenant, is no longer entitled to sit as deputy. He sends in his protest on this matter to his friends in Berlin. They shrug their shoulders, and answer by asking him why he had left Pomerania. In angry mood, Bismarck goes to see his betrothed, and, resigning himself, laughs the whole thing to scorn.

Then (at last!) one of the Saxon knights in Berlin falls sick. Even though the man gets better, Bismarck's friends induce him to withdraw in the substitute-deputy's favour. No doubt Bismarck himself had a hand in the game, for he declared that it was his "most heart-felt wish to become a member of the Landtag." He hastened to Berlin, and entered the hall of assembly. It was in May 1847, and Otto von Bismarck was thirty-two years old.

Here he finds all the provinces from the Rhine to the Memel represented; the first symbol of a united Prussia. Yet what animates the leading intelligences in this hall is not the thought of Prussia but of Germany. All men of spirit, all who looked towards the future, were in those days liberal in sentiment, and full of a longing for German unity. The king, who also now seems smitten with the great ideal of united Germany, that ideal which his father had detested, is supported in this by the people, and by an overwhelming majority; but the pillars of the throne are still exclusively Prussian in sentiment. In the united Landtag, out of five hundred members, only seventy are conservatives, and not one of these seventy is a champion of united Germany.

Bismarck felt himself isolated. His social position made him wish to side with the king, but his personal sentiments from youth upwards had been antagonistic to the liberals. The result was that he could not make common cause with either of the two parties. The basic elements of his nature — pride, courage, and hatred — were inflamed to passion. In the third sitting, when the proposal to found an agricultural bank with a State guarantee was under discussion, and the conservatives were opposing the scheme, Bismarck made his first speech in the assembly, defending the government against the conservatives, and the conservatives against the liberals. This maiden speech was an attack, and the attack was delivered in two directions at once. Contemptuously and passionately he writes to his betrothed: "It is strange how much confidence orators show, as compared with their capacity; and to note with what shameless self-satisfaction they venture to make their futile speeches in so great an assembly. . . . The business moves me far more than I had expected." Again he speaks of "this political excitement which grips me much more strongly than I had anticipated."

Never before, not even in the days when he had been ardently in love, had Bismarck put his scepticism so thoroughly to sleep; never before had men or things made so strong an appeal to his interests. Why is he so deeply moved to-day? Not because of the problems under debate, since he cares little about the peasants, and whether they can or cannot secure credit on advantageous terms. Thoughts of Prussia will never give him a bad night, and thoughts of Germany still less. What stirs his pulses is that at length he is upon the battlefield, is in the arena where he can fight in the grand style. When he is about to set out for the meeting of the Landtag, he writes again and again to his betrothed, with perfect seriousness: "Now I must go to the battle." Hitherto his self-esteem had found expression only in contempt for his fellows, which had secured vent in mocking letters, or at most in a few duels; there had been no reverberations; his intense vital energy, his extraordinary keenness of understanding, had not yet known the stimulus of competition. Too proud to become an official, too independent to become a soldier, lord only over peasants, and supreme in a society where a man of his parts could reign without effort, Bismarck had, so far, met no worthy antagonist. — Now, at length, he has discovered the platform on which fighting is worth while. He does not champion any specific ideals; he does not strive to realise specific plans of economic or political reform. He simply runs atilt against persons and groups. To be a representative of the people means, for him, to unsheathe his sword.

His first long speech is made at the fourth sitting he attends. "A man at the beginning of the thirties, tall and strongly built, his head firmly set upon broad shoulders, his face distinguished though not finely chiselled, mobile without inertness, firm without stiffness. He had a fresh-coloured, rounded face, with red whiskers; he radiated strength and health. The lower part of his face was somewhat fleshy, and he had a mocking smile; his nose was ill-formed; his eyes, surmounted by lofty brows, were clear, shrewd, and crafty; his forehead was straight, strongly moulded, and wide. The impression that here was a man who liked to live comfortably was outweighed by the sense he gave of intellectual confidence and controlled energy." Even though this description by an eyewitness was probably touched up with reference to the history of Bismarck's subsequent career, it still conveys a good general impression. Only one point has been forgotten. Both now and during subsequent decades there was a peculiarity which struck all hearers. This giant of a man spoke in a high-pitched, gentle, and faltering voice. The paradox brings us up against the whole enigma of his being. What led him to-day to the tribune?

A liberal nobleman (for there were such) ventured to say in the Landtag that in the year 1813 the Prussians had not been moved to take action by hatred for the conqueror, since so noble a people could not have known anything of national hatred; that things must have been better then than now, for then the government had based itself upon the people. Unexpressed in this remark is the thought, in vogue at the time, that the people had risen, in the War of Liberation, on behalf of its own liberation, and had in 1813 been fighting for popular government. Bismarck had written against any such idea. Now, in what appeared to be a sudden outburst of anger, though it had in truth been carefully prepared (the draft of what he said is extant), he exclaimed:

"It is absurd to suppose that any other reasons for the folk movement of 1813 need be sought, or that any other motives could be found, than the disgrace inflicted on us by the presence of an enemy in our land. It is, I think, an affront to the national honour for any one to assume that this maltreatment . . . was not sufficient to make people's blood boil, and to make hatred of the foreign invader overpower all other feelings. A man must lack a sense of honour if, in order to explain why he is up in arms against blows he has received, he speaks of doing a service to some third person, as if that were his only reason for self-defence."

Bismarck's friends listen to him unsympathetically. His first blow in the battle is a blow in the air, for the previous speaker had said nothing that could warrant the implication. All those

who had been volunteers in the War of Liberation, and all the
sons of such volunteers, even among the conservatives, were outraged. "Repeated expressions of dissent; turmoil," says the report. Another speaker replies, saying that what had stirred the
people to action was not hatred, but love of country; Herr von
Bismarck was too young to have any knowledge of the matter. —
A personal opponent! Now his heart beats joyfully, and once
more he mounts the tribune. "Much disturbance; the president
begs for quiet; renewed hooting." Thereupon he, the youngest
member of the assembly, turns his back upon it in its wrath, takes
a newspaper out of his pocket, and reads it to himself until quiet
is restored. Then, beginning to speak, he says it is quite true that
he was not alive in the days of the War of Liberation; yet his
unceasing regret at this fact would now be diminished by the
declaration he had heard to-day, to the effect that Prussia's en-
slavement had not been imposed by the foreigner but was a
domestic product.

A second blow in the air. "It seems incredible," said a friend
of his afterwards, "that so able a man should make himself so
ridiculous." A relative who had been awarded the iron cross, said
to the speaker: "Of course you were perfectly right; still, that
is not the sort of thing that ought to be said." Blanckenburg
remarked: "The lion which has here licked blood will soon roar
in a very different tone!" Sybel, then a young historian, criticised
the speech in his newspaper by saying that reforms and liberties
could not be separated from one another by such hair splitting.

Sybel was right. All the critics, including Blanckenburg, were
right. But not one of them was then able to recognise the inner
reason for his making such a splendid laughing-stock of himself;
namely that genius, at its first encounter with the crowd, always
has a collision with it. No doubt, he had prepared his speeches,
and that was the very reason why he lost his grip; no doubt, he
had failed to understand the laws of the epoch, and had set his
own friends against him. But there was something behind all this:
the force of hatred, directed far less against the French than
against those who repudiated hatred of the French; the courage

with which this unknown man, amid all the tumult, mounts the tribune a second time; the contempt with which he turns his back on the assembly! In the fight, he showed himself a champion fighter. Writing to his betrothed, he said: "Yesterday I aroused an unprecedented storm of disapproval by an utterance, which certainly lacked clarity, concerning the nature of the folk movement of 1813, an utterance which was an offence to the vanity of many of my own party, and naturally made the whole pack of the opposition howl in chorus against me. They were exceedingly bitter, perhaps for the very reason that I told them the truth. . . . My youth, and various other things, were cast in my teeth."

For the rest, his letters to Johanna, while no less affectionate than of yore, tend, increasingly, to assume the tone of a report. When she falls seriously ill, he prays for her, but remains "at his post"; promises to come and see her at Whitsuntide and fails to keep his word, writing: "I need not give any explanation of why I cannot come; . . . now that one vote may often enough turn the scale as regards matters of the utmost importance to our country. . . . It is a grief to me that a distance of fifty leagues or more separates the Landtag from you. . . . You women are strange people, and it is better to communicate with you by word of mouth than by letter." The marriage must not be postponed. Johanna need not trouble if she has to begin her wifehood as an invalid. "At Reinfeld I should be an idler. Until we are married, I cannot associate with you as freely as I should like."

Thus within a few months of the beginning of the engagement, the lover has begun to write in the resolute tone of a husband. The warmth of his affection is undiminished, but firmness and an assumption of leadership quickly become conspicuous; his will is already the ruling one. For the first time in his life, Bismarck begins to reverence time, speaks of being an idler; for the first time in his life, he regards something as really important. He actually declares that politics annul hunger and drive away sleep. "I am infuriated by the calumnious dishonesty of the opposition." Soon, however, he begins to long for the open country and for Johanna. After a fortnight's experience of the Landtag, he tells her that his interest in political affairs has increased to an unexpected pitch. Five lines later we read: " If I could but put my arms around you in good health, and take you with me to a hunting box far away in the green forest, where I should see no human face but yours! That is my hourly dream. The rattle of the political carriage grows more repulsive to me day by day. . . . If only I could be alone with you, enthusiastically contemplating nature. Perhaps it is only the perpetual spirit of contradiction in me which makes me long for whatever I have not got."

Here we have it once more. Quite recently, when he had no experience of politics or public life, he was telling his betrothed to prepare herself for the great world. Now, when he himself has entered that world, he raves about a hunting box in the forest. He knows the reason, names it himself, will bewail it for forty years to come. Here is the core of the matter, his enigmatical nature, which is never satisfied by any situation. He is Bismarck, the wanderer.

X

A restless man with a high-pitched voice, unsoldierly, vain, and unstable, caressed if not permeated by the grace of God — such was Frederick William IV. Already he had been nicknamed " the rope-dancer ", and certainly the part he played between people and throne was but a mummer's part. A romantic and cloudy enthusiast, in some ways overburdened with intelligence, he imagined at the outset that he would solve all difficulties, that he would be able at one and the same time to further the cause of the eastern powers and that of France, to work with the Holy Alliance and promote the unification of Germany, to serve both reaction and liberty. When, with a specious appearance of liberalism, he was fulfilling his father's solemn pledge, he said after the opening of this first Landtag: "You will certainly ruin the whole affair!" He was always missing opportunities when he ought to have given with lavish hand; had absolutely no understanding of the spirit of the age; was mulish and arrogant, and believed himself capable of playing the autocrat. These were premonitory signs of a mental disorder which was soon to be plain to all men's eyes, although he was to be allowed to work mischief to his country for nearly two decades before being officially pronounced insane. He gave the people an instrument, and then hurled threats at any one who dared play on it. While saying, "I bid you a cordial welcome", he would, in the same breath, forbid any one to approach him. He was the last but one of the kings of Prussia who could say: "There are things which only a king can know."

It would have been difficult, in those days, to find any one whose character could be more uncongenial to Herr von Bismarck-Schönhausen, than that of this monarch. Nevertheless, in the year 1847, Bismarck often went to court. He took part in the cruises on the Havel. "Before Easter we visited our friend the king, and the distinguished folk at court made much of me." The princes congratulated him on his speeches in the Landtag. The king refrained from doing so, wishing to avoid arousing doubts as to the independence of his youngest champion, and knowing Bismarck to be still independent. The king's advisers, Leopold and Ludwig von Gerlach, the general and the president (two brothers with a great knowledge of the world), were Bismarck's advisers also. They were twenty years older than he. Ludwig was a pietist, who had met Bismarck at the Thaddens', and liked him exceedingly; and Ludwig gave Bismarck the king's hints (that is to say, the king's wishes) for a great speech.

Thus there began to ripen in him, though at first only in broad outline, a twofold endeavour. He wished to be useful, both to the king, and to himself; to increase his own influence, by being loyal to the king; to improve his own prospects, by supporting the king's views; to lay the foundations for his own future power, by strengthening the king's power for the time being. In this first contact with the intimates of the throne, the inborn sentiments characteristic of a member of the knightly order were strengthened by ambition. They speedily became intensified into a legitimism which was appropriate to his origin, and which in later days he liked to refer to as " feudal sentiment."

This sentiment, which he subsequently cultivated for his own purposes, was deeply rooted; for, writing confidentially to his wife, he assumed a tone unusual to him: " Do not speak lightly of the king. We are both inclined to err in this respect. We should not talk of him irreverently any more than we should talk irreverently of our parents. Even when he makes mistakes, we must remember that we have sworn to show fealty and to pay homage to his flesh and blood." The seriousness of this reproof finds no parallel in the whole correspondence. He insists that his wife must honour his king, just as she insists that her husband must honour her God; throughout life he clung to this dogma of his, just as she clung to her dogma. The ancient memories of his ancestors are here surging up anew in his blood; memories of those ancestors who certainly defied their kings often enough, but never played them false: and, while he compares the kings to his parents, concerning whom he alone is entitled to harbour sceptical thoughts, his gaze is fixed on the great family, which lives in solitary grandeur above, while the rest of the people inhabit the lower floors. To-day this attitude, which is at one and the same time deliberately chosen and a product of his class conscientiousness, demands no sacrifice from his pride. He is still free to choose his party or to change it; he is still courted, still a critic, still without responsibility. Woe to his pride, when, in days to come, he will be the king's adviser and leader, and yet at the same time the king's vassal!

Already the dilemma begins to press. At any cost, the young deputy wants and needs the tribune, the fraction, the parliament. Where else can he carry his powers and his intelligence to market? If he is to demand yearly sessions of the Landtag, he must vote with the detested liberals. What is he to do? To put pressure upon the king would be disloyal, and therefore Bismarck's counsel is that the main problem shall be left undecided. When the Jewish question comes up for discussion, Bismarck would like to absent himself, for in this matter he is not at one with the government. Ultimately, however, he puts in an appearance; and, since he has already become, in a sense, one of the leaders of the extreme right, he takes up his parable against the "tedious humanitarian twaddle" of the left, which is striving to secure equality for all the king's subjects.

"I am no enemy of the Jews," he declares arrogantly; "and if they are hostile to me I forgive them. I love them under every circumstance. For my part, I would grant them all rights, save only the right of holding the chief offices in a Christian State. . . . To me, the words about God's grace are not empty ones. . . . But I can only regard as God's will that which is revealed in the Gospels. . . . If we withdraw the religious foundation of the State, then the State remains nothing more than a chance aggregate of rights, a sort of bulwark against the war of all against all. . . . It is not clear to me how, in such a State, the ideas of the communists, for instance, concerning the immorality of property could be disputed. . . . For this reason we ought not to encroach upon the people's Christianity."

Such has always been the tone of absolute monarchs and absolutist ministers; and had Bismarck's grandfather, Mencken, spoken in like manner, his kings would not have taken it amiss. Had not old Mencken brought up his daughter in the ideas of the enlightenment, she would not have tried to instil them into her son; and then, perhaps, young Bismarck, simply out of opposition to his unloved mother, would have become a liberal — if she had imbibed reactionary ideas from her father! This much, at least, is certain, that the man who in youth had envied Mirabeau and Peel, who had been charmed with Byron's lyrics and had admired England, had become better fitted, thanks to his education and his natural scepticism, to overcome race differences than class differences. When, for the first time, he publicly emphasised class differences, he was not influenced by pietism, for neither now nor later did pietism exercise the least influence upon his politics. He may, however, have been moved by consideration for pietists. For whereas he had, a year earlier, defended the separation of Church and State in opposition to President von Gerlach, it now pleased him to please this group of pietists. There was nothing Jesuitical about this. It was only half consciously that he achieved an approximation of his convictions and his aims, until, like lovers that seek one another, they clasped one another spontaneously and unembarrassed. Otto von Bismarck was a statesman.

As a statesman, five minutes later, he summoned the lowest strata of society as his witnesses. "When, as representative of the king's sacred majesty, I fancy myself having to obey a Jew, I must admit that in such circumstances I should feel myself profoundly humiliated. . . . I share this sentiment with the mass of the lower strata of the population, and I am not ashamed to be in their company." As a matter of fact, he had never been willing to obey any of the king's representatives, whether Jewish or Christian; and he had done great violence to his own nature in forcing himself, even as one of the king's representatives, to obey at least the monarch himself.

This untamable pride grows less fierce only when he meets his betrothed, or thinks of her. When she is ill, he would fain give the go-by to all the good Christians at Reinfeld, who can only put their trust in God, and will have nothing to do with medicines. He insists upon the need for medicines, his remarkable reason being that God has provided them. When she has recovered, she compares her uneventful life with his interesting one, with which he has made her acquainted by his letters and of which she reads in the newspapers.

"When my thoughts follow the course of your present life, flitting from one of your joys to another, and through the unending turmoil, . . . I often grow moody, but I lay a finger on my lips and my hand on my heart, quietly praying for you. . . . I almost fear that they are making you too proud, . . . and that in the end you will despise our modest Reinfeld." With such timid phrases she sometimes masks a genuine terror, and one of her letters breaks out in tragi-comical fashion: "Otto, you are frightfully hot-blooded!"

He grows more and more cheerful as the date of their marriage draws near, and writes with masterful gallantry: "Do you expect

me, on a mild evening, wearing a black velvet coat and a great
ostrich feather, to come and twang a zither beneath your window,
singing 'Fly with me', and so on (which, indeed, I could now sing
most heartily, and in most melting tones: 'And re-e-est on my',
etc.); or shall I, at high noon, turn up in a green riding coat
and red leather gloves, to put my arms round you without either
singing or speaking?" When he advises her to invite several
friends to accompany them on their wedding journey, she emphatically refuses.

The marriage took place six months after the engagement had
begun. A friend had sent her the bride's pocket-handkerchief, and,
in accordance with the language of flowers spoken in this circle,
had wrapped a white rose in it. Then, when the bridegroom was
sitting at table, and had imbibed a fair quantity of champagne,
he seized Johanna's handkerchief. His mature, unromantic, realist
eyes lighted on the symbolical flower, and, before his anxious
bride could prevent him, he had set fire to it with his cigar. The
implication was: "Here endeth Jean Paul together with the
mysticism of girlhood."

He takes a paternal delight, on a lengthy honeymoon tour, in
showing his beloved the world. "As far as I am concerned," he
writes to his sister — and no one would imagine that the writer
was only thirty-two years old — "I have grown too old to be
impressed by novelty, so that my chief pleasure has been derived
as a reflexion from Johanna's." Even more sceptical in his report to his brother: "The thick end came last, and Johanna had
to supplement my hundred gold fredericks with nearly two hundred talers of her own which she had laid aside for the purchase
of silver plate. No matter for that, since tea out of Wedgwood
tastes just as good, and we have had plenty of wedding presents.
The whole journey cost about seven hundred and fifty talers for
the two of us. Since it lasted fifty-seven days, this works out at
about thirteen talers per day. . . . Less agreeable news is that,
while away, I have lost six cows and one bull from anthrax —
the best of the herd."

How tame has Bismarck the adventurer become! Certainly,

when he is travelling, alone or with his wife, everything must be of the best, and he is never penurious. But when we see him, just back from his honeymoon, dividing the total by fifty-seven, and closing his first report with the story about his six cows and one bull, we realise how readily he is accommodating himself to narrow horizons — precisely because wide horizons are opening to him.

XI

On March 19, 1848, Bismarck, who is visiting a neighbour, is probably discussing political affairs with his friends, for the situation is a lively one. Unexpectedly a carriage arrives. The ladies step down, and, full of excitement, they tell the astonished Bismarck and his friends that they have fled from Berlin, for revolution has broken out, and the king has been taken prisoner by the people. Bismarck, since the Landtag is not sitting, has been spending the winter with his young wife at Schönhausen — the only quiet six months in his married life. For the last fortnight he has, like every one else, been uneasy, for recently the Parisian populace has risen, driven the king away, and declared a republic once more. The result has been to strengthen similar wishes in Germany, so that in various countries throughout the fatherland the governments have dismissed reactionary ministers and appointed comparatively liberal ones. Too late! On March 18th, the Berlinese assembled in the streets and came into collision with the soldiers, until the king, quite needlessly, from cowardliness rather than from sympathy with the popular movement, ordered his officers to withdraw their forces. On receipt of this news, Bismarck hastened back to Schönhausen.

Now it seems to him that his very existence is threatened; for whom will the excited populace be more likely to expropriate and perhaps decapitate than himself, who is one of the spokesmen of reaction? Naturally his thoughts turn to his heritage, which his instincts as husband and prospective father make him wish to safeguard. Furthermore, his pride is touched, and his courage is stimulated, so that it seems to him the first need is to hit back against the Reds. Temperament and interest therefore combine to make him think chiefly of the use of force, and he promptly sets to work gathering the means that are under his hand. When, next morning, commissioners arrive at Schönhausen from the town, and call upon the peasants to raise the black-red-and-gold standard, the lord of the soil charges them to resist and to drive away the townsmen, "which was promptly done, the women taking an active share." He has a white flag bearing a black cross run up over the church tower, collects arms, finds twenty fowling pieces in his own house and another fifty in the village, and sends men on horseback to fetch gunpowder from the town.

Then, taking his intrepid wife with him, he makes a round of the neighbouring villages, and finds most of the people ready to accompany him to Berlin in order to set the king free (for, as has already been said, the current report was that Frederick William was a prisoner). When one of his neighbours, a liberal, threatens to agitate on the other side, Bismarck's answer, reported by himself, is:

"If you do, I shall shoot you."

"You would not do that!"

"I give you my word of honour that I would, and you know that I am a man of my word. So you had better not!"

After this romanticist overture, he becomes the politician once more, and sets out alone for the capital; visits Potsdam on the way; learns from generals of his own persuasion what has really happened. They tell him they want potatoes and grain for their soldiers, but that peasants are of no use to them. They are furiously angry because the king has forbidden them to take Berlin. When Bismarck hears this last item of news, he gives up the king as hopeless, wants to get to work on his own account, and moves to secure active orders from Prince William of Prussia. He is referred to the princess.

Augusta was four years older than Bismarck, and had at this date been married for nearly twenty years — married, and therefore waiting. The more plainly the king's madness became evident,

the better grounds had she for hoping that, since Frederick
William was childless, she and her husband would ultimately sit
on the throne of Prussia. Now it seemed as if the hopes of her
lifetime had been shattered at one blow, and that both the
brothers had forfeited all prospect of further power. William had
gone into hiding on Pfauen Island, and had kept his place of retreat a secret even from the most loyal. This gave his handsome
and dictatorial wife a chance to make the most of her Weimar
culture, and to play the part of one of the great queens of an-
tiquity, for she now staked her head on a hazard. She wanted to
secure the succession for her son, and negotiated about the matter with Vincke, the leader of the old liberals. While she was
engaged in this intrigue, she was informed that the new royalist
leader had arrived. It would not be safe to receive him in the
drawing-room, where all the walls had ears.

"She received me in the servants' hall in the entresol, seated on
a deal chair; refused to let me know where her husband was; and
declared, obviously much excited, that it was her duty to defend
her son's rights. What she said was based on the supposition that
the king and her husband could not retain their positions, and
she made it clear that her plan was to be regent during her son's
minority."

There stands the Junker, loyal to his king, uneasy in his mind,
eager to find the vanished prince, and to find in him a man who
will have the will and the courage to resist the popular movement.
He is faced, in this servants' hall, by Prince William's wife, sitting on a plain deal chair. She has long since given up all hope
for her husband and the king; her only wish, now, is to save the
crown for herself and her son; and she discloses this design, which
borders on high treason, to a member of the Landtag who is almost a stranger to her, and whose own schemes run counter to
her plans. We do not know exactly what Bismarck said to
Augusta, but we can infer the tenor of his words from what,
shortly afterwards, he said of Vincke. "In the name of the members of his party, and presumably under instructions from higher
quarters, Vincke craved my support for an endeavour to induce

the Landtag to ask the king to abdicate; the prince of Prussia was to be passed over, presumably with his own consent; the princess of Prussia was to be regent for her son during his minority. I . . . declared that I should counter any such proposal with one to take proceedings against its authors for high treason. . . . Vincke abandoned his plan in the end quietly, . . . and readily enough, with the remark that it would certainly not be possible to move the king to abdicate without the support of the extreme right, whom he looked on me as representing. This interview took place in my room on the ground floor of the Hôtel des Princes, and contained far more than it is expedient to record in writing."

The concluding sentence, which was written nearly forty years after the events to which it relates, enables us to read between the lines a great deal which the old man does not actually report, and he is well aware why he concludes by saying: " I never told Emperor William anything about this affair, not even in the days . . . when I could not but regard Queen Augusta as my opponent — although to keep silence was the hardest test to which my sense of duty and my nerves were put at any time in my life." Augusta was never able to pardon this Joseph his political chastity.

The scene just described was the first, and at the same time one of the most remarkable, of the occasions when Bismarck fought for his king simply from a sense of loyalty, and unmoved by personal interest; moreover, this happened at the very moment when he was filled with contempt for Frederick William. At such critical instants, his sentiments, compounded out of courage, out of hatred for the mob (to whom no one ought to yield), out of the hereditary pride of the knightly order, out of a somewhat romanticist conception of an ideal paladin, were apt to overpower his cold reason. From a purely circumstantial point of view, Vincke was right in describing his own proposal as a "politically needful, carefully considered, and sedulously prepared measure." In those days of revolt, Bismarck, as an ambitious man, might well have acted more prudently if he had allowed his sense of loyalty to Frederick William and the prince of Prussia to be outweighed by the thought of what Princess Augusta would do for him in return for his support of her wishes; he might well have been excused for taking sides with these younger members of the royal house, against whom there was no black mark in the popular mind.

According to Bismarck's own account, the fate of the family was then in his hands. If even the conservatives had been in favour of Frederick William's abdication, the adhesion of this smaller party to the plan would have decided the matter, since the king was in any case alarmed at his position; and there can be no doubt that the Landtag, which was predominantly liberal, would have welcomed this way out of the difficulty. In that case, Prince William would never have mounted the throne, and Frederick would have become king of Prussia at eighteen instead of at fifty-eight. But Bismarck could not foresee either Frederick's future development or his own. The line he took, first in the servants' hall at Potsdam, and then in the hotel in the Leipziger Strasse, probably decided his own career, and certainly played a great part in deciding the destiny of Germany.

He had refused to depose the king; his endeavour now was to checkmate Frederick William. That very day he asked Prince Frederick Charles, "since His Majesty is not free to act", to give orders that the troops should be led to Berlin despite the king's orders. Since Frederick Charles refused to give the order, and the general in command (whom Bismarck likewise incited to disobey) was also refractory, Bismarck drove off to Berlin to see if he could make better headway with Frederick William. On arrival in the capital, he was by no means inclined to be provocative in aspect. He had his beard shaved off, put on a broad-brimmed hat with a coloured cockade; thus rigged out, since he was also wearing a frock coat in the hope of an audience of the king, he made so exotic an impression that people called after him in the street: "There goes another Frenchman!" However, when his cousin wanted to put some money in a collecting box on behalf of the barricade fighters, he said out loud (so he tells us):

"Surely you won't let yourself be frightened by a blunderbuss, and give money to these assassins!" For at the citizens' guard-post he had recognised a judge of his acquaintance, who, turning, himself recognised Otto, in spite of the absence of the beard, and exclaimed: "Good God, Bismarck! What a sight you are! There is a foul business going on here!"

When refused admittance to the palace, he writes a letter to the king on a scrap of paper, informing Frederick William (though he has no special sources of information, and merely writes as he does to encourage the king) that nowhere in the country districts of Prussia has the revolution found support. Frederick William will be master as soon as he leaves the capital.

All is in vain! He makes his way back to Saxony, in order to put the general in command there in touch with the Potsdam forces. In Magdeburg he is advised to leave at once, for if he stays, there will be no option but to arrest him for high treason. Now he has to cool off at Schönhausen, and must content himself with returning to Potsdam accompanied by a remarkable deputation of peasants who want to speak to the generals themselves. At Potsdam, he hears Frederick William tell the officers of the guard: "I was never freer and safer than under the protection of my burghers." Bismarck reports: "Thereupon there were murmurs, and rattlings of scabbards, such as a king of Prussia had never before heard when among his officers, and one may hope, will never hear again. Sore at heart I went back to Schönhausen."

Thus did Bismarck's counter-revolution end in vexation and disappointment. Later, when the new liberal ministry laid before parliament the electoral law which the March rising had extorted, he succeeded, with considerable difficulty, in having the congratulations to the barricade fighters expunged from the document. This seemed to appease him. In the new speech from the throne, the German question was mooted once more, the king declaring that henceforward Prussia must play her part in Germany. Bismarck was opposed to the idea, but the question was not yet acute. When the address was now to be voted, he unexpectedly mounted the tribune, and then, suddenly, disclosed his anger and sorrow in an elemental and extremely impolitic way. It seemed as if he no longer realised where he was. His speech was faltering.

He began by saying that he would vote for the king's programme, and went on: "But what leads me to oppose the address is that it contains utterances of joy and thankfulness for what has taken place of late. The past is buried, and I regret far more than many of you that no human power can resurrect it, now that the throne itself has cast earth upon the coffin. . . . If it should really happen that a united German fatherland should be attained along the new road, then the moment will have come when I shall be able to express my thanks to the originator of the new order of things. But as yet it is not possible for me. . . . " Here he was seized with a fit of sobbing, was unable to continue, and left the tribune without finishing his speech.

Thus do the man's wounded feelings overcome him when everything seems to him lost and betrayed. He compromises himself and he compromises the king in the very hour when Frederick William has made peace with the people. With the scepticism of one who has been conquered, and at the same time with the foresight of a political genius, he already feels that not thus and not now can Germany be united. He speaks in rhetorical fashion, and full of obvious doubts; he expresses his thanks to the originator of the new order; and quite unconcernedly, in so doing, hits back at himself. At this very moment, as if his perspicacity were taking its own revenge, and as if he did not dare to look farther forward into the obscurity of the future, all the passion and bitterness of these days rises from his heart into his eyes. He bursts into tears, and has to break off his speech.

XII

Two months later, Prince William can venture to return from England, whither he had fled for refuge. When he is on his way back, Bismarck is waiting for him at a wayside station, but is careful to remain in the background. The prince (whose wife, in giving him an account of Bismarck's visit, has told him only of the latter's intentions without saying a word about her own designs) recognises him, goes through the crowd to him, shakes hands, and says: "I know that you worked actively in my behalf, and I shall never forget the fact!" A strangely logical misunderstanding leads to the first cordial handshake between these two men, who, almost severed by the princess' rancour, were subsequently to be united on the platform of universal history.

Having been invited to Babelsberg, Bismarck tells the prince about the anger of the troops which had been withdrawn in the March days, and pulls out the militarist stop, reading aloud to William a poem written in those days, which ends as follows:

> Then to their loyal ears there came the trait'rous call:
> "No longer Prussians be, henceforward Germans all!"
> Black-red-and-gold, the new-made banner waves;
> Dishonoured the Black Eagle's humbly furled,
> And Zollern's glories sink into their graves,
> A king dethroned — not battling 'gainst the world!
> We do not care to trace the path of fallen stars!
> Prince, you will rue the day, the deed, done here;
> None will you find so leal as Prussians were.

Thereupon the prince bursts into tears, as Bismarck will see him do once again in days to come. This form of emotion, in two men both of whom are personally courageous, betokens kinship — not indeed in respect of temperament, but in respect of their behaviour at certain supreme moments. William was then over fifty. He had lived a dull, comfortable life; except for certain obscure episodes in youth and for certain love renunciations, he had never encountered any serious obstacle. Now, after a danger had been overcome, when he was being humbugged by courtiers, he recognised in Bismarck's report the first plainly spoken truth, which was aptly conveyed to him in the form of a soldier's song.

Just as vigorously and boldly, in these same July days, did the Junker withstand the king. Much embittered, he would no longer go to court; and when the king sent a body-servant to his hotel, commanding his presence, Bismarck replied that his wife was ill, and that he had to leave for the country at once. This was something new in the king's experience; he promptly sent an aide-de-camp, inviting Bismarck to dinner; placed a royal messenger at his disposal to bring news as to Johanna's health; and thus compelled him to come. After dinner, Frederick William walked with Bismarck on the terrace at Sans-Souci, asking, in friendly fashion:

"Well, how are things in your part of the world?"

"Not at all good, Your Majesty."

"I thought that there was a good mood there?"

"The mood was excellent, but since revolution has been innoculated among us by the royal authority under royal seals, it has changed very much for the worse. There is no confidence in the king's support."

Now, as Bismarck tells us, the queen came out of ambush, saying:

"How can you speak in that way to the king?"

But Frederick William said:

"Leave us, Elise, I shall deal with him myself. — What do you reproach me with?"

"The evacuation of Berlin."

"I did not want this."

Whereupon the queen, who was still within earshot, intervened once more, saying:

"In this matter, the king is not to blame. He had not been able to sleep for three days."

"A king must be able to sleep."

"You men of the legislative assembly always know better than any one else. . . . Reproaches are not the best way of reestablishing a shaky throne. That needs support, activity, and self-sacrifice; not carping criticism."

By this tone, the guest is suddenly made to feel himself "completely disarmed and won over."

Such was the course of Bismarck's first political conversation with a king of Prussia. In actual fact, his position was an easy one, for it was as a royalist that he was campaigning against the king. From the formal point of view, it was a difficult one, for he had entered this palace in order to chide. Since he was treated with the utmost consideration, he was won over. The king accepted his criticisms with a sort of paternal benevolence; but when, shortly afterwards, Gerlach recommended Bismarck for a ministerial post, Frederick William wrote across the written recommendation: "Only to be used when bayonets are supreme." Though the judgment was false politically, it was psychologically accurate at the time when it was made, for Bismarck certainly seemed resolute to defend his order with any and every means.

When the government wishes to take a step which has long since been taken in other lands, and to abolish the exemption of the landed gentry's estates from taxation, Bismarck, grossly exaggerating, writes a private letter to the king: "This confiscation . . . is an arbitrary attack on landed property such as only conquerors and rulers by force have ever before attempted. It is an illegal act of force . . . directed against a defenceless class of subjects who have been loyal to the throne for centuries. . . . We, in conjunction with the great majority of the Prussian people, will hold Your Majesty responsible before God and posterity, if we have to see the name of the king whose father was known as the Just, written beneath laws which will indicate an abandonment of the road along which the kings of Prussia acquired a perennial reputation for immaculate justice, and made the mill of Sans-Souci an historical monument." Thus threateningly, and in a most unreasonable spirit, does he confront the king, whose father was by no means entitled the Just.

At the same time, he writes, for peasant consumption, articles directed against the revolution; tries to counteract the influence of the progressive newspapers and of revolutionary pamphlets; becomes one of the founders of the new agrarian party and its organ, the "Kreuzzeitung" (for which he writes much during the next few years); does his utmost to secure election to the Prussian National Assembly; when he fails to achieve this, plays a considerable part in the intrigues which, in November, lead to a coup d'état by which the assembly is forcibly dissolved. Before this dénouement, he safeguards his own position, for, as he writes sophistically to his wife: "I have no need to await the progress of events here, nor do I propose to tempt God with having to protect

me in dangers which I have no occasion to seek. . . . If the affair
breaks loose, I should like to be in the king's neighbourhood; for
there you may be quite sure (I say this regretfully) there will be
no danger."

Then he does everything in his power to secure reelection, running for two circles. He even humiliates himself so far as to sing
his own praises. He writes to Bodelschwingh, asking the latter, in
the event of his having, thanks to election in two circles, to vacate
the seat for Teltow, to recommend the electors there to vote for
Professor Stahl as substitute. "Or, if this gentleman's marked
ecclesiastical tendencies should arouse dissatisfaction here and
there, perhaps you will use your interest on my behalf. I have
good reason to believe that, in such a case, Your Excellency's
recommendation would be decisive. . . . For the nonce I am can-
vassing in the Brandenburg Havelland, but without much hope
of success. . . . Your obedient servant, Von Bismarck."

Thus does he do his utmost to secure election, and yet he has
never had to do anything more distasteful than in these February
weeks of 1849, when he has to play the part of Coriolanus, flattering the common people whom he despises so profoundly. He is
strongly moved to throw up the whole business, which is repugnant to his nerves, his education, and his taste. "To-day I have
to make some more electors' acquaintance; messengers innumerable have been sent out in all directions; two patriotic orators
are going to Werder. . . . It is like being at military headquarters — messages and despatches every few minutes. . . .
Many thanks for your letter, which came to hand yesterday when
I was amid the reek and noise of four hundred people. . . . I
read it by the light of an evil-smelling lamp. 'If the tones of a
well-loved voice had summoned me out of the hateful confusion,'
I should instantly have shaken myself free of all these futile
activities. . . . If I am elected, this having to live without inward
repose will be a difficult business. . . . Now the electors are casting their votes. I have left the matter in God's hands, and am
awaiting the result with equanimity, although hitherto I have
been in a state of febrile excitement."

Directly he is elected, he hastens to withdraw himself from contact with those whose favour he has been wooing. "Again and again I have scorned myself," he writes to his brother, "during this week, . . . when I have been doing my best to win votes by personal amiability. . . . After the election there was a banquet attended by four hundred persons. The usual songs: 'Now all give thanks to God', 'Hail to thee, crowned with victory', and the 'Preussenlied.' Next day I had a headache, and all the muscles of my right hand were aching from the continual hand-shaking. The day after that, some of my friends had their windows broken, and a few of them were roughly handled, when I was already safely at home with Johanna." These comments, in the Wallenstein vein, disclose the contempt felt by the Junker who, in his climb to power, is obliged to court the favour of the populace. As lord of the soil, this man had done his best to avoid quarrelling with his peasants. Now that he has become a politician, he mocks at the plebeians whose only use, as far as he is concerned, is to vote for him and to become his tools in the work of the counter-revolution.

It is his Junker sentiments, too, which, during these days, decide his position as between Prussia and Germany. His feelings are absolutely opposed to Germany. "What the devil do I care about the petty States?" he exclaims to his friend Keudell. "My only concern is to safeguard and increase the power of Prussia!" When, in the Landtag, some one calls him a lost son of the German fatherland, he rejoins:

"My fatherland is Prussia, a fatherland which I have not yet forsaken, and never shall forsake!" Indeed, his Prussianism is even stronger than his monarchical feeling; for his king, though hesitatingly, had recently announced the merging of Prussia in Germany. His opposition to the unification of Germany is the outcome of his conservatism even more than of his Prussian sentiment. It was the revolution which had reawakened the idea of German unity among the people; and at the very time when in Frankfort the tribunes are endeavouring, from beneath, to build up the imperial realm of the Germans, the eternal jealousy of the dynasts is imperilling and their anti-democratic spirit is destroying the work from above; the petty princes are fighting against Prussia's dominance, and the king of Prussia is fighting against the dominance of the parliament of Frankfort.

Forty years later, Bismarck, having passed through notable transfigurations in the interim, will write about these matters in his memoirs, saying: "I think that if the victory of that day [March 19, 1848] had been firmly and shrewdly turned to account — the only victory that was then gained in Europe against the rioters — German unity might have been achieved in a more consolidated form than was ultimately achieved when I was a participator in the government. Whether this would have been more useful and more durable, I will leave open. . . . Unity achieved through street fighting would have been of a different kind and of less significance than the victory ultimately achieved on the battlefield. . . . It is dubious whether unity reached by the shorter and quicker path of the March victory in 1848 would have had the same historical effect upon the Germans as the extant form of unity, which produces the impression that the dynasts, even those who aforetime were exceptionally particularist, are more friendly towards united Germany than are the fractions and the parties."

We, who live a generation later than the days when that old man, writing a great epilogue, cast up his accounts, cannot but be greatly impressed by his reflections. He tells us that that which he achieved by force of arms in prolonged combats, could have been achieved quickly and in a more consolidated form without wars. Barricades and street fighting had alarmed him; he preferred the battlefield; and he does not seem to have struck a balance between the hundred or two hundred that fell in the March Days, and the hundreds of thousands that were slaughtered in the three wars. Bismarck did not live to learn that the unity of Germany would endure after the dynasts had vanished, and he would have emphatically repudiated the possibility. He did not survive until the day when the dynasts whom he describes as friendly to the idea of a united Germany (though in other respects he often made mock of them) fled from the German realm at the moment of its greatest danger, leaving to the fractions and the parties the task of saving Germany.

For the moment, he fully shares the views of his king, in so far as they are known. On April 2d, the Frankfort Deputation, and even Count Brandenburg, minister president of State, believed that next day the king would accept the offer of the imperial crown. But when that day came, the king, whose actions were incalculable, in a speech composed by himself refused the crown in such vague terms, that in the evening Prince William had an argument with Simson (the disappointed leader of the Frankforters) as to whether his brother had or had not refused it. Greatly surprised, too, were the Junkers, who the day before in the Landtag had signed the following address to the king: "The confidence of the representatives of the German nation summons Your Majesty to the glorious task of becoming the supreme ruler of resurrected Germany. . . . Reverently but urgently we implore Your Majesty not to ignore the appeal of the German National Assembly."

Though very few persons seem to be aware of the fact, and though all Bismarck's biographers ignore it, among the signatures to this address were those of Von Bismarck-Schönhausen, his relatives Kleist and Arnim, and two titled ministers of State. (See the shorthand report, pages 355–357.) Thus did Bismarck recognise the detested Paulskirche [the Frankfort National Assembly] as the voice of the German people, and advised his king to accept a crown handed up from the gutter — simply because he believed that his king wanted it! His signature to the address was written on April 2, 1849. On April 2, 1848, he had made that impassioned speech against the king whom he had regarded as unduly democratic, the speech which sobs had prevented his finishing. The budding diplomatist's loyalty had certainly grown in the course of a year!

As soon as the king, to every one's astonishment, had refused the imperial crown, the Junkers were immensely relieved; and on the 21st, Bismarck, speaking from the tribune, said: "The illegal

decisions with which the Frankfort National Assembly has tried
to give expression to its dictatorial lusts [interruptions; the
president rings his bell] are such as I cannot recognise to be
existent for us." He called the whole negotiation "constituted
anarchy, offered from Frankfort"; and refused "to lend the
Frankfort lust for sovereignty the support of our approval."

He goes on to say: "I find it inconceivable that two constitutions can continue to exist . . . side by side in Prussia and in
Germany; especially in view of the fact that the German nation
of the narrower confederation [without Austria] would contain
very few persons over and about Prussian subjects." He concludes as follows: "Every one wants German unity. . . . But I
do not want German unity at the cost of such a constitution. . . .
If the worst comes to the worst, I should . . . prefer that Prussia should remain Prussia. . . . Perhaps the crown which Frankfort offers may shine brightly, but the gold which will make the
glitter real is to be supplied by throwing the Prussian crown into
the melting-pot: I am by no means confident that the re-casting
would be a success under this form of constitution."

Thus, in the year 1849, Bismarck dismisses the idea of united
Germany with a reductio ad absurdum which he himself will annul
twenty years later. But when Radowitz becomes minister, and
persuades the king to espouse the cause of a lesser Germany,
developing his plans in great detail, Bismarck, writing anonymously in the "Kreuzzeitung", makes mock of Radowitz's "voice
gravid with bravos. Amid thunderous applause, this minister,
like a ghost from the tomb, stalked back to the ministerial bench,
and Herr von Beckerath pressed him by the hand in the name of
Germany."

Neither in Berlin nor in Erfurt, where Radowitz is having the
so-called Union Constitution discussed, does Deputy Bismarck
want anything positive to be done, either as regards Germany or
other concerns. All he wants is defence against the revolution. He
publicly repudiates the right of the Landtag to refuse the voting
of taxes; thunders against comparisons with England and
France, whose rulers received their crowns from the bloody hands

of the revolution; rails against freedom of occupation, civil marriage, and especially against great towns, "the hotbeds of democracy." Of the towns, he says: "I do not find there the true Prussian people. Far from it; it is the true Prussian people which, if the great towns should again rise in revolt, will enforce obedience upon them, even if it be at the cost of razing them to the ground!" His demeanour is so revolutionary that in Erfurt he is compared with the radical leader, Karl Vogt.

In private he makes fun of the chamber in which he has worked with so much fervour, as a hall where "three hundred and fifty persons are deciding the fate of our fatherland, though hardly fifty of them know what they are doing; and even among these fifty, thirty are ambitious and conscienceless rogues, or comedians puffed out by vanity." He deplores that there should still be extensive risings in southern Germany, and he says to Lerchenfeld: "I pray to God that your army, wherever it is unsteady, may desert. Then the struggle will become a fierce one, and the outcome will be all the more decisive when the ulcer shall have been healed. . . . We shall carry our cause and yours through: if with more frenzy, so much the better!" He is completely mastered by un-Christian hatred, and when he has been to visit the graves of the champions of freedom at Friedrichshain a year after the March Days, he writes to his wife as follows: "I cannot even forgive the dead, . . . seeing that every inscription on their crosses boasts of liberty and right, in a way shameful to God and man!"

Simply from hatred for a revolution which wishes to abolish the nobility as well as other things, he now for the first time begins to write before his name the "von" which has hitherto been absent from his signatures. He says to one of the liberals: "I am a Junker, and want to enjoy the advantages of my position!" Nevertheless, in sittings of the committees, he prefers to sit among his opponents, saying: "I find it very tedious over there among my friends; here it is far more amusing." He makes a speech proclaiming the merits of the nobility in Prussia, but does so with a knowledge and moderation which render it most effective.

He visits the battlefields where the Prussian nobles had fought and fallen, and remarks: "It is true that the Prussian nobility had its Jena, . . . but when I survey its whole history I can find no justification for the attacks that have been made upon it here during the last few days." Then he sets up the nobility against the kings, studies the history of the order in Venice, Genoa, and Holland; and regards the present instability of most of the States of Europe as the outcome of the period when the dominant princes oppressed the independent nobles — a tendency which in Prussia found expression in the utterance of Frederick William I.: "I am stabilising sovereignty comme un rocher de bronze."

In this way, Bismarck links himself on to the tradition of his own insurgent forefathers, and, to the amazement of his more obtuse colleagues, challenges monarchical authority. He is more of a feudalist than an elected representative of the people.

Class feeling and politics are intertwined for him. When, after he has made this speech, the "Kladderadatsch" asks: "Where, we wonder, was a certain Herr von Bismarck commanding in the year 1813?" Bismarck promptly answers with a challenge. What touches himself, he says, he will answer through the columns of the press. But as concerns his ancestors, four of them [though not indeed his father] were fighting in 1813 as officers. "When insults to my family are uttered, I assume — until I have proof to the contrary — that your well-born way of thinking does not differ greatly from mine, and that . . . I may expect you to give me the satisfaction which, in my opinion, no gentleman can refuse another."

Sometimes the two principles, force and Christianity, come into conflict — though this only arises in family affairs. When his mother-in-law, a highly cultured woman, a very independent one, and therefore often at odds with him, espouses the cause of the champions of liberty in Hungary, and censured Haynau, who is drowning their aspirations in a blood-bath, Bismarck (who as a rule writes to her only on her birthdays) delivers himself with much excitement by letter:

"You have so much sympathy for the relatives of Batthyány. Have you none for the thousands upon thousands of innocent persons whose wives have been widowed and whose children have been orphaned through the crazy ambition or monstrous presumption of these rebels who, like Karl Moor, want to enforce happiness on the world after their own mad fashion? Can the execution of one man provide a sufficiency of even earthly justice as retribution for the burnt cities, the devastated provinces, the murdered populations whose blood cries from the ground to the emperor of Austria whom God has entrusted with the sword of authority? Such compassion as yours for criminals is responsible for most of the bloodshed of the last sixty years. You say you are afraid that the Austrian government will point the way to the democrats! But how can you possibly put a legitimate authority and a party of traitors upon the same footing? The former is responsible for protecting with the sword the subjects God has entrusted to them; the latter, the rebels, remain murderers and liars when they dare to have recourse to the sword; they can kill, but they cannot righteously condemn to death. Luther expressly declares: 'Secular authorities must not forgive those who have done wrong, but must punish them.' . . . Forgive me for writing to you at such length about these matters; I felt myself personally affected by what you said, for if it should be my mission, some day, to exercise supreme authority, I should not like Johanna to feel towards me as you are feeling towards Haynau. . . . Farewell, your loving son, Von Bismarck."

The writer of this epistle seems to regard it much as if it were a ministerial note. Now, when he is beginning to recognise what his future will be, or at any rate is striving to secure it, he finds it necessary to steel his breast against compassion. He is in truth tender-hearted, and Christian influences have deprived him of some of his armour. The wife whom he loves is a danger to him in this respect, even though she loves him; for she is also her mother's daughter, and she spends many months of the year with her mother, amid sentimental country gentlefolk who dislike dictators just as much as they dislike liberals.

The lines quoted mutter a warning. He wants to insure himself against foes in his own household. He is entrenching his camp before he takes up his quarters in it.

XIII

Bismarck has become a parliamentarian. Between the ages of thirty-three and thirty-six, he is wholly devoted to this profession. If his lively tempo therein seems astonishing, we must remember the explanation, must picture the eagerness with which he applies his titanic will to making up for a wasted decade. His wife and his landed property begin gently and imperceptibly to recede into the background. Frenzy has seized him; and this, in conjunction with his native ambition, drives him forward to action. He is now in splendid health, eats voraciously and drinks abundantly. "I must stop, for I have just eaten so gigantic a supper . . . that I can no longer sit still." Again: "When we went to bed, we ate the Wurst, without any bread, in three helpings, cutting it up with a hunting knife. The thin end was not so good as the thick, but the general impression was extremely satisfactory." Once more: "To-day, I have eaten such a lot of figs that I must have some rum to drink." Yet again: "Then I ate my supper walking up and down the room, devouring almost all of the thick Wurst, which tasted delicious; I drank a whole stone pitcher full of Erfurt beer; and now as I write to you, I am putting away a second boxful of marzipan. . . . I am really very well, only at the moment my stomach is rather too full of Wurst."

Whatever he does, is done vehemently. After "too long a walk", he comes home dead tired; he takes long rides at full gallop with a friend; sleeps always for a very long time, and is furious if he is wakened too soon. He spends the day shooting woodcock. "Overnight I ate a great many trout and drank a lot of small beer." He sallies forth in the rain and tramps from one to four o'clock, having to rest three times, "for more than once I was almost dropping with fatigue, so I lay down in the wet heather and let the rain fall on me. . . . I was absolutely resolved to sight a woodcock. I saw several, but they were out of range. . . . By five o'clock I was home again, . . . broke my fast of twenty-four hours with a very good appetite, and drank two glasses of champagne; then I slept for fourteen hours, until one in the afternoon, and now feel very much better than I did before the expedition, and am delighted with the memory of the wonderful scenery God was good enough to show me." He studies elocution, manages "to overcome initial shyness"; speaks — like Goethe at the age of thirty — of an accession of mental peace now that he is playing a more active part in life. If he is in the least out of sorts, he is unable to speak to his satisfaction, and is afterwards extremely mortified on account of the defects in his speech. "I had a wretched morning because I was suffering from a cold. . . . I forgot the best of what I wanted to say, for I was quite stupid." He makes a general confession: "In the evening I am always restless in my loneliness unless I am thoroughly tired out."

He complains bitterly of having to lead a bachelor life in Berlin, rails at the whole affair as senseless, and yet often stays in the capital longer than he need. If he takes a flat there for the winter months, he gives his wife a precise description of all the room; tells her exactly where the couch on which he sleeps is situated; says that what he pays in rent amounts to a third of his allowance as deputy. Throughout life, Bismarck is greatly concerned about the place where he lives and eats. "My things are strewn all over the floor, and I have no one to arrange them for me. I wonder, darling, when we shall again be sleeping quietly together behind our red curtains, and able to drink our tea together!"

His married life runs a tranquil course, does so for forty years to come. The fires of erotic adventurousness seem to be quenched; not because Johanna excels all other women, but because he has taken her to wife when his years devoted to the battle of the sexes are over, and when he has transferred his energies to the contest with men. To begin with, they write alternately in a diary. On his wedding day, he makes the entry "Married!" Once when she has written, "Scoldings the whole day, two days' silence", he puts his pen through the entry, and, with a happy metaphor, writes over it, "Fine weather!" Or he writes to her: "We have only been separated for forty-two hours, and it seems to me as if a whole week had passed since I saw you standing among the pine trees on the hilltop and waving to me, . . . and since some of my tears ran down into my beard. I think this was the first time since the days when I had to go back to school after the holidays, that a parting brought tears to my eyes. My look into the past makes me thank God that I still have something from which I find it hard to part."

When she gives birth to their first child, a daughter, he tells her that he is "glad that it is a daughter, but even if it had been a pussy-cat I should have thanked God on my knees that Johanna was through her trouble!" During her lying-in, he sleeps behind the curtain in her room, for his wife has more confidence in him than in the monthly nurse. "Thus . . . I spent part of my time, at my writing-table, busied with political struggles and plans, and the rest of it playing sick-nurse. It seems to me I am making a pretty good hand at both."

If wife or children are ill, or illness threatens them, he promptly loses his nerve, and has no more Christianity left than will enable him to pray God that all may remain in good health, and no one may die. "For these last four days, darling," he writes, "since the child fell ill of scarlet fever, I have been desperately uneasy, as I could not fail to be after receiving your last letter. If you are ill, I think some one might have been kind enough to write me a line. I cannot endure this uncertainty. All sorts of dreadful possibilities have been passing through my mind during the last few days." When the wet nurse's child dies in Berlin, he writes three letters to the country, giving directions as to how the news can best be broken to her, so that the shock may not have a bad effect upon the nursling.

His affectionate tyranny grows. After he has left his wife alone for months, he forbids her to stay in her parents' house for her confinement. "For you to be confined in Reinfeld will be half way to a divorce. I cannot and will not be so long without you; we have been parted often enough." When she encloses a letter he is to send on to one of her friends, he begs her next time "to address it prosaically. With thick broom-handle strokes, I wrote over the address to 'Your Elizabeth' a new one. Never mind how fond you are of her, you should be coldly polite on the outside of the envelope. That is usual custom."

Although in the early days of their courtship he had wanted to train her for the great world, at a time when his own return thither was still dubious, now, when he himself has returned to that world, he does not care for her to participate in his life there. He writes: "No doubt this news will interest your father very much, but you will not understand it." Yet he monologises in his letters, mixing international politics and domestic affairs in a strange medley. "Certainly, if the child is no longer thriving with the nurse, you had better do as you suggest. . . . The speech from the throne is free from revolutionary admixture; if the king sticks to this, . . . of course everything will remain as of old, for Austria and the others will never give way to the Frank-forters. . . . I can't count my washing, I should have to stoop too much, it all lies higgledy-piggledy in the portmanteau. For-give me, perhaps I will do it on Sunday." In one letter after an-other, he says that he is coming home soon; yet he does not come. When she reproaches him on one occasion with having a good time of it in society while she has to lead a dull and lonely life with her parents, he answers in lively fashion: "I must have dinner and supper once a day, anyhow, and I hope you do the same thing where you are."

Speaking generally, he is tolerant in family life, but if domestic concerns have to be paraded before the public, his tastes and his caste feeling are outraged. When Herbert, the elder son, has been born in the third year of the marriage, and when they all are to travel together, his annoyance finds vent in a humorous letter to his sister: "I already picture myself with the children on the platform at Genthin, then both of them in the railway car-riage, incontinently satisfying their needs and making a nasty smell. The other travellers sniff pointedly, Johanna is ashamed to give the baby the breast, and he screams until he is blue in the face. . . . Then behold us with the two little howlers upon the platform at Stettin. . . . Yesterday I was in such despair at the prospect of all these annoyances, that I positively made up my mind to give the idea of the journey the go-by. Then, in the night, Johanna attacked me, carrying the baby in her arms, and, making use of all the feminine arts which cost our race the privilege of living in paradise. She was naturally able to talk me over, so that we have gone back to our original plan. But I seem to myself a person to whom a terrible injustice is being done. Next year, I shall certainly have to travel with three cradles, nurses, swaddling clothes, and so on. . . . If only my allowance as deputy were larger because I am a family man! Fancy squandering the remnants of a once fine property upon travelling with a pack of infants! I am very unlucky!"

But he now lives thriftily, having no expensive taste save his fondness for wine. Who could believe that this was a correspondence between blue-blooded brothers, when Bismarck writes to his elder brother: "The state of the wool market here was just the same as in Stettin. . . . The sellers lost courage after twenty-four hours. In the good old days, father used often to sit for five days or a week quietly upon the woolsack. The day before the market opened, I sold for seventy-three talers, though I ought to have got seventy-five. . . . In my opinion you let yours go five talers too cheap." Bismarck is still continually short of money. The failure of an expected seventy talers to materialise is an embarrassing circumstance; the saddle horses have to be harnessed to the carriage. Schönhausen, let on lease, brings him from three to four thousand talers. "So far, during the present year, the garden has cost one hundred and three talers, and up till Christmas will certainly cost from forty to fifty more. . . ." He sends his wife an exact account, as follows: "oil, talers 8·8; sugar, vegetables, and salt, talers 9·20. He estimates what his servants cost him, and then says it is an under-estimate, for part of the cost of their maintenance is hidden in the wages of the gardeners, since they consume garden produce." He sends her from Berlin twenty-two pounds of tea, saying: "You must add the cost of carriage if you pass any of it on."

He is delighted when he can save something on his allowance as a deputy.

When he comes home, it is in the mood of a schoolboy on the holidays. "I am leading a gloriously idle life. Smoking, reading, going for walks, playing with the children; I only learn about politics when I read the 'Kreuzzeitung'. . . . I greatly enjoy this idyllic solitude; I lie in the grass, read poems, listen to music, and wait till the cherries ripen." He behaves like a townsman, and is filled with the secret pride of the intellectual worker, just as if he had not lived a countryman's life for a whole decade, very recently too!

If he comes home alone, only the first three days are as charming as he had expected while he was still in harness. There is Odin, the great Dane, whose predecessors and descendants never leave him; he regrets that his wife is not there to see the Turkish wheat, "three feet higher than I can reach with my hands"; and he rejoices at the growth of the young trees in the new plantation. After a very few days, since Johanna is staying with her parents, and he must put in his time on duty at the dike, he grows, first annoyed, and then bored. The cook must be sent away, despite Johanna's objection, for she is dirty, and nevertheless sends an incredible amount of clothing to the wash. "The kitchen is positively filthy. Besides she is half-crazy, and burns wax candles, presumably ours. I do not know where they are kept and how many there were." Soon, all sense of rest and satisfaction have disappeared, and he feels utterly miserable because he is alone. Bismarck positively must have his wife with him unless he is engaged in active and productive work. Thus, during three October weeks, he writes to her a whole sheaf of letters; the tone of former days recurs in them. We hear the distant rumblings of his alarm lest he be condemned once more to solitude and a dull existence.

"I am so frightfully bored, that I can hardly stick it out here.

I am more than half inclined to send in my resignation (let the dike look after itself!) and come to Reinfeld. . . . Be sure you write often, even though the postage should come to a hundred talers. I am always anxious lest you should be ill, and in my present mood I could make my way to Pomerania on foot, I long so much for the children, for Mutsch and Väterchen, and above all for you, my darling. . . . I can no longer rest. What do I care for Schönhausen without you? The deserted bedroom, the empty cradles, the foggy autumn silence, . . . it seems as if you must all be dead. I am constantly thinking that your next letter will bring bad news. . . . In Berlin, I can get along even though I am alone there, for I am busy the whole day, and with plenty of people to talk to. Here it is enough to drive a man mad. I must have been quite a different being in those days when I was able to endure it." Then he has to make up a parcel for her, and as he does so, and goes through the items, he feels a little better: "Next there is a dress of tulle, or something of the sort, with a red band, stockings for the children, all very pretty. . . . This makes me feel so much as if I were with you, . . . that I have become quite cheerful; then I remember the seventy leagues that lie between us, for thirty-five of which there is no railway. Pomerania stretches out to such a terrible length. . . . Countless books have come from the bookbinder. . . . The tailor declares that he has only been able to make five pairs of drawers out of that piece of stuff. I suppose he is wearing the sixth pair himself. God's grace be with you. Your most loving, Von Bismarck."

Through all the warmth and tenderness, we see that this enigmatic man is continually oppressed by the dread that his happiness is fleeting; and the more his contempt for his fellows grows, the more strongly does he become attached to his wife and children. During these weeks, when they are perfectly well and cheerful, his anxiety about them borders upon the hysterical. Because there is no letter for two or three days, he is so much alarmed, "that I can do nothing but sit in front of the fire. I stare at the glowing fuel, and turn over in my mind a thousand possibilities of illness, death, letters gone astray, plans for travel, maledictions upon dike-reeve and overseers." He goes on: "Suddenly I find that my cigars have run out. . . . Now for the first time do I feel how much a part of me you and the babies are, and how you fill my whole nature. No doubt that is why I seem cold to every one except you, even to Mother. If God were to visit me with the fearful affliction of losing you, I think that then . . . I should cling so much to your parents, that Mother might well complain of being pestered with love."

So fiercely does this egocentric man cling to his nearest and dearest, that he has safeguarded himself even in the event of losing them, and will then fling his heart to persons whose company has hitherto been of no importance to him. He is always fleeing from his unresting ego.

His new-found faith in Christ does not save him. Already in the first three years of his married life and his religious belief, God is nothing more than the authority to whom he appeals for help on behalf of his dear ones; and when he tells his wife that he always prays for them "at night, when it strikes two, and alas with more earnestness than I pray for the salvation of my soul", we feel that the words are fraught with meaning. There is not a letter in which he does not commend his wife and children to God's care; there is, likewise, hardly one which discloses any other evidence that he is a believer. "I pray in my room and in the street that he will not take from us what he has been so gracious as to bestow." This is when one of the children is seriously ill, and is no doubt absolutely true. But when Bismarck hears some one, a professing Christian, condemn the execution of Robert Blum, he passionately exclaims: "Wrong, utterly wrong! If I have an enemy in my power, it is my duty to destroy him!"

In a birthday letter to his mother-in-law, writing in the vernacular of the pietist he is addressing, he analyses the cleavage which separates him from the faith: "If only, with God's help, I could banish anger from my heart. . . . However, nothing but God's grace can unite into one the two men within me; and so fortify His share in me, the saved share, that it will slay the devil's share. Unless this happens in the end, things will go ill with me. . . . No doubt God will stand by his part and remain master of the house, so that the other will only be able to show his face in the basement — though he sometimes behaves as if he were really the master."

This humility is the utmost concession his pride can make. For the rest, he merely glimpses a higher power from the vantage ground of his domestic hearth. When, on one occasion, his wife is out of humour, he says to her imploringly: "Do not let anything shake your belief that I love you as a part of myself. . . . I am afraid that I should not be able to please God unless I had you; you are my anchorage on the safe side of the harbour; if that anchorage ceases to hold, then may God have mercy on my soul." So closely interwoven for him are peace and faith, marriage and prayer, that in one hemisphere of the world he cultivates each upon the soil of the other. Thus he hopes that, in the second hemisphere, he may win freedom for his passions.

Questions of taste also influence his moods of piety. Just as he values pietism in women only, so do we find that the congregational singing of Protestant churches is distasteful to him. He writes: "I would rather have good church music, sung by persons who know how to pray for me; Mavrovlachian masses said by white-robed priests, amid the vapour of candles and fumes of incense, would be even finer. . . . Büchsel had a boys' choir; they sang a hymn without any organ accompaniment, sang it out of tune, and with a very vulgar Berlinese accent."

Sometimes, however, the two worlds which he wishes to keep apart venture to mingle. Then he is in a strange dilemma, for he tries to harmonise ambition, duty to the State, and conjugal love. He is summoned to Magdeburg as juryman; on the same day, the king has invited him to a hunting party, and he is eager to go; he has also promised his wife to visit her at Reinfeld. Good resolutions, passions, and sophisms, strive for precedence. We seem to be hearing the argumentation of an adolescent.

"I was casting lots about the matter just now, and did not know whether, while doing so childish a thing, I ought to think about God or not. In the end, my thoughts turned to him, simply because I cannot refuse the invitation without telling a falsehood. Really I want most of all to come to see you, but I could not allege this excuse (though it is as good as any other) since it is certainly not a courtier's excuse. If I tell a lie, and have to stay here after all, it will serve me right. If I speak the truth, then I can at any rate say, 'God's will be done.' Certainly the king wants to have a talk with me. . . . I am writing down for you how my thoughts have been vacillating for the last two hours: showing you how I sometimes conceive of myself as one who courageously carries out God's commandment and renounces the idea of seeing you again soon; now as one who goes to Magdeburg, while lusting after the hunting party as the fox after the grapes; and now as one who is afraid of being detected in having given a false excuse." In the end, he slips out of the net of conscience by accepting the invitation while tacitly reserving the right of crying off. "Besides," he writes, "it may well turn out that by Thursday I shall not have finished my work as dike-reeve."

Though he thus tries to leap over his own shadow, he almost always in the sequel repents whatever choice he makes. Besides ambition, there slumbers a contempt for the results whose worthlessness he had in youth foreseen; and this contempt is ever ready to awaken. If anything goes amiss, if anything irritates him, he promptly speaks of a longing "to lay aside politics and parliamentary life, and to live quietly with you at Schönhausen; life always reminds me of the way in which my dear old father at Kniephof used solemnly to draw his coverts with men and hounds, and always watched for the breaking away of the fox with keen interest — even though he knew as well as I did that there was no fox there."

All the same, though he cannot free himself from this sense of disillusionment, Bismarck will never abandon his political activities again; and the only compensation he finds, the only escape from his contempt for men and things, is to run away from time to time, back to nature and solitude. Then his feelings find free

vent, his heart secures expression, his childhood revives. The poet
in him finds expression: "I was sitting in the Tiergarten on our
bench beside the swannery. The cygnets, which when I was there
with you were still within the egg on the little islet, were now
grey and fat, swimming about unconcernedly among the dirty
ducks. . . . The foliage of the great maple is already dark
red. . . . The paths are covered with the rustling yellow leaves that
have fallen from the limes and the alders and the other trees. . . .
My walk reminded me so keenly of Kniephof, of woodcock shooting and of setting snares there; and of that other time when
everything was so green and fresh, and I went there with you, my
darling." Such moods exhibit his genuine and unsophisticated
sympathy with all created life. After writing to her about the
sale of timber, he suddenly surprises us with the remark: "For
the moment, I have left our little bit of wood standing, for I
couldn't bear to have it cut." Or he goes out shooting, and suddenly finds himself unable to pull the trigger, "for I could see
nothing but mothers and babies."

These are the ups and downs of a profoundly emotional nature,
which has no need of dogma. Again and again, his adult life is
linked on to the days of his youth. That is the Gulf Stream which
flows through Bismarck's heart, when he chances to visit his first
school (which he had left at the age of ten), and when his customary scepticism is replaced by a gentle regret. "How small is
the garden which was my whole world! I cannot realise what has
happened to the great space through which I used often to run
breathlessly; my little garden with its vegetables; . . . and all
the birthplaces of ruined castles-in-the-air, and the blue haze of
the mountains that then lay just outside the wooden fence. . . .
How I used to long in those days for life and the world; the whole
variegated world, as it then existed for me, with its forests and
cities, and all the experiences which awaited me there. . . . This
surged up in my mind as I stood in the garden, and I could have
wept if prosaic Hans had not called me. . . . Then, of course,
I remembered that I now knew perfectly well that the garden was
nothing more than a tiny spot in the Wilhelmstrasse, and that

there was nothing remarkable outside the wooden fence; . . . and that the Dornberg at Kniephof measures sixteen acres; and that we had business to attend to with General Gerlach."

XIV

German unity had been locked up in the Federation coffer at Frankfort under Metternich's protection. Nevertheless, the great flame at which, since the War of Liberation, all the German patriots had warmed themselves, was still glowing in silence, secretly cherished in the small, and the very tiniest fatherlands instead of being boldly fanned; surrounded by stifling vapours which fumed up from the "lead chambers of the Viennese governmental system." For a second time, revolutionary ardour had made its way across the Rhine from Paris; and Europe, greatly astonished, saw political passion manifest itself even among the Germans. Now or never was the time to create, not freedom alone, but German unity as well!

It was a stupendous undertaking, this wresting of liberty and unity out of the graduated mass of dynastic and territorial servitudes. The princes, the military caste, the bureaucrats, and all the wielders of authority, were opposed to liberty. As for German unity, to this the opposition between the newly German Prussia and the three-quarters un-German Austria was an obstacle. Thus the great movement of '48, though uplifted with a wealth of ideas, though winged from within, ended, ere long, with the foundation of spurious freedoms in the " constitutions " of the various German principalities, with the quarrels between the monarchists and the democrats, between Great Germans and Little Germans. Before two tumultuous years were over, the old German local idols had been set up once more.

Of the activities of the Frankfort National Assembly, of its German bill of rights, of the ordinances of this first of our national parliaments, of the cloudy ideas and the abstractions of its constitution, nothing now remained but a parchmented fragment without an executive. From the very first, this was sabotaged by

Austria and all the other enemies of Prussia. Again attempts at
the unification of Germany had come to naught. The old Bundestag under Austrian patronage had been reestablished. In the
summer of 1850, formal invitations to its opening were issued.

What of Prussia? Frederick William IV., refusing the offer of
hereditary empire, had timidly sought refuge in his romanticism.
What was left of his claims to the leadership of Germany was
concentrated in the precarious federation of the small and middle-
sized States of northern Germany, in the so-called Union. The
Erfurt parliament melted away in face of the threats of Austria
and Russia; and the refusal to send delegates to the Frankfort
Bundestag (which had been unanimously broken up in July
1848) was tantamount to provocation.

But Prince Schwarzenberg, the new ruler of Austria, would not
tolerate any equivocation. When the elector of Hesse, weary of
having his doings in his little territory subjected to constitutional control, introduced the Viennese system of government, so
that discontent grew in Hesse, Schwarzenberg, through the instrumentality of the Bundestag, gave him assurance of protection. Was it possible to conceive of a more impudent challenge so
soon after the revolution? Prussia, as head of the Union (to
which Hesse belonged), protested. War seemed imminent, and
Prussia was the guardian of liberty! For a moment, Prussia was
almost popular throughout Germany. Radowitz, general, and
minister of State in Berlin — not a Caesar, but a man — took all
risks. Austria and Bavaria had their men under arms, within
range of the Prussian troops. It seemed as if the hour were at
hand when the rivals would measure their strength in a fight for
the leadership of Germany, and would sweep the old Germanic
Federation into the dustbin. This was in November 1850.

Bismarck, being an officer in the Landwehr, was summoned to
his troop, and was at the same time called to his duties as a
deputy. When he was on his way to Berlin, an old village magistrate came up to the post-chaise to speak to him. This man had
fought in the War of Liberation, and his question was: "Where
are the French forces?" The old warrior was greatly disap-

pointed to learn that on this occasion the enemy was not French, but Austrian. On reaching Berlin, Bismarck's first visit was to the minister for war. He learned that the Prussian troops were so widely dispersed that in the event of war Berlin would have to be surrendered to the enemy. He therefore promised, before the chamber met, to do what he could to promote the spread of moderate views, for fiery speeches might easily precipitate a conflagration, and Prussia must gain time. Lieutenant von Bismarck, with the minister's approval, postponed joining his regiment.

Prince William is passionately in favour of war. He admires Radowitz, who resigns at this juncture, and is actually supposed to have unbuckled his sword and flung it with a curse at the king's feet, saying: "It is no longer possible for a man to serve you with honour!" Even Moltke, chief of general staff, thinks that Prussia has four hundred thousand men ready to fight. "The worst government in the world cannot destroy this nation. Prussia will, in spite of everything, come to the headship of Germany. . . . But it is certainly true that there is no more pitiful nation than the German on the face of the earth!" Radowitz, just after his fall, and immediately before his death, writes "A Vision of 1900", in which we read: "I see a restored German empire, with Prussia at the head; France brought back to her natural frontiers and made harmless by the loss of Alsace." Yet the man who thus foresaw the results of Bismarck's policy, described Bismarck as "le mauvais génie de la Prusse."

Why was Bismarck on the side of peace? Did he believe that Prussia lacked military strength? Perhaps in his case, as in that of the conservative ministers, the real reason for hesitation was dread of the liberal powers. Perhaps he and the ministers, and the king as well, preferred to make common cause with Austria and the reaction, rather than to accept the revolutionary idea of unification. As regards Bismarck, he was continually ordering and then countermanding horses and boots for the campaign, thus showing his inner vacillations. He complained to his wife that intrigue, and nothing else, was deciding the destiny of seventy millions. If peace were to be kept, perhaps he had played his part in the matter. "War, at this juncture, would be utterly absurd, for its outcome would be that our government would move a couple of leagues farther to the left."

Suddenly he drops into the style of a speech which he expects to make next week; says it would be criminal to bring about the death of hundreds of thousands without any need; forgets (for ordinarily he is the most natural letter writer in the world) to whom he is writing, and says: "That is what Prussia has come to. These are the men for whom we shall conquer, if we do conquer; and every democrat with whose help we conquer will display his wound to the king as an unpaid bill. I cannot restrain my tears when I think what has happened to my pride, my joy, my fatherland; and how the loyal, valiant, and honourable Prussian people is drunken with the heady wine it calls 'the honour of Prussia'!" Never in his life has this master of a simple style written, even to a stranger, in such a tone; still less to his wife. He is penning a draft of his speech! When, a few days later, war seems once more imminent, he orders his horse and his arms, closes his epistle in the style of a cavalryman who rejoices at the prospect of a campaign, and for the first time signs himself to his wife: "Ever thine." On another occasion he writes to her: "It is not long since I was greatly looking forward to the distractions of a campaign."

"These are the men for whom we shall conquer, if we do conquer." That is the real reason why Bismarck, the swashbuckler, is opposed to war, a war that is to unify Germany under Prussia's leadership, against Austria. A few days later, peace is definitely decided upon, for Russia has brought pressure to bear. The reason is (as Bismarck explained in old age) that "the Russian tsar likes the young emperor of Austria better than he likes the king of Prussia." Manteuffel, the new minister, goes to Olmütz and tells Schwarzenberg that Prussia renounces the claim to hegemony. The Bundestag, which Prussia had forsaken two years earlier, shall be reestablished, and Austria shall resume the leadership in Frankfort.

The whole of Prussia, on this occasion we may say the Prussian people, is roused. There is a widespread demand for the dismissal of Manteuffel, and for war. In no one should we expect enthusiasm for the national honour to flame up more passionately than in Bismarck. Always he has been an adversary of Austria, always exclusively devoted to Prussia. Now, after such a reverse, how can he help hating his opponent, and desiring his enemy's annihilation? Bismarck was a good hater! He could never come to terms with a conqueror; only with the conquered.

Soon he learns of a detail which wounds his pride. The Austrian prince is quartered in the first storey of the hotel at Olmütz, and has a great suite of attendants, whilst the Prussian representative is housed on the ground floor, has only two servants, and must play the underling. Bismarck realises Schwarzenberg's designs — designs which Schwarzenberg avowed to his friends. The Austrian aim was first to humiliate Prussia, and then to destroy her.

But what happens? Bismarck, the fighter, is up in arms. And for what purpose? In a great speech he defends the government and Olmütz before the Landtag! This is the last and the most important of his speeches as deputy.

"Why do great States make war nowadays? The only sound reason why a great State goes to war, being thereby distinguished from a small State, is egoism and not romanticism. . . . It is easy for a statesman to blow the war trumpet, warming himself at his own fireside the while! It is easy for a statesman to beat the big drum at this tribune, while leaving to the musketeer who is bleeding in the snow to decide whether victory shall be won and fame acquired. . . . Woe unto the statesman who makes war without a reason which will still be valid when the war is over! After the war, you will all look differently at these questions. Will you then have the courage to turn to the peasant who is contemplating the ashes of his farm, to the man who has been crippled by a wound, to the father who has lost his children, and say to them: 'You have suffered greatly, but rejoice with us, for the Union constitution has been saved!'"

After these sarcasms, he turns to the left. He says that people are ready to talk of the honour of Prussia, and that, strangely enough, the liberals are especially fond of doing so. "But you will

not be able to transform the Prussian army, which on March 19th
. . . accepted the rôle of the conquered, into a parliamentary
army. It will always remain the king's army, and find its honour
in obedience. God be thanked, the Prussian army has no need to
prove its courage. . . . I find the honour of Prussia in this, that
Prussia shall, above all, hold aloof from any shameful alliance
with democracy." Then he goes on to speak in behalf of Austria.
He says that Austria is " a German power fortunate enough to
rule foreign nationalities which in old days were subjugated by
German armies. . . . I regard Austria as the representative and
heir of an Old German power, which has often and gloriously
wielded the German sword."

Thus did Bismarck speak at the age of thirty-five, concluding
with a curse against all who would shed human blood on behalf
of the Union constitution, that is to say on behalf of a German
realm without Austria — the very realm for which, sixteen years
later, he was to shed that same blood. Thus did Bismarck defend
Prussia's subjugation at Olmütz; and we do not possess any
private documents to show that this speech was a mere diplomatic
effort, behind which warlike and anti-Austrian designs may have
been hidden. Why did he take this step? The two Gerlachs, Manteuffel, and Brandenburg, all councillors and ministers of the
king, were opposed to the war and on the side of Austria; their
reason was that Vienna was the citadel of reaction. Bismarck
had to march shoulder to shoulder with them, so long as he wished
to use them as a means for his own advancement. Now was the
moment when, by one great speech on behalf of the government
and the king, he could ensure the support of both. His chief aim,
just then, was to win a share of power. Having acquired this, he
would use it for the benefit of his country according to the dictates of his own mind. The Junker sentiments traditional in the
Bismarck family, and the new ambition introduced by the Mencken
strain, were jointly operative in making him the defender of Olmütz.

His calculations were sound. The effect of his speech was to
open for him a diplomatic career. The man who, in this crisis of
national shame, actually ventured to defend that shame, must be

the very man to represent the country at the Bundestag, where, after all, it had again become necessary to cooperate with Austria. He had already laid his plans two years earlier, when he had said: "Things will be worse before they are better. In two or three years from now, there will be a place for people like Kleist and myself in State service." Now the hour had come. Four weeks after his speech he is offered the post of minister in Anhalt. He writes to his wife in the usual style: "I have not hitherto made any push in the matter, but have left it to God. The position is attractive. The duke is an imbecile, and the minister is duke. It would be pleasant enough to rule there as independent duke, . . . and, right in the Harz, to govern the whole valley of the Selke."

Never before has he written this word "rule!" Now he strikes a blow with it as if it were a hammer, and it resounds through the romantic forest region which he would fain upbuild. Since the Anhalt scheme comes to nothing, he hesitates as to his next step, wonders whether he shall keep his Schönhausen coachman, or dismiss the man; treats for the sale of Schönhausen. Then, thinking as a landlord, he adds ironically: "To sell seems to me rather a reckless procedure, though perhaps I take this view for reasons which would have no weight before the Lord."

He enumerates the positions his party friends have secured; proposes to resign the office of dike-reeve; announces that he "will only become Landrat in Schönhausen, Kniephof, or Reinfeld. . . . If we were quite certain to stay in Schönhausen, it would suit me to have another coachman. But if I am sent somewhere else in service, I am used to Hildebrand, and it would be more agreeable to have him."

In service? We seem to be listening to one who has just lost a situation, and is seeking a new one as a means of livelihood. Yet we really have to do with a landowner in easy circumstances, who could never serve a community, who has always done his utmost to avoid having to obey any one. So wholly, now, has he become involved in the wheelwork of political activity, that he can no longer picture himself living a private life. The thought of having to spend a single day at Schönhausen without his wife seems to him "so horrible" that he will not go there, although he has important business to transact. He cannot have enough of Berlin, and especially of the court, and he cannot talk enough about them. He takes up dancing again, though he has not danced for years, with the result that Johanna, alone at Reinfeld, grows jealous; but he soon makes his peace with her, and tells her that after the dance the king had said: "The queen has been making eyes at you for the last half hour, and you never even noticed it!" Another time, Bismarck writes to Johanna about the fairy-like beauty of the White Hall, thronged with a thousand ladies and with men in uniform. "To sit in the gallery, upon a white divan, among palms and plashing fountains, listening to the music, and watching the waves of vanity beneath — this is poetical, and gives one something to think about."

In truth Mephistopheles has not been driven out of him, but has been turned into a tolerably good courtier. He plays the courtier even in his letters home, and when the military attaché from St. Petersburg conveys flattering messages to him from the tsar and tsarina, he reports the matter to his wife with the following gloss: "That is all very fine, but I wish we could both sit quietly in this house, and that it were situated in Kniephof, for that would be more agreeable to me than all the favour of the potentates." He is writing from and writing about the king's castle in Brandenburg, and there is nothing to prevent him and her from living quietly in Kniephof. But court life, after all, is not to be despised; and the dream of the Bismarckian heart would be best fulfilled if he could take the king's palace home, so that in one wing he could install politics and power, and in the other wing tranquillity and Johanna. It is characteristic enough that, writing to her from Berlin, he should complain that his life is a perpetual drive, although the last thing in the world he wants is to be freed from this drive. "To give you a picture of my existence: on Saturday, from ten o'clock in the morning till five in the afternoon, an Ordensfest; at seven, a conference with the president of the department of maritime commerce; documents and accounts until ten; then to see Manteuffel; tea and intrigues till midnight. On getting home, two letters to my constituency, and to bed at two in the morning. On Sunday, up at six o'clock; from seven till nine, negotiations about the ministerial post in Anhalt-Bernburg. Büchsel's sermon till eleven; with the minister for home affairs till noon; visits till three; at six an appointment with Goltz on an affair entrusted to me by the prince of Prussia; at my desk writing about this matter until nine. Then to see Stolberg. To bed at one in the morning."

At length, in the spring of 1851, General Gerlach induces the king to send Bismarck to Frankfort. Gerlach speaks of this appointment as entirely his doing, so we may presume that he has discussed the matter fully with his friend beforehand, especially since he designs to pursue his own policy at the Bundestag through Bismarck's instrumentality — and he regards Bismarck as his political nursling. This appointment, which Bismarck has been thinking about for months (for he has pulled many strings in the hope of obtaining it) is more important than he can reasonably have expected, though much less important than his pride might have demanded. But in Prussia, if a man, be he never so great a genius, wished to force his way into the upper levels of the bureaucracy, a great deal of work upon the "gouvernement occulte" was requisite, suggestions must be plied year after year, there must be court and cabinet intrigues.

Now, writing to his wife with ultra-diplomatic naivety, he represents the appointment which had been the outcome of so much deliberate effort as a chance affair, as something which had come to him much as the offer of a crown had come to Henry the Fowler one day when out bird-snaring. "Every one here is talking about the Frankfort appointment," he writes to Johanna just after he has come back to Berlin from a visit to her. "To-day the matter is mentioned in the 'Vossische Zeitung', but I know nothing about it." Next day: "They really intend to give me some sort of diplomatic appointment. . . . Besides, I want a position which I can regard as a lasting one, so that I can settle down somewhere with you, my angel. . . . It is possible that the affair will be shipwrecked on these wishes of mine. . . . I should very soon give up a position in which I could not enjoy family life." Furthermore: "If I were to put my neck under this yoke, I should have to give up for an indefinite period all the comforts of life, and the hope of living quietly with you and the children as we did during our first winter. God will decide matters as may be best for our souls. . . . I have not expressed any wishes of my own, and am not pushing in any particular direction." Next day: "My poor darling, it now becomes highly probable that I shall go to Frankfort for the nonce, without any fixed position, but with a salary."

For "God", who plays the part of destiny in Bismarck's account of the matter, we may read "Gerlach." What he writes about house and family, about his desire for a permanent appointment, and especially about the goal of his desires being a "yoke" at the very moment when he is arriving there — all these are genuine enough, for he is just as little able to carry on a life of affairs without a yearning for tranquillity as he is able to endure tranquillity without a longing for a life of affairs. When, next day, Manteuffel asks him whether he will accept the appointment, he answers simply: "Yes." Directly he has secured it, his pride, which has long been dammed up, breaks loose. He goes to the king.

"You are a bold man, to take a foreign post like this without previous experience."

"The courage is on Your Majesty's side, for entrusting such a post to me. Your Majesty is under no obligation to maintain me in the position, if I do not show myself worthy of it. I myself cannot be certain whether the task may not prove beyond my capacities; I cannot be certain until I have tried. I have courage enough to obey, if Your Majesty has courage enough to command."

"Very well, then, we will make the attempt."

Thirteen years before this conversation, which reopens for him the door into State service, Bismarck had quitted that service by telling the lord lieutenant's porter that he was going away and would not return. To-day he writes to his wife: "You have

complained that the people at the head of affairs could find
nothing for me to do. Now, beyond my expectations and wishes,
comes this sudden appointment to what is, at the moment, the
most important post in our diplomatic service."

Although in this very letter he has disclosed the fact that his
wife had urged him to seek advancement, and that she had been
vexed because he had not hitherto been given an appointment,
he goes on tranquilly: "I did not seek this position. It is the
Lord's will, and I must comply. I can do nothing else. . . . It
would be cowardly to refuse. . . . I pray devoutly that a merci-
ful God is ordering all things without risk to our temporal welfare, and without harm to my soul." During the next few days he
modifies these ideas, and orders the silken coat and the pistols
without which he cannot enter upon a diplomatic career; he also
tells her that he is only to hold the subordinate position for a few
months, and that then he will become envoy.

Now Johanna begins to voice complaints. "Why are you unhappy?" he rejoins. "Certainly it will be very pleasant in a
foreign land, but I am almost ready to weep when I think of the
rural stillness with you and the household, which, now that it is
far distant in the land of dreams, seems to me more attractive
than ever. . . . You must get used to the idea that next winter
you will have to enter the great world. How else can I keep myself
warm? It is likely enough that for years to come I shall only be
able to get home on short leave from time to time. . . . I am
God's soldier, and I must go wherever he sends me. . . . What
God does is well done; let us face the future with that thought in
our minds. . . . I am homesick, so homesick for you all, and for
the green springtime, and for country life; my heart is heavy.
To-day . . . I went to see General Gerlach, and while he was
giving me his instructions about treaties and monarchs, I was
looking through the windows into the Vossische Garden beneath,
where the horse-chestnut blossoms and the lilacs were waving in
the breeze, and I was listening to the nightingales, and was thinking if only I were standing with you in the window of the dining-
room and looking out over the terrace! I was so absorbed in these

thoughts that I did not follow what Gerlach was saying. . . .
Your letter arrived yesterday evening. I was so unhappy and so
sick with longing for you that I shed tears as I lay in bed. . . .
My salary at Frankfort to begin with will be three thousand
talers. I have to become a privy councillor — a piece of irony
with which God is punishing me for all the abuse I have showered
upon privy councillors. . . . If only I could hold you in my arms
for a minute and tell you how much I love you, and how rueful
I am, Sweetheart, for anything I may have done amiss towards
you. . . . I am sore at heart at this sudden distinction, and more
than ever do I long for you and Teifke, or Freichow. . . . I love
you more than ever, Sweetheart!"

Such are the conflicting thoughts which course backwards and
forwards through his mind. God and redoubled tenderness are to
deaden the pangs of conscience, the pangs which this Christian
feels now that he has attained his end. He cannot bring himself
to acknowledge his purposes candidly, though they are reasonable enough, soundly moral, and suitable. Of what, then, is Bismarck afraid? Certainly he is not afraid of power, and still less
is he afraid of the fight. Perhaps his fears are aroused at sight
of the bureaucratic ladder, a glimpse of which scared him in
youth. He is afraid of it, although as yet he has by no means
climbed to the topmost rung. He is afraid of his superiors, afraid
of being under compulsion, afraid of having to make reports and
to come and go as his chief may command. His pride is afraid of
having to obey. That is why he is suddenly inspired with a passion for rural tranquillity, which he has not cared about for
years; that is why he has these stormy desires to find happiness
and peace in Johanna's arms. But Gerlach is at hand, instructs
his pupil, urges a speedy departure, though he has not finished
the course of instruction. With strangely mingled feelings, the
newly appointed diplomatist adds this postscript to the letter
to his wife:

"Henceforward write to Frankfort-on-the-Main, addressing
your letter to the Royal Privy Legation Councillor von Bismarck, Prussian Embassy."

BOOK TWO: 1852–1862

THE STRIVER

*His genius, which is manifest in every sentence he utters, is continually
making me throw caution to the winds; but he is never wholly
to be trusted.*

—FONTAINE.

I

"I find it incredibly tedious here. . . . The Austrians are continually intriguing under the mask of a rough geniality. . . . The representatives of the lesser States are, generally speaking, diplomatists of an antediluvian type, who think it necessary to assume a professional manner if they are merely asking you for a light; and who choose their looks and their words with Ratisbon punctilio when the only thing they want is the key of the privy. . . . Could I ever become independent in this place, I should clear my field of weeds, or should suddenly make my way home again. . . . I feel myself shelved here, and robbed of my freedom to no purpose. Let's hope there will soon be a change for the better. . . . Besides, I don't know whether and how far I can identify myself with our German policy, unless its main threads pass through my hands. . . . It seems to me that in the domain of Prussian diplomacy, there is very little which can satisfy the ambition or occupy the activities of a fully grown man, unless it be as king, as adjutant-general, or as minister for foreign affairs.

Thus, in the early days of his diplomatic career, does Bismarck's mood oscillate between impatience and boredom, mockery and arrogance. It is but a few weeks since a long-standing wish has been fulfilled, since he has attained a position of power in which he can influence all Prussia — and already he declares there is nothing in what he is doing worthy to occupy the activities of a grown man; he already regards his colleagues as ridiculous, and tugs at the chains he has riveted on himself. If he had been asked whether he would be willing to wait another eleven years, if he had been told that not before 1862 would he have the main threads in his own hands, he would promptly have retired, would have withdrawn under the guns of Schönhausen.

This much is certain, that he had no desire to become adjutant, but would fain have been king. Then, the German problem would have been solved in the twinkling of an eye, and no doubt also the problem of the enigmatical Bismarck.

For what disturbs his nerves now is that for the first time in his life he has to serve, has to have a master over him, a master who is himself a servant. " I must get used," he writes to Johanna from Frankfort on the very first day, " to being a dry man of business who keeps regular hours, must have fixed times for work, must work long spells, and must be content to grow old; playing and dancing are over for me; God has placed me in a position where I must be an earnest man." Thus solemnly does he address his wife. In reality she is no more inclined than himself to believe that hitherto he has not been an earnest man, or that he will become a dryasdust. He remains what he has always been, a man of strong passions. Restless by temperament, he speedily comes to despise whatever he has acquired; his perpetually unsatisfied spirit allows that to crumble away in Mephistopheles' hands which Faust has produced by long endeavour.

" Last spring," he writes to Gerlach, " my appointment to the most unimportant post of chargé d'affaires in Germany, as an apprenticeship, would have exceeded my expectations." In very truth, anything seemed to him better than the wretched babble he had had to listen to for the last three years from the deputies he had always derided. But the diplomatists, with whom he is associating for the first time, promptly seem to him " far more ludicrous than the deputies to the Lower House in their sense of self-importance. . . Now I know perfectly well what we shall succeed in bringing to pass, in one, two, or five years; and I myself will undertake to bring it to pass within twenty-four hours if only the others will retain their senses and be reasonable for a whole day." But hardly is he back again in the Berlin environment, which he has just been extolling, and to the bustle of which he has looked forward longingly throughout his years at Frankfort, than he begins to rage once more at " these sterile disputes in the chamber, where there are all sorts of absurdities to try one's temper. I really find myself longing for the tedious but courteous debates in the Bundeshaus."

Thus syncopated is the rhythm of Bismarck's heart: not only because his clear vision and masterful reason enable him to solve most problems far more quickly than an assembly can solve them; but above all because the daemon in his nature dooms him to despise a thing as soon as it is acquired. When he cannot fight, he is lost. As conqueror of the world, Bismarck would have been bored to death.

He trembles lest Frederick William, under Austrian pressure, may, after all, withhold the definitive appointment as envoy; what a delight for his enemies! He writes to Gerlach: "I am far from being so ambitious as your brother is apt to think me; but if . . . my intended appointment were taken as a party move, the cancelling of it would be regarded as implying that the powers-that-be have, after all, decided that I am unfitted for the post. . . . That is why I now really have an ambition for it." Thus does he press one of the Gerlach brothers, at the very time when he is telling the other that he has no desire in the world but to become envoy. He wishes both of them to hand on to the king what he has told them. But in his private thoughts, he has already made sure of his future, for he writes to his wife: "With the salary of three thousand talers and our own little income, we shall be able to live here, though we shall have to cut things rather close. If, therefore, I do not become envoy to the Bundestag by the summer, I must see if they will grant me an increase of salary. Failing this, perhaps I shall give up the whole affair."

However, his friends persuade the vacillating king, and Bismarck, only thirty-six years of age, who has never before served the State, becomes envoy in defiance of all precedent, because as deputy he was the king's paladin, and because he is a friend of the king's chief paladins.

The first thing he does is to furnish his establishment, making all the arrangements himself, for his wife is inexperienced and moreover is not with him. Now, just as in youth and as in old age, he likes to make himself comfortable and to have plenty of possessions round him. His salary as envoy starts at twenty-one thousand talers, and he has never had the spending of such a sum before, so he begins, though thriftily enough, to make the most of it. "Who would have thought, a year ago "— he is writing to his brother — " or even six months ago, that I should rent a house for five thousand gulden, and should be keeping a French cook in order to give dinners on the king's birthday! . . . I have already spent from ten to twelve thousand talers on furnishing, and have not finished yet. The most expensive requirements are plate, bronzes, glass, and porcelain. Carpets and furniture don't cost quite so much. Since no one here eats two courses with the same fork, for a dinner of thirty persons at least one hundred sets of knife and fork and spoon are needed. . . . Now I have to give a dance for three hundred persons. . . . Work-folk and the shop-people are all on the make; the useless expenditure is enormous; . . . not to mention the cost of twelve servants, half of them men, half of them women! I would much rather have to keep thirty country servants in order."

In this society of pushing people, we may well suppose that no one else began his career with such perfect naturalness. But when we hear Bismarck, after so many journeys and so many visits to court, discussing the number of knives and forks; or when he reports that his old coachman looks like a count in the new livery — such remarks to his brother show how narrow were the circumstances in which the Bismarcks had been brought up; and the " great man of the world ", as the Farther Pomeranian girls had called him, is disclosed as nothing more than a country gentleman of the second magnitude who is suddenly called upon to represent the State. These peasant traits; this thrift as a transfiguration of earlier extravagance; this desire to increase his heritage, to pay off the burdens on his landed estates, to get new properties, to accumulate forests and villages for the benefit of his great-grandchildren — such characteristics remained with Bismarck to the end of his days. Sometimes they were a nuisance to him, but in general they were a source of strength, for they made him as careful an economist in public life as he was in private, and developed from being the qualities of the paterfamilias to become the qualities of the father of his country.

His pride of caste, too, is typical of the Junker who has suddenly made his way into the best society, for it is greater than that of a certain Count Thun, who is not above inviting the rich Frankfort merchants to dinner. Bismarck reports to his chief, Manteuffel, the minister for foreign affairs: "I had the pleasure of dancing a quadrille with the wives of most of the men who have been supplying my house-furnishings, and the civility of these ladies helped me to forget my bitter feelings anent the high bills and the bad wares of their husbands. My vis-à-vis was the wife of the gentleman who is kind enough to provide me with cigars; and the lady next me had as partner the man who the day before yesterday was providing my wife with window hangings." All this is quite in keeping with the character of a man whose first business, in domestic policy too, will be to wage the class war.

In these matters, the only person who can understand him is his brother; though even the latter finds it difficult to understand him in anything else. The brother was "Bismarck translated into the harmless shape of a landowner of the March of Brandenburg." Although, as had been arranged between them, the brothers keep their monetary affairs quite distinct, and although there is no evidence that Bismarck the diplomatist ever gave his brother the squire any important commissions, one sends the other financial reports from time to time. To the local government, to which he himself now really belongs, he complains about supplementary payments, dikes, etc., demanded by the present master of Schönhausen. "Now that I have received the arrears of rent from Schönhausen, I am full of plans for the paying off of debts, and have grown as avaricious as any other capitalist." When he and his wife are invited to visit a duke one day and a grand duke the next, he calculates that "such expeditions, with baggage and servants, tips and carriage hire, cost almost as much as a moderate dinner party in my own house." Then he enumerates the dinner parties which his position compels him to give. "To pay for all these, demands more care from me than I have previously been accustomed to give to monetary affairs. We are now living most thriftily in order to make up for all the expense of the previous winter. By July 1st I shall have my finances in order once more." When he has to defray out of his own pocket a sum of one thousand talers which, prior to this, he has been able to charge up to the State as expenses, he is so greatly annoyed that he becomes "much more stingy in social matters." There is a great deal about his dinner parties, not only in the early letters, but even six years later. "These dinner parties, of which the broken meats are a great nuisance to me! If I eat all that is left, quite by myself, I ruin my digestion; but if I invite gourmets young and old to join me in getting rid of this remnant of the feast, I drink more than is good for me."

Speaking generally, he finds his life in service monotonous. "My time," he writes to his mother-in-law, "is usually spent from morning tea until noon in receiving the visits of envoys and in hearing the reports of officials; . . . then I have to attend sessions, which end at various times between one and four. After that, until five, I have time to get out for a ride, and also to attend to necessary correspondence. . . . We usually have dinner in the company of one or both of the attachés, and the after-dinner hour (though often enough I am called away before I have finished the last mouthful) is usually the most agreeable in the day. I take my ease in the great tiger-skin chair, smoking, surrounded by Johanna and the children, and fluttering the pages of about twenty newspapers. By nine or half past, we are usually told that the carriage is waiting, and, in ill humour, full of bitter reflections concerning society's conception of pleasure, we must dress to play our part in European high society. There, Johanna gossips with the matrons, while I dance with the daughters, or talk grave nonsense with their fathers. Towards midnight or later, we get home, and I read in bed till I fall asleep, to be roused by Johanna's third enquiry whether I am never going to get up."

In the house there is a sort of formless comfort, rather a muddle, for ease always takes precedence of etiquette. Motley, the American, who visits his old friend in Frankfort, says: "This is one of the houses where every one does as he likes. . . . The private rooms are at the back of the house, looking on the garden. Here they are all cheek by jowl, young and old, grandparents and children and dogs; here they eat, drink, smoke, and play the piano, while pistols are being shot off in the garden, all at the same time. In this house you can get anything edible and drinkable; porter, soda-water, small beer, champagne, burgundy, or claret, are perpetually on tap; and every one smokes the best Havanas at all possible times." When Bismarck can wear his flowered dressing-gown till fairly late in the day, perhaps till noon, he is in a good humour. When he has to go out, however, everything must be tip-top. "Instead of ten starched shirts, I would rather have five of better quality; you can't get a decent shirt for two talers."

This sort of life rejuvenates him to some extent, as the oil painting by his friend Becker shows. Now that he has shaved off his beard, he has lost a certain ponderousness of aspect which existed before his days as envoy, and which recurs later. The shaving of the beard had been a sacrifice to diplomacy, for although he assured his wife it was at her request that he had shaved in Berlin, he had really done it owing to a hint from Nesselrode, for he was about to be introduced to the tsar, and Nicholas was supposed to have a prejudice against beards. A sedentary life is new to him, and often harassing. He complains of "a perpetual succession of dinners and parties, which follow one another ever more closely, boring me to distraction and wasting my time. Owing to the mass of sophisticated dishes people take in order to spin out their meals, I find that my liver is being ruined — to say nothing of the evil effects of the lack of exercise." But when his doctor advises him to get up at five in the morning and to wrap himself in a wet sheet, he says he would prefer "some more natural mode of dying, if one could be found."

He can only keep down his weight by riding and shooting. He is always in a fury if business interferes with a shooting expedition. "Shooting is, after all, the best way of spending one's time; and the thickest of forests, where there is no one about, and where there are no telegraph wires, is the only place where I feel really comfortable. I am often homesick for country life. . . . Age is creeping on, and I want to have a quiet time." He begs his brother to find him a saddle horse, "up to my weight, and pretty good to look at. I don't mind how spirited the beast is; on the contrary, I need vigorous exercise." In this matter of ordering a horse, the change wrought by ten years is shown: in those days, horses and women could not be wild enough for him; now he does not want to tame any one, but merely to ply the spurs. Only when, off the coast of Denmark, he can spend the night on deck in a storm; only when in Hungary he hears how his friends have had an affray with robbers in the forest — only in out-of-door life— does he sometimes grow fiery once more, and complain "in tedious Frankfort one has no experiences of that kind."

In very truth, his new occupation ages him quickly. During his years as envoy, from the time he is thirty-seven to the time he is forty-eight, Bismarck's vital energies decline. It is not that he grows more easy-going. Far from it, he becomes increasingly nervous. He sees how time is passing away. Although for a whole decade he is malcontent with all that happens in Prussia, he can alter nothing, and his energy is dissipated in an endless series of reports and letters. "I could never have believed," he writes after two years, "that I should get used to regular work as I have done here. . . . I am continually wondering to what extent I shall be able to constrain my inborn disinclination to penmanship and my natural laziness." If we think of what Bismarck was, we shall realise that he has been effectively tamed when he accuses himself of youthful levity because he has been without newspapers during a fortnight's journey. After three years at Frankfort, he grumbles "because there is a lull in affairs."

Of course he is only referring to high political affairs, and not to everyday matters, which he leaves to his inferiors. At the sittings of the Bundestag, when tedious speeches are being made, he passes the time writing letters to his family. But when, on one occasion, he finds that it is incumbent on him to order the arrest of a young man who has compromised himself politically, he goes early in the morning to see the youth, climbs three flights of stairs, and says: "You'd better leave for foreign parts as soon as possible!" The youth hesitates, and Bismarck goes on: "Apparently you don't know me. Perhaps, too, you are short of funds. Here is some money for you, and you'd better clear out quickly, cross the frontier, or people will say that the police work more efficiently than the diplomatists." In St. Petersburg, again, when a criminal on the run is recognised at the embassy, Bismarck helps the man to escape, provides him with a change of clothing as a disguise, lets him out at the back door — and then goes to scold the police for allowing the malefactor to slip through their fingers! Such irregularities are rare, but when they happen they reverberate with the adventurousness of his youth.

His brain works double tides when he is dictating. His attaché describes him as walking up and down clad in a green dressing-gown, thinking aloud, as it were, in sentences that burst forth impatiently, interspersed with comments. When it suits him, and he can get hold of a secretary, he will dictate from midnight till morning. As a chief, he is, before all, straightforward and genial. He cannot bear a secretary "who grovels with respect so that we are not on comfortable terms together." He invites his secretaries to go out shooting with him, and to drink with him. In respect of circumstantial details, he inspires dread. When he is having a piece of work elaborated, he is never content. As two of his secretaries report in almost identical terms, he treats them like refractory schoolboys. When one of his orders has not been carried out, he says: "I think you yourself must regret this, for I am sure that you must share my opinion that what a man of honour has undertaken to do is as good as done." These and similar remarks, uttered in a gentle tone, chill the hearers to the bone. When an historical blunder has been made, he enquires with cutting politeness: "Is it possible that you have never read page so-and-so in Becker's *Universal History?*"

II

Austria was the chief adversary. He hated Austria, and Austria was already the main objective of all his campaigning, before he had experienced Hapsburg arrogance in Frankfort. To his innate dislike of that country, mistrust was now superadded, thus intensifying his inherited antagonism. For, just as during these twelve years of waiting in Frankfort, his four chiefs at the Foreign Office become suspect to him one after another, because they occupy the place he wants to fill, so does his suspicion fall upon every power that wishes to occupy Prussia's place. To him, all Germany outside Prussia is foreign territory, and especially does this apply to Austria. The staging of affairs at Olmütz had mortified him even more than the conditions of the treaty. He had not defended the treaty in order to avoid war, but merely in order to postpone it; and no doubt, at the moment, feelings of personal ambition may have played their part in deciding his course of action.

At the very outset, the irritation of the man who cannot occupy the first place was keen. Neither as Otto von Bismarck nor as a Prussian was it compatible with his sense of self-importance that he should have to sit at a table cheek by jowl with a dozen other envoys, and where another than himself was president. The man who took the first place was, for this born hunter, his quarry. In self-importance and craftiness, Count Thun was fully equal to Schwarzenberg. Bismarck describes him as "presiding in a short jacket, which, . . . buttoned up, conceals the absence of a waistcoat. There is but a faint intimation of a necktie. He carries on the business in a conversational tone." The wording shows the newcomer's supreme contempt for the man of whom he is speaking; and we cannot believe him when he declares that he contemplates this strange specimen with all the dispassionateness of a man of science. "Thun plays hazard at the club till four o'clock in the morning; dances from ten till five without a pause and with obvious enjoyment, consuming meanwhile an abundance of iced champagne, and ostentatiously paying court to the pretty women of the mercantile community, doing so in a way which suggests that he is quite as much concerned with the impression he is making on the spectators as he is with his own pleasure. . . . He is a mixture . . . of aristocratic nonchalance and Slav peasant cunning. Cautious disingenuousness is his most salient characteristic." Of Thun's assistant, a baron, Bismarck writes: "From time to time, the man is a poet; he is sentimental, readily provoked to tears by a drama; he is outwardly amiable and obliging, and drinks more than he can carry."

These sarcasms have a devastating effect; but they do not disclose what were the initial words and the glances which aroused so strong an animus. Bismarck, when he was still only a secretary of legation, had paid his first visit to Thun. He had been accompanied by another Berlinese official. The Austrian, who knew that Bismarck's appointment as envoy was imminent, deliberately left him out of the conversation as much as possible. On leaving, Bismarck said to his colleague, "his voice trembling with excitement": "Did you see how Thun treated me?" As far as the men's personal relationships were concerned, matters were decided once for all by this interview. We are rather surprised to learn that on a subsequent occasion Thun should have received Bismarck, who paid an official call as envoy, seated, smoking, and in his shirt sleeves (ostensibly because the weather was very hot); and that Bismarck, at his second visit, should have astonished his colleague by lighting a cigar. He was careful that all the world should know this next day.

During the sittings of the Bundestag he writes private letters: "My position is rendered rather difficult by the cross-fire of breath to which I am exposed from my neighbours X. and Y. You will remember the smell of the former, which is a powerful mixture of his uncleaned decayed teeth, and of his rank armpits when he unbuttons his coat. As for the other, his smell before meals gives unmistakable evidence of a disordered digestion, the inevitable result of a combination of too many heavy dinners and insufficient exercise. This is the natural odour of diplomats and marshals of the household."

It was not entirely Bismarck's fault that all problems here in Frankfort assumed a personal aspect. This was part of the atmosphere of the Bundestag, where ostensibly all were equals and Austria was only the primus inter pares; it was the outcome of recent history. How could it be expected that the Austrian representative should not wish, at this table, to humiliate the Prussian envoy before all the world, seeing that Prussia had three years earlier departed from the place declaring her intention to establish a new confederation from which Austria was to be excluded — and had now come back in the guise of a penitent? Austria could reckon upon the support of most of the other States, whereas Prussia could only count on the votes of four of the northern German petty principalities. All the others were suspicious of Prussia, for they believed that she wanted to subjugate them in her Union, and, with the aid of an ill-starred Germany, to carry out the idea of revolution; whereas the mighty land of Austria attracted all the legitimists, this meaning nearly all the princes, to her side.

Thus in Frankfort Bismarck finds nothing to surprise him, but only confirmation of his previous views. Right on into old age he speaks of friendship between Austria and Prussia as nothing more than "a dream of youth, arising out of the after effects of the War of Liberation . . ." He had come to Frankfort as an opponent of Austria, but he was certainly astonished at the intensity of Austria's hostility to Prussia. It was here that he first learned of Prince Schwarzenberg's despatch concerning Olmütz, to the effect that it had rested with him (Schwarzenberg) "to humiliate Prussia or magnanimously to forgive her." It was during the very days when that arrogant report had been sent, that Bismarck, in the Prussian Landtag, had defended the Olmütz treaty. Was it not inevitable that his pride should be outraged at the sight of these words?

Within six weeks of his arrival in Frankfort, he expressed himself as follows: "The Austrians are, and will remain, people who cheat at cards. In view of their overwhelming ambition, and of their home and foreign policy, which is not guided by any ideas of right, I think it impossible that they will ever enter into an honest alliance with us."

In November he used his first chance of hitting back: " Count Thun spoke in the same sense as Posa, expounding Great German fantasies. I supplemented his exposition by saying that, according to such an outlook, the existence of Prussia, and still more the occurrence of the Reformation, were regrettable facts. . . . There did not exist in Europe any such Prussia as that which, to quote his expression, ' repudiated the heritage of Frederick the Great'; and before I could advise on such a policy at home, matters would have to come to the arbitrament of the sword." There is a fragment from the dialogue between these two friendly allies. A dozen veils are torn aside, and our only wonder is that Bismarck's war did not arrive for another fifteen years.

These strictures, sedulously reported to Vienna, naturally increased the jealousy between the two powers. Nor was the mood in Berlin rendered very conciliatory when Gerlach read aloud to the king a passage from one of Bismarck's letters, in which the latter declared that all their misfortunes were the outcome of the surrender to Austria, "for one who shares my bed can much more easily thrash me, poison me, or strangle me, than a stranger can, . . . especially when the man who shares my bed is ruthless and a coward." It does not help matters much when Count Thun is recalled, and is replaced by the statesman who has up till now been the Austrian envoy in Berlin.

Count Prokesch-Osten, a more interesting man than Thun, well-informed about the Near East, highly cultured, a better European, makes his Prussian Colleague uneasy by other characteristics. Prokesch-Osten calls on Bismarck too often, stays too long, is too amiable in the way he plays with the children, talks to him too long during the sessions. "In other respects, my position in relation to him is plainer than it was in relation to Thun, for Thun sometimes spoke the truth, but Prokesch never does." Still, said Bismarck, one could always read the true state

of affairs in the man's face. Unfortunately, Prokesch was careless enough to leave anti-Prussian documents in a writing-desk
which he sold. These were drafts of revolutionary articles to be
inserted in Prussian newspapers, such articles as had hitherto
been ascribed to the democrats. Thereupon Bismarck advises
offensive and defensive measures of the same calibre. It would be
a mistake to render the Austrian envoy's position untenable by
denouncing his tactics to Vienna. The best course would be " to
make him uneasy as to his position, and to tell our allies about
the matter confidentially, so that our forbearance may appear
to them in an advantageous light." It would be a good thing to
reprint some of Prokesch's spurious articles, with the implication
that the government's suspicions have been aroused for the first
time by the discovery of these documents in private hands.

So cunningly does Bismarck go to work, Bismarck who is
always ready to complain of his opponents' sincerity! But Prokesch has a good knowledge of men. Here is his striking characterisation of Bismarck: "Herr von Bismarck declared that
Prussia was the centre of the world. . . . He represented an
endeavour to destroy the Federation. If an angel had come down
from heaven, Bismarck would not have admitted this angel unless
he had worn a Prussian cockade. . . . As clear-headed as Machiavelli, he was too shrewd and too smooth to despise any means
that came to his hand, and we must admit that he was never a
man for half-measure. . . . Thus did he indefatigably try to
paralyse the Federation; . . . and, making a lavish use of the
press, he knew how to imply that Austria was the guilty
party. . . . So impressed was he with the importance of Prussia's mission, that he more than once declared to me that the
unification of Germany under Prussia was indispensable. Never
before have I met a man so secure in his convictions, so self-
confident in his will."

Bismarck would have admitted the soundness of this judgment,
and it is one which has been confirmed by posterity. At the slightest affront to his Prussian attitude he was ready to draw his
pistol. When Count Rechberg of Vienna lost his temper after one

of the sittings, declared that he really must demand satisfaction, and that they would fight in the wood near Bockenheim, Bismarck answered quietly: "Why should we bother to go so far? There is plenty of room to exchange shots in the garden here. Some Prussian officers live hard by, and you can find some Austrians easily enough. All I would ask is that you will allow me to describe the origin of the quarrel, for I do not wish my royal master to look upon me as a swashbuckler who is over-ready to conduct diplomacy by force of arms." Thereupon he begins to write his report. Rechberg sees that he is making a fool of himself, takes himself off, and allows the whole matter to lapse.

A journey to Vienna strengthened the mutual hostility between Bismarck and the Austrians. The German Customs Union, the forerunner of a united German realm, was the strongest tie between Prussia and the other States of Germany. Now that the time had come for the renewal of this Customs Union, Austria wished to blunt its political edge by joining it. The entrance of all the Austrian States into the Union would have given Austria the lead in tariff questions as well as in political. Bismarck, who offers a commercial treaty instead, will not budge from his position, and goes home from Vienna leaving matters as they were. This is his first great success, for, notwithstanding all the intrigues of Austria, the Customs Union is renewed without the admission of that power. The only person who pleases him in Vienna and in Ofen [Buda], and the only person pleased with him, is the young emperor, now twenty-two years of age; and when he reads a letter from the king of Prussia aloud to the emperor of Austria, it is likely that nothing in the letter pleases him more than the statement that his family has lived in the March longer than the Hohenzollern. Of Francis Joseph, in those days, Bismarck said commendingly that the emperor had "fire, dignity, thoughtfulness, a frank expression, candour, and openness, especially when he laughs."

As the king's favourite, he has during all these years a peculiar relationship to his chief, who naturally detests him. Bismarck's appointment had been displeasing to the minister president, for it had been engineered by the Gerlach camarilla, with which Manteuffel was on terms of acidulous friendship. Petty, cold, cunning, aspiring, vacillating, liberalising — such was Manteuffel's rule during the eight years in which Bismarck acted as his subordinate in Frankfort. In reality, Bismarck often had more influence on the leadership of affairs than Manteuffel, and was always a disturbing influence. Inasmuch as Manteuffel knew that Bismarck was likely to be his successor, and was aware that Bismarck was both able and impatient, he could not venture to play the chief, and rarely went so far as to withstand Bismarck, though at times he would show strange obstinacy in small matters, and would succeed in counteracting Bismarck's influence with the king. When a wire came from Frankfort to the effect that the baggage of a certain suspect consul should be seized, Manteuffel made a cabinet question of the matter by inviting this same consul to a court dinner. On another occasion, when Bismarck wanted an incompetent official in the Frankfort chancellery to be pensioned off, Manteuffel refused. When Gerlach summoned Bismarck to Berlin, Manteuffel wrote acrimoniously that he must not stay away too long.

Bismarck, on the other hand, tells us that he is "much lazier than last year, for my diligence finds no echo in Berlin and has no results there." Although the relationships between the two men were outwardly civil, and although they exchanged innumerable letters, nay although Manteuffel actually stood godfather to Bismarck's son, the chief employed a famous secret agent to get hold of the portfolios in which the king's, Gerlach's, and Bismarck's letters went to and fro. When, after some years, the king sent an enquiry to his envoy through Manteuffel, asking whether Bismarck would like to become minister for finance, the premier took it upon himself to reply to the king: "Bismarck simply laughed in my face!"

The centre of these intrigues, the leader of the "gouvernement occulte", is Leopold von Gerlach, adjutant-general and the king's friend, the man who has secured Bismarck's appointment in order to strengthen his own party against Manteuffel. Except for Bismarck, whom he wished to train for his own purposes, Gerlach despised all those with whom he came in contact. He spoke of Manteuffel as a man without principle, and as an untrustworthy minister. The king was "a very strange person, not to say quite incalculable" — this meaning, in plain terms, that Gerlach regarded the king as insane. Experienced, pious, and a master in the art of intrigue, twenty-five years older than Bismarck, he regarded the latter as his own discovery, looked upon himself as an adoptive father, and scarcely realised how soon this adopted son, though so much younger than himself both as man and as official, had come to excel, not Gerlach only, but the king and Manteuffel as well, in mastery of intrigue. With no one did Bismarck go more cautiously to work than with this friend of his king, so long as Frederick William was on the throne. But as soon as William became regent, the relationships between Bismarck and Gerlach grew far less intimate, for William could not endure Gerlach.

To no one else did Bismarck write so many letters and such notable ones. They are of the same inestimable value, as evidence of his political ideas, as his letters to his wife are valuable as evidence of his domestic sentiments. They sparkle with lively thoughts and sarcasms, with crackling expressions of enmity, and with far-reaching and thunderous schemes of power. These letters, many of which occupy twelve pages of print, were usually read aloud to the king, and were therefore for Bismarck a means of directly influencing the monarch; and they perhaps worked more powerfully than the spoken word would have done, seeing that they were written by a master hand and were carefully thought out. At first Bismarck writes to Gerlach as " your excellency ", signing " your most obedient friend and servant." Later, the superscription is to "honoured friend", and he signs " yours sincerely." Countries are humorously spoken of by the names of villages, and individuals are alluded to as Shakespearean characters. Some of the letters are extremely lively. Some are entirely filled with malicious gossip and quaint anecdotes of court life. All these are obviously designed to interest and amuse, not only

Gerlach, but also the indirect recipient. All the same, the adoptive father sees to it that his adopted son shall not wax too strong for him. In 1854, he prevents the king from appointing Bismarck to a ministerial post, and takes care that his protégé shall not get too much influence in the conservative party. In other cases, Gerlach assumes the ecclesiastical manner in the most delectable way. When Bismarck wants "in the interests of the service, to employ a rogue", Gerlach thinks it necessary to remind him "of the apostle's warning against doing evil that good may come." In such times of tension it is always Bismarck who swallows his pride lest he should lose this indispensable go-between. To Gerlach, the old gladiator, Bismarck replies in a pious tone that will go to his correspondent's heart:

"I endeavour . . . to win back . . . to community with you . . . daily, with the aid of prayer, and submission to the leadership of the Lord, who has appointed me to this post." Again: "I shall be utterly uprooted if I get out of touch with you. . . . If I am to serve the king joyfully, I cannot get on without the consciousness of an intimate and trustful intercourse with you, whose comrade-in-arms I have been, not only in evil times, . . . and from whom no difference concerning the common principles and aims of our activities can ever separate me." Again, ending a letter: "Farewell. Doubt that the stars are fire, etc. (see *Hamlet*), but never doubt my love!" Again: "Do not let anything shake your confidence in me! For the king and for you I am to be trusted à toute épreuve." When Bismarck, in later days, himself received such letters, how he mocked at the motives of the senders!

But he has to build the bridge leading to power; and one who aspires so high, must grasp at all available means to make sure of the support of the king, who is almost an absolute monarch. Frederick William was in love with Bismarck for several years. He liked to plume himself on having discovered this statesman. "He saw in me the egg which he had himself laid and hatched." At the same time, Bismarck was always useful to him as a bogey to frighten his ministers; or, as he said, to bring Manteuffel to heel. As his mental disorder increased, it became common enough

BISMARCK IN 1855

From a painting by Jakob Becker

for him to cheat his own ministers. He would have urgent and important despatches drafted by the camarilla instead of by Manteuffel; he would then send the draft to Bismarck in Frankfort; thereupon Bismarck would get into touch with Manteuffel about the matter; and Manteuffel would look up one of the French émigrés, and would wait several days until this gentleman had found the best French phrase "which would hold the mean between the obscure, the ambiguous, the dubious, and the alarming." At other times the king would ask Bismarck to write memorials to counteract those emanating from the Foreign Office. Favourite though he was, Bismarck would complain, now and then, of Frederick William's autocratic paroxysms; would speak of "his terrible uncertainty of opinion, of his irregularity in business matters, of his accessibility to backstairs influences."

Again and again, during the early years of his Frankfort life, Bismarck was summoned to Berlin by the king or by Gerlach. In one year, he travelled more than two thousand leagues between Frankfort and Berlin. Occasionally he went to Berlin against Manteuffel's wish, because the king wanted him. If, as sometimes happened, his coming to Berlin was delayed by the needs of the service, Frederick William would not receive him on arrival, and yet would not give him permission to return. "This was a kind of educational method, such as is used in the schools, when a pupil is expelled from a class, and then readmitted. I was, as it were, interned in the palace at Charlottenburg, a state of affairs which was rendered more tolerable to me by an excellent and admirably served breakfast." When the king wanted to make him envoy in Vienna, and Bismarck rejoined that he would feel this equivalent to being handed over to his adversary, and that he would only go upon express command, the king said: "I will not command you. You ought to go voluntarily, and to beg me for the favour. . . . You ought to be grateful to me for undertaking your education, for thinking that you are worth so much trouble."

The typical relationships between potentate and favourite, when the favourite has to endure the caprices of the weather! Once the king summoned him to Rügen in order to redraft a note

of Manteuffel's, which did not satisfy Frederick William. The re-
vised note was despatched, Bismarck was praised for its tenor,
and was still kept dancing attendance, although for days past he
had wanted to get back to his wife who was ill. At length Bismarck departed without leave, and the king thereupon punished
him by sending a telegram to countermand the note. He got it
back into his own hands and altered it from Bismarck's wording.
Thus was the kingdom of Prussia ruled in those days.

Bismarck was never inclined to overestimate the value of these
activities. He was well aware how fleeting is the favour of princes.
"Now all is sunshine when I arrive. The court forgives me; great
folk flatter me; lesser folk want something of me, or to gain something through me. But it is not very difficult for me to remember
that these gilded glories may be gone in twenty-four hours, and
that then, at a court festival, I shall have the opportunity of seeing just as many cold backs as I can now see friendly faces."

No doubt, therefore, he is not surprised when, five years later,
he writes in almost the same words to Gerlach: "There has been
a change of scene. Either the king has discovered that I am just
as ordinary a person as all the rest of us, or else somebody has
been carrying evil tales of me — true enough, belike. . . . Anyhow, he has less need to see me than of yore; the court ladies'
smiles are less cordial than they were; the men no longer give me
a fervent hand-clasp." He continues, with a change of tone:
"You, my most honoured friend, are comparatively free from this
pettiness of the courtiers; and if your confidence in me is less im-
plicit than it was, I beg you to give me other reasons than this
change in court favour."

With so delicate a touch can Bismarck key up the elegy of a
favourite who is now out of favour, key it up to suit the ears of
a pious courtier; thus gently can he glide from a tone of modest
reproach into one of adulation addressed to a philosophic mind.

III

Tsar Nicholas was the mightiest man in Europe. Only in his gigantic empire had everything remained quiet. There only did serfdom persist unchanged and apparently unnoticed. When the revolution broke out in Hungary, the tsar was able to send young Francis Joseph a considerable corps of auxiliaries, a force big enough to turn the scale. Thenceforward, Nicholas was inclined to regard the emperor of Austria as a sort of vassal. Now was the moment to take charge of Constantinople and to partition Turkey, the land which he was the first to describe as the Sick Man; but Napoleon did not wish to surrender the key of the Holy Sepulchre. He wanted to take personal revenge for his uncle's defeats in the years 1812 and 1814. Moreover, he had been affronted because the arrogant tsar, when writing to him, had addressed him, not as "mon frère", but only as "mon cousin." Such were the farcical considerations which then decided the destinies of Europe. In the beginning of 1854, war was imminent between Russia on the one hand, and an alliance of the French, the British, and the Turks, on the other. Austria, dreading Russia's expansion in the Balkans, had determined to join the alliance of the western powers. The same question was under discussion in Prussia.

All Prussians with liberal sentiments wanted to fight on the side of the western powers, against Russia. Even among those who stood nearest to the king, many favoured war, and the leader of the war party was Prince William. Manteuffel had already approved the idea of sending an ultimatum to St. Petersburg. Only the old conservatives, led by Gerlach, were opposed to the idea of attacking the Russian citadel of reaction, for, they said, Russia had been Prussia's ally in 1813. In March, when the crisis was at its height, Gerlach recalled Bismarck to Berlin. Thereupon, William promptly sent for him. Not that he liked the man, but he knew that Bismarck had great influence over the vacillating Frederick William. Besides, he and Bismarck were on fairly good

terms, and Prince William had recently, side by side with Manteuffel, stood sponsor to Bismarck's second son Wilhelm, later
known as Bill.

"You see before you two conflicting systems," began William,
"one of which is represented by Manteuffel, and the other (Rus-
sophil) by Gerlach here and by Münster in St. Petersburg. You,
being a new arrival, are summoned by the king in some sort as
arbiter; your opinion will turn the scale, and I implore you to
express it in the following sense: 'Russia's attitude is ranging the
whole of Europe against her, and she will ultimately be defeated'." The actual fact was that William had a friendly feeling
for his nephew the tsar, and wanted to take a strong line against
Russia in order to intimidate Nicholas, who, he thought, would
then give way before a united Europe, and be saved.

"I can't do that," rejoined Bismarck. "We have no ground for
war, nothing to fight for, and should only arouse bitterness and
a thirst for revenge in a conquered neighbour. Out of dread of
France, or in order to serve England, we should be assuming the
rôle of an Indian vassal prince who has to carry on war for the
benefit of his English patrons."

"There is no question of vassals or of fear!" exclaimed the
prince, reddening with anger. In his voice, Bismarck hears the
tones of Augusta (Bismarck believed her to be anti-Russian in
opposition to her Russian mother — a psychological counterpart
to the antipathy he felt towards his own mother). He also considered that Augusta "had more interest in all foreign matters
than in those which lay near at hand." In Coblenz, where William
and Augusta now lived, a rival court to Sans-Souci had already
formed.

This was the second time that William and Bismarck had met
as adversaries. Four years earlier, William had wanted war
against Austria, whereas Bismarck had wanted to go to Olmütz;
and William had considered the appointment of his opponent as
envoy to Frankfort a further mark of subjugation to Austria.
Now the prince is afraid of humiliation by Russia. Is he to look
upon Bismarck as a coward? "In any case," he writes furiously to

Manteuffel, "this man's political activities are like those of a senior schoolboy."

In actual fact, for the first time in his life, Bismarck was engaged in political activities on the grand scale. During the Crimean War he became a European statesman. Whatever Prussia did, so he thought, would in the end redound to Austria's advantage. For that reason he did not wish "to couple our smart and seaworthy frigate to Austria's worm-eaten battleship. Great crises constitute the weather which favours Prussia's growth, provided that it is fearlessly (perhaps even ruthlessly) turned to account by us. . . . Anyhow, as things develop, the value of our support will increase." Vienna ought only to be given Prussian support in return for admitting Prussia's predominance in Germany. But the vacillating king does not know what to do, enters to-day into an offensive and defensive alliance with Austria, to-morrow dismisses the advocates of this policy, for the second time sees his brother leave him in a passion, and knows that the Berlinese are saying: "In Sans-Souci he goes to bed with France and England, and gets up next morning with Russia."

During the next year, Bismarck severed himself even more widely from court opinion, and this time from the king as well. Without any special commission, he went on a visit to Paris, and returned with the impression that there was no reason why Prussia should not work hand in hand with Napoleon, provided the circumstances were such as to be advantageous to Prussia. This idea aroused horror at Sans-Souci. Gerlach wrote pious letters against this "consorting with the evil one." The king's disfavour was manifest! A second visit to Paris, an official one this time, confirmed Bismarck in his views.

Between 1857 and 1861 he had four intimate conversations with Napoleon III., each of them more astonishing than the previous one. Napoleon let his tongue wag too freely, and perhaps Bismarck did the same. Their last meeting was to be at Sedan. For the nonce, however, after the Crimean War and after the peace signed in Paris, Napoleon could regard himself as the arbiter of Europe, whereas the Prussian envoy who appeared before his throne seemed a man of minor importance. None the less, Bismarck's reception is a brilliant one. The empress makes much of him, and he is captivated by both emperor and empress. He says that Napoleon is a very intelligent man and most friendly. Eugénie is even handsomer than her portraits, most gracious and amiable. He tells us that he "admires her greatly, . . . she is really a most remarkable woman, not in looks only." (Of him Eugénie says: "Il est plus causeur qu'un parisien.") Such are the words, repeated both privately and officially, of the man who had written mockingly and disparagingly of the rise of this parvenu, and had railed at the revolution which had in the end made Napoleon emperor. These are the words of Bismarck, Prussian through and through, monarchist and legitimist. This is the man who now writes so enthusiastically of Paris and of the two upstarts! All the same, both now and later, the French are as alien to him as the English are congenial. Although Paris fascinates him to-day, he will soon find fault with it. Why not with the emperor too? Has he really become so much fired because Napoleon has paid him honour?

Bismarck is a man of ice. The fire which animated him in the Landtag when attempts at revolution or democracy were being made in the homeland, has long since been extinguished. Coldly, and with a clarity which liberates him from the sway of principles, he contemplates the interplay of forces. He knows that Napoleon is eager to enter into an alliance with conquered Russia; and that Austria, too, is wooing the tsar. What course must Prussia take, if she is not to be left isolated in the middle, in danger of destruction? An alliance with France! The emperor meets him half way, admits that he would be foolish to demand the Rhine frontier, says that only in the Mediterranean does he wish to advance.

"The Frenchman is a land fighter, not a sea fighter; and for that very reason his fancy is tickled at the thought of conquests by sea. Prussia must expand; must annex Hanover, Schleswig, and Holstein; then become a sea power of the second magnitude, in order to join with the French and hold the English in check.

With that end in view, I should like to be able to count upon Prussia's benevolent neutrality if I should ever become involved in complications with Austria on account of Italy. I wish you would sound the king about these matters."

Bismarck: "I am doubly pleased that Your Majesty should make this declaration to me: first of all, because it is a proof of your confidence; secondly, because I am, no doubt, the only Prussian diplomatist who would venture to keep these declarations to himself when he gets home, and would not reveal them even to his sovereign—for it is quite out of the question that His Majesty would entertain such proposals for a moment. It would, indeed, be indiscreet to let His Majesty know of these proposals, for that might endanger the good understanding with France."

Napoleon: "That would be more than an indiscretion; it would be treachery!"

"You would sink in the mire," said Bismarck. Napoleon accepted the hint; thanked Bismarck for his frankness; and promised to hold his tongue about the matter.

The first time Bismarck is put to the test in the European arena, he shows himself at the very climax of his powers. Instead of answering, as an ordinary diplomatist would, that he has no instructions, and will duly report what has been said, he has sufficient presence of mind, courage, and sense of responsibility to annul at the very outset this foreigner's plan for interfering in German affairs. He tramples out the flame before any one else can catch sight of it. He does this although he is Austria's enemy; although, almost alone among Prussian statesmen, he is determined to advise an alliance with the emperor! "Thou com'st in such a questionable shape," he says to himself—and indeed we are amazed that the shrewd Frenchman should make so heedless a proposal. Are we to suppose that he understands and sees through the Prussian's new diplomacy, and that he wishes to enforce frankness by frankness?

If so, he errs fatally; for Bismarck is frank when he wishes to terrify or to bluff, but never when his adversary trusts him. By the form of his answer to Napoleon, he wishes to gain the latter's confidence; and he does so. Furthermore, as he has promised, he suppresses details in his report; though directly he gets home, he tells both Gerlach and the king all about the matter. Although to Napoleon he has described himself as the only Prussian who would venture to conceal the latter's proposition, at home he is the only Prussian who has nerve enough to advise the king to invite Napoleon to Berlin — at the very time when the "Kreuz-zeitung" is persistent in its abuse of the emperor of the French. For the first time, in the course of his development, the great realist stands up against the Potsdam romanticists, the man without principles stands up against the legitimists; for the first time we see him liberated from the principles of a party to which he had never given a sworn adhesion. In lengthy correspondence with Gerlach, he now parts company from his master, on utilitarian grounds; sacrifices the fundamental principle of legitimacy to which he was supposed to be devoted. The party man has become a statesman who is willing to abandon his own obsolete judgments.

"The man [Napoleon] certainly does not impress me. I have very little capacity for admiring men, and it is perhaps my weakness that I have a keener sight for defects than for merits. . . . If you are referring to a principle applicable to France and to his legitimacy, I certainly agree that I fully subordinate this to my specifically Prussian patriotism. France only interests me in so far as it reacts upon the position of my fatherland; and we can only enter into political relationships with the France which actually exists. I look upon that country as nothing more than a piece, a necessary piece, upon the chessboard of politics. My only mission in playing the game is to serve my king and my country. My sense of duty in the foreign service of my country is such that I can find no justification for sympathies or antipathies, either in myself or in others, towards foreign powers and personalities; such sympathies and antipathies are the germ of disloyalty towards king or country. . . . In my view, not even the king is entitled to subject the interests of the country to his own feelings of love or hatred towards foreigners. . . .

" I ask you whether there is any cabinet in Europe which, more than the cabinet of Vienna, has a born and natural interest in preventing Prussia from growing stronger and in diminishing Prussia's influence in Germany. . . . As far as foreign countries are concerned, I have never in my life had any sympathy except for England and its inhabitants, and even at the present day I am not free from this. But people will not accept our friendship; and as soon as any one can show me that it will be in the interest of a sound and carefully considered policy, I shall be equally satisfied to see our troops fire at the French, the Russians, the English, or the Austrians.

" When have any of these powers given signs, and what signs have they given, of ceasing to be revolutionary? It seems that we are to forgive them their illegitimate birth as soon as we are in no danger from them; and that we are not, on principle, to find fault with them when they continue, impenitently and even glorying in their shame, to acknowledge that they are rooted in illegality. . . . If we are to find a terrestrial origin for the revolution, we should seek it rather in England than in France, unless, indeed, even earlier in Germany or in Rome. . . . How many existences are there in the modern political world which are not rooted in revolutionary soil? Consider Spain, Portugal, Brazil, all the American republics, Belgium, Holland, Switzerland, Greece, Sweden, . . . England. Even as regards the territory which the contemporary German rulers have won, in part from the emperor and the empire, . . . and in part from their own estates, no fully legitimate title of ownership can be established; and as regards our own State, we cannot claim that we are perfectly free from the utilisation of revolutionary foundations. . . . But even if the revolutionary manifestations of the past have not yet attained the degree of prescriptive right which would enable one to say of them, like the witch in *Faust:* 'Here I have a flask out of which I myself sip at times, and it has now no evil smell whatever ', — still, we have not always been chaste enough to abstain from loving caresses."

Here for the first time we encounter Bismarck the statesman.

In this letter to Gerlach we trace the fundamentals of his political career. When he is eighty-two, he will still hold the same opinions that he holds at forty-two. Let us suppose that the liberals had had as efficient a spy service as the government, and had been able to get hold of this letter. What would one of the left-wing deputies have said about the phrases it contains, when he recalled that a few years earlier this same Junker had been railing against the territories and the crowns which owed their position to bloody revolutions and street fighting? " Is that so? " he would say. " Essentially, then, we are all of revolutionary origin; and what matters is, not the revolution, but how long ago it took place! The crowns which are said to be worn by the grace of God, do not come from God, after all; the rebellions of peoples and the ambitions of princes, the class war and the rivalry among the dukes, forcibly decided, of old, the ownership of land, and developed it into property. They do the same thing to-day. Why, then, is a Hohenzollern more legitimate than a Bonaparte? Why is a Romanoff tsar better entitled to rule than a prince of the house of Savoy? What justification is there for the privileges of the nobles? " Is this the first time one waging the class war has uttered truths concerning kings and nobles?

By no means. Bismarck knew all this seven years ago quite as well as to-day. To-morrow he will deny it officially; just as he denied it seven years ago when, in his own land, he wished to fortify the prerogatives of his own class. That is what he does at home. Abroad he feels free to act precisely in the way he thinks will be advantageous to his own country. He has no prejudices as regards foreign affairs. What was dogma at home, becomes sentimentalism abroad; what were reasons of State at home, are ridiculed as romanticism abroad. Bismarck's fundamental idea is to apply different standards to the measurement of home policy and foreign policy; and we may say that it was he who, à la Richelieu, introduced such a double standard into Germany. Out of this cleavage arose all those mistakes thanks to which the Germans at home were allowed to pine and languish, what time, abroad, the power of the State grew as Bismarck's own sense of power grew.

Here we have them, the greatness and the limitations of Bismarck's influence. We have a will untroubled by principles or by sympathies, directed exclusively towards increasing the power of his own land, ridiculing the ideas which, none the less, were driving Europe and the nineteenth century forward. At the very time when the will of this fighter was winning victories abroad, at home it was trampling the rights of the nation under foot — rights which no statesman can coerce with impunity, can coerce instead of establishing an equilibrium by the use of opposing influences. He will be just as well pleased to see the soldiers fire upon foreigners or upon Germans, provided he thinks it useful to Prussia. In days to come, when he wishes to use the army against Prussian rebels, merely because they wish to rule their land in a different fashion from his, his power will be broken.

IV

"Really it is a madcap notion," writes Bismarck to his brother, with an eye to the cost, when the king has summoned him to the Upper House. "But it is for a life term, and will give me a strong position, will furnish me with influence upon the government. Whether it is useful and agreeable to exercise such influence is a debatable question, which as a rule I am inclined to answer in the negative — though there are moments when, moved by ambitious or patriotic considerations, I would give my ears for the chance of being able to carry out my political plans. . . . If I could only have the tiller in my hand for six months." Soon he leaves the party and the chamber in the lurch, refuses to seek reelection, and takes advantage of his duplex position in Berlin to absent himself when his friends must vote against the government or he must vote against his friends.

He excuses himself for that course of action when he comes across some liberals in a Berlinese restaurant. He sits down at their table for a quarter of an hour, and is able afterwards to relate with satisfaction: "I certainly spoiled their appetite. I stroked one fellow's cheek, pressed another's hand, was amiable to them all. It was a delight to see the spleen peeping out of their eyes!" But he is on bad terms with his own party. He declares himself strongly opposed to any breach of the constitution, for "it no longer interferes in any way with the work of government, and tends more and more to become a vessel to which the personality of the ruler supplies a content." Thus he has modified his tactics, and even in home affairs has given his formal blessing to what he had spoken of as an abomination. He actually enquires whether it is wise to remain a reactionary for ever, if the only result of this is to drive some of the petty States into the arms of Austria instead of making them friendly towards Prussia by a liberal policy. Although the Berlinese chambers are democratically inclined, he thinks it will be as well to let them go on talking about Germany, so that the idea of Prussia as the leader of the German realm may become popular.

For this Prussian has now begun to think that it would be well for Prussia to assume the leadership of Germany (in the narrower sense). He says as much with productive cynicism: "Strongly as I am disinclined to sacrifice right to policy in my fatherland, I have none the less a sufficient store of Prussian egoism to be less conscientious where the right of Hanover is concerned." Great Germany is a dream, the Germanic Federation is dead or moribund, the "German will" of the lesser dynasts is a mere phrase, the Confederation of the Rhine looms once more on the horizon, and he asks Gerlach: "What justifies your belief that the grand dukes of Baden and Darmstadt, the kings of Würtemberg and Bavaria, are ready to play the part of Leonidas? Can you imagine King Max telling Napoleon in Fontainebleau that the emperor of the French shall only enter Germany or Austria over his dead body?"

Meanwhile he has become acquainted with Germany, for when he accepted his post he stipulated that he must be allowed to visit all the German courts. Within a few years, his personal knowledge has become wellnigh complete. He knows the princes, the

ministers, the newspaper editors, and other intriguers — taking
particular delight in this form of public service. Even when he
writes home from the turmoil of Berlin, it is in the cordial vein of
an amused bachelor.

He has become fond of travelling, travels more than he need,
always alone. Although his letters to his wife usually end with
the expression of his longing to be with her, Bismarck only writes
this because he is a man who must perpetually emphasise his mood
if he is to retain it. He visits Brussels, Amsterdam, Copenhagen,
Budapest, and Paris. Now that he is able for the first time to
travel as a great man, moneyed and titled, received everywhere
as a distinguished foreigner, he enjoys himself immensely. When
Johanna is in Switzerland with the children and her parents, he
is lying on the shore at Norderney, "smoking, dreaming, or
thinking about Interlaken." His greatest pleasure is when he is
invited to shooting parties, in Denmark, for instance, or Cour-
land. "If I shoot an elk to-morrow, I think I shall be able to find
time to make a trip in your direction. But I cannot come away
until I have been successful in this — or not until need drives."

In such weeks his joy of life reaches its climax, for he feels
young again, and can write cheerfully from Ostend: "Only the
consciousness of being a model of manly beauty can make a man
of my sort bold enough to strip himself before the whole world
of women — and though, of course, I am well satisfied with myself
in this respect, I generally prefer the more remote 'paradis', . . .
where there are none but men bathing, in the costume I have just
implied. I cannot endure wet clouts on my body." Or, again, on
a July evening, he will go boating on the Rhine, will swim in the
moonlight to the Mäuseturm, enjoying the romanticism of the
exploit and declaring he would like to have such a swim every
evening. Afterwards he sits down with a colleague to drink
Rhenish, and philosophise about Rousseau and God.

Music provides him with another way of relaxing tension. He
smokes and walks to and fro while Keudell plays to him. This he
enjoys, though all his life he has detested formal concerts. "Music
must be freely bestowed, like love; and I cannot endure to sit

cooped up." Nor does he care to listen to quartettes; there is too much constraint about them. Also he dislikes variations. Enjoyment comes to him only when the player is without music, and begins to talk to his instrument. Then he sees pictures; essentially, it is always himself whom he sees, for when, after the music is over, he describes what he has been thinking about, it is invariably a man of action. " It was like the striving and sobbing of a whole human life. . . . If I often heard music like that I should always be valiant." This is what he says after listening to the Appassionata. Or in imagination he sees " one of Cromwell's troopers, riding into battle, the reins loose on his horse's neck, and thinking that he is riding to his death." After listening to Mendelssohn: " The man is really having a very bad time." After one of Bach's preludes: " The man was hesitant to begin with; but by degrees he fought his way through to a firm and joyful profession of faith."

This enigmatical creature, in the end, always came back to Beethoven. He says: " Beethoven is my preference; he is most accordant with my nerves." We see deep into Bismarck's heart when he confesses: " Good music is apt to drive me in one of two opposite directions: to anticipations of war, or to an idyll." In those days, he bowed reverently before things musical. Once when Keudell was playing, the pianist saw in a mirror how Bismarck came into the room behind him, and stretched his hands for a few seconds over the player's head: " Then he sat down by the window and looked out into the gloaming while I went on playing." Such seconds of inexplicable emotion, of relaxation and self-surrender, rare moments of tender self-denial, are in the line of succession to the paroxysms of melancholy in earlier days, the ecstatic melancholy he used to experience in his loneliness.

Only on very rare occasions does he allow his youth to come to life once more. When he revisits Wiesbaden, where twenty years before he had lived so riotously, there seems to be no kindly thought in his mind of the women who had then been his lively companions. He speaks merely of " the days when the champagne of youth was fruitlessly effervescing, and was leaving empty in-

BISMARCK IN 1859
After a photograph by Elise Wolff

clinations as its sequel. I wonder where Isabelle Loraine and Miss Russell are now, and in what sort of way they are living. . . . I cannot understand how a man who reflects about himself, and yet knows nothing or will know nothing of God, can endure his life instead of dying of self-contempt and boredom. . . . I simply cannot understand how I used to endure it. If I had to live now as in those days, without God, without you, without the children — I can really see no reason why I should not lay aside this life as one takes off a dirty shirt. . . . I feel as one feels on a fine September day when one looks at the foliage beginning to turn; healthy and cheerful, but a little melancholy, somewhat homesick, longing for forest and lake and meadow, for you and the children, all mingled with sunset and Beethoven's symphonies."

Religious belief and family faith are now more strongly interwoven than ever. When he is afraid of unbelief, he is afraid of his old solitude. He looks back at the days of his youth with a strange animus, a peculiar hostility, which helps him to bear the oncoming of age. "I am a little afraid of the forties," he writes to his brother. "By that time one has crossed the pass, and is on the down grade leading to the vaults of Schönhausen. Yet one still tries to persuade oneself that one is at the beginning of life, and has its essentials still before one. . . . It is so difficult to dismiss a certain claim to youthfulness. When one writes one's age with a 3, even though the 3 is followed by a 9, there is still something which assists this illusion. Life is like a clever tooth-extraction. We think that the real tug is still to come, until we wonderingly realise that it is already over. Or perhaps in view of my occupation here in Frankfort, a better comparison would be to a dinner, at which the unexpectedly early appearance of the roast and the salad arouse an expression of disappointment in the faces of the guests." In one case, sarcasms; in another, self-reproaches — attempts to constrain himself to a patience and a renunciation which conflict with his burning thirst for life; for his Faust nature makes it impossible for him to forgive God that the core of life has always to be waited for. What he has done so far has been nothing worth. To rule! That would bring deliverance! When he is forty-two, Keudell asks him: "Don't you feel that the waves of life beat higher to-day than when you were a student?" Pause. At length he answers: "No. — I would say 'yes', if I could dispose of the whole as I pleased! But it is a dreadful thing to have to waste one's energies under a master whom one can only obey with the aid of the consolations of religion."

This intimate confession, which will be followed by others of the same kind, does not only lay bare the inner unrest of his soul, but it likewise discloses the character of his faith, which he always props up with his loyalty, so that each may support the other. "Nothing but Christianity," he writes at about this time, "can deliver rulers from that conception of life which leads them, or many of them, to regard the position to which God has appointed them as nothing but the means that provides opportunities for enjoyment and the exercise of arbitrary power." Thus does Bismarck, who has just been laughing the legitimists to scorn and proving that all the governments of Europe had a revolutionary origin, set up God once more when he happens to meet God, and cast God down when God happens to get in his way. Arguing with his pious wife, he now ventures to say: "I might be willing to feed my enemy if he were hungry; but as for loving my enemy, such love would be very superficial if it existed at all." When he wants the new navy to make an attack, although there is no real reason for it, he excuses his wish with the cruel words: "The lives it will cost are the lives of men who will be dead anyhow forty years hence."

Ludwig von Gerlach, the pietist, is frankly alarmed when he sees his spiritual foster-child taking this Machiavellian turn, and conveys a warning through the instrumentality of his relative Kleist-Retzow: "Keep Bismarck's faith warm. Do not allow him to fall into worldliness. He is made of noble Carrara marble. . . . He would be a luscious morsel for the world and for Satan, who is not easily persuaded to loose his prey. . . . Put him through his catechism!" Yet all these years he himself has been teaching Bismarck worldly politics.

The dilemma of the Christian knight is most perplexing when

he becomes involved in a duel. Vincke, his rival in the chamber, has, at the tribune, described him as a diplomatist whose whole performance in history has been determined by Count Thun's cigar, and as one who has no discretion. Bismarck retorts that Vincke is ill-bred. Thereupon Vincke sends him a challenge. In later years, Bismarck declares that the underlying cause of the enmity and the duel had been the somewhat acrimonious conversation of March 1848, concerning Augusta's mischievous plans. At evening prayer that day Bismarck asks the pastor a strange question. He asks whether, next morning, he will be right to take careful aim, as well as to fire his pistol. "It was lovely weather, and the birds were singing sweetly in the sunshine, so that all my gloomy thoughts vanished as soon as we entered the wood." There, a further attempt was made to compose the duellists' differences. It had been agreed that they were to fire two shots each; now the number was reduced to one, and the whole thing would have been dropped if Bismarck had been willing to express regret for his words. The duellists take their places. "I fired, without feeling any anger, and missed. . . . I cannot deny that when I could see through the smoke, and realised that my adversary was still standing, I was by no means inclined to join in the general jubilation. I was annoyed that the number of shots we were to exchange had been reduced, and I should have been glad to go on with the combat. . . . But it was all over, and we shook hands. . . . Well, God knows what use he expects to make of Vincke."

In this report, whose pugnacious passages are doubly true (since the letter is written to his mother-in-law in pious phrasing), the whole contradiction is displayed between Bismarck as fighter and man of force, on the one hand, and as Christian, on the other. To shoot is permissible, but to take aim is of dubious morality; the hunter must therefore have no anger in his mind, and yet it is extremely annoying to him if, when the smoke of the shot clears away, he sees his quarry still standing unharmed! No question enters his mind as to why he himself is not hit. After the shots had been exchanged, he wonders for what purpose God can have spared Vincke, but does not trouble to ask why God left himself, Bismarck, alive. In this case, as in so many others, it is plain that his hatred for his opponent is stronger than his love for himself.

Johanna takes some time to forgive him. She loves peace just as much as he loves war. She lacks all the essential qualities which fit him for such activities; lacks ambition, worldly-mindedness, and health. She is often ill, not only after the birth of the children, whom she has to care for by night, and to whose education (neglected by her husband) she has to devote hours and months in the year. She has eye trouble, which gets worse; she has to visit health resorts; on journeys, and in social life, things must be made easy for her; and, since she is not strong enough to manage all the housekeeping unaided, Bismarck has to keep the servants in order, to discharge some and engage others, to see to the buying of furniture and plate—matters which he is glad enough to attend to as a change of occupation, and for which his early experiences fit him. He, though he is so much busier than she, is the better correspondent; again and again he asks why she does not write; she is capricious about the matter, and does not know how to allot her time.

All that he strives to do, and all that he succeeds in doing, impresses her very little; and she does not hide her disapproval of his worldly life. "If we could only go to Schönhausen," she writes to her friend Keudell at a time of crisis, "not bother about anything but ourselves, our children, our parents, and our real friends—what a delight that would be. Then, I am sure he would soon be strong and fresh once more, just as he was . . . when he began this wretched, stormy diplomatic life, which has brought him no good, nothing but vexation, enmity, disfavour, ingratitude. . . . If he would only shake from his dear feet the dust of this useless turmoil, would escape from the futilities in which, with his honourable, upright, essentially noble character, he is quite unfitted to play a part—I should be perfectly happy and content. But, alas, he will not do this, for he fancies that he owes a debt of service to his 'beloved country'."

In this letter, we not only discover the desires of her clear and pious mind, but we also discern the account he has given her of his own motives. There is no humbug about what he says, for what can be more natural to him than the depiction of his own imminent moral superiority, for his own benefit and that of others, and the declaration that his adversaries, his colleagues, or his chiefs (who are merely less clever than he), are craftier! In the long run, indeed, he would find it intolerable to have a wife who was cunning enough to control him psychically, or was so ambitious as to spur him on in the game of general intrigue. His knowledge of character was not at fault when he chose Johanna Puttkamer for his wife. She loved him and him only. And the feelings of her frank nature never misled her into either criticism or idolisation of the man she loved. Since she had his heart, she asked nothing more from him — not even genius.

He finds it easy to teach her the things she really must do, but nothing more. "And you, my poor child, must learn to sit stiff and dignified in a drawing-room, and to be clever and wise when you associate with excellencies " — thus had he written to her in the early days. It becomes absolutely necessary that she should learn to speak French, and that she should learn to ride. She manages both. But if he finds that anything he asks is too much for her, he promptly withdraws his demand, and even speaks angrily of himself for having made it. " I married you to love you in God according to the needs of my own heart, and that amid a world of strangers I might have a place for my own heart, where all the harsh winds of the world could not chill me, and where I could warm myself at the domestic hearth. Thither do I always come when there is cold or stormy weather outside." But the diplomatist in him is ever ready to peep out. When, with her natural integrity, she writes passionately and plainly about certain individuals, he replies, with an eye to the possibility of her letters being read on the way through the post, that she should be careful " not to write so strongly about particular persons, for I, as a man, shall be held responsible for what you have written. Besides, you are unjust to those of whom you write. Do not write anything which the police had better not read, anything which they might pass on to the king . . . or to a minister of State. . . . Do not forget that what you whisper to Charlotte in your bathing hut is as likely as not to be served here or at Sans-Souci, warmed up and with a sauce added."

Her début at court miscarries, though not by his fault or hers. He is invited to a trip on a Rhine steamboat, and makes her come too, that she may be presented to the king and the queen; but "their majesties ignored her entirely, although we spent several hours together on the steamboat en très petit comité; the queen was not very well, and therefore had very little energy to spare for her, and the princess of Prussia snubbed her deliberately. . . . Although the prince, in the most amiable way, tried to make up for the marked neglect of my wife, her unspoiled Farther Pomeranian royalism suffered under the test, so that she was on the verge of tears. . . . Your chivalry [he is writing to Gerlach] will make it easy for you to understand that I feel this humiliation of my wife more strongly than I could feel anything which might happen to myself. . . . Of course I tried to convince her that she was not slighted in any way, that these were the manners usual at court."

We can reconstruct the whole scene when we read his fairly plain statement of grievances made to the king's friend. We cannot doubt that on the homeward journey Johanna must have done her best to prove how futile this sort of life was and how unsuited to him; and we may infer that the Princess of Prussia's behaviour must have been insufferably arrogant. The real Bismarck is disclosed in the resoluteness with which he quits the royal vessel at the first stopping-place. Still, we may suppose that he had his thoughts about brilliant and high-born women at whose side he might have made a more creditable appearance in these circles.

Bismarck provides Johanna with everything she wants; and, having from old experience a good knowledge of women, he attends carefully to details. When he writes to his colleague in Paris, commissioning the latter to buy a cashmere shawl, he gives precise directions as to the colour. Again, he asks his sister to get a dress

for Johanna, and says it is to be of moiré antique, twenty ells of
stuff, pure white; also a gilt fan, which must rattle briskly when
it is used (although he himself hates the noise). He hunts all
Paris for bluethroats, because she has taken a fancy for these
birds. He is even so complaisant as to wear a chain with dangling
medals, a gift from her, "for she would be very much grieved to
discover that I do not really like to carry all these fal-de-rals
about on my person".

He always includes her parents among his intimates; speaks
most affectionately of her father; is glad to have them on visits
for weeks together; and writes of "the little State of seven souls
we make up together. . . . In our earthly life, we cannot be free
from troubles and sorrows, and it is better to be cold in the street
than in one's own house."

V

The king's mental condition was growing worse. The ten years
that followed the revolution were characterised by so much contradiction, caprice, and exaggeration on the part of Frederick
William that those who surrounded his person often found it
difficult to keep up an appearance of continuity of policy. While
Augusta's hopes rise, while she poses as a liberal, the king speaks
of the abominable stench of the revolution, refers to the imaginary
circlet of the imperial crown as made up of "filth and clay",
refers to it as a "dog collar", wishes again and again to replace
the constitution by a charter. In an address to Francis Joseph,
he says, "I exist only to hold the stirrup of the emperor of Austria", and in an address to the tsar, "May God preserve for you
the continent which God has given you as heritage." The natural
result is to increase the contempt which both these potentates feel
for him.

It was not until the year 1858 that his mental disorder became
so pronounced as to jeopardise his position as head of the government. The very fact that there was no outbreak of frenzy, that
his powers of thought simply faded away, suffices to prove that

he had really been insane for many years. During the critical weeks, Bismarck, riding at the king's side, found it necessary to hold his master's bridle. When the king, who could not even bear the smell of sealing wax, and whom the odour of tobacco made positively ill, was travelling in the tsar's company in a closed saloon carriage (the tsar was an inveterate smoker), he collapsed in a fit of apoplexy. Thereupon the struggles of the parties at court became acute. The adherents of the king, who wished to maintain their own position, wanted to govern by perpetually renewed representation (the temporary appointment of a "deputy"); the adherents of the prince of Prussia wanted a regency, which would bring them to the front.

Bismarck happened to be in Berlin at the time. He was not alarmed at the course of events, which he had long foreseen, but his bridge to power had become shaky, for what Prince William thought of him was plain enough.

At Olmütz, eight years before, and in the time of the Crimean War, four years before, the wishes of the warlike prince had been frustrated by the opposition of Bismarck, who in both these crises had influenced the king in a direction contrary to William's desires. Since then, Prince William and Bismarck had met often enough. Their mutual dislike had never kept them apart, for political interests made it necessary for them to be on speaking terms. Now, when the king was lying unconscious, Prince William invited the envoy to take a long walk with him. Bismarck, asked for his advice, said that William, if he took over the government, would do well to accept the constitution as it was, and not to demand a revision. Bismarck was also in favour of a regency, since this would stabilise conditions. Are we to suppose that he expected, in spite of everything, to become minister? Hardly! Still less did he think it likely that he would be recalled from Frankfort. What would be the best way of cementing an alliance with the new ruler?

After William's position as deputy had several times been renewed, Bismarck learned from private sources that there was a proposal to reestablish the insane king as ruler, under the queen's control. He promptly made his way to the heir to the throne, who was then in Baden, and disclosed the design. William, perfectly frank and wholly the officer, was content to exclaim:

"In that case I shall withdraw."

"You would do better to summon Manteuffel," answered Bismarck, "and destroy the whole intrigue!" He knew that Manteuffel was aware of the scheme, and was awaiting results at his country seat. The prince sent for Manteuffel, and, as the latter had trembled for his own position since the king's stroke, he was alarmed, and wanted Bismarck to accompany him. Manteuffel was promptly dismissed from office; and, in the autumn of 1858, the prince, who had been inspired with some of Augusta's energy, had himself sworn in as regent. A liberal cabinet was appointed. Bismarck's friends believed, and Johanna hoped, that he would now have to resign his post. But Bismarck, aware that his new master was indebted to him for an important service in the critical hour, rejoined that matters would go on all right, that the new premier, Prince Karl Anton von Hohenzollern, was a conservative. "I shall stay in Frankfort, greatly to the annoyance of the gossip, Frau Usedom, who would like to come there herself!" Nevertheless, in view of Augusta's hatred and William's weakness, he safeguards his retreat.

"Change is the soul of life," he writes at this date to his sister. "I hope that I shall feel rejuvenated by ten years or so if I find myself once more in the same fighting position as in 1848 and 1849. If it should prove impossible to combine any longer the rôles of gentleman and diplomatist, the pleasure or the burden of spending a high salary will not influence my choice for a moment. I have enough of my own to satisfy my needs; and if God continues to grant health to my wife and children, I shall say 'vogue la galère', whatever the course of events. After thirty years, it will be a matter of indifference to me whether, in these days, I play the part of diplomatist or that of country squire; and hitherto the prospect of a vigorous and honourable struggle, without being hampered by any sort of official fetters—in political bathing drawers, so to speak—has almost as much charm for me as the prospect of a persistent régime of truffles, dispatches, and grand crosses. 'Everything is over at nine o'clock,' says the actor." When there is talk of his being transferred to St. Petersburg, he writes: "I think there is likely to be bad weather here, politically speaking; and I shall be glad to await the issue in a bearskin, eat caviare, and hunt the elk!"

In Bismarck's case, such letters are simultaneously advertisements and reinsurances — while he bides his time! There is really no question of his ever becoming the Schönhausen squire again and nothing more, although, in reiterated growls, he expresses his longing for such a consummation. That is all over. What he really has in view, should he lose his present post, is the immediate resumption of the fight in the chamber. Everything may be changed once more within a few years. Although the prince regent is not so old as the king, he is over sixty. Even Augusta is not immortal. For the nonce, she is able to induce her husband to summon her liberal friends among the nobility. Bismarck is cashiered, Usedom and his eccentric wife are sent to Frankfort, and, in the end, Bismarck is to go into "exile" in St. Petersburg. As soon as he learns his fate, he wants to be beforehand with the regent, and, as he himself reports, depicts the situation with remarkable freedom: "It is a great pity that the capital which has been accumulated during my eight years in Frankfort through my knowledge of persons and things should, for no good reason, be destroyed. Count Usedom will make himself impossible there on account of his wife."

"That is precisely the point," says the regent. "Usedom's notable talents cannot be advantageously utilised elsewhere, for at any of the courts the presence of his wife would make trouble."

"It seems, then," rejoins Bismarck, "that I myself made a mistake in not marrying a tactless woman, for if I had done so, I suppose I should have the same claim as Herr von Usedom to a post in which I feel myself at home."

"I do not understand why you are so bitter about the matter. St. Petersburg has always been regarded as the chief post in our diplomatic service, and you ought to accept your appointment as a mark of the highest confidence."

"Of course if Your Royal Highness puts it in that way, there is nothing more to be said."

When he goes on to express his concern about what is likely to happen in Frankfort, the regent answers:

"Do you think I shall go to sleep? I shall be my own minister for foreign affairs and my own minister for war. These are departments I thoroughly understand."

"Nowadays the most competent Landrat cannot govern his circle without an intelligent secretary. . . . Without intelligent ministers, Your Royal Highness will find no satisfaction. . . . Look at Schwerin's profile, for instance. Above the eyebrows, he shows the signs of a power of rapid concentration; . . . but he has not enough forehead, the region in which the phrenologists tell us that circumspection is centred. As a statesman, Schwerin lacks vision, and is more competent to destroy than to build." Bismarck then proceeds to take a survey of all the members of the cabinet.

In this very first official conversation between Bismarck and William, we see plain indications of what divides them. It is difficult to say whether we are to admire most the boldness, the astuteness, and the logicality of the man, or the adroitness with which he shifts responsibility on to his adversary's shoulders and then ticks off his rivals. At the same time we are struck by the quietude of the master who thinks he is promoting his servant.

Hitherto, William has never had any political grasp of the necessities of a situation; he has only had a soldier's sense of them. He has nothing behind him but a lengthy career as an officer; disciplined and narrow. In all respects superior to his brother (whose fantastic schemes served only to show forth his incompetence), William had more solidity and less imagination, and was well ballasted with the old Prussian virtues which were lacking to Frederick William. William was regular in his habits, diligent to excess, precise, just, benevolent, extremely pious, and a legitimist both for himself and for others. He was simple, and (to repeat) narrow.

Bismarck did not possess any of these qualities. He was irritable, venturesome, dissatisfied; cunning, sceptical, relentless; towards his God and his king, his sentiments vacillated, for he would be a legitimist one day and a revolutionist the next; he was enigmatical, but a man of genius.

Both men were proud and courageous, and it was only their kinship in the matter of personal courage that made it possible for them to work together. Their pride, on the other hand, tended to bring them into conflict. William's pride was that of the born king, whose piety and cult of ancestry made him regard himself as higher than all with whom he came in contact, though he did not for this reason overrate his own intelligence. His self-esteem was now hardening into an old man's obstinacy, so that he could never at any price endure the recognition that his ministers were guiding him; his sense of royal superiority made this intolerable to him. Bismarck was always driven forward by his pride, fighting as he went, always on guard; and although he was not in the least vain, he was continually comparing himself with his associates — to his own advantage! William, therefore, would not admit to himself that Bismarck guided him, whereas Bismarck was incessantly saying to himself that he guided William. Without these two mutual reserves, the two men could never have cooperated.

Bismarck always wanted to be up and doing; William, who was almost twenty years older, wanted only to exist and to rule. William had no wish to conquer anything for Prussia, not even in Germany; Bismarck wanted to aggrandise Prussia through Germany. The king had, as a rule, the equable pulses of an heir; but he would become excited at critical moments, and give way to furious passion. The statesman had always the syncopated rhythm of a primitive, who is perpetually in movement, driven forward by an inner urge; but in moments of crisis he was ice-cold and clear-sighted. Thus in later days he towed the quiescent old king in his wake, wearing himself out by devoting his gifts to the service of another — the tragical figure of a genius enslaved.

VI

Tsar Alexander II. was William's nephew, and, so long as the latter was alive, this blood relationship was a safeguard for the friendship between two lands whose interests conflicted as rarely as they do to-day, and which had, in view of the long stretch where their frontiers march, excellent reasons for remaining good friends. William and his sister, the dowager tsarina (abler than he), were both endowed with strong family feeling, and were both simple in disposition. So long, therefore, as William reigned, there were, despite a hundred difficulties, ample guarantees against war between the two countries.

All the same, Alexander II. was by no means easy to get on with. He was now forty years of age, with a strangely vacant expression of countenance. He was fanatical, brutal, and obscene —the walls of his private apartments were hung with lecherous pictures which have only become known to the world in our own day. All the same, he could be charming and impressionable, when the fancy took him. Sometimes it would be his ambition to play the liberal, and at other times to play the vengeful oppressor. He was a mighty hunter, though no soldier, for he was essentially timid. Thus he can be aptly described as a Russian translation of his uncle Frederick William IV., an abler and weaker man, but equally hysterical. His ukase liberating the serfs was inspired at once by cowardice and by caprice, and for these reasons remained no less void of effect than (for long years) did the constitution granted to Prussia by Frederick William IV. The nephew now delighted, as formerly the uncle had delighted, in the gigantic Pomeranian baron. In Alexander's case, as in that of Frederick William, a sense of the contrast between himself and Bismarck may have been at work, an agreeable feeling of amusement produced by the man. No doubt Bismarck's originality was pleasing to the tsar, who welcomed him as a sort of family envoy, preferred him to the other foreigners at court, and singled him out for distinction by going on smoking when he received the

Prussian envoy in audience. This was regarded as a special honour, and made all Bismarck's colleagues jealous.

Furthermore, there was a sense of political kinship between
Bismarck and the tsar. The new envoy was a royalist, and was an
enemy of Austria. At the time when Bismarck went to St. Petersburg, Napoleon had set going the long planned war of Sardinia
against Austria, which was justified by the terms of his alliance
with Cavour. Once again, as five years earlier in the days of the
Crimean War, half Germany wanted to take up arms on the side
of "German" Austria against the man who was spoken of as the
hereditary enemy. The third Napoleon, it was said, just like the
first, wanted to destroy Austria to begin with, and then make an
end of Prussia. The Rhine must be defended on the banks of the
Po; as a safeguard, Alsace and Lorraine must be seized. The
"Kreuzzeitung" thundered against the child of the revolution;
Moltke, whom the regent had appointed chief of general staff,
counselled war. But William was afraid of repeating his father's
blunder, perhaps to find himself in the end, like his father, standing alone against the French conqueror. Would it not be possible
to revive the Holy Alliance under another name? With soldierly
emotion, he recalled the bravura of his entry into Paris as a youth
in the year 1815; and he allowed old Gerlach to offer him the
sword, since it was a case of attacking the French once more.

Bismarck is alone among statesmen of repute in advising
against war, even at the risk of seeming to share the sentiments of
the liberals, who are ardently opposed to the Habsburgs, and
ardently favour the cause of the Poles and the Italians. To-day,
just as in the days of the Crimean War, he does not wish to help
the Habsburgs; speaks openly of Austria as "a foreign country";
insists that at least Prussia should remain neutral, and declares
that it would be better for her to espouse the side of France;
speaks of the views advocated by the "Kreuzzeitung" as "lunacy"; utters warnings against supporting Prussia's enemy; and,
with finely chosen words, expresses to his brother his fear "lest,
in the end, we shall allow ourselves to be made tipsy by Austria,
under the impression that we are back in 1813."

When, in June, the Austrians are beaten at Magenta and Solferino, William wants to march to their help, and mobilises his
forces. The enemies, however, are driven quickly into one another's arms, for both are afraid of the intervention of an intact
army. Napoleon does not wish to risk his new-won military
glories; and Francis Joseph does not wish to risk his position in
Germany. In July, therefore, the adversaries make peace. The
Prussians, the regent at their head, are furious. Only Bismarck
is delighted that Prussia has not been involved in the fight. The
tsar claps his hands at Austria's defeat, and envelops the new
envoy from Prussia in a denser cloud of tobacco smoke than ever.

Received in so friendly a fashion, and wishing to strengthen
the threads of union between Prussia and Russia, Bismarck is
in his element. He takes the dowager tsarina by storm, and makes
himself so charming, that, as he reports, a four-year-old princess
says of him in Russian: " He is a dear." Of a general whom the
same child refuses to notice, she says: " He stinks." The dowager
tsarina is ailing. Bismarck sits at her bedside talking and listening, and learns from this friendly gossip much more than he can
learn by formal audiences or through his spies. He knows, too,
how to get on with Gorchakoff, the cunning, pious, elderly premier, in whose presence he plays the respectful disciple, and whose
vanity (even more overweening than that of most diplomatists)
he knows how to tickle. Withal, he does nothing but growl at
his master because the latter has not yet promoted him as a
soldier — in consequence of which (says Bismarck) at big reviews
" his envoy figures as a corpulent lieutenant among all the bottle-
nosed generals "; and although Bismarck continues to see the
tsar pretty often, he tells Berlin that it is now his purpose " to
renounce this one opportunity of seeing the tsar anywhere else
than at the winter festival. I am not really at home in this
service."

From time to time, Bismarck was fairly content in St. Petersburg. He had what was always essential to his satisfaction, a
comfortable dwelling, having been busied about the details of this
matter even before his arrival. The furnishing of his residence

cost him more thought than his official service. Writing to his wife, he said the house he proposed to rent had rooms for the children into which the sun would shine during the winter until noon; and he even told her all about the servants' quarters. Just as when he was an impoverished Junker, he takes a personal interest in all these little things. His wife, who is still in Frankfort, is to have certain articles of furniture covered in Darmstadt, for in Russia everything is dearer. "The silk-and-cotton patterns look like silk, and will perhaps do for all the furniture, but especially for the green furniture in my room, and also for portières. . . . . The bookcase is unsuitable. The pedestal is good, but it must stand higher. I shall see if I can find some other piece of furniture on which to place it." Postscript: "Why bother to have the children's milk-teeth stopped? They'll have good new teeth in a year or two." He has his wines from the old cellar shipped by the Baltic to Russia, "for who knows who will drink them in Schönhausen?" He boasts that his house on the Neva is a very large one, rather too fine, with excellent stables, and a private manège. He orders for his own use " a much larger writing table ", and "very large and thick toothbrushes, as hard as stone." The more his income grows, the more thrifty does he become. He declares that on his salary of thirty thousand talers he will have to economise carefully; gives no parties, merely keeps visitors to luncheon if they happen to be calling at the time; gets his brother to ship him apples and potatoes from Pomerania; asks Bernhard to see to irrigation and other farming details on his estates; and is delighted that he is able to save his private income.

Nothing impresses him more in Russia than the grand scale of things, especially when he goes out shooting. A country in which it is still possible to hunt bears is from the first congenial to Bismarck. Worth more to him than the friendship of the tsar, perhaps even than Austria's defeat at Solferino, is the moment when " a bear that had been shot at, rearing up on his hind legs, made for me open-mouthed. I let him come within fifty paces, and then gave him two bullets in the chest, whereupon he fell dead. Not for a minute had I any sense of danger. Behind me stood a huntsman holding a second double-barrelled rifle ready loaded. . . . There is nothing finer than primeval forest. Russia is a hunter's paradise. A young bear which I am taming, and which I shall send to Reinfeld, has bitten my finger. For that, I shall give him a wife, and banish the pair of them to Pomerania." Coming back from the chase, he writes a similar account to his friend Keudell, and ends by saying dogmatically: "A hunter's life is really the natural life of man." At such moments as that when the bear was charging him, and when he had no sense of fear, the old robber knights' blood surged up in him. Comparing the story of this incident with similar ones, we are astonished when we recall that, none the less, Bismarck was an accomplished man of the world, and could play his part well at court.

He is intensely delighted when he can send his sister a bear's ham. He apologises for the quality with the amusing phrase that the ham "belonged to a small bear only one year old; you may find it rather salt, but I hope it will be as tender as bear can be." When, after a grand duke has called on him, he unpacks the cigars this dignitary has brought him as a gift, he estimates them as worth fifteen groschen apiece. A generation later he relates in his memoirs that when he went to visit the dowager tsarina "for the other gentlemen of the embassy, on that occasion two, and for me three, dinners were provided from the imperial kitchen. . . . On one occasion all the table furniture and accessories were laid out for me in my quarters. The second time, the same thing at the tsarina's table, for me and my companion, and after all I did not dine with him, for I was specially served with a small company at the bedside of the ailing tsarina, my companion not being present." The Russian autocratic tone comes easily to him, and he says cold-bloodedly after a review when forty thousand men had been marched past: "Very fine material, men, horses, and leather."

Everything here is on the large scale. Even "the daily quarrels of Frankfort have . . . given place to greater and more interesting ones. . . . Federal animosity and presidential poison seem childish from this distance. . . . When we drive home, and the words 'Prussian ambassador' are called upstairs, all the Russians have a benevolent smile on their faces, as if they had just swallowed an extra strong dose of vodka!" Expanse, power, and autocracy have impressed him in sleeping Russia. He was already sympathetic towards the country. These new impressions strengthen his Russophile tendencies, and influence his policy in the future. During the next thirty years, that policy undergoes frequent changes, but the Russophile trend remains unchanged, the only constant. Even on into old age, in anecdotes of the kind already given, he continues to show the influence exercised upon him " by the elemental vigour and tenacity of Russia, upon which the strength of the Russian temperament as contrasted with that of the rest of Europe depends."

This mental and bodily comfort in Russia was disturbed for Bismarck by two mischances, the like of which he had never experienced before, and was never to experience again. On arrival at St. Petersburg, he found there a secretary to legation who, though only second secretary, had under Bismarck's predecessor been really in charge of affairs. This man seemed to know everything and understand everything; for several days he sat talking matters over and smoking with Bismarck. But when the latter then wanted to dictate a long despatch, the secretary said: " It is really quite beyond my powers to write a despatch to another man's dictation." Kurd von Schlözer was neither a genius nor a statesman; he was highly cultured, an excellent official, perspicacious, sprung from a humanist family, and was only two years younger than his new chief. He shared two qualities with Bismarck, courage and self-esteem. That was why he promptly declined to allow himself to be used as a machine, and, as Bismarck's subordinate, gave Bismarck this characteristically Bismarckian answer.

What does the chief do in this unwonted situation? Nothing of the kind has ever happened to him before, and in his secret heart he may have respected Schlözer the more. But there is too little of the philosopher about him, and too much of the autocrat, for him to let matters rest there. For the moment, Bismarck has nothing more to do with Schlözer, and gets an attaché to take down the despatch while he himself "like a pasha", marches up and down the room. A few days later he sends for the secretary to write in cipher, having deliberately chosen an unusual time in the evening. Schlözer turns up an hour later, finds his chief already at work with the attaché, and has a very cold reception. Thereupon Schlözer gives Bismarck "a piece of his mind", adding that the chief was not used to such plain speaking. Two days later a written ukase is sent unsealed through the embassy, and Schlözer has to countersign it: "I request Herr von Schlözer to come to me daily at eleven o'clock, in order to discuss current affairs." He comes, very stiff and proud, and asks: "What is there for to-day?" Nothing. Bismarck, somewhat embarrassed, says: "I did not mean it that way. I only requested you to come when there was something on hand."

Bismarck now puts his back into the quarrel, and it remains to be seen which of the two men will be more persistent. Official business is duly dealt with between them, "but he does not get any friendly looks from me. . . . I've never had anything to do with a man like this before! It is very disagreeable, but better to put up with disagreeables than to give way." They exchange angry letters. At the same time Bismarck writes to the premier, his chief: "Herr von Schlözer takes his duties very lightly, and he is amazingly uncivil." At headquarters in Berlin, they think highly of the secretary, and regard the envoy as a dangerous man, so they make no move. Schlözer, who expresses his sentiments in letters and in a diary, writes after a week: "This perpetual chivvying at the hands of a relentless chief, who seems to think that all other men are weaklings, who veils his own plans in darkness or suddenly tries to bluff his auditor, who trusts no one — is by no means agreeable. . . . I have as little to do with him as possible, . . . for one must be always showing one's teeth or else one is lost. Squeeze a lemon and throw it away, that is his policy." Then he goes on to say that there is a network of intrigues, "and in the background the giant warrior, Bismarck! . . . I was so plain with him that he wanted to challenge me. So far he has not made much headway in the diplomatic corps."

Three weeks later: " Every time I enter the pasha's room, I say
to myself: ' Don't be soft! Don't let him take you by surprise!'
He would like to play the comedy of a reconciliation, but I won't
have it. Although I am fully aware of his overwhelming intellectual power, and although an inner voice keeps on telling me
that there is something in him which I might call 'master', I will
not listen to this voice. He must admit that he has been unjust
to me."

After the lapse of another month: " The pasha has been touching the strings softly, playing the agreeable. I have remained extremely distant. But there is a change in him; he praises me behind my back, . . . and no longer corrects my drafts. He has
been ill for a week; . . . this makes him gentler and milder."
Soon afterwards, at the chief's request, there comes to join the
embassy staff a certain Prince Croy, who soon shows himself incapable, and makes himself ridiculous. Thereupon, nothing can
please Bismarck better "than to make fun of the man. But I am
not having any; I will not show him any friendliness; I have refused his invitation to lunch, and have several times rejected his
offer of a cigar. The fact is that every one is afraid of him except
me, and that is why he is so angry with me!"

Six months later, when the chief, having fallen seriously ill, has
been away for a long time, Schlözer, writing to his sister-in-law,
and apologising for having left her so long without a letter, says:
" It is all the fault of this pasha. He upsets me so thoroughly that
I did not want to let you know." In February, the chief writes to
him about furniture and servants, since no one else is competent
to deal with these matters. " Thus the pasha has had to bite the
sour apple, and write me a private letter. . . . I answered civilly,
and have twice at his request sent him some caviare." At the same
time, Bismarck writes to his chief in Berlin, saying: " I have
nothing but praise for Herr von Schlözer, so that I have completely changed my first opinion of him, which was so unfavourable." This is nearly a year after the first meeting.

Six months later still, in the summer, Schlözer writes: " I am
getting on famously with Bismarck. In Berlin I heard that he had

been praising me to the Wilhelmstrasse, and that he had loyally taken back everything he had said against me at first — when he was in poor health, irritated by political contrarieties, and perhaps influenced against me by certain persons. . . . That chapter is closed. Politics are another story; there he is the very devil, but — what is he driving at?" A little later: " I dine every day with Bismarck by special invitation. I have had no further disputes with him. He is the embodiment of politics; everything ferments in him, drives to activity. He wants . . . to bring order out of the chaos in Berlin, but does not yet know how to do it. . . . A remarkable man, full of contradictions." Two years after going to St. Petersburg, Bismarck writes to Berlin in order to secure the withdrawal of Prince Croy, and to get Schlözer appointed first secretary. Before he sends the laudatory letter, he reads it over to Schlözer. It contains the words: " Schlözer is a difficult man in his relationships with his superiors, and at first I had a disagreeable time with him, but his efficiency and conscientiousness in the service have completely altered my opinion of him."

This was an isolated experience in Bismarck's life. Hardly ever again did he have an independent underling, and never again did he come to terms with any one who proved refractory. Very fine is the astonishment with which each of these men recognises the greatness of his enemy, Bismarck admitting that Schlözer is thoroughly efficient, and Schlözer admitting that his chief is a man of genius. The official relationship begins for both to become phosphorescent; it is the exercise ground for the pride of two noblemen, neither of whom can bow before seniority or position, and who can only be overcome by genius and character. Since both are men of genius, and both men of strong character, both are in the end victorious and neither of them sustains a defeat.

VII

One July day, two months after his arrival in St. Petersburg, the new envoy, who has been riding in an overheated manège, returns home without a cloak, is seized with pains in the legs,

sends for a German doctor who puts a plaster on the left leg.
During the night, when the pain grows intense, Bismarck tears
the plaster off, and finds next day that there is a damaged vein.
What makes him especially furious is that he cannot discover
" who was the poisoner ", the doctor or the chemist. A celebrated
Russian surgeon declares that an amputation is necessary.
" Above or below the knee? " asks the patient. The surgeon points
to a spot well above the knee. Bismarck refuses the operation,
and, ill though he is, takes ship for Germany.

His career, his life's work, is at stake. A one-legged Bismarck
would not be deprived of his intelligence, but would have lost all
that the successes of this intelligence have brought him in the
way of bearing, imposing presence, boldness. As matters stand,
nothing but his titanic nature has saved him; for when, half
cured, and on the way back to St. Petersburg, he has a brief rest
with his family at a neighbour's country seat, he is suddenly
forced to take to his bed once more. A clot in the damaged vein
has become detached; an embolus lodges in the lung, for several
days his life is despaired of; and he makes his will. In old age he
reports: " I would have met death gladly, for the pain was intolerable." But he does not say a word about religion. His last
growl in this hour is directed against the bureaucracy; for, himself a high State official, he objects to any kind of State interference in the guardianship of his children.

In Berlin, where he stays as a convalescent for nearly six
months, he pays more attention to politics than to the doctors.
William keeps him there, although the regent would much rather,
if he could, let Bismarck return to his post. The regent is afraid
of the fights in which Bismarck seems likely to involve him! Nevertheless, though Bismarck is little to his liking, he has no wish to
part with the man who may prove his last resource in the coming
struggle with the liberals. Bismarck does not find this betwixt-
and-between position distasteful. Being at the centre of things,
he can pull more strings on behalf of his appointment as minister
for foreign affairs than he can from the honourable banishment
to the Neva. As for the long waiting, he can satisfy his pride by

putting it down to the doctors. With delicious humour he writes to his wife: "I am sitting here on the Balcony Rock like the Lorelei, watching the ships on the Spree going through the lock; but I am not singing, nor do I bother much about combing my hair. I amuse myself by thinking that I am growing enormously old in the hotel here, that the seasons and the generations of travellers and waiters pass by me, while I remain always in the little green room, feeding the sparrows and losing my hair."

The regent, who is waiting for his brother's death, gets on meanwhile with Schleinitz as premier. Bismarck speaks of Schleinitz as a courtier dependent upon Augusta. William goes through the comedy of summoning Schleinitz and Bismarck to a conference, as if wishing to steer a course between the two extremes. Bismarck is asked to develop the programme upon which he has insisted since the days of the Crimean War, to speak of Austria's futility and Prussia's strength, and of the friendship of the Russians; the programme in which he has compared Prussia to a hen which does not dare to cross the magical chalk line. Then the regent tells Schleinitz to take up his parable. The minister, thereupon, reminds William of his father's testament, "a string which never failed to strike an echo in William's heart." This string was attuned against Paris and in favour of Habsburg. When Schleinitz had finished, William, without a pause, answered in a speech which had been manifestly prepared for the occasion, saying that he adhered to these old traditions. Thereupon the sitting was closed. This scene had been planned by Augusta, who wished to show the reactionaries the seriousness of the alternatives. According to Bismarck, she was not influenced so much by positive aims as by certain dislikes: dislike for Russia, dislike for Napoleon, and "dislike for me, because I am temperamentally independent, and because I have again and again refused to put this exalted lady's views before her husband as my own."

Now, in 1860, it was not Augusta alone who kept him away from the leadership; the chief factor was his German programme. The war of the previous year had once again aroused a sort of nationalist feeling among the liberals and the champions of the ideas of 1848. Again, as in that revolutionary year, there were numerous orations, festivals, brotherhoods. Among the statesmen, the more advanced wanted, at most, to dispose of the alliance with Austria in exchange for hegemony in Germany; that is to say, they wished to keep the Germanic Federation in being. Bismarck wanted to destroy that federation, regarding it "as an infirmity, which, sooner or later, must be made good by the use of fire and sword, unless, at some favourable opportunity, a cure can previously be found." There it was, for the first time in black and white, penned by an envoy to his minister: "with fire and sword." Only in that way did it seem to him that a united Germany could come into existence. Soon afterwards he declared: "I should not be willing to see the word 'German' inscribed instead of the word 'Prussian' on our banner unless we were more intimately and purposively united with our other fellow countrymen than has previously been the case; the word loses its charm if . . . it is used too much and prematurely."

At the same time, and to conclude, his breach with legitimacy (which had now become complete) severed him from the regent. At this date he wrote a secret letter of farewell, in which he expressed, to the now powerless Gerlach, the truth as he saw it: "For me, France remains France, whether Napoleon or Saint Louis rules there. . . . As far as political calculations are concerned, the difference is, of course, extremely important; but . . . as far as questions of right and wrong are concerned, such differences have no meaning for me; I feel no inner sense of responsibility for foreign affairs. . . . If you are talking about the difference between right and revolution, Christianity and unbelief, God and the devil, I cannot argue with you. I can say no more than: 'I am not of your opinion, and you are passing judgment on something that is within me, something that is outside your jurisdiction.' . . . I shall be willing enough to thrash France until the dogs come and lick up the blood — but I shall not do so with any more sense of personal enmity than if I were attacking Croates, Bohemians, Jesuit confessors or Bambergers."

That was not the tone Bismarck had used when Gerlach was

still powerful because he was the king's friend. Now, when the regent has no use for Gerlach, Bismarck, whose international realism has grown more decisive and whose self-confidence has increased, speaks his mind freely to the statesman who has fallen from power. Soon, however, he forgets Gerlach, and seeks other contacts. Crises increase in severity and succeed one another more frequently. He goes back to St. Petersburg. Thence he watches events from a distance, disappointed once more, febrile with excitement, making his combinations. That is the picture of him we get from Schlözer, his daily associate during the autumn:

"My pasha is now terribly excited. His stay in Berlin, the perplexity and confusion that prevailed there, have set his blood boiling once more. It would seem he fancies that his hour will come soon. Schleinitz will resign, and then Pasha expects to have his chance. The great question is, will he suit Prussia? Will the Prussians suit him? The sudden introduction of this volcanic spirit amid such narrow and restricted circumstances! . . . They don't like him, and they behave as if he did not exist. He therefore plays his own game. He won't settle down here, continually complains of the rise in prices, sees very few people, does not get up till eleven or twelve, sits about all day in a green dressing-gown, never stirs, drinks all the more for that, and curses Austria. . . . He talks to me a great deal, is incredibly frank, interesting, fitful, revolutionary, contemptuous of theory. Imagine him in the Wilhelmstrasse! Thunderweather! Recently he said that Schleinitz must become treasurer of the household. 'Then the king can choose between Bernstorff, Pourtalès, and myself as minister for foreign affairs.' Ipsisissima verba Pashae! Night and day he dreams of portfolios!"

A caged tiger, always ready to spring, cut off by the bars from those he would fain make his victims, no longer interested in his old amusements, seeing nobody, never going out shooting, his mind circling always round one great question: "When shall I be in power?" This is the real Bismarck. Here he is far more genuine than in his letters to his wife, where he plays the part of tormented Christian.

At length, in January 1861, the mad Frederick William dies, and William comes to the throne. He has waited a whole generation, is already sixty-three, and everything seems to him in a muddle. He is so much disturbed by the liberals' attack on his new army plans, and so wearied by his contest with wife and son, that he is half in mind to abdicate, and to let Frederick (now thirty) assume the reins of power. All the conservatives (meaning the whole court) are atremble; for, had this happened, Frederick, greatly influenced by his English wife, would instantly have entered into an alliance with the liberals. The king's chief supporter is Albrecht von Roon, a soldier of the right sort, the most upright personality in William's circle. He is manly, serious, modest, devout, careless of appearances and applause, unenvious, and distinguished, guiding his own life in accordance with his motto, "Do what you should, and bear what you must." Such is the man who forges the weapons of Prussia. He is strongly opposed to war, but has grown up among those accustomed to think in terms of military power, and thinks in those terms himself. The new king is a soldier too, and while still regent he has summoned Roon to renovate the army. It is Roon who, reminding William of his great ancestors, gives backbone to the king. Roon advises William, at the coronation, to exact an oath of fealty, like his ancestors, who had reigned as absolute monarchs. The other ministers, weaklings, are opposed to this idea. Roon knows of only one man whom he considers resolute, the only man fitted to take Schleinitz' place, the only man with the stamina to insist upon the oath of fealty, and to carry through army reform even in a constitutional State and in a time of conflict. That one man is Bismarck.

The king would fain evade the issue. The most he will concede is Bismarck's appointment as minister for home affairs, for here he needs a fighter and oppressor. But the man shall never be chief at the foreign office, for he is a "Bonapartist." Bismarck protests against this accusation in a private letter: "If I am to be falsely described as a devil, at least let it be as a Teutonic and not as a Gallic one!" For the first time he avoids the use of the word "Borussian"; for the first time Bismarck acknowledges himself a German, and in doing so he uses the classical phrasing which he had made fun of when he was a youth. Roon, meanwhile, lays all possible stress upon the oath of fealty, which is to establish a royal precedent. He invites Bismarck to Berlin, and asks him to wire his decision, for "the king suffers terribly. The nearest members of his family are against him, and advise an ignominious peace." Bismarck, who in the winter was longing for a portfolio, is now, six months later, disappointed by a proposal which will shut him out from the main object of his desires. He does not wire, but answers cautiously by letter:

"Your command 'To horse' sounds amiss when my feelings run towards young woodcock on the one hand and the seeing of wife and children on the other. I have become inert, dull, and faint-hearted, now that the necessary foundation of health has been withdrawn from me." The oath of fealty seems to him of little importance. He has no inclination for the portfolio of home affairs, for the Prussian régime is too liberal at home and too conservative in foreign relationships, when it ought to be the other way about. With these thoughts in mind, he pens one of the profoundest phrases ever uttered about the Germans: "We are almost as vain as the French. If we can persuade ourselves that we have prestige abroad, we will put up with almost anything at home." He adds: "I am loyal to my sovereign even as far as La Vendée, but as regards all others, I feel no disposition to raise a finger on their behalf. Such being my mood, I fear I am so far from the way of thinking of our gracious lord that he would hardly find me a satisfactory adviser." Then, with a sudden revulsion, he concludes as follows: "If the king can move a little towards my way of thinking, then I shall be happy to take up the work."

This half-refusal, this pusillanimous tone, is explicable rather on the ground of obstinacy than on that of illness. He is well enough to get up at midnight in order to go out shooting woodcock, and henceforward we shall find that his health is one of the weapons in his political arsenal. The fact is that he sees through the uncertainty of this extremely unofficial summons, and doubtless feels that it puts him in a rather undignified position. When he at length comes to Berlin, Augusta, his old enemy, has won the game; the king has given way, and is to be content with a simple coronation, " for which the robes were already ordered in February."—" The king," declares Roon, " is more than ever at the orders of the queen and her satellites. Unless he becomes more vigorous physically, everything will be lost, and we shall move further towards putting ourselves under the yoke of parliamentarianism and the republic."

Nevertheless, Bismarck promptly goes to Baden to see the king. At his advent William is " disagreeably surprised, believing that I had come because of the ministerial crisis." The king is not friendly in his manner until he is sure of Mephisto's views. At this time, a German student makes an attempt on William's life, the reason being that the king takes no steps on behalf of German unity. Bismarck shares the would-be assassin's views, though he himself shoots at the king only with ideas. He seizes his opportunity. The king has been deeply moved, both by his escape and by the assassin's avowed motive. Bismarck explains his own views to William, and then embodies these views in a memorial which is penned during a summer holiday at Reinfeld, where Johanna copies the document. It contains evidence of a decisive and valuable change in his ideas, for it develops no less an idea than his fundamental thought of a German empire:

" Prussia cannot accept in Germany the role of a subordinate minority. . . . A federal State, which disposes of more power than all others, must have a predominant influence upon joint affairs. . . . In order to approach such a goal, a national representation of the German people in the federal central authority is perhaps the only means of connexion whereby a counterpoise can be established to the centrifugal tendencies of the separatist policies of the dynasties. As soon as popular representation . . . exists in every German State, it becomes impossible to regard a similar institution for Germany as a whole as essentially revolutionary. . . . The intelligence and the conservative behaviour of such a representation might perhaps be guaranteed if its members were not elected directly by the population but by the various Landtags. . . . The subordinate disputes of the diets would give place to a more statesmanlike handling of German interests in general." As for home affairs, each State must retain its authority unimpaired. Since Austria, of a surety, would reject the scheme, it could not be carried out by means of the existing Bundestag. "A more hopeful possibility, perhaps, would be an attempt to establish some other kind of national institution by following the road on which the Customs Union was brought into being." An announcement of these plans "must be designed so as to produce a twofold effect: first of all, to tranquillise the German princes concerning the scope of our designs, so that they may realise that we are not aiming at their mediatisation but at a voluntary understanding among them all; and secondly to counteract the discouragement that is general among the people, owing to the belief that Prussia considers the course of German development closed with the formation of the existing Bundestags."

These ideas concerning a customs parliament which is to develop into a German Reichstag, when contrasted with Bismarck's speeches and letters of the year 1840, show his development from a partisan into a statesman. It is he, now, who wants to realise the basic idea of the revolution, and therewith the unification of the Germans, which in those earlier days he rejected on account of its revolutionary origin. "Every one wants German unity, but I will not have it with this constitution," he had exclaimed. Even to-day, though he does not want this constitution, he is willing to adapt one of its main elements. He considers that its origin has been hallowed by the years; that it has thereby become legitimate and "cannot possibly be termed revolutionary." He even recognises and declares that it is not only permissible, but necessary, to admit Germans to a share in the governing of Germany — necessary as a counterpoise to the jealousies of the princes!

The document above quoted is penned in a forensic style. The same great turn in his policy finds a more vigorous and Bismarckian expression in the letter he writes simultaneously to a friend against the conservative programme: "It has come to this, that the unhistorical, godless, and lawless delusion of sovereignty of the German princes (who use our federal relationships as a pedestal on the top of which they disport themselves as European powers), is to become the spoiled darling of the conservative party. . . . For my part, I cannot see why we should shrink so fastidiously from the idea of popular representation, whether in the federation or in a customs union parliament. . . . It would be possible to create a thoroughly conservative national assembly, and yet earn thanks for it from the liberals."

Ten years after these utterances, Bismarck opened the first German Reichstag.

VIII

William I. stood in front of the altar; he picked up the crown from the Lord's Table, and with his own hands set it upon his head. This was a token that he received the emblem from God, and not from the people. Then there was a great review of the troops. Among the brilliant train was a giant figure wearing a blue uniform. Familiars at the court would have supposed it to be Bismarck, had it not been that this tall man had a head well covered with hair. But it was Bismarck after all, as they realised when they came near, and he said with a laugh: "In the courtyard of the palace, I was thoughtful enough to provide myself, not only with a military uniform, but also with a wig which puts Bernhard's into the shade. Without it, I should have had a bad time spending two hours in the open air bareheaded." Such was the rig-out in which Bismarck attended the crowning of the king, whose crowning as emperor he was to achieve a decade later. At the first coronation, the king shuns his vassal, just as he will ten years hence. This time the reason is that William wishes to avoid appearing reactionary. The queen's behaviour is very embarrassing both to her husband and to Bismarck. She meets her enemy with more civility than for years past. In the middle of one of the ceremonies, she halts in front of him to begin a talk about

German policy, "the king, who was leading her by the hand, vainly endeavouring for some time to make her break off the conversation."

But the receipt of the crown at God's hands did not tranquillise the king's heart. The confusion in his realm grew steadily worse. At the end of the year, the progressive party gained the victory in the elections. Parliament refused the new soldiers the king wanted. The following spring, as a punishment, the liberal cabinet was dismissed, and conservatives were appointed to assist Roon. Count Bernstorff, a clever and active man, fairly modern in his views, though not strong enough to enter upon a new road, replaced Schleinitz, who, however, continued to rule in the background, so that when Bismarck was at length recalled from St. Petersburg, the latter remarked that there would soon be three ministers for foreign affairs. The folly of the elector of Hesse, who, when his subjects refused to pay taxes, sent military locksmiths to break open their money boxes, seemed to give the desired excuse for intervention, and Bismarck said to Bernstorff: "If you want war with Hesse, make me your under-secretary; within four weeks you shall have a domestic war of the first quality." He was already "strongly opposed to the catchword of fraternal warfare."

So eager for action has he become in this spring of 1862, that he is ready to accept the post of minister without portfolio. He is again humiliated by the king's decision that there is one post he must not hold, that of minister for foreign affairs, which Bismarck regards as his specialty. He cannot endure to be kept waiting as he was two years earlier, and in the end he presents his chief with an ultimatum: office or resignation. Within three hours he is appointed envoy in Paris. This was the first of a series of tugs of war, in which Bismarck threatened resignation in order to force the king's hand. The post in Paris had just become vacant; so had the London embassy, to which Bernstorff wished to withdraw. Bismarck, regarded with ill-will, detested by the queen, looked upon by the king as a sinister statesman, nevertheless, when presenting this ultimatum, took the risk of being told to resign from the service. It was Bernstorff's merit that he advised against so risky a course. The only man upon whom Bismarck could count for personal support was Roon, and Roon was indispensable to the king.

In St. Petersburg, Bismarck had always felt his position to be temporary, and he had only spent half of his three years at his post. To Paris he went as if on a visit. At any moment, the crisis might become acute, and then Roon would send for him; that was the private understanding between the two friends. Though formerly he had liked Paris well enough, now nothing there could please him. The embassy was frowsty; the French were provincial, were too fond of posing, and yet had too many reserves. Since, for the last two years, all his thoughts had turned towards the holding of power, he was bored by everything else, and sometimes sank into a nihilism which recalled that of the most unhappy period of his youth.

"Since my illness, I have become lethargic mentally," he wrote in a letter to his sister when transferred from St. Petersburg. "I have no longer vigour enough to deal with lively circumstances. Three years ago I might still have been a fairly useful minister of State; now I seem to myself nothing better than a sick circus rider. . . . Without regret and without pleasure I would go to Paris, or to London, or stay here, just as might please God and His Majesty; it would be all the same to me, and would make no difference to our political life. . . . I dread ministerial office like one shivering before a cold bath. I would rather accept any vacant post, or return to Frankfort, or even Berne, where I was very comfortable. . . . Varnhagen" — Bismarck has been reading Varnhagen's memoirs — "is vain and malicious, but who is not? The differences between people only depend upon the way in which life ripens one person's disposition or another's — so that the fruit becomes maggoty, or flourishes in the sunshine, or suffers from wet weather; becomes bitter, sweet, or rotten."

All the same, he does not suffer. It is true that his wife, his children, and the other members of the household, are continually ailing; and a certain softness of mood is shown in Bismarck by the increasing cordiality with which he writes to Pomerania, especially to his sister. When he himself had been seriously ill, he had recognised the relativity of all his political feelings, and had written to his wife in a Hamlet mood: "There is nothing in this world except hypocrisy and hocus-pocus. No matter whether, in the end, fever or a bullet tears off the mask of flesh, soon or late it must be torn off. When that happens, there will be so much likeness between a Prussian and an Austrian (if they are the same size, like Schreck and Rechberg) that it will be hard to distinguish between them. The foolish and the wise, when there is nothing left of either but their skeletons, will look very like one another. Such an outlook frees a man from the burden of a specific patriotism."

Henceforward, when he lets himself go (and he does so at times even towards his pious wife), the vestiges of a religion whose forms seem to him ever more paradoxical are analysed away by reflections of the foregoing kind, by truths which smack of the diabolic. He writes home less often than of yore, and much shorter letters, though they are always affectionate. He goes to the heart of things only when he is describing nature — then he is a poet.

When he has been bludgeoned by fate, he consoles himself with thoughts of providence. When his nephew is killed out hunting, he writes to his sister: "In twenty years, or in thirty at most, we shall both of us be beyond the cares of this life; and by that time our children will be where we are now, and will be astonished to find that their lives, which had seemed to them only just begun, are already on the down grade. It would not be worth dressing and undressing if that were all. . . . The circle of those whom we love is continually growing smaller, and never enlarges until we have grandchildren. At our age, we form no new associations which could replace those who are taken from us by death." Even here we see how family feeling gets the better of religion.

But in the ordinary moods of life, when both pathos and weakness are absent, he pens the truth. For instance, after attending the funeral of a prince, he writes: "When the church, hung with

black, was emptying itself, I stayed behind with Gorchakoff. We
sat down beside the coffin, which was covered with a velvet pall,
and talked politics. . . . The preacher, in his sermon, had taken
his text from the hundred-and-third Psalm (grass, wind, gone),
and there we were, planning and plotting as if we were immortal!"
Such contemplative moods, proper to the born self-analyst, were
much rarer in his Christian decade than they had been in youth.
Henceforward they become common once more, for they summon
truth to stand in front of the mirror.

In a similar frame of mind he now roams through the streets of
Paris. He has not set up house properly there; his wife is not with
him, he has practically no associates, and anyhow most people of
his class leave the town at midsummer. His uneasiness because he
is not reaching his goal increases until it takes the form of contempt for the goal. He writes to Roon: "I have lively accesses of
the enterprising spirit of that animal which dances on the ice
when the world goes too well with it." He and his correspondent
discuss the family reasons which may lead Bernstorff to postpone
his departure, and may thus put off the crisis until the spring.
Bismarck ends by saying: "Maybe we are reckoning without
our host. Perhaps His Majesty will never make up his mind to
appoint me, for I really cannot see why he should do so now, since
he has not done so during the last six weeks." In August, when he
urges Roon to give him some definite news, as he would like to
know where his writing-table will be next winter — whether in
London or in Paris or in Berlin — Roon answers characteristically: "The king will understand such motives, and therefore
they may have more effect than political considerations."

His incessant longing for home, and for a fixed residence, makes
him nervous, and this reacts on his friends in Berlin. "My things
are still in St. Petersburg, and will get frozen-in there; . . . my
horses are in the country near Berlin; my family is in Pomerania;
I myself am on the road. . . . I should like nothing better than
to stay in Paris, but I must be assured that I am not taking the
trouble to install myself merely for a few weeks or months; my
household is too big for that." Then he goes on: "I am ready,

even to-day, to take office without portfolio, but I see no serious prospect of it." After his usual manner, he leaves a line of retreat open, writing to his brother to the effect that if he were to secure ministerial office it would not be for long; then he would go for a time to the country, in order to plant nurseries. "My fixed idea is to grow oaks for the bark, in sandy areas. Even on the worst and most gravelly wastes, the Dutch make at least twenty to thirty florins the acre in this way." Another time he writes to his brother like a lieutenant after a night out: "Separation from wife and children and a surfeit of apricots I had yesterday make me feel rather depressed, and I have a longing for some fixed place where I could look forward to ending my days in peace."

The only good thing he gets out of these two months in Paris is a conversation in Fontainebleau. Just as five years ago, but more urgently than before, the emperor plays the part of Bismarck's tempter. It would almost seem as if Napoleon had an inkling that this man, who seemed likely to rise to power ere long, was the enemy destined to destroy him, and as if the emperor hoped in some way to avert the disaster. When the two men were out walking together, the Frenchman said unexpectedly to the Prussian: "Croyez-vous que le roi serait disposé à conclure une alliance avec moi?"

"The king has the most friendly feelings towards Your Majesty's person, and the prejudices in public opinion as concerns France have pretty well vanished. But alliances are only fertile when circumstances are favourable, when the alliances are necessary and useful. There must be a motive for an alliance; there must be a purpose."

"That is not quite true," says the emperor. "Some powers are more friendly towards one another, and others are less friendly. In view of the uncertainty of the future, it is necessary to guide confidence in a particular direction. I am not talking in any adventurous fashion about an alliance. It seems to me that there is an identity of interests between Prussia and France, and that this can provide the elements for an intimate and lasting entente, unless prejudice should impose hindrances. It would be a great

mistake to attempt to create events; they come of themselves,
without our being able to foresee their trend and their strength.
That is why we must, in advance, make sure of the means whereby
we shall be enabled to meet them when they come and to turn them
to account." He develops this idea of a diplomatic alliance, then
suddenly stands still and says: "You can't imagine what amazing
offers Austria has made me these last few days. . . . Vienna
seems to be in a panic. Metternich has spoken to me of plenipotentiary powers, powers whose extent he scarcely dares to
mention. He says that he is empowered to treat with me about
all questions without reserve, that he has such powers as no sovereign has ever before given his envoy. This declaration has
embarrassed me. I don't know what to answer. He insists upon
his desire to arrange matters with me at any cost and without
reserve. But for my part, to say nothing of the conflicting interests of the two countries, I have an almost superstitious dread
of becoming involved in Austria's destinies."

The first thing that astonishes us so in this conversation is
the emperor's unceremoniousness, which is a departure from his
usual custom, and which in this instance is shown to the very
statesman who is already noted for his cunning assumption of
frankness. It might be thought that Napoleon spoke as he did
from caprice and levity, but the man's character and previous
history seem to preclude this hypothesis; he knew that diplomatists are prone to gossip, so he was not likely to invent the story
of Metternich's offers out of whole cloth; and his conception of the
nature of an entente was more accurate and more modern than
Bismarck's. What Bismarck said was not his real view. It was a
mere pretext. Nothing can be more remarkable than his chaste
refusal, which in his own report he compares to Joseph's refusal
of the advances of Potiphar's wife: "He had the most improper
proposals for an alliance on the tip of his tongue; if I had gone
to meet him half way he would have spoken far more plainly."

What would Bismarck have risked by attempting to get any
more information out of the emperor? Principles did not hinder
him, for he was not a legitimist; and if he had brought home with

him a positive proposal from powerful France, the king might
in the end have been willing to discuss matters. Besides, we know
that in his letter to Bernstorff he amplified his official report of
the same day by saying that the emperor was "a strong supporter of the plans for German unity, that is to say he is in
favour of a lesser united Germany, without Austria. Just as five
years ago, when he was talking matters over with me, he wanted
Prussia to become a sea power, at least of the second magnitude,
and said that she must have the necessary ports for this. He considered the boxing up of Jade Bay . . . an absurdity." But
Bismarck said nothing to his chief about the answer he had given
the emperor in the matter of the Austrian proposals. He was
content with the general conclusion that it would be inexpedient
to enter into an alliance with France upon specific terms, but also
undesirable to become Austria's associate against France, for
Austria would never "voluntarily agree to an improvement of
our position in Germany, but would be willing enough to sacrifice
Venetia and the left bank of the Rhine"; and, speaking generally,
"would be willing to enter into any combination which might help
to make her preponderant over Prussia in Germany."

Bismarck's silence towards his chief is noteworthy, for he had
been quick to recognise the profound historical significance of
this conversation in the park at Fontainebleau. It is plain that he
was considerably more frank towards the emperor than he was
towards the minister for whose shoes he was waiting. He hoped
that ere long Bernstorff would be envoy in London, while he himself would be minister in the Wilhelmstrasse, and therefore chief
of the man whose subordinate he now was. Why, then, should he
tell Bernstorff the whole truth about this almost unexampled conversation? It is likely enough that Bismarck concealed the purport of the talk even from the king; and although he himself said
nothing but generalities to the emperor, we may be sure that he
got some further confessions out of Napoleon. Four years later,
during the Austrian war, when he is again in touch with Napoleon, he will perhaps remind the emperor of these matters.

During this time in Paris, Bismarck met Thiers, the leader of the opposition. He also made a trip to London. After a dinner at the Russian embassy, he is said to have alarmed Disraeli and some of the other leaders by his frankness — though no doubt the traditional report of what happened must be regarded as apochryphal. He was asked what he would do if he came into power. "My first care would be to reorganise the army. As soon as it was strong enough, I should take the first opportunity of settling accounts with Austria, dissolving the Germanic Federation, . . . and establishing a united Germany under Prussia's leadership." Accustomed to bluff, Bismarck was convinced that people always believe a bluff when it is false, and never believe it when it appears to be a bluff and is honestly meant. This time, however, he erred, for one of his auditors was his own equal in intelligence. Disraeli, repeating Bismarck's words, added with a flash of genius: "Take care of that man, he means what he says!"

The German problem turned on the Prussian army. Every party — there were three of them — wanted the Prussian army on its side. The liberals wanted Germany under Prussia's leadership; the conservatives who were Germans first and foremost did not want to be ruled by Prussia; the conservatives who were Prussians first and foremost did not want to become Germans. The cleavage went right through people and society, the court, the officialdom, and the royal family. There were waves of feeling, just as there had been during the revolution.

The king was the only person who heard two voices speaking to him. For thirty years he had been aiming at the reorganisation of the army; here was his unique interest, and this was a subject in which he was at home. Since the War of Liberation, there had been no change in the constitution of the army, no modification in the age at which men were called up to service, although the population of the country had doubled. William, now that he had at last risen to power, now that his vacillating brother had passed away, wished for a new army law according to which a larger number of recruits would serve for a term of three years; on the other hand, the Landwehr, which consisted of married men, was to be reduced in size. Thus the total military force would remain the same, but the number of men actually with the colours would be raised from 400,000 to 700,000, and the army would consist of much younger men. This sparing of the older men sounded like a popular measure; and perhaps the king, soldier though he was, had nothing more in mind at first.

But he was soon to find that, politically speaking, there were other ways in which his scheme could be interpreted; that it could be attacked from either of two sides. The liberals rightly looked upon the Landwehr as the last stronghold of the people, the one which they had continued to occupy since the year 1813. It was their fathers, the "people" in the literal sense of the word, who had won the War of Liberation — not the nobles, whose attitude had been undecided, and not the king, who was hostile to the people. Now, it seemed that the people's army, which Scharnhorst had created in those days, was to degenerate into a king's army. Moreover, like William, the liberals wanted to strengthen the army; they wanted a united Germany, and that was why they were in favour of a two years' term of service. What they were averse to was that the influence of the nobles over the army should be increased. They objected to the proposed enlargement of the officers' corps and of the military colleges; and they did not wish to see the officers of middle-class origin transferred to the Landwehr. Everything else had slipped back into the power of the nobility, for the diplomats, the lord lieutenants, and the Landrats were all nobles. But if the army could be kept as a people's army, something would still be left of the spirit of 1848.

It was Roon who brought the conflict to a head. Far more royalist than the king, he declared in the chamber that, at important moments, the crown must not be dependent upon changing majorities and partisan speeches. Thus he openly expressed himself opposed to the constitution, and, as he had wished, made the left turn at bay. Until the establishment of the constitution, the king had decided the numerical strength of the army at the dictates of his own will. Was Prussia now to be a constitutional State, or a military State as of old? No soldiers without pay!

Refuse to vote money for the three years' term of service! If you do that, the chamber shall be dissolved! Thus did the conflict rage.

During these weeks of crisis in Berlin, Bismarck went for a swim every morning and every afternoon in the waters of the Atlantic, where the waves strike most mightily on the coast of France. He was at Biarritz, close to the Spanish frontier, far from railways, couriers, and German newspapers. Enjoying his daily bathes, he stayed there for weeks instead of for three days as he had at first intended. He lay about on the sand dunes, "smoking, watching the sea, doing target practice. . . . I have quite forgotten politics, and read no newspapers." Important letters from Bernstorff and Roon followed him to the foothills of the Pyrenees; Bismarck lolled at ease in the sand, and exclaimed: "If only there is no direct summons to Berlin! I am nothing but sea-salt and sunshine. . . . I stayed over half an hour in the water, and feel there as if I could fly, except that I have no wings. After dinner we went for a ride along the sands. The moon was shining, and the tide had ebbed. Then I went on farther by myself. You see that my old vigour has returned."

It is ten years and more since Bismarck has been so happy as during these weeks; and because he is happy, he is in love — honourably, of course, as becomes a man of strict principles. A man who knows women, in daily letters he raves to his wife about the other woman, and, comparing her to that dead friend of theirs, he throws fresh light on his own youthful affection: "Out of sight of every one, lying between two rocks on which heather is blooming, I look at the sea, which is green and white in foam and sunshine. Beside me is the most charming of women, whom you will be very fond of when you get to know her; she reminds me a little of Marie Thadden, . . . but has a very original personality — gay, clever, amiable, pretty, and young." Princess Orloff, née Trubetzkoi, whom he meets at the seaside resort, she and her husband, form the worldly foreground which Bismarck, as years advance, comes to prefer to savage forests and beetling cliffs: "I am ridiculously well, and am as happy as I can be when away from you." He goes to bed early, rises early and briskly. The charming Russian lady plays the piano to him at night, as he sits by the open window looking over the sea; plays his beloved Beethoven, also Chopin, and Schubert's *Winterreise.* " She is a woman to whom you will be devoted when you know her." They visit a lighthouse, and find that the wife of the keeper is expecting to be confined. A romantic fancy seizes the lovers. They will hand down their intertwined affections to the unborn being, and they offer themselves as godparents. In actual fact, when the boy is born, he is christened Othon Lafleur, their joint names. For the nonce, Bismarck forgot his wedding day; the Russian woman made a conquest of this man of much experience, who was always susceptible to the charm of foreign women. Never again was he thus stirred.

For now, in the handsome lady's train, he travels towards his greatest passion: power.

After many postal and telegraphic vicissitudes, a warning reaches him at Avignon. At length, when he is back in Paris, comes the definite summons for which Roon had prepared him by letter a fortnight earlier. The message runs: " Dépêchez-vous. Periculum in mora." This comes to hand on September 18, 1862. The telegram is dated September 17th. Early in the morning of September 19th, he is in the train on his way to Berlin. His mood is like that of fifteen years before, when, after long waiting, his peasants had ridden hell-for-leather to the gate of Schönhausen, shouting: " The ice has begun to break up. Come quickly, Herr Baron! "

In the Lower House, the progressives had refused to pass the army bill, unless the term of service were to be limited to two years. Roon, his hands forced by his weaker colleagues, rejoined that he would think the matter over, for he was in these days prepared to make concessions. Bernstorff had resigned because he would not face the need of ruling unconstitutionally without parliament, in the event of the refusal to bow to the wish of parliament about the two years' term of service. But now the king stood firm, supported by Moltke. Thereupon, when everything was at stake, Roon, on his own initiative, sent for the statesman who was to provide these three generals with their troops.

When the call to arms reached Bismarck in Paris, the king, at Neubabelsberg, was in a state of great excitement, since for the second time he was at the parting of the ways between law and conviction. As he was not a politician but a nobleman, he again wished to evade the issue, and withdraw. The most terrible moments of his life surged up in his memory: his flight to Memel in childhood; his flight as a grown man to the Pfaueninsel, and to London; Olmütz; the day before the Crimean War. All had been in vain. On September 18th, he sent for his son, and laid before Frederick his act of abdication still unsigned. The crown prince, much too weak a man, and far too averse from action, to seize the crown his father offered him, refused even to read the document, declaring that he could not begin his reign by retreating before the chamber. Abdication, he said, would only intensify the conflict; the politicians of the right would play off the father against the more liberal son. The name of Bismarck cropped up.

"He is a partisan of France," says Frederick.

"All the more reason why I do not want him as minister," says William.

When Roon again urges the appointment of Bismarck, and Bernstorff backs up the general, old William, driven into a corner, exclaims:

"He won't accept it now! He is not here! We can't talk matters over with him!" This was the king's last effort to avoid the inevitable. On the 20th, early in the morning, Bismarck turned up. An acquaintance describes him as arriving: "lean, well, and sunburned; like a man who had been riding a camel across the desert." Bismarck finds everything in confusion. They all have something to say to him, and each of them gives him different advice. The ministers still think that an abdication is imminent, and dissuade the king from the step. The crown prince tries to escape from the chaos, travels to a neighbouring spa, sends for Bismarck on the 21st, but finds him extremely reserved, for the envoy has not yet talked matters over with the king. The king hears of this visit to Frederick, and when, on that same day, Roon has audience, the king, very much out of humour, says:

"There is nothing to be done with Bismarck. He has already been to see my son!" In these words, recorded by Bismarck himself, William's whole personality is expressed. The king would rather abdicate than yield to the chamber, for he is a soldier. If his son refuses to accept the throne, so much the better, for, after all, William would rather continue to hold the power he has waited for so long. But when he finds that the man he was yesterday willing to summon seems to have been coquetting with his son, the king is full of suspicion — even though the man be Bismarck. There must be a conspiracy. Roon had summoned Bismarck on his own initiative. Roon is in it too! Unfortunately, however, the man is here now; William cannot refuse to see his own envoy; no use letting matters drift on any longer. Besides, none of the others are any good, and what William wants more than anything else in the world is the new army.

Well, let him come, give him a trial. We must use what weapons we have.

On the 22nd, at an early hour, Bismarck enters the king's study at Babelsberg. The king, who is less inclined towards abdication than he was three days ago, nevertheless tells Bismarck about this intended abdication, and shows him the document which he has shown also to Roon as well as to Frederick. Although he is fully satisfied that he is king by God's grace, and regards as sacred the crown he took from the Lord's Table, in the realism of the struggle he is the army officer once more, saying again and again:

"Then I shall resign."

"I will not reign unless I can do so in such a way as I can answer to before God, my conscience, and my subjects. . . . I cannot find any ministers who are ready to carry on my government, and I have therefore decided to abdicate." Bismarck was expecting this declaration, and the king knew that he was expecting it, for all the ministers had been made aware of his intention. The envoy rejoined:

"As Your Majesty knows, I have been ready to take office since May."

Following his usual tactics, Bismarck is throwing the responsibility on the other, who should, he implies, have summoned him sooner. Roon, continues Bismarck, must remain in office, and others must be found.

"Would you yourself be prepared to insist upon the reorganisation of the army in spite of the adverse majority?"

"Yes."

"Then it is my duty, with your aid, to attempt the carrying on of the struggle, and I shall not abdicate."

The whole form of the conversation shows us that the king, before the door had opened, had made up his mind to continue his reign with the aid of this undismayed statesman, so that he could retain his position with honour. His questions suggest the answers he wants, and yet they are an appeal to conscience. He is too simple and straightforward to make a theatrical gesture, to tear up the act of abdication, to shake the new man by the hand, and to begin a new era. He is like Bismarck, who for the second time in his life makes a great decision in a single word. The king invites him for a walk in the park, and questions him further. Now William shows Bismarck a holograph memorial, eight closely written folio pages, dealing with all the questions at issue, from the concessions to the liberals to the reform of circle administration. Thus has the king armed himself to meet his formidable servant. The programme is to protect William against Bismarck's adventurous follies. Bismarck, as he glances through the document, infers that it has been inspired by the queen.

Thereupon he changes his tone. The sense of the presence of his invisible enemy, and the feeling of security given him by the recent informal appointment, restore his whilom self-confidence, and with his first word in this dangerous alliance he stabilises at one and the same time his own policy and his rights. He refuses to discuss the details of the programme.

"The question now at issue is not between conservative and liberal, but whether the régime in Prussia shall be monarchical or parliamentary. If needs must, parliamentarianism should be withstood by a period of dictatorship. In this respect, a programme would only tie our hands. In such a situation, I shall express my opinions to you frankly, even if Your Majesty commands me to do things which I do not consider wise; but if you remain of your own opinion, I will rather perish with the king than leave Your Majesty in the lurch in the struggle with parliament."

A new tone! Bismarck has deliberately chosen it, because in this hour he wants to win William's confidence. Yet at the same time he has given a vow of obedience, precisely because he feels capable of disobedience and autocracy. At the same time we may be sure that, with Mephistopheles, he is thinking to himself: " I will drag him through the perplexities of life!"

He has accepted the summons as liegeman and officer, but also as diplomatist. A minute later he shows his realistic foresight when the king makes a motion to throw the now worthless programme into a dry ditch. Thereupon the monarch's companion checks him, having an eye to dangerous possibilities. This is the first advice that Bismarck as minister gives his king. Often, in future, he will warn William against dry ditches.

On his way back from Babelsberg, Bismarck meets Schlözer. To this man, who has won his confidence by such devious routes, he says (so Schlözer reports), "in a very strange tone ":

"I think I have been taken into custody."

BOOK THREE: 1862–1871

THE BUILDER

Not without punishment can we eat of the tree of life

— ROON

I

"Here in the Landtag, while I am writing to you, I have to listen . . . to amazingly foolish speeches delivered by amazingly childish and excited politicians, and this gives me a few moments of involuntary leisure. . . . When I was an envoy, although an official, I had the feeling that I was a gentleman; but as minister one is a slave. . . . The men here differ as to the motives which bring them together; that is what the quarrel is about. . . . They slaughter one another con amore, that is the necessary outcome of affairs of this sort. . . . These chatterers cannot really rule Prussia; I must resist them; they have too little wit, and too much comfort; they are stupid and arrogant, . . . and yet 'stupid' (in its general sense) is not the right term. They are fairly clever in a way, have a smattering of knowledge, are typical products of German university education; they know as little about politics as we knew in our student days — nay, less! As far as foreign politics are concerned they are, taken individually, children; in other matters they become children as soon as they meet together in corpore."

Thus does Bismarck write to Motley, the friend of his youth; and such are his sentiments during the first months of his reign. He despises these men as a group, these ideologues whom he is fighting, though he recognises unreservedly that individual leaders among them are men of culture. As regards European affairs, he feels himself to be without qualification their superior. At the same time he suffers from having to struggle unceasingly against his sensitive feeling of honour; he has to learn not to hit back as of old. Hitherto he could attack his opponents openly, throwing all his forces into the battle: fighting, when a deputy, from the tribune; and when a diplomatist, in reports and letters. Henceforward he has to conceal his thoughts and plans from the elected of the people, for otherwise they would come to the knowledge of the nations, and new plans would be needed. With his rise to power, his loneliness begins.

He has no reason to be surprised when a Berlinese newspaper greets his elevation as follows: "He began his career as a country gentleman of moderate political information, one of those whose views and acquirements do not exceed what is common to all educated persons. The climax of his parliamentary fame was reached in 1849 and 1850. In his speeches, he showed himself rough and ruthless, nonchalant to the pitch of frivolity, and sometimes witty to that of grossness. When, however, has he ever uttered a political idea?" It was true that he had been little in the public eye; and only a few initiates knew all that he had done during the last decade on behalf of peace. Though his activities were not of a priestly character, they were esoteric. "Even a man of greater power," wrote Gustav Freytag in the "Grenzboten", "would be shipwrecked against the firmness of the chambers. We may give Herr von Bismarck a year." Poeta propheta! He held power for twenty-eight years.

One who at this date watched his work from close at hand questioned his sanity: "Bismarck suffers from a severe nervous disorder," writes one of his underlings after a few weeks, "and it seems to me at times that he is not wholly responsible for his actions. For example, when he issues instructions for the press, his thoughts sometimes gallop in such a way that it is hardly possible to follow them. The diplomatists of Berlin are for the most part inclined to believe that . . . he will not live long, for he never spares himself."

Nevertheless, after his scientific manner, he was beginning gently and slowly, being determined to take action only after extensive analyses and experiments, and to proceed carefully. A little while before, he had written to Roon saying that if he came to power people would exclaim: "Now there will be the devil to pay!" He was resolved to disappoint his enemies' expectations of violent and foolish behaviour. Immediately on accepting office, he withdrew the budget for the year 1863, thus offering a truce to the chambers; entered into negotiations with the old liberals with the offer of seats in the cabinet; and astonished them even more by the manner than by the matter of his proposals. What was Twesten, the deputy, to tell his friends when the man whom he was inclined to despise rather than to fear, in a long conversation, had spoken almost intimately and very critically of the king whose unthinking supporter he was supposed to be? Oetker, a liberal, describes how, at the first visit, he had expected to find "a servile Junker, an idle sportsman and gamester; but within a few minutes I had formed a very different picture of Bismarck. There was no trace of what I had expected. . . . A man of great stature, powerful but lithe, came to the door, greeted me in a most friendly fashion, shook hands with me, drew up a chair for me, and said with a winning smile: 'Well, so you are out of favour with the democrats, too!' Then he went on to say that times had changed since the days of his active opposition to the men of the barricades — in Frankfort he had learned a great deal." He abused the "Kreuzzeitung" in terms stronger than any his visitor "had ever said or written."

Thus masterly is his management of opponents who have expected to find him arrogant and reserved. They are received with the utmost civility and with a semblance of frankness. Oetker is not a petty official or small tradesman, the sort of man who talks politics in a provincial club; he is one of the Hessian leaders, a lawyer, well educated. He is flattered by the way in which the great man comes to the door and greets him and draws up a chair for him — not because of Bismarck's official position as premier, but because this affable prime minister is also a Prussian Junker. Arrogant, at that date, was the traditional demeanour of the Prussian landed gentry; and Bismarck, who is supposed to be the very embodiment of such class feeling, breaks through all the forms, behaves naturally, and in the presence of his opponents, rails against the excesses of his own party, shows that he is neither stiff because he is now styled "Your Excellency", nor doctrinaire like a Junker. He shows himself a man of the world; original and unusual, indeed, but anything other than the typical Prussian official.

No one was keener to note these experiments of early days in office than Schlözer, who had the pleasure of drinking a glass of wine with Bismarck several times at this period. Schlözer writes: "Bismarck plays his comedy thoroughly, trying to intimidate the king and all the parties. It amuses him to take every one in. He is trying to induce the king to give way about the period of military service. To the members of the Upper House, he paints in such dark colours the reaction he proposed to install that, so he fancies, they are positively alarmed. . . . He sometimes takes a very strong line as regards the members of the Lower House; at other times he behaves in a way designed to encourage them to come to terms. As for the German cabinets, he makes them believe that the king finds it difficult to hold his new minister's Cavourism in check. This much is certain, that he has, so far, made a great impression by the brilliancy of his genius. C'est un homme!"

For the time being, he practises the utmost politeness, even when he is sorely tried. He had hardly been minister a week before he took advantage of a sitting of one of the Landtag committees to make some personal admissions. In the course of the debate he opened his cigar case, and showed his opponents a small olive branch, saying: "I recently picked this at Avignon, intending to offer it to the people's party in token of peace. I see, however, that the time for such an action has not yet arrived." Rather supercilious, perhaps, but said with a courtesy which he seems to have brought back with him from the land of the olive branch. A moment afterwards, the virtuoso changes his tone, and declares that the accusations levelled at him by the press (which asserts that he designs to make war in order to distract attention from the confusions at home) are false, and goes on to say:

"It is true that we can hardly escape complications in Germany, though we do not seek them. Germany does not look to Prussia's liberalism, but to her power. The South German States would like to indulge in liberalism, and therefore no one will assign Prussia's role to them! Prussia must collect her forces and hold them in reserve for a favourable moment, which has already come and gone several times. Since the treaties of Vienna, our frontiers have been ill-designed for a healthy body politic. The great questions of the time will be decided, not by speeches and resolutions of majorities (that was the mistake of 1848 and 1849), but by iron and blood."

At a green table, addressed to the ears of one or two dozen deputies and a few ministers of State, without provocation, a monologue conciliatory in tone, ostensibly an impromptu but unquestionably prepared — such is the way in which these sentences fall from his lips. No shorthand writer took them down, but when they ran like wildfire all over Germany, when press and people had changed the rhythm of the phrase to "blood and iron" and had expressed real or feigned alarm, the speaker did not repudiate the words.

Nevertheless, he deplored having used them. Like the first thrust of Bismarck as deputy fourteen years earlier, his first thrust as minister president was a blow in the air. This time, likewise, he outraged every one, friends as well as foes. "Phrases like that are racy digressions," said Roon, his friend and discoverer, when the two were on their way home together; and Roon found fault with him for what he had said. "Everything is sport to this man; no responsible minister talks like that," wrote the liberals. Bismarck himself explained matters to a deputy as follows: "All I meant was that the king needs soldiers. I was not making a speech designed to help the German problem forward a stage. It was only a warning to Vienna and Munich. By no means was it an appeal to force against the other German States. 'Blood' only means 'soldiers.' I see now that I should have done better to choose my words more cautiously." This most noted of all Bismarck's sayings was his last tactical blunder.

The king read the words with alarm. Being exposed at Baden to the queen's criticisms, and, when her birthday came, being subject to those of the crown prince and princess, it was natural that he should cherish gloomy thoughts concerning his new premier, who had sworn fealty to him only a week before and whom he had promised his wife to keep under a tight rein. The royal family was greatly incensed. There was talk of Louis XVI., of Strafford and Polignac — and on the queen's birthday, too! All the joy of the festival had vanished. Bismarck, in Berlin, foresees the effect his speech will have in Baden; he enters into the king's inward struggles, although William has neither written nor wired to him. In imagination, he sees William travelling home alone a few days later, his ears filled with warnings and reproaches. Now, therefore, Bismarck begins his management of the king by a secret journey, disclosed beforehand neither to the king nor to the cabinet, and designed to influence William before he reenters the capital. Bismarck sets forth to meet William.

At the booking-office, Herr von Unruh, the liberal, recognises him. Bismarck enters the same compartment with Unruh in order to get suggestion to work upon him, cautiously discusses the situation, and, on stepping off the train at Jüterbog, says he is going to visit a relative. Then he sits down in the unfinished station, "in the dark, upon an overturned wheelbarrow", among workmen and other people of no importance. He is spoken to gruffly by the guard when he asks for the royal carriage; he does not give his name; no one knows him. Thus he, who insists upon the utmost respect being paid to his class, seems not to demand any respect for his position. The man of blood and iron, about whom, in these days, all the world is talking for the first time, and whom all the world is abusing, sits in the dark upon an overturned wheelbarrow, waiting for his master.

In those days of fable, the king of Prussia still travelled in an ordinary train. He was sitting alone in a dimly lighted compartment. There the minister found him, obviously depressed. When Bismarck asked permission to explain the situation, the king cut him short, saying:

"I see well enough how all this will end. In the Opernplatz, under my windows, they will cut your head off — and, a little later, mine!"

Bismarck, who sees the shade of Augusta behind the king, is content to answer: "Et après, Sire?"

"Après, indeed! Then we shall be dead!"

"Yes, then we shall be dead! We must die sooner or later, and could there be a more respectable way of dying? I should die fighting for the cause of my king and master. Your Majesty would die sealing with your own blood your royal rights granted by God's grace. Whether upon the scaffold or upon the battle-field makes no difference to the glorious staking of body and life on behalf of rights granted by God's grace! Your Majesty must not think of Louis XVI. He lived and died a weakling, and does not make a fine figure in history. Think, rather, of Charles I.! Will he not always remain a distinguished personality, the man who, after fighting for his rights and losing the battle, went unmoved and with kingly mien to his death? Your Majesty has no option but to fight. You cannot capitulate. Even at risk to your person, you must resist the attempt to force your hand!"

"The longer I went on talking in this fashion, the more was the king invigorated, and the more did he come to feel himself playing the part of an officer fighting for kingdom and country. . . . The ideal type of Prussian officer, the man who goes to certain death unselfishly and fearlessly, saying simply 'at your orders'; but who, when he has to act on his own responsibility, fears the criticism of his superiors or of the world more than he fears death. . . . He felt that he had been put on his mettle as an army officer. Thus he was guided on to a road which was congenial to his whole mode of thought. In a few minutes he had recovered the confidence which he had lost in Baden, and had even become cheerful. . . . Before we had reached Berlin, he was in a fighting as well as a cheerful mood, as he showed plainly enough to the ministers and officials who came to meet him."

This scene, whose dramatic force gives it the stamp of truth, though it was not described until thirty years later, is one of his masterpieces. Here he is not forcing an opponent to surrender, or urging his master into a war; he is merely trying to cajole the justly angered king into approving a speech which the man who

made it himself regards as injudicious. Bismarck sitting on the
wheelbarrow had an uneasy conscience. Even though he had admitted to an opponent that he had made a mistake in talking
about blood and iron, he was by no means inclined, when he had
been premier for a week, to make the same admission to his king.
That was why he whipped both himself and the king into a fighting mood which had been lacking at their first consultation; and
this combative frame of mind in William, suggested by Bismarck,
became a reserve of force for future occasions.

Even if all this could be attributed to the man's innate shrewdness and calculation, it was also a true expression of his deepest
feelings. From the days of his first duel, Bismarck had ever been
ready to die fighting; nor was there any hour in his life when
he was afraid to risk his body. The minister's personal courage,
whose genuineness the king could realise through all the pores of
his own veteran soldier's skin, was a powerful means of suggestion.

That was the magical potion with which Bismarck could always
cure his master in hours of weakness.

II

"I don't suit His Highness, who must be handled very delicately!" Those were the words with which, when William became
regent, four years before his own appointment as premier, Bismarck had pointed out to Gerlach the difficulties, as far as he was
concerned, involved by the change of rulers. Whether he suited
Prussia, that was the great question, which Schlözer (in his
mingled love and hatred) had not ventured to answer in the
affirmative. The king was the only Prussian who could give him
Prussia as the object of statecraft. First he had had to get hold
of William; now he had to hold William fast. Bismarck handled
him as a skilful lover manages the mistress of whose affections he
can never be wholly sure, as an inventor manages the capitalist
who is to finance his invention — for Bismarck was a master
craftsman. In the struggle between the two men, neither of whom
could get on without the other, in the wordless and often silent

struggle between the two whose characters were so utterly different, in the struggle not for power but for self-conquest, in this
unending and royal rivalry, each of the combatants had half the
merit and half the burden. It is difficult to say whose was the
harder task. Was it harder for an elderly gentleman of moderate
gifts though of royal blood to put up with a comparatively young
man as minister, a man who was only a Junker, but happened to
be a genius; or for a bold statesman to put up with a perpetually
hesitating king? The veteran rider was always mistrustful of the
spirited horse; and the horse was always chafing at the bit.

Again and, again, after a discussion in which the king and the
minister held divergent views, the two would part in bad humour,
each of them wishing one thing above all, to be quit of the other.
But when, tired out (or, more often, as a shrewd manœuvre), the
subordinate told his chief he intended to resign, the chief was
alarmed, and promptly gave way. There were hours of furious
strife, hours of which only faint echoes have found their way into
the memoirs.

Bismarck had foreseen all this, years before; long, long before
either of them rose to power. In his days as envoy, he had always taken it into his calculations. When he now came into contact with the king in daily work, he set himself to play his part
in the grand style. In general, he had a profound knowledge of
men; in particular, he was a courtier; occasionally, he was a
soldier: but always he must make himself out to be religious, for
otherwise he would alarm his master, now verging on seventy.
Even at this age, the king would at times get into such a passion
that he would crumple up State papers in his hands, papers
which, after the crisis, Bismarck would contemplate with a smile,
finding them all the more interesting for their creases, as a great
portrait painter finds a face more interesting for its wrinkles.
The only way to meet these storms was by composure, and this
quality was one which Bismarck had but recently acquired. He
did not take offence, for he knew his master to be straightforward, and not double-faced like Frederick William — who
would cheat his ministers, and play them off one against the other.

William I. gave his confidence unconditionally to a man who accepted the fullest responsibility.

Bismarck, when he took up the reins of office, knew the king, and for him therefore no surprises lay in ambush; but the king only made acquaintance with Bismarck very slowly, and did not lay aside his prejudices until years had passed and his minister had won many successes. He had entered into this relationship reluctantly, and during its first years his relatives and his friends did everything in their power to break it off. At first, the old-liberal politicians sent trusted emissaries to the king, begging for the dismissal of the new minister. It was with regret that the old gentleman saw the sympathies of his people flow away from him. In early days, when he had been detested as the " cartridge prince ", he had despised these sympathies; now, in the so-called liberal era, he had begun to win them again. Four months after Bismarck's appointment, the king read in a letter from an officer who was an old friend of his: " The people are faithful to Your Majesty, but they also cling to their rights. . . . May God, in his grace, avert the unhappy consequences of a terrible misunderstanding! "

Such words incensed him. Contradiction made him more obstinate. Underlining salient passages twice or thrice, and writing with the passion of a youth, he rejoined: " I have never ceased to repeat that my confidence in my people is unshaken, for I know that my people trust me! But I condemn those who wish to rob me of the love and confidence of my people. . . . Every one knows that those who wish to do this are prepared to use any means. . . . Have I not conceded four millions — unfortunately! Have I not made other concessions — unfortunately! . . . One who makes such use of his rights, that is to say reduces the budget in such a way that all the work of the State is arrested, is fit for a lunatic asylum! Where is it stated in the constitution that only the government shall make concessions and the deputies never??? "

A king writing to a subject who is not in official employment can only write with such fury when his conscience disturbs him o' nights; and we may be sure that the pious man has been wrestling with God for his minister.

In times of crisis, Bismarck does not allow any letter to the king to leave his hands without calling upon God; and when, at Christmas, the king sends him a walking-stick, he compares it to Aaron's rod, although the comparison is hardly an apt one. Before great decisions, which must invariably be first of all suggested to William by slow degrees and subsequently wrested from him, Bismarck keeps close watch on the king's moods. Thus, he writes to his friend Roon: "The king's heart is in the other camp. . . . The king's feelings are against me." Before an order for mobilisation is issued to Roon: "It is very much to be desired that the king should give his definitive order to-morrow, for by Maundy Thursday he will no longer be in the same mood." A few years later: "I am again at the end of my resources. It is really too much for me to keep up these contests with the king."

Bismarck did not repay in kind William's original dislike for him. He was content, to begin with, with his general sense of superiority. That was Bismarck's way. In youth, he was wont to examine the physique of every one he met, and when he grew older to study the mental qualities, in order to make sure that he was superior in all respects to this possible antagonist. In the case of William, first as crown prince and afterwards as king, he had no difficulty in convincing himself of his own superiority; and it was not until after their relationships became those of king and minister that the latter began to cherish two new feelings, without which he could never have endured his position. Bismarck came to regard the king as his liege lord and as a sort of father. In the early days of his marriage, Bismarck had written to his wife: "We have sworn fealty to his blood." Now, when Bismarck was in daily contact with William, was called upon to protect him and to act as his shield-bearer, this sentiment of feudal loyalty took on wider proportions. Furthermore, these symbolical feelings were strengthened by the venerable aspect of the white-bearded elder. In old age, Otto von Bismarck spoke of his relationship to the king, who was often in a passion, as having been like that of a son to a father, whose fits of temper and caprices must be accepted as vis major. He forgot that in his own youth he had never been inclined to pay this reverence to his real father.

In the course of the slow process of subjecting the king to his will, he gradually acquired a sympathy for the man who thus surrendered power; and, after William's death, this sympathy became intensified into a feeling of love, which was the obverse of his hatred for William II., and was made the most of with an eye to subsequent generations. During the crises of the first decade Bismarck was always attracted towards his headstrong master when he had the opportunity of witnessing William's personal courage — on the battlefield, and later when attempts were made on the king's life.

The only thing William was afraid of was the "manœuvring criticism of his wife." In this matter, nothing mitigated Bismarck's hatred, in general for women who wanted to play a part in politics, and in especial for Augusta. His dislike for the queen dated from that fateful conversation during the March days in the servants' hall at Potsdam. No monarchical sentiment tempered this dislike; nor was it modified by a respect for what, in an occasional tolerance of women, Bismarck spoke of as "ladies' rights."

His conflicts with Augusta were spoken of by Bismarck as "the hardest-fought battles of my life." Augusta's influence was exercised in the form of curtain lectures, and the effect of these upon the king was the subject of Bismarck's complaints to his own wife. This Augusta, who had fruitlessly "looked in Goethe's eyes", could only bear to meet Bismarck's eyes under the protection of her position. Had she possessed any political ideas or impressions to set up against his, she might have been admirable even in defeat; but she had nothing to put forward against him beyond vague humanitarian phraseology, behind which was concealed her dread of a new '48; and when, among her intimates, she compared King William and his ministers to Louis XVI., Strafford, and Polignac, Bismarck was in her eyes the head and front of the evil influences at work upon her husband. She forgot that he and not she had been right in those March days; that it was he, by his refusal to enter into her plans, who had preserved the crown for her; and she was readier to ascribe the basest motives to him than to support him or to honour him as the champion of monarchical rights.

Bismarck's general mistrust and misanthropy led him often enough into the erroneous belief that he was being persecuted. But for what he had to bear during twenty-six years from Augusta's intolerable "accessory and opposition government", we must certainly commiserate him; for here, faced by a woman and a queen, the champion was weaponless and had to bear her blows in silence. Whenever his master had been affected by Augusta's influence (often at breakfast, by letters written for that express purpose), he traced the king's mood to its origin. In the early years, if he ventured to make any allusion to the fact, the only result was " a very sharply worded denial. The king . . . set his face against the belief that this was so, even if in truth it was so."

When he wants to influence the king against the queen, he has to wrap up his medicine in a quantity of grotesque and courtly verbiage. At Gastein, in 1865, the agreement with Austria is under discussion. Once more, all the other factors are working against Bismarck's policy. Then the king tells him that he (William) has just made a confidential communication to the queen. Bismarck, having gone home, is in despair concerning the effect of family gossip, which he foresees, and which will threaten the destruction of his schemes. He therefore sits down and writes a holograph letter (for he could not entrust so delicate a matter to another hand), a long request:

"Your Majesty will graciously forgive me if a perhaps excessive care for the interests of your exalted service induces me to return to the communications which Your Majesty has just been good enough to make me. . . . I share Your Majesty's belief that Her Majesty the queen will keep your communications secret; but if from Coblenz, in reliance upon blood relationships, any intimation were to reach Queen Victoria or Their Highnesses the crown prince and princess, or were to reach Weimar or Baden, the mere fact that the secrecy to which I . . . pledged myself has not been preserved, would awaken the distrust of Emperor Francis Joseph, and would bring the whole undertaking to shipwreck. The result of that shipwreck would almost inevitably be a war with Austria.

" Your Majesty will ascribe it, not only to my interest for your exalted service, but also to my devotion for your exalted person, if I cannot avoid thinking that Your Majesty would enter upon a war against Austria with a different sort of feeling and with a much freer mind, if the necessity for this step should arise out of the nature of things and out of monarchical duties, rather than that there should be room for the arrière pensée that a premature announcement of the intended solution might have withheld the emperor from offering Your Majesty the last acceptable expedients. Perhaps my concern is foolish, and even if it were well grounded and Your Majesty should choose to disregard it I should think that God was guiding Your Majesty's heart, and should not for that reason perform my service any less joyfully. But, to satisfy my own conscience, I venture respectfully to ask whether Your Majesty will not command me to summon the courier back to Salzburg by telegraph. Urgent ministerial business could serve as a pretext for this, and early next morning another courier could be despatched, or the same one could start again. . . . I have such respectful confidence in Your Majesty's proved graciousness as to feel assured that Your Majesty, even if you do not approve my proposal, will pardon it, and ascribe it to my honest endeavour to serve Your Majesty, not only dutifully, but also to your exalted personal satisfaction."

No more than half a century has elapsed since a great statesman deemed it necessary to write such a letter to a king who, but for that statesman, would have figured merely as a number in history! While we read, do we not imagine that a courtier must be begging for an order of distinction, or for a pardon? What is going on here in Gastein concerns matters on which the writer of the letter has pondered long in the hope of carrying them through, and has secured his master's assent by long struggles. Neither

God nor his conscience, neither duty nor the needs of the service, have anything whatever to do with these affairs of State. We have here only a great chess player who, by unsearchable detours, is driving his opponent into a corner that he may checkmate him in the end. Now, in the midst of the most difficult negotiations, this man, wearied out by the struggle with his master, sees that his work is endangered because his schemes are likely to be prematurely divulged by court gossip. He has to think over the ways by which a plan can be blabbed from one realm to another: if Augusta tells the secret to Princess Victoria, the latter may pass it on to her English mother, and the queen of England may write to Vienna or to Dresden, so that, amateurishly, or with hostile hands, they may shatter the whole plan. Can we be surprised that Bismarck's contempt for crowned heads should increase day by day and year by year? What astonishes us is that he remains a royalist!

For among all these Hohenzollern there is not one who supports him. Frederick, who is apt to be up in arms against the king's cautiousness, is here under the thumb of his wife (his intellectual superior); he brings excellent English ideas over to Prussia, but lacks the power and the courage to fight for their acceptance in his native land. Only once does he venture. The conflict has become more acute. Bismarck has issued ordinances against the liberty of the press. The crown prince, making a tour of inspection, accompanied by his wife, has a public reception in Danzig. He plucks up courage, and at a reception in the Town Hall, declares: "I deplore that I have come here at a moment when there is dissension between the government and the people, dissension of which I have learned with great surprise. I knew nothing of the ordinances which have led to this. I was absent. I have had no part in these measures."

The king reads his son's speech (which is reported in all the Prussian newspapers), and is in a great rage; not because his heir is playing the demagogue, but because, a disciplined soldier, he believes that obedience, the foundation of his army, is imperilled. True that, ten years before, he himself had been in a like situation; but he had not allowed his wrath against Frederick William to go beyond the four walls of his room. The memory of his own dumb submission in the days of the Crimean War makes him now all the fiercer against the son who publicly proclaims dissent. What does Bismarck do? In the king's present mood, the premier could easily persuade him to inflict humiliation on Frederick. Recall, disciplinary transfer, even imprisonment in a fortress, are within the king's competence to inflict; and he has meditated all of them. But the minister president advises him to forgive his son. Does he want to ingratiate himself with the heir apparent? Hardly! Far more probably, Bismarck thinks that punishment would equip Frederick with a halo! "Walk warily in your dealings with the young man Absalom," he says to the king, who is fond of Biblical phraseology. "Take care to decide nothing in anger. Be guided only by reasons of State. If there were a quarrel between young Fritz and his father, popular sympathy would be entirely on the side of the son." By such carefully chosen words, he manages to bring about a reconciliation.

Privately, however, the crown prince is free to say what he thinks; and, as he now detests Bismarck more than ever, he condemns the latter's anti-democratic policy in set terms. Frederick also refuses to take any further part in the ministerial sittings, "for I am definitely opposed to Bismarck." After a while, when the two men meet again, Bismarck asks Frederick why he absents himself from a government which, within a few years, will be his own. Surely the prince would do well to expound his differences, and thus facilitate the transition.

Transition? This electrifies the crown prince. "He definitely refused; in the belief (so it seemed to me) that I wished to pave the way for my transition to his service. For years I was unable to forget the hostile expression of Olympian loftiness with which he spoke. I can still see [Bismarck is writing thirty years afterwards] his backward-tilted head, his flushed face, and his sideward glance at me over his left shoulder. I suppressed my wrath, thought of Carlos and Alba, and answered that when I spoke of transition I was referring to an application of dynastic sentiment. . . . I hoped that he would dismiss from his mind the thought that I was looking forward, some day, to becoming his minister. I never would be anything of the kind. His anger passed off as quickly as it had arisen, and he closed the conversation with friendly words."

We picture the two men standing in a chilly parqueted hall. They are clad in uniform, and both of them wear swords. A terrible moment for Bismarck, a terrible affront to his pride! Never before has any one dared to look at him over the shoulder. But he, who would fain draw his sword, has to swallow his pride, has to pretend to be pleased with what does not please him. He divines his adversary's thoughts, and, forcing himself to speak in a subdued tone, he says: "I never would be anything of the kind."

III

Besides the enemies who were hostile because of the ties of blood, Bismarck had many enemies who were hostile from sentiment, and some who were hostile for intellectual reasons. In later days he classified them as enemies of the first, second, and third class.

Complete harmony prevails only with one man, with Roon. There is no real confidence between Bismarck and any of the ministers, generals, courtiers, or leaders of parties. Fundamentally, he has no party. The "Kreuzzeitung" and Ludwig Gerlach are too extreme for him, and he himself is looked upon as an ultra by the old-liberals. He is at open war with the left. Only to Roon, the military Hotspur, does he continue to show a virile friendship, which is not disturbed by differences of opinion upon intellectual matters. Most unwillingly does he, on one occasion, grant Roon six months' furlough: "I cannot get on without the support of your political authority, for no one has eaten so much salt with the master as you have."

He has summoned Keudell, the musician, Johanna's friend, to collaborate with him, for the two men have confidence in one another; but within a few weeks they come into collision. Keudell writes to him recommending that in the Danish question he shall make sure of the support of public opinion; and says that if Bismarck cannot agree with him, he would like, in all friendliness, to return to his musical career. Next morning Bismarck summons him to an interview, and speaks "in subdued tones, but obviously excited", saying:

"I wish you would tell me why you wrote that letter. If you fancy you can influence my decisions, I may as well tell you that a man of your years cannot do any such thing. . . . Is it possible that you, who have known me long and well, can think that I am entering upon so great a matter light-heartedly, like a subaltern, without having a clear view of the course for which I shall be responsible before God? I cannot bear to think it; the mere thought has disturbed my sleep for two nights. There is no reason whatever for your resignation. . . . I want you to realise how grievously you have wounded me!" Keudell asks pardon, and takes back this letter. Bismarck says: "That puts everything straight. . . . If you should ever differ from me again, don't write; talk the affair over with me. . . . "

Thus solitary is Bismarck. A man who has been on intimate terms with him for fifteen years, and has known his wife even longer, a man who is now one of his underlings, gives, with all due respect, advice which coincides with the general view of the matter; this is enough to disturb the sleep of the statesman who is unruffled by all the abuse of the press. Et tu, Brute! And although matters are patched up between them, their relationships do not return to the old footing. Keudell could not win from him the respect which Schlözer had won; he never was anything more than a talented assistant and a man full of music; he was not a factor with which Bismarck reckoned in action.

In so far as the Foreign Office thinks, it is as a whole opposed to its chief. But "that does not bother me." When, however, he finds that the foreign envoys are working against him, he has to adopt the defensive in a new field. Usedom in Florence and Goltz in Paris would both of them like to occupy his post, and they write directly to the king traducing the foreign minister's policy. But the king is loyal to his minister. Instead of betraying him, as Frederick William would have done in a like case, he hands Bismarck the letters to answer. Although Bismarck for eight years had worked against the policy of his own chief by sending private letters to the king and to Gerlach, this does not make him tolerant now that he himself is prime minister. With characteristic conviction, the man of genius considers that he stands above morality; what Usedom and Goltz have done is not on the same footing with what he used to do, and he forbids his envoys a practice which had been his own when he was an envoy. The way in which he forbids it, however, especially in a letter to Count Goltz, whom he himself had sent to Paris, is a brilliant example of the way in which he can combine the official tone with the familiar, for he writes a holograph letter as follows:

"No one expects reports which reflect only the ministerial view. But yours are not reports in the customary sense of the term. They resemble, rather, ministerial lectures commending an opposite policy to the king. . . . Such a conflict of opinions may do harm, and cannot be of use, for it may give rise to hesitation and indecision, and I think any policy is better than a vacillating one. . . . I set a high value upon your political insight. . . . At the same time, I do not regard myself as stupid. I am prepared to hear you say that this is self-deception! Perhaps you will think better of my patriotism and my discernment when I tell you that for the last fortnight I have been working along the lines of the proposals which you make in your report.

"But how can I make up my mind to unbosom myself to you as to my deepest thoughts, when you, . . . more or less frankly, avow your intention to fight the present ministry and its policy, that is, to reverse it if you can? . . . Yet I, as minister, if the interests of the State are not to suffer, must be absolutely open, down to the very last word of my policy, in my relations with the envoy in Paris. The friction which every one in my position has to overcome in his relations with the ministers and counsellors and at court, the friction with occult influences, with the chambers, with the press, and with foreign courts, must not be increased by an undermining of the discipline of my department through rivalry between the ministers and the envoys. . . . I can seldom write as much as I am able to this Christmas Eve, when all the officials are away on leave; and I would not write any one else a letter one fourth as long. I do so because I cannot make up my mind to write to you officially, . . . and in the distant tone of your reports. . . . If you want to overthrow the ministry, you must do that here in the chamber and in the press, at the head of the opposition, not from your present post. In that case, I shall be guided by your own maxim that in a conflict between patriotism and friendship, the former must be decisive. I can assure you that my patriotism is so strong and pure that a friendship which cannot be measured against it may still be a very cordial one."

This is a letter likely to disarm the recipient! In how masterly a fashion is the genuine anger reenforced by measured doses of respect and menace, and by the intimation that a good friend has been wounded to the heart. Furthermore, although the threats do not grow loud, he lets his rival know that a rough time may be expected by Goltz if he should seriously attempt to overthrow the writer. Since Bismarck knows that Goltz is on a good footing with the king, he sugars the pill of official rejection in such a way that Goltz will pay more heed to subtle indications that his chief is animated by personal respect and admiration for him. This will please Goltz, for the envoy suffers from vanity. The letter (of which only one fourth has been here transcribed) has so much artistry that we can examine it again and again, much as when we walk round a classical statue; and we are fain to admit that one such letter would suffice to establish the writer's fame as a notable diplomatist.

Others try to annoy the keen-sighted chief by offering to resign. The governor of Schleswig, an old acquaintance of Bismarck and a friend of the king, begs leave to resign on the ground that he is weary of the perpetual interference of the Foreign Office in matters of detail. Bismarck writes in reply: "I am perfectly willing to lay before the king the order of release from office you ask for; but I beg you to note that if the king were to appoint you foreign minister and me governor of Schleswig, I would pledge myself to carry out your policy strictly, . . . and not to do anything to increase the difficulties of the ministry. . . . If I, in such cases, had been prone to declare myself tired out, I should long since have won back to the outward semblance of peace in private life, whilst the inner peace which I derive from the knowledge that I am serving my king and country would have been lost. . . . I ask you, therefore, to accept this letter as an expression of friendly confidence, which I would much rather have given you by word of mouth."

Is this the man of blood and iron? It is Bismarck, the seducer.

Very different is his tone towards his enemies, the liberals. Here he varies between contempt and irony. Like every nineteenth-century dictator, Bismarck wishes to keep the semblance of justice and legality on his side. He therefore begins with "interpreting" the constitution which he proposes to violate in favour of the army; splits hairs in a way that he very likely laughs at in private; and manages to poke a hole in the place where the three factors of the constitution do not coincide. Since he speaks of crown rights which are not stated in the constitution, he substantially reerects the absolutist State whose collapse he angrily watched in March 1848. In the Landtag, too, he says frankly, as a solution of the dilemma: "Since the State machine cannot stand still, legal conflicts readily become conflicts for power; the one that has power in his hands then acts as he thinks best."

Immediately this phrase is twisted to mean that "power transcends right"—which Bismarck certainly believed in decisive hours, though he was never such a fool as to say it. His rejoinder to this interpretation was: "I did not give any solution. I merely pointed to a fact."

With such a breakneck leap, he only reached the edge of the abyss where he wishes the conflict to take place. Then he arranges for the Upper House to pass the unmutilated budget. Thereupon the Lower House declares the decision unconstitutional. Now Bismarck rises in his place and invites the deputies to come to the palace at three o'clock. Here he announces that the king has none the less decided to carry out the reforms, and dissolves the Landtag. All the Prussian newspapers raise a clamour at this. Some demand that the minister shall be put under restraint. Even the conservatives think it would be better he should be dismissed. After all, there are only eleven of them left! As the Berliners were wont to say, the whole pack of them could get into one omnibus.

Next session, six months later, he takes stronger measures. Meanwhile the conflict has been intensified in the press and in speeches. "He was still wearing civilian attire;" thus Lucius describes him. "His heavy moustache was still auburn, like what remained of his hair. At the ministerial table, his tall figure looked vigorous and impressive. The nonchalance of his pose, his movements, and his speech, made his demeanour somewhat provocative. He kept his right hand in the pocket of his light trousers, and reminded me strongly of the blustering seconds in a students' duel." His words are just as provocative as his demeanour. He speaks more fluently than in the first week, when he was still uncertain whether he would rule with the Landtag or against it— for then, writes Schlözer, "he stammered, and lost the thread of every sentence, since he was still trying to ride two horses!"

Now he speaks loftily: "The government will conduct any war it regards as necessary, whether the House approves or not." Another time: "The kingdom of Prussia, an heir to whose throne was by a remarkable coincidence born four years ago this very day, has not yet fulfilled its mission. It is not prepared to function as a mere ornament of your constitutional building." He is speaking on January 27th. The heir to the throne, to whose future power Bismarck seems to be referring, became afterwards William II.

Bismarck was, in subsequent years, to show himself unquestionably superior to those who were now fighting him in this hall. The proof is to be read in the history of the half century that followed—years which now belong to the past. Everything which Europe had hitherto striven to achieve, and everything which has

taken place in all lands before and since the World War, was essentially contained in the programme of the young progressive
party of Prussia, which demanded nothing more than a " republic
with a monarchical head ", that is to say British popular government. They and their allies (the first social democrats) were the
men whom Bismarck, in the above-quoted letter to Motley, had
described as able enough, though unskilled in foreign policy. A
lack of training among a people which till yesterday had been
under an absolute monarch, and in a nation where the State and
culture had walked in separate paths, seemed natural enough in
these early days of the liberal parties. Their members were able
and highly cultured, but unpractical, and, unfortunately, lacking
in originality. Ideologues with their gaze fixed on the future sat
on these benches; facing a realist who scrutinized the present with
a penetrating eye, and endeavoured to master it with means drawn
from the past.

The most interesting of the progressives was Virchow. A few
years younger than Bismarck, small and frail in physique just as
Bismarck was tall and vigorous, sprung from a humanist circle
in the lower middle class, eager to learn, more ambitious in youth
than Bismarck had been and quite as analytical — such was Virchow. If we compare the letters he wrote in the third decade of
his life with those written by Bismarck at the same age and dealing in great measure with the same affairs, the young, rapidly
rising doctor, the man noted for his scientific researches, compares most unfavourably with the idle, nihilistic, essentially fainé-
ant Junker. In Virchow, everything is vague, fantastic, rash; in
Bismarck, everything is carefully thought out. Again and again
does Virchow declare to his father that he has feelings but conceals them — so much does he yearn for feelings. A strong feeling
of self-confidence is continually being swept away by unpractical
ideas taken bodily from others, and rolls along beneath the surface of the flood. "As a man of science I am necessarily a republican; for the realisation of the demands determined by the
laws of nature, and the demands that arise out of human nature,
is only possible in a republican form of State." (It is true that

these same laws of nature led him to the scandalous conclusion: "I have made thousands of post mortems, but have never come across any trace of the soul.")

Whereas young Bismarck's letters were full of things and persons seen, sifted, usually despised, always deeply felt, Virchow's were full of catchwords. His promise to give up political agitation for the sake of his post in the State service is as reasonable as was Bismarck's conduct when he disguised himself by shaving off his beard in the March Days of 1849. At the age of thirty, both men have become dilettantes in politics. Bismarck is, however, only a second-rate farmer, whereas Virchow is already an authority on pathological anatomy. Moreover, while still a young medical man, he has made himself famous by social criticism on the grand scale. Thereafter, Bismarck studies politics from the inside for fifteen years. Virchow, in the interim, has been studying cellular pathology; and, even though he may possess a measure of political genius, he must not be surprised when he is defeated by a man with an expert knowledge of European affairs.

Their controversy in the Landtag is a credit to neither. We are amazed that men of genius can waste their own time and that of their fellow-citizens upon such follies.

Bismarck: "Does not the honourable member deem it possible that, in the domain of his specialty, one to whom anatomy has been only a side issue, one addressing an audience politically sympathetic towards the speaker and personally well-disposed towards him, but not as profoundly versed in the science as the honourable member himself — that before such an audience, such a speaker (with less eloquence than the honourable member has displayed) might with conviction put forward anatomical statements of whose inaccuracy the honourable member, being himself an expert, would be fully convinced, but which he would only be able to refute before an audience as fully conversant with all the details as he himself is?"

Virchow: "I wish the minister president were likely to win among the diplomatists of Europe a position so highly esteemed as my own among the specialists of my profession. His policy is indefinable. We might even say that he has no policy, . . . and, above all, not the slightest inkling of a national policy. He has no understanding whatever of national concerns."

Bismarck: "I fully recognise the honourable member's high position in his own specialty, and I admit that in this respect he has the advantage of me. But when the honourable member forsakes his own province, and, uninstructed, trespasses upon my field, I have to tell him that in political matters his opinion weighs very little with me. I really think, gentlemen, I do not exaggerate in saying that I understand these things better. [Loud laughter.] The honourable member charges me with a lack of understanding of national politics. I can throw back the charge while suppressing the adjective. To me it seems that the honourable member has no understanding of politics of any kind."

Two actors, quarrelling in the dressing-room about their respective importance and popularity, could not produce an impression of greater pettiness than do these two voices in the Prussian Landtag, though they are the voices of Virchow and Bismarck. Another time, when Virchow expressed his doubts as to the minister's truthfulness, Bismarck sent him a challenge. Virchow's answer was at first a vague one. Then one of his fellow progressives declared that he ought not to fight a duel, and thereupon he sent a refusal. This challenge was the last ebullition of Bismarck's youth. He was then fifty years old.

When he keeps himself in the background, his work as minister is more effective. Simson: "This policy is the chance poem of a man who is no poet. We may compare Herr von Bismarck with a rope dancer, whom we only admire because he does not fall off his rope. Such admiration as we give to every rope dancer would not be to every one's taste." Bismarck: "I do not feel called upon to enter here into a discussion of the questions of good taste and propriety."

Such were the ups and downs of his personal management of his enemies. But when he was handling the apparatus of State, the much experienced man was perfectly plain. There force reigned. The possibility of exercising a dictatorship seemed to

Bismarck the most desirable outcome of the conflict, for in truth he had no wish, or no longer had any wish, for the rôle of Peel or O'Connell of which he had dreamed twenty-five years earlier. Such self-confidence and such will-to-power as his were the qualities of a dictator. That was why, in subsequent decades of constitutional government, he never felt so much at home as during these four years of conflict. Where the rights of the people were concerned he had no scruples; he felt just as he had felt when out bear hunting, and had no more sense of danger now than then. He congratulated himself that such adventures were still obtainable in "so dull a country as Prussia."

Vengeance now overtook the enemy of the privy councillors. No chief of the government before him had ever taken so much pains as Bismarck concerning the personnel of the great hierarchy of those who ruled the State, for any one whose way of thinking was at all irregular was dismissed. Immediately after his appointment, he began to remove from the judiciary and the executive all persons who held, or were suspected to hold, liberal views. Within the first four years, more than a thousand officials suffered in this way. When the members of the progressive party espoused the cause of the victims, they were persecuted in their turn. Liberal officers of the Landwehr were cashiered by courts of honour. Burgomasters, town councillors, lottery collectors, bank agents, public vaccinators, were put on half pay. Officers of the judiciary were punished, had their salaries cut down, were deprived of their old-age allowances.

Last of all he deals with the press. In the Russian style, press ukases, stricter than Napoleon's had been, are issued. He is not content to suppress a newspaper for a brief period on account of some offending article, but will suppress it permanently because of its general tenor. All this is adorned with moral motives, and supported by the quotation of paragraphs from the constitution, so that "the passionate and unnatural excitement which has of late years affected people's minds owing to partisan feeling, shall give place to a more tranquil and unprejudiced mood." Bismarck, in the last resort, appeals to the principles of morality and to God in order to convince the king that such measures are essentially just. It is likely enough that he gets the same explanations to work in order to satisfy Johanna, for her mother is still living in full possession of her faculties, and Bismarck doubtless remembers what the old lady had written to her daughter anent the Hungarian revolution, and remembers his own reply likewise. He needs no such excuses to appease his own conscience. He despises the many, and is perfectly satisfied if he wields the power wherewith to tame them.

Bismarck was always fonder of power than of liberty. In this matter, as in others, he was a German.

IV

All Germany rejoiced over the conflict in Prussia, although it seemed to strengthen the government month by month. Reactionary lesser States laid stress on the fact that they allowed debates upon the budget. In Saxony, even Beust allowed a popular festival to take place in honour of the Battle of the Nations, because in Prussia this historic struggle could only be acclaimed by the military bands; and young Treitschke was allowed to make an ardent speech upon German freedom in order to annoy his colleagues in Berlin. Vienna was especially delighted. Schmerlingh patronised a plan for a constitution; Rechberg discovered the solution of the German problem; an ex-revolutionist, a "plain citizen", was given rope for the development of a scheme for liberty and legitimacy — a scheme whereby Austria and Germany were to be reconciled in ten minutes.

The Habsburg heart began to beat in favour even of the revolutionary Poles, when it was seen that Russia and Prussia were allied. In actual fact, the new rising of Poland against the tsar in the beginning of the year 1863 was successful because Gorchakoff himself led the friends of Poland in St. Petersburg, and because the apostles of liberal trends in the west were able to mask their Russophobe interests behind the catchword of national freedom. Half Europe began to talk about a buffer State. Even

Napoleon III. showed enthusiasm for liberty because French-
women were fond of Chopin's erotic nocturnes. Soon the crisis
became so acute that there were threats of a new ultimatum as in
the year 1854. Perhaps Prussia had the final decision in her
hands. What did Bismarck do? He promptly entered into a military convention with the tsar, wishing to seize his opportunity
of binding that potentate to his side.

"Europe will never allow Prussian troops to aid the Russian,"
said the British envoy to Bismarck.

"Who is Europe?" asked Bismarck quietly.

"Various great nations."

"Are they united?" enquired Bismarck. There was no answer!
For twelve years he had been thinking out this situation. It was
the one which in three great crises had led to identical or similar
combinations. In a hundred memorials, reports, and letters, penned
through the long hours of the night, he had weighed all the
possibilities of the position. Now he could develop his game with
the rapidity and confidence of a master chess player.

In the Landtag the liberals shouted: "The government is giving
over an area of five hundred square leagues to the horrors of war
as the Russians wage it! . . . Prussian blood must not be shed
for such a policy! . . . Quite needlessly we are being burdened
with complicity in a terrible man-hunt, which is regarded by all
Europe with abhorrence!" When speeches of this kind were delivered by Twesten, Waldeck, and Virchow, Bismarck politely
asked: "Would an independent Poland leave her neighbour Prussia in possession of Danzig and Thorn? . . . The inclination to
make sacrifices to foreign nationalities at the expense of the
fatherland is a political disease peculiar to Germany."

Here is the antithesis clearly stated. As far as power politics
are concerned, Bismarck is right. What he wants to do at this
moment is not so much anti-Polish as pro-Russian. A resusci-
tated Poland would be very likely to enter into a dangerous alliance with Russia and France. But if Prussia relieves the tsar
of the long-standing dread of risings in Poland, by giving him
the help he needs, then it will become difficult for Alexander to

take the side of Austria in the imminent settlement of accounts between Prussia and that country. Bismarck can buy the tsar's friendship cheap. His decision does not cost a war, or any bloodshed; only a signature, and the hatred of the Poles. From Warsaw, he receives a sentence of death, sent to him in a casket bound in a black-and-white ribbon. Another comes from Barcelona: "The undersigned committee of revolutionary propaganda has summoned you to the bar of judgment. It has unanimously condemned you to death, and has fixed the execution for the first week of next month."

Bismarck is fearless. Fearlessness is the best, the never obsolete, heritage of the knight. Without it he would not have been able, at any rate in the sixties, to march straight forward, all lonely as he was, unaffrighted to his goal. Without it he would never have been able to disregard as he did the threats of the chambers, the king's mistrust, the queen's influence working against him, the malice of the courts, the intrigues of the envoys, the death sentences passed on him by foreign revolutionists, and, ere long, the revolvers of fanatical idealists. Had nothing of what he built proved stable, had everything he did been erroneous, still he would have remained for the Germans the necessary exemplar of a brave civilian, a model possessor of that courage for lack of which the chiefs of his class, the princes, were to perish in later days.

In Vienna, where intrigue was as much a matter of course as courage was in Potsdam, people were inclined to regard the new tone as bluff, and the Austrian statesmen made up their minds to laugh when their North German brother growled. They had smiled already when they read Bismarck's programme. " Our relationships," he had said to Karolyi shortly after taking office, "must inevitably grow better or worse. Prussia's wish is that they should grow better. But if the imperial cabinet does not meet us halfway, we shall have to consider the alternative possibility, and to prepare for it. . . . Austria can choose, either to abandon her present anti-Prussian policy, or to renounce the idea of an honourable agreement. You believe that we stand in

greater need of protection than you do. Our business will therefore be, should you not pay heed to our words and wishes, to
convince you that you are wrong in that assumption." Not since
the days of Frederick's youth had any Prussian spoken in such
terms to the envoy of the Habsburgs. But Karolyi was, at bottom, an admirer of the hostile minister; and besides, he was too
much the Hungarian to raise a needless clamour. He therefore
answered by the polite question:

"And where shall we find compensation?"

"The most natural would be for you to remove your centre
of gravity to Budapest." With this shrewd thrust he checkmates
the count, for Karolyi, being a good Hungarian, must certainly
cherish such a wish, though he dares not express it. Shortly afterwards the minister says to another envoy from Vienna: "I am
absolutely opposed to the use of such a phrase as fratricidal war.
The only policy I recognize is an unconciliatory one, blow for
blow, and stark." What is the effect of this sort of language in
Vienna? "The man is suffering from severe nervous disorder,"
they say with a smile.

Habsburg's plan is to refashion the Germanic Federation once
more. There are to be five directors, with Austria as president and
Prussia as vice-president; and, in addition, a powerless assembly
of delegates from the German parliaments. When Bismarck threatens Prussia's withdrawal, and Austria is in a minority, the attack is renewed from the other side. Austria now proposes to
summon all the princes; they will sit and deliberate in Frankfort; all will feel uplifted thereby. Is not Gastein a spa for elderly
gentlemen? We princes by God's grace will settle matters among
ourselves. Suddenly Francis Joseph comes to see King William,
is his guest at Gastein. He proposes that there shall be an imperial
parliament, with princes, and a people's house. The emperor invites the king of Prussia to follow him to a diet of princes, which
is immediately to be held in Frankfort, and to which the other
princes have already been invited. Old King William seems inclined to accept, and Francis Joseph is delighted.

The pity of it is that this wretched minister president will not leave his master alone even in Austria's mountains. "In Gastein," wrote Bismarck in his old age, "I was sitting under the fir trees on August 2, 1863. Above me was a long-tailed tit's nest, and I had my watch in my hand, for I was reckoning how many times a minute the birds brought a caterpillar or other grub to their fledglings. While contemplating the useful activity of these little creatures, I noticed that, across the ravine, in the Schillerplatz, King William was sitting alone on a bench." When he got home, he found a letter from the king asking him to come to the Schillerplatz and discuss the emperor's visit. "It was too late. If I had spent a little less time studying natural phenomena, and had seen the king sooner, it may well be that the first impression made upon him by the emperor's proposals would have been a different one.

"To begin with, he had not noticed that this surprise invitation, . . . this invitation à courte échéance, was disrespectful. Perhaps the Austrian proposal pleased him because of the solidarity of the princes which it implied. . . . The queen dowager Elisabeth, too, urged me to go to Frankfort. I rejoined: 'If the king decides on this course, I will go there, and do his business for him; but I will not come back as minister.' The queen seemed very much disquieted at this prospect, and no longer tried to set the king against my view. It was not easy for me to induce the king to stay away from Frankfort. . . . I thought I had convinced him by the time we got to Baden. But there we found the king of Saxony, who renewed the invitation in the name of all the princes. My master found it hard to stand up against this move. Again and again he repeated: 'Thirty reigning princes — and a king as courier!' . . . Literally in the sweat of my brow I persuaded him to refuse the proposal. He was lying . . . on the sofa, and had burst into tears. I myself, when I at length succeeded in making him commit himself to a definitive refusal, was so utterly exhausted that I could hardly stand. When I left the room, I was staggering, and was in such a nervous and excited condition that as I shut the door from the outside I actually broke off the handle!" In handing over the letter of refusal to be sent to its destination, he knocked down a salver with glasses on it. "I had to smash something! Now I can breathe again!"

Here we have the first of the series of hours that make up the history of the conflicts between Bismarck and William: the threat Bismarck utters to the queen dowager; the slow bringing of light into the mind of the worthy monarch, who has utterly failed to see that Austria is getting the better of him. While his minister is watching the long-tailed tits, and, half naturalist, half playing the sovereign ruler, is calculating how many grubs are needed for the nourishment of the bird state, the king is talking to his cousin of Austria, and in four weeks (if Francis Joseph gets his way) William will again become no more than the second among German rulers. Old William burst into tears at having to refuse, for a king has come to him as courier. Even the man of iron has a fit of hysterics, and must smash something before he can breathe freely, although he has won the trick. One of them is a dynast, and the other is bound to him in fealty. When they now begin to build the House of Germany together, it seems impossible that they will ever be able to finish the work, so many are the obstacles.

This was the last attempt of Austria to remain the leading power in Germany. Then came the Schleswig-Holstein affair; a satire preluding tragedy.

V

At that time Bismarck had no rival in Europe for intelligence. The kings and the emperors could not think or could not act. Francis Joseph lacked experience; Napoleon was worn out; Alexander was too dense; William, Victoria, and Victor Emmanuel were mediocrities, incompetent to carry out policies of their own; neither Gladstone nor Disraeli had yet attained the summit of power; Gorchakoff was too vain; Cavour, notable after his fashion, died just at the time when Bismarck came to the front. Only in Prussia was there yet another political genius. His name was Ferdinand Lassalle. Though he had no considerable party to back him up, though he was a revolutionist, though he could not allure his great opponent either by kinship of ideas or by power, Lassalle speedily won recognition from Bismarck. It was the magnetism of genius, nothing else, that drew Bismarck and Lassalle together.

Massive and heavily built both in body and mind; a dome-shaped head; a man who had come to the front slowly, after a long overture, looking forward to many decades (like the great German bronze founders, who, in works crowded with figures, represented a whole generation), curbing imagination by realism, weighing words and preparing deeds, reckoning by preference with magnitudes rather than with ideas — such was Bismarck, the realist, on the threshold of his great work, when he was on the verge of fifty. Slender, elegant, quivering, like an Arab steed but half broken in, was the man of Semitic stock who confronted him; a man with a long and narrow head; scintillating; little over forty, and yet approaching the end of an impetuous career; a great draughtsman, whose formative impulse exhausted itself in dazzling sketches; an imaginative and thoughtful man; an escapee from the school of ideas into the world of deeds; fighting even in this world of deeds with eloquent words rather than with blows; his eyes directed towards the future — such was Lassalle. Bismarck had grown out of the soil, was the champion of his class. After an adventurous youth, he had returned to the conventional forms of life and property characteristic of the stratum from which he had sprung; as a statesman he was unsentimental, ready to work hand in hand with every nation and to collaborate with every form of State which might be useful to his own. Lassalle was a Jew, a man without nationality, who had scrambled his way upwards in a strenuous youth, who fought his class and was in conflict with his heritage, his emotional nature inflamed for the cause of the nation to which he did not belong by race, and for the cause of the class to which he did not belong by station. Bismarck made no sacrifices when he began his career; Lassalle staked everything. Bismarck consolidated his position by his rise; Lassalle lost liberty and health in prison. Whereas Bismarck had begun at thirty-two to live in the style warranted by his birth, Lassalle, at the same date, when twenty-two, had begun to repudiate in all respects the manner of life of those to whom by birth he belonged.

Nevertheless, both were animated by the same impulse. The Jewish socialist and the Pomeranian Junker were alike spurred to action by pride, courage, and hatred; in both of them, these motives engendered the will-to-power; neither knew the meaning of fear, neither could put up with a superior, neither really loved. Just as Bismarck hated powerful Austria more strongly than he loved the less powerful Prussia, so was Lassalle less inspired by sympathy with the fourth estate than by dislike of the third. That was why Bismarck neither sought nor found friends among the Prussian Junkers, and that was why Lassalle neither sought nor found friends among the leaders who had risen from the ranks. Bismarck did not live the life of a courtier, and Lassalle did not live the life of the people. Both of them were filled with splenetic feelings towards the limitations of their respective classes; and they resembled one another in irony and cynicism.

Bismarck was compelled to life-long service by the career he had chosen: he had chosen to serve the king, whereas Lassalle had chosen to serve the many. Although Bismarck dwelt in a strong castle, he always heard over his head the footsteps of a man under whom it was his destiny to live. Lassalle heard no one over him, but his castle was built of air, and his nerves trembled more in the wind of the future than through the frictions of reality which were so deadly to Bismarck's nerves. Both men were of the artistic temperament; but the elder was playing chess against the other powers, whereas the younger was rather an actor contemplating his own performance. That was why Bismarck was influenced chiefly by ambition, Lassalle by vanity. Thus it was that Lassalle could luxuriate in successes and prospects in which he visioned a more distant future than Bismarck could see; whereas Bismarck wanted less, but wanted tangible realities, and therefore he cultivated patience. That was why Bismarck lived twice as long as Lassalle, and also why Lassalle was richer than Bismarck in moments of happiness.

No sooner did they meet than they recognised one another's

worth before that worth had become known to the world. Had
Bismarck fallen in the year 1863, in the duel to which he challenged Virchow, his name would never have ranked higher than
that of Radowitz, who has long since been forgotten by the people. Lassalle, though ten years younger than Bismarck, was
killed in a duel at the very outset of his work, which seemed at
first in danger of extinction; yet now that name is honoured by
millions upon millions of all nations. He fell, and became famous
throughout the world, because he wished to realise the ideas of
a day that has not yet dawned; Bismarck achieved his next day's
aim, and his monument remains purely German.

The thing that brought the two men together was the fight
against the bourgeoisie. Bismarck wanted power to use against
the constitution; Lassalle wanted to mobilise the masses. Bismarck had weapons in his hands, weapons with which he forcibly
equipped men; Lassalle had men at his disposal, men who were
vainly clamouring for weapons. Each of them essentially desired
a dictatorship under his own guidance; each of them detested
free trade in goods and ideas, and detested no less the champions
of free trade, the liberals. Their very aphorisms were alike. Bismarck, September 1862: "Questions of right readily become questions of power." Lassalle, April 1862: "Constitutional questions
are not primarily questions of right but questions of power.
Written constitutions are only valuable and durable when they
are the expression of the relationships of power existing in society." When Lassalle was attacked for this utterance, his answer was just like Bismarck's. He said he was not putting might
before right. He was not laying down an ethical postulate, but
was merely recording an historical fact. So strongly did Lassalle's
feelings, like those of Bismarck, turn towards the politics of power,
that in a play he made Sickingen (his own image) announce:

> All that is great, all good for which we strive —
> The sword alone has power to make it thrive!

We need not be surprised, then, that Prussian counts should
have agreed with him in the Upper House; or that the "Kreuzzeitung" should have written: "These are real men; whereas the

liberals have at their disposal neither bayonets, nor fists, nor the charm of genius." For the aim of the reactionaries, in these days, was to win over the working class to their side, to lure the working class away from the progressives. "Can we be surprised," asks a conservative association, "that members of the working class show no inclination to support a government that does nothing for them?" Bismarck promptly takes up the idea; appoints a committee to study the problem of old-age pensions, and improvement of the conditions of the working classes; and recommends "a discussion of the question whether the State, in its position as employer, could not set an example to other employers in the regulation of working conditions." He goes on to speak of the need for long notice before discharge, the regulation of wages, profit sharing, working-class dwellings, arbitration in labour disputes, working-class societies for cooperative distribution and the mutual provision of credit, State-supported sick clubs and life insurance societies for the working class. Such is his social programme five months after he has become premier, and it is unexampled anywhere else in the Europe of the sixties. All these measures are in conformity with Lassalle's demands.

Bismarck is not moved in this direction by love of the people; he is inspired by hatred of the middle class. Since the nation repudiates his policy, he endeavours to win it over to his view by introducing social reforms. While the wealthy employers in the Landtag were proclaiming themselves the friends of the people, Lassalle, in his letters and speeches, was railing against them for their double moral standard, and was pleasing no one more when he did this than the premier. It was already being declared that Lassalle, who had just founded the General Union of German Workers, was a tool of the reaction. Lothar Bucher warned him: "Take care! In actual fact, you are helping the government at this juncture. You will be given your head for a time, and then a heavy hand will be laid on you!"

Lassalle, like Bismarck, grew to manhood in the days of the revolution. This has left an indelible mark on his character. He spurns caution, does not ask the political complexion of his allies, joins hands with any one who is the enemy of his enemy. He, the socialist, dares, in full view of the public, to approach the detested minister for foreign affairs. The two men's outlook on foreign policy has always been identical, except that Lassalle was beforehand with Bismarck in wanting a united Germany. He made mock of the frock-coated men who in the year 1849 travelled from Frankfort to Potsdam to petition a king on behalf of Germany, instead of simply decreeing the existence of Germany. Since his eyes were directed towards the masses and not towards the princes, to him German unity was a racial and not a dynastic question. The decade from 1850 to 1860 made Bismarck more of a parliamentarian, and led him as early as 1860 to write his memorial concerning a German parliament; Lassalle had come to recognise at the same date that a united Germany was possible even without ridding the land of its princes. He and Bismarck were at one in making a decisive stand against Austria-Hungary, whose twenty-six millions of non-German inhabitants were an obstacle to united Germany. Each took his own road to this conclusion, for Lassalle had no insight into the policy at which Bismarck was working through his envoys; and Bismarck did not need to study Lassalle's pamphlets in order to form his own views upon the Austrian question.

Lassalle was like Bismarck in his attitude towards Napoleon. Although he was an enemy of Napoleon's despotism, in times of crisis he would rather march shoulder to shoulder with France against Austria than with Austria against France. Lassalle wrote in public to precisely the same effect as Bismarck had written in private: "If Napoleon should revise the map of Europe in accordance with the principle of nationalities in the south, we should do the same thing in the north; if he were to liberate Italy, we should take Schleswig; thus Prussia could expunge the disgrace of Olmütz. . . . If Prussia hesitates, that only shows that the monarchy is no longer capable of a national deed." The only thing which distinguishes him here from Bismarck is that he pulls out the nationalist stop, which he needs as an agitator, whereas Bismarck, as a diplomatist, does not need it. At the same time,

Lassalle, being a pupil of Hegel and Fichte, bases his demands upon grounds that are more philosophical than Bismarck, as a pupil of Machiavelli, needs: "The metaphysical nation, the German nation, thanks to its whole development and in full conformity with its subjective and objective history, is vouchsafed this great prize, this supreme historical honour, that it is able to create for itself a territory out of the simple spiritual national idea, that it is able to generate being out of thought. Such an act resembles God's creation of the world! ... This has to-day become a religion, and under the popular and dogmatic name of German unity it animates every noble German heart. On the day when the belfries throughout Germany announce the birth of the German State, on that day we shall also celebrate the true festival of Fichte, the wedding of his spirit to reality!"

Bismarck was ready enough to forgive the affectations of style. He bore the text in mind and drew his own conclusions. He also read what the new leader said of him in public meetings that were fiercely hostile to him: "Beyond question Bismarck has a very accurate knowledge of constitutional matters. His views harmonise fully with my own theory. He is perfectly well aware that the real constitution of a country is not to be found in the sheet of paper on which it is written, but in the actual objective circumstances." Soon, Lassalle went so far as to say publicly at huge meetings in Rhineland: "The progressives are flirting with the princes in Frankfort in order to make Bismarck uneasy. . . . If we had to exchange volleys with Herr von Bismarck, justice would compel us to say, even while the shooting was in progress: 'He is a man, and all the others are old women'."

Before Bismarck had read this love avowal, he had received a telegram from Solingen, where Lassalle's meetings had been prohibited: "Progressive burgomaster, at head of ten gendarmes armed with muskets and bayonets, has just dissolved, without legal justification, a workers' meeting summoned by me. Protest ineffectual, have with difficulty restrained the people, numbering five thousand, from resorting to violence. Urgent request for the promptest legal satisfaction. Lassalle."

This came very much apropos, for, a few days earlier, Bismarck, playing a trump card against the congress of princes, had demanded the introduction of universal and equal suffrage for the Germanic Federation. The premier hands on the complaint to the legal authorities. Lassalle calls on him "to express thanks." Then, in the winter of 1863–4, he visits Bismarck about a dozen times, perhaps oftener, having a long interview on each occasion. Many years later, when it was in Bismarck's interest to make light of this political intercourse with Lassalle, he said in the Reichstag: "There was something about Lassalle which attracted me immensely as a private individual. He was one of the most talented and amiable persons with whom I have ever associated; he was ambitious in the grand style. . . . Our conversations lasted for hours, and I was always sorry when they came to an end. . . . I fancy he had an agreeable impression that I was an intelligent and ready listener."

These conversations, between the two strongest German statesmen of that epoch, concerned the great question whether Germany would have to be unified dynastically or could be unified on the popular plane. From the alternatives as stated by the radicals they had both moved away. Lassalle now considered that a German republic was unattainable, and Bismarck did not expect to realise the creation of a league of princes and nothing more. In private, moreover, neither of them now regarded the solution he was supposed to favour as ideal. There is fairly good authority for the accuracy of a fragment of their conversation as recorded by Lassalle.

Bismarck: "Why don't you join forces with the conservatives, since you have very little prospect of getting your candidates elected? Our interests march with yours, you fight from your standpoint just as we fight from ours against the attempts of the bourgeoisie to win power."

Lassalle: "For the nonce, Your Excellency, it may seem as if an alliance between the labour party and the conservatives were possible; but we should only be able to go a short distance along the road together, and should then be more fiercely opposed than ever."

Bismarck: " I see what you mean. The question is which of us is the man who can eat cherries with the devil. Nous verrons ! "

As far as matters of fact are concerned, their debate centres round two points in Lassalle's programme, both of which Bismarck would like to realise on behalf of his own interests. Before this, he had written about universal suffrage: " In a country with monarchical traditions and loyal sentiments, it would make an end of the influence of the liberal bourgeoisie, and would lead to the election of monarchical representatives. In Prussia, nine tenths of the people are loyal to the king, and nothing but the artificial mechanism of the elections prevents the expression of their true opinion." Bismarck thought it was too soon for the introduction of universal suffrage into Prussia. If he moved too slowly, Lassalle moved too quickly. The latter tried to persuade Bismarck to introduce universal suffrage, not only into Germany (in due time — for both men were convinced that there must be war before the reconstruction of the Germanic Federation could be effected), but into Prussia, immediately, by an ordinance. Thus the radical democrat advised a coup d'état. Bismarck doubted whether the time was ripe.

" Above all I blame myself," wrote Lassalle to Bismarck, " because I forgot yesterday to insist once more upon the fact that the eligibility of election must be extended to all Germans. This would be an immense instrument of power ! The real moral conquest of Germany ! As far as electoral technique is concerned, last night I read again the history of French legislation ; but I found little of value to our own position. However, I have been thinking matters over, and am now in a position, your Excellency, to give you what you want, a ' charmed recipe ' to prevent abstention from the polls, and the dispersal of votes. I have not the least doubt in the world that what I propose would be effective. I therefore await an appointment with Your Excellency one evening. My urgent request is that you choose an evening when we shall not be interrupted. I have a great deal to discuss with Your Excellency concerning electoral technique and other matters as well."

This letter, which is half-intimate in its phrasing, shows plainly enough who has the initiative. We might infer that a young man is writing to an old one, and yet the younger is over forty and the elder not yet fifty. We picture Bismarck on the previous evening, buried in his armchair, listening through the cigar smoke to the words of his energetic visitor, and then vainly attempting to annoy Lassalle with such a phrase as "charmed recipe." There are indications in the letter of the spiritual duel in which both take pleasure. Events come to break off their intercourse. Five days after the letter just quoted was written, the attack on Denmark began. Lassalle grew more urgent:

"I don't want to be importunate, but circumstances press, so you must excuse me if I seem importunate. I wrote to you last Wednesday saying that I had the charmed recipe you wanted, a most effective one. Our next conversation will, I think, lead to definite conclusions; and since, in my opinion, these definite conclusions must be reached without delay, I shall venture to call on you to-morrow morning at half-past eight."

How ardent the man is! How the matter lures him on; how near he feels himself to realisations such as, till now, he had scarcely dared to hope for! But Bismarck is just beginning his war. Suffrage must wait!

A few weeks later, Lassalle is being tried for high treason. He says when before the supreme court: "I do not merely wish to overthrow the constitution; perhaps I shall have overthrown it in less than a year. Strong games can be played! Cards on the table! . . . Therefore I tell you in this solemn place that perhaps a year will not have passed before Herr von Bismarck will have played the part of Robert Peel, and universal and direct suffrage will have been established!" The name of the English statesman has a dignified sound, though no one in the court of justice will understand its significance. So brilliantly does Lassalle's clear intelligence analyse the inaccessible minister, that he mentions as Bismarck's exemplar the very man to whom Bismarck had referred in a letter twenty-five years earlier, justifying his withdrawal from the State service on the ground that in Prussia he could never expect to play Peel's part. No one but a few of Bismarck's relatives know of this letter. Perhaps the writer has forgotten it. Still, he knows that Peel, O'Connell, and Mirabeau were much in his mind of old; and when he reads how boldly this Jewish revolutionist is defending himself against the government, and how easily Lassalle can read his heart, his respect for Lassalle needs must grow.

Bismarck follows Lassalle's lead in two of his plans. The socialist induces the reactionary minister to support productive cooperatives, with the aid of State credit to the tune of a hundred millions, and to inaugurate State enterprises on a large scale. Lassalle's aim is to found a socialist State in accordance with the new Marxist doctrine; Bismarck's aim is to strengthen the monarchical State by the extension of its powers. Just as in the question of universal suffrage, so here, they are using the same means to secure different ends. A good many years later, Bismarck spoke of these methods as " serious and shrewd things"; for the moment, however, he was content to thank Lassalle for sending him a pamphlet which developed the ideas.

This was too much for Lassalle's vanity. Bismarck ought to have given the pamphlet to the king, so that William could learn " what kingdom still has a future." He became really importunate now, demanded to see the minister about the matter. The urgent tone annoyed Bismarck. He did not break off relationships with Lassalle, but postponed attending to the matter. For this reason he never saw Lassalle again, since the fatal duel occurred that year.

In the spring, however, Lassalle was able to arrange for the reception of a deputation sent by the poverty-stricken weavers of Silesia to the king. This was a great event, for nothing of the kind had ever before happened in Prussia. When the hungry weavers came away from their audience, Bismarck was standing in the anteroom. He asked them a good many questions, and then said: "I am afraid you won't be able to eat roast goose for dinner so soon as next Sunday!" There stand the poor fellows, trembling, a crowd of beggars, who are terribly afraid of tum-

bling down on the slippery floor of the king's golden palace. Then
the prime minister encounters them, and, with his terrible witticism, widens the abyss which he might have taken the opportunity of gently bridging over. Even in Lassalle's luxurious rooms
in the Bellevuestrasse, among Turkish rugs and marble busts,
the workmen who went to visit him felt embarrassed; and they
were not pleased at the sight of the fancy waistcoats the demagogue wore on public platforms. He was not one of their sort.

Bismarck, however, took energetic measures to restrict the
social privileges of the bureaucrats. He wanted to get the recently
formed workers' party on his side, and made advances to four
other socialist writers besides Lassalle. Lothar Bucher the tax-
resister, who had been exiled and then amnestied, became a member of the staff of the "Norddeutschen", Bismarck's newspaper.
So did Brass, who had written a verse: "We paint red, we paint
well, we paint with tyrants' blood!" Liebknecht followed Brass.
Bismarck commissioned Bucher to ask Karl Marx, likewise, to
join the staff. Marx refused. Liebknecht soon broke away, for
he realised that Brass was being corrupted. Bucher stayed twenty
years. In these adventurous attempts to recruit from the enemy's
camp, we see once more the Mad Junker.

Furthermore, Bismarck is a State socialist. When one of the
Landrats listens only to what the employers have to say about
the poverty of the Silesian weavers, and is actually content to get
the employers' point of view through the mouth of a policeman,
Bismarck asks him furiously why he does not adopt an impartial
standpoint, from which these difficult matters can be rightly understood, instead of identifying himself exclusively with the employers' interests. Indeed, he actually proposes to cashier this
Landrat because of the man's lack of judgment. Then he appoints
a committee to study the question of wages, vital needs, and means
of helping the workers. Their side of the case is to be "listened to
by reasonable men, who will be capable of defending the interests
of the working class against the employers." At the same time
he induces the king to pay privately a sum of seven thousand talers
for the experimental foundation of a productive cooperative in

according with Lassalle's plans, in order thus "to gain experience concerning the possibility, the cost, and the results of a more extensive application of the principle." This cooperative is to be registered; it is to have the power of unhampered activity "which is necessary for the sale of the goods, and which will enable the weavers to secure the profits of the sale in addition to their wages." Thus Bismarck, in his hatred of the liberals, and in his hope of securing a new ally, becomes the first State socialist in Prussia.

That summer Lassalle, from a false sense of honour, fights a duel, and is killed by the bullet of an idler. For the time being his work remains without a leader. A year later, when the ministry of State declares itself opposed to all attempts on the part of the State to interfere in social problems, Bismarck has the following passage interpolated into the report: "The food of the weavers, which consists mostly of potato soup, gruel with salt, only a very small quantity of fat, and coffee made of chicory, has been reduced to the minimum quantity essential for the maintenance of life." When he reads in the report that, since equally urgent claims might be put in from all quarters, the State can give no help, Bismarck writes in his bold handwriting in the margin:

"Then, for that reason, the State is to give no help? The State can!" With these three words, Bismarck's productive will vibrates once more against the walls of the great cage in which he is imprisoned with the other members of his class, and even with many of the liberals. These three words are the echo of the discussions in which Lassalle, the ardent spirit of the future, had that winter endeavoured to beguile him.

VI

"Now I am minister here, the last arrow in the quiver. If you will undertake to weld Scandinavia into an empire, I will in like manner unify Germany. We will then form a Scandinavian-German league which will be strong enough to rule the whole world. We have the same religion and the same culture; nor are our languages very different. Pray tell your countrymen that if they are not inclined to fall in with my plans, I may be obliged to put them out of action, lest I should have an enemy in my back when I come to attack other points."

In this amazing letter, Bismarck seems to be jesting with the old friend to whom it is written, a Dane, his sometime companion in the chase. We may suppose that the recipient in Copenhagen, Baron Blixen, reads it twice over, for he is Danish premier, and the Danes have good reason to watch the German weather just now. If he knows Bismarck, he must know that Bismarck has never been a megalomaniac or a dreamer, but always a calculator and a realist. After all, the idea is by no means so foolish as it might seem at the first glance. Less than five hundred years ago, the three Scandinavian lands were united, and their ruler was a man from Pomerania. The letter is more than a jest; perhaps it is a warning. Since Bismarck never aims at anything that is absolutely out of reach (and for that reason will never impress the imagination of posterity like the great Napoleon), his warning to-day is only uttered because of Schleswig-Holstein.

These two little territories are a thorn in the side of Germany. For the last fifty years, the mood in Schleswig-Holstein has been an index to the intensity of the German longing for unity. Since the two little countries wanted to remain "up ewig ungedeelt" (for ever undivided) the whole of Europe rummaged through treaties which were four centuries old, and really interested no one, not even the Schleswigers and the Holsteiners themselves. People racked their brains about male and female heirs of Danish kings and Holstein dukes. When, now, one such king died, and it behooved his successor to swear fealty to the new constitution in Schleswig and Holstein as well as elsewhere, the rival nationalisms came into conflict. A certain duke of Augustenburg had sold his territory for two million talers. This worthy's son found a flaw in the deed, and, availing himself of the extant dispute, slipped back into the land of his fathers. He wrote an address beginning "to my liege subjects", and had himself proclaimed duke of Schleswig-Holstein.

Ambushed near at hand was the formidable Prussian. He cared little or nothing about the Germanity of the two territories, which, as members of the Germanic Federation, would only increase the anti-Prussian forces. But he cared a great deal about enhancing Prussia's power. While he knew how to make a good use of the genuine zeal for German unity which animated some of these northlanders, the core of his thought was: "How can the duchies be made into Prussian provinces?" His classical summary of the matter runs as follows: "Down to the very end, I was always firmly convinced that a personal union with Denmark would have been better than what existed; that an independent ruler would have been better than the personal union; and that union with Prussia would have been better than an independent prince. Only events could show which of these was attainable." Being a disciple of Machiavelli, he therefore treated first with Denmark, then against Denmark with the Augustenburger, and then actually with Austria — always in the hope of coming out victor in the end.

Even if this was not the outcome of a plan thought out in all its details beforehand, it was at any rate a string of pearls for which he had spun the string in readiness. When the question became acute in the middle of the year 1863, and when all Germany was acclaiming the young duke of Augustenburg for his determination to wrest a German land from a foreign power, Bismarck rose to his feet at the sitting of the Council of State and recommended the annexation of the territories. The king looked up and said: "But I have no rights in the duchies."

"Had the Great Elector, had King Frederick, any more right in Prussia and Silesia? All the Hohenzollern have been enlargers of the State."

The king makes no answer, and the crown prince lifts his hands towards heaven as if doubting the speaker's sanity; the ministers are silent, not excepting Roon; the council passes on to the order of the day. When Bismarck reads over the minutes he finds that there is no mention of his proposal. The secretary explains that the omission was made by the king's orders. His

Majesty had thought that Herr von Bismarck would prefer to have no note made of what he had said. "His Majesty seemed to have believed that I had lunched, not wisely, but too well; and that I should be glad to hear nothing more of what I had said. But I insisted upon the inclusion of my proposal in the minutes."

At about this time he writes: "My method in foreign policy to-day is like my method in old times when I used to go snipe-shooting, and when I would not put my weight on a fresh tussock until I had tried it carefully with my foot." This much is certain, that, thanks to the ups and downs of the Schleswig affair, he was able to manœuvre Austria — first to his side, then away from it, and ultimately out of the Federation. Had it not been for Düppel, Königgrätz would hardly have been possible. But this road led along the edge of the European abyss. Always he had one eye watching the moods of the great powers; while his other eye, like a lion tamer's, rested on his king. More than once, he seemed to have lost the game, which he himself described as resembling one of Scribe's involved plots. If there be truth in the Turkish proverb that luck is in love with the virtuous man, Bismarck must have been supremely virtuous, for he was almost always lucky, and never more lucky than in this particular coup.

If forthwith, and alone, he had attacked Denmark, he would have had Austria in the rear and Europe in front. Instead, he informed Count Rechberg, the minister for foreign affairs in Vienna, that he would undertake single-handed the so-called liberation of the duchies, the most popular thing that could then be attempted in Germany. By this threat, he compelled Rechberg to rally to his side. Then, having so strong an ally, he ignored the Germanic Federation. He had now assuaged the anxieties of Europe, which believed that the inherent hostility between the two German great powers gave security against too overwhelming a success on the part of either one of them. Thus with one stroke he had made Austria his ally, and Europe neutral. The danger of worldwide war was averted, for Prussia and Austria had jointly declared war against the Danes. This is what Bismarck was able to write before the war had actually begun:

"Is it not the most complete victory possible that Austria, two months after attempting to refashion the Germanic Federation, should be delighted when nothing more is said about the matter, and that she should write to her former friends notes identical with ours? This summer we have achieved that which we have been vainly striving to do for twelve years. Austria has adopted our programme, which she publicly made mock of last October. She has preferred the Prussian alliance to the Würzburg alliance. She accepts assistance from us; and if to-day we turn our backs on Austria, the Austrian ministry will fall. Never before has Viennese policy been thus directed from Berlin, both wholesale and retail. We are courted by France. Our voice has an authority in London and St. Petersburg which it has not had for twenty years past. Our strength must be based, not upon the chambers and the press, but upon power politics, upon the strong hand. We have not sufficient and sufficiently enduring strength to waste it upon a false front, phrases, and Augustenburg. . . . Not that I have over-much trust in Austria; but I think that just now it is as well to have her on our side. Whether the time will come to break away from her, and what the reason will be, must be left to the future."

The foregoing sentences are in a long letter which Bismarck writes to Goltz in Paris, at Christmas in the year 1863. We can hardly take it amiss that he should strut about in this way before his rival; at the same time his letter is a soliloquy, perhaps the deliberately muted echo of a hundred soliloquies, for when he says "we" he means himself. He feels that his hour as statesman is at hand. In a few days, the year 1864 will begin.

The silent struggle with the king is preceded and accompanied by a noisy contest in the Landtag. The debate with the democrats shows how difficult it is to carry on foreign policy in conjunction with a parliament — unless all States are doing this, and even then it is sometimes impossible.

Virchow: "The king must be told how imminent is the danger. The minister president has within a comparatively short time adopted such a number of different standpoints, . . . he is speed-

ing without a compass into the sea of foreign complication . . .
he has no guiding principle. . . . That is his weakness. . . . he
has no understanding for what issues from the heart of the people,
. . . and, by his violence he damages the most sacred interests of
Germany and Prussia. He is given over to the Evil One, from
whose clutches he will never escape."

Bismarck: " An assembly of three hundred and fifty members
cannot, nowadays, in the last resort, direct the policy of a great
power, prescribing to the government a programme which must
be followed out to the end. . . . The politician who is not a spec-
ialist at the work, regards every move on the chessboard as the
end of the game. Hence his illusion that the goal is continually
changing. . . . Politics is not an exact science. . . . I am not
afraid of democracy; if I were, I should give up the game. [A
member cries: "A game! A game!"] If the house refuses to vote
supplies, we must take them where we can find them." Thereupon
the house rejects the proposal for a war loan. The Landtag is
dissolved, and does not meet again for a year.

Now that the conflict is at its height, antitheses are struck out
from him like sparks: most sacred interests; political dilettantes
without a compass and without knowledge; principles; games of
chess! The fact that Virchow, man of science and atheist, delivers
over his enemy to the Evil One, when we might rather have expected that the Christian politician should take that course with
the man of science, restores to the dialogue the natural humor
which the ceremonious phrasing hides.

While in the chamber he lays stress on the royal authority,
Bismarck tries to frighten the king with the chamber, saying
that nothing but a strong foreign policy, war in fact, will silence
the opponents of army reform. He also casts his spell over Karolyi in Berlin, and terrifies Rechberg in Vienna by telling him of
the revolutionary trend of national German sentiment. In the
Viennese Reichsrat, however, people are better informed, and
one of the deputies there laughs at Rechberg's report of the
matter, saying: "We are going into the war hand in hand with

the Prussian cabinet, which is condemned by all the world! Bismarck's triumphs are keeping the men of other States awake! In Prussia, the need for expansion is openly proclaimed. Hardly has she digested the stolen territory of Silesia, when she stretches out her claws to grasp the duchies, and we are actually sending our regimental bands to make music for the Prussian march! What tune shall we play?"

The king of Prussia, urged one way by Bismarck and another by the warnings of his nearest and dearest, hesitates. He looks at the prey, and is afraid to seize it. He asks his minister with a serious mien: "Are not you also a German?" Moments come when Bismarck is in despair. "I have a presentiment," he writes to Roon, "that the cause of the crown against the revolution is lost, for the king's confidence is given more to his opponents than to his servants. As God wills. Twenty or thirty years hence, it will be a matter of indifference to us, but not to our children. . . . In default of a miracle, the game will be lost, and we shall have to bear the blame. . . . As God wills. He knows how long Prussia is to continue in existence. God knows I shall be sorry if Prussia comes to an end." Thus he talks of winning or losing the game, and continually invokes the name of God, which he only mentions when he is in great difficulties.

When at length he has persuaded King William and Emperor Francis Joseph to make war, Bismarck is still uncertain for whom the foreign land is really going to be conquered. He may yet find that, despite himself, he is waging a so-called " just war", one which will only liberate the duchies, and will only redound to the advantage of the Germanic Federation. The diplomatist does not hold his peace even after the first shots have been fired. He sends a hurried note to Roon: "Is not the force in F., two companies, far too small? . . . Our companies will be in a mouse-trap if our artillery does not command the aforesaid sound. We have soldiers to spare in Holstein. Why should not we occupy the island more strongly? Forgive my sending you these observations about military matters." What would he have said if Roon had sent him political advice? But his responsibility is greater than that of any general can be. The war is of his contriving. It is his bold hazard.

Within three months the entrenchements of Düppel have been stormed, all the country as far as Alsen has been occupied. London calls a conference, and there is a truce. Bismarck's eyes are always turned towards Paris. He makes vague promises to Napoleon. If only France will stay quiet now! At present, he can do nothing but join with the others in advocating the claim of the Augustenburg duke. He hunts up yellowing documents to support this worthy's claim, has recourse to lawyers' tricks, and compels the duke to accord Prussia rights enough to make himself powerless from the first.

As soon as the increasing discords of the London conference make it possible, he summons the duke to Berlin once more, has an interview with the man towards midnight (this, too, is a means of suggestion) after the duke has, by this contrivance, spent the day with the king and the crown prince. Fresh demands: the duchies are not to become an asylum for liberal agitators. The duke, who has hitherto agreed unhesitatingly to all the stipulations (since his sole desire is to reign), now feels that his position has been strengthened by his interview with William and Frederick. For the first time, he expresses an opinion of his own. He says that, in accordance with the terms of his " constitution ", he must get the assent of his estates to all the conditions. Has the fool been drinking too much champagne at the king's table? Attach provisoes to his assent and thus render it worthless? Bismarck makes up his mind. The territories are to become Prussian. He promptly devotes his ingenuity to proving that all the Augustenburg rights are null and void. He feels, perhaps enjoys, the irony of the situation, for he writes: " The longer I work at politics, the less faith I have in human calculations."

The second part of the war, which occupies no more than a couple of weeks in July, brings a definite victory to the allies. The territories are in their hands, and the only puzzle is what to do with them. There is a meeting in the palace of Schönbrunn. The two rulers, with Bismarck and Rechberg, sit round a table together. Four allies smiling at their success. King William has an uneasy conscience, and so perhaps has Rechberg, who is too simple and straightforward for such policies. But Francis Joseph and Bismarck are quite easy in their minds, each being resolved to cheat the other.

Bismarck: "Now that history has summoned us into political community, we shall do better for ourselves and one another both dynastically and politically if we hold together and take over the leadership of Germany, which will remain in our hands so long as we are united. . . . If our joint acquisitions were in Italy instead of in Holstein, and if Lombardy were at the disposal of the two powers, it would never occur to me to try to persuade my king that our wishes should be set up against those of our allies."

Francis Joseph: "Are the duchies, then, to become provinces, or is Prussia merely to acquire certain rights in them?"

A pause. The king says nothing.

Bismarck: "I am delighted that Your Majesty has asked me that question in the presence of my exalted sovereign. I hope that I shall now learn his views."

William, hesitatingly: "I have really no rights over the duchies, and cannot claim any."

What a scene! Two monarchs who have no idea what they are to do with conquests which their ministers have forced upon them, and their military commanders have won at point of sword. They display mutual distrust which can only find expression in courtly phrases, until the elder of the pair, in a state of profound moral perplexity, says that he has no rights, thus disavowing his own minister, who has just implied the contrary. With a false friendliness, the monarchs say "thou" to one another; "Majesties" and "Excellencies" are bandied about. The discussion ends with a breakfast upon gold and silver plate, and the disappointed minister tries to drown his annoyance in the excellent wine from the Habsburg cellars.

VII

The internal conflict has not been solved by the Danish war. It has only been intensified. The government could point to the successes of the army reform to which the deputies had refused their assent; but the liberals had no difficulty in proving that the reform had scarcely yet begun. The fundamental problem was whether might or right was to rule. This remained just as uncertain after the victory in the field. When, in January 1865, the representatives of the people met once more in the chamber, Bismarck was extremely polite, and was less sarcastic after the victory than he had been while the struggle was in progress. Yet the liberals cannot leave matters alone. " The government," they cry, " has only followed the trend of public opinion!" Bismarck flashes back at them: " If your refusal of the first loan led to the conquest of Düppel and Alsen, then, gentlemen, I hope that your refusal of the present loan will give birth to a Prussian navy." The dispute continues.

So does the dispute between the allies. Austria, who does not wish the conquered territory to become Prussian, would like to make the duchies into a German federal State. Count Mensdorff, the new minister for foreign affairs in Vienna — an aristocrat rather than a statesman, a man of refined sensibilities, and an optimist — is, despite all his politeness, as much of an intriguer as Count Thun was in Frankfort ten years earlier. " Look here," says Bismarck to Karolyi in Berlin, " we are standing in front of the duchies like two guests before whom an admirable banquet is spread; but one of them, who has no appetite, sternly forbids the other, who is hungry, to fall to. Let us wait, then, until the moment comes; for the present we can get along pretty well as we are."

In the summer, the uneasiness in Vienna becomes so great that a breach with Prussia seems imminent. Bismarck's pulse quickens. The aim of the first war, the aim of his fifteen years' work, seems to be on the verge of achievement. " The moment is favourable for a war," he says with scientific coolness in the council of

State, "but the ministers cannot advise to such a step. The resolve can only come from the king's free conviction."

William shakes off the evil dream of a fratricidal war. He goes once more to Gastein, and commands Bismarck to patch up matters again with the hostile friend. This is in August 1865, a year after the Schönbrunn conversations, and two years after the conference of princes. Now "the cracks in the structure are plastered up", and the spoils are shared. Austria will take Holstein and Lauenburg, Prussia will have Schleswig; the sovereignty in both territories will be a joint one. The Augustenburg duke is dropped; and Europe, half amused and half annoyed, asks: "Up ewig ungedeelt?" Bismarck says: "That was the very last time I ever played quinze. I played so recklessly that every one was astonished. Count Blome had said that the best way to understand people's character was to play quinze with them, and I thought I would show him mine! I lost several hundred talers, which I really should have been entitled to draw as part of my allowance for expenses of the service; I succeeded in fooling him, for he believed me to be more venturesome than I am, and gave way." After signing the agreement, Bismarck is supposed to have said to Blome: "Well, I could never have believed that I should find an Austrian diplomatist willing to sign that document!" At the time, Austria was in a condition of internal unrest, and she had no allies among foreign powers; that was why she signed a document which was greatly to the advantage of Prussia. When, finally, Austria sold Prussia the duchy of Lauenburg for two-and-a-half million Danish talers, Bismarck was delighted: "Austria fell in public estimation owing to this deal. One who buys is a man of distinction; one who sells for a ridiculously low price is looked upon with contempt!"

After this first "expansion of the State", the king created Bismarck a count. When, after the Danish war, William bestowed on the minister the order of the Black Eagle, Bismarck expressed his true sentiments in a letter to his wife: "and, which was even more gratifying to me, the king cordially embraced me." To him the highest order of distinction William could grant was of little account. Not so as regards the new title of nobility. His family feeling, the strongest of all his inherited qualities, was gratified. He had always been proud to look at the ancestral portraits of the Bismarcks hanging on the walls of Schönhausen; and, in his pride of birth, he had said that the Bismarcks had lived longer in the marches than the Hohenzollern. Among his fellow Junkers and acquaintances, there were many who had more distinguished escutcheons, and when ambition was driving him towards high office he always had in mind the faces of these privileged persons. An accessory motive with him was the desire to be able to make a good showing before the members of his own caste. As an actual fact, the arrogance of the titled nobility made them look down upon those who were simply gentry.

He himself had no need of coats of arms. He was Bismarck, a man who already had a European reputation. But it mattered to him a good deal that his wife, the daughter of a Farther Pomeranian squire, his wife, who had been slighted in exalted circles, could now write herself countess, and that his sons, and their sons' sons, could write themselves Counts Bismarck. This brought the Junker more satisfaction than all the titles and offices he had received in the past, and more than the friendship of queens and empresses. His near ones and dear ones, the only people he cared for in the world, had been given a step upwards. Bismarck was now fifty years of age. At five-and-twenty, when he had resigned from the public service, he had sketched his future in a letter to his friend, writing: " And if in the wool market they call me ' Herr Baron ', I will sell three talers cheaper."

When he read the friendly explanation King William gave for conferring this title upon him, he could not help laughing inwardly at the king's pride. For two years he had been leading his reluctant sovereign forward step by step, but now the old man spoke of the conquest "as an outcome of my governance which you have followed with such great and distinguished circumspection. . . . Your affectionate king, William."

Meanwhile the great settlement of accounts was drawing ever nearer; and, as it became imminent, Bismarck kept more and more attentive watch on Napoleon. The emperor of the French and the nation he ruled looked askance at the reconciliation between the two rival German powers, for their chronic quarrel had been pleasing to Europe. England, indeed, was already beginning to consider the desirability of forming a powerful league against united Germany. To Bismarck it seemed that the only way of learning what Napoleon really thought would be to have a personal interview. The man who had just been talking to one emperor in Gastein, hastened from that watering place to another watering place, Biarritz, to weave his spells there around another emperor. In truth it felt almost like a journey into a hostile country. He took lodgings near the imperial Villa Eugénie, where Napoleon had established his summer court. Bismarck had given it out that this extraordinary journey had been undertaken for the sake of his wife, who was in poor health. Johanna alone believed this. She wrote: "At first terribly depressed, for I reproached myself because I had cost poor Bismarck so much without any prospect of benefiting by the journey! . . . It seems to me that I should have been much better off in Homburg." These naïve words show how, after the first years of his marriage, Bismarck had ceased to tell his wife anything about his political aims.

Had he not been much happier in the previous year, when he had been alone in Biarritz? After peace had been signed with Denmark, he had made a brief visit to the Biscayan coast. No emperor there then, and his wife had not been with him. His only companions had been, once more, the charming Madame Orloff and her husband, with whom he had spent the time bathing, riding, and enjoying the charms of music. During the two years that had elapsed since Roon's fanfare had summoned him from Biarritz, he had met the handsome Russian lady half a dozen times. In letters she is spoken of simply as Kathi, a name which does not suggest a Russian princess. Now the happy hours were renewed. Twice he wrote to his wife in a tone of reverie which might seem utterly foreign to his nature: "Here I really am, darling, as if in a dream; in front of me is the sea, upstairs

Kathi is practising Beethoven, such weather as we have not had all the summer, and not a drop of ink in the house! . . . If they send me any despatches, I shall run away into the Pyrenees. After all, I shall not buy Lubben, but Ishoux, or some land near Dax. When I think of how we had to keep fires going in Baden and even in Paris, and how here the sun makes us lay aside overcoats and tweeds; how yesterday we lay on the shore in the moonlight until ten o'clock; and how to-day we are breakfasting in the open air —I must say that God has been wonderfully gracious to these southern lands in the matter of climate. . . . I am anxiously awaiting news of you."

So light grows the heavy heart of this German when he is in the society of foreigners, when he can loaf for week after week on the seashore in the company of a handsome woman whom he admires; when he can enjoy himself in a way which is no longer possible to him in the forests of his homeland. Distant horizons; brilliant days; clear, blue skies; sparkling seas; brighter the sunshine; gayer the women's dresses; more sprightly the lilt of the language—that is a German's dream.

This time, however, when he is accompanied by his wife and his daughter (both of whom are ailing), when the Russian lady is no longer there, and when his mind is heavy with plans, the shore has a different look. Prosper Mérimée, the famous writer, is at Biarritz. As a foreigner, he has more insight into Bismarck's character than many a German, writing: "Bismarck is wittier than becomes a German; he is a diplomatic Humboldt. . . . C'est un grand Allemand très poli. Il a l'air absolument dépourvu de Gemüth [geniality] mais plein d'esprit." A year later: "This great man is so well prepared that it would be unwise for us to pick a quarrel with him. We shall have to swallow a good many mortifications at his hands, until we too have needle-guns." One cannot but admire the art of the statesman even more than that of the man of letters. Bismarck is a quick-change artist. In a moment he can assume the complexion of the country which he wants to turn to his service. Will he be able to trick the emperor likewise?

There they stroll up and down the terrace, close to the sea. Bismarck is strong, healthy, has a keen and questing glance. As he strides along, he is careful each time they turn to move to the emperor's left. Napoleon is sallow, bent, and prematurely old, though he is but a few years the German's senior. He walks with short paces, and his eyes are uneasy. The dog, Nero, follows at their heels. Any one who could foresee that five years hence the two men would be at war, would infer the upshot simply from their looks.

But a listener would have remained doubtful whether matters would ever come to blows. Neither of the two wants a fight. The emperor, weakened by bladder trouble, dreads nothing more than he dreads a new war, whereas in the days of his prime he wanted "an active campaign every few years." If he has to fight now, he would rather fight on the shores of the Mediterranean or in Venetia in order to strike a blow for Italy and on behalf of the fashionable cause of national liberty — and at the same time win a little power for himself! Thus the wishes of the French would find both a real and an ideal satisfaction. Since these aims can only be fulfilled by going to war against Austria, the emperor considers that it will be to his advantage to support Prussia. What shall he demand of Prussia in return for this inestimable service?

What will Napoleon demand? Bismarck asks himself this question repeatedly. He cannot give away any German territory, and the Frenchman has no fancy for Austrian. He therefore talks of Belgium, and, since Napoleon is reserved, he sums up the situation with Mephistophelian brevity by saying: "It is difficult to offer foreign territory to any one who does not want it." Then he goes on to speak of French Switzerland, also of German territory on the Rhine, also of Treves and Landau. All this as the two men walk up and down, and with the implication: "We cannot make you an offer of territory, but if you take it for yourself, we shall not stand in your way." The emperor, too, leaves the annexations unexpressed. He talks in general terms: "We should welcome a greater Prussia, freed from any kind of serfdom."

"An aspiring Prussia," rejoins Bismarck, no less vaguely, "would regard the friendship of France as of supreme importance; a discouraged Prussia would have to seek alliances against France. Besides, we cannot create events; we can only allow them to ripen."

"As soon as circumstances make a closer and more intimate entente desirable," says the emperor, "your royal master can approach me with confidence."

He makes no further advances, nor can Bismarck go any further, for King William has strictly forbidden any talk of an alliance. Will Bismarck report the whole conversation to the king? He will only relate as much as he thinks fit, and only in terms which the king will be able to understand. On attaining power, Bismarck has speedily ceased to be frank. He discloses only so much as the hearer is fitted to understand. He treats the king in this way just as he treats others, and he does not think that King William is nearly ready for war against the Habsburgs. "My general impression is that the present mood of the French court is entirely favourable to us." Thus his report is couched in the ambiguous terminology appropriate to the conversation just recorded. Through the veil, we see the lightning-flashes of his soul. We see how this statesman purposes to make war against his German brethren, in defiance of the wishes of his people, of his king, of Europe; and we see how he tries to appease the great and ambitious land of France by half-promises.

Since both he and Napoleon purposed to cheat one another, it remains uncertain which of them was really humbugged at Biarritz. The victory of the artillery in 1870 ended the duel between these two, though it did not decide it.

VIII

In the middle of the sixties, Bismarck the Prussian began to become a German.

I do not mean that either now or earlier he was driven forward by another wish than that of beating Austria within the Federation. Hatred and self-assertion were in this matter, likewise, stronger than love and the desire for order. To put Prussia in Austria's place, to fight and conquer his rival — these were the elemental impulses of his nature, not "The German idea." The liberals, to whom Germany had become a sort of religion, were right when, in those days, they denied that Bismarck shared their faith. He had then felt no closer kinship with Rhinelanders and Bavarians than with Viennese and Salzburgers. Why should he trouble to classify the Germans across the frontier? To-day, just as when he had written to Gerlach ten years before, he was ready to shoot down any of these folk if his general policy made such a course of action desirable. A few months hence he will, without turning a hair, see Saxons, Hessians, and Hanoverians fall by thousands in his war. They are all foreigners. Prussia alone is his fatherland, his homeland.

The form of patriotism which the history of German lands has made peculiar to the Germans, is in Bismarck remarkable rather for its breadth than for its narrowness. For, as he himself declared in old age, the German is faithful to the dynasty of the land in which he is born, and for the most part loves only a corner of land. Thus Bismarck's affection is mainly given to Pomerania. Prussia, a land of chance conquests, and in those days having a narrow body, was too large and illogical a structure to arouse dynastic sentiments. There was no community of feeling between Cologne and Memel. Bismarck was one of the few who, nevertheless, were resolved to love Prussia as such, whatever its shape might be; the reason being that the conquests of the royal house were for him a dogma, whilst questions of racial stocks were of no importance whatever. As a liegeman of the king of Prussia, as a knight of Brandenburg, his only concern was with the expansion of Prussia; and he would much rather, after the manner of earlier centuries, have conquered German princes in order to enlarge Prussia, than have troubled himself about the problems of the Germanic Federation. "Primus" was what he wanted to be, and only perforce "inter pares." That was the logic of his blood! But his sinister intelligence, his profound knowledge of history, and his clear view of reality, overpowered these wishes, natural though they were. He kept his eyes fixed on what was attainable, ignored what was merely desirable, and determined after the victory over Austria to ensure that his Prussia alone should be leader in Germany. True, a few more provinces were to be added to Prussian territory, but conquest was no longer the aim.

A new ambition awakened in him. Keudell, a trustworthy witness, to whom Bismarck had said ten years earlier, "My only interest is in the crown of Prussia", now records the saying, "My greatest ambition is to weld the Germans into a nation!" Ten years before, when Bismarck the partisan became a diplomatist, he shed some of his reactionary prejudices, and began to reckon with magnitudes without troubling himself about principles. Now, when from being a Prussian minister, he was becoming a German statesman, he began to think in terms of German territories. It was his inborn peculiarity that he should think in dynasties and not in tribal stocks. Neither now nor later could he rid himself of that primitive outlook. That was why Bismarck was nothing more than the greatest statesman of his time; that was why he never became a seer.

At the present juncture, he is glad that Austria's position is difficult. Austria finds that the administration of the distant province of Holstein involves difficulties like those of colonial administration. She would like to sell Holstein to Prussia, and Venetia to Napoleon for four million lire. Since she does not venture to dispose of both, she allows the duke of Augustenburg to recommence his agitations in Holstein, thus infringing the treaty of Gastein, which gives Prussia a joint voice in both the duchies. Now Bismarck is able to show his king that Prussian rights are being infringed; now he is able to spur Frederick William on. He utters his designs with amazing frankness. "The king is so constituted," he says to the French envoy Benedetti, "that if I am to induce him to claim a right, I must prove to him that others are disputing it. When any one dares to put limits upon his authority, he may be expected to form energetic resolves." A formal complaint is lodged in Vienna. An indignant answer is returned.

The Privy Council meets in Berlin in February, 1866. The king speaks firmly: " We do not wish to provoke war, but we must not shrink from war." All the ministers agree, the crown prince being the only dissentient. The king: " The ownership of the duchies is worth a war. We must negotiate and wait. I want peace, but am resolved to make war if needs must, for I regard the war as a just one, now that I have prayed to God to show me the right path." Eighteen months earlier, in Schönbrunn, God had made it plain to him that he had no rights in the duchies; as far as he is concerned, now, the Germanic Federation and the rights of Austria have become things of the past.

Bismarck's hopes rise. He has a controversy with the crown prince, which " becomes acrimonious." The same evening, after dictating to one of his secretaries, he sits at the window and delivers himself to Keudell as follows: " If Mensdorff goes back to the old policy, we must flaunt a little black-red-and-gold before his face. The Schleswig question and the German question are so closely interconnected that we must solve them together if it should come to blows. A German parliament would keep the remainder of the middle-sized and petty States within bounds." Then, after a pause: " If, perchance, there should be an Ephialtes, the great German movement would crush him and his master!" Then " he stood up quickly and left the room." Thus does Bismarck form resolves. He thinks them out slowly, part by part; then an historical parallel suddenly leaps into his mind out of the past into the present; with it he crushes his opponents; then, by jumping to his feet, he expresses the resolve which is hidden in his mind.

As the war draws near, he puts this resolve in operation. The dictatorship now becomes more rigid. As long as the deputies can say whatever they please, the mood in the country will not ripen to great resolves. Consequently the public prosecutor must take proceedings against the liberals for misuse of the right of free speech, and two trustworthy assistant judges are appointed to deal with the matter. The Landtag is furious: " You may decorate your judges with all the orders of distinction at the disposal of the Prussian State. Your stars do not hide the wounds these men have inflicted on their own honour, cannot hide them from their contemporaries or from posterity! Alas, they have wounded, too, the honour of the fatherland. . . . Such proceedings arouse a mood of pessimism which is a danger to the State. Even quiet folk begin to think that the future can only be a season of revenge!" Thus does Twesten, one of those against whom a prosecution has been instituted, thunder from the tribune, his closing words pointing straight to revolution, on the very eve of the war.

Bismarck replies: "In this way we should make the chamber a court of appeal higher than the supreme court. In this way we should give the deputies privileges over other citizens, such privileges as even the most imaginative of Junkers has never dreamed of for the members of his class! If you had your way, the deputies would be entitled to utter the crudest insults and calumnies!" The conflict has become insoluble; and yet such a conflict is the only thing which can make the king back up a fighting minister. The Landtag is dissolved. Bismarck is satisfied with the situation.

The next step is to make sure of France and Italy. The king must now write to Napoleon the letter which the emperor had stipulated for when circumstances should become critical. The envoy will tell Napoleon everything; the moment has come. Goltz says to the emperor: "We do not simply wish to have the duchies. What we want is to found the North German Union under Prussia's leadership." The emperor agrees to remain neutral. But since he is suspicious with regard to Prussia's further plans, he declares that in the event of any further enlargement of Prussia he will put in a claim for certain territories on the Rhine. Bismarck cautiously carries on the negotiations. He sends Bleichröder, in whom he has especial confidence, to Paris. Bleichröder conveys his wishes to Rothschild, who is to transmit them to the emperor. Thus does Bismarck make use of private relationships, and even of the Jews. Soon afterwards, in the chamber, Thiers speaks about the imminence of the unification of North Germany, and says that the preponderance of France can only be maintained by maintaining the disintegration of Germany. There are storms of applause from all sides. Napoleon is alarmed. Henceforward he deliberates whether Austria should not perhaps be compensated in Silesia for the loss of Schleswig, lest Prussia should grow too powerful. One cabinet after another, one house of parliament after another, plays at carving out new frontiers. There is a busy exchange of cipher despatches concerning the demands which the great powers think of making after a war which, perhaps, will never take place.

When, at this juncture, an Italian general appears in Berlin, Bismarck finds it expedient to allow the negotiations with Florence for a secret treaty to become known in Vienna, so that sharp notes of protest may be made by the Austrians. These will be useful to him in order to goad on the king to action. With this end in view, he confides his plans to old Wrangel, whose way it is promptly to blab all confidences. To the Italian general, Bismarck says: "I hope that I shall be able to make the king consent to the war, but I cannot pledge myself positively." Although all the other foreigners in Berlin warn the Italian general against Bismarck's wiles, there is no misunderstanding in Florence; and when the expected complaints come to hand from Vienna, Italy decides on an alliance with Prussia. The Italians are to invade Venetia as soon as the Prussians invade Bohemia. This bill of exchange is payable in three months. Bismarck, the German royalist, is not in the least disturbed by the fact that he is getting foreign arms to assist him in the fight against the German House of Habsburg.

Now at length, when his allies are ready to sign, King William refuses his assent! Bismarck has a nervous breakdown. "The day before yesterday," writes Roon, "our friend, who has been exhausted by his Herculean labours both by night and by day, . . . suffered from such intense pains in the stomach, and was consequently in such a terribly depressed mood, so irritable and disturbed, . . . that I am still anxious to-day, for I know what is at stake, and that he has the utmost need at this very moment of all his strength of mind, undisturbed by bodily ailments." During these weeks, both he and Roon seriously consider the prospect of resigning. At length Roon recovers confidence, and persuades his friend to go ahead. "You know from your own experience what life is like," writes Bismarck to an acquaintance. "You know its happenings, its tasks, its deprivations, the lack of time and energy. . . . Do not imagine that discouragement makes me write like this. I believe in the war without knowing whether I shall see it; but I often feel overcome by exhaustion." Such a tone is unusual in this fighter: philosophical, renunciative, tired.

When his enemies form a ring round him, he is reinvigorated. Now most of the conservatives have deserted his cause. In their eyes, an attack upon the legitimate Habsburg ruler seems impossible. In their eyes, the man who had resisted Radowitz sixteen years earlier has become a second Radowitz. Ludwig Gerlach, his sometime friend and protector, sitting by the fireside in the evening over soda water and cigars, threatens him with God's curse. When Gerlach attacks Bismarck's policy in the "Kreuzzeitung", Bismarck grows angry: "I am no hothead, who is eager to involve the country in wars!" Such are Bismarck's surly words to the old pietist. "In this matter I must follow my own course. I thought matters out in solitary communion with God, and did not consult the members of my party." He is "blunt, pale, passionate, has no friendly words." When Gerlach says he hopes that these differences in political matters will not disturb their friendship, Bismarck is silent. Silence, here, means refusal. Never again does Bismarck speak to Gerlach.

Simultaneously the crown prince and his wife are at work, and Augusta more than all; they do their utmost against the war, this meaning against Bismarck. A friendly duke procures pacific letters from the Austrian minister, in order to send them to the king. Letters and deputations pour in on King William from the most loyal of his subjects: Prince Charles, Senfft-Pilsach, Bodelschwingh, Gerlach, all the pietists. Even the Holy Alliance rises like a ghost from the tomb. There is general effervescence. One man alone remains quiet amid the turmoil. When Bismarck's war trumpets sound, Moltke declares that the reports of Austria's military strength are greatly exaggerated. Nevertheless, Bismarck continues to do all he can to induce Austria to take the offensive, being certain that the king will not strike the first blow — for William is afraid of his wife. According to Bismarck, Augusta's tactics in those days were so definitely anti-national that "when fighting had already begun on the Bohemian frontier, very questionable negotiations were going on in Berlin . . . under Her Majesty's patronage."

The crown princess' conduct was even worse. "My dear Mama," she wrote at the end of March to her mother in London, "it is important you should know that the wicked man is beside himself with wrath because the king wanted Fritz to write to you, . . . that would not do at all, would interfere with his plans, was a needless intervention, and so on, . . . in a word, he was very angry indeed, and is now . . . doing everything he can to prevent any other sort of interference. I think you ought to know this, and that is why I write to you direct, although it may seem like intrigue, which I detest." It was not intrigue, it was treason; and even if Princess Victoria had not ceased to be an Englishwoman, she ought to have learned from the tradition of the English ministers, who at all times have refused to allow immigrant princes to interfere in their affairs.

Bismarck is in a fever of excitement. Sometimes, so an eyewitness records, he clasps his forehead when he is at dinner, saying in low tones: "I think we are all going mad!"

What will the German princes do? Will the other German stocks allow themselves to be led by Prussia? Now, with a premonition of such good fortune, he has recourse to the most surprising means in order to influence public opinion in the desired direction. He proposes to the Germanic Federation the summoning of a German representative assembly, to be elected by direct and universal suffrage! Lassalle is dead, but here one of his great ideas is resurrected. "In view of the necessities of the occasion," wrote Bismarck in his old age, "and struggling against great odds abroad, I should not have hesitated in case of need to have recourse to revolutionary means, and should have been willing to throw universal suffrage (then the strongest of the liberal artifices) into the scale, if thereby I could have scared monarchical foreign lands from attempts to poke their fingers into our national pie. . . . In such a fight, when life and death are at stake, a man does not look too closely at the weapons he uses. The only question then is what will be successful, what will ensure that other powers will keep their hands off?"

Eighteen years earlier, Von Bismarck-Schönhausen, the deputy, declaiming against universal suffrage, had said: "A pound of flesh and human bones affords no standard of measurement!" Vincke had shouted back: "Souls!"

Now, with this bolt from the blue, Bismarck announced the German war. The echo was laughter! He, who for four years had ruled his own land unconstitutionally, without a budget, as a dictator—did he dare to mock the Germans by an offer which was generally considered to be the outcome of fear? If the words of the crown prince in those days had been made public, they would have been received with acclamation: "Bismarck handles the most sacred things impiously. A bellicose minister cannot solve the German problem." Not even the crown prince knew that this same man in the year 1860, in his Badenese memorial, had recommended the king to summon a German parliament! "Not thus," writes Treitschke, and half Germany applauds him; "not as a spirit conjured up to meet an urgent need, but maturely prepared by a strictly constitutional régime in Prussia, and for that reason supported by the firm will of the Prussian nation and received with the jubilant assent of the German people—that is how the idea which the nation has cherished in its heart for years should enter the arena of practical politics! . . . The nation is stupefied as it contemplates the sudden reversal of Prussian policy!"

German sentiment overpowers reason! While the ideologues of Germany moralise, and exclaim "Not thus!", Bismarck, mastering his sentimental dislike of parliaments, is guided solely by reason.

But this popular negative is less alarming to his ears than a call for peace from Vienna. In that quarter, too, there has been a sudden turn, and peace is in favour. There is a proposal for mutual disarmament. Thereupon Bismarck, whose body is subject to the tension of his nerves, becomes really ill, and is only able to communicate with the king in writing. Then Victor Emmanuel decides to take the field, doing this under Napoleon's patronage. In response, Austria mobilises, not only the army corps necessary to meet the Italian forces, but the whole Austrian army, for she has long known about the secret treaty. At this news, Bismarck quickly gets well again, and points an accusing finger at the "cheats" in Vienna. In the Privy Council, the king now takes a stronger line than ever before. Spur him a little more and he will leap.

"Your Majesty will rest assured that it is opposed to my sentiments, I can even say to my faith, to attempt, in any urgent way, to influence your exalted and sovereign decisions in matters of war and peace. I am content to leave it to Almighty God to guide Your Majesty's heart for the welfare of the fatherland, and I am more inclined to pray than to advise. But I cannot hide my conviction that if we keep the peace now, the danger of war will recur, perhaps in a few months, and under less favourable conditions. Peace can only be lasting when both parties want it. . . . One who, like Your Majesty's most faithful servant, has for sixteen years been intimately acquainted with Austrian policy, cannot doubt that in Vienna hostility to Prussia has become the chief, I might almost say the only, motive of State policy. This motive will become actively operative as soon as the cabinet of Vienna finds that the circumstances are more favourable than at the present moment. Austria's first endeavour will be to mould circumstances in Italy and France, so that they may become more favourable."

Once more: prayer, God, and religious faith have to be mobilised in order that the king may be mobilised. Bismarck strikes home. He reminds the king of Olmütz days, he who, sixteen years earlier, had quarrelled about Olmütz with the man who is now king. Old William trembles at the prospect of being again defeated. He writes: "You can tell . . . Manteuffel that, if a Prussian now whispers Olmütz in my ears, I shall at once abdicate!"

At length, in the beginning of May, the king orders the mobilisation, though in such a way that it does not yet mean war. Augusta, protesting, leaves Berlin. The crown prince, who is an officer of high rank, declares that the fratricidal war is unjustifiable, and will probably turn out ill; Silesia and Rhineland are likely to be lost. The queen dowager, a Bavarian by birth, is furious. Even some of the older officers, whose fathers have told them of the Battle of the Nations, are adverse. Now, when both Bismarck and the king are agreed upon war, they stand alone. "I know," says the king to his reader, "that they are all against me. Every one of them! But I shall myself draw my sword at the head of my army, and would rather perish than that Prussia should give way this time!" Bismarck simultaneously declares: "I know that I am generally detested . . . fortune is as fickle as the opinions of men. I am staking my head, and I shall play out the game though it bring me to the scaffold! Neither Prussia nor Germany can remain what they have been; and, in order to become what they must, they will have to travel along this road. No other course is possible."

Yes, his head is at stake. An assassin lies in wait for him, and will strike as soon as the detested minister (who has been ill) appears again in public. On May 7th, when Bismarck leaves his house for the first time since his illness, and has been to see the king, he is walking back along the central alley of Unter den Linden. He hears two or three shots close at hand, turns swiftly on his heel, and sees a young man who is about to fire again. Bismarck leaps at him, seizes the assailant's right wrist with one hand and his throat with the other. But the assassin is just as resolute as the man he wants to kill, takes the revolver from his right hand to his left, and fires two more shots point-blank. One misses, scorching Bismarck's coat; the other apparently finds its billet. Bismarck, rallying his forces, continues to grip his assailant by the throat until a passer-by, with the aid of two soldiers, seizes the man. Bismarck is amazed to find that, though he has a little pain, he can walk quite well, so he returns home on foot. Johanna and some guests are waiting for him at table.

Entering unnoticed, he goes first to his study, examines his clothing carefully, and then writes a brief report to the king. After that, he joins his wife, and kisses her on the forehead: "Don't be alarmed, darling, a man has tried to shoot me, but by God's grace I am uninjured." At table he relates the story as if it had been an adventure out hunting: "Being an old hunter, I said to myself: 'The last two shots must have hit, I am a dead man.' Still, I was able to walk home all right. I have looked into matters since getting home. There are holes in my overcoat, my coat, my waistcoat, and my shirt, but the bullet slipped along outside my silk undervest without hurting the skin. One of my ribs ached a little as if it had been struck, but that soon passed off. It happens sometimes with wild beasts that a rib can bend elastically when a bullet strikes. One can see afterwards where the hit has been, for a few hairs are rubbed off. I suppose this rib of mine bent in the same way. Maybe, too, that the shots did not develop their full force because the muzzle of the revolver was pressed against my coat."

He tells his tale with all the calm of a man of science, without explaining that he has just saved his own life by his resolute courage, by the way in which he attacked his assailant. Only to the innate energy with which he gripped the assailant by the throat does Bismarck owe it that in this hour he can raise his wineglass composedly. Soon the king comes to embrace his minister. The princes appear with mixed feelings. A crowd begins to gather in front of the house. Bismarck steps on to the balcony, his wife by his side. He has been the most hated man in Prussia. Never before has a crowd applauded him. To-day, because a democrat has taken pot shots at him and failed to kill him, democrats cheer him to the echo. He speaks a few words, and cries: "Long live the king!" Next day the assassin commits suicide in prison. His name was Cohen-Blind, a student from Tubingen, half English by descent, who had hoped to kill the enemy of the people and thus prevent a war. No doubt Bis-

marck regretted that his revenge thus escaped him. If this
man's bony structure had really been of iron and not elastic
like his spirit, if he had fallen, the political struggle between
Prussia and Austria might have been intensified for a time, but
the German war would not have taken place. This was not a people's war; it was not even a war made by the cabinets; it was the
war of one minister, who dragged along the cabinet, the king, and
the generals, in his wake. Had he merely been put out of action
by illness during these weeks, Roon tells us that "in my view
this would have meant that the Prussians would have lost the
battle of Kollin a second time."

According to Keudell, after the attempt on his life Bismarck
"felt himself to be God's chosen instrument, though he did not
express the thought in words." Keudell was a keen observer, and
saw the minister from day to day; we cannot doubt his testimony.
Bismarck has been in deadly peril, immediately before the war
of his own making and when he is uncertain how it will end. He
is saved from this peril in a way which seems to him miraculous.
Even Bismarck's realism fails for a moment, and he fancies
that the finger of God is at work.

IX

Five weeks elapse between the last shot fired by the idealist
at the enemy of the people and the first shot fired by the realist's
orders at his German brethren. "Compensations!" Paris exclaims
even before the German army stirs. Napoleon, who is fiercely
attacked by Thiers, begins to regret his policy. Perhaps he still
believes in the words conveyed to him by Bismarck, more or less
in confidence, through an emissary: "If it rested with me alone,
I should, perhaps, be willing for the sake of the good cause to commit a small act of treason, and, since I am far more a Prussian
than a German, to cede to France a fragment of Rhenish territory
south of the Moselle; but, you see, the king will not allow me to do
this." During these weeks, Bismarck humorously compares himself to a lion-tamer, and Napoleon to an Englishman " who every

evening presents himself before the lion's cage, waiting unmoved for the coming of the hour in which the beasts will eat the tamer."

When, two or three years later, the unsuspecting king is astounded by certain revelations, Bismarck admits their accuracy, "even though my personal policy is placed in an unfavourable light by them. . . . I could only keep the Napoleonic policy in check by continually giving Benedetti and the Italians to understand that I myself was prepared to step aside from the paths of virtue, but that my gracious sovereign was not, and that they must give me time in which to convince Your Majesty. As Your Majesty is well aware, I have never tried to do anything of the kind. . . . The belief of the French that I was trying to do it has been most useful to us."

During these last weeks, all kinds of people are still trying to influence the king against Bismarck. Letters of warning from old confidants pour in. Bethmann-Hollweg, whose grandson was in later days to give similar advice to the grandson of this same king, went so far as to deny that the wicked Bismarck could be regarded as a true Prussian: "No understanding is possible so long as this man stands at Your Majesty's side, and enjoys Your Majesty's confidence — the man through whose actions all the other powers have lost confidence in Your Majesty. . . . This is the eleventh hour, and when once the bloody dice have been thrown, it will be too late." The writer does not know that it has already struck twelve, and the king does not know that he is in the toils. For when, in the beginning of June, the Austrians summon the estates in Holstein, Bismarck is able at length to accuse them of a breach of faith, and King William is wrathful! "Austria follows up perfidy with falsehood, and falsehood with a breach of faith," exclaims the king in answer to a warning from one of the princes of the Church. "I have wrestled with God in prayer in order to learn His will. Step by step I have kept Prussia's honour before my eyes, and have acted according to my conscience!" The good king really believes what he says, although Bethmann-Hollweg, in consultation with the same German God, is convinced that German honour is being sullied.

Southward, the gentry on the Danube invoking the same deity, though with somewhat different rites, commend to him the protection of their Habsburg honour.

Even Bismarck, who is overwhelmed with work, uneasily opens the Bible haphazard one morning in search of an oracle, and hits upon the following passage (Psalms, ix., 2, 3, 4): "I will be glad and rejoice in thee: I will sing praise to thy name, O thou Most High. When mine enemies are turned back, they shall fall and perish at thy presence. For thou hast maintained my right and my cause; thou sittest in the throne judging right." Johanna is not at all surprised that her husband should be "comforted and filled with new hope" by these words. Even Keudell, who records the incident, does not appear to ask himself whether on the same morning Mensdorff in the Ballhausplatz or Beust on the Brühlschen Terrasse may not have been practising sortilege, may not have discovered the same words, and may not have an equally genuine conviction that God is on their side. Nor does any one remark how this good Christian (Dürer's Knight, Death, and the Devil, all rolled into one) is, simultaneously with his search for the divine approval, treating with a Hungarian general about the possibility of a Hungarian accessory legion being raised to fight against the legitimate ruler of Hungary; or that Bismarck actually persuades his own master King William to condone this joining hands with the revolutionists of 1848.

When Bohemia is invaded by the Prussians, he incites the Czechs to high treason. A proclamation is issued addressed: "To the inhabitants of the glorious kingdom of Bohemia." They are assured that in case of victory "perhaps the time will be propitious for the Bohemians and the Moravians, so that, like the Hungarians, they will be able to fulfil their national desires."

Meanwhile most of the German princes have taken up arms on Austria's side. Prussia withdraws from the Germanic Federation. An ultimatum gives the rulers of Electoral Hesse, Nassau, Hanover, and Saxony, twenty-four hours in which to make up their minds. In these days Bismarck invites to dinner a journalist from Paris whose acquaintance he has not previously made.

He has a long talk with the man, is witty, discusses Parisian memories, and assumes a confident pose, which his guest hastens to describe in a telegram sent to Paris that evening. In the night of the ultimatum, Bismarck walks up and down the garden of the foreign office, accompanied by the British envoy. He speaks of Attila, and would seem this very evening to have discovered him for Germany. "After all, Attila was a greater man than Mr. John Bright in your House of Commons!" Twelve o'clock strikes. He takes out his watch and looks at it, saying: "At this moment our troops are entering Hanover and Hesse. The struggle grows serious. Perhaps Prussia will be beaten; you may be sure that we shall fight bravely. If we are beaten, I shall not come back. I shall fall in the last onslaught. A man can die but once, and if one is conquered it is better to die."

Two weeks later, everything has been settled in the north, and now, since the news of victories comes in, a change of mood begins. After the attempt on the premier's life, there had been very little stir. The corpse of the would-be assassin, the idealist, had been secretly decked with laurels — a thing which would hardly have happened to Bismarck's body had he fallen in Unter den Linden. Caricatures had been sold, depicting a proud avenger with features, like those of Wilhelm Tell, shooting at Bismarck, and only hindered from being successful by the intervention of the devil, who thrusts in between, exclaiming: "He belongs to me!" Now, six weeks later, crowds surge in front of the palace, acclaiming William, who, in the March days, had had to flee from this palace to an island in the Havel. The king stands beside Roon and Bismarck, thanking his subjects, and when Bismarck drives home, people want to unharness the horses from his carriage and draw it themselves. Then thousands assemble before his house, and a well-meaning man shouts: "Hail to the general who does his valiant deeds in the battlefield of diplomacy!" Bismarck stands at the window with his wife, speaks to the people, and is able to venture upon saying: "It is plain, after all, that the king was right!" There is a thunder clap, and his last words are drowned by the noise from the skies. He shouts: "The heavens are saluting us!" Such conceits, which are soon bruited abroad through the capital, make Bismarck better understood by the man in the street. They give a more credible demonstration of his views than any proclamations can.

Bismarck had never sought popular favour. To-day he can afford to despise it. He is in search of securer grounds for the solution of the conflict. He decides that there shall be new elections, and three days after the first shot has been fired he summons two of the leaders of the opposition. Twesten, the very man who has recently been prosecuted, at Bismarck's instigation, for his speeches in the Lower House, now comes to visit his enemy; and we may be sure that in doing so he enjoys the Prussian sentiment of obedience when the country is in danger — and that his pride therein is no whit abated though he is kept waiting many hours. Bismarck discusses the new situation with him, and also with Unruh, the liberal. The talk with Unruh takes place in the garden, the two men walking up and down during the cool hours of the summer night. Bismarck has had no time in the daylight hours. Unruh points out that the proclamation contains no mention of a return to constitutional government. Thereupon Bismarck speaks with strong emotion:

"People think I can do anything! I am faced with difficulties such as few are able to realise! I cannot persuade the king to do everything I should like. We had taken that for granted. Then the king said: 'This proclamation is just as bad as the constitution. On the strength of it, after the war, they might take away some of my regiments! I won't have it!'"

This is no mere pretext, for the frankness with which Bismarck speaks of the king to this opponent and anti-royalist, shows how hard put to it he still is in his contest with William.

Unruh: "Our situation to-day resembles that of Prussia before the Seven Years' War. . . . Yet with all due respect to the king. . . . "

Bismarck: "The same situation, but without Frederick the Great! Agreed! Still, we have to make the best of it. . . . I am proud that I have been able to persuade a king of Prussia to such an act as the summoning of a German parliament. But such a policy cannot be waged by speeches and resolutions. It must be decided by half a million soldiers. . . . A war with Hungary, Ruthenia, and Slovakia is not a fratricidal war!"

Unruh: "Every one is surprised that the flag is still flying over the palace."

Bismarck: "Several times I have asked the king when he proposes to give orders for the start, and he has answered snappishly that he would decide that for himself. You see, therefore, that I cannot always arrange things as I please. The king is close upon seventy years old, and the queen works against me!"

Unruh: "What will happen if we sustain a reverse?"

Bismarck: "Then the king will abdicate."

These answers, which are uttered "explosively", show all the wild impetuosity of a swimmer after he has sprung into the water. The one thing that matters now is to reach the farther shore. That is why his answers are so curt. Three times in this half hour he gives the king away. He knows perfectly well that next morning Unruh will pass on what has been said. He also knows what a defeat in battle would mean, and what the king's abdication would mean, for himself. When the crown prince speaks to him of the possibility of a catastrophe, he answers with like fierceness: "What does it matter if I am hanged? Enough if the hangman's rope should tie your throne firmly to the new Germany!"

Three days after the start, Bismarck is with the king on a hilltop near Königgrätz. What chiefly moves us of a later generation, when we read the account of this battle, is the story of the fate of the beaten commander Benedeck, upon whom Emperor Francis had played so scurvy a trick. The battle was decided in favour of Prussia by the opportune intervention of the corps commanded by the crown prince. Keudell writes: "Bismarck was mounted on a huge chestnut. Wearing a grey cloak, his great eyes gleaming from beneath his steel helmet, he was a wonderful sight, and reminded me of the tales I had been told in childhood about giants from the frozen north." This mythological hero vanishes, and a man with human feelings appears, when Bismarck, riding amid the shattered corpses, says in low tones to Keudell: "It makes me feel sick at heart to think that Herbert may be lying like this some day."

Amid the bursting shells, he vainly implores the general to send the king out of the firing line. Roon answers that the king can ride whithersoever he pleases. "The generals were all a prey to the superstition that, as soldiers, they must not speak to the king about danger, and, since I was a major, since I was also an army officer, they sent me to him. . . . A squad of ten cuirassiers and fifteen horses was weltering in blood close at hand." He gallops up to the king, and says: "If Your Majesty were to be struck down here, all the joy of our victory would be lost! I urgently beg you to retire from the field!" The king slowly moves leftwards into a road which runs through a cutting, and is soon hidden from the enemy's guns by a line of hilltops. He is seventy years old, and it is more than fifty years since he has seen a battle. No doubt Bismarck is animated by mixed feelings when he induces the king to move out of danger. He probably thinks of the timidity of the late king, Frederick William; his mind will have turned to the man who will succeed if William falls; and no doubt he thinks of God, for, after the battle, he writes tranquilly and beautifully to his wife about the king: "I would rather he should be like this, than that he should be over-cautious."

When the enemy begins to yield ground, Bismarck rides up to Moltke and asks: "Do you know the length of the handkerchief of which we have grasped a corner?"

"Not exactly. At least three army corps. Perhaps it is the whole of the hostile army."

When the victory has been won, an aide-de-camp makes an observation which admirably summarises the whole of Bismarck's problem: "Your Excellency, you are a great man . . . now. If the crown prince had come too late, you would now be the greatest of rascals!" Bismarck does not take it amiss; he bursts out laughing.

X

"Il mondo casca!" exclaimed the State secretary in the Vatican when, next morning, the news reached Rome. Thenceforward, Prussia was the ally of the robber prince Victor Emmanuel, and, having with him gained a victory over His Apostolic Majesty, was in a state of mortal sin. In Prussia, on the day of the battle, and before the news has come, one hundred and forty conservative deputies are elected. Next day, Bismarck has a talk with the crown prince about the peace; the speech from the throne will be conciliatory. "For the rest, we shall establish a North German Union, as a step on the way towards German unity." The plan was clear in his mind, and he appealed to the heir to the throne for help in carrying it into execution. These two men who, working together in spite of themselves, had achieved a great deed, were deeply moved. The wonder of the hour brought them together; there was a tacit reconciliation; the prince accepted Bismarck's invitation to dinner, the first invitation of the kind Bismarck had given him for years.

Bismarck has now a chance of seeing what the common people are really like, those of whom he has known practically nothing since Schönhausen days. What does he make of them? "Our men are splendid." They are so courageous, quiet, obedient, orderly. They have empty stomachs, wet clothes, sleep on the damp ground (what little sleep they get): but they are friendly to every one, no plundering or burning; they pay for things as far as their money goes, and eat mouldy bread. The fear of God must be deeply rooted in the hearts of our common people, for otherwise these things could not be." Such are the words he writes to his wife. They are perfectly truthful, and inspired by direct observation. It is as if he were speaking of his peasants, a kindhearted gentleman who demands above everything obedience and self-sacrifice; who thinks that the virtues that astonish him can only be the outcome of the fear of God, can be explained in no other way among Prussians. He is honestly touched, but there is really no bridge between him and the common people. And yet, though he is prime minister, he asks no special consideration for himself. His sleeping accommodation the first night after Königgrätz is "a trifle better than a manure heap". It was in Horic. All around him are the wounded. At length some duke or other discovers the minister president, and takes him along to better quarters.

His relationships with the generals make him irritable. He finds it hard to bear that these men should issue orders while he has to keep silence. When, during one of these nights, some one wakes him to tell him that the king wants to ride out at four o'clock in the morning in order to see a skirmish, he calls furiously from his bed: "That must be the generals' unhappy excess of zeal! They want to arrange a rear-guard skirmish in order to show off to the king, and that is why I am to be robbed of the sleep which I need so much!" His struggle with the military arm begins with this comical prologue. Immediately after the victory, he writes to his wife: "If we are not excessive in our demands, and if we avoid believing that we have achieved the conquest of the world, we shall secure a peace which will have been worth the trouble. But we are just as easily exhilarated as depressed, and it is my thankless task to water the fermenting wine, and to remind people that we do not live alone in Europe, where there are three other powers which hate and envy us!"

While he is on the alert to hear what Europe is saying, the generals are rattling their sabres and marching on Vienna. There is a council of war in Czernahora. He arrives rather late. The king gives him the news. The heavy guns are expected in a fortnight. Then the army will make for Vienna. Bismarck trembles: "A fortnight!" He is only a major. His epaulettes do not shine brilliantly. There is no question of a red stripe. He sits looking at the map, and (while the generals listen to him sarcastically) advises that the bombardment of Vienna should be avoided. It will be better to go to Pressburg, and to cross the Danube there. Then the enemy would be in an unfavourable position fronting eastward, or else would withdraw into Hungary and would abandon Vienna without striking a blow. The king asks for the map, looks at it, and then backs up Bismarck's proposal. " The plan was accepted, though reluctantly. . . . My chief concern was to avoid anything that would impair our future relationships with Austria, anything that would give rise to mortifying memories. . . . The victorious entry of the Prussian army would, like any cession of anciently held dominions, have been a terrible blow to Austrian pride. . . . Already at that time I had no doubt that, like Frederick the Great, we should have to defend the acquisitions of this campaign in subsequent wars. . . . It was historically inevitable that a war with France should follow the war with Austria."

A few days later, at another council of war — this time in Brünn — the proposal to make the peace in Vienna is again pressed. Bismarck says quietly, in the king's presence: " If the enemy's army abandons Vienna and withdraws into Hungary, we must follow. If we once cross the Danube, our proper course will be to remain on the right bank, for on this mighty défilé one cannot march à cheval. But once we are across, we shall lose touch with the rear. Then the best thing would be to march on Constantinople, to found a new Byzantine empire, and leave Prussia to her fate!"

Seldom has the brilliant coldness of Bismarck's intelligence been plainer. He alone has invented, he alone has enforced, this war; but as soon as it has been won by a single battle, he refuses to continue it. Abruptly he cuts it short because on the horizon he sees another war, one that, willy nilly, he will be compelled to fight. Ten days after the battle, he has made up his mind. Peace with Austria without indemnities or annexations. What lures the generals towards Vienna is simply the urge of their hearts. If Major Bismarck finds a better way, it is not because he is a better strategist than the generals, but because he is a statesman and not a strategist. At the same time, he has to carry through his plan without displeasing the king, a man of soldierly instincts. In fact, William is not best pleased when his generals tell him how spiritless Major Bismarck is. Thereupon the statesman, left to his own resources, tries another means, and endeavours with the aid of sarcasms to strengthen the position which, at the previous council of war, he had won by an equivoque.

For the Frenchman is already pressing him hard. On the eve of Königgrätz, Vienna had offered Venetia to Emperor Napoleon if he would stay the Italian advance. The emperor, instead of intervening with the other powers, is negotiating single-handed; and at Prussia's Bohemian headquarters he offers to intermediate on behalf of peace. Bismarck draws a deep breath! Prompt acceptance; ask nothing from Austria; settle the German question through Goltz in Paris. He is prepared, so he says, "to swear a Hannibal oath to this Gaul." Benedetti, allowed to pass by maladroit sentries, suddenly appears, and stands by Bismarck's bed. A veritable spectre! Now begins an exchange of telegrams with Paris. Already the danger seems to have been overcome, for to outsoar the great powers is Bismarck's aim. Then a great power he had not thought of intervenes. The king of Prussia!

True, William had entered upon the campaign "only for defensive purposes." Now having tasted victory, and urged on by his generals, this prince of peace has developed an appetite for land. Although without Bismarck's pen no one would have drawn the sword, the king indignantly declares that the pen shall not destroy what the sword has won. Through Napoleon, as mediator, he demands Schleswig-Holstein, Prussia's leadership in Germany, a war indemnity, the abdication of the hostile rulers (including the king of Saxony), the annexation of all these territories. That is the arrow William shoots off towards Paris. But Bismarck shoots a second arrow drawn from his own quiver. The envoy is to report the impression which these demands arouse at Fontainebleau. "I am convinced that we can come to an agreement with the emperor if I can keep the terms reasonable, when they will be adequate for us."

Napoleon, hard pressed by his ministers, is "shaken, indeed quite broken." What is to be done? He has made a mistake. Austria and Saxony must be preserved. France rages against the establishment of a German empire. The essential thing, therefore, is to keep the south severed from the north, if only to outward seeming. At the same time, the tsar wants to take a hand in the game, and proposes a congress. This means that he, too, wants his pickings. The infection which the great physician had hoped to hold in check has begun to spread; annexation fever has seized all the cabinets of Europe. Meanwhile, infection of another kind has broken out in the Prussian army. Perhaps the cholera will decide the upshot of the great war which seems imminent.

Peace with Austria. Not to-morrow but to-day! The victory must not be again endangered by disputes about square miles and millions of money. "Anything that will hinder a speedy settlement, in the hope of securing minor advantages, will be done against my advice." Here is Benedetti once more. He begins to talk of the left bank of the Rhine. Instead of attacking him, the conqueror weaves spells. Instead of being iron, he is brilliant. "At the moment I cannot accept an official declaration, though we can discuss whatever you please. France is perfectly right. We must seek means for the realisation of this idea. Since victorious Prussia cannot cede territory, we must see whether anything can be done with the Rhenish Palatinate. The simplest thing will be for France to fix her eyes on Belgium." Benedetti, delighted, wires to Paris, advising concession. An agreement is reached. On July 27, 1866, there is a council of war in Nikolsburg Castle. Everything is ready. The only thing that remains is to win over the king.

"After considering all the circumstances, I had determined to make the acceptance of the peace offered by Austria a cabinet matter. The position was a difficult one. The generals were disinclined to stay their victorious progress, and in those days the king was continually exposed to the influence of his military advisers. He was more amenable to their counsel than to mine. . . . I was no better able than any one else to foresee how the future would shape itself, and what the judgment of the world would consequently be; but I was the only person present whose legal duty it was to have an opinion, to utter it, and to advocate it. . . . I knew that in the general staff I was spoken of as the

Questenberg in the camp, and this identification of me with the member of the imperial council of war in Wallenstein's camp was not flattering."

These were the most critical hours in Bismarck's life. Not the council of war, but the days which preceded it, the loneliness in which he had to form his decision, his sense of historical responsibility. It was then that for the first time, and really for the only time, he was completely independent. Four years later, in Versailles, so many other factors were at work that he could not decide solely on his own initiative. In the Austrian affair, however, he was alone; and, while his days were fully occupied with negotiations (for everything had to pass through his hands), he lay awake at night deliberating what it was best to do. If he were to give way to the king and the generals, he could safeguard himself by putting in a report, and, in case of need, by tendering his resignation, thus saving his reputation before the country and before posterity. But if he were to insist on getting his own way, he alone would be responsible for what was done, as if he had been an absolute monarch. He knew that in that case nothing but success could ensure forgiveness.

At this time Bismarck was ill, and was therefore unable to make imposing appearances in his blue uniform and wearing a sword. He had to keep his room, in mufti, and had to receive the king and the generals in the stuffy sick-room when they came to him fresh from a ride in the morning air. Still, he ventured to maintain his own opinion, and set forth all his reasons for it. The soldiers wanted to march forward; the king agreed with them; Bismarck was quite alone. "My nerves were not equal to the strain which had lasted for so many days and nights. I stood up in silence, went into my bedroom nearby, and there burst into tears. Meanwhile I heard the council of war dispersing in the next room."

The last time he had been so much affected had been seventeen years before, when speaking from the tribune. The last words on that occasion which he had uttered to the assembly had been these: "If it should really happen that a united Ger-

man fatherland should be attained along the new road, . . .
then the moment will have come when I shall be able to express
my thanks to the originator of the new order of things. . . .
As yet it is not possible. . . ." For seventeen years Bismarck
has been wrestling with this problem. Now he has looked at it
from close at hand, now from a distance. He has untied the
knots, retied them, untied them again; never aiming ideologically
at one single idea, nor even idealistically at one single thought;
always desperately labouring, with mockery and sarcasm, with
suggestion and logic, to undermine this stumbling block of an
Austria, the land where seven languages are spoken. To-day the
stumbling block has been rolled away, and the path is open.
Enough has been done with hatred, the destructive element; now
is the time for reconstruction to begin.

Once more his king stands in the way. Seventeen years before,
the king had forbidden him to conquer the revolution, against
which he had offered to lead his peasants from Schönhausen —
and had offered to use something far more powerful than this
symbolical troop: the forces of his determined will. The ruler of
those days had been a coward, had become insane, was dead and
gone. William had taken the place of his brother. He was neither
mad nor a coward, though he had not wanted to fight. Hardly
was the war he had so reluctantly entered upon brought to a
successful issue, when the king was seized with a lust for conquest, and did not wish to begin the work of construction. Bismarck sat there facing them, a sick and elderly civilian; and no
one, neither the king nor the generals, could recognize in him "the
originator of the new order" to whom they owed their thanks.
He did not break forth into passionate protest; he did not
threaten to resign. Silently he went away into solitude, away out
of sight and hearing of his opponents, and burst into tears, just
as he had done seventeen years before. Who is there in the castle
able to understand the dramatic force of the scene, one worthy
of classical tragedy.

But there is no time for any display of sentiment. The king,
nonplussed, rises to his feet, and his generals follow him out of

the room. Bismarck, in his bedroom, broken with sobs, listens to the sounds of their departure, and, with his fine diplomatic sense, he knows what it signifies. He pulls himself together and writes. Once more he elaborates the reasons which influence him, and appends to them a request to be allowed to resign if his wishes are not followed. Next day when, with this document in his hand, he goes to the king, he hears in the anteroom the latest reports of the spread of the cholera, foresees that it will be raging in Hungary that August, when water will be scarce and there will be a superfluity of over-ripe fruit, so that his political reasons are reenforced by military and hygienic considerations. Admitted to audience, he represents to the king that Austria, seriously damaged, will very soon join forces with France and even with Russia in order to seek revenge on Prussia; that the destruction of Austria will make a gap, and will open the way for fresh revolutionary developments. He shows that Prussia has no need of German Austria. "An amalgamation of German Austria with Prussia would not be a successful one. Vienna could not be governed as a dependency of Berlin. . . . We must settle matters quickly, before France has time to exercise further diplomatic influence upon Austria."

The king declares that these considerations are insufficient. He insists that Austria must cede Silesia, and that fragments of territory must be taken from the other German States. The minister parries all this, warns William against mutilating the countries named, and against the vengefulness of untrustworthy allies. But the king is an army officer and nothing more. The essential point is that he is loath to stop the victorious progress of the army. Since he can find no arguments against what Bismarck says, he squares his shoulders and exclaims:

"The main offender must not go unpunished! Those whom he has led astray may get off more easily."

Bismarck rejoins: "It is not our business to hold an assize. We are concerned with German policy. Austria's rivalry of Prussia is no more worthy of punishment than Prussia's rivalry of Austria. Our business is to establish German national unity under the leadership of the kings of Prussia, or to take the first steps toward this." These three sentences in their supra-national justice and their constructive insight have never been excelled by Bismarck, nor ever again formulated by him. He knows just as well as we know to-day what it means to bar eight million Germans out of a realm to which they have belonged for ten centuries. Is he also aware that thereby he is beginning to break up Austria — that Austria upon which, in days to come, he will depend too much? His most passionate desire, at any rate, is to heal the wound. He wants neither annexations nor indemnities. His only wish is to bring about a reasonable union among allied stocks; he renounces reliance upon artillery; he esteems prudence more than power. Here in Nikolsburg, and here only, does Bismarck draw near to the political thought of the twentieth century.

But the man facing him was born in the eighteenth century. William cannot understand Bismarck, and becomes so much excited "that continuance of my exposition was impossible, and I left the room believing he had rejected my plea." Bismarck's first thought is to join his regiment as a military officer, and thus, sword in hand, to continue the war which he regards as foolish. This will show, at least, that he has no lack of courage. When he is back in his room, he is "in a mood in which I was ready to wonder whether it would not be better to fall out of the window, which was four storeys from the ground; and I did not look round when I heard the door open, although I guessed that the person coming in must be the crown prince, whose room I had passed in the passage on the way to mine. I felt his hands on my shoulder and he said: 'You know that I was opposed to the war. You considered it necessary, and you are responsible for it. If you are now convinced that the aim has been achieved, and that peace must be made, I am ready to support you, and to back up your opinion in conversation with my father'."

Less than half an hour afterwards, Frederick comes back in the same tranquil mood, and says: "It has been a hard tussle, but my father has agreed." This espousing of his adversary's cause does honour to the crown prince, and also shows how de-

BISMARCK IN 1866

From a photograph by G. Linde, Putbus

pendent the king is upon his minister. For upon the margin of Bismarck's statement of reasons, William writes the following irate comment: "Since my minister president leaves me in the lurch in face of the enemy, and since here I am not in a position to replace him, I have discussed matters with my son. As he is of the same opinion as the minister president, I am, to my sorrow, compelled, after such brilliant victories won by my army, to bite into this sour apple, and to accept so shameful a peace."

It is like a comedy. The elderly gentleman would fain go on dancing, but his doctor forbids him to do so, and threatens to throw up the case. Since the old gentleman cannot find any other physician, he has no resource but to accept his son's advice. He nods to the orchestra and the music stops.

XI

In the train from Prague to Berlin, a week after the Nikolsburg crisis, a fresh struggle breaks out between the pair. The king has not been allowed to take vengeance on the enemy abroad; at least he will take vengeance on the enemy at home. All the extreme reactionaries whom Bismarck has been fighting for so long have now flocked to headquarters, declaring that the moment has come to overthrow the constitution, or at least to alter it. Now is the time to draw the teeth of the small number of liberals who have survived the recent elections. Conservative deputations wait on the king, and spur him on to action.

Bismarck sums up the matter thus: "All of those in Germany who are dissatisfied with the victory would, in that case, draw away from an absolutist Prussia; the new provinces would join the opposition; we should have waged a Prussian war of conquest, but Prussia's national policy would have been hamstrung." With such far-reaching considerations did Bismarck, on the homeward journey, try to persuade the king that now was the very time for emphasising the constitution, and for, in accordance with the English custom, going to the popular assembly to be indemnified after unconstitutional action.

Indemnification? Exculpation? Is he to ask for this after such a victory? Must not the king look upon his minister as a coward? "I cannot admit for a moment that I have done anything wrong!" he exclaims, becoming a moralist once more, and not seeing the joke. The minister patiently gets to work, in order to prove that this merely signifies "the recognition of the fact that the government and the king, rebus sic stantibus, have acted rightly. The demand is a demand for the recognition of this." That is a topsy-turvy statement but it is one the king can understand. Time presses. To-morrow a sentence to this effect must be incorporated in the speech from the throne. "The conversation lasted for hours, and was very exhausting to me because I had to speak so cautiously. There were three of us in the compartment, the king, the crown prince, and myself. . . . The crown prince did not support me, openly, although the mobile play of his features indicated that he was quite of my way of thinking, and this strengthened me in my attitude towards his father. . . . At length, the king gave way, though reluctantly."

There has been a change of fronts. Four weeks ago, the crown prince was Bismarck's enemy and the king's opponent. Now Frederick will not speak in so many words against the indemnification, because his father knows him to be a liberal; but he makes signs to the enemy of yesterday, and thus urges Bismarck to stand firm. Shortly afterwards, in the Landtag, the minister says: "We want peace. We shall solve the immediate tasks in cooperation with you. In this connection, I am far from excluding the fulfilment of the pledges made in the constitution." Now, for the first time in his life, Bismarck hears vigorous expressions of approval from all sides. In great curves of thought, he continues: "The immediate problems of policy are still unsolved. The brilliant successes of the army have merely, as it were, increased our stake. We have more to lose than we had before. . . . So much is certain, that hardly anywhere in Europe will you find a power glad to further the establishment of this new and generalised life for Germany. . . . Therefore, gentlemen, our business is to ensure the unity of the whole country, both in fact and in appearance. . . . I beg you to keep your eyes turned abroad, and not to forget how necessary it is that we should stand shoulder to shoulder, facing outwards." Metallic words! The indemnification is voted by a large majority. This means that the house renounces its right to impeach the government for the illegality of its actions.

Even some of the liberal leaders, Lasker and Vincke, for instance, vote for the indemnification. Bismarck has foreseen this, and has done his utmost to split the liberals. Those liberals who have supported him on this occasion constitute henceforward the National Liberal Party. But the radicals, at this juncture, have just as little sense of humour as the king. Waldeck: "We protest against a repudiation of that for which we have been fighting!" Virchow: "Let us be careful to avoid the idolisation of success!" Are politics, then, really nothing more than applied philosophy? Bismarck describes them as the art of the possible. If, in that art, nothing succeeds like success, then politics mean the idolisation of the principles that are destined to triumph. The guns of Königgrätz have done something more than solve the dispute between power and liberty in Bismarck's favour. Did not the idolisation of success begin at that moment when the aide-de-camp rode up to Bismarck and said: "If the crown prince had come too late, you would now be the greatest of rascals!"

Not until ten years later, when these struggles were already matters of history, did Bismarck admit in face of Virchow: "I have great respect for the resoluteness with which the popular assembly of those days did what it believed to be right. You could not then know what was the aim of this policy, nor was I certain of its upshot. . . . Even if I could have told you, you might have answered: 'We value constitutional right more than foreign policy.' I am, therefore, far from wishing to reproach any one — at all events now, although in the heat of the moment I may sometimes have been reproachful."

For the nonce, the wind changes in the Landtag too. Both in the house and at the court, all the conservatives wrathfully declare that he must annex more, for the peace is not yet signed.

Now, at the last moment in Germany, the king would like to snatch back what his minister had snatched from him in Austria. The very man who a year before in Schönbrunn had declared that he had no rights in Schleswig, the very man who three months before had prayerfully wrestled for God's approval of the war, has now been so much rejuvenated by his successes that he actually says to Roon: "This makes me want to begin a new war at once!" The chasm between the western and the eastern provinces must at length be filled in! We must "round off" our possessions by Hanover and Electoral Hesse. Since the Würtembergers have swallowed the little princedom of Hohenzollern, we must make a fragment of their northern territories Prussian. At all costs Ansbach and Bayreuth, which belonged to our ancestors, must be restored to our house!

Bismarck rejects half of this, though not in a spirit of opposition to the king. The Badenese come to the territorial mart in Berlin in order to prove that a great Bavaria can hinder the unification of Germany. The only thing, they say, to safeguard perpetual peace, will be to establish an equilibrium among the southern States — this meaning that Baden is to be enlarged by the gift of a part of Bavaria. As soon as the man from Baden has gone, a Hessian appears, demanding compensation with scraps of Bavarian territory for a portion of Hessian land that has been ceded. When this envoy complains that if Prussia were to ask for Homburg, Princess Charles would weep, Bismarck the royalist exclaims: "If here in Berlin we were to bother ourselves about the tears of princesses, we should get nothing at all!"

Bismarck is especially civil in his dealings with the southern States. He looks upon them as the loveliest beauties in his forthcoming harem, and caresses them in advance. He wants Bavaria for his own. "Sentiments and family claims are of little concern to me. Nor do I want to play the part of Nemesis; the king may leave that to his minister for public worship and instruction!" At first he demands money and land from the Bavarian minister. When he has sufficiently discouraged the Bavarian, he says: "You might have peace on very easy terms, without ceding any land at all."

"On what terms, then?"

"The immediate signing of an offensive and defensive alliance."
Thereupon, so Bismarck tells us, the Bavarian embraced him,
and began to weep. He had like successes with the other southern
States. Bismarck found his reward in these private conversations,
and in documents which only two or three people saw. When he
had locked them up in his safe, he knew the taste of happiness.

In the western sky, the weather looked threatening. No one
knew how soon the storm would burst. When, in August 1866,
Napoleon suddenly became incisive in his manner, and demanded
the frontier of 1814, Bismarck countered by changing his tone
towards Benedetti:

"If you insist upon this demand, we shall use any and every
means. We shall not merely appeal to the whole German nation,
but we shall make peace at any price, leaving South Germany
to Austria, and even accepting the Bundestag once more. Then,
joining forces, we shall march to the Rhine with eight hundred
thousand men and seize Alsace. Both our armies are mobilised;
yours is not. You had better weigh the consequences!" Thus does
he bluff the Frenchman. Yet so unstable is the equilibrium during these summer weeks of 1866 that Hohenlohe, the Bavarian
premier, believes that Bismarck proposes (inter alia) "to cede
part of the Bavarian Palatinate to Napoleon. The king is opposed to the idea. If he does not give way, there will be war between Prussia and France." Then France makes advances from
another direction, endeavouring to form an alliance with Prussia in order to mop up Belgium. Even Goltz is in favour of this.
In the beginning of September, he treats about the matter in
Berlin for a whole week. Bismarck tacks hither and thither. Perhaps he would have agreed to the proposal had he not had distressing premonitions with regard to the instability of the new
Napoleonic dynasty. In any case, he wants the proposals in
writing, and asks Benedetti to draft a treaty in which France
makes sure of Belgium for herself. At an extremely awkward
hour, he will take this document out of his safe.

Thus he holds the Frenchman in play until peace is signed at

Prague, and until the North German Confederation is founded. For beaten Austria, in the peace treaty, has to recognise, not only the annexation of three German principalities and the dissolution of the Germanic Federation, but also the formation of a new union northward of the Main; furthermore, Austria must agree " that the States southward of this line shall enter into a union whose national consolidation with the North German Confederation shall be left open to arrangements for an understanding between the two unions, and the southern union shall have an international existence."

That was the aim of the fighting statesman at Nikolsburg — not annexations or indemnities. "Austria is a foreign land," he had written twelve years earlier. Now Austria was to admit before all the world that she was foreign to Germany.

After the war, the king wants to reward his minister. Bismarck is already a count. What more is he to have? The rank of general and four hundred thousand talers. Just as "mobilisation" was used as a euphemism for "war", and "indemnification" as a euphemism for "exculpation", so this gift of money is dignified by the name of "dotation." The gift comes in very conveniently, though Bismarck cannot enjoy it at the moment, for he is on the verge of a breakdown. On the September day when the army reenters the capital amid the jubilation of the populace, Bismarck rides beside the king. William and his generals are sunburned and look younger than when they set out; but Bismarck, in his cuirassier's uniform, is pale and suffering, "as if he had risen too soon from a sick bed." He is aware of his own physical weakness, complains of feeling exhausted, and says: "The best thing would be for me to send in my resignation. I should do so in the consciousness that I have achieved a certain amount of good for my country, and that I should leave this impression behind me. I doubt whether I still have the power to do what remains to be done."

"Go and spend the winter in the Riviera, and you will pick up your strength there," advises Keudell.

"The women in Pomerania have a saying, when the hour of

childbirth is at hand: 'Now I must face my danger.' Next spring, the exalted mood of the people will probably have passed off. Unless I go right away for good, and hand over the affair to another, I must peg away at it myself. Nor do I know any one to recommend as my successor. I must put my own shoulder to the wheel once more, as soon as my nervous energy is restored. I shall just go and spend a few weeks on the Baltic coast."

Immediately after the entry into Berlin, he goes away; in Putbus he collapses in an inn, and some friends take him into their house. Johanna hastens to him. She finds him in a dull and melancholy condition, just as wretched as he had been at the time of the attack of phlebitis. She writes: "Politics makes him both melancholy and angry. But if he keeps quite still, gazing at the blue sky or the green fields, and fluttering the pages of a picture book, he gets on fairly well."

He has to lie about on a sofa, away from home, weeping or cursing if any mention is made of his affairs. At the very time when the nation is beginning to admire Bismarck as the man who had planned and won this victory, at the very time when all are ready to congratulate him, he has been put out of action by the hardships of the service, and is fit for nothing but to turn over the pages of illustrated books!

XII

One afternoon in September 1866 Bismarck, having returned home in better case, has dictated to Lothar Bucher, the friend of Lassalle, the new German constitution. Overnight, Bucher touches up the style. Next day it is to be discussed in the Privy Council, and, as soon as possible, to be laid before the plenipotentiaries. "The copies were only just off the press, some of them being brought in still damp, during the sitting." This constitution of the North German Confederation, which was little altered by the first Reichstag or subsequently in the year 1871, remained for fifty years, down to 1918, the constitution of the German realm. After a decade of deliberation, its creator had dictated it in five hours. In it were mirrored his thoughts of statecraft, and it may be called an image of his soul. It was Bismarck's constitution, and has nothing more to say about the Germans than that Bismarck, too, was a German — this meaning an individualist.

It was, therefore, a constitution for the strengthening of the monarchy, not of the people. It was the victory of that revolution from above which for four years he had been carrying on against the people, the revolution whose enemies he crushed for half a century to come. It may be true that the German people was not then ripe for self-government, but this did not decide the issue at that time any more than fifty years later. The only thing certain is that it was not such a conviction which guided Bismarck's decision. What moved him was his supreme contempt for the many and their leaders, his loathing for demos.

This loathing and contempt were not, in him, set off by any fondness or veneration for kingly power; at bottom he had no greater confidence in the wisdom of a crowned head than in that of an elected head. His self-esteem and his misanthropy led him, in all affairs of everyday life and in all affairs of State, to run counter to the decisions of the crowd. Since he had no capacity for working in harness, he always wanted sole responsibility; and since he had good reason for regarding his own intelligence as the best in the country, he believed that he knew better than any one else. These basic feelings of pride, hatred, and courage were the determining factors of Bismarck's wish for sole personal responsibility, and of his antagonism to joint decisions. These motives cooperated in bringing about his rejection of responsible parliamentary government, the modern form of rule which all the liberals were demanding for the new State. Inasmuch as he (with good reason at that time) could only contemplate the powers of State as incorporated in himself, this masterful man heaped upon himself all the responsibilities which another would have preferred not to shoulder. The master builder designed his castle as if he himself were to be the castellan for ever. Thus he resembled Lassalle, for Lassalle had imperilled the validity of his organisations in the same way, by an excessive accentuation of the personal element.

Bismarck's scheme set up the Bundesrat and the Reichstag as rival champions. In the Bundesrat "the sovereignty of the princes was to find uncontested expression." As in the old Germanic Federation, their envoys were to sit in the Bundesrat, headed by the federal chancellor, who represented "nothing more than the postman" of the Prussian minister for foreign affairs. By this device, Bismarck was able to ensure that the princes, who had been unwilling to subject themselves to the Frankfort emperor or to merge their supremacy in the Frankfort realm, should in their totality become sovereigns of the new realm—though this served only to veil Prussia's real supremacy. Legislative and executive powers were ostensibly given to the Bundesrat, but really remained in the hands of Prussia. Thus equipped, thus watertight and strongly armoured, the ship of State could proudly and without risk be launched into the parliamentary ocean.

The spirit of the time was opposed to his scheme. The new party of those who went over to their old opponent desired that in the new confederation there should not be two fronts as in Prussia, but a unity of people and government; that there should be ministers of the realm who should be responsible to the Reichstag. That idea, above all, was odious to him. "In such a scheme of government, no one will be responsible. If any mistake is made, one will receive a box on the ear from an invisible power. In this mysterious . . . collectivity there is a power like that of a Vehmgericht, which always keeps one dependent."

Thus Bismarck, wholly a fighter, a man who has hitherto reigned with absolute power, begins his experience of the parliamentary institutions that have been forced upon him. He is doubtless aware what struggles he will have to face, though he can hardly have an inkling of the frame of mind in which he will close that experience. For the system could only work (and even then it worked with difficulty) if a king who had not an unduly high opinion of his own intelligence were willing to allow him-

self to be guided by a statesman of supreme ability. If there
should be arrogant kings, and chancellors lacking independence,
under such a constitution the unified nation would vainly seek
for rights, and rulers and ruled would checkmate one another.
Bismarck foresaw all this, but he had to choose. Either he could
ensure his own power to-day, or he could ensure the impotence
of his successor to-morrow. He could not ensure both. Had he
loved the State, or even the crown, like Roon, he would, when
faced by this alternative, have chosen like a king who thinks
of his heir. But, being an official who could be dismissed at any
moment, it was necessary for him to safeguard his own power
(which he felt to be the best thing for the State) against the
caprice of the parties. He could not but regard the vacillations
of the king, despite all the vexations they might involve, as less
dangerous than the vacillations of a Reichstag.

It is true that attempts were made to resist him. That the
constitution might have the semblance of a modern State authority, a formula was incorporated to the effect: " The ordinances and dispositions of the federal presidency shall be issued
in the name of the confederation, and will only become valid when
signed by the federal chancellor, who thus assumes responsibility
for them." Responsibility before whom? The Reichstag? The
Bundesrat? The king? The supreme court of judicature? All
enquiries as to this matter were ignored by the Reichstag. Bismarck laughed, and in order to fill in the gap which might separate him, the master of Prussia, from any federal chancellor,
he decided to appoint himself chancellor in place of Savigny,
who was too good a man to be fobbed off with the position of
postman alias chancellor. The federal chancellor rolled into one
with the Prussian minister president — that was the expedient
whereby Bismarck turned his enemies' criticisms to his own advantage, for now all the official positions of the federal realm
were logically dependent upon the federal chancellor; all the officials became his officials.

Thus he stood forth as the only responsible person. To whom
responsible no one could say; presumably to God. It is true that

he also stood in the focus of all the rivalries which the Reichstag was to direct against him for the next twenty-three years. Why did the Reichstag accept the minister's scheme? If the house had wished, it could have rejected it! A majority of the members were prepared to vote in favour of their own salaries: only fifty-three votes were registered on behalf of parliamentary control, on behalf of popular government. Our party, the people's party, was like the General Union of German Workers in its clear demand for "the unification of Germany into a democratic form of State; no hereditary central authority; no Little Germany under Prussia; no Great Germany under Austria."

Inasmuch as this constitution was not imposed from above like the Prussian constitution, but was voted by the elected of the people, the "people" itself is historically responsible for its momentous consequences.

The Reichstag had actually been elected by universal and equal suffrage; and, indeed, by secret ballot, although Bismarck had objected to this on the amazing ground that it was opposed to the frankness and openness of the German character. Lassalle, through whose influence on Bismarck universal suffrage had first become a question of practical politics, was dead; he had lost the wager which the two men had tacitly entered into, for in fact Bismarck's hopes were centered in monarchical Prussia. The democrats saw it coming, but could not, without making themselves ridiculous, renounce the universal suffrage they had so long been fighting for. Bismarck said: "If universal suffrage does not make good, then we must do away with it"; and, despite the wishes of the majority, he ruled out the proposal to pay salaries to members of parliament, for he wished to favour the influence of property in the Reichstag. With contemptuous feelings, he watched the majority of his liberal enemies coming over to his side merely because Roon's and Moltke's armies had realised his policy. Only nineteen of the liberals voted against his constitution as "defective, as one which circumscribes and endangers the rights of the people." With the recalcitrant minority voted the only social democrat who represented Lassalle's ideas in this house. Constitutional, State, and popular rights, had receded into the background since the victory of blood and iron; old conservatives like Gerlach had taken a back seat now that German unity had been achieved without Austria.

The strongest party was the new National Liberal Party. Its twofold name was the expression of a compromise between two worlds. Lasker, Twesten, Forkenbeck, and Unruh, the members of the Prussian Landtag, and Bennigsen from Hanover, were its leaders; heavy industry and shipowners supplied it with funds; professors furnished it with formulas. Bismarck numbered the heads, yielded ground in a few formal matters, and was happy to see that the soul of the new realm was all-powerful in his Bundesrat. For, although he could command only seventeen out of forty-three votes, he had in it a presidency far more powerful than Habsburg had ever possessed in Germany. "The form," wrote Bismarck to Roon, "in which the king of Prussia holds sway over Germany has never seemed to me a matter of much importance; but to the substance of his power, to the actual fact that he should hold sway, I have devoted all the energies that God has given me."

King, chancellor, and army: these were the trio whose power Bismarck wished to enhance. In the new Reichstag the struggle began just where it had left off in the old Landtag: the right of the representative assembly to refuse money for the army. Now, indeed, that dispute became furious in the Landtag as well: "When a man has been fighting hard for five long years to achieve what now lies before you, when a man has given the best period of his life and has sacrificed his health in its behalf, . . . then gentlemen who know little about all these struggles behave here in such a way, . . . that I can only recommend them to read one of the first scenes of *King Henry IV.*, where we are told what Harry Percy felt like when a certain courtier came to him asking for some prisoners, and, when Hotspur was wounded and tired, bored him by a lengthy discourse about firearms and inward bruises." Then, when the right of voting supplies was demanded for the Reichstag, a right which, if conceded, would have meant that parliament had the power of deciding the strength of the army, Bismarck declaimed stormily from the tribune: "What would you say to a man who had been disabled at Königgrätz if he were to ask you what had been the result of this mighty combat? You would say to him: 'Oh, well, as far as the unity of Germany is concerned, that is not yet achieved, but will no doubt come by and by. . . . However, we have established the right of the Lower House to vote supplies, the right which year by year will endanger the existence of the Prussian army. . . . That was why we wrestled with the emperor of Austria outside the walls of Pressburg!'"

Sixteen years earlier, on the same tribune, had stood Deputy Von Bismarck-Schönhausen, protesting against the war with Austria which all the liberals were clamouring for because of the disgrace of Olmütz. Then Bismarck had shouted: "Will you have the courage, after such a war, . . . to turn to the man who has been crippled by a wound, to the father who has lost his children, and say to them: 'You have suffered greatly, but rejoice with us; for the Union constitution has been saved!'" Surely there must be in the assembly now some who heard what Bismarck said in those days, and who will remind the minister of his former words, saying: "Precisely what Radowitz wanted, a German union under Prussia, Austria being excluded, is what has been achieved after sixteen years, and Bismarck, who was then neither a count nor a State official, who in those days had unjustly made mock of 'the orator's voice pregnant with bravos, his mystical phraseology, and the brilliant mosaic of his verbose speech', can now, at bottom, find nothing better to do than to repeat Radowitz' speech?" For the war which he had opposed in former days, and this war which he has so recently brought about, had the same aim, a new German constitution; and to men who had been wounded at Königgrätz Bismarck's cabinet war would bring no better consolation than Radowitz' war would have offered to the wounded had that war ever taken place.

For, even now, German unity had not been achieved. It is true that the democrats of South Germany were striving in its be-

half, but every one of the German princes seemed hostile to the
idea of union. The only exception was the Badenese ruler, who
was King William's son-in-law. When Bismarck summoned the
South Germans to a customs union parliament, they were all up
in arms, considering that this "must be a preliminary stage to
the formation of a German realm"; and when the Bavarian envoy had to start a cheer on behalf of his king's Prussian rival,
he did it with a wry face. Prince Chlodwig Hohenlohe, the then
leader of Bavaria, who records this incident, is opposed to the
idea of Bavaria's entering the confederation; so are the Bavarian court and Bavarian society. Bavaria is Catholic, but the
protestantism of the north is not the only objection. Owing to
the "historical position of the house of Wittelsbach", Bavaria
wants nothing more than a German "federation of States" (not
a "federal State"), and would rather join with Austria than
with Prussia. After Königgrätz, Hohenlohe, writing with reference to the possibility of a war between Prussia and France, had
said: "In that case, Bavaria and Austria will fight on the side
of France." Even as late as the beginning of the year 1870,
Würtemberg would "rather become French than Prussian", but
here the opposite motives are at work. The Würtembergers would
like their army to become a militia after the Swiss model, so
that "it cannot be misused as a weapon for the massacre of the
peoples." At the same time the queen of Würtemberg, who is of
Russian birth, is intriguing against Prussia. But the sovereign
who gives the finest demonstration of his German sentiments is
the grand duke of Hesse. This worthy, in the autumn of 1868,
backed up by his minister Dalwigk, informs the governor of
Strasburg that now is the moment for France to attack Prussia. At the same time the grand duke offers the port of Hesse
lying westward of the Rhine, if Napoleon will give him appropriate compensation at Baden's expense.

Bismarck bides his time. The progress of events will decide.
States and men will be won over in due course. "Strategically
considered," he said to the Würtemberg minister as late as the
spring of 1870, "an alliance with the South will not strengthen

us; nor, politically speaking, have we any need for a union with the South. It is difficult to say which are Prussia's worst enemies, your particularists or your democrats. . . . For sound politicians, the first things that come are the necessary things; desirable things come afterwards. . . . When I have laid bait for deer, I don't shoot at the first doe that comes to sniff, but wait until the whole herd has gathered round."

XIII

For the last ten years, and especially during the last ten months, Bismarck's gaze has been directed towards France. Here is the only power able to step between him and his goal. The diplomatist's ambition was to unify Germany without having to conquer France, for there was nothing on which he prided himself so much as upon the art with which, during the last war, he had prevented France's intervention. It is true, that, since he was a man of violent disposition, war seemed to him "the natural state of mankind"; but, just as little as from his hostility to the common people he drew the practical conclusion that he should rule only with the aid of Junkers, just so little did his delight in dangerous sports and wild forests, in duels and manœuvres, make him at any time inclined to promote war as a means for improving the quality of the nation. There is not one among the ten thousand written or spoken sentences of his which have been quoted, in which he extols war because it steels youth. Never in his letters about war did he speak of the greatness of war, but only of its seriousness. Since, moreover, he had, in Bohemia, studied war with his own eyes, Bismarck had become adverse to war — all the more now that his sons were growing up. Again and again he insisted (not only to foreigners whom he wished to appease, but also to his own confidants) that the sight of the battlefields, and still more the sight of the hospitals, had made him more cautious.

An additional factor in this change of outlook was his growing consciousness of his own handiwork. The more widely his name became famous in Europe, the vaster the circle embraced by his cynicism, the less was he inclined to esteem the art of the military commander. "People are much stupider than I had imagined!" was his generalisation after the first few months of his premiership. Since he had never known fear — in this one point resembling Siegfried, and even more closely Hagen — he fearlessly placed war in his medicine chest, and determined to use this strongest of poisons if no other drug would serve his turn. What made Bismarck almost unique among the Germans was that he excelled both in intelligence and courage.

Since, furthermore, he had no interest to serve by conquests in France, it seemed far more attractive to him to defeat France himself in the diplomatic field, rather than to have the country vanquished by Moltke on the battlefield. Again and again, there were periods in which he believed that war could be avoided. In a retrospect addressed to the Landtag at the close of the year 1866, he said: "We have nothing to gain by a war with France, even though it should turn out well for us. Emperor Napoleon, differing in this from earlier French dynasts, has recognised in his wisdom that peace and mutual confidence are to the interest of both nations; that they are not called upon by nature to fight one another, but, as good neighbours, to walk along the path of progress side by side. . . . France cannot regard it as desirable that in Germany a preponderant power, . . . unified under Austria's leadership, should come into existence. An empire with seventy-five million inhabitants, an Austria extending up to the Rhine — even a France extending up to the Rhine — would not form a counterpoise to that. . . . Only in a Germany detached from Austria do the points of contact which are likely to lead to hostile relationships become less numerous. . . . I opine that France, if she judges her own interests shrewdly, would be equally unwilling to witness the disappearance of the Prussian and the disappearance of the Austrian power." Ten years before, conversing with Napoleon in the park at Fontainebleau, he had said: "You would sink in the mire."

For five years, Bismarck had been keeping Napoleon in play

with talk of Belgium. When he felt strong enough, he recommended the emperor to take Luxemburg as a Belgium of the third class, for the fact was that the land hunger of the Frenchman, who was becoming more and more anxious on account of Prussia's growth, concerned nothing but square miles — whether in Nice, Brussels, Treves, Landau, or Luxemburg, was a matter of indifference. What can give a better indication that Napoleon's claims were based mainly upon a desire for prestige, than this lack of fastidiousness on his part? He did not resolutely demand what France most needed, but vacillatingly tried to snatch what took his fancy at the moment. Bismarck was especially liberal in his offers of Belgium. Now, when the Germanic Federation had been dissolved, he could be equally liberal with the offer of Luxemburg, and hastened to declare that Prussia's right to occupy Luxemburg was extinct. It would have seemed to him the cheapest and most convenient way of satisfying France that the king of Holland, who (by inheritance and exchange) had for thirty years been sovereign lord of Luxemburg, should sell the little country to Napoleon for a few million francs. " Sign the deed of purchase quickly, and then let us know about it," that was what Bismarck had implied to Benedetti, wishing to confront the Reichstag with an accomplished fact.

At the first news of the scheme, a clamour was raised throughout Germany as great as that which had been made over the affair of Schleswig-Holstein. " A land that is essentially German must not fall into the clutches of our hereditary enemies." The general staff, too, wanted war, because France was not ready. Bismarck prevented the war. He warned his adversary by the publication of the offensive and defensive alliance with the southern States; and at the same time he played on the fears of the king of Holland, to whom he would never explain clearly what his own wishes were. Nor would Bismarck allow himself to be taken by surprise when a ready-witted Hungarian general suddenly turned the conversation to the prospects of war against France. " I can still recall how his eyes flashed when he realised that his secret thoughts were known to me. He retained his self-control in a way which I could not but admire, and said affably: 'I have absolutely no desire for a war with France'." Then he begged the Hungarian to ask Napoleon to recall Benedetti. "Besides, His Majesty knows my views about Belgium from the draft treaty which I have talked over with Benedetti. As far as Luxemburg is concerned, I will not ask whether the majority in that country is on the side of France, but will simply say: 'Take it!'" When the Hungarian related this in the Tuileries, the emperor said: "I can quite understand that he finds Benedetti a nuisance; he has made us too many promises. Furthermore, Bismarck is fond of offering us what does not belong to him."

Bismarck wishes to avoid war with France. In conversation with a deputy, he puts the matter in this way: "I cannot regard the war as absolutely inevitable, for I do not discern any serious interest, either for ourselves or for France, which can only be decided by force of arms. . . . No one is justified in beginning a war unless it be necessary for the honour of the country (not to be confounded with what is termed prestige), or for its most vital interests. No statesman has the right to begin a war merely because he personally believes war to be inevitable within a specified time. If ministers for foreign affairs had always had to follow their sovereign or their military commanders into the field, there would have been fewer wars recorded in history. I myself have been on the battlefield, and, which was much worse, in the military hospitals. I saw young men dying there. When I look out of these windows, I see many cripples making their way along the Wilhelmstrasse. Such a poor fellow, as he goes by, looks up at the Foreign Office and thinks: 'But for that man sitting up there who made the wicked war, I should have all my four limbs and be in the best of health.' I should never have an easy hour, if I had to reproach myself with involving the country in war on frivolous grounds, or from ambition, or in pursuit of glory for the nation."

His confidant Keudell records similar conversations; over the writing-table, or in the evening when work is done. These are truths; more deeply felt than the calculated utterances from the tribune. At such times, when there is no talk of God or king, we see into the depths of a human heart; we see how the calculations of a chess-player ruffle it and control it; and we may well fancy that, in a quiet and lonely room in an observatory, we are standing in front of a seismograph whose incorruptible pointer is recording the tremors of the inner earth.

The king of Holland was afraid of these subterranean convulsions, and disclosed the Frenchman's offers. The excitement in Germany grew. Every one was talking about the cession that was shortly to be made. On April 1st, Benedetti called on Bismarck in the morning, to offer birthday congratulations. The envoy wanted "to make an important communication", but Bismarck cut him short, saying:

"I have no time now to attend to business. I must go to the Reichstag to answer the interpellation concerning Luxemburg. If you will come with me, I will tell you the substance of my answer. I will not hear of the breaking off of negotiations, for that would mean a breach with France. If I am officially informed of the sale of the territory, I shall be compelled to announce it in the Reichstag. Well, here we are, and I must go in. Has Your Excellency a despatch to give me?" The augurs smile.

Within, Bennigsen is making himself a reputation by a sonorous patriotic speech. In order to display before France the power of the German national movement, he has been careful to proclaim that he stands shoulder to shoulder with Bismarck. He concludes as follows: "Is the Prussian government resolved, as the Reichstag unanimously wishes, to safeguard for all time, in conjunction with Prussia's federal allies, the union of the grand duchy of Luxemburg with the rest of Germany; and, in especial, to safeguard the Prussian right to occupy the fortress of Luxemburg?" This can be nothing more than a rhetorical question, for it is followed by an amazing announcement to all the parties. Bismarck rises to make one of his cleverest speeches. To-day he might become popular. Nothing would be easier. He need merely sound the note of national honour, and all would throng round him. This would have meant war. Instead, in face of the excited House, he dares to play the cautious man instead of the man of iron:

"Out of regard for the sensibilities of the French nation, and with due consideration for the peaceful and friendly relationships between the Prussian government and the government of a neighbouring great nation, . . . I leave unanswered the question which has been addressed to His Majesty's government." An astonished silence follows. "His Majesty's government has no reason to suppose that a decision as to the future destiny of the territory has yet been arrived at. Of course the government cannot certainly know that the opposite is true; cannot know whether such a decision, if not yet arrived at, may not be close at hand."

When, that evening, the king of Holland learns the tenor of this speech he revokes his promise to sign the contract for the sale of Luxemburg; Napoleon, a sick man, draws back in alarm; the cabinets of Europe hum like disturbed hives, cipher telegrams are freely exchanged, plans of invasion are drawn up. At length the tsar proposes a conference (his solution for all difficulties). This is held in London. Luxemburg is declared neutral territory, and is instructed to raze its fortresses to the ground. Futile attempts are made in Paris to describe what has happened as a Prussian retreat, and in Berlin as a French retreat. The mischief is done. Both parties remain in a bad temper. Three years hence they will fight out their quarrel.

From now onwards, Napoleon is Bismarck's enemy, without qualification. For the second time he feels that he has been duped. He begins to negotiate vigorously with Florence and Vienna. The three powers draw together in their joint dislike for Prussia. From 1867 to 1870, statesmen grow increasingly nervous, and general staffs redouble their preparations — as before the war of 1914. After the close of the conflict just described, the flames of artificial hatred spread from Paris across the frontier. I say "artificial", because the French nation as a whole has not been any less peaceful than the German. Only now does Bismarck give the watchword to the German press. The papers must be "much saucier, much more threatening and aggressive. . . . Revolver in pocket, finger on trigger, we must keep close watch on our suspect neighbour's hands; and he must learn that we shall have no hesitation in shooting instantly and with intent to kill, as soon as he spits across our frontier."

This sharpness of tone against France is new in Bismarck. Hitherto he has only spoken in such a way against Austria. The document quoted above is an instruction to his under-secretary of State, and beneath it is written: "You seem all to have gone to sleep!" We may infer from this that Bismarck had slept out and was in an angry mood.

From the time of these Luxemburg negotiations, he counts upon the coming of war. In the year 1868, he says to a visitor that Napoleon's uncertain situation will make war inevitable, and probably within about two years. At the same time, to another visitor, he discloses the fundamental motive which makes him glad that war will be inevitable: "A more extensive union of the majority of the Germans could only be attained by force — or else if a common danger should rouse them all to fury." Then he shifts his ground once more. In private conversation with his friend Keyserling, he describes the horrible impression the last war has left upon his mind. In a prophetical summary, he says: "After all, if Prussia were to gain the victory over France, what would be the result? Supposing we did win Alsace, we should have to maintain our conquest and to keep Strasburg perpetually occupied. This would be an impossible position, for in the end the French would find new allies — and then we might have a bad time!"

XIV

"When I threaten to resign office, the old gentleman begins to sob and to shed tears, and says: 'Now you, too, want to forsake me! What on earth shall I do?'" Thus, in conversation with Karl Schurz, a complete stranger to him, does Bismarck describe his relationship to the king. No doubt he has a motive. He wants the fact that he is indispensable to be widely known in the United States. He gains this end by sacrificing the royal dignity. To the Saxon minister, that it may be retailed in Saxony, Bismarck says:

"Despite his great sense of duty, my master lacks culture. His father was content to provide a satisfactory education for the eldest son alone. For this reason, King William has no opinion of his own in important matters; he is dependent upon the advice of others — advice which he seeks in various quarters." At the same period, Bennigsen, who then saw a good deal of him, wrote in a private letter that Bismarck despised all the ministers except Roon. "The king and he have more hatred than friendship for one another. His relationships with the heir to the throne are extremely cold."

The expression "hatred" is erroneous. He has grown used to the king; and, more difficult, has made the king accustomed to him. By forcing success on the king, he has tamed the only power which he has to tolerate over himself. Though at first he had been the horse carrying a royal rider, he has now become the rider. Speaking of the Seven Weeks' War, he says with good reason: "At that time I used the spurs vigorously, to compel the old race-horse to take the jumps and risk the hazards." The way Bismarck used to behave when the king was refractory is shown in tragi-comical fashion by the request for leave to resign with which, in the beginning of 1869, he extorted the dismissal of Usedom, whom he suspected as a possible successor — for the king was in close touch with Usedom as a freemason.

"My sole motive is the insufficiency of my powers and the inadequacy of my health for the performance of the sort of services required by Your Majesty. . . . The totality of the duties incumbent upon me can only be performed by the expenditure of all my energies, and only then if Your Majesty is willing to grant every alleviation which can be derived from the choice of my collaborators, in the fullest measure of your exalted confidence, and in the freedom of movement resulting therefrom." His discouragement "is increased by the circumstance that in personal questions Your Majesty's exalted personal benevolence towards every one of your servants in face of the strict needs of the service has a weight which is prejudicial to the interests of the one who has to make up for the inadequate performances of others. . . . The struggles I have had to undertake in my official life have entailed upon me the disfavour of highly placed persons and the dislike of influential persons. . . . Your Majesty will make due allowance for this weakness since it is the outcome (even though a morbid one) of love for Your Majesty's person. . . . I have not the feeling that a long life will be vouchsafed to me, and I am afraid that my constitution inclines towards an end like that of His Majesty of blessed memory. I have no right to expect that Your Majesty will in official matters make allowance for my physical infirmities."

This is a masterpiece! We learn from his account of the matter, that for several days before sending the letter he had practised, fruitlessly, a sort of "stay-in strike." Then he sent the letter, in which he catalogued all the king's offences. For personal reasons, he said, William was giving a preference to individuals who were interfering with his (Bismarck's) work, and were exposing him to general dislike. In this way he was losing his powers of body and mind, and would in the end be driven insane like the late king. There was only one thing which could relieve him: freedom of movement!

The good king is terrified: "How could you think for a moment that I would accede to your request? My greatest happiness is to live with you, and always to enter into a closer and closer understanding with you! How can you be so hypochondriacal that one difference of opinion can lead you to so extreme a step! . . . Your name stands higher in Prussian history than that of any other statesman. And I am to let this statesman leave my service? Never! Rest and prayer will settle all your difficulties. Your most faithful friend, W." The word friend is thrice underlined. Usedom is thrown overboard. The intensity of the king's feelings at having to dismiss his brother mason can be gauged by the fact that he makes good the difference between Usedom's official income and his pension out of the privy purse. Indeed, he is so much mortified, that in a second letter, which expounds the matter at issue, William ventures to say: "I am sure that even you will not expect me to close my ear to the voices of

those who, in important moments, turn confidently towards me."
When he goes on to ask whether he, who feels just as weary as
Bismarck, is not entitled to lay down his kingly office, Bismarck
writes in the margin: "No! But accept in good faith what one
cannot oneself see among thirty million, and believe what a minister officially assures you!" The king signs for the first time with
the handsome phrase: "Your eternally grateful King William."

Bismarck gets on tolerably well, now, with the crown prince.
The victory has softened both men's asperities. Frederick's liberal
confidant, Duncker, has been able to draft a constitution, even
though Bismarck has not accepted it; and the national liberals
are in the running for ministerial posts. But Princess Victoria,
who is more passionate and arrogant than her husband, seizes
the opportunity of dinner-table conversation to make an onslaught upon the minister — though "in a teasing and amiable
tone."

"It seems clear, Count Bismarck, that it is your ambition to
become king, or at least president of a republic!" Bismarck replies to this persiflage with perfect seriousness as follows:

"I should not make a good republican. In accordance with my
family traditions, I need a monarch for my earthly well-being; but,
praise be to God, I am not compelled, like a king, to live upon a
salver. It may be that my personal convictions will not be uni-
versally inherited. Not that I suppose that royalists will die out,
though perhaps kings may become extinct. If no king were forthcoming, the next generation might be republican." Three thoughts,
each of them a spear thrust, and the last of them a deadly one —
for he tells the lady that her husband lacks all the qualities proper
to a king.

If the number of such flashes of genius — characteristic of the
born diplomat — seems henceforward to increase, this is only because, henceforward, every one commits to paper what Bismarck has said to him. Karl Schurz, a revolutionist in the days
of 1848, a refugee who had made a career for himself in the United
States, had now, after the lapse of twenty years, come back to
Berlin as an American general, filled with all the prejudices

which, in his private capacity, he could not but cherish against this Junker. Though he was an unbending man, he was taken by storm when he met Bismarck. "His lively flow of speech, his flashing wit, his laughter (sometimes pleasantly contagious, sometimes bitterly sarcastic), his sudden transitions from cheerful humour to deep feeling, his delight in his own talent as an anecdotist, his impetuous tempo — and, behind all these, his forceful personality." Schurz is invited to late dinner next day. The other guests are tedious elderly lawyers. He is asked to stay when they leave. Now, becoming personally cordial, Bismarck questions him, asks him about America.

One of the premier's diplomatic tricks is the use he makes of his health. If he wishes to pass as a weakling, as uninfluential and uninterested, he gives himself out to be an invalid. At a review, he says within the hearing of dozens of people: "I feel wretchedly ill. I cannot eat, or drink, or laugh, or smoke, or work; my nerves are bankrupt. . . . There is no brain left behind this forehead of mine, nothing but a mass of jelly." In the company of royalists, he plays the loyal subject. To a professor of constitutional law, he says that if the Hohenzollern had used their power against the refractory nobles, "then my family belonged to that section of the nobility which would have fought beside them on the left bank of the Elbe in order to force obedience upon the nobles on the right bank of the Elbe" — although this was the precise opposite of the truth.

When a Stuttgart politician comes to see him, he poses as a democrat, and talks at table about the blessings of compulsory military service, saying: "I too was my mother's spoiled darling, and it did me a lot of good to have to shoulder a musket, and to sleep on straw from time to time. You would hardly believe what an effect it has when a peasant can say: 'I used to stand in the ranks beside Squire!' Besides, it is an excellent thing for the officers' corps. When there are so many cultured persons among the rank and file, the officer has to put his back into his work." Before this man from Würtemberg, he wants to put a democratic gloss upon compulsory military service, although in actual fact he had been anything but his mother's spoiled darling, and although he had detested service in the ranks, and had never slept upon straw except for his own amusement when out shooting.

"He believes," said Roon in those days, "that he can win over everybody by diplomatic dialectics and kindly shrewdness, thus leading every one by the nose. With the conservatives he talks conservatism, with the liberals he talks liberalism. In this way he either displays a sovereign contempt for all his associates, or else he is giving himself up to such incredible illusions as horrify me. He wishes à tout prix to be all things to all men, now and in the future. This is because he feels that the edifice he has begun to build will collapse amid the scornful laughter of the world as soon as his hand is withdrawn. He is not so far out, there; but does the end justify the means?" Such is the uneasy question of Bismarck's affectionate friend, a man of steel, to whom duty is a god. Roon shudders before the spirit he has conjured up.

Whilst Bismarck, by his personal variations, calculates the working of every sentence he utters (even in private), he is indifferent to fame, and remains so throughout life. He is indifferent to fame because he despises it; he calculates the effect of his words because this effect is important to his policy. Since he is free from vanity, he finds it nothing but a nuisance "to be stared at in every railway station as if I were a Japanese", or to have every one looking at him when he is in the Viennese Volksgarten "as if I were a new hippopotamus destined for the Zoo." He regards titles and orders as ridiculous. In his official letters, he does away with certain customary flourishes, not troubling to conceal his originality. On one occasion, when he is summoned to audience with two other ministers, he asks the aide-de-camp on arrival: "Have not the other two swindlers arrived yet?" At court balls, to begin with, he finds it amusing to dance, but ere long the king forbids the princesses to choose him as a partner, saying: "Already, people are only too much inclined to blame me for having appointed a frivolous-minded man as premier." On one occasion, the broad ribbon of his Red Eagle is continually slipping down. He allows a court official to fasten it properly for him. While constraining himself to patience as this is being done, he points to one of the princes, saying: "Orders are all right for gentlemen like that. I think that they are born with suckers on their skin, suckers which keep these things in their place."

When "Kladderadatsch" caricatures him as a hunter, he says to Hohenlohe wrathfully: "I don't mind their attacking my policy. That only makes me smile. But there is no joke about sport. It's a serious matter!" Though his wife is of a frugal disposition, he will not allow her to play the part of thrifty country-woman — at any rate when she is visiting a spa. He is prone to mock at the formalities of official life; yet wherever he goes (in parliament and at home, for he is seldom seen anywhere else), he displays the imperturbability of the born aristocrat. Only to his intimates, most of whom are relatives, and to his secretaries, does he display his nervous peculiarities so that such persons have a chance of telling posterity about them.

Already he has a European reputation. The diplomatists in Berlin speak of him as the great wizard and as Sarastro. Letters and memoirs penned in foreign capitals are filled with his name. Mérimée writes again and again that this or that will happen "unless Monsieur de Bismarck has decided otherwise." Zola gives a splended picture of him as a guest in the Tuileries: "When Saccard, the company promoter, strode through the hall in triumph, arm in arm with his mistress (whom he shared with the emperor) and followed by her husband — Count Bismarck, who, a sportive giant, was amusing himself with some of the guests, burst out laughing, and followed the unsavoury trio quizzically with his eyes."

At this date his reputation is more realistic than it becomes later. He is regarded as the great amoralist, as one whose mingled frankness and cunning are an amazement to connoisseurs. "He has tricked the French in a most extraordinary way," says Bennigsen of the Luxemburg imbroglio. "Diplomacy is one of the most mendacious affairs in the world, but when it is practised in the German interest, as by Bismarck, with such splendid powers of deception and with such stupendous energy, we find it impossible to withhold our admiration." Without giving him the lineaments of a hero, the diplomatists of that epoch talked to one another, and wrote to one another, freely, about his coups. Beust, for instance, declared: "'The last thing we are thinking of is of acquiring German Austria for the German realm,' said Bismarck in Gastein. 'We should be more likely to think of Holland.' A few months later the Dutch envoy, who was transferred from Berlin to London, told me that Bismarck had assured him no one had any thoughts of Holland, and that the German-speaking province of Austria was more likely."

The truth was that Bismarck never wanted either the one or the other. What he wanted was to keep his neighbours and opponents uneasy, and thus to make them afraid. This had already been his way in his student days. It is likely enough that he made both the observations above recorded with the deliberate aim of having them passed on, as they actually were. No matter who might be present, he never hesitated to use the strongest invectives in his vocabulary. He was particularly fond of speaking of his adversaries as miscreants. When he was in the best of humours, he would say of one or another — and this was quite a friendly opinion — "he is a stupid idiot!" The freedoms he now allows himself in these matters are the necessary outcome of his pride and misanthropy, and they are a delight to him. Perhaps the feeling that he can say what he pleases about any one, even the king, gives Bismarck the most agreeable moments of his life.

Hostile but noteworthy was Gustav Freytag's opinion: "Bismarck is only possible in an epoch which is passing out of the night into the clear light of day. . . . Between the romanticists and the æsthetics comes a narrow cultural stratum of tourist dilettantes, Junkerdom in its elegant types. . . . Bismarck seems to me . . . a belated survivor from this vegetative period. His most noteworthy characteristic is a lack of veneration, a tendency to judge everything capriciously and by personal standards, together with the first beginnings of a fresh and impudent vital energy. That is why this man will not be the founder of a school; his faults are not especially the faults of our time. . . . The present king will not get quit of him unless Bismarck wishes it; to sulk on the quiet will be of no help. . . . A man less certain of himself, a more wayward man, one of less distinguished social antecedents thus rising to the top, would have been able by recklessness and by truly sublime qualities to identify himself with the glory and greatness of Prussia in such a way that any one who struck at him would simultaneously strike the State."

So anomalous did he then seem to all the world! Though many would have agreed that he possessed the sublime qualities of which Freytag spoke, and that they were useful to the country, still on the whole, at this epoch (which followed one and preceded another of his great partisan struggles), he was estranged from all the parties and all the classes — especially from his own party and his own class. It was inevitable that his public appearances, namely his speeches (from which alone the nation formed a picture of him), should produce estrangement. "I want what you want, but I want it in a different way," was, more or less, what he ventured to say in the new Reichstag. "If I should cease to react against your opposition in one way or another, you would draw the conclusion that I was indifferent about the matter. I think you ought to be pleased that I never display such indifference." (Sensation.) Again, when he is urged to accept Baden as a member of the North German Confederation: "Do not press forward so eagerly, gentlemen, towards farther stages. Be content, for the moment, to enjoy what you have got, and do not covet what you have not got. . . . I may be mistaken, and you may be mistaken. All I can tell you is that I differ from you, and shall act in accordance with my own views of the situation."

One who treats the representatives of the people in this fashion will play the autocrat among his colleagues. Since he regards the North German Confederation as his own handiwork, he claims the right, literally, to rule it, and Prussia at the same time. Already in those days his most intimate friends were inclined to complain about "Otto's dictatorial ways, which have become quite intolerable since Roon's retirement, so that he will no longer bear the slightest contradiction." Roon, whose retirement was temporary, writes of Bismarck: "In the sittings, he is too uppish, almost monopolises the conversation, and seems to be entangled in the old error, the belief that by intellectual alertness . . . he can overcome all the difficulties of the situation. . . . Politically, I belong to the conservative opposition, because I am not content to have my eyes bound and to be led against my will, the Lord knows whither. Now, as before, Bismarck neglects his most faithful and devoted friends, and does not hesitate to be rude to them." Thiele, under-secretary of State, writes: "The chief is as opinionated as usual, always grumbling, sometimes intervening in matters of little moment where he is not fully informed, and sometimes obstinately refusing any interference in matters of importance. Never mind! If his health is satisfactorily restored, we can confidently ask: 'What price Europe?'"

Since they all dread the tyrant, no one ventures to make even the most trifling decision. This drives him to fury. "You would hardly believe," writes Johanna from the country to Keudell (and we are listening to her husband's voice), "how indignant Bismarck is because of the babyish anxiety which prevents the folk in Berlin from accepting any responsibility, and which makes them refer every trifle to him for approval or decision. . . . You know the great helmsman of our State very well; you know what distresses and annoys him." If, when he is absent, everything does not go exactly as he wishes, he writes: "I regret that my representations in the second section have had so little effect. It seems to me that I very seldom trouble these gentlemen, and to compel an invalid to return to such a matter three times over really verges on contempt."

While he thus develops into a soloist, and plays a star part, the chorus grows mute. No one is eager to associate with this most powerful and most interesting of the Germans. Even before the new German realm is ready, intellectual Germany withdraws from it almost involuntarily, without programme or definite intention to oppose. Never, in letters or in conversations, do we find distinguished intellectuals mentioned as Bismarck's guests. If some of the documents are placed at Treitschke's disposal, if a new novel by Spielhagen is mentioned, or if Fritz Reuter is thanked for his books — this exhausts the list for years. Even Eckart, a shrewd observer, visiting the house for the first time, finds that the only guests there are Junkers, who address Bismarck as "thou", though elsewhere they are often his opponents. Eckart enquires: "How are we to explain that such men as these form the intimates, the customary associates, of this first of Germans, what time the intellectual leaders of the nation are strangers to the house, or only come there on rare occasions?"

The only people to whose conversation Bismarck refers with pleasure in these days are Jews. He speaks of Lassalle as one of the most brilliant of men, as one from whom he is loath to part even when they have been talking far on into the night. Bleichröder, whom he employs as confidential agent, always has the entry; receives a power of attorney for the administration of Bismarck's property, and, at the premier's instigation, is raised into the ranks of the hereditary nobility. For years a certain Doctor Cohen acts as both friend and physician, the relationship continuing till Cohen's death. Thus Bismarck entrusts both his health and his property to Jews. "My intercourse with Simson is a real pleasure to me. . . . He is a man of genuine talent. When he came to visit me he was most entertaining — a thing I cannot say of the majority of my visitors. He is filled with genuine patriotism; is a noble vessel into which the most sublime sentiments have been poured." That characterisation cannot be paralleled among all those penned by Bismarck. Yet, twenty years earlier, as secretary in the Erfurt parliament, he had made fun of this same Simson. "My father would turn in his grave if he saw me here, acting as clerk to a Jewish professor." In a dispute, Simson had actually called the minister a rope-dancer. Bismarck had certainly not forgotten these things. At a later date, he was full of praise for Disraeli. We cannot but ask why it was that he should make so much of Bleichröder instead of Hansemann; of Cohen instead of Frerichs; of Lassalle instead of Liebknecht; of Simson instead of Richter; of Disraeli instead of Salisbury.

By this date, Bismarck had long since discarded anti-Semitism,

together with the other reactionary prejudices of his youth. Even
in the strictest privacy, he never appears to have given vent to
any more expressions of antagonism to the Jews, although we
can hardly doubt that — reason notwithstanding — the traditional prejudices of his class in this matter must have, to some
extent, persisted to the last. Twenty years after his speech
against the admission of Jews to positions in the State service, it
was he who carried through a law for the emancipation of the
Jews, insisting that since Prussia had no State religion, the government could not take sides in such matters. In the Reichstag he
extolled the Jews on account of their "especial capacity and
intelligence for affairs of State"; in private he spoke of respect
for parents, conjugal fidelity, and benevolence as their crowning
virtues. He advocated marriages between the nobility and the
Jews; and he referred to the Lynars, the Stirums, the Kus-
serows, and other houses, in which Jewish alliances "have led to
the birth of extremely sensible, excellent persons. . . . Con-
versely, it is better still when a Christian stallion of German stock
enters into a union with a Jewish mare. Money must be freely
circulated, and there is no such thing as a bad race. I do not
know what I might advise my own sons to do in this matter." In
old age, he summarised the social and biological value of the
Jews in the following epigram: "The mingling of Jewish blood
with the various German stocks introduces a certain sparkle
whose value must not be underestimated."

At bottom, he is cold towards all: Christians and Jews; ministers and party leaders; the princes of his own nation and the
princes of foreign nations. Even among his old comrades, almost
the only one towards whom he retains a certain amount of cordiality is Roon. Touching, though somewhat comic, is the way
in which, during the year 1869, these two friends seize one
another by the collar, each dragging the other back into office
on the manifestation of any sign of a wish to escape. When Roon,
with characteristic seriousness, takes the prime minister's
above-quoted tender of resignation at its face value, he writes:
"Since I left you yesterday evening, my honoured friend, I have

been incessantly thinking about you and your decision. It leaves me no rest. Do compose your letter in such a way as to leave a loophole. . . . You should bear in mind that the letter you received yesterday from the king has the stamp of genuineness. . . . Make due allowance for the fact that anything in it which may not ring true is only the copper of false shame, which will not make any admission, and perhaps, in view of the writer's position, cannot do so — will not admit wrong-doing and determination to improve. You really must not burn your boats. . . . If you do so, you would ruin your position before the country, and Europe would laugh. . . . People would say that you had resigned because you despaired of being able to complete your work. I need not labour the point. Enough to sign myself your unchanging and devoted friend. . . ."

How striking is the nobility with which he finds excuses for the king, while in no way defending the royal master's conduct! How accurate is his insight, historically speaking! How impressive is his reserve! When, a few months later, Roon himself, mortified by Bismarck's opposition in a naval question, wants to resign — quite in earnest, and without arrière pensée — Bismarck writes to him warningly from Varzin: "When, in September 1862, I unhesitatingly shook hands with you on our bargain, I certainly had thoughts of Kniephof, but none of the possibility that, after seven glorious years of campaigning together, we should have a serious difference of opinion about a naval question. . . . You should read the watchword of August 14th with a secular interpretation. . . . Above all it seems to me that this question is not so important as to justify you in giving the king (now in his seventy-third year) the go-by under the eyes of God and the fatherland, or in throwing a shadow upon your colleagues, myself included, by your resignation." Here every word is calculated for its influence upon the recipient's sense of duty and upon his piety. Quite egoistically, and in a typically Bismarckian vein; the responsibility from first to last is thrown upon the shoulders of the man who had years ago summoned Bismarck from a quiet life into an active one, and whose resignation will now prove injurious to the writer.

Forty-eight hours later, and the man who so recently was laying all possible stress upon the importance of duty and self-control, the man who wrote like a parson, sits down at the same table and pens the following furious epistle to the same correspondent: "No one has any right to ask me to sacrifice my health, my life, and even my reputation for honesty and soundness of judgment, to a caprice. I have not slept for thirty-six hours; I have been vomiting bile all night; and my head is burning like fire, though it is wrapped up in cold compresses. All this is enough to drive me crazy! You must forgive my being so much moved, but the document bears your signature, . . . and yet . . . I cannot believe that you have . . . really probed the matter thoroughly. If the cart on which we are driving is to have a smash, at any rate I want people to know that I have no share in the responsibility. . . . Perhaps we are both too hot-tempered to be able to row the boat together any longer. A man would need to have heart and conscience as tough as parchment to enable him to bear it!" What had happened? Had the king arranged a foreign alliance after talking the matter over with the ministers in Berlin, or had he announced his intention to enter into such an alliance? Had the Reichstag been dissolved, had a proposal of Bismarck's been withdrawn, had a minister been dismissed?

The premier had recommended that a postal official from Hanover should be appointed director general of the post office, and the cabinet had refused to accept the recommendation.

XV

"When I have breakfasted and read the newspaper, I wander through the forests in my hunting boots, climbing hills and wading through the marshes, learning geography and planning nurseries. As soon as I get home, I have my horse saddled and . . . go on with the same work. . . . There is very thick undergrowth here, also a great deal of felled timber, waste land, nurseries, streams, moorland, heath, gorse, roe-deer, woodcock, impenetrable thickets of beech and oak, and other things in which I delight, when I am listening to the trio of pigeon, heron, and kite, or to the tenants' complaints of the depredations of the wild sows. How can I give you any idea of all this?"

He writes from Varzin, not far from Reinfeld. When Bismarck rambles over the estate at his first visit, he feels that he has been amply rewarded by the nation for all his struggles and victories. The only strange thing is that he took the money with which he bought these forests. "It ought not to have been given in money," he declared a few years later. "For a long time I found it very difficult to accept, though at length I yielded to the temptation. What made matters worse was that it did not come to me from the king but from the Landtag. I did not wish to take money from persons with whom I had been quarrelling fiercely for so many years." The liberals had at that time proposed that no donations should be given to the ministers Roon and Bismarck who, they said, had had enough done for them by the indemnification. That Bismarck should, none the less, accept the money was an indication that, with advancing years, he had a growing taste for wealth and family estates — though as regards his private concerns he was never a good man at business. At any rate, he lacked time and the requisite concentration for the increase of his private means by judicious investment.

The wish for money was in conflict with his pride. When, at the beginning of the struggle, the Landtag had decided that the private property of ministers of State should be liable to attachment in order to secure a refund of unconstitutional expenditure, Bismarck had considered the desirability of making over his estates to his brother. "Such a cession to my brother, in order to escape a confiscation which was not absolutely impossible in the event of a new accession to the throne, would have given an impression of anxiety and pecuniary embarrassments which I was reluctant to produce. Furthermore, my seat in the Upper House was dependent upon the ownership of Kniephof." Despite his objections to this cession, he certainly wanted to carry it through, although the loss of his seat in the Upper House would have made the affair public and would have aroused caustic comment. At this time he actually offered the estate to his brother, and gave the following remarkable reason: "I find it hard to abandon the thought of spending my old age there. I am, however, superstitious, and certain considerations move me to sell. . . . My pecuniary circumstances, or those of my children, are such that I cannot ask you very much less than I should ask from a stranger." Enigmatic motives! This much is certain, that the sale was not then effected.

Now, four years later, when the Landtag has lavished money upon him for the very deeds which have previously been regarded as misdeeds, and when he has become rich, he hastens, none the less, to rid himself of this same Kniephof. Yet he had spent all his youth there, from the age of two to the age of twenty-eight. When he first let the place, long before, did he not feel extremely rueful about it? Even now, when he rides over from Varzin, "they never leave me alone, though I have much more to say to the trees there than to the human beings." Right on into old age, this home of his childhood will be paradise for him. All the same, he promptly writes to his brother from Varzin, saying that he wishes to sell Kniephof at once; "preferably to Philipp or to you, but not much cheaper than the market price." He says nothing more about his superstitions, nor anything more about his close attachment to the land and to the house, such as had characterised him both at Schönhausen and at Kniephof.

True, he delights in the forests at Varzin; but they will never mean as much to him as the others. Nor can the house at Varzin compare with the great mansion of Schönhausen. "Its outward aspect is that of a hospital. That is to say, it has two long wings. In general, it is commonplace, with a great many windows, and no look either of a castle or of a Roman villa." Such is Keyserling's description of the place when he is staying there. Since the forests do not bring in any income, it is necessary to install steam sawmills and a paper factory. "These will cost a hundred thousand talers, but day by day every fir tree can be transformed into a great number of sheets of paper." How practical has the man who was once an enthusiast for nature now become; a political economist, a paterfamilias!

Since he cannot rest and must always be at work, at the very first visit he sets his hand to livening up both the forests and the house of Varzin. "Send over from Schönhausen the red glasses, the carved chairs, one or two bureaus that can be locked up, and whatever beds remain. . . . The tables can be brought here from Berlin, and instead of them you can put in my study the roll-top desk which is in the anteroom. Why should we furnish His Majesty's rooms? . . . Now I am going out for a drive, to see the forest, the roe-deer, and the sunshine. . . . I cannot write much. Ink gets on my nerves. . . . Come here soon, and let the young folk follow you. I suppose there are beds to be had in Köslin. Don't bring any maids with you except your own girl. Perhaps you won't want even her, for there is a young laundrymaid here who has worked in the laundry at Bumenthal for three years. . . . You need not, therefore, bring either the cook or the maidservant, unless you yourself want them. Send some thick, dark-green stuff for window curtains and for covering the inner sides of glass doors, so that we can have a little privacy. I do not think it likely that I shall be in Berlin again before you come here. Tell people that I am pretty bad, though improving, but that I do not want to undertake a journey, thanks to which I might lose what I have gained. Come soon."

We see Bismarck at his happiest. He has got away from business. He is expecting his wife, has no guests, no telegrams, only gamekeepers and foresters; horses; accounts fairly satisfactory. In such circumstances he finds life pleasing enough, maybe for a whole week. Then the lust for affairs seizes him once more; or, if this fails to awaken, the lure of habit gets to work, and he wants once more to act and to command. Even in his country retirement, he is not free from the will-to-power. His words, when he points to a neighbour's estate, are profoundly symbolical: "Every evening I am overwhelmed with the longing to annex that piece of land; next morning I can look at it quite calmly again." Bismarck's passion and his moderation, all the rhythm of his policy, are incorporated in that one sentence.

Here in the country, he is more struck than ever with the

stupidity of his guests. Of course, if he wished, he could summon the best intelligences in Germany. But unless a minister of State, a secretary, or a party leader comes to see him, he sits "among a dozen relatives, three of whom are deaf, so that the others shout to make them hear. There is always a chorus of voices. Nevertheless," says the writer, "he was so extraordinarily amiable to them all that they were delighted, and did not leave for home until half past ten." Sometimes Keyserling comes. Then "we sit together upon the camp bed, . . . and, amid cheerful converse, we listen to the music made for us by Herr von Keudell."

Bismarck is so often overwrought that he confesses to Keudell how he finds even Keyserling, the friend of his youth, fatiguing, and he looks forward to his guest's departure.

Now, and always, his favourite is Motley. The way in which Bismarck has given the love of his heart to this cheerful and plain-spoken American, to this man who is in every respect shrewd and highly cultured, is an indication of his yearning to appease his own inborn unrest by the contemplation of one whose nature is more harmonious. Neither the king nor Johanna can serve his turn here, although to both of these he has allotted special places in his esteem, exempting them from the contempt he feels for almost every one else in the world. But both the king and Johanna lack freshness, stimulating personality, initiative. His wife is too tender and inexperienced. William is old and thick-headed. Comparatively tranquil though they are by nature, they cannot bring him tranquillity. Motley is the essence of tranquillity; is manly and content with the world; is natural and yet distinguished; is devoted to Bismarck yet makes no claims upon him. Above all, Motley is more independent than any one else he knows. In the medley of malicious and stupid folk, Motley is a man upon whom he can build; he is Bismarck's friend. To no one else does Bismarck write in such terms as to Motley decade after decade. Bismarck, whose way it is to let people wait for an answer, even his nearest and dearest, writes again and again to Motley in the following strain — usually in German, but sometimes (as here) in English:

"Jack, my Dear,—Where the devil are you, and what do you do that you never write a line to me? I am working from morn to night like a nigger, and you have nothing to do at all—you might as well tip me a line as well as looking on your feet tilted against the wall of God knows what a dreary colour. I cannot entertain a regular correspondence; it happens to me that during five days I do not find a quarter of an hour for a walk; but you, lazy old chap, what keeps you from thinking of your old friends? When just going to bed in this moment my eye met with yours on your portrait, and I curtailed the sweet restorer, sleep, in order to remind you of Auld Lang Syne. Why do you never come to Berlin? It is not a quarter of an American's holiday journey from Vienna, and my wife and I should be so happy to see you once more in this sullen life. When can you come, and when will you? I swear that I will make out the time to look with you on old Logier's quarters, and drink a bottle with you at Gerolt's, where they once would not allow you to put your slender legs upon a chair. Let politics be hanged and come and see me. I promise that the Union Jack shall wave over our house, and conversation and the best old hock shall pour damnation upon the rebels. Do not forget old friends, neither their wives, as mine wishes nearly as ardently as myself to see you, or at least to see as quickly as possible a word of your handwriting. Be a good fellow and come or write. Your, V. Bismarck. Haunted by the old song, 'In good old Colony Times.'"

When his friend has been appointed United States ambassador in London, and is therefore close at hand, Bismarck writes to him from Varzin: "You ought to give us the pleasure of transporting your wigwam to the Pomeranian forests. For an ocean traveller such as you are, this means no more than the journey in old days from Berlin to Göttingen. You will give your wife your arm, get into a cab with her, be at the station in twenty minutes, in Berlin thirty hours later, and from there only half a day's journey more. . . . It would be splendid. My wife, my daughter, I myself, and the boys, would be crazy with delight; we should all be

as merry together as in the old days. . . . I am so taken with the
idea, that I shall be positively ill if you refuse, and that would
have a very bad effect on the political situation. Your affectionate
friend."

To Motley he has given the real love of his heart. His affection
for wife and children is tinged with the jealousy of the owner,
whereas he loves this American without reason or purpose. The
intimate friendship between the two had begun when Bismarck
was only seventeen, and his fondness for the American persisted
unchanged for two generations. Obviously, Motley must have
signified for him the satisfaction of an elemental longing, just
as Zelter did for Goethe. He was, among men, that which among
women no one but Malwine seemed to Bismarck — the harmonious
human being, who is intelligent as well; the cheerful person, who
is at the same time experienced and serious-minded. It was not a
chance matter that this archetypal German should have found his
chief friend among the offspring of a younger world.

Johanna is ailing. In the period of conflict, her dread of attempts on her husband's life has robbed her of rest. He often
speaks of her as "sleepless, suffering from palpitation, depressed." He sends her by herself to one spa after another, being
nervous all the time about her and himself. By the time she is
forty, she signs herself, writing to her children, "your old
mother." When the young folk grow up, so that they have done
with the frequent maladies of childhood, she takes to mothering
her husband. Her sole concern during the latter half of her life
is to care for his health, to mitigate his troubles, to tend him
and protect him. She gives up everything, her wishes, her hobbies,
her own opinions; never ventures to advise him; does not even
risk writing to him at Königgrätz about a wish she cherishes, but
enquiries indirectly through her friend Keudell whether she cannot come to Vienna and take part in the "entry" into that town.
Keudell does not think it wise to pass on Johanna's enquiry to
the formidable chief. Thus does she obliterate herself through
love. Once, when Bismarck and Johanna are out for an excursion
in Keyserling's company, and Bismarck asks her whether she

would like to drive farther or to turn back, she answers: "Do as seems best to you; I have no other will than yours." When he is out of sorts at Varzin, she remains "continually with him day and night, except for the brief intervals of breakfast and dinner; quiet, reading or working, or doing something for him. Every word spoken is a distress to him, and I am half dead with anxiety."

The children, too, are passive. They venture nothing; he asks nothing. When he complains that Marie ought at least to write, he soon gives way when he is told that she, a girl of sixteen, finds it so difficult. Bitter memories of his own youth haunt his mind and lead him to spoil his children. The rancour of this most successful of men, his enduring mistrust of the world, is disclosed when he says to Keyserling that he does not propose to have his sons educated for the State service, "for they would, in the end, be badly provided for, and have to bear their cross in the world." At Nikolsburg, when he knows the whole of Germany is expectant, he writes to his younger son on the lad's birthday, a letter which begins with political news. Soon he becomes aware of the dilemma in which he is placed by occupying the joint positions of states-man and educator, for, he says, "in politics one must, if one has many opponents, first rid oneself of the stronger by knock-out blows, and then skin the weaker — which in private life would be regarded as a mean kind of behaviour." What he wants for his sons is health and energy. If he ever praises them, it is for physi-cal prowess. A young guest is "astonished to see the size of the helpings consumed by Bismarck and the children; the lion with his cubs!"

His own health is wholly dependent upon his nerves, and these in turn are dependent upon the progress of affairs. His remedies are as violent as his life. Just as he would never carry an umbrella or wear galoshes, and just as he always drove in an open car-riage, so, when ill, he had no use for doctors, and was his own physician. "His illness will prove incurable," writes Blancken-burg from Varzin, "if he continues to live as unhealthy a life as before. He gets up very late, and then, until five o'clock, roams the woods like a forester. He has dinner (such a dinner!) beginning at five, six, or seven. Then he plays billiards for half an hour. After that he does absolutely essential work until ten or eleven o'clock. He ends the day with the familiar cold supper, and is naturally unable to sleep on account of indigestion. . . . He spoke almost tearfully of his troubles, saying that everything was going awry; but he did not give me a chance to get in a word edgewise. . . . The result of his exciting himself in this way was an acute attack of indigestion." When, in a matter relating to Hanoverian finances, he gets his way with a majority of only five, he is " profoundly shaken, and immediately begins to suffer from pains in the feet, discharges of bile, and face-ache." Roon warns him fruitlessly: " I think you should have sufficient self-control to curb the extravagances of your nature, and to impose upon yourself the orderly life of a worthy German paterfamilias! You must surely be able to do this!" Roon, trusty companion, risks even the word " must." In vain!

Bismarck's inborn irritability makes him suffer more in the daily frictions of the service than in the rare hours of great decisions. When, at Gastein, it rains for two or three days in succession, he complains that the atmosphere of the place is like that of a wash-house. The waterfall near the inn gets on his nerves. Whenever he is in mountain country he suffers from the lack of wide horizons. When his wife writes to tell him that the children have had their teeth scraped, he replies: " You make me terribly anxious, and I feel quite upset!" One of the Hessian leaders asks him about the future of Hesse. Thereupon, " his face, not a handsome one, yet expressive, became convulsed with a storm of thought. . . . Silently, broodingly, he fidgeted, now with a pencil, now with a paper knife. For a little while, a fairly cheerful smile played about his mouth; soon it passed away; his features assumed a truly demoniacal aspect, and he knitted his bushy eyebrows."

While his body is thus ageing, and while his mode of life betrays the passing of the years (although his native energy wrestles with time), he tends to return to the incredulity of his youth. With giant strides he goes back towards the scepticism of the first phase, retaining little more than formal gestures from the days when he had been inspired with religious faith. When a pious neighbour accuses him of being unscrupulous, he replies in a long Christmas letter, assuming a Christian attitude: "I am perfectly willing to admit that I ought to go to church oftener than I do . . . what keeps me away is not so much lack of time as regard for my health — especially in winter. . . . Any one who describes me as an unscrupulous politician, does me an injustice, and had better search his own conscience first in this field." If forgiveness and repentance are two of the main props of Christianity, we can but smile when we hear of Bismarck's delight when informed of an old Wendish motto adopted by an officer on his coat of arms: "Never repent, never forgive!" Bismarck's comment is: "Long since, I have found that principle most useful in practical life!" A few days before the beginning of the war against Austria, in a letter to a friend, he pens the following satanic phrase: "The dice have been thrown; we look forward confidently towards the future; but we must never forget that God Almighty is capricious!"

To-day, as long ago, he superimposes his royalist notions upon the formulas of his Christianity, as a man may hang his shield upon a tree and camp beneath its shade. Bismarck's pride is so great that he must either perish, or make a revolution, unless he is continually suggesting to himself that monarchical power has a divine origin. "If I were no longer a Christian," he says at dinner in the presence of a large company, "I should not serve the king another hour. . . . I should have enough to live upon, should be satisfied with my position in the world, and should have no need of him. . . . Titles and orders have no charm for me. I firmly believe in a life after death; that is why I am a royalist, for otherwise, if I followed the bent of my nature, I should be a republican. Indeed, I am a republican, to the uttermost! Nothing but the firmness of my religious faith has enabled me to be steadfast for the last ten years. . . . If I did not possess the miraculous foundation of religion, I should long since have told the court to go to hell!" Some one present rejoins that a great many people serve the king simply out of a sense of the State. "This self-denial, this self-sacrifice on behalf of duty to State and king," rejoins Bismarck, "is, among us, a vestige of the faith of our fathers and grandfathers—a faith that has been transformed, so that it is obscure and nevertheless effective, no longer a faith and yet a faith after all. How glad I should be to retire! I delight in country life, in forests and nature. Take away from me the relationship to God, and I am a man who to-morrow would pack his trunks, set out for Varzin, and grow oats. In that case, a fig for the king! Why, except under divine command, should I subjugate myself to these Hohenzollern? They come of a Swabian family which is no better than my own, and whose welfare is no special concern of mine. I should be worse than Jacoby, whom one could put up with as president of the republic. . . . He would in many respects be a more reasonable person and would certainly cost less."

On many occasions Bismarck has given utterance to such a train of thought, but he has never more consistently reduced it to absurdity than here. By describing the sense of the State as the last vestige of religious faith, he stabilises a general sentiment of duty which he does not accredit any individual with possessing! Just as he discovers personal motives for even the most trifling actions of all the great figures of history and of all his contemporaries, so is he himself solely lured into the political arena, driven into the State service, elevated to supreme political power, by ambition and the will-to-power. The elemental forces of his nature lead him into these paths; he is not driven into them by humility towards God, like Luther; by eagerness to help the king, like Roon; by a sense of duty towards Germany, like Stein.

In view of his avowal that he is a republican, we must suppose that his revolutionary sentiments would have induced him, had he been born in Motley's country, to aspire to the presidency. His sense of self-esteem made him wish to see his own nation, his own class, his own family, in the position of honour: that he should need, for the attainment of these ends, to serve a Swabian family whose forefathers were more efficient or luckier than the Bismarcks; that he must subordinate himself to persons whom he excelled in intelligence and temperament, in fervour and genius — this was only made possible to him by the autosuggestions of his faith, thanks to which he was able to believe that this crowned family ruled by divine grace.

How otherwise can we explain the Junker sentiments of his youth, when he declared himself a pantheist and mocked at Christianity? Why did the unbelieving aristocrat detest the liberals, who were aiming at a moderate republic, whereas the believing minister was willing to-day to govern with their assistance? If, then, he was God's enemy, he ought, in accordance with his artificial logic, at least to have been an adversary of the king. If, to-day, he is God's servant, he ought to honour the monarchy. Does he honour it? He is asked what a prince ought to learn, and he answers confidentially: "A prince ought really to be educated in the Persian manner, that is to say he must learn to ride and to fight. If, over and above this, he wants to make a special study of his own profession, then he must learn how to stand for long hours, how to say something pleasant to every stranger, how to lie. He need never utter disagreeable truths, for that is the business of his ministers. Our king does not know how to lie. We see this at the first go-off, whenever he makes the attempt."

Now hear how he speaks of the royal family! "If I go hunting with the king in Letzlingen, it is in a forest which used to belong to our family. Burgstall was snatched from us by the Hohenzollern three hundred years ago, simply because it was a good hunting ground, for in those days there was twice as much forest there as now. It used to be valuable enough, apart from the chase; and to-day it is worth millions. It was taken away from us by force, in defiance of our legal rights. The then owner was locked up and fed on salted food without anything to drink, because he was unwilling to part with the land. The compensation paid for it was not a fourth part of its value." Here we learn the nature of Bismarck's belief in the divine grace which has set up the Hohenzollern over him.

When we see him as a good hater, we know our man. He is fond of quoting Mephistopheles aptly enough. He knows by heart long passages from the first part of *Faust*, and recites them admirably. Bismarck is responsible for the following remarkable literary judgment: "For the mere asking, I'd give you three fourths of what Goethe wrote! As for the rest, with seven or eight volumes out of the forty, I should be glad enough to pass the time on a desert island." Then he describes Goethe as a journeyman tailor: "'Happy the man who, without hatred, shuts himself away from the world; without hatred, who has a friend of his bosom with whom he can enjoy things,'—a man who can write like that is a journeyman tailor! Just think of it, 'Without hatred', and always some one cleaving to your bosom!" When, on another occasion, Keyserling's daughter speaks enthusiastically of tragedy, in which it is so delightful to imagine oneself as playing the heroic rôles, he comments with characteristic bluntness: "Would you really enjoy being murdered like Wallenstein, in a wretched tavern, by a rapscallion?" Keudell speaks of fear and compassion. Thereupon Bismarck rejoins, "furiously": "Yes, I feel fear and compassion so strongly that when I am in the theatre I am always ready to take the villain by the throat!" Keudell, the humanist, clings to the "victorious idea" in the drama. Bismarck thereupon begins to talk of roast goose, and asks: "Do you know whether in the Baltic provinces people eat goose with potatoes or with apples? I like it better with potatoes."

He now listens to music only as an accompaniment to his reading or to his work. In later days, when he has become imperial chancellor, he gives up listening to it at all, because it makes him sleep badly.

Speaking generally, the fundamental tone of his soul becomes more and more that of the wanderer. With growing success, with the attainment of power such as he had hardly dreamed of to begin with, his internal unrest increases. It is as if he had expected the realisation of his wishes to free him from these Faustian feelings, and now found himself more disillusioned than at the start. "Faust complains of having two souls within his breast; but I harbour a whole company of them, and they quarrel with

one another. They behave just as if they were in a republic. . . .
I disclose most of what they say, yet there are whole provinces
of which I never allow any one else to get a glimpse." These
words, which are uttered when he is driving in company with two
of his assistants (one of whom is quite out of sympathy with
him), are the expression rather of dissatisfaction than of loneliness, for in the latter case he would keep them to himself. On gala
days, he writes more frankly to his nearest and dearest: "The
unrest of this existence is intolerable. . . . It is no sort of life
for a properly constructed country gentleman. . . . I am homesick for quieter days, for the days when I was master of my own
time, and when (as I often fancy now) I was happier — although
I remember perfectly well that the phrase 'post equitem sedet
atra cura' was perfectly true of me when I was riding old Caleb."
These tones of impotent resentment directed against his own inborn character sound most clearly in a letter which he writes to
his sister on the occasion of her silver wedding:

"I should have been so glad to exchange with you once more
. . . reflections concerning the visionary fugitiveness of life. It
is so long before we lose the illusion that life is soon going to
begin, and we go on so long making ready for that beginning, that
we need such milestones as this of the silver wedding to remind us
to look backward, and see clearly how long a traverse we have
made, how many good and bad stations we have passed. Is it a
proof of our inadequacy, . . . or is it only my own mistake, that
I should always feel the present station more uncomfortable than
any of the earlier ones, and that I should never cease striving
restlessly forward in the hope of reaching a better one? I heartily
wish that you . . . may celebrate your festival in so happy a
mood that you will be inclined to call out to Postilion Time:
'Drive gently, friend.' I myself am quite ungrateful to God in
that I have never attained this mood of content, notwithstanding
the fact that I realise I have many reasons for content, when I
think of wife and children, and above all of my sister, and of so
much else I have striven for in the public service and in private
life — and have not valued on gaining it."

How delicately does this cruel analysis spin itself out into melancholy! How fine is his touch in these ironies! With how much reserve is the whole of his life's work compressed into a syllable! And yet, how dispassionately is Bismarck here dissected by his own pen, exposing the eternal wanderer. All the victories, all the struggles, the great results of twenty years of incessant fighting, are described as nothing more than uncomfortable stations, from which he presses forward in search of a better one!

XVI

Napoleon did not want war, but he needed war. It is difficult to know what France wanted; whether French ambitions were incompatible with German unity, which was obviously close at hand. Probably there was no widespread feeling about the matter, for the indignation that was manifested during the July days was confined to Paris. The displays took place only in a few of the streets of the capital, and even these displays were organised by certain newspapers in the service of the government. The only definite indication we have to show the feelings of the French people is afforded by the May plebiscite, in which, despite pressure and corruption, only seven million votes were cast in favour of Napoleon, whilst one and a half millions voted against him, and three millions showed tacit hostility by abstaining from the polls. Inasmuch as Napoleon's rule was, in popular parlance, supposed to be devoted to maintaining the glory and the greatness of France, the adverse voters and the abstinents showed their desire for a continuous policy of labour and peace. The French nation, quiet and pleasure-loving by nature, spurred on to passion only by a brilliant leader, or by bitter need, had obviously no desire to quarrel with any one. This mood was dangerous to a conqueror who had to shine in the public eye if he hoped to retain his position. There was a general wish for peace and a republic. The emperor gambled upon the chance of a victory, although, ailing as he was, he trembled before the possibility of defeat.

After the dispute about Luxemburg, Napoleon regarded war as inevitable, and Bismarck was hard put to it to prevent war immediately after that imbroglio. Napoleon had come to an understanding with Italy and Austria. During the spring of 1870, in consultation with an Austrian archduke, he drafted a joint plan for the campaign against Prussia. At the same time he made the duke of Gramont minister for foreign affairs, for, though he detested Gramont personally, the empress and the anti-Prussians at court insisted upon this appointment. The story runs that in 1866, when Gramont had wished to attack Prussia, Bismarck's saying, "Gramont is an idiot", had come to his ears, and he had sworn vengeance. Thus everything was ready for a cabinet war. Nothing was lacking but a pretext. This came soon!

The Spaniards had driven out their queen. After a vain search elsewhere for a new ruler, they turned to Germany, whose princely houses supplied half Europe with kings. Enquiries were addressed to a lateral line of the Hohenzollern which had just furnished Rumania with a ruler. King William, as head of the family, was asked his permission; he was adverse. Bismarck, however, was guided by the policy of opening as many branches of his firm as possible. It would be foolish to suppose that his direct aim was to bring about a breach with France. The most we are entitled to say is that he considered it would be more advantageous to have a Hohenzollern on the throne in Madrid than to have Paris appeased; that a diplomatic victory would be better than a Hohenzollern monarchy in Spain; and that an understanding would be better than a diplomatic victory. Since he had neither reason nor desire for a war (to secure Alsace, for instance), though he saw that war was coming for the sake of the unification of Germany and was prepared to accept war resolutely on this ground, he did not seek any pretexts on his side, being certain that France would find a sufficient pretext in the Spanish affair. Even now, his main determination was to wait.

When, therefore, Benedetti, in May 1869, before the official proposals had been made, announced that a conflict of the first order was imminent if a Hohenzollern should accept the Spanish

crown, Bismarck avoided inducing the king to forbid the acceptance of the Spanish offer. He treated the whole affair as a family
matter in which the lateral line was free to do as it liked. He would
give no formal undertaking, for he wanted to keep his opponent
on tenterhooks. He was quick to recognise that the question was
a thorny one. How was he to induce the king, who had already
been adverse to the acceptance of the Rumanian offer, to become
favourable to the Spanish offer?

"The Spaniards would probably be most grateful to Germany
if Germany were to free them from the imminent danger of
anarchy. As regards our relationships with France it would be
an excellent thing to have on the other side of France a country
upon whose sympathies we could rely, and with whose sentiments
France would have to reckon." Furthermore, the plan would save
Prussia one or two army corps. It was the two army corps that
decided the king's mind.

Bismarck knew that this step might bring on war. He was
prepared to take the risk. Since he was working solely for Prussia's power, and for this only in order to further political ends
(for to-day he cared as little about Alsace as in 1866 he had
cared for Austrian Silesia); since he neither now nor at any time
wanted to conquer German or foreign lands for Prussia, but,
as before, merely wanted to secure his own political leadership in
Germany — he prepared for war against Napoleon, just as
formerly he had prepared for war against Francis Joseph.
To the unification of Germany now, as to the formation of the
North German Confederation then, these potentates would give
only an extorted consent. The reasonable desire of a German
statesman to bring his fellow countrymen together, even against
their will, was the determining cause of both the wars. There was
not really an Alsace question in Germany, nor was there really
a left bank of the Rhine question in France; these "questions"
were invented on both sides by a few braggarts who wished to set
peaceful folk at one another's throats. The politicians in Vienna
and Paris had just as much right to prevent the formation of a
united power adjacent to their frontier as the German stocks

and princes had to strive for such a unification — though they strove for it by fits and starts, and in accordance with very varying plans. Bismarck's epigram in Nikolsburg to the effect that Austria's war against Prussia was no more immoral than Prussia's war against Austria, applies in all its cold clarity to the French war as well. As long as little Europe suffers from the infatuations of leadership and hegemony, of great powers and alliances, no nation will be allowed by the others to achieve unity, and thereby to acquire enhanced power, except at the cost of war.

Bismarck, whose aim was always the possible, and never the merely desirable, was a prey to conflicting motives, thanks to the disintegration and hostility of the Germans. If he had been a Bavarian, he would, with his powerful will, have hindered any sort of unification under Prussia. Being a Prussian, he wanted such a unification, and was moved thereto by the basic feeling of his pride — pride of person, pride of caste, pride of nationality. At the same time, as a statesman, he recognised that his desire was a reasonable one from the general German point of view. This platonic recognition was associated with his natural desire, made that desire morally presentable, and rendered it easier for the man to square with his historical sensibilities the unacknowledged coercion he was exercising over the southern States. If it were true that the nation " could only be consolidated in a fit of universal wrath ", how could this wrath be more readily aroused than by foreign intervention? Such were the psychological detours whereby the policy which threatened France became congenial to Bismarck the analyst, and whereby the war which he did not seek came to seem desirable to Bismarck the statesman.

In the Spanish affair, he scented the possibility of bringing matters to a head. His diplomatic zeal was stimulated by the knowledge that there were obstacles to overcome. Now he sent two agents to Spain, Bucher and an army officer, to revive the proposal when it had already been half abandoned. This was done secretly, for he wanted to confront Napoleon with an accomplished fact, and to put the emperor in the wrong as soon as any objection was raised. Spain was an independent country! Why

should she not seek her king wherever she pleased? The formal
proposal was sent. It was accepted in Sigmaringen, behind William's back. In the end, unwillingly, "after severe internal struggles, the king of Prussia gave his assent."

Then, shortly before the official announcement, the affair became known in Paris. The fat was in the fire! In a semi-official
article, Gramont started a baying which was promptly taken up
by the hounds of the Parisian press. With wrath, real or assumed, the newspapers expressed "surprise at the choice of a
German king." In reality, Gramont, knowing that Bismarck had
spoken disparagingly of him, wished to give the Prussian minister
a slap in the face, publicly, for all the world to see!

Bismarck is taking his ease at Varzin. There has been a frost in
the middle of the summer. He describes it in a letter to his wife:
"I have been eating pike and mutton; to-day pike and veal; also
asparagus, which we get better here than in Berlin. The frost has
nipped the young beeches at Waldecken, and has blackened many
of the sapling oaks. Your roses have come off still worse. Six or
eight of the standards have given no sign of life since the frost.
The rye has suffered, too, in patches; but the potatoes, Pomerania's consolation, seem to have escaped. I have had to take my
meals in melancholy isolation. Climbing the hills in the heat, I
could think of nothing but Grätz beer. Alas, there is none left!
The Klette is also finished. . . . I have nothing to fall back upon
but Breslau beer; but there is some wormwood in that, so it is
not agreeable for regular use. After dinner I walked through the
park and the preserves, saw four roe-deer, three of them bucks. . . .
Your alder plantation on White Moor is growing up finely, but
has been touched by the frost. The black ground beneath the
pines was whitened with flowering shrubs three feet high, like
blossoming myrtle (I enclose a specimen)—sedum palustre, called
in Pomerania 'Schwiene-Pors'—also wild rosemary. . . . I go
to bed at ten o'clock."

Shortly afterwards (for meanwhile the bomb has burst in
Paris), he is pacing up and down his room, dictating, inspiring,
what he wants to have printed as an answer to the hubbub raised

by Paris. He dictates "whole heaps of notes for articles, and detailed essays." In official utterances all is to be stated quietly; but in semi-official utterances the presumption of France is to be treated scathingly. "It seems as if the empress, who is fanning the flames, must want to see a new War of the Spanish Succession. . . . The French are like a Malay who has got into a fury, runs amuck in the street, foaming at the mouth, kris in hand, stabbing every one in his path. . . . " On July 7th he reads the speech Gramont has made in the Chamber of Deputies the day before: "We do not think that respect for the rights of a neighbouring nation makes it incumbent upon us to endure that a foreign power should establish one of its princes upon the throne of Charles V., thus disturbing to our detriment the balance of power in Europe and endangering the interests and the honour of France. If this should happen, we should do our duty without hesitation and without weakness!" Thunders of applause! When Bismarck reads it, he says to Keudell: "It looks as if there would be war! Gramont would not talk like that unless he had made up his mind. . . . If we could only attack France instantly, victory would be certain! Unfortunately we cannot — for various reasons."

That very day, acting on Gramont's instructions, the French envoy seeks audience of King William. This course is in order, for Bismarck has refused to deal with the family problem by the ordinary official channels.

The king is in a complaisant humour. The good man does not wish his summer in Ems to be disturbed; he discusses matters with Benedetti instead of, as Bismarck would like, abruptly dismissing him. On the 9th, the king, to whom the whole matter seems sinister, tells the French envoy that, as chief of the Hohenzollern family, he is prepared to advise his cousin to withdraw. He despatches an aide-de-camp to Sigmaringen. "I hope to God," writes William to his wife, "that the Hohenzollern will listen to reason!" When Bismarck learns the news at Varzin, he is furious, and exclaims: "The king is beginning to draw back!" He feels that he has been let down, that William's action will be interpreted as a Prussian surrender. He promptly wires for leave to wait upon the king. An answer does not reach him until the 11th. There has been a terrible day of waiting! On the 12th he is with Keudell on the way to Berlin, for he has to pass through the capital. When, after a ten-hours' journey, he drives up to the Foreign Office, and is handed a telegram, he is in such a fever of excitement that he opens it before getting out of the carriage. He is told in this wire that Benedetti has made further attempts in Ems, and that the king has again given a civil answer. Moltke and Roon, hastily invited to supper, soon join Bismarck. While they are at their meal, comes another telegram, to the effect that Hohenzollern aspirations to the Spanish throne have been withdrawn.

"My first thought," writes Bismarck in retrospect, "was to leave the service. . . . I regarded this enforced yielding as a humiliation of Germany for which I would not be officially responsible. . . . I was extremely depressed, for I could see no way of repairing the hurt which would be inflicted upon our national position by a timid policy unless I were deliberately to pick a quarrel. . . . I therefore gave up the idea of going to Ems, and asked Count Eulenburg to go thither and explain my views to His Majesty. . . . Thanks to his inclination to conduct affairs of State personally and on his own responsibility, the king had thrust his way into a situation to which he was not equal. . . . My exalted master . . . had so strong an inclination, if not to decide important questions for himself, at any rate to have his fingers in the pie, that he was unable to make a proper use of the device of acting behind cover. . . . This mistake must be largely ascribed to the influences which the queen kept at work upon him from the neighbouring town of Coblenz. He was seventy-three years of age, a lover of tranquillity, and disinclined to risk the laurels of 1866 in a new campaign. When he was free from petticoat influence, a sense of honour was . . . always dominant in him. . . . The queen suffered from feminine timidity and a lack of national sentiment, and the king's power of resisting these influences emanating from her was weakened by his chivalrous sentiments towards women."

It is twenty years after the events to which he refers, when Bismarck passes these strictures upon the king and the queen of Prussia. He makes them, not like Gramont (who fills his descriptions of the same days with reproaches against the emperor and the court), when he has lost a political battle, but when great deeds and great victories might be supposed to have expunged the feelings aroused in him by the king's lack of a sense of honour and the queen's lack of national sentiment. His rancour is persistent because of his wrath that the king should have allowed himself to act independently in this "family affair." Writing home that night, he said he would soon be back, but whether he would come as minister, he could not tell.

Hours of insomnia; a night of combinations and plans, of pride and hatred! On the morning of the 13th he gets news, not indeed from Ems, but from the Russian embassy, and learns that Paris is not yet satisfied. What a relief! Now, in conversation with the English ambassador, he can assume the pose of righteous indignation, saying: "If Paris makes any further demands, the world will see that what France really desires is a war of revenge. We are determined not to tolerate any insult, but to take up the challenge. . . . We cannot look on passively while France outstrips us in military preparations. . . . We need trustworthy guarantees against the danger of a sudden attack! Unless Gramont's threatening speech be withdrawn, Prussia will have to demand satisfaction."

Matters had been going awry. Now he has got everything in train once more. His short-sighted adversary, blind and altogether his inferior, puts the trumps into his hand. Yesterday, while Bismarck was travelling, and the Hohenzollern prince was renouncing the Spanish crown, Gramont, on his own initiative, had wired instructing Benedetti to ask the king of Prussia for an official utterance concerning this renunciation. At the same time, he had urged Werther, Prussian ambassador in Paris, to write to King William saying that Napoleon wanted from him a letter declaring that Prussia would do nothing to injure the interests or the dignity of France. Gramont hoped that when he had both these documents in his portfolio, he would be able to win a brilliant victory in the chamber. That evening, at Saint-Cloud, he showed himself angry and excited. Four days earlier, Emperor Napoleon, extremely ill, had refused to undergo the operation urged by his advisers, being afraid that it would prove fatal. Three years later he was to succumb to this operation. Had he undergone it now, he might have perished under the knife, but a great many other people would have been saved from death on the battlefield.

When Bismarck heard of the proposal that had been made to his envoy, he was in a fury because the latter had been content with courteous dissuasion. Werther was promptly recalled. The king at Ems received a threatening wire wherein Bismarck declared that if William should receive Benedetti again he, Bismarck, would resign. In the afternoon, Moltke and Roon came to dine with him. To these generals, who yesterday had still symbolised war for him, he uttered further complaints, and announced his intention to resign. Roon said that this was equivalent to backing out, whereas soldiers must stick to their posts. Bismarck drew himself up and replied: "You, as soldiers, act under orders, and cannot share the outlook of a responsible minister. It is not possible for me to sacrifice my sense of honour to politics." Then a new cipher telegram from Ems was brought to the table. It came from Abeken:

"His Majesty writes to me: 'Count Benedetti accosted me on the promenade, in order to demand of me—most importunately, at last—that I should authorise him to telegraph at once that I pledged myself for all future time never again to give my assent if the Hohenzollern candidature should be revived. I repelled him in the end somewhat severely, for one may not and cannot make such engagements à tout jamais. Naturally I told him that I had received no news as yet, and, as he had later news than I by way of Paris and Madrid, he could again realise very well that my government had no hand in the matter.' Since then His Majesty has had a despatch from Prince Charles Anthony. Inasmuch as His Majesty had told Count Benedetti that he was awaiting news from the prince, His Majesty, in view of the above-mentioned exacting demand, determined, in accordance with Count Eulenburg's advice and mine, not to receive Count Benedetti again, but to let him know through an aide-de-camp that His Majesty had now received from the prince confirmation of the news which Benedetti had already had from Paris, and therefore had nothing more to say to the ambassador. His Majesty leaves it to Your Excellency to decide whether this new demand of Benedetti's and its rejection had not better be communicated without delay to our envoys and to the press."

Divested of the wrappings of the court style, the wording of this telegram showed intense indignation; Eulenburg's advice, following upon Bismarck's instruction had been the last straw! As Bismarck's emissary, Eulenburg had informed the king of the federal chancellor's anger, had reported the mood of Moltke and Roon, had made no secret of the fact that the chancellor had been much mortified by the king's behaviour — and, on the top of this, had come Bismarck's refusal to visit Ems and his threatening despatch! To the Frenchman, the king had been outwardly civil, though " rather severe." In camera they must all have given free vent to their fury — for if the fastidious Abeken (a man who would not hurt a fly, and still less be rude to a duke) could speak officially of an " exacting demand ", and of a " rejection ", we may infer that in the conference much stronger words had been used. Why, even the aide-de-camp was to tell the ambassador of a great power that the king would not receive him again, and had nothing more to say to him! Finally the old gentleman, perhaps at the instigation of Eulenburg or of one of the aides-de-camp, happens upon the idea that this rejection should promptly be made known to the public, and in the most incisive way — through the embassies and the press! Once more, as in the year 1862, when travelling back from Jüterbog to Berlin (but this time through an intermediary), Bismarck had made his royal master feel that he had been put on his mettle as an army officer, and must try to act with less irresolution.

At Bismarck's table, the despatch has, to begin with, a crushing effect. Both the generals lose their appetite. They " refused to eat and drink. In repeated examination of the document, I dwelt upon the authorisation from His Majesty which it contained. . . . I put a few questions to Moltke, asking him what he thought about the state of our military preparations, and how long would be required to get ready in view of the imminent danger of war." Moltke answered that a prompt outbreak would be more advantageous to Prussia than a postponement. Thereupon Bismarck picked up his monster pencil, and, in presence of his guests, condensed the cipher despatch for publication in the following terms:

"After the news that the hereditary prince of Hohenzollern had renounced all pretensions to the Spanish crown had been officially communicated to the imperial French government by the royal Spanish government, the French ambassador in Ems made a further demand of the king, asking for authority to telegraph to Paris to the effect that His Majesty the king pledged himself for all future time to withhold his assent if the Hohenzollern candidature should be revived. His Majesty the king thereupon refused to receive the French ambassador any more, and instructed the aide-de-camp on duty to say that His Majesty had nothing further to communicate to the ambassador."

No new words have been introduced into the despatch. It has merely been edited. Some have been left out, but there are no additions. Even the blunt phrase "nothing more to say to the ambassador" has been modified into the politer form "nothing more to communicate." Publication to the envoys and to the press (a step likely to have a prodigious effect) was suggested by the king, recommended by him, for practical purposes commanded. The man who has just been reediting the despatch can, in imagination, hear the words of its French translation, can picture his "refusal" as shouted along the boulevards by the sellers of extra-special editions of the Paris papers. Yet there is nothing falsified, nothing more than compression. From a long and shapeless balloon, containing too little gas and therefore unable to rise in the air, an empty portion has been ligatured off; the remainder is now a round and well-filled bag which will rise quickly into the firmament and become visible to thousands of eyes. As thus edited, the despatch merely embodies the answer which Bismarck would rightly have made to the Frenchman, thus forcing him to choose between the alternatives of war or submission. Though Liebknecht subsequently called this despatch " a crime almost without parallel in history ", the crime was not Bismarck's. The crime lay in this, that the forms of society and government were such as to allow two or three men to start a war without asking the opinion of the people.

Furthermore, Bismarck wanted to take William by surprise. He was thinking of the king when he made this lightning resolution which, as always throughout his life in similar cases, was the fitting crown to years of thought. Bismarck wished to strike when the iron was hot, for to-morrow the king's wife, and the day after to-morrow the king's son, would speak in favour of peace. In actual fact, by publishing this despatch, Bismarck made war inevitable without having even asked his master. That, for a brief time, the king had been bellicose we learn from a second Ems telegram, despatched after the first had already been sent out to the world. This second Ems telegram reports a third refusal to give audience to Benedetti, a refusal couched in the following terms: " What His Majesty said this morning was His Majesty's last word in the matter, and His Majesty can only remind you of his previous statement." Thus was Bismarck's editing of the first telegram confirmed!

The chancellor's action was logical, seeing that the commander-in-chief had declared the moment favourable, and seeing that the developments of the last few years had shown war to be inevitable — if the creation of a real Germany were to be achieved. Since, as psychologist, he knew that in great measure his success would depend upon the mood of Europe, he seized his opportunity as the best likely to offer; for, not only in substance, but also in form, he appeared to be the challenged party. If to us of a later generation it can ever seem that the future unification of a people can be worth fighting for, it is certainly true that our French neighbours could not have been in a worse plight morally than they were when a war which they themselves wanted in order to prevent German unification was thus forced upon them.

Above all, however, that afternoon, Bismarck had been able to find a motive and a situation which would inflame even the last Francophil Bavarian and the last Prussophobe Würtemberger to common wrath. Three days later, the myriad mouths of the people had created a legend about the peaceful old king taking his morning walk at the spa, and the wicked Frenchman lying in wait for him, ambushed in a thicket like an assassin. All this, Bismarck's prophetic eyes had seen in a flash when he was editing the despatch which, ere midnight tolled, was to fire so dread a shot in the capitals of Europe.

XVII

A week later, speeches from the throne, issued simultaneously in Berlin and Paris, informed the world that an enemy had forced the nation to unsheathe the sword. God, who sustained the righteous cause of our forefathers, will sustain our righteous cause also: and so on, and so on. Both parliaments called their electors to arms, voted their electors' money, gnashed their teeth — without really knowing, or even hating, the enemy. For the first time in modern history, there appeared during these July days in both countries certain persons, groups as yet rather than masses, who opposed the war. An appeal to the workers of all nations, issued from Paris, contained the following words: " In the eye of all the workers, a war to redress the balance of power or to support a dynasty can be nothing else than criminal folly." A number of addresses and manifestoes sounded the same note. Echoes from the utterances in the Saxon and Bavarian legislative assemblies came back across the Rhine. Only in Prussia did no one venture to speak in this way. All that the socialist orator could bring himself to do there was to take the French under his wing for protection against Napoleon, thus recommending war against the emperor.   Then the General Council of the International Work-

ingmen's Association declared that the workers must take part
in the German war of defence, but must resist any attempt to
extend it into an offensive war.

The feeling that the French were the attacking party influenced the radicals in the chambers. In Paris, after Thiers' and
Gambetta's fiery speeches, ten men refused to vote the war
credits. In Berlin, Liebknecht and Bebel abstained from voting,
for they wished to avoid defending either Bismarck's policy or
Napoleon's. Among the Social Democrats, there was criticism
of this attitude. At first, in one of the socialist papers, we read:
"Napoleon's victory would signify a defeat of the workers
throughout Europe, and the complete break-up of Germany. . . .
Our interest demands Napoleon's annihilation, being here in harmony with the interests of the French people." Three days later,
in the same journal: "Let German Cæsarism and French Cæsarism fight matters out in the company of the dividend hunters.
We proletarians have nothing to do with the war." Next day a
manifesto was issued in the opposite sense. People even went so
far as to talk of a "Liebknecht monarchy", although he had
favoured the refusal to vote the credits.

With European breadth of view, Karl Marx wrote to Engels
in the very first days: "The singing of the *Marseillaise* is a
parody, like the whole of the second empire. . . . In Prussia,
there is no need for such monkey tricks: *Jesus my Confidence and
Hope*, sung by William I., Bismarck on the right and Stieber
(chief of police) on the left, is the German *Marseillaise*. The
German philistine seems positively delighted that he now has a
chance of giving free scope to his inborn servility. Who would
have thought it possible that twenty-two years after **1848** a
national war in Germany should find such theoretical expression
as this?" But there was, as yet, no echo to the conversation
between the two exiles!

Europe's sympathies were with France, for every one was
afraid of Prussia. In order to mould British opinion in the way
he wanted, Bismarck sent the "Times" a facsimile of the draft
proposal which he had secured from Benedetti during the Lux-

emburg negotiations — the proposal in which Napoleon had agreed to the unification of Germany on condition that he should be free to annex Belgium. Benedetti answered officially to the effect that the idea had been Bismarck's, and that the document had been written from Bismarck's dictation. Bismarck rejoined that he had frequently discussed the matter with Napoleon, and that had he not now published the document, the emperor, after completing his military preparations, would certainly have proposed, in face of an unarmed Europe, and with the aid of a million soldiers, to gratify his wishes at Belgium's cost — just as Bismarck himself had proposed before the first shot had been fired in the year 1866.

Benedetti's main point is sound; and if Europe believes him, this merely shows that people are aware of the cunning with which Bismarck does his work. "There is only one good thing about the matter," wrote Engels; "that now all the dirty linen will be washed in public, and that there will be an end of the trickery between Bismarck and Bonaparte."

What no one in Germany then knew (for the fact only came to light in 1926 when the correspondence of Queen Victoria was published) was, how blind hatred for Bismarck led, not only Princess Victoria of Prussia who was of English birth, but also her husband, into intrigues against the fatherland. When the war was over, the crown prince paid a visit to England, and Queen Victoria wrote in her journal:

"Osborne, July 31, 1871. — A very fine day. Breakfast in the tent. Afterwards met good Fritz and talked with him of the war. He is so fair, kind, and good, and has the intensest horror of Bismarck, says he is no doubt energetic and clever, but bad, unprincipled, and all-powerful; he is in fact the emperor, which Fritz's father does not like, but still cannot help; as for the treaty which Bismarck published, said to be proposed by Benedetti, Fritz thinks it was quite as much Bismarck's as the emperor Napoleon's doing. That he felt they were living on a volcano, and that he should not be surprised if Bismarck some day tried to make war on England." Such was the gratitude of the heir of the Hohenzollern to the man who six months before had won for him the much desired imperial crown!

Once more, as in the year 1866, every one goes over to Bismarck's policy as soon as the guns, which he does not himself aim, seem to justify his course. Once again, as on the evening after Königgrätz, immediately the first battle was over, that officer might have repeated his remark, with an adaptation to the new circumstances: "Since the attack has been successful, you are a great man; but if the enemy had made his way across the Rhine, you would now be the greatest of rascals!"

This time, too, the statesman had to intervene within a few weeks. When, during the night after the battle of Sedan, the unhappy Wimpffen begged Moltke to spare the French army, and urged him to win over the French nation by his magnanimity, Bismarck interposed: "One can count upon a prince's gratitude, but not upon a nation's, least of all upon the gratitude of the French nation. In France there are no permanent relationships. There is a continuous change of governments and dynasties, and the extant government is not bound by the pledges of its predecessor. The French are a jealous people; they took our victory at Königgrätz amiss, although it did them no harm. How can any magnanimity be expected from them, such as would lead them to forgive us for Sedan!" Unconditional surrender of the whole army, without weapons or colours, is demanded.

With such austerity does Bismarck open his policy against the French republic (foreseeing that to-morrow there will be a republic); and he will remain equally harsh during the negotiations of the next six months. His policy is an inexorable one, a conqueror's policy, quite different from that which he pursued at Nikolsburg. One of his reasons, the inconstancy of Parisian governments, has just been named, others will follow. This policy leads him to the annexation of Lorraine, and has incalculable consequences.

When, early on the morning of September 2d, he is summoned to Napoleon, and meets the emperor in the road, driving, surrounded by officers on horseback, "I had my revolver buckled on, and when I found myself quite alone facing him and the six officers, I may involuntarily have glanced at the pistol. Perhaps I instinctively moved my hand towards it, and this, I suppose, was noticed by the emperor, for he became ashen pale." At this instant the characters of the two men and the nature of their meeting are summed up as if in an epigram. The victor suddenly finds himself face to face with his enemy, one against six, and, with a natural movement, grips his revolver, which he has with him in case of need; the vanquished, in his carriage, notes the movement and turns pale; both know perfectly well that there will be no shooting, and yet they react instinctively as if a shot might be fired at any moment.

Except for this prelude, the interview, the conversation between the two men in a poor cottage by the roadside, is of little importance. Bismarck, who was chivalrous and cautious, subsequently spoke of it as a " cotillion conversation", and in it, all too late, agreed with the emperor that neither of them had wanted the war. At this hour, our great hater did not experience any of the voluptuousness of revenge such as he had enjoyed in other circumstances. The interlocutor, the man who pitifully bemoaned his impotence, was not Gramont, but Napoleon, whom Bismarck, thirteen years earlier, had described as a man of little account, yet possessed of a kindly disposition. Bismarck had never hated Napoleon; sometimes he had been afraid of the emperor, but had always tried to win him over. Now he may well look upon his defeated adversary as a man may look upon a long courted, at length conquered woman, for whom his only feeling is one of sympathy.

Substantially, this captured emperor is a nuisance to him. On the very evening after the battle, and after Napoleon's surrender, he had said, with one of the lightning flashes of his thought: " Now we shall have to wait a long time for peace." So much perturbed is he by the turn things have taken that he would fain have pursued the same course as after Königgrätz, have avoided any further military advance, and have been content to hold in pawn that part of France which had already been occupied! For the enemy army had been annihilated, captured, or completely encircled; the leaderless nation would break up into parties, and would yield in its weakness. Had Bismarck carried out this idea then as he had done four years earlier, he would have put the crown upon his statecraft at Nikolsburg. But if it had been difficult to keep the king and the generals from making a triumphal entry into Vienna, it was impossible to persuade them to renounce this triumph over Paris. The general staff was fore-armed against such civilian follies, and the civilian knew that his promotion to the rank of general since the days of Königgrätz counted for nothing. When Bismarck was getting into the train which was to carry him to the front, he had overheard Podbielski's remark: "We have taken our precautions this time, so that Bismarck shall not be able to have things all his own way!"

Above all, what now forced his hand was the call that came from the whole German nation. After Königgrätz, Germany had feared the occupation of Vienna rather than desired it. Now the German press demanded the annexation of Alsace "as a guarantee against a future attack by our hereditary enemies."

The only Germans who declared that the war had been ended with the fall of Napoleon were the socialists. On September 4th, the republic had been proclaimed in Paris. On the 5th, in many German mass meetings, sympathy with this republic was expressed. Henceforward, the working-class papers headed every issue with large capitals: "A just peace with France! No annexations! Punishment of Bonaparte and his accomplices!" A manifesto penned by Karl Marx was circulated throughout Germany, prophesying that the annexation of Alsace would lead to "mortal enmity between the two countries, to a truce instead of a peace." Thereupon some martinet of a stay-at-home general had the members of the party committee arrested, and sent in chains to a fortress. When Johann Jacoby, who had made a speech in Königsberg condemning the idea of annexations, was likewise arrested, stalwart democrats were greatly stirred. "The craving for Alsace-Lorraine," wrote Marx as early as the middle of August, "seems to prevail in two classes, in the Prussian camarilla, and among the pot-valiant patriots of South Germany. It would be a terrible misfortune, likely to divide Europe, and more specifically Germany, in twain. . . . The Prussians might have learned from their own history that permanent guarantees against a war of revenge by a beaten opponent cannot be obtained by dismemberment, etc." At first, Bismarck seemed to be of the same way of thinking.

"The German people, and the French people as well," he had insisted in the speech from the throne at the outbreak of the war, "both of them enjoying and desiring the blessings of Christian civilisation and increasing prosperity, are summoned to a more wholesome rivalry than the bloody rivalry of arms. The rulers of France have known how to exploit, by a deliberate misguidance on behalf of personal interests and passions, the justified and sensitive self-esteem of our great neighbour nation." No citizen of the world could have spoken more clearly or with more dignity than Bismarck thus, on the first day of the war, spoke to the enemy, and at the same time to Europe. Never did any statesman more plainly distinguish between a nation and its government. The only thing which Bismarck, in the urgency of the hour, may perhaps have failed to allow for, was the likelihood of so speedy a collapse of Napoleon's rule and personality. If he did realise the imminence of such an eventuality, he certainly forgot or failed to appreciate the impression which it was likely to make upon some of his fellow countrymen.

Nay more! In the middle of August, when King William set foot upon French soil, Bismarck began his proclamation as follows: "After the Emperor Napoleon had by sea and by land attacked the German nation, which desired and still desires to live at peace with the French people, . . . " At the same time, Frederick Charles issued an army order: "The French people was never asked whether it wished to fight a bloody war against its neighbour; there was no ground for hostility."

But what happened now? When, five weeks after the issue of these manifestoes, the first republican minister for foreign affairs entered the conqueror's headquarters, in order to ask for a truce during the election of a national assembly, had not Jules Favre good ground to hope that this sharp differentiation between Napoleon and the French people was something more than a phrase? Could not the opponents of the war, in both countries, count upon a recognition of the peaceful sentiments which the French had shown by the overthrow of the former bellicose government and by the elevation of their opponents to power — by the sudden and radical transformation of the empire into a republic? Had not Thiers and Favre, at the critical moment, condemned the war; had not they and their friends refused to vote the war credits; had they not now become leaders of the republic?

Theory, alas, does not always realise itself in fact, and the winning of half a dozen battles had made a difference. This very Bismarck, who in the speech from the throne had expressed his sympathy with the great neighbour nation because it had been misled by those who were pursuing personal interests, the very Bismarck who in his manifesto of the middle of August had said that the Germans still wished to live at peace with the French, now issues two circulars to the envoys in which he declares that the whole German nation is responsible for the war of conquest. When Favre explains to him that the French have driven out their war-making emperor, that they want peace, and offer compensation, Bismarck, to whom an adventurous emissary from the Empress Eugénie has also made his way, rejoins:

"We have no concern with the form of your government. If we find that it suits our interest to restore Napoleon, we shall bring him back to Paris. . . . Were I certain that your policy is the policy of France, I would induce the king to withdraw without asking for a fragment of land or for a single farthing. But you represent nothing more than an insignificant minority. We have no warranty either from you or from any government that may come after you. We have to think of our own future safety, and we shall demand the whole of Alsace together with a part of Lorraine and the town of Metz."

There stands Jules Favre, Parisian lawyer, pale of face, his great beard in disorder. He picks up his "dusty overcoat and

crumpled hat ", saying : " We will not cede one inch of our territory
or one stone of our fortresses ! " Yet the angry Bismarck pleases
him. He speaks of the German statesman as " imposing and harsh
but his harshness is mitigated by a natural and almost kindly
simplicity. He received me civilly and seriously, without any affectation or stiffness, promptly assuming a benevolent and frank
demeanour, which he retained to the end."

Bismarck's change of mood has decisive results, which entail
disastrous consequences for half a century thenceforward. There
really has been a change of mood; for the happenings of the next
few months show that, despite all the generals, he can get his
way with the peacefully disposed king. His demand that the
German realm shall be safeguarded by the surrender of Alsace
and Lorraine, that peace shall be guaranteed in this and no
other way, shows that his understanding must be clouded. It is
but a year since, in confidential talk with Keyserling, he said :

" Besides, if Prussia were to gain the victory over France,
what would be the result? Supposing we did win Alsace, we should
have to maintain our conquest and to keep Strasburg perpetually garrisoned. This would be an impossible position, for in
the end the French would find new allies — and then we might
have a bad time ! "

Here we have another version of Karl Marx's idea : a truce
instead of a peace ! Bismarck had seen that war was coming, and
had been glad enough to see this, for in those days the only
gain he wanted from the war was the establishment of the German realm. Never had Bismarck's thoughts and wishes turned
against a neighbour merely because that neighbour was an un-
quiet one. During the lapse of fifty-five years, the French had
half forgotten the last invasion of the Germans. Only for four
years had the growth of Prussia got upon French nerves. In
none of the memorials or speeches, in none of the private letters
or conversations, of the previous twenty years, had Bismarck
given utterance to such a motive. He had never talked about
" hereditary enemies." He did not love the French — but whom
did he love? Now, suddenly, and in a way which no one could

have expected after reading his last proclamations, he finds that one of the objects of the war is to safeguard a realm which has only been brought into existence through this very war. There is a complete reversal of the essential trend of his international policy. All in a moment, Bismarck, the architect, develops into a conqueror.

Why, asks Europe, should not these territories become neutral, since that is what they themselves wish? "In that case," replies Bismarck, later, in the Reichstag, "there would have been forged a chain of neutral States extending from the North Sea to the Swiss Alps, which would have made it impossible for us to attack France by land. . . . We are accustomed to respect treaties and neutralities [hear, hear!]. . . . France would have been provided with a protective girdle against us; but we, so long as our navy was not able to cope with the French navy, should not have been protected against an attack by sea. This was one reason, though only a secondary one." The main reason was that Belgium and Switzerland really wished to be independent and neutral States; whereas Alsace and Lorraine did not. "We could only expect that the strong French elements which will long remain in the territories — elements which, by their interests, sympathies, and memories are bound to France — would, in the event of a new Franco-German war, have influenced this neutral State . . . to attach itself to France again. . . . There was, therefore, nothing else for us to do than to take these areas of land, with their fortresses, wholly into German power, so as to defend them as a strong glacis of Germany against France, and in order to remove the starting-point of a prospective French onslaught several days' marches farther away.

"The first obstacle to the realisation of this idea was, . . . the hostility of the inhabitants. . . . There were one and a half million Germans who were endowed with all the merits of the German character while living as members of a nation which has other merits, but not these: their qualities gave them a privileged position. . . . It is part of the German character that every stock wants its own peculiar kind of superiority, es-

pecially as against its nearest neighbours. Behind the Alsatian
or the Lorrainer, so long as he was French, stood Paris with its
splendour and France with its unified greatness. He confronted
the German with the feeling 'Paris is mine'. . . . It is an actual
fact that this hostility existed, . . . and that it is our duty to
overcome it by patience. We Germans have many means. On the
whole it is our practice to rule, sometimes less skilfully, though
in the long run more benevolently and humanely, than do the
French statesmen [laughter]. . . . But we must not be too ready
to flatter ourselves that the end is close at hand, that in Alsace
as far as German sentiments are concerned the conditions will
soon be like those that prevail in Thuringia."

Through all these reasonable and just considerations breathes
the careful concern of the statesman. If, after a victorious peace,
he ventures to tell his fellow countrymen, with regard to the
spoils of war, that he had had no choice but to take them, this
gives us yet another proof that he had not taken these spoils
without long and anxious thought. Why, then, did he take them?
Several years afterwards, he will assure representatives of the
new provinces that Alsace and Lorraine were annexed by him
reluctantly, and only under pressure from the military chiefs.

The first reasons are to be found in the mood of the army and
its leaders. There have been great battles, heavy losses; the enemy is ill-prepared and can no longer defend his fortresses; the
princes and the generals are drunk with victory. Besides this,
Bismarck has acquired a definite hostility towards his arrogant
neighbours, who will not tolerate a power equal to their own
across the Rhine. Last of all there was a German nationalist
consideration. He felt that Germany was unduly exposed to attack from France, for the king of Würtemberg had once explained to him that the country's weakness in this respect would,
as far as South Germany was concerned, be a permanent hindrance to unification. "The wedge which the corner of Alsace
drove into Germany near Weissenburg," thus did Bismarck
formulate the matter in the Reichstag, "really separated South
Germany more effectually from North Germany than did the

political line of the River Main." But this realist consideration concerned only Alsace, and no more than a part of that province.

Moreover, Bismarck himself laughed at the Pan-German phraseology with which the country behind the fighting line fanned the flames of its moral enthusiasm. "What we want are the fortresses. The idea about Alsace having been primitively German is an invention of the professors." He knew that the attitude of the Great Elector towards Louis XIV. had been the main reason for the loss of Alsace, and that therefore the Hohenzollern had the slightest possible claim to the province. Nor was he slow to realize the danger of the annexation of Lorraine, for he said as early as September 6th: "I do not want the annexation of Lorraine, but the generals consider Metz indispensable, since it represents the value of a force of a hundred and twenty thousand men." Shortly afterwards he remarked to an English diplomatist: "We have no desire for Alsace or Lorraine. France may have these provinces upon conditions that will make it impossible for her to use them as a platform from which to begin war against us. What we must have is Strasburg and Metz."

But the most far-reaching of the grounds upon which Bismarck forced himself to accept the necessity for an annexation that seemed so risky was the thought of the unified German realm which was about to be created. It seemed to him that people's rigid minds would only become fluid and pliable under the influence of "a common wrath." Now the allied Germans had a pledge of their union, this joint possession. He was convinced that the need for wedding North Germany and South Germany would become obvious to both when they had to join hands in the rearing of this new shoot.

It was on the day of the battle of Sedan that Delbrück, Bismarck's confidant, coined the epigram: "Out of the Reichsland [the imperial provinces of Alsace and Lorraine] will grow the Reich [the German empire]."

XVIII

Bismarck marches forward towards his empire with the tranquillity of a master. When, after the first battle, in which Prussians were slain side by side with Bavarians, people began to write in the Berlin newspapers that William must become emperor, Bismarck had the Bavarian envoy informed that he was indignant at such utterances, and that no one had any thought of limiting Bavaria's independence. "On the contrary, we shall be eternally grateful to our glorious ally. There is no need to seek or to make the unity of Germany, for it already exists." The policy he will pursue for the next three months will be that of a wealthy firm which allows lesser ones to seek amalgamation. When he sends Delbrück to Dresden, it is only to accept the proposals from that quarter. To the Würtembergers he says: "We are awaiting your offers." He was determined to listen to all the voices, and then to do as he thought best.

In very truth, when our nation of individualists tried to get together, every one had a different plan. All the tribes, all the classes, all the parties, and finally all the different "philosophies", were in conflict, each of them resolute that there should be no Germany if Germany could only come into existence in accordance with some one else's recipe. The Prussian nationalists wanted a federation of German princedoms in which the Hohenzollern would rule supreme; the liberals would only have a Germany in which the people were supreme; the king would hear nothing of emperor and empire, and aimed only at the drafting of treaties for a joint army; the crown prince wanted the empire, and the subjection of his royal cousins to the authority of the imperial crown. Only in Baden did prince and people wish for an empire under Prussian hegemony. In Bavaria, the government desired a South German Federation including Austria, while the great towns would fain have joined the North German Confederation, and the king would have preferred that there should be no federation of any kind. In Würtemberg, the queen intrigued against Prussia, and the liberals wanted only to join a

democratic North Germany. In Hesse, the powerful minister proposed a constitution for the German realm of a kind which he
did not himself want; he proposed it because he knew that the
chancellor did not want it either, and that his proposal would
introduce general confusion. Finally they all made their way to
Versailles, for there Bismarck was sitting beside the furnace and
was making ready homunculus in his phial.

The crown prince of Prussia seemed to be the man of the
future, and was thus in a sense the most important figure, seeing that the first emperor was in his seventy-fourth year. Since
the outbreak of the war, there had been grave differences between Frederick and Bismarck. The crown prince had a romanticist dynastic-democratic dream of the new empire. He wanted
Prussia to be merged in Germany. Nothing was to be left to the
other German princes beyond titles, right and honour, and seats
in an Upper House. The Hohenzollern were to have the imperial
crown and the essential authority; the government was to be
carried on by an imperial ministry responsible to the Reichstag.
As early as the middle of August, during the German advance,
he had disclosed this scheme to his confidant, Gustav Freytag,
when the two were together in a Vosges village. " He was strongly
moved, his eyes shone, and he said: 'I must become emperor!'"
Freytag goes on: "I looked at him in dismay. He had wrapped
himself in his general's cloak in such a way that it enveloped his
tall figure like a royal mantle. He had put on the golden chain
of the Hohenzollern (which it was not usually his way to wear
in camp), and he strode proudly up and down the village green.
Obviously, his mind filled with a sense of the importance of the
imperial idea, he had dressed himself for his imaginary part."

His friend, the man of letters, vainly warned him of all the
dangers that impended, prophesying as follows: "The simple
blue uniform of the Hohenzollern will in the end become nothing
more than a memory of the past. . . . With the general increase in well-being, it is already difficult to maintain the old
discipline and simplicity in the officers' mess. That will only be possible in the future if our rulers continue to set us a good example

of simplicity. . . . And, as has happened before, a servile spirit
will spread among the people, a spirit of courtly adulation which
will be quite out of keeping with our old Prussian loyalty. . . .
Every movement towards an extreme evokes its opposite, and
there is a strong democratic undertow running in our century.
If, owing to great disasters and to misrule, differences tend to
spread throughout the people some day, even the most venerable
among the ruling families will be in great danger. Already our
princes have come to resemble actors upon the stage, facing,
amid loud applause and overwhelmed with bouquets, the approval
of an enthusiastic audience, while hidden beneath the trapdoors
are waiting the demons that will annihilate all these splendours!"

The crown prince let Freytag have his say, and, at the end of
this wonderful forecast, broke out with: "Now, you listen to
me!" What was the answer to so notable a warning? Nothing
more than this, that King William, when asked by Napoleon
which ·monarch should have precedence at the Paris exhibition
—the tsar of Russia or the king of Prussia—had said that the
tsar must have the premier place. "No Hohenzollern will have to
say that again! It will no longer apply to any of the Hohenzollern!" Such was the crown prince's fierce conclusion. "These
words," said Freytag, "enabled me to see deep into his mind.
He was filled with sovereign pride, so that I felt it would be useless to utter another word of dissuasion." A dozen similar scenes
convinced the man of letters that such feelings held unrestricted
sway in the prince's mind.

After the battle of Sedan, the crown prince mooted the imperial question in conversation with Bismarck, but Bismarck was
evasive. As soon as they had all reached Versailles, the sight of
the Roi Soleil's ornate apartments roused in the mind of Frederick William IV.'s nephew the idea "that this would be the very
place for celebrating the reestablishment of emperor and empire." Soon, however, he became resigned: "I had, indeed, ere
this, been compelled to recognise that Count Bismarck, 'our great
statesman', had never had a genuine enthusiasm for the German
question. . . . When I found that even such victories of ours

. . . had failed to awaken in him the sacred fire, what was left but to yield to the inevitable? Prussian officials in the royal service can never rise higher than Berlinese parochialism! . . . Woe unto those who cannot learn the truth even from such mighty times as our own; whom nothing can teach; who can never learn wisdom!"

That is the judgment which the heir to the throne of Prussia confides to his diary concerning the Prussian minister president, at the very time when the German empire is about to be established. The great statesman whose greatness is thus derided by the use of quotation marks, is "an official in the royal Prussian service." Woe to him because he has not learned anything from the German war! Frederick's opinion of October 1870 and his indiscretion of August 1871 give plain proof of the progressive decay of the dynasty. The good old king seems a hero beside the son.

Soon afterwards the heir to the throne comes into personal conflict with the statesman. Frederick insists that Bismarck must force the rulers of the southern States to make up their minds at length, must threaten them, and thus bring about a union. "No danger will arise from our showing these States that we are determined. If we deal with them resolutely and in the proper spirit, you will see that you have not yet fully realised your own power!"

Bismarck: "We are in the field side by side with our allies, and, were it only for this reason, we cannot threaten them. That would merely drive them into Austria's arms."

Frederick: "What matter? There could be nothing simpler than to proclaim the empire by a majority of the princes here present, and simply announce a constitution! All the kings would have to submit to this pressure!"

Bismarck: "King William himself cannot be moved to such a course."

Frederick: "If you don't wish it, Your Excellency, that is certainly enough to make it impossible to move the king to a step."

Bismarck: "For the moment we must leave the development of the German problem to time."

Frederick: "For my part, since I represent the future, I cannot regard such hesitation with indifference!"

Bismarck: "The crown prince would do well to refrain from expressing such views."

Frederick: "I protest in the strongest way possible against having my mouth closed in this fashion. No one but His Majesty has the authority to tell me what I may or may not say!"

Bismarck: "If the crown prince orders me, I shall act as he directs."

Frederick: "I have no orders to give Count Bismarck, and I protest against this utterance!"

Bismarck: "I shall at any moment be ready to make way for any other person whom you think better fitted than myself to carry on affairs."

The crown prince was fully entitled to criticise. He was nowise pledged to bend to Bismarck's will. His father had given power to a man whose ideas of statecraft ran counter to his own. Because part of the bourgeoisie wanted a more independent Germany, that was no reason why the heir to the throne should not want the same thing. His ideas of statecraft, however, should have been the outcome of personal experience, should have been intimately felt, should have been his own religion. In actual fact, they had been instilled into his mind by some one cleverer than himself. The general design of the web is not his. It is a blue English web, planned by the wife he so greatly admires, whose homeland naturally impresses him. But it is shot throughout with a purple Prussian thread, the imperial thread. This thread is introduced by Frederick himself. Even though the Hohenzollern wishes, after the English manner, to admit his people to a share in the government, he is at the same time determined to mediatise the members of his own order, the princes, and to reduce their powers to titles and formulas.

Frederick wants to rule, wants to wear the imperial purple and an imperial crown, wants his wife to share these honours;

but he does not want to be primus inter pares. Yet this should
have been his motto. In his arrogance, he degrades the other
German kings to the position of rebellious nobles who are to be
threatened and coerced; and when he tells Bismarck that the
latter underestimates his own strength, we hear a reproach which
Bismarck himself can never have heard before, and we cannot
but smile. It never occurs to this military officer that he is
betraying his companions-in-arms when he proposes to turn
against them the power he has gained with their aid; in such
faithlessness he is quite different from his father. How much
more sterling than this pseudo-democrat appears Bismarck, the
Junker, who has in the past mocked at the "godless and lawless
megalomania of the German princes"; who would gladly have
deposed the whole lot of them, just as the rulers of Hanover and
Nassau had been deposed—not for the sake of insignia, but
for the sake of actual power, which he would never allow to be
infringed by any Reichstag. At such moments, when characters
are revealed, the times become "tremendous", not in respect of
cannonades and attacks—for we are not speaking of the violence
of armies, which is not to be compared with the tactics of a
mighty intelligence.

None the less, the man of genius is sailing against the wind
of the time, whereas the heir, a weakling, is being driven along
by it! For it is this same crown prince who, aptly summarising,
writes on New Year's Eve: "It seems at the moment as if we were
neither loved nor respected, but simply feared. We are regarded
as capable of any crime, and mistrust in us continually increases.
That is not the outcome of this war alone.—To such a point
has the theory discovered by Bismarck and acted upon by him
for years, the theory of blood and iron, brought us! What is
the use of power, warlike renown, splendour, if hatred and mistrust meet us everywhere? . . . Bismarck has made us great
and powerful, but he has robbed us of our friends, the sympathy
of the world, and our peace of minds. I am still firmly convinced
that without blood and iron Germany could have made moral
conquests, could have become united, free, and powerful, simply

through her own good right. . . . The bold Junker, a man of violence, had other views. In 1864, his quarrels and intrigues made the victory of a good cause difficult. In 1866, he defeated Austria without unifying Germany. . . . How difficult it will be to counteract the blind idolisation of rude force and outward success; how difficult to enlighten people's minds; how difficult to guide ambition and competitive zeal back towards beautiful and healthy aims!"

These are words suited to Aristides the Just, or Abraham Lincoln. They are such as Freytag or Liebknecht could speak here and now. But they ill become the leader of an army who has such a man as Blumenthal among his field marshals, who wants to coerce his fellow princes and allies into submission, who does not wish to consult the people, but proposes simply to proclaim the constitution and then to wear the ermine with dignity and charm — after the manner of his rehearsal on the village green. Besides, he has not understood the history of the last decade, for why was the Danish war a "good cause", unless because the duchies had come to Prussia? Why was Austria defeated, Austria for whose preservation he had himself supported Bismarck's demands in Nikolsburg? Why did the chancellor of the North German Confederation delay the accession of the South, which he had at last brought to pass, thanks to his policy of blood and iron? No doubt German unity could have been achieved without the force of arms! But then the dynasties, at least, would have forfeited their power, and there would have been left to this New-Year's-Eve critic nothing more than the ermine which his twenty-two royal cousins likewise wore. Happy the fate of this prince, for the patriarchal age to which his father survived saved him from being put to the test of practice, and enabled him to go down to history wearing the halo of the untried idealist!

By the side of this Anti-Machiavel, the great realist strides resolutely forward towards the goal of his statecraft. The democratic crown prince wants to have the constitution "proclaimed" in the camp. The reactionary minister thinks of sum-

moning the whole German Reichstag to Versailles; and although
this primarily seems nothing more than a threat directed against
the hesitant princes, Bismarck is the man to change his threat
into earnest; indeed, he has already allotted the quarters in the
palace. Meanwhile, the ministers of the four southern States
come and go. Bavaria, however, objects to twenty-two points in
the draft. Bismarck is obdurate. The ministers go back to Munich.
Everything is at a standstill as before.

Now Bismarck makes as if he proposed to come to terms with
Baden and Würtemburg alone, Baden being very ready to do
this seeing that Bavaria seeks aggrandisement at the cost of the
Badenese Palatinate. Then the postal service, the railways, and
the telegraphs, raise their voices! The armies of the different
German territories want to have distinctive uniforms; German
unity is near to being shipwrecked on the colour of a collar! One
of the Badenese ministers says of Bismarck: " He displayed most
wonderfully tender sensibilities towards the interests of the
States, not infringing these without good reason; whilst he was
ready to ignore the most important of Bavarian interests when
the higher interests of the German realm made this necessary."
Since he wants the empire to come into being, he gives way as
regards the details of uniforms and suchlike bagatelles. Unity
is reached. Except for Bavaria, everything seems ready, and
the parties to the negotiation wish to sign. Then the queen of
Würtemberg, a Russian, intervenes. Under pressure from an intriguing baron, she makes her husband, who is weak of will, telegraph dissent, saying it will be better to wait for Bavaria.
Bismarck, outwardly calm, shows his anger when he is among his
intimates, falls ill, and deliberates whether it may not be advisable
to mobilise the South German masses against their governments.

Now the Bavarians have cocked their crests again. When
they put in an appearance a fortnight later, much more has to
be conceded to them. Provision for a diplomatic committee under
the presidency of Bavaria is made in the constitution. The Bavarian postal service, railway system, and telegraphs, are to be
independent; so is the Bavarian army in peace time. When,

finally, Munich gets its way in the matter of taxes upon beer and spirits, Bismarck has at length secured what he wants — "a satisfied Bavaria, which signs the agreement."

This November evening, after the conference, Bismarck, glass in hand, comes into the salon and sits down among his collaborators: "The Bavarian treaty is ready and signed. German unity is achieved, and the emperor will reign. It is an event. The newspapers will not be satisfied; and any one who writes history after the usual manner . . . will be able to say, 'The silly idiot might have asked more, for they would have had to give way', and such a historian might be right about the 'had to.' But what use are treaties if one 'has to'? I know they have gone away satisfied. The treaty has its defects, but it is all the more firmly fashioned for that; what is lacking can be made up in future. . . . I consider it one of the most important achievements of recent years."

Then he goes on to speak in sceptical terms about the king of Bavaria. Abeken, who is always loyal, says: "But he is such a nice man!"

Bismarck looks at him with astonishment, saying: "So are all of us here."

With such straightforwardness does Bismarck characterise the great settlement on the eve of the completion of his work. But when he has been sitting a little longer over his champagne, always in a mood of pensive survey, regardless of his audience, he says, without transition: "I shall die at the age of seventy-one." He deduces this from a calculation whose elements are incomprehensible to those present.

"You must not die so soon as that! Too early! We must drive the angel of death away!"

"No," says Bismarck quietly, "in the year 1886. I have still sixteen years. It is a mystical number."

XIX

While engaged in his realistic work at Versailles, Bismarck occasionally passes under the spell of historical sentiments. "A marvellous world we are living in to-day," he says on one oc-

casion. "Everything which used to stand on its feet is now standing on its head. Perhaps the pope will soon be living in a Protestant German town; the Reichstag will come to Versailles; there
will be a corps législatif in Cassel; Garibaldi will be a French
general, and there will be papal Zouaves fighting side by side
with him!" When King Louis is expected, he says: "I should
never have thought that I should come to be a steward of the
household in the Trianon. What would Napoleon, what would
Louis XIV., have thought of it?"

Speaking generally, his life during these five months is spent
in petty detail work. His moods, which are recorded in hundreds
of conversations, show that he is in rather a depressed frame of
mind. When he is asked how he enjoys this period, his only answer is: "In political life there is no summit from which a satisfactory retrospect is possible. I do not know what will be the
outcome of all that is being sown to-day." Once more we have
an avowal between Faust and Mephistopheles. On the whole
there is more vexation and hostility in his talk than sublime emotion and wit. At table, he monologises. When to-day and to-morrow are done with, and when the anecdotes of his own life are
exhausted, the conversation nearly always turns upon hunting,
travelling, cookery, and wines. We hardly hear a word of the
cultural and political problems which all Germany is discussing;
there is no mention of such matters as the interchange of letters
between Renan and Strauss. Mushrooms and fish, roast meats
and Wursts, Médoc and Deidesheimer, champagne and sweet
wines — the frequency with which these are mentioned shows how
important a part they play in Bismarck's daily life. He does not
need quantities only, but refinements as well; in these things,
too, we see that his nature is a dangerous mingling of strength
and nerves.

When he is invited to dine with the king, he has a good meal
in his own house before or after, for "we get lean fare at the
king's table. When I note the number of cutlets, I help myself
to only one, being afraid that if I take two some other guest
will go hungry, for only one apiece is provided. I can't sign a

satisfactory peace unless I get a satisfactory amount to eat and drink! That is part of my profession. Therefore I prefer to dine at home." He repeats this remark several times when one of the king's aides-de-camp is present. At dinner he actually displays nationalist sentiments, declaring: "A French hare is not to be compared with a Pomeranian hare. The French hare has no gamey flavour, quite different from ours, with its lovely taste of heather and thyme. . . . In our family, we are all good trencherfolk. If there were many with as good appetites as ours, the country would go bankrupt, and I should emigrate."

He goes on to complain that he cannot sleep. After a gigantic supper, he does not go to bed before midnight, sleeps for a little while, but usually wakes towards one o'clock. "I begin to think of all kinds of things, especially when any wrong has been done me. . . . Then I write letters and despatches — without getting up, write them in my head. Years ago, when I had first become a minister of State, I used to get up at night and write them down. On reading them over in the morning, they seemed the crudest platitudes — worthy of his Serene Highness of X. I would much rather go to sleep, but I can't help myself. Something goes on thinking and speculating in me in spite of myself." It becomes essential to him to sleep on late in the morning. No one dares to call him before ten or eleven, and thus he misses the military reports.

To put the cap upon the unhealthiness of his life, he now rides very little. The only exercise he takes (provided his feet do not hurt him) is a lonely walk at night in the garden, surrounded by high walls. On one of these occasions he sees a ladder leaning against the wall. "At once I felt an irresistible desire to climb to the top of the wall. Would there be a sentry there? In the end I had a talk with the man on guard, and asked him whether he thought we should make our way into Paris." When he goes out, he does not wear a sword. "I always take my revolver, for, though I am quite willing to be assassinated in case of need, I do not wish to die unavenged!" He is, in fact, well hated in France, and during the advance there had been a plot to assassinate him. He writes to his wife: "The people here seem to regard me as a sort of bloodhound. Old women, when they hear my name, fall on their knees and beg for their lives. Attila was a lamb compared to me."

The fanciful moods of old days seldom recur now. There is only one record of such a mood. He writes: "I fled from my worries to-day, to gallop in the soft autumn air down the long straight avenue of Louis XIV., past rustling foliage and clipped hedges, quiet ponds and marble gods and goddesses. There was nothing human near me, except the sound of Joseph's clattering sabre as he galloped behind me. I brooded in the homesickness natural to this season of the fall, when one is alone in a foreign land. Memories of childhood came back to me, memories of clipped hedges which no longer exist." There is no other indication of such imaginative moods, though here at Versailles he is leading a life outwardly more tranquil than that of Berlin.

At the outset of the campaign he issued orders to his sons: "If either of you is wounded, let him telegraph to me at the royal headquarters, . . . not to your mother until I have been informed!" When he is with the king in August, on the evening after the battle near Mars-la-Tours, an officer comes up and in low tones makes a report to Moltke, who is also there. The general looks alarmed. Bismarck says instantly: "Does the matter concern me?"

The officer: "In the last attack made by the first dragoon guards, Count Herbert Bismarck fell, and Count Bill was mortally wounded."

"Where does the news come from?"

"From the general in command of the tenth corps."

Thereupon he has his horse saddled, rides off without a word, and in his cousin's company ransacks the field hospitals. During the night he finds Bill with nothing amiss, for the lad had merely been thrown; but Herbert has been wounded by a lance. These hours of search were Bismarck's most distressing experience since the days of his illness in Russia. If he had found his sons dead, as he had feared, his vital force would have been spent, just as it would have been if he had had his leg amputated. He would have died as soon as the war was over. A life without sons would have seemed to him aimless. He could never have found compensation in his work. Although he troubled himself very little about their upbringing, his knightly sentiment needed the certainty of having male heirs, just as his misanthropy made him need an object of affection, and just as his blood needed a guarantee of permanence.

During the war, therefore, he thinks more than usual about his sons. From Versailles he carries on the administration of Varzin simultaneously with the administration of the kingdom of Prussia. He sends a letter to his wife, and subsequently wires to have the delivery of the letter delayed because he learns that she has gone away from Reinfeld, and he is afraid that it will be opened by his father-in-law (a man of eighty), shown to the pastor, and so find its way to the press. In this letter, wondering whether Bill will not be too cold, he asks his wife whether the boys have plenty of warm underclothing. He is annoyed that they have not long ere this received the well-merited Iron Cross, though he carefully avoids saying anything about the matter to the king. At Christmas, when Herbert has recovered from his wound, Bismarck sends the young man a fine sword, but takes care that he shall not be ordered to the front once more — this precaution being suggested by Roon, whose own son has been killed in the war. When we hear how Bismarck, in the king's company at Gravelotte, had lost his composure because he knew that his sons were in the midst of the fray, and when we are told that "he stood stooping forward, his usually impassive face working with excitement", we feel sure that the chancellor's political desire to hasten the coming of peace is intensified by his own paternal feelings.

Under the pressure of these manifold influences, the nerves of the man who is responsible for all, suffer, and his subordinates suffer from his nerves. On one occasion, when some pencilled comments of his in the margin of a document are not inked over as they ought to have been before sending the document to press, he bursts out at the privy councillors: "You do not keep the office in proper order. We are not here on a pleasure trip. If you all leave me in the lurch and drive me crazy, you choose a bad time for it, seeing that I am very difficult to replace." At table, when he is monologising, a certain baron interrupts him. He says cuttingly: "When any one is speaking, it is wrong to interrupt. You have quite put me out. What you wanted to say could have been left till afterwards." Even the worthy Abeken complains to his wife: "The worst thing is when he will not listen while one is telling him simple facts which he has to be informed about. . . . Often he does not answer, or answers quite irrelevantly; pays no heed to what I am saying, but thinks only of what he wants to say to me; and this often happens . . . of set purpose." At the same time, Bismarck feels that he is misunderstood and hated. He complains to his wife: "How the chilly morass of dislike and hatred rises gradually higher and higher up to one's heart; one makes no new friends; the old ones die off or withdraw in dudgeon; and the cold from above increases, for this is natural to princes, even the best of them. . . . I freeze with the cold, and I long to join you, to be alone with you in the country."

At headquarters he shows caution only in his dealings with foreigners. He assures an American general that he himself from youth upwards has been "all toward republicanism", but has been diverted from following up this trend by family influences — Germany is not yet sufficiently advanced to become a republic. He has frequent talks with the "Times" correspondent, and often learns more from the newspaper man than the newspaper man learns from him. When he hears that a representative of the "Neue Freie Presse" is at Bucher's quarters, he drops in unexpectedly. The correspondent is a Pomeranian nobleman who had been condemned to death in the days of the '48, though the sentence had been commuted to six years' imprisonment. Here is an opponent to be won over. Bismarck's first move is to pretend recognition of the man, though he has never seen him before. Then he goes on to say: "We are of the same age and you are wonderfully well preserved."

"I can tell you a good way of keeping youthful looks," replies Corvin, cheerfully. "You only need to spend six years in a prison cell!"

This amuses Bismarck. In a friendly way, he asks Corvin about various relatives. Then he draws the following parallel:

"You and I grew up in pretty much the same circumstances. Like you, when I was quite young I aroused alarm in my family by my liberal trend; like you, too, at an early age I became inspired with enthusiasm for the idea of a unified Germany, but was disgusted by the incompetence of many of the leaders of 1848. In youth one is more passionate. From a certain altitude, the party colours become confused. Besides, as you know, one can never quite shake off one's Junker heritage. . . . You see how fate disposes. The same sentiments brought you behind prison bars, and brought me to the place where I stand to-day."

The journalist listens with astonishment. What consummate art to seduce a political opponent by distorted comparisons and false inferences. How ingenious to welcome Corvin as a fellow Junker, and to flatter the journalist likewise by allusions to the similarity between them in youth, to his own early liberalism! Bismarck achieves his end, for Corvin tells us that a great impression was made upon him by the chancellor's cordiality, sympathy, and appreciation.

Bismarck's enemies in Versailles may be divided into men in mufti and men in uniform; into bureaucrats and princes. The only persons with whom he is on reasonably good terms are Frenchmen. "Never before have I known such bitterness displayed against any one," writes Stosch from headquarters, "as is displayed to-day against Bismarck, who is now ruthlessly trying to get his own ideas carried out." He is on especially bad terms with the general staff. "The ingratitude of these army men is abominable," he exclaims, "seeing that I have always done my best for them in the Reichstag! They shall see what a change they have wrought in me. I went into the war a pious champion of army interests, but I shall return home a thoroughgoing parliamentarian; they'll find out when my next budget comes — there 'll be no iron in that one!" In after years, he speaks of the "militarist boycott" against him; and in actual fact the army men do their utmost to keep him out of their counsels, and when possible discuss matters while he is asleep. Russell, the "Times" correspondent, "was, as a rule, better informed than I about their plans and doings, so that I found in him a useful source of information." The general staff took careful note of the federal chancellor's intimates, keeping an eye on any one who might openly or privately give him news. Bismarck was watched by the generals as shrewdly as if he had been an untrustworthy neutral. There were two reasons why the army men pursued this foolish policy of concealing from the statesman who was at the head of affairs the operations by whose course his calculations must be partly determined. The first reason was nothing better than jealousy of his power. The second was pique on account of his autocratic determination to have all the strings in his own hands. "It is monstrous," said Manteuffel, "that a politician should have more influence than the leaders of the army!"

It was a decade now since he had had to allow things to be done close at hand without his having any voice in the matter and even contrary to his wishes. He was compelled to let the king, whom he would have liked to keep always under his own eye, associate unwatched with the generals, who influenced William in political as well as in military affairs. His pride, his dictatorship, his habit of deciding all matters in the overweening strength of his own intelligence, made him revolt against this isolation, just as they made the generals wish to isolate him. While the army men criticised his peace policy and his imperial policy, he saw to it that they should learn his open censure of their conduct of the campaign. "The strategy of our supreme military command has been armchair strategy, and the common soldier has won all the victories. We owe our successes to the fact that our soldiers are physically stronger than the French soldiers; that they march better, have more patience, are inspired with a keener sense of duty, are more spirited in attack.

If MacMahon had had Prussian soldiers under his command and if Alvensleben had had French soldiers, victory would have been the other way about." At table, he blames Steinmetz and Alvensleben. He invites Eulenburg into the camp, "that I may see a congenial man among all these wearers of uniform." On one occasion, when he is feeling ill and is in an overheated room, he complains to Waldersee: "Important operations are being concealed from me, and I learn only by chance of events which are of the greatest moment to me." We are told that when he was saying this, "his eyes grew larger and larger; drops of sweat formed on his face; he was smoking a strong cigar, and, as I could see from the bottle, he had been drinking strong wine."

He bluntly tells Prince Hohenlohe that after Sedan the army had made nothing but blunders. "Of course I am a man of no great intelligence or capacity! Still, there is one thing that I really do understand, and that is strategy. Instead of concentrating all our forces in the forest of Argonne, and waiting there for the enemy to attack us, we foolishly advanced straight on Paris without knowing why. I protested, but Moltke would not hear reason." For Bismarck's keenest opponent during the siege of Paris is Moltke; the antipathy that has been growing for years finds vent at last.

In the portraits of these two men in youth, at an age when people still look as if they might make of themselves what they will, the contrast is plain. Bismarck is all muscle, substance, will; Moltke is all bone, outline, thought. During the middle twenties, when Bismarck was penning letters full of arrogant and ironical self-analysis, Moltke was describing himself in an autobiographical novel as follows: "Blond locks surrounded a rather pale and very expressive countenance, which, though it could make no claim to good looks, was animated by extremely serious and noble features. His deportment was elegant; his features were only moved by what was going on within him; he was like a deep river which rolls ceaselessly onward beneath a smooth surface, and only breaks into a turmoil of foam where rocks im-

pose an obstacle to its course." Bismarck's soul, ever in movement, even in youth, already resembled a storm-tossed sea.

Kindly, gracious towards every one, positive like Roon though
cooler, moderate in all things, almost disembodied, Moltke never
needs work in order to appease an inner unrest, for he is equally
serene in work and in repose. He is chary of words, not from
profundity or from misanthropy, but simply because he has
no occasion to complain, no urge of egoism driving him to speak,
nor anything which he need hide behind a cloud of clever words.
His silence is not the outcome of either arrogance or melancholy.
He is silent merely because he would rather look on than take
a hand in the game; because, when he does take a hand, he has
no need of an audience. Even in the forms of his recreation, even
in sleep, in drink, and in reading, his is in all respects an equable
temperament, a morning nature. He prefers his park to the forests; completes all his work with his own hand, whether he is
writing reports to the king, sawing down trees, or grafting. A
childless man; always thinking of others; having no use for a
servant; a novelist, a lover of Mozart, a translator of foreign
poetry — such is Moltke. If we were to reverse every one of his
characteristics, we should have the precise image of Bismarck.

The antithesis is intensified by the fact that he has no homeland. He is as much a German as Bonaparte is a Frenchman.
True, he was of German birth; but his father had been natural-
ised as a Dane when the future general was a boy of five, and
young Moltke was a Danish lieutenant of twenty-two when he
returned to his German fatherland. Forty years later he made war
on Denmark with no more emotion than a condottiere would have
shown, directing his guns against the very Danish heroes, colours, and troops which he had once sworn to defend. He reckons
with figures, whereas Bismarck reckons with magnitudes; in the
service he is wholly the professional expert, whereas Bismarck is
wholly the personality; that is why Moltke can justify his conduct in this respect to himself far more easily than Bismarck can
justify his own determination to shoot at men of German birth.
For Moltke, his movements, his lines of attack, are foreordained.

Bismarck, on the other hand, makes decisions, and thereby makes himself responsible. Moltke loves to travel, spends many years in foreign lands; when he is over forty he marries an English-woman young enough to be his daughter. He features the German neither in personal appearance, nor in character, nor in mode of life. Had chance made him a lieutenant in the Russian army, he would have been just as much at home there as he will be in the Silesian estate he will presently buy with his dotation. In Russia, as in Prussia, his genius for strategy (the most international of all gifts and occupations) would have brought him to the forefront of his profession.

Such symmetery in attributes and conduct, such moderation and taciturnity, could not fail to make him even more uncongenial to Bismarck than Bismarck was himself to Moltke. Their only common trait was that each of them had the profoundest mistrust of the other. Moltke was unable to understand how any one could live so stormily, and Bismarck could not understand how any one could live so tranquilly. That is why neither of them ever said such a friendly word to the other as Roon often exchanged with both. To-day, when they have to work together, opportunities for friction are multiplied. In the evening after the battle of Sedan, Moltke invited the weary Bismarck to dismount and to join him in his carriage. As the two drove away together, the troops cheered their leader Moltke lustily. Bismarck said: "Strange that they should all know me so soon!" Moltke kept his own counsel at the moment. A few days later he related the incident with a smile.

In October, the chancellor complains that the general has failed to listen to a statement of his, "looking all the while more and more like a bird of prey"; whereas others describe him as appearing "almost virginal."

When the question is mooted whether Paris shall be bombarded, and when "interloping English humanitarians and sovereign ladies" declare that it will be kindlier to starve the French capital out, instead of shooting it into submission; when weeks pass in which, with wearisome iteration, the report from Paris runs "no news"—then the statesman begins to tremble as he did in Nikolsburg lest neutrals should intervene. Now his wrath is concentrated upon Moltke, who has declared that great cities surrender without a blow if they are encircled.

This theory, which is subsequently rejected by masters of the science of war, infuriates Bismarck. He fiercely complains to Blumenthal about the king and Moltke, saying in a rage: "They have kept me uninformed, have treated me most discourteously. . . . I shall resign the instant the war is over. I can no longer endure being treated so contemptuously. It has made me quite ill, and will kill me unless there is an end of it. I have always been opposed to the investment of Paris, which I regard as a great mistake. What I should like best is to restore Napoleon with his armies, for he is a sick man and no longer dangerous. . . . The king won't hear of it. I was a royalist when the war began, but shall not come out of it a royalist." To Bennigsen: "I shall not look on much longer. If this arrest of operations continues, I shall set off with my groom for the German frontier!" At this same period Moltke complains about Bismarck to the crown prince, saying that Bismarck "wants to decide military matters as well as civil ones, without listening to what the responsible experts have to say. Besides, Count Bismarck addresses questions to the general staff relating to such secret strategical problems that I have several times had to refuse an answer. I am the king's military adviser, and cannot allow myself to be diverted from my purposes by Count Bismarck's opinions."

In the middle of December, Bismarck has recourse to his favourite method. He goes on strike, remains invisible for a whole week, and allows a journalist to know enough of the quarrel to send information about it to America. He does not reappear until the bombardment has finally been decided upon. The crown prince then asks Bismarck and Moltke to dinner, in order to bring about a reconciliation. Again and again Frederick has to intervene in order to guide the conversation back into calm waters, for Bismarck takes the opportunity of passing his strictures upon the whole conduct of the campaign since the battle of Sedan.

At headquarters, next to the generals, it is the German princes who reduce Bismarck to despair. Eight days after the outbreak of the war, he writes querulously to his wife: "It is really outrageous, the way in which these royal onlookers occupy all the best places, so that Roon and I find our work hampered, and are deprived of room for our best subordinates, in order that the royal highnesses with their servants, horses, and aides-de-camp, may be comfortably housed." During the advance, he does everything he can to avoid them. Should he have no choice but to meet them when he is visiting the king, he describes the whole scene afterwards to his collaborators: "There were so many princes that there was no room for ordinary mortals. . . . Such an empty-headed fool with his nonsensical talk, . . . full of his princely self-importance, though I am his federal chancellor! . . . The mayor of X. comes to pay his respects: 'Delighted to see you, Mr. Mayor! What is the chief occupation in this good town? It makes tobacco and hosiery? . . .' At the king's table, . . . they put me between the prince of Bavaria and the grand duke of Weimar, and then the conversation is insufferably humdrum."

One of his chief tribulations is this same grand duke: "Since negotiations are now in progress," says the grand duke of Weimar to Bismarck, "I hope that you, as my federal chancellor, will give me the necessary information, so that I can pass on as much of it as I please to Russia." This is precisely what Bismarck wishes to avoid, and he bows, remarking with veiled irony: "I shall leave nothing undone which my grand duke could wish to have done." When, subsequently, the grand duke sends a minister to him, Bismarck says he is astonished that the gracious ruler can make such claims upon his time and health. The Coburg prince writes him a letter of twelve pages concerning German policy, and is informed that of all the proposals there is only one which has not already been carried out, and that this exception is really not worth talking about.

When the grand duke of Weimar wires to his wife in the style of King William, "My army has fought bravely," Bismarck, through whose hands the despatch passes, sends for his secretary late in the evening, and shows him the telegram in order that this piece of folly may be bruited abroad. When the duke of Saxe-Meiningen makes an excessive use of the overburdened wires for private purposes, Bismarck sends a message to the petty potentate to the effect that the use of the field telegraph to send messages anent the concerns of the State theatre cannot be permitted; that he seems to have nothing better to wire about than forest nurseries, chorus girls, and horse dealing. The prince of Coburg is even worse in this respect. The elector of Hesse, another German patriot, who in July had wished to preserve the freedom of independent decision, writes in November saying that he will come to Versailles if they will guarantee that at the triumphal entry into Paris he will not have to join the procession on horseback.

On another occasion, Bismarck meets all the German princes at the king's: "Their highnesses flocked round me like crows round an owl, . . . and each of them plumed himself on getting two or three minutes more of my free time than the others. . . . At length, somewhere in a neighbouring room, they were told that there was a surviving leg or the back of an old coronation chair, so they all went away to look at this wonder, and I seized the chance to make my escape." When, in his own quarters, he is summoned from dinner because the grand duke of Baden has arrived, he returns ten minutes later in a fury, saying: "This is too bad, they will not even let me alone at meal times. They will end by pursuing me into my bedroom! In Berlin, people give me notice by letter before they come. Why should they not do so here? . . . I will have any one who comes without notice placed under arrest. There is no end to such vexations! I suffer from bilious vomiting if anything makes me lose my temper when I am eating! They seem to think that I am here only for them!"

After such comedy scenes, after such manifestations of this "royalist's" contempt for the princes, there is a poignant re-

currence of the lamentations of a born dictator who is doomed
to service. On a November evening, after long consultations with
the South German ministers, he comes late into the salon, sends
for beer, sighs, and then says: "Oh, dear, I was just thinking
once more what I have so often thought before. How splendid it
would be if only for five minutes I had the power to say: 'This
shall be done, and this shall not be done!' If I had no longer
to torment myself with wherefore and therefore, with proving
and haggling where the simplest matters are concerned! There
was much less waste of time for people like Frederick, who were
themselves soldiers, knew something about the course of affairs, and acted as their own ministers of State. Napoleon was
like Frederick in this respect. But here one has eternally to
talk and to beg!" Soon afterwards: "I can hardly breathe
under it all! . . . Oh, to be a landgrave! I am confident I should
know how to be severe—but I am not a landgrave!"

The enigma of his position, the tragedy of his life, is here
summed up by the weary man in a few words of complaint, uttered in the evening over his beer. He is born to rule, and appointed to serve. The world, therefore, seems a sorry place.
Things he would like to do, things he ought to do, seem within
his grasp; but when he reaches out his hands, a prince lets down
a glassy wall from above, the statesman is shut away, and has to
wait outside.

Oh, to be a landgrave!

XX

"The position is no longer that of last September. If you still
say 'not one stone of our fortresses', there is no use discussing
matters." These are Bismarck's first words to Jules Favre, who
pays him a second visit at the end of January, when the Germans have already been three months besieging Paris. He goes on:
"Your hair has got much greyer since last I saw you. Anyhow,
you have come too late. Behind the door, there, a new envoy
from Napoleon is waiting. I shall treat with him. . . . Why

should I negotiate with you at all? Why should I give your republic a semblance of legality? At bottom it is nothing more
than a few rebels! When your emperor comes back, he will have
the right to shoot you as a traitor."

Favre: "Then there will be civil war and anarchy."

Bismarck: "Are you sure of that? Besides, I don't see how
your civil war will do us Germans any harm!"

Favre: "Are you not afraid to drive us to despair? Are you
not afraid of making our resistance even fiercer?"

Bismarck: "Your resistance! . . . You have no right — please
listen to me carefully — you have no right, before man and God,
for the sake of so pitiable a thing as military renown, to give
over to famine a town with a population of more than two millions! . . . Don't talk of resistance. In this case it is a crime!"
He turns towards the door behind which, as he has told Favre,
Napoleon's emissary is supposed to be waiting.

Favre: "Not yet! Do not, after all our disasters, force upon
France the shame of having to endure Bonaparte!"

Five minutes later, the essentials of the cession and the war
indemnity have been agreed upon. Dinner follows, and all watch
to see how much the envoy from the starving capital will eat.
Now the preliminaries are discussed. Bismarck offers Favre a
cigar, which the Frenchman refuses.

"You are making a mistake," says the German statesman.
"It is better to smoke when people are beginning a conversation which is likely to become acrimonious. No smoker wants to
drop his cigar, and therefore he avoids violent bodily movements.
Besides, smoking soothes our minds. The blue vapours of burning tobacco rising from our cigars will exercise a charm upon
us, will make us more accommodating. Eyes are occupied, hands
have something to do, the odour is pleasing, people are happy
when they are smoking." When, very soon after this utterance,
he begins to grow hot about Garibaldi, the French count who
has accompanied Favre, and to whom we owe the story of this
conversation, smilingly offers him a cigar.

Perfect mastery, in conjunction with unfailing courtesy, with

which latter the French accredit him! Of course he is playing
with them as a cat plays with a mouse, but in his present company he plays with Gallic wit in order to charm his adversaries
— for he wants peace almost as much as they do. If he were negotiating with Englishmen, his tone would be a very different one.
When, later, Thiers has an interview with him, and makes fine
speeches, Bismarck demands six milliards. Thereupon Thiers exclaims: "C'est une indignité!" Bismarck immediately begins to
talk German, and says he must send for an interpreter: "My
knowledge of your language is so slender that I cannot understand
Herr Thiers' last words." As soon as they begin to discuss practical details once more, Bismarck drops back into French.

"As a political man of business," says Favre, "his ability was
almost inconceivable. He would only reckon with the actually
extant; his gaze was fixed solely on practical solutions. . . .
Accessible to every impression, highstrung, he cannot always
master his impetuosity. I marvelled, sometimes because he was so
considerate, and sometimes because he was so ruthless. . . . He
never deceived me. Often enough he hurt me and angered me by
his severities, but in great matters and in small I always found
him upright and precise."

Lengthy consultations with the king and the generals hindered
the negotiations. All sorts of unauthorised persons offered advice, Augusta in the van. "I am fully informed regarding these
discreditable intrigues," said Bismarck. "At my request, the king
has written her a lengthy epistle, so that she will not be in a
hurry to write again!" When he wants to use two hundred millions levied from the town of Paris for the repayment of what
had been extorted from the German princes, now Prussia's allies, in the year 1866 — the king refuses. Every one except Bismarck insists upon the fortresses being handed over. At length,
he agrees to demand Alsace with Belfort, and part of Lorraine
with Metz. He only consents to this because Moltke insists that
the cession is indispensable to the safety of Germany. He also
asks for six milliards as indemnity, and the entry of the Germans
into Paris. He abates his demand to five milliards, this sum being

proportional to the amount paid per head of the population by
Prussia as indemnity in 1807. The calculation is made by Bleichröder, whom he has summoned. In the end, he gives his adversaries the choice between the surrender of Belfort and agreeing to
a German entry into Paris. Thereupon, the French promptly
decide to save the fortress by accepting the humiliation, a decision which is little in keeping with the customary estimate of the
French character.

While all are rejoicing, the statesman remains sceptical. He
is uneasy about this annexation, and says to the crown prince:
"Nothing but consideration for the views of our army men has
made me agree to keep Metz. Besides, the king has let fall remarks which lead me to think that he would be inclined to continue the war to make sure of getting this fortress." To his wife
he writes: "We have gained more than, as far as my personal
political views go, seems likely to be useful. . . . I have to heed
voices from above and voices from below, the voices of those who
lack foresight. We are taking . . . Metz, with some extremely
indigestible elements."

When matters have been finally settled with Thiers and Favre,
he draws a breath of relief. For the last few days he has been
suffering from severe neuralgia; now the pain vanishes. He goes
into the room where the officers are waiting and whistles the
death halloo. In the evening, he has the Bavarian minister and
Bleichröder to dine with him: symbols of unity and finance. When
they have gone he asks for some music, after long deprivation.
The first thing he wants Keudell to play is the Hohenfriedberger
March.

Next day, when Thiers comes to sign the agreement, the beaten
minister has been retransformed into the dispassionate historian.
He eyes the victor and says: "C'est nous, du reste, qui avons fait
votre unité!"

The shaft strikes home. Bismarck looks shrewdly at the learned
Frenchman, and is content to answer in a single word: "Peut-
être."

After the struggles and intrigues, the lies and subterfuges, of the protracted negotiations, this brief dialogue lifts us above the atmosphere of figures and interests into the pure air of the spirit. The whole problem which had been at issue between these two neighbours, one of whom grudged the other the attainment of unity, a unity which that other would not have been able to attain without taking up arms; the dependence of the national advance in Germany upon the international enmity between Germany and France — after all the bombardments with shells and reasons, these essential facts suddenly appear in the limelight, and the more fortunate of the two combatants does not deny that they are facts. Thiers, a much older man than Bismarck, is also a clever man. The German does not wish to be rough in manner towards the Frenchman, nor does he want the Frenchman to suppose that he himself lacks insight. Still less, however, does Bismarck wish to put himself in pawn to Thiers by any admission which Thiers can subsequently flourish from the tribune of the chamber as new and unexpected laurels. Bismarck sees all this in a flash, weighs and calculates, knows how to get out of the difficulty. With the confidence of genius, he answers: "Perhaps."

By the end of November, when the preliminaries of German unity had been arranged, the only thing lacking was the crown. In this matter there continued a struggle of all against all, degenerating into a farce such as the history of empire in Europe had not known since the first Caesar thrice refused the crown. All those who held liberal views were opposed to the idea of an empire. Even Freytag objected to the assumption of this title of world dominion, which would be, he said, "the revival of a false idealism." All the German kings and most of the German lesser rulers were likewise opposed to it, from corporate jealousy. More than all, the chief person in the drama was averse. Had he ten years earlier crowned himself with his own hand in order that now a chorus of princes, and in the end the people, should offer him a second crown which his own brother had refused, calling it a crown of filth and clay? "I am a Prussian," exclaimed King William, thinking of his ancestors and his seventy-four years; determined to resist any such usurpation. "What do I care about such a title as a man sports at a fancy-dress ball?" said the king, who was, before all, an army officer. Bismarck, with sly humour, could but answer: "Surely Your Majesty does not want to remain neuter for all time, to be a mere 'presidency'?"

"The most objectionable, the most distasteful matter to me is the question of title," said the modest king as late as New Year's Eve to his son. "I cannot but remember how the question of a greater unification of Germany was the chief purpose of His Majesty of blessed memory, and how the — paper — crown was offered to my brother, and how, thank God, he would not accept it!... Yet I, a man with a Prussian heart, . . . am to see the title which has been so glorious recede into the background, and am to give the premier place to another which . . . for a whole century was borne by the enemies of Prussia! . . . The fates are conspiring against me."

A thousand years earlier, Charlemagne had felt as William now feels; for Charlemagne had been taken by surprise, had been reluctant, when the pope had crowned him with the imperial crown, saying afterwards, "se eo die, quamvis praecipua festivitas esset, ecclesiam non intraturum, si pontificîs consilium praescire potuisset."

Bismarck himself, always a realist, had at first been opposed to this idea of "emperordom." As late as October, he had spoken to the crown prince about the greater glories of the old Prussian court. But by degrees he had warmed to the imperial idea, recognising that the imperial title would promote unity and centralisation.

A considerable proportion of the German stocks favoured the formation of an empire; so did the grand duke of Baden; so, above all, did the crown prince of Prussia. Of the latter, Freytag (who at this time held frequent and intimate converse with him) says: "To Prince Frederick, the provision of a new crown and a new weapon for himself and the crown princess were very serious concerns. I mean that he was the prime originator of the new configuration of Germany, and the chief motive force in its construction." It was Frederick who, when the first German Reichstag was opened, arranged for the introduction of the ancient coronation chair of the emperors of the Saxon house into the modern ceremony — much to the astonishment of the deputies.

But neither the son nor the son-in-law of the king of Prussia was now in a position to make the proposal. This had to come from the most powerful of the German kings — and he sat in his castle of dreams, charmed by music, sailing, as Lohengrin, across the shell-girt sea. His cousin of Baden's fine letters remained unanswered, for King Louis had no use for emperor or empire. It was only when he was told that he might be staying in a still more beautiful palace, in the Trianon, that he paid heed to what was going on, and sent his grand equerry to the seat of war to bespeak lodgings and stables outside Paris.

Bismarck took a firm grip of this chief equerry, Count Holnstein. After all his trouble, were his plans to be frustrated because one king would not accept the imperial crown, and the other would not offer it? He wrote three of his most brilliant letters "then and there, at a dining-table from which the food had just been cleared, upon paper that was little better than blotting paper and with reluctant ink." He shows King Louis (a naïve man after his own fashion) that it would be intolerable for Bavaria if the king of Prussia were to exercise any influence within that country; a German emperor, however, would not be a mere neighbour to Bavaria, a neighbour belonging to a different class, but would be a fellow countryman; therefore King Louis could make the concession only to the German emperor, and not to the king of Prussia. If this argument should not prove convincing, there was a stronger one. Would it not be possible (thinks Bismarck) to strike up an alliance between the Wittelsbachs and the Bismarcks? There used to be such an alliance three hundred years back! In a second letter, therefore, enclosed in the same envelope, he thanks the king " for the remarkable kindnesses which the Bavarian dynasty, throughout more than a generation, showed my ancestors, at the time when the Wittelsbachs ruled in the March of Brandenburg."

Here we have an argumentum ad regem and an argumentum ad hominem! What will King Louis answer, should he write? If he should make the proposal in a different form from that recommended by Bismarck, if he should do anything to arouse the dynastic touchiness of King William, all would be lost, for the king of Prussia is only waiting for a pretext to refuse. William too, in Bismarck's opinion, "is not free from the desire to parade before the other dynasties the superiority of his own, . . . being more concerned to emphasise the preponderant prestige of the Prussian crown than to bring the imperial title into recognition."

Thus Bismarck has to play the neurologist, to give the same medicine to his two distinguished patients, but to administer it in a different manner in the two cases. He does the cleverest thing possible. With all humility, when sending the letter to King Louis, he encloses the draft of the reply he suggests that Louis shall write to King William ("Your Majesty need merely be good enough to copy it"). The chief equerry journeys back with the three letters. But King Louis is out of sorts. At Hohenschwangau, he wants to hear only of King Henry, to the length of three Wagnerian acts, and not to hear about an Emperor William; besides, he has a toothache. Still, Holnstein manages to get on with his job. King Louis reads the letter twice, and, as Bismarck had calculated, is flattered by it. He makes one of his grooms bring ink and paper, and promptly, sitting up in bed and without consulting any of his ministers, he writes the letter of solicitation which the representative of the solicited monarch has dictated. Holnstein hastens back with it to Versailles.

There the birthday of some princess or other is being celebrated. A Bavarian prince "takes over the extraordinarily agreeable commission of presenting the letter to the king immediately before the banquet." — "A state despatch? Bismarck must read it first, for this matter comes within his province." So, after dinner, King William hands Bismarck the letter, requesting him to read it aloud to himself and Frederick. With a serious mien and a fine emphasis, Bismarck thereupon reads the letter he has himself composed. What will the recipient say to it? William need pay no heed to the susceptibilities of the writer, who is far away. There are no strangers here, so the old gentleman indignantly exclaims: "This comes at a very inconvenient time!" Frederick tells us that King William was "beside himself with annoyance because of the contents of this letter, and extremely depressed by it." William dismisses Frederick and Bismarck without detecting the conspiracy. Outside the room, the crown prince, feeling that his deepest wish is likely to be fulfilled, shakes hands with Bismarck. That evening he writes in his diary: "To-day emperor and empire have been irrevocably reestablished. Now . . . the emperorless, the troublous, time is over. This proud title is a sufficient guarantee."

At first the emperor elect is a passive resister. No one dares to speak to him of the new crown. He will have nothing to do with it. But all has been made ready, and now even the nation can say "Amen." The second act of the comedy is played in the Reichstag. A deputy is permitted to ask whether the German people is not to have a supreme overlord. Thereupon Delbrück, "in a strident voice, read aloud the king of Bavaria's despatch. . . . It looked as if the unfortunate German imperial crown was being pulled out of his trousers pocket, wrapped up in a piece of newspaper." Bismarck said: "This imperial comedy ought to have had a better stage manager; there should have been a more effective mise-en-scène."

All the same, thirty representatives of the Reichstag are invited to Versailles, to present, not the imperial crown, but simply an address. Meanwhile, the Bavarian Landtag shows a strong inclination to refuse its consent to the treaty. King William is furious about the "Emperor Deputation." On the evening when it arrives, he declares he will not receive it until the demand of all the princes has been formally presented to him in black and white, "for otherwise it would seem as if the proposal to reestablish emperor and empire had proceeded rather from the

Reichstag than from the princes." According to the crown prince, gentlemen of the court openly ask: "Why on earth have these fellows come here?" Stieber, chief of police at headquarters, writes to his wife: "The court party and the military party were cool; I represented the German people here." Since Stieber had in former days passed as a communist, it was quite in order that he should add: "Extraordinary times!"

In the end it appeared that the representatives of the Reichstag would have to be received, but the princes and the generals did not make up their minds to attend until an hour before the ceremony, and for this reason the scene was improvised in the prefecture of police. "Unfortunately no use was made to-day of the fine marble staircase," complains the crown prince. The worthy Simson delivered a speech. He probably remembered the speech he had made twenty-one years earlier to the late king, William's brother, when he had offered the same crown, and, to his astonishment, had been met with a refusal. Next, Simson read an address containing the words: "In unison with the ruling princes of Germany, the North German Reichstag approaches Your Majesty with the request that he will consecrate the work of unification by accepting the German imperial crown." The king's answer left the legal position just as "nebulous" as the address had done. William said: "Only in the unanimous voice of the German princes and free cities and in the wish of the German nation and its representatives duly accordant with that of the princes, can I recognise the call of Providence which I shall be able to follow in the confident hope of God's blessing." Thus the sovereign princes had voices, while the subjects had only wishes, and thus the "filth and clay" were gilded. On this occasion, Germany was represented by two Jews, for what Simson read had been written by Lasker, and the king said afterwards: "Indeed I have to thank Herr Lasker for a very great honour!" In these days when the empire was being established, Bebel and Liebknecht were arrested on a charge of high treason. They had openly criticised the forms of the new constitution, and, in conjunction with six others, had refused to vote the new war credits

on the ground that they were for a war of conquest. The aim of
the arrests was to exclude the socialist leaders from the electoral
campaign.

The old gentleman had still to play the third act, which was
more trying than the others. On January 18th, the office of the
marshal of the household issued the following invitation: "The
Ordensfest will be celebrated in the glass gallery of the palace
of Versailles at noon; there will be a brief prayer, and then the
proclamation will be made." This invitation, which is equally
remarkable for the German in which it is penned and for the
word "Glasgalerie" in it which has been mistranslated from the
French, avoids naming the giver of the feast. The day before,
the king had refused to become "German emperor", declaring
that it was his set purpose to become "emperor of Germany",
or not to be emperor at all. Vainly did Bismarck endeavour to
convince him that the term "emperor of Germany" implied territorial sovereignty, quoting the example of the Russian emperor,
who was not called emperor of Russia. The king disputed this
assertion, basing his objection upon a false translation. Bismarck showed him a taler upon which Frederick was described as
Rex Borussorum, not as Rex Borussiae. Then he came back to
the wording of his own letter, which the king of Bavaria had
copied to send it to the king of Prussia. Thence the conversation passed to the relative positions of emperors and kings, arch-
dukes and grand dukes. He spoke of the pavilion in which a
Prussian king had met an emperor; and was ready with a pleni-
tude of historical examples to show William that the morrow's
ceremony would certainly not imply an accession of rank for the
king of Prussia. The old gentleman grew angrier and angrier,
and exclaimed: "No matter how these things have been in the
past. It rests with me to say how they shall be to-day! The arch-
dukes . . . have always taken precedence of the Prussian princes
and so they shall in the future!"

Suddenly he begins to sob and to shed tears, lamenting "his
desperate position, because he would next day have to bid farewell to dear old Prussia. In a surge of excitement he exclaimed:

'My son is whole-heartedly in favour of the new order of things, whereas I do not wish to move a hair's breadth in that direction, and cling only to Prussia!' . . . At length he sprang up in a fury, broke off the discussions, and declared that he would not hear a word more about the festival fixed for the morrow." This was the last boding cry of the last king of Prussia. It came from the man who, during the German advance, had had his camp-bed set up in the ornate bedroom of one of the palaces of the Rothschilds, and had used the bathroom as his study; the man who was enraged when he was spoken of as a veteran hero; the man who, when people mentioned the Hohenzollern eagles, said angrily that the Hohenzollern had no eagles in their coat of arms. In 1848, William had wished to retire in order to save his brother; in the year 1862, he had wished to retire in order to save his honour in the struggle about the army; now, in 1871, for the third time, he wishes to retire, to abdicate "and hand everything over to Fritz", because all his affections are centred on Prussia, and because, with a seer's vision, he dreads the boastful new title.

"After this scene," writes the crown prince, "I felt so ill that I had to take medicine. Subsequently I learned that the king would not appear at the tea table in the evening." What was going to happen next day? No one knew. But the office of the marshal of the household is stronger than kings, and William's training as an Old Prussian officer makes him comply in spite of himself. Next morning, under the stage management of the crown prince, the dignitaries appear in the Hall of Mirrors, sixty standard bearers, six hundred officers, a certain number of rankers; followed by the German ruling princes — King William in their wake. Since no one knows under what symbol he intends to become emperor, the most important point, the placing of the princes, has to be improvised by him then and there. He does it ceremoniously, and with chivalrous modesty. In his straightforward way, he subsequently described the affair in the following terms:

"I had not troubled myself about the military arrangements; nor did I know where the banners would stand. They wanted to set up a throne for me, but I forbade this. I wished to remain among the princes in front of the altar throughout the ceremony. When I saw that my colours and standards had been placed on the haut pas I naturally went thither, for where my colours are there must I be also. The haut pas was so crowded that the princes had hardly any room, and they would have had to stand beneath me. I therefore let them get up on it first, and was content to order that the colours of the first regiment of the Guards (the regiment I entered when I joined the army), the flag of my own grenadier regiment, and the flag of the Landwehr battalion (whose commanding officer I have been for so long), should be placed immediately behind me. My intention to stand in front of the altar, and there to take the new and weighty pledge, was frustrated by the colours upon the haut pas. My only regret was that the colours of all the Guards regiments were not there!"

After the throne had been thrust aside by the altar and the altar by the colours, and when the new emperor had called his crowned cousins to stand upon the same level as himself and had been separated from them by his standards, the pastor, instead of uttering the brief prayer that had been prescribed, delivered a philippic upon Louis XIV. and a discourse upon January 18th, which infuriated Bismarck by its "Prussian self-idolisation." Then the chancellor stepped forward, and read the proclamation, which began as follows: "We, William by the grace of God king of Prussia, after the German princes and free cities have unanimously appealed to us to renew the imperial dignity which has been in abeyance for more than sixty years, to reestablish the empire and to take charge of it, . . . hereby inform you that we regard it as our duty to the whole fatherland to respond to this summons of the allied German princes and free cities and to assume the German imperial title." This address is directed "To the German people." But the people is no more than audience, has only a passive rôle, while the Reichstag is not mentioned at all. Thus, in the latter part of the nineteenth century, a solemn announcement is made to the world that the German princes have

BISMARCK IN 1877

From a photograph by Loescher and Petsch, Berlin

chosen an emperor, as they had formerly done in the Middle Ages, and have informed their faithful subjects of the fact.

"When Bismarck uttered the first words, . . . his breast was heaving with excitement, his face was pale, and his ears were so bloodless that they were almost transparent." This description is given by a doctor who was present on the occasion, and it may well be that the chancellor was greatly moved at having turned so dangerous a corner. The crown prince, however, gives a different account of the matter, saying that Bismarck was "business-like, without any trace of warmth or of solemnity of mood." With regard to the applause that followed the announcement, Frederick says: "This moment was intensely moving. I bent my knee before the emperor and kissed his hand, whereupon he raised me to my feet and embraced me with strong emotion. I cannot attempt to describe my own frame of mind." Still, the crown prince was not so deeply moved but that he could watch the effect of his actions, and he says that "even the standard bearers showed unmistakable signs of emotion."

The veteran monarch soon pulls himself together, for this theatricality is not to his taste for long. He leaves his platform, and the direction of his steps and glances show that he is making for the men who have achieved so much. The generals are standing in the front rank, beside the princes. In the place between the two groups is one figure. The chancellor stands erect there, the proclamation still in his hands, waiting — for the exchange of hand-clasps which must now follow is a symbol, and Bismarck will never bend the knee like Frederick. He pays homage by his actions, not by idolisation; by tension, not by relaxation. Assuredly he must be expecting that thanks will be silently rendered him before the hundreds of onlookers. Nevertheless, after all that has gone before, he still does not know his aged master. William had not wanted to become emperor at all; or, if emperor, to be not German emperor but emperor of Germany. The chancellor has spoiled all his pleasure in the festival! William, therefore, ignores the offender, stalks past without noticing him, and gives his hand to the generals only.

This is the weakest moment in the life of William I. Not because he thus publicly ignores the man whose creative mind, as he well knows, has brought all these things to pass, but because he allows an old man's obstinacy to get the better of an inborn sense of what is fitting. It is his weakest moment because, on this solemn occasion, before all the princes and standard bearers, before all the journalists and generals (most of whom are the chancellor's enemies, or regard him with jealous dislike, or are at least the possessors of gossiping tongues which to-morrow will spread the news abroad), he shows whom he prefers, and whom he cannot endure. Since the minister stands alone in symbolical isolation, it is impossible for any of those present to overlook the affront. To-day, the emperor's studied slight is reflected in the hundred mirrors of the hall; to-morrow the scene will be re-enacted in thousands of imaginations.

Bismarck accepts the affront stoically, merely placing it on record, saying that it did not affect political relationships, and that after a few days " we gradually found ourselves upon the old footing once more." The king (let us continue, for a little while, to speak of him by this finer title which Bismarck never ceased to use) accepted the emperordom which had been thrust upon him. It was his frugal way, when sending back a document which had been submitted to him, to use the envelope in which it had been sent. This very evening, when he was discharging his customary duties, he dealt with the papers relating to that day, which had been sent to him by Bismarck. Reading upon the envelope the words: " To His Imperial Majesty, from the Federal Chancellor " —he ran his pen through the word " Federal " and wrote over it " Imperial."

Thus circumspectly, thriftily, and unostentatiously, did the German empire begin.

Roon, who had kept away from the proclamation ceremony, wrote to his wife: " I had hoped that the successful laying of the imperial egg would have given Bismarck temporary satisfaction. Unfortunately this is not so." Bismarck to Johanna: " Forgive me for not having written to you for so long, but this imperial childbirth was an extremely difficult business, and kings at such times have strange cravings, just like women before they give to the world that which they cannot retain within them. I, who had to play the accoucheur, felt often enough like a bomb which was about to burst and lay the whole structure in ruins." Two nights after the ceremony, when at his dinner-table there was a dispute about "German emperor", "emperor of Germany", and similar matters, Bismarck held his peace for a while. At length he enquired:

"Do any of you happen to know the Latin for Wurst? Farcimen? Farcimentum?—Nescio quid mihi magis farcimentum esset!"

BOOK FOUR: 1872–1888

THE RULER

Bismarck makes Germany great and the Germans small
—G. VON BUNSEN

I

" Count Bismarck-Schönhausen will be at home to Deputy
Blank from April 24th onwards at nine o'clock every Saturday
evening during the session of the Reichstag."

This invitation, circularised for the first time after the opening of the North German Reichstag, arouses uneasiness among
the representatives of the people. Some of them are delighted with
the innovation; others strongly object to it. Simson says: "Certainly we shall have to wear evening dress, to keep up the dignity
of the occasion." Bismarck wanted neither evening dress nor
dignity. His aim was to establish a sort of weekly political stock
exchange at which "in ten minutes, in the corner of a drawing-
room, matters could be settled which would otherwise necessitate
a question in the Reichstag."

For his own part, he had long since ceased to accept invitations; very rarely went even to court, preferring as a rule to wear
a long coat beneath whose collar his necktie almost disappeared;
or else to sport a pot-pourri of fragments of uniform which made
Moltke smile. He was growing old, and was used to getting his
own way. His aristocratic pride made him fonder of being host
than guest. He hated having to thank any one. These considerations, in conjunction with business sagacity and the desire for
opportunities of exercising personal influence, led him to invite
his chief enemies to assemble week by week beneath his roof.

During the decade of the wars, Bismarck had regarded Virchow and Duncker as more cordially hostile than Napoleon or
Francis Joseph. Now, when the second decade of his power opened,
the decade of peace, the whole Reichstag formed front against
him. The fact that he stood alone against hundreds of enemies
invigorated Bismarck's lust for battle. He had not been satisfied
with simply locking up his enemies' house and putting the key

in his pocket. He wanted open contradiction; he was not at ease unless he had something to grumble at; even if he had been an absolute monarch, he would have ferreted out causes of friction. During the next twenty years we shall see Bismarck always discontented, always complaining, and we shall know that this sense of perpetual friction is what keeps the fighter's vital forces at the stretch. The ever-renewed internal conflicts gave him fresh resolution to cope with external adversaries.

This unwearied combativeness is the deeper explanation of his mistakes. Because Bismarck's misanthropy grew with the years, because he could never concede anything either to the position or to the talents of an opponent, because he inclined less and less to negotiate, and more and more to command, the changes the time spirit was undergoing were hidden from his eyes, and he was blind to the logical thoughts and wishes of other men than himself and other classes than his own. In foreign relationships he had never under-estimated an opponent; had never risked an entry into action without superior forces, heavier guns, or stronger coalitions to back him. But in home affairs, now, he begins to make hazardous ventures. Because his unconstitutional régime has been successful, he is filled with contempt for old and new opponents, who will in the end overthrow him. Roon's cannon, Moltke's needle-guns, and the discipline of obedient Prussians, had forced Europe to condone Bismarck's action in setting might above right; in the end, his own people took vengeance on him because he set might above spirit.

Projecting his own character into his country, he succeeded in making the Reichstag an enemy instead of an instrument to his hand, and in estranging all the parties one after another, so that a contemporary caricaturist depicted him as Cronus devouring his own children. In home affairs he made and broke alliances with the same pitiless realism as he had found necessary from time to time in foreign affairs. As time went on, he made all classes of the nation distrust him, since every five years, when the elections came, he ran atilt against another class of the population. Although his genius as a European aroused the wonder of the whole continent, and at last extorted a kind of veneration, at home his autocratic policy embittered the common people, who were unable to understand his skill in foreign affairs. In these latter, he could sit alone playing chess with great powers, silently, responsible to no one but the aged king whom he dragged along in his wake. At home, every measure had first to be proposed, and then to be defended; and he would often refuse concessions to the Reichstag solely from hatred for this or that leader, just as, because it hated him, the Reichstag would refuse to bend before his will. A man can be a dictator or a parliamentarian; he cannot be both.

On Saturday evenings, the big rooms of the chancellor's mansion were thronged by representatives of the people. Some of the members of the opposition came thither, lured by the magnetism of their great adversary, and also by the exceptionally rich fare which the host provided as a political calmative. He welcomed his guests with extreme courtesy, and sometimes with studied ceremony. He knew them all individually, though he could not always remember their names, and this led him to say that his eye worked with the precision of a modern rifle, whereas his memory was slow and uncertain like a flintlock. Except for the greeting on arrival, there was no formality. Nobody was introduced. You went up to the cask of Munich beer and turned the tap yourself to draw a bumper. Ladies were seldom present at these free and easy gatherings. As midnight drew near, the host would generally be found soliloquising, the centre of a large circle, telling anecdotes of the past, sketching the future, always assuming the pose of a star performer among those who could expect, in good time, to soar to his altitude.

See him sitting there, half reclining in a long chair, holding a great German pipe in his right hand, surrounded by the invariable litter of newspapers, a soloist facing the chorus. He gazes searchingly into the eyes of his guests, paying special attention to his principal opponents. Since, even when he is wearing a military tunic, he has no weapons, it is as well that he should have some trusty guardians. The two great Danes are always there, close at hand, ever on the watch, ready for instant battle; and on these parliamentary evenings, when their master is entertaining a hundred or more of his enemies, they are very much on the alert. "He ate and drank freely on these occasions," writes a friend of the family; "and, when he called for his pipe, he looked like a patriarch among his disciples."

Those assembled here have very different heads, which have given them very different destinies.

There is a slender man, quick in his movements. His face is red, framed in a dark beard. He has a high forehead and is almost bald. With his clever eyes, his friendly and serious expression, one might take him for a humanist; but some of his gestures, and a wide scar across the face, suggest that he is an officer and a man of family. He is in fact all three of these things — Rudolf von Bennigsen, one of the best and ablest men of his day. Reserved and virile, noble-minded and faithful like Roon, natural and modest though he does not underrate his own abilities, he seems made for the guidance of the whole country. Since, at the decisive moment, he hesitates to enter the cabinet, his life is devoted to the leadership of a party, in which he plays the born mediator, favouring its activities by his rare and usually formal orations, his diligence upon committees, and his continuous association with all his colleagues. The party is itself a middle party, that of the national liberals, and therein he himself occupies a position between the two extremes.

Bismarck regards him as too soft, is repelled by his æsthetic sensibilities and by his lack of passion; and Bismarck is right in regarding Bennigsen as a German idealist, as one who thinks better than he acts. Even when he is seventy years of age, Bennigsen will sit once more among the students at Göttingen to learn. He is the son of a general from Lower Saxony, a man whose family is as old as Bismarck's, so the chancellor has a certain respect for him. He has given up Hanover, his homeland, for Germany, without loving Prussia; and Bismarck, the man who annexed Hanover to Prussia, can understand this. At times, Bismarck will even address Bennigsen as "honoured friend." Bennigsen leads a party which does not unconditionally break with him when it no longer follows him — and this is a thing that Bismarck can never understand. When it happens, he calls Bennigsen a stupid fellow.

Of rougher and cooler type is the man next him. The long well-knit figure expresses a firmer will; and the untidy, grizzled hair gives him a defiant stamp. A fighter, like Bismarck, proud and gruff, is Wilhelm von Kardorff. He is a younger man than the chancellor, and when he does not wear glasses his grey-blue eyes are as keen and piercing as Bismarck's. But when we look at his bronzed features, our gaze is arrested by the bluish-white tint of his nose — it is an artificial one, for he had lost his nose in a student's duel.

His temperament and his abilities had attracted Bismarck's attention, and it was only his determination to be independent which had saved him from Bismarck's claws. By remaining independent, he can remain on friendly terms with Bismarck; and he will continue to be faithful to the house of his friend when the other Junkers turn to the new sun. A man of more mobile mind than most of the members of his class, Kardorff sat among the parties of the right, and would often venture an excursion into more liberal air; in economic matters, he clung to the ideas that prevailed eastward of the Elbe, and was instrumental in promoting Bismarck's adoption of a protective tariff policy.

In the midst of these German aristocrats stands a Jew, a lean, dark man with somewhat pointed features. Of the same age as Bennigsen, Eduard Lasker had, like the other, learnt to ride and to fence when living on the family property. As a boy he had studied the Talmud in a small town in Posen, and had translated Schiller's *Teilung der Erde* into Hebrew verse. No wonder, then, that he, as the better lawyer, the cleverer man, the leader of the radical wing, should soon have become Bennigsen's rival. As critic, debater, and orator, he excelled Bennigsen. His ideal was the constitutional State, whereas Bennigsen inclined towards the ideal of the national State. He had socialist leanings, but was no less patriotic than Bennigsen. He was concrete in his aims, a man who had few wants; was of an autocratic temperament, and was therefore not congenial to Bismarck — who, besides, preferred to have corpulent and easy-going folk around him rather than lean and eager ones.

A man of Lasker's race, and a member of the same party, is listening to him with a pallid visage and a sceptical air. Ludwig Bamberger is growing old, is narrow-chested and round-shouldered. To look at him nowadays, when he is lean and wasted, no one would believe that he had been so active in the days of the '48, or that he had once been a man noted for physical prowess. You would think that such a man could have played small part in practical life, that his zeal must have been chiefly rhetorical. But in those days Ludwig Bamberger, consumptive though he was, had been driven into the ranks of the radicals by his internal fires. Because of his doings, he had had to flee from Prussia, had thought of going to America; in the end he had stayed in London, living with rich relatives. At twenty-six he became a junior assistant in their bank, grew rich, and before the war had removed to Paris, where his roaming spirit found anchorage, and where he was charmed with the French wit, the French style, French irony, and the elegant women of the City of Light. There all circles were opened to him as a patron of the arts.

Thenceforward, this man who had once played so active a part in life, came to regard life as a spectacle, in which only at times, when he was in a good mood, he would himself figure on the stage. A homeless man, a welcome guest in all civilisations, he could speak and write French as well as his mother tongue, so that his supple talents for observing and participating could find full scope in Paris. Returning to Germany after the amnesty, he became a national liberal, retained an almost neutral poise during the war, and wrote to a private correspondent: "In Paris, the flower of Catholic romanticism blooms; at Versailles, in the German headquarters, the radicalism of an upstart prevails. Paris is the Bastille which is being stormed; Favre and Gambetta are legitimacy, whereas William and Bismarck are the revolution." None the less, he is summoned to the German headquarters, because Bismarck can turn his expert knowledge of banking to account. Dispassionately, Bamberger describes Bismarck as "a compound of Stuart cavalier, Prussian lieutenant, German feudal magnate, and Spanish Don Quixote." Both now and later, he recognises the chancellor's greatness, although Bismarck cannot endure him.

Here is a man whom the chancellor hates far more than Bamberger, a bearded man, still quite young, a rare visitor. We may be sure that Bismarck will sleep little to-night, because Eugen Richter, standing somewhat aloof from the crowd, has been eyeing him keenly and critically through his spectacles. Richter has health, youth, and lust of battle — a combination which makes the older man jealous. He has an uncanny knowledge of facts, is incorruptible, adheres uncompromisingly to his principles. During the years of conflict, he was disciplined as one of Bismarck's victims. Dismissed from his post as Landrat, deprived of office and income as burgomaster, because he wrote condemning the arbitrary measures of the police, he had become a journalist, and had opposed Lassalle, because Lassalle negotiated with Bismarck. He has a passion for the commonweal; seeks, not his own aims, nor yet power, but only the advance of the good cause. He therefore kept close watch on Lassalle, and now keeps close watch on Bismarck. He will neither abase himself before the Junker caste, nor before the great position of this particular Junker. That is why, when Richter begins to speak in the assembly, Bismarck leaves the hall. When, at breakfast next morning, he reads the report of Richter's attack — perhaps a criticism of the army estimates, supported by figures and illuminated by revelations — Bismarck promptly drives to the Reichstag in order to hit back: "Unfortunately Herr Richter has always lived in houses and among newspapers, and knows little of practical life; this autocrat of the democratic party thrives upon exaggerations and alarums; there is always a sting hidden in his speeches." Thereupon Richter, with wounding tranquillity, replies: "Is the imperial chancellor aware . . . ?"

Perhaps behind the back of this guest, the imperial chancellor now sees looming the shades of two others, who appear only as shades, like Banquo's ghost, and not in the flesh — for between them and Bismarck there can be no circumstantial debates, only the voiceless and angry contention of two conflicting and irreconcilable worlds — a conflict of antipodal outlooks. I or you; for "we" is impossible. Yet Wilhelm Liebknecht, one of these shades, can reckon up his ancestors for as many generations back as Bismarck, and when he does so can trace his lineage to a man who is more like Bismarck than Bismarck's own robber knight ancestors are — back to Luther. Moreover, he can trace back his lineage to a number of German men of learning, as whose descendant Liebknecht had become a student and a member of the Burschenschaft. Orphaned early, after a strenuous youth, nevertheless to this aspiring lad life would have been easy enough if he had followed in the footsteps of others of his class! But he has an idealist bee in his bonnet, wants the welfare of all mankind and not that of his own class alone. At twenty, therefore, he is exiled as a communist. Zurich; Paris; eighteen forty-eight; the Badenese rising; thus at twenty-two he hoists the flag of the republic, and it is only by chance that he escapes being shot with his confederates — just as seventy years later his son is to be murdered for the founding of the republic.

What a life do such men have to lead! Always faced by hostile judges, unfeeling prison warders, penned in narrow cells, free only in exile. Yet their mission is in their fatherland, which they love no less ardently than do the legitimists. Bismarck's nerves, doubtless, have many worries to endure in the forty years of struggle, and we have heard the lamentations of the born ruler who is called upon to serve; yet day by day and year by year he grows more prosperous in the circumstances of his material life. He owns forests and castles; can keep a good table such as suits his good appetite; while the king and the nation vie with one another to shower gifts and honours upon him. Hear, now, what Liebknecht says proudly to his judges: "If, after unprecedented successes, I am still a poor man, I pride myself on the fact." In very truth, when he returns to Germany after twelve years' exile, he is poor in material possessions, and his life is lightened only by the things of the spirit: not by wealth, not even by power; solely by faith.

If the two men, knowing nothing of one another, had met on a forest path in some distant land, Bismarck and Liebknecht would soon have been on good terms. Both of them love trees, know birds; and, if we speak of Germany, they both love their country. All too soon would the realist recognise the agitator; the cynic would discern the man of faith; the calculator would perceive the man of dreams — if the path were narrow, neither would give way to the other, and neither would turn back; they would come to blows, for essentially both of them are autocrats.

August Bebel is less of an autocrat. Among his forbears there is no revolutionist and no humanist. By his heritage, he should be obedient, for he was born in a fortress, the son of a non-commissioned officer. He should have been a champion of order. It is nothing but a thirst for knowledge that drives the turner's apprentice into the Workers' Educational Society. Once he gets there, his clear intelligence soon enables him to understand why he and those like him are in such evil case. Anger loosens his tongue; he spurs on his comrades, makes his way into the Reichstag, while trying at the same time to continue his manual craft. It is Bismarck who gives him the opportunity of extending his studies. Sentenced to imprisonment in a fortress (which, since he was born in a fortress, does not alarm him), he meets there, as fellow prisoner, Liebknecht, a much older man than himself. From this companion, he learns the theoretical foundations of the cause for which he has already been fighting under stress of his passions, and for which he has already forfeited his freedom. Liebknecht and Bebel have to cool their heels in prison for two years, and this is long enough for Bebel to make himself familiar with the teachings of Karl Marx, at whose feet Liebknecht has sat in London.

The son of the people remains more practical and more plastic than the son of a line of scholars; his intelligence is more stalwart and clearer, his critical powers are simpler and more popular than those of the man with whom he now strikes up an enduring friendship. The two are brothers in faith, brothers in self-sacrifice, in their readiness to risk their liberty and their health. Bebel, who has followed a sedentary occupation for more than five years, suffers at times from nervous insomnia. He says: "When this happened, I used to think about Bismarck, who also suffered from sleeplessness and neuralgic pains."

At Bismarck's, the shades disperse, the guests take their leave, after shaking their host by the hand. There rises from an armchair to which he has been glued throughout the evening a tiny figure. He looks like a dwarf, now that he is standing up. Stepping forward with tiny strides, he confronts his host: the gnome before the giant. The hands of the big man could crush those of the little one; the gnome's hands might overpower the giant's by magical forces; instead, they join in a friendly farewell. But, in the moment of parting, the colossus speaks to elicit an oracle from the dwarf. This dwarf is Windthorst. His pitiful, shrunken body is surmounted by a huge head. He has a large mouth, which he rarely opens to speak. From grey, sunken eyes he peers into vacancy through his thick spectacles. Bismarck, glancing down at the mannikin, whose right hand is thrust into the breast of his long black coat, watches the light of intelligence playing over Windthorst's features; and when the little man speaks in answer, it is with a firm and somewhat harsh voice that he replies to the unduly high and thin tones of Bismarck.

Since the little man's sight is bad, he has redoubled the sharpness of his ears and his memory. In the Reichstag he can recognise the voice of every one who speaks from the tribune, and even interpolates an observation. When he himself speaks, since he can use no notes, he keeps all his points clear in his head, and will, in the end, certainly succeed in making his opponent look ridiculous. He derives full advantage from being son and heir of a long line of lawyers. His small stature and the congenital weakness of his sight have but spurred him on to train his mind in order to replace what is lacking in his body. Thus at Göttingen young Windthorst studied diligently, spent only a few coppers on his dinner, was strictly temperate; whereas at the same time and in the same place young Bismarck, trusting in his bodily energies and his high spirits, was spending the money of his impoverished father on riotous living. The result was that, at thirty, Windthorst had already become a judge of the High Court of Appeal, when Bismarck was still trying to make an impression upon Pomeranian countesses by revelry, and by feats of horsemanship which frequently led to disaster.

According to his friends' account, Windthorst was a religious man, though never intolerant, and was endowed with far too keen a sense of humour to play the prophet. His irony, which in controversy became intensified to mockery, was not held in check even when he contemplated his own peculiarities. He would make fun of his own "diminutiveness", his own "ugliness", and would laugh roguishly when speaking of them. He was fond of light music. He was inclined to speak teasingly to women, taking such liberties of speech as used to be characteristic of deformed jesters in ancient days; but, instead of the traditional malice of the hunchback, he showed nothing worse than an infallible understanding of the weaknesses of his fellow men — though he did not, like Bismarck, despise them. Perhaps he had as much self-esteem as the chancellor. In the political party of which he was the leader, he was regarded as autocratic. He was inclined to consider himself a statesman, yet he was, as one of his friends said, less the statesman than the parliamentarian; within these limitations, he was unequalled as a tactician. He seemed almost incorporeal, and did not need for the defence of a barely existent body such qualities as Bismarck had in the form of personal courage; but, precisely because of the spiritualisation of his essential personality, he seemed born to act as counsel for the intellectual powers. He was cautious to a fault, scarcely ever writing a letter, and when he did so imploring the recipient to burn it instantly. Since he did not wear a cowl, he had no need for humility, and could be a fighter without having to affect the possession of prophetic fire. When the Reichstag was sitting, so that he had to spend his Sundays in Berlin, he would go every Sunday morning to the Hedwigskirche, and then to visit Bleichröder. The way this extremely secular champion of the faith spent the day of rest was characteristic. He never tried to gain any private end.

Windthorst was the only man who effected a personal conquest of Bismarck, and that was why the conquered champion never got over his defeat. "Hate," said Bismarck, "as a spur in life, is no less important than love. Two people are indispensable to me; one is my wife, and the other is Windthorst."

II

As a result of three victories, threatening clouds gathered in the skies. Bismarck saw the coming dangers from time to time, and believed he would be able to avert them. Twenty years before, the king of Prussia had said that Bismarck would only be possible as minister president "when bayonets are supreme." Ten years ago, the present king had appointed him in spite of misgivings, wanting a strong man for the management of home affairs. Bismarck had used his dictatorship to win three victories abroad. Need we be surprised that such a man should return to his starting point, and should feel himself strong enough to play the dictator at home? Need we be surprised that his attempt to do so should have failed? Proud of his independence of all doctrinaire theories, he failed to recognise the danger of having no philosophy. Looking down with contempt upon the numerous parties which confronted him, he failed to notice that he had no party to back him up. Coming fresh from the fields of battle, and having no basic sociological ideas, this great architect was not really competent to set his own house in order.

His absolute self-confidence was a deeper reason for his failure. As long as he was thinking in terms of States, Bismarck was confronted with opponents of his own type, and as a chess player he always saw to it that he had sufficient power to outwit or to destroy his adversaries. But in home affairs, before the game opened, he was sure that he outmatched his opponents in knowledge, energy, and skill. Across the frontier were great powers, which had to be won over; at home there were only small fry, people who dared not answer back. Abroad, he stood among equals, who were entitled to be Germany's opponents; at home, he knew better than any one else. If he, as master, chose to point out the roads along which his country might advance towards greatness, let no man dare to suggest there was a better way. As regards the statical problems of Germany in Europe, he was an artist; as regards the social problems of Europe, when they presented themselves in Germany, he was a dictator. Accustomed to reckon with magnitudes and not with ideas, with forces in uniform and not with forces in civilian dress, he would make no concessions, and in home affairs was rigid in his assumption of absolute sovereignty.

His first conflict was with the Church.

At Versailles, one day, the bishop of Mainz sat facing the chancellor, a cowled Junker over against the Lutheran Junker in military uniform. The prelate wanted certain articles protecting the Roman Catholic Church to be introduced into the imperial constitution. Unable to get his way about this, he turned the conversation towards doctrinal matters.

"After death, as Your Excellency knows, the prospects for Catholics are brighter than for those of any other persuasion."

Silence, and a smile.

"But perhaps, according to your way of thinking, a Catholic cannot be saved?"

Now the Protestant takes up his parable.

"A Catholic layman, certainly. I have my doubts about a cleric. He has committed the sin against the Holy Ghost. The words of Holy Writ condemn him."

The bishop answers this jest with an ironical bow. Two statesmen in fancy dress, one garbed as a general and the other as a bishop, look at each other smilingly; but Bismarck's anti-Catholic sentiments are stirring angrily beneath the sportive smile. At that time, he had it in mind to invite the pope, now threatened by the "robber king", to Cologne or Fulda, in the belief that "nothing could more effectively disillusion the Germans, nothing could enlighten them more quickly, than to see the priestly cuisine close at hand."

In this, as in other matters, we see that Bismarck lacks an understanding of moral powers. He has a profound knowledge of history, but we discern gaps in his acquaintance with ecclesiastical history.

Here, however, we are not really concerned with a Kulturkampf, a struggle between two rival cultures, that of the Catholic Church and that of the secular State. Bismarck was fighting for power, not on behalf of ideas — counters which for the last twenty years he had changed as occasion demanded. Besides, he was tolerant in all matters which cost nothing. When he fought the Church, it was as a power, and not as an exponent of a particular type of culture; he was its enemy only where it threatened to weaken his State. He had recognised the coming of this struggle twenty years before, in the Frankfort days, declaring a fight "against the lust of conquest in the Catholic camp" to be inevitable. Since Austria's concordat, he had held that some of Prussia's enemies were always to be found in that camp. After he had risen to power, he had (as he knew) actually been characterised in the Vatican as "the incarnation of the devil." At a later date Windthorst said: "The Kulturkampf dates from the battle of Königgrätz." In very truth, at that time, the Prussian heretics in clerical gowns, and especially a court chaplain at Berlin, had said and written: "Europe, including Turkey, must be evangelised!"

But the crisis did not come until the Vatican Council met in Rome, concentrating there anew all the powers of Catholic Europe. In the middle of July 1870, when the war was beginning, the dogma of papal infallibility was proclaimed, affecting Bismarck's sentiments as much as his calculations. It was intolerable to him that any one should call himself infallible. Why, he did not even believe that Otto von Bismarck was infallible! It was monstrous that all the Germans of one confession should be dependent upon a foreign power. When he was setting out for France, he warned the German bishops against assenting, and warned the pope against using compulsion. At the same time he brought all possible opposing influences to bear, in the hope of protecting his State against Roman powers. If this new dogma were accepted, "the bishops would, vis-à-vis the government, be the officials of a foreign sovereign."

Thereupon, while the war is still in progress, Windthorst's friends founded the Centre Party, as a fighting Catholic party. Bismarck, having failed to establish a German Catholic Church, promptly assumes the offensive. The archbishop of Cologne has forbidden the students at Bonn to attend the lectures of liberal theologians. Bismarck declares this pronouncement invalid. Because he is upbuilding the empire, and while he is doing so, he stigmatises the ecclesiastical dispute as an attack upon the empire, and insists that Rome is the rallying-ground of all the foes of the empire. When he gets home, he finds that the new party has marshalled fifty-seven men, and that all the malcontents are concentrating round it.

One with far more equanimity than Bismarck might well have been infuriated. For twenty years, he has been thinking over his work. For eight years, he has been fighting on its behalf. At length, in a few strenuous weeks, and in defiance of adverse winds, he has piloted his ship into port. Now, weary and weather-beaten, with overwrought nerves, he comes home to consult with the people. What does he find? A phalanx of hostile deputies, held together by a religious faith, whose chief, far from Germany, must necessarily be averse to the new Lutheran emperor, being a mourner for the old apostolic emperor. The sceptic in the chancellor, who has just delivered his testimony regarding the perishability of his handiwork, cannot fail to see that this group wields an invisible hammer which will smash the laboriously fashioned structure. Who expects a man of passionate temperament to be just at such a moment? Determined to protect his work, still full of the spirit of the battlefield, the marksman miscalculates the range, and, aiming at a few German Catholics, hits the great power in Rome, without injuring it seriously. The militant mood of the conqueror and the anxiety of the architect explain this realist's misconception, explain his dread of a Catholic league against his young empire.

Not only is the party arrayed against him. At home, all the dispossessed, the Guelphs, the Poles, and the Alsatians, join forces. Abroad, the Austrians and the French join his antagonists. The social democracy, as young as the empire and as weak as Europe, comes to an understanding with the Centre Party. Among all the "enemies of the empire", the Centre Party was merely "the first to take the field." Confusion only grows worse confounded because some of the theologians at German universities (including even Cardinal Hohenlohe) are opposed to the dogma of infallibility; because the Catholic king of Bavaria endorses their protests; because the German Centre Party is at the outset censured by Rome. Mortified leaders who really have no concern with the matter join in the fray — Savigny, for instance, whose ambitions Bismarck had thwarted a few years earlier.

Outbursts of wrath notwithstanding, Bismarck is never forced to a decision by his prejudices and his moods. He does not act until he has calculated the political consequences of what he wants to do. He considers that by carrying on this campaign, he may be able to fortify the anti-clerical tendencies of the new Italy, and to sunder Italy from France; he may be able to strengthen the ties between Germany and Russia, since Russia is in general hostile to Rome, and is especially antagonistic to Roman Catholic priests as promoters of rebellion in Poland. At home, this policy will make the crown prince friendly, and will overcome the discontent of the liberals with the constitution, for the crown prince and the liberals are guided by a rationalistic philosophy, and will like nothing better than a fight against the Church.

Bismarck opens his campaign immediately after peace has been signed in May with a vehemence which recalls the tempo of the military camp. "The German government," he writes as a semi-official announcement, "will in the very near future have to decide upon aggressive action. . . . Three hundred years ago, German sentiment was stronger in Germany than Roman Catholic sentiment. Far more is this true to-day, . . . when Rome is no longer the metropolis of the world, and when the German imperial crown is worn by a German prince instead of by a Spaniard." Bismarck does not, at this time, unconditionally desire separation of Church and State; all he wants is a "strongly defensive attitude against the aggressions of the Catholic Church." To carry out this policy, he begins, in the empire, by issuing the "pulpit paragraphs", which make every reference to State matters from the pulpit an offence punishable with imprisonment. Soon he is driven forward by the impetus of the movement, so that within a year or two he issues, in Prussia, the "May laws", which have important consequences. He abolishes the Catholic department of the ministry of public worship and instruction, and expunges from the constitution the paragraphs protecting the Church. He interferes in the administration of the bishoprics and with religious instruction in the schools; banishes the Jesuits and kindred orders from the empire; makes civil marriage compulsory; threatens religious zealots with exile, fine, imprisonment, or detention in a fortress; confiscates their incomes; deprives many parishes of priests; sows discord between bishops and priests, priests and laymen; sets the members of families at odds; thrusts problems of conscience upon clergymen, laymen, students, and women. A chaos of sentiments and interests is produced. In a way which he had never foreseen, there is now realised his own most vigorous threat: "Acheronta movebo!"

"You need not be anxious," he cries to his opponents. "We are not going to Canossa, either bodily or spiritually!" He will have occasion to regret his words, which soon fly across Germany and over the Alps! A prince of the Church compares the German government to a man who enters a river without knowing its depth, and who, as he steps forward, encounters unexpected abysses. Another describes Bismarck as a "boa destructor." Windthorst recalls the persecutions of the early Christians. The Prussian bishops declare themselves opposed to "the principles of a pagan State." The pope forbids the German Catholics to obey the new laws. Bismarck stands armed upon the tribune, and speaks with unwonted emotion:

"We are not concerned with the fight . . . of a Protestant

dynasty against the Catholic Church; we are not concerned with a struggle between belief and unbelief. What is here at stake is a struggle for power, a struggle as old as the human race, the struggle for power between monarchy and priesthood. That is a struggle for power which began long, long before our Saviour appeared in this world; the struggle for power which, in Aulis, Agamemnon had to wage against the seers, which cost him his daughter and delayed the start of the Greeks; the struggle for power which has filled the whole of German history, . . . which found issue in the Middle Ages when the last representative of the sublime Swabian imperial race perished on the scaffold beneath the axe of a French conqueror, what time this Frenchman was in alliance with the pope of the day. We have been near to an analogous issue from the struggle, allowing, of course, for the changed customs of the time. If the French war of conquest, whose outbreak coincided with the publication of the Vatican decrees, had been successful, who can say what history would have had to tell with regard to our ecclesiastical domains in Germany, as concerns the Gestis Dei per Francos?"

Thus did Bismarck, in general so chary of words, five times thunder the phrase "struggle for power" at his hearers, disclosing his true motive so openly that he falsified the historical situation by a splendid parallel. There is no question of culture! Why, then, speak of a "Kulturkampf?"

From very different motives, Bismarck's oldest enemy and latest ally, Virchow, defends the same cause — Virchow, who had introduced the word Kulturkampf which he had borrowed from Lassalle. Virchow said: "The Protestant trend, in the spirit of free research, opens for mankind wider horizons in all directions, and urges us forward to independent work. Do your utmost to lead your bishops onwards to greater freedom and your officials to more independent activities, and then everything will be different. . . . You must oppose this un-German Roman system. . . . If you think that you are entitled to extend the domain of faith to the sensual, to the things of this world, . . . then we are lost, then you will break the whole course of German development!"

Liberty and Science? Were we not hearing a few moments ago of a struggle for power? To-day, just as ten years before, two different worlds, Virchow and Bismarck, have (by the grotesque saltations of politics masquerading as intelligence) been reconciled for the duration of a masked ball, and are dancing together. Now the contentious Mallinckrodt, one of the leaders of the Centre Party, rises, and drives back the soulless pathologist.

"Where, then, does the greater intellectual force of the Protestants show itself? Perhaps in the fact that among them there is hopeless confusion because every one has his own opinion of what is right! . . . With us it is a fundamental proposition that the Church is the bearer of the truth. . . . When the Church arrives at a decision, the Catholic has to recognise this as true. Here we have the simple difference between our authoritative principle and your principle of individual judgment. That is why, after nineteen centuries, we are still firmly united, and as strong in the world as ever, whilst you have to look on mournfully as the stones of your building crumble!" What can the imperial chancellor think when he reads this speech? Does he not feel himself to be much more closely united with this adversary than with his own allies? The Catholic orator has caught Bismarck's own rhythm, Bismarck's own style, and thunders against Virchow words closely analogous to those which the pathologist, in an earlier controversy, had had to hear from Bismarck's own lips!

The champions fight skilfully; their speeches in the Kulturkampf form the climax of German political debate; but Windthorst always carries away the palm of victory. When Bismarck rails against him once more as an embittered Guelph, warns the Centre against this leader who is hostile to the empire, mockingly speaks of the Hanoverian Christian's humility and impassivity, Windthorst rejoins: "I have many faults, but not that of showing passion in parliamentary debates. Here, my pulse beats sixty to the minute just as it does outside the walls of parliament. Furthermore, my honoured opponent reproaches the Centre because my small person belongs to it. Is that a compliment to me, or a censure?"

When Windthorst says that Bismarck wants to transfer the preponderance of State authority to parliament, Bismarck nervously grips the glass on the table in front of him, and hastily gulps down several mouthfuls. Windthorst goes on: "If the Church is thrust out of our schools, who will undertake religious instruction? Is the State competent for this task, and has it the instruments wherewith to perform it? If so, I beg you to let me know your new State catechism! It will either be a heathen State, a godless State, or else it will be God himself here on earth." At the moment, Bismarck neither will nor can answer; he merely rejoins, with a sense of personal irritation: "I have given my proofs during long years of service to the monarchical principle in Prussia. I trust that a similar experience awaits the honourable member for Meppen."

When he hits back, next day, it is with fierce invectives: "The oil of your words is not of a kind to heal wounds, but of a kind to nourish the flames of anger. I have rarely heard that the honourable member for Meppen has been inclined to persuade or to conciliate. . . . May the God in whom I believe safeguard me against the evil fate that would be mine if the honourable member could decide what would be my share in God's grace. . . . You will more readily be able to live at peace with the State if you repudiate Guelph leadership. Guelph hopes can only be realised when discord and revolution prevail in the State."

Windthorst replies on the spot: "I am nothing, and I can do nothing. But you, gentlemen, apparently wish to make something out of me. . . . I will not say what I think of the minister's attack on me, for I am subject to the authority of the president of the assembly, which does not altogether seem to be the case with the ministers. Yet I do not retreat before any one. The honourable gentleman asks me whether I still retain my loyalty to the Hanoverian royal family. It will last until I die, and nothing in the world, not even the powerful premier of Germany, will alter my sentiments. In accordance with the words of Holy Writ, I believe myself to have performed my duties as subject conscientiously. . . . When secret plans are ascribed to the Centre, when attempts are made to intimidate it by throwing suspicion upon a deputy, we are near to a terrorism which suppresses freedom of speech. Let me assure the honourable gentleman that it is easy enough to support the monarchical principle when fortune is favourable; but it is not so easy in evil days, when obedience is imposed!"

Thus brilliantly does Windthorst do battle. Subsequently he discloses the kernel of this struggle between might and spirit: "The honourable gentleman is more successful in realising his views because he has more soldiers and more money than I have. . . . One who is backed up by two million soldiers has little difficulty in carrying on his foreign policy!" Bismarck leaves the house while Windthorst is speaking, and Windthorst smilingly sends a shaft after him: "In the case of such attacks, it is a chivalrous custom to accept the answer personally. . . . I should have greatly esteemed the privilege of conversing with my honoured adversary before Germany." Thus proudly and supplely, thus wittily and fiercely, does David sling his stones at the head of Goliath.

But he cannot hit the mark! Bismarck speedily recognises that he has made a mistake in this religious question. He takes advantage of the death of the quarrelsome Pius and of the accession of the diplomatic Leo XIII. to make a veiled withdrawal, and thrusts upon the shoulders of his subordinates the responsibility for a campaign he had himself ordered. In home affairs, he suddenly abandons the struggle. As late as the end of 1873 Andrassy wrote: "Bismarck's eyes become bloodshot whenever he speaks of the pope; his words sound like maledictions. He calls the pope a danger to all countries; a revolutionist and anarchist whom Europe must resist if any prince is still to be secure on his throne." Soon afterwards he realises that Rome is invincible. Thereupon he lays all the blame upon Falk, his minister for public worship and instruction. In conversation with Mittnacht, the Würtemberg minister, he makes merry in brilliant metaphors of "the State as gendarme, stealing, sword in hand, after light-footed priests." He declares that when the law concerning civil

marriage was promulgated, he had been away at Varzin. To the
Saxon minister, Friesen, he says officially:

"The struggle was entered into in opposition to my plans.
I only wanted to fight the Centre politically. It is not my fault
that the whole Catholic population has been incensed. I was
opposed to it, . . . but Camphausen and Falk threatened to
resign, so I had to give way. Now I regret that I did not at least
read these laws before signing them, for there is far too much
nonsense in them. . . . I want you to be good enough to tell your
king that he should not hold me responsible for what has happened in Prussia during the last two years."

Such is the utterance of the man who, only a year before, had
spurred on one half of his fellow citizens against the other half
by saying: "It is the infallible pope who threatens the State!
He arrogates to himself whatever secular rights he pleases, . . .
declares our laws null and void, levies taxes, . . . in a word, no
one in Prussia is so powerful as this foreigner!"

He fancies that Dresden has forgotten his words long since;
but he is wrong. Europe remembers it, and Rome remembers it
above all. Nor is it forgotten that twenty-five years earlier he had
exclaimed in the Landtag: "I hope I may live to see the ship of
fools of our time split on the rock of the Christian church!"
When old Gerlach reminds him of the words he had uttered in
his pietist days, Bismarck coolly replies that he had meant the
Protestant Church. The Roman augurs could not but smile.
Pius, shortly before his death, described his great enemy as a
Protestant Philip, and uttered the following prophecy: "In the
end, a rock will roll down the mountain side and break the
colossus!"

III

On March 18, 1848, William had run away from Berlin, fleeing
before the revolution. On March 17, 1871, twenty-three years
later, he entered Berlin as a victorious emperor and was received
with acclamations. Next day, the Commune was declared in Paris,

and throughout Germany the masses proclaimed their sympathy with the popular uprising. Bismarck was alarmed: "This cost me another sleepless night." Bebel, the only socialist in the first Reichstag (elected immediately after the victory), speaking from the tribune a fortnight after peace had been signed, said: "The Commune of Paris was only an outpost skirmish! Before many years have passed, the motto of the Commune, 'War to the palaces, peace to the huts!' will have become the battle cry of all the proletarians of Europe!" [Loud laughter.] Bebel went on to appeal to the Alsatians and Lorrainers to participate in Germany's struggle for freedom, so that, at length, the day might dawn when the peoples of Europe would have secured the right of self-determination which could only be realised in a republic. Thereupon Bismarck said: "You need not be afraid that I shall answer the last speaker. You will one and all agree with me that his speech needs no answer in this assembly!" Later, however, he described Bebel's speech as a flash of light suddenly illuminating the situation. The State and society were imperilled, and must defend themselves. This enemy must be annihilated.

Long after Lassalle's death, Bismarck had kept in touch with his successor, and had never completely forgotten Lassalle's State-socialist ideas. Now, after the Commune, he lets socialism drop. According to his calculations, he no longer needs a counterpart to liberalism. His policy, therefore, is to pass new laws protecting property, and he wants to punish every socialistic speech with imprisonment. When the Reichstag rejects his proposals, he utters a warning: "Social democracy has made immense progress. . . . Within a few years, the bourgeoisie will be clamouring for penal measures." After the next elections, the young Social Democratic Party has twelve deputies in the Reichstag, and he appeals as a remedy to the rod of correction which God holds over mankind. Utterly failing to understand the new thought-trend, he speaks of "utopian nonsense, the ideas of those who believe that roast pigeons will fly into their mouths"; and proposes to treat this "criminal madness with fresh air and sunshine." He does not succeed in instituting forcible measures against the socialists, for the Reichstag is afraid of passing exceptional laws against a particular section of the community.

Now a shot discharges the tension.

In May 1878, a man fires at the eighty-year-old emperor who is out driving. The would-be assassin is an out-at-elbows student, a mauvais sujet, who has been expelled from the Social Democratic Party. When the news comes to Bismarck, he thumps the table, exclaiming: "Now we've got them!"

"The socialists, Your Excellency?"

"No, the liberals!"

In a flash he has made his combinations. To-day, the excitement about the attempt on William's life must influence the liberals to vote an exceptional law. In this way it will be possible to get quit, at length, of the liberals, who, now that the Kulturkampf has been laid aside, are no longer necessary. The very same day he asks the minister for justice to draft the new law. Next day, it is sent to the other ministers. Ten days later, the long-desired measure (vamped up in a hurry, and containing numerous technical errors) is laid before the Reichstag. The pretext for its introduction is: "We can only fight social democracy effectively if we are able to transgress the barriers which the constitution, in its unduly doctrinaire regard for the protection of individuals and parties, has established in the so-called fundamental laws." Twenty days after the attempt on the emperor's life, the law is rejected by the whole Reichstag, the conservatives excepted. Bennigsen prophesies that if it is passed there will be secret intrigues far more dangerous than open ones; and that the classes attacked by the exceptional law will be greatly embittered. "Otherwise law-abiding people will say: 'If the possessing classes have recourse to such means, if hundreds of thousands of citizens stand outside the protection of the laws, why should we, in our turn, respect the laws?'" Such a law, continued Bennigsen, could not fail to arouse widespread agitation. Richter took the same line, declaring that the exceptional law would provide a number of otherwise insignificant persons with a crown of martyrdom.

Three weeks later, from a window in Unter den Linden, a second shot is fired. This time the aged monarch, driving by in his carriage, is seriously wounded. Three hours after the attempted assassination, Privy Councillor Von Tiedemann brings the news to Prince Bismarck in Friedrichsruh Park. "At length I caught sight of him, accompanied by his great Danes, striding slowly across the grass in the sunshine. I went up to him. He was in a cheerful mood, told me where he had been walking, and how much good the fresh air had done him."

" Some important telegrams have arrived."

" Are they so urgent that we need bother about them here in the open country? "

"Unfortunately they are. There has been another attempt on the emperor's life, and this time the bullet has found its billet. The emperor is severely wounded."

Abruptly, Bismarck stands still. Striking the ground vigorously with his oaken walking stick, he draws a deep breath and says:

" In that case we will dissolve the Reichstag! "

Quickly he made his way across the park to the house, Tiedemann telling him details the while. On entering, he ordered preparations to be made for his return to Berlin.

Never will any one see Otto von Bismarck better pleased than he is to-day. After his own fashion, he is fond of the veteran monarch, who placed him in a position of power sixteen years ago, and enabled him to find free scope for his genius. He is often restless and plaintive because of the old man's mulish obstinacy, but he does not despise William as he despises others. At any rate, he puts up with the emperor's whimsies much as a son who has long since taken charge of affairs will put up with the tantrums of an aged father. For himself, Bismarck wishes a long term of office; he therefore wishes for his master many years of life. The crown prince is his opponent. Perhaps to-morrow Frederick will be king, and then Bismarck's day will be over. One would think that sentiment and self-interest would lead him, at the outset, to enquire after the condition of the wounded man.

But Bismarck is, above all, a fighter, a good hater. He hates during the night, calculates during the day, always with his gaze fixed on his enemy, and always on a new enemy. What? This Reichstag, which he set up, is to veto his plans? These Richters and Windthorsts, these Laskers and Bennigsens, are strong enough to forbid him his fight against the disturbers of order, the stealers of property? So recently the "chatterboxes" have struck the weapon out of his hand! A saving shot, this, no matter by whom it has been fired! He does not yet know to what class or to what party the unknown assassin belongs; he knows nothing about the severity of the wound, and whether an old man of eighty will be able to recover from it. All he knows is that the emperor's wound at an assassin's hand will be as invaluable to him as a victory on the field of battle, will be worth a fortune to him in an electoral campaign! Now we can lay all our domestic enemies low! We will dissolve the Reichstag!

Nine days later, the dissolution had taken place; and, within a few weeks, the second attempt on the emperor's life had provided a new majority for Bismarck.

What does the statesman care when he learns that the man who fired the shot is insane, has never belonged to any political party, and (before his death from a self-inflicted wound) declares that he had not wished to quit the world without taking a great man with him as companion? Fill the newspapers with Nobiling's confessions, with the tale of Nobiling's sins. Day after day telegraph all over Germany the story of conspiracies and discoveries! Declare a state of siege in Berlin! "The wisest course will be to promote the inevitable collision, to suppress the rising forcibly, and then, when the public is thoroughly alarmed, to pass severe laws in the Reichstag." Thus, after half a generation, does the lawless minister return to the point from which he set out. Blood and iron had been successful abroad. They are to enforce success at home. The crown prince objects to these measures. He is acting for his father during the latter's period of incapacity, and he does not wish to begin his reign with a deluge of blood. All the liberals hope the emperor will die, hope for the son's accession; but Frederick dares not speak openly against the exceptional law, since ostensibly this law is proposed in order to protect his father's life. The conflict of feelings within the crown prince increases.

Then the unexpected happens. The old man gets better. The only thing that had saved him was the helmet, which, that day, he had been wearing contrary to his usual custom. Now, victor in spite of himself in three wars, he has brought his own old skin to market. That is the sort of thing the common people can understand. The ruler who aforetime had been hated, becomes extraordinarily popular. Restored to health, he rises from his bed and humorously declares that Nobiling has treated him more successfully than the doctors, for what he had really wanted was to be blooded. All Germany rejoices, and even Bismarck finds that his master is more jovial and livelier than for a long time since. Bismarck, the German people, the crown prince and his wife, nay all Europe, begin to realise that William is predestined to enjoy a glorious old age like that of a king of fable, to attain a romantic position such as no ruler has known for centuries. Thus did the shot do its work. Seizing the favour of the moment, Bismarck ventured upon the most dangerous of his undertakings.

At the elections which followed the attempted assassination, elections during which Bismarck was continually reediting the watchwords, the forces of the left were greatly weakened, whilst the conservative right grew very much stronger. Now, the master could force his exceptional law through the Reichstag, and he took the opportunity of making its provisions more stringent than ever. Once again he thunders at the liberals as of old, accepts the help of Windthorst (who smilingly announces the bankruptcy of the ecclesiastical policy), changes his front, and is able to utilise the centre and the national liberals alternately in order to secure a majority. In accordance with the terms of the new law, adopted first for two years, and then renewed for another four years, the authorities were entitled on their own initiative to suppress and punish all activities which aimed at " overthrowing public order." Printers, booksellers, tavern-keep-

ers, could be expelled or arrested; any one could be banished
for merely uttering socialist doctrines; socialists were denied freedom of the press and the right of public meeting; every lord
lieutenant could declare a state of siege within the territory over
which he ruled.

During the debates on this measure, the lineaments of a new
century manifested themselves from time to time, as if illuminated by summer lightning. Bismarck, all Junker and Holy Alliance, as if he had never drawn near to Napoleon, thundered
to the socialists: "When you make brilliant promises to people,
scornfully and mockingly assuring them that all they have hitherto regarded as sacred is a lie, . . . faith in God, faith in our
monarch, patriotism, family ties, property, inheritance, earn-
ings, . . . when you take all this away from them, it is not very
difficult for you to lead comparatively ignorant persons to say
with Faust: 'Cursed be hope, cursed be faith, and cursed above
all be patience.' . . . What is then left for such a man beyond
a frantic hunt for sensual enjoyments which alone can now rec-
oncile him to life? . . . If we had to exist under the tyranny
of a society of bandits, existence would lose all its value!"

Here is Bebel's answer: "The attempt to make the deed of a
lunatic the occasion for a long-prepared reactionary coup, the
determination to do this even before the judicial enquiry concerning the attack on the emperor is finished, . . . the determination to hold accountable for it a party which condemns
murder in every form, and which regards economic and political
developments as independent of the will of individuals — such
attempts are self-condemned. . . . It is not our aim to abolish
property, but to ensure a juster distribution of property for
the benefit of all." Then, to astonished Germany, he discloses the
details of Lassalle's intercourse with Bismarck.

Now begins a period of hatred and corruption, of spying and
wanton cruelty. Throughout the country there are domiciliary
raids, arrests, banishments. In defiance of his own formal promise to the national liberals that he would only declare states of
siege and order expulsions "in case of the utmost need", four

weeks later Bismarck declares Berlin and environs in a state of siege and expels sixty-seven of the socialist leaders from Berlin. When the elections in the free city of Hamburg do not go according to his taste, a state of siege is declared there likewise. Ere long, the sentences of imprisonment pronounced against fifteen hundred persons totalled more than a thousand years. Within a few weeks, in the confines of the empire, two hundred associations have been put under the ban, and two hundred and fifty books or pamphlets suppressed. Within six months, the number has risen to six hundred, while thousands of persons have had their livelihood taken away from them. Bebel is justified in his comparison of these happenings to those of the Middle Ages: "The men of our way of thinking have been deprived of their livelihood, have been abused and calumniated, described as dishonourable and lawless. The authorities have wished to provoke disorder. . . . These days of murderous attacks and lèse-majesté are among the most tragical of modern German history."

Bennigsen's warning is fulfilled. At innumerable secret meetings, in forests and in quarries, the leaders confer with their followers. They meet their brethren in Switzerland at public or private conferences. "Bismarck's restless and destructive activities are playing into our hands," writes Bebel to Engels. Speaking from the tribune, Liebknecht says triumphantly: "The socialist law is the iron hoop which holds our party together, and safeguards the moderates and the radicals against secessions. The man who has planted this seed will reap bitter fruit. Somehow or other, we shall prove victorious. Let them do their worst, for it will redound to our advantage! The more frenzied their activities, the more speedily will it be all up with them!"

IV

When Bismarck became a count, he had welcomed the rise in his family fortunes, not without a sly glance at his fellow Junkers, who were unwilling to believe that their order could produce a man of genius. When, after the return from France, the king created him a prince, he was alarmed. He had made up his mind to advise his master against such a step, but was taken by surprise, received by the king as a prince, congratulated by the whole royal family (all of whose members were hostile to Bismarck), so that he had no option in the matter. When Prince Frederick Charles reproached him with ingratitude, he made a fine answer to this officer, saying: "I have always felt myself to be a nobleman."

Why does Bismarck dread his new rank? "A man who is merely well-to-do can get along as count, but a prince must be rich. This rise in rank involves an extremely uncongenial change in my mode of life. Besides, it is really a pity; I had rather hoped to found one of the oldest lines of counts!" These remarks were uttered in private. The king tried to meet his wishes in one respect by bestowing on him the Sachsenwald near Hamburg, thirty thousand acres, valued at three million talers. William can neither understand nor silence Bismarck's pride of ancient nobility. Surely he might have remembered his own frame of mind so recently at Versailles, where like feelings, a similar sentiment of respect to his own ancestors, had made him dread a rise in rank.

If Bismarck should compare that moment of his master's glory with this moment when he, the servant, is enjoying like glory, he will recognise that he himself is animated by the same profound doubt as the king — by the dread of the members of his own order. How long will the kings of Bavaria and Saxony put up quietly with the unexampled ascent of their cousin of Hohenzollern, how long will the Pomeranian and the Brandenburg Junkers tolerate the unexampled ascent of their cousin of Schönhausen? Will not their sense of rivalry grow? Will it not be found in both cases that envy will lead to political intrigues? Jealousy on the part of dear relatives, who ascribe to evil fortune what is really due to their lack of talent, will prove the innermost motives of the secession with which the members of Bismarck's class disgrace themselves before the tribunal of history, instead of being content to enjoy a reflexion of the glories of the man of genius who has sprung from among their number.

Political enmities aggravated the tension to a breach which kindly sentiments would have prevented. These Prussian Junkers, conservatives one and all, who had never before produced any man to equal Bismarck in intelligence and strength of will, fell away from him. Thus the last of the great political parties seceded from the chief of the State, injuring thereby its own interests by facilitating for Bismarck a cooperation with the liberals which was not natural to him. The Junkers played the part of an affronted wife, who, when her husband displays a rejuvenated humour, holds aloof from him menacingly, and thus leads him to seek his enjoyments elsewhere, when, by complaisance, she could have prevented anything of the kind.

Already in the year 1868, Bismarck had warned his party, saying that incontestably it would be necessary from time to time to rely on the aid of a group which was not altogether pleasing to this party; for otherwise " the government would have to manœuvre and to enter into compacts against the constitution, . . . and would thus lapse into the weakness characteristic of coalition ministries." Roon, himself a hard-shelled conservative, complained about the " envious and malicious arrogance of some of the conservatives. The party must in the end realise that its views and aims need to be very different to-day from what they were in the time of the conflict. The party must become a party of conservative progress, and must abandon the wish to be nothing more than a brake."

Now that Cousin Bismarck has become prince and dictator, the breach widens. " Ote-toi que je m'y mette," says Bismarck. In his memoirs, written long after the before-mentioned struggles are over, he mentions Arnim and Goltz as adversaries of the second class. The third class, he says, comprises " the members of my own caste of the territorial nobility, who were out of humour because, in my exceptional career, I had transcended the traditional idea of the equality of the territorial nobility — an idea which is Polish rather than German. I might have been forgiven if, from country squire, I had merely risen to the position of minister; but my dotations and the title of prince, which was bestowed upon me much against my will, could not be forgiven. That I should be 'Your Excellency' was not beyond the bounds of customary attainments; but that I should have become 'Your Highness' aroused acrimonious criticism. . . . I should have been better able to endure the disfavour of my former friends and class associates if there had been anything in my own mood to justify it." The psychological insight with which he appraises the mentality of his own class cannot be excelled. As early as the year 1872, one of these Pomeranian Junkers wrote: "We shall make Bismarck so small that he will have to eat out of the hand of any honest Pomeranian country squire!"

The trouble began with the ecclesiastical dispute, in which the Lutheran pietists were the enthusiastic champions of the pope. Bismarck was suspected of atheism because he was allied with the atheist Virchow against the Church. He was compelled, in his own defence, to speak from the tribune in unwonted super-latives on behalf of "Protestant edification, the most primary and the profoundest reason for this struggle, a reason inti-mately connected with our soul and our salvation." In this attack on Bismarck, it is not the older men who are the most acrimo-nious. When the veteran Gerlach says, "Bismarck is treating me badly, but I love him all the same!" we are listening to the music of the heart. Senfft-Pilsach, too, Bismarck's other pious patron, behaves like an honourable man when he now, half cour-teously, half prophetically, warns the chancellor, apostrophising him as follows: "Your Highness should take heart in humility, should take heart in God, who loved you so much that he gave up his life for you, and who even to-day stretches his pierced hands towards you. If Your Highness should continue stub-bornly to withstand God's warnings, he will show you that his work endures; your great and fine work will suffer, and you will undoubtedly become subject to his judgments."

This sort of thing makes the knight don his harness. Directly he reads it, Bismarck makes a fierce answer: "I should have been glad if I could feel certain that your warning voice would also be directed against certain persons standing near to you who are the opponents of His Majesty's government, persons to whom our Saviour's humility (of which you do well to remind me) has become so foreign that, in wrathful and arrogant self-conceit and in heathen partisanship, they regard it as their business to set themselves up as masters over the country and the Church. . . . In honest contrition, I continue to do my daily work without Your Excellency's exhortations; but while I, fearing and loving God, serve my king loyally and by exhausting labour, the pharisaical misuse of God's word, peculiar to my Pomeranian opponents as well as to my Roman Catholic opponents, will not shake my faith in Christ. Let me beg Your Excellency to take care lest your own arrogance should bring upon you the judgments of God against which you warn me." In conclusion, Bismarck recommends his correspondent to ponder the following text: "Arise, O Lord; save me, O my God: for thou hast smitten all mine enemies upon the cheek bone; thou hast broken the teeth of the ungodly. Salvation belongeth unto the Lord: thy blessing is upon thy people. Selah."

Bismarck's Christianity breathes its last in this Biblical capriccio.

His younger enemies advance towards their goal without circumlocution. The only use they make of the cross is that they fight under the sign of the "Kreuzzeitung", of which Bismarck had been one of the founders. As the chancellor tells us in his memoirs, this newspaper, "under the Christian symbol of the cross, and under the motto 'With God for King and Fatherland', had for years past ceased to represent the conservative fraction, and had got even more out of touch with Christianity." In the "Kreuzzeitung" and in the "Reichsglocke" (specially founded by the Junkers for the attack on Bismarck) begins, in the year 1872, the campaign of calumny against the honour and integrity of the chancellor. "The Delbrück-Camphausen-Bleichröder Era" is the name of the first series of anonymous articles — signed, in compliance with the law, by some casual member of the staff. The real author is Baron von Loë, a diplomatist who has quarrelled with Bismarck.

"I propose that the next number of the 'Reichsglocke' should be a benefit number for the chancellor. From the point of view of psychological medicine, it seems to me very important in this series of articles to emphasise first the serious and then the comic side. The main point is that, to begin with, his digestion should be upset for several days, and that can be brought about only by passionate excitement." At the same time, one of the Manteuffels writes to the other, Bismarck's sometime chief and opponent who has recently spoken against the chancellor in the Upper House: "You do not need any cure at a spa in order to become minister president." Such is the tone of these gentlemen behind the scenes. Before the footlights, in the published articles, they say:

"There is reason to believe that, before Prince Bismarck became minister in Prussia, he was in close touch with exalted circles in the world of finance. The intimate relationships between Herr von Bleichröder and the prince, which, indirectly at least, date from the prince's pre-ministerial era — in the days when, upon the meagre allowance made to a Prussian envoy and without notable private means, he was able to represent his sovereign in St. Petersburg, Paris, and Frankfort, must have helped to provide Prince Bismarck with good counsel in financial matters. . . . Of course the prince, like every one else, is entitled to demand that we shall assign none but good motives to him until he has been proved to have acted from bad motives; yet it cannot be denied that this powerful statesman has conferred favours upon suspect despoilers of the people. . . . There is hardly any mistake which the present government has not committed, simply in order to hide its scandalous relationships with the financiers of Berlin." Baron von Loë wrote that, in July 1870, the day before the declaration of war, he had met Bleichröder in the ministry: "We can hardly suppose that Herr von Bleichröder and Herr von Bismarck came together in order to talk about the weather. I do not know if, that day, Herr von Bleichröder bought or sold securities, in a word, speculated upon war or peace. Still, I cannot doubt that the friendship between Herr von Bleichröder and

Herr von Bismarck has been advantageous to the latter — intellectually advantageous, I mean."

Further it was said that Bismarck had placed government orders with a Jew named Behrend, the tenant of his paper-mill at Varzin. A certain Captain von Puttkamer wrote that Bismarck had only promulgated the law concerning the Farther Pomeranian fiefs in order to ensure his wife's inheritance of a Puttkamer fief.

Could meanness go further? The members of Bismarck's own order describe the man before whose greatness they are dimmed as a vulgar financial intriguer, doing him great harm in a period of company promotion, and making the Jews in all cases the centre of their invectives. Above all, they harm their country, for Europe is delighted at these charges of corruption. Whilst this class is prone, during the speculations of an all too victorious epoch, to avail itself of the services of Jewish banking houses (because the Jews are clever financiers), the very same persons who turn the Jews to account calumniate them before the eyes of foreigners, and declare that Bismarck, who was the originator of the national impetus, is really responsible for these excrescences of financial speculation, " for corruption has assumed colossal dimensions. . . . We live under an evil régime, and its name is Bismarck." Only the last sentence was actionable. The anti-semitic author of the article fled to escape being jailed, and wrote henceforward from Switzerland.

Such calumnies, if directed against Windthorst, who also met Bleichröder from time to time, would only have aroused a smile, for Windthorst remained a poor man to the day of his death. Bismarck, on the other hand, was determined to use his genius and his power to secure personal advantages. He often referred to the great gifts made by the British nation to its statesmen, considered that his rank as prince could only be worthily upheld thanks to such gifts, and, during thirty years of power, acquired great wealth.

Nevertheless, he was much too shrewd a man to risk his position as chancellor or to risk his personal reputation, even to gain millions. What did he do? As a political genius, he discovered the only path along which he could attain his goal without running any risks. Among the bankers of his empire, he sought out the man whom he regarded as the boldest and the most upright, put this man under an obligation by occasional conversations in the course of business, and at the same time ensured the greatest possible growth of his own property by a single signature, giving his friend a general power of attorney.

There was a widespread animus against him because of what he did in this respect, especially in those days of company promotion, when every man on the make was a spy on all the others. Among the nobles who were acquiring wealth there was current talk about "the dangers to the general welfare of the State, in that the first statesman of the German empire should have given a general power of attorney for the management of his property to the leading banker, who was a great Jewish financier." Moltke and others of the generals tried by indirect means to separate Bismarck from Bleichröder. Old intimates warned him by letter. "I cannot refrain from telling Your Highness that a witticism is current to the effect that Bleichröder is the government's partner. . . . Old Prussian honesty is discredited . . . because a company promoter finds favour in high places." Bismarck would not listen to any advice. When some one wrote to warn the emperor, Bismarck arranged for Bleichröder to pay William a visit on his estate. Moreover, the emperor's own property was thriving like Bismarck's in the hands of another "Jewish financier."

"There is no question in my mind," says Bismarck in old age, "as to what I owe to Bleichröder and his sons. He was my banker. It is false to say that I ever gave him any political tips which could have enabled him to make advantageous deals on his own account or on mine. It is quite true that in the year 1866 he provided me with the means for carrying on the war, which no one else would supply. That was an action for which I owed him gratitude. As a responsible man I could not allow even a Jew to say of me that I had used him, and had then failed to recompense him for services which, as a statesman, I could not but esteem highly." Here, in retrospect, we see the interconnexion of gratitude and self-sacrifice.

During the first ten years, Bismarck attended personally to certain details, for he tells us that it was not until the year 1877 that he sold his last foreign securities. "When I learned that Shuvaloff had been appointed envoy in London, I had a sleepless night during which I reasoned that if the Russians were sending away their cleverest man at such a moment it was ten to one that they would commit some blunder. For that reason, I instructed Bleichröder next day to sell my Russian State securities. Subsequently, he complimented me upon my foresight in this matter."

Thenceforward, he bought no more foreign securities, for he wished to be able to play his game of chess against Europe without regard to personal financial interests. Neither then nor at any other time did Bismarck (like Holstein and others in later days) guide his actions either in business affairs or in political matters in accordance with prices on the stock exchange. Certainly, year by year, he had better reason to be satisfied with Bleichröder's management. It is true that his paper-mill at Varzin put in a tender for certain State supplies, and that his tenant secured the order because the Varzin tender was the lowest. This could not bring any personal advantage to Bismarck. Nor is there the slightest warrant for the charge brought against him by Captain von Puttkamer.

Thus in the Reichstag, from the safe harbourage of his general power of attorney, he could hit back against his enemies with deadly precision. "If such a newspaper as the 'Kreuzzeitung' . . . has the audacity to utter the most shameful and false calumnies against men who are highly placed in the world, to utter them in such a form that they . . . are not actionable, and yet arouse the impression that this or that minister had acted dishonourably — we have to do with a shameful calumny against which we should all form front, and no one ought to participate in the bringing of such charges even indirectly by subscribing to

the newspaper. . . . Every one who takes in the newspaper is
. . . a party to uttering the lies and calumnies it contains."

Still, his fellow Junkers defied him. Forty-six of those who bore
some of the oldest names, subsequently joined by several hundred
pastors, described themselves in the "Kreuzzeitung" as loyal adherents of the monarchical and conservative flag, determined not
to desert their newspaper. "If the imperial chancellor doubts the
genuineness of our Christian sentiments, we scorn to argue with
him, just as we scorn to accept advice from him in matters of
honour and decency." This was signed by a number of persons
bearing such names as Wedel, Zitzewitz, Marwitz, Seherr-Toss,
and Gottberg; likewise by Bismarck's oldest friends and cousins,
Blanckenburg and Kleist-Retzow; finally, "with profound sorrow" by old Thadden-Trieglaff.

Thus do those who had supported young Bismarck in his
adventurous youth show themselves hostile to him in his late
maturity, when he, the mightiest man in the empire, takes up his
parable against them. He prints this list of "declarers" in the
"Reichsanzeiger", thereby proclaiming an attack on his person to
be an act of hostility to the State. After this outburst Bismarck
is severed for years from the caste to which he belongs.

Bismarck the class-proud Junker is wounded more sorely than
Bismarck the statesman. He has no special affection for any of
the signatories individually; but, as a commander, he regards the
group, the class to which they belong, as his staff, and considers
that they have betrayed him. His pride is touched. "When intercourse with those whom one has regarded as one's equals . . . is
suddenly broken off, from motives which are personal rather than
material, malevolent rather than honest, and, in so far as they
are honest, utterly vulgar when the responsible minister concerned is boycotted by all those who have hitherto been his
friends, is treated as an enemy, and is thus isolated, . . . this
onslaught cannot but intensify his official troubles, upset his
nerves, and disturb his habits. . . . At my age, and feeling convinced, as I do, that I shall not live much longer, the loss of all
my old friends and the breaking of all my old ties causes pro-

found discouragement, which is tantamount to utter loneliness when the anxiety about my wife is superadded."

In every one of these enemies his wrath discovers the basest motives. When, in the company of an intimate, he scans the list of the Junkers who have voted against his ecclesiastical law, he ticks them off with his huge pencil, and delivers the following monologue à la Wallenstein: "Gottberg? He is out of humour because he has not yet been appointed lord lieutenant. Rosenberg votes against me, the man whom I have saved from so many dangers! Gruner? Frustrated ambition. Puttkamer? The man has never got anything out of the Church, would like by factiousness and opposition to show that he is just as good as I am! These fellows are angry because I have been made a prince, and also because I have not invited them to dinner! I know my neighbours of Pomerania!"

He is especially wrathful with Moritz Blanckenburg, for having first of all refused the offer of a portfolio, and for having afterwards carelessly handed on some misunderstood remarks made in a conversation concerning a negotiable stock — remarks which another of the signatories has subsequently repeated in a law court. Such is the end of the friendship which had been entered into so enthusiastically; such is the end of the song of Marie von Thadden's love and death. They end in gossip about some securities which Bleichröder is said to have bought for the imperial chancellor, but has not bought at all.

There is a hopeless breach, too, between Bismarck and Herr von Kleist-Retzow, a relative of Johanna who had been Bismarck's stable companion in the days of Landtag, the little man of ascetic inclinations who had been a candidate for ministerial office at the same time as himself, had subsequently stood godfather to Bismarck's daughter, who had been used to write to him as "My darling Bismarck", and whose religious exhortations he had long patiently endured. Now they face one another angrily in the Upper House. When they rail against one another in their speeches, they may perhaps be thinking of the days of twenty-five years back when they would privately rehearse to one another their forthcoming orations against the democrats. The chancellor invited his friend to come and see him once more, hoping to talk Kleist-Retzow over. When, at this final interview, Kleist refused to give way, Bismarck used his table knife as if he were cutting the cloth on the table, rose to his feet, bade farewell to his whilom friend, and soon afterwards spoke of him mockingly from the tribune, saying: "The previous speaker has spent much time upon the study of theology, and will, no doubt, at some time or other, have pondered the question whether it might not be to the advantage of his soul if he were to turn Catholic."

Later, Kleist made a further attempt at reconciliation, sending Bismarck a poem on the occasion of the chancellor's silver wedding. But Bismarck forbade his wife even to write to Kleist, and, in the presence of witnesses, told his servant: "I am not at home to Herr von Kleist."

V

It was with a mingling of bitterness and ecstasy that Bismarck, at the age of sixty, was confirmed in the misanthropical attitude he had adopted in his twenties. He said to Lucius: "When I am lying awake at night, I often turn over in my mind the unatoned wrongs that were done to me thirty years back. I grow hot as I think of them, and, half asleep, I dream of retaliation. For instance, I think of how badly we were treated in the Plamann Institute, where they used to wake us with a rapier thrust." One who after the lapse of fifty years will, when half asleep, leap at his teacher's throat, is one whose natural enmities will be cherished till they become fierce longings for revenge. As Bunsen, a keen observer, remarks of him, he is "even more inclined than most despots to hatred and vengefulness, and in small matters is petty."

He now heaps persecution upon all who are of another way of thinking than himself. During the seventies, every offender is prosecuted. He has specially printed formularies to be used in charges of slander. He calls it "territion." Rarely does any one venture to resist him. Even Mommsen, accused of slander, is weak enough to deny having uttered the words which he is charged with uttering in an electoral speech. Thereupon Bismarck is able to crow over his adversary, saying: "Perhaps the accusation was a mistake; but since Mommsen has demeaned himself so far as to lie about the matter, we have really won the trick."

When the editor of "Kladderadatsch", with whom he is fond of jesting in private, publishes a harmless shaft directed against him, he suddenly has the journalist prosecuted and clapped into jail. In conversation with a Russian statesman, Bismarck makes an amazing admission: "It is quite true that anger gets the better of me sometimes, and, which is worse, it often overpowers my better judgment." When Lasker dies in America, and Congress passes a formal resolution expressing its sympathy with the German nation, directing that the resolution shall be wired to the chancellor, he refuses to transmit to the Reichstag this homage to his dead adversary, and sends it back to Washington. He is so overburdened with suspicions that on one occasion when he is walking in the garden of the chancellery and sees a light in a cellar, he stops abruptly and enquires: "What's that light there for? Nobody lives there. D' you think that is a coiner's den?"

He can recognise only two reasons why any one should differ from him in opinion: malice or place-hunting. It is true that the courts, the embassies, and the ministries of State, become ever more dangerous centres of intrigue. When, in old age, he pens his memoirs, the longest of all the chapters is the one entitled "intrigues." The Arnim affair is the most famous of these.

How can one help sympathising with poor Arnim, a companion of Bismarck's youth? Vain and affected, hysterical, unstable and cowardly, was this shrewd diplomatist: a lion of the drawing-rooms and a brilliant performer on the piano, ambitious since the days of his rich marriage, an actor, prone to feign scrupulousness, fond of quoting Machiavelli, and talkative in many languages. When the wine had got into his head one night, he confided to Bismarck: "I regard every one who stands in advance of me in my career as a personal enemy, and I treat him accordingly. But I am careful not to show it so long as he is my superior!" Bismarck, who is his chief, and regards him as a man of talent, first sends him as envoy to the Roman Curia, and subsequently makes him envoy in Paris. Meanwhile he has become a count, and thus his advancement is speedier than that of all others. He has no doubt that he will become chancellor, and therefore courts the favour of Empress Augusta. She regards Arnim as a friend of the Catholics and of the French, and prizes him as a brilliant conversationalist — such as Bismarck could have been had he wished, though he never did wish to distinguish himself in Augusta's presence. Since Bismarck has upheld the republic in France, and would not like to see that country strengthened by a renewal of monarchy, in court circles (as usual), opinion runs counter to his, so that the court favours the legitimists. In Paris, therefore, Arnim works against Thiers and the other republicans, and writes private letters to influence Emperor William. The simple and incorruptible monarch hands the missives over to the chancellor, just as in earlier days he had handed over the letters of Goltz.

Bismarck instantly decides Arnim's fate, will not receive him when he comes to Berlin, leaves the capital, does not answer Arnim's letters. The emperor, meanwhile, gives audience to the envoy several times, with the declared intention of making up to him for the chancellor's neglect. Arnim is so foolish as to think that in the German empire he can collaborate with the emperor against Bismarck. He bases upon his definite grievance against their joint master a request to be allowed to resign, which the emperor refuses. According to Arnim's account of the matter, Emperor William said: "There is nothing wrong but the prince's rancorousness. Rancour is his predominant characteristic. It is a pity that I should have to say this about so excellent a man." Feeling that his position has been strengthened by the conversation, Arnim now ventures into the lion's den for a talk which both he and Bismarck have recorded.

According to Arnim, Bismarck begins "in a wounding tone of indulgent, tranquil superiority." Then, in answer to Arnim's question why the chancellor persecutes him, Bismarck breaks out into a flood of reproaches. "For eight months you have injured my health, disturbed my peace of mind! You are conspiring with the empress! You will never rest until you yourself come to sit at this table. Then you, too, will see how futile it all is!"

Rarely can we see into the twilit depths of Bismarck's heart so clearly as at this moment, when the will-to-power lures from him so remarkable an admission, when (his tongue running away with him) he discloses all the worthlessness of his position as ruler to the man who would fain replace him.

Instead of leaping to his feet and hurling his resignation at his chief, Arnim complains in gentle tones:

"Has Your Highness no longer any confidence in me?"

Thereupon Bismarck looks at him "with wooden eyes", and rejoins: "None at all!"

Arnim holds out his hand, saying: "Won't you shake hands with me in farewell?"

"Within my own house I won't refuse to shake hands with you, but I will ask you to be good enough not to offer to shake hands with me anywhere else."

After this interview, Bismarck finds it easier to place before Emperor William the old alternative: "He or I." He writes in menacing terms to the effect that he will not wrestle for his master's confidence "with an ambassador whose character is so little worthy of trust." He goes on: "I suspect (nor do I stand alone in this matter) that his official activities are sometimes directed by his personal interest. It is not easy to prove such an assertion, but now that suspicion has entered my mind I find it hard to remain responsible for the way in which this high official carries out his instructions."

Arnim is supposed to have delayed certain negotiations relating to the payment of the French war indemnity, with the express purpose of advantaging certain speculations in which he was engaged with Baron Hirsch. There is a ludicrous similarity between the accusations which Bismarck and Arnim, both Pomeranian Junkers, both leading servants of the empire, each of them guided in business matters by an ennobled Jew, levy against one another. Each accuses the other of pursuing private interest to the detriment of the State; for Arnim, though his name does not appear, is one of the group of Junkers who are attacking Bismarck. Both calumnies are unproved; both are incapable of proof; but their wording is practically identical. Only the stronger of the pair will be able to strike his charges home.

The most that Emperor William is inclined to agree to is to put his envoy upon half pay. This does not suit Bismarck, who dreads Arnim free to intrigue in Berlin more than Arnim in Paris. He therefore has his adversary exiled as envoy to Constantinople. Thereupon Arnim commits a blunder. Instead of resigning, that he may be free to join the party in the Upper House which is making war against the chancellor, he bows before the hostile chief who within the last few months has scourged him with the most insulting official despatches: "I must ask that you show more regard to my instructions and less inclination . . . to follow your own political views than has been witnessed by your reports and your official behaviour hitherto." Now Arnim has certain documents printed anonymously, documents designed to bear witness to his own foresight as contrasted with Bismarck's lack of perspicacity; and he himself is so shortsighted that he overlooks the certainty of discovery. Bismarck has his enemy in the hollow of his hand! No longer can the empress protect Arnim. The chancellor can dismiss him for a breach of official duty. Up till now the fight has been one between two rivals, the weaker of whom, by his foolishness, makes victory easy for the stronger.

Then Bismarck shows his cruelty, which is so marked that " the Arnim affair" enlists half the nation against the victor. His contemporaries and posterity cannot forgive the chancellor for having wanted to annihilate the foe he had already checkmated. When Arnim's successor reports from Paris that certain documents are missing, Arnim, declaring them to be private papers, refuses to hand them over. His brilliant career has been broken.

He, who had hoped to be chancellor, is nothing more than a pensioned official. Relying on his exalted protectors and on his high birth, he defies his all-powerful rival, who thereupon, legally within his rights, has the offender arrested forthwith. After trial on a charge of embezzling official documents, Arnim is sentenced to nine months' imprisonment, and flees to Switzerland. Bismarck's reason for having Arnim publicly tried is that he wishes to have the case thrashed out in court once for all, and thus to prevent a dropping fire of " revelations." He says that the emperor has even more interest than he himself in seeing to it that the affair shall not be spun out. Privately, he advises Arnim to sue for pardon.

By now Arnim is beside himself. In exile, he publishes foolish and unwarrantable pamphlets. Thereupon there is a fresh trial, in which the offender is accused of treason, insult to the emperor, and libelling Bismarck, is sentenced by default to five years' penal servitude, and legally declared to have behaved dishonourably. When, four years later, he is about to take measures to exculpate himself before the Imperial Court of Justice, he dies in Nice, before he can start for Germany, a " dishonoured " and homeless man.

In this trial there appears in public for the first and last time a man whose profession it is to shun publicity. Baron Holstein, whose acquaintance Bismarck had made in St. Petersburg, had been employed by the chancellor as a spy attached to the Paris embassy. His real mission had been to watch Arnim, whose adversary he was, and to send Bismarck secret reports concerning Arnim. That was how the chancellor had received definite information concerning Arnim's aspirations towards the chancellorship. Bismarck made Holstein give evidence in court, and this publicity, this disclosure of the nature of his avocations, was extremely harmful to the spy. Holstein himself tells us that that was why he came to hate Bismarck, with a hatred that was not to be disclosed now, but in later years, with consequences of world-wide historical importance.

VI

There was only one among those in contact with Bismarck who combined loyalty and criticism, friendship and power of independent judgment. This was Roon. Even his friendship with Bismarck was imperilled by the storms of the seventies, and the only thing that saved it was Roon's chivalry. With that seriousness of mood characteristic of the man who aimed always at serving his king and his country, indifferent to his own advantage, to position, and to party considerations, Roon recognised that storms were brewing in home affairs. As early as 1872, he wrote: " The successes of 1866, or rather the illusions coupled with these successes, the false impression that political antagonisms would thenceforward be reconciled, were the first things to trip us up; . . . and the heroic leaps of 1870 did not save the situation. Indeed, the intoxication consequent upon the victories of that year retarded our return to sobriety, so that we staggered farther into the abyss."

Nevertheless, Roon stood firmly shoulder to shoulder with Bismarck when almost all the chancellor's old associates had turned against him. Nothing would induce Roon to sign the declaration, although Blanckenburg was his nephew and had been his political confidant for decades. His love of country, which was more ardent than that inspiring any other Prussian of the day, conjoined with his faith in Bismarck as a greater man than himself, sufficed to keep him free from jealousy. A shrewder and kindlier man than the other Junkers, satiated with power, he was not ashamed to admit that he was no more than a second. He was accustomed to speak of himself as the shield upon which Bismarck had been uplifted.

Perhaps it was this veneration for the chancellor which actually tended to sever Roon from his friend. It was because he admired Bismarck so much, that Roon, when friction came, decided to resign. The king, all of whose old servants had gone except these two, was horrified at Roon's resolve, and did everything he could to induce him to remain. Bismarck succeeded in doing more than this. By a stroke of genius, he kept the last of the faithful by his side, and at the same time shifted some of his own burdens. He appeased Roon's weariness of office by raising him to the position of Prussian minister president, and thus, at the height of the struggle with the conservatives, transferred responsibility from himself to Roon. This was all done in a moment, immediately after receiving Roon's communication; and on New Year's Eve, 1872, he hastened back to Berlin in order to settle matters. The same day, before leaving, he wrote to his friend saying that he himself was ailing, and could no longer conduct affairs as he had been used:

" As long as the king commands it, I shall be glad to go on serving him as minister for foreign affairs. . . . I cannot transmit to any one else the fruit of my twenty years' experience in matters of European policy, and the confidence of foreign courts. But the foreign affairs of the strongest of the great powers require the undivided attention of the person responsible for them, and it is an unprecedented anomaly that the foreign minister of a great empire should at the same time be responsible for home affairs. My occupation is one in which a man makes many enemies and wins no new friends. On the contrary, he loses his old friends if he pursues his course for a decade straightforwardly and fearlessly. . . . In home affairs, I have lost the platform I desired, owing to the desertion of the Conservative Party. . . . My energies have been paralysed by overwork. The king, who sits in the saddle, hardly realises that he has been riding a mettlesome horse until it has foundered. The lazy ones last longer." That is why he wishes to hold only the posts of chancellor and minister for foreign affairs.

"In my present mood of discouragement, I can no longer accept responsibility . . . for such of His Majesty's wishes as I cannot share. The influences which conflict with mine are too powerful, and since last spring my delight in the struggle has vanished owing to the deplorable arrogance and the political ineptitude of the conservatives. Nothing can be done in conjunction with the conservatives, . . . and I do not want to do anything in defiance of them. . . . In accordance with these considerations, I shall, the day after to-morrow, hand in a partial resignation to His Majesty. . . . If God grants us life, we shall be glad to remember the great days in which we worked together as old friends. . . . In cordial and immutable friendship."

Thus in the grand style does Bismarck deck out as a prompting of the heart the partial retreat which is really the outcome of cold political calculation. Ere long he tells his confidants that he will soon come back, and that he is only awaiting a new summons. Roon, however, is his moral prisoner. The new Prussian minister president will only remain in office nine months, for, while it is difficult to work under Bismarck, it is impossible to work beside him. The chancellor has divided his power. As chancellor, he has to ask another man's permission if, as premier, he wants to do something. Bismarck is the empire, and Roon is Prussia. All the frictions which could only be avoided by the personal union, by the mingling of rôles, all the fundamental defects of the imperial constitution, now become manifest, and wreak vengeance on the body of their maker.

We are in February 1873. The Junkers' campaign of calumny is at its height. They have detected old Wagener, Bismarck's confidant, once a journalist and now a privy councillor, in a corrupt practice, and they are trying to prove that Bismarck was privy to it. Bismarck vents his spleen about this matter in the presence of Roon and others. Both the friends grow hot. Bismarck feels that Roon is not doing enough to defend him, and does not conceal his irritation. In the evening, he is surprised to receive the following letter:

"Unhesitatingly recognising your superiority in many respects, I have always . . . tried to remain on the best of terms with Your Highness. Even to-day, when the tone of your remarks made it very difficult, I tried to avoid a breach. Obviously your 'explosiveness' underestimated mine! . . . Perhaps it will be better in both our interests, and certainly it will be better for me, to avoid similar encounters in the future. Therefore, remembering the ties of friendship which have bound us together for so many years, and the decade in which we have worked together, I beg Your Highness to feel assured that you can always count fully upon me as long as you call upon my activities in a suitable way; but that if you give utterance to remonstrances or to actual reproaches as regards my official conduct, you can do so only when you take all the risks involved in my own 'explosiveness.' I shall certainly not pit my ageing forces and my feeble influence against you; I am neither foolish nor self-assertive enough for that. So much is certain! But it is equally certain that I cannot permit you any more, in complete misunderstanding of my nature, to treat me in so inconsiderate and hostile a way, and actually as if I were a refractory or negligent subordinate — such as I never have been nor will be." He goes on to beg Bismarck to regard his letter as an attempt " to enlighten Your Highness fully as to my views concerning our mutual relationships, and the indispensable conditions on which alone their continuance will be possible. It is my wish to give you one more proof (whether we part or not) of how gladly I remain your old friend, Roon."

Does there exist in the German tongue a more splendid letter penned by a man of lesser genius to a man of greater genius, as the outcome of wounded friendship and mortified pride? What could the recipient do but hasten to the writer, to answer him with a cordial handclasp and a friendly glance? Bismarck, who has written plenty of angry letters himself and has never received such a letter as this, takes a weak middle course, writing:

"Dear Roon, I am sorry that you have written me so cold a letter, for I think that I have had to bear stronger explosions from you than mine to-day, or have speedily forgotten them. Moreover, as regards to-day, my impression is that the contagious outburst of wrath began sooner in you than in me. I do not think that you are able to put yourself in my place as fully as so old a friend should, and as I should try to put myself in your place if you had been publicly attacked in so base a way. . . . I should certainly have imagined myself sure of the eager sympathy of my colleagues when my honour and integrity were pub-

licly impugned. . . . Perhaps you have too much to do to be able
to spare time and nervous energy in making allowance for the personal sensibilities of another. The fact is that, as far as I am
aware, not one of my colleagues, no newspaper, not a single friend,
has voluntarily taken any steps to support me in face of this
undeserved and gross insult. . . . I have had to take official
measures in order to secure the aid which friendship and personal
affection have failed to give me. . . .

"In any case, my sentiments were less overbearing than you
assume. They were merely those of a colleague who, when suffering from severe and undeserved mortifications, encounters business considerations and angry refusals where he had good reason
to expect friendly help. . . . Be patient with me, recollecting our
ten years of work together, and remembering even more our association in still earlier days. You will not need to be patient long.
I shall fight for my reputation with the last remnant of nervous
energy which God leaves me. . . . After that, I shall not give
you any occasion, by such conversations and letters as to-day's,
for regarding as imperilled the long-standing friendship which I
hope will endure after my term of public service has come to an
end."

Roon, minister president, lives close to the chancellor. Perhaps
from his window he can see Bismarck pacing up and down the
garden, cooling off after the despatch of this letter. How can
Roon help smiling when he reads the assurance of the unparalleled
egoist, who declares himself always willing to defend a friend, and
says that anyhow he is soon going to resign? Roon is so much
kindlier than Bismarck that he forgives the latter's reiterated
accusations; forgets, though he is an army officer, that he has
been affronted before witnesses, who will certainly not be slow to
tell all and sundry how the chancellor had scolded the minister
president. Roon takes pen and paper and begins his letter: "Dear
Bismarck."

Never before has Roon begun a letter to Bismarck with such
a superscription. At most he has written "Honoured friend."
Often there has been no superscription at all, because Roon could

not make up his mind to respond in kind to Bismarck's habitual mode of address: "Dear Roon", which to the latter seemed unduly cordial, or to make too many claims. Thus addressing him for the first and last time as "Dear Bismarck", Roon tries to atone for the "Your Highness" of yesterday's letter — shows that he has a feeling of love for the man whom yesterday he had held at arm's length by addressing him as "Your Highness." Lovingly and yet with dignity he continues, himself describing yesterday's scene:

"While it is true that I had to write a 'cold letter' to you yesterday, you must know that when I did so I was deeply grieved. You cannot fail to realise how great is my esteem for you. You must remember that, feeling for you as I do, I have opportunity day by day to break lances on your behalf, and that I seize these opportunities valiantly, whenever and wherever I come across enmity towards you. That was why your assumption that, in chill disregard of your honour and your reputation, I was disposed to be lukewarm in your behalf, hurt me deeply, . . . and yesterday, you coupled serious and causeless menaces with what you wrote. When I gave expression to my astonishment that you had let yourself go against me in this way, the result was to arouse fresh outpourings of unwarranted lack of confidence in my zeal, and repetitions of your angry doubts as to my sympathy with you. . . .

"Enough of yesterday and of what lies behind us! You say that I am to show patience towards you. . . . You know me well enough to be sure that I always try to guide myself by the scriptural injunction: 'Bear ye one another's burdens.' But I am only a weak mortal, who finds this beyond his powers when he is misunderstood, and when he believes himself misused, by those whom he esteems and loves more than all others. . . . You, too, must have consideration for me, and must not expect me to be nothing more than a dumb target when, without warrant, you choose to direct the shafts of your wrath against me. Coming to what you say about the shortness of the time for which I shall need to show patience towards you, let me tell you that it is my cordial wish and hope that you will continue to guide the fortunes of our country to the general advantage long after my bones are resting in the tomb."

Thus did a nobleman write to his friend.

But the weather has not cleared. Friction continues, and since Roon wishes to keep Bismarck as his friend at any cost, he resigns in the autumn. He writes to his nephew, saying that he might have been able to go with Bismarck against the liberal current, but that "to fight against both, exceeds my powers." To Bismarck, Roon writes, in words of virile renunciation: "Allow me, once more, to call to you from a full heart 'Adelante, adelantador, atrevido!' [Forward, brave hero!] I shall continue to do so until the end of my life, which perhaps is near; shall continue to do so whether I am on the stage or in the auditorium."

Bismarck's answer is no less fine. When he has no underlying purpose to gain, and when he is free from mistrust, the chancellor knows how to read the human heart. He does not underestimate the loss which he has brought upon himself: "In public life I stand in the breach, and my earthly master gives me no line of retreat. So be it. Vexilla regis prodeunt. Ill or well, I shall continue to bear onward the standard of my feudal lord, against my factious cousins no less firmly than against the pope, the Turks, and the French. If I get tired out, I shall have been used up for a purpose, and any audit office would justify the expenditure. I shall be rendered lonely by your withdrawal, for among all the ministers you are the only man with a feeling heart. . . . In the yellow sessions-room, no one can fill the gap where you used to sit on the sofa, and when I look at your place I shall think: 'I once had a comrade'." This great duet of two male voices records the end of old-world Prussia. Eleven years earlier, the pair had sallied forth together to slay the dragon of democracy. It seemed, for the nonce, as if the two knights had succeeded only too well. They threw their lances at the time spirit again and again, until at length he cried "Hurrah" and fell. But now the dragon has come to life again, with three heads in place of one, and roars out of the abyss. Can it be supposed that the unaided strength of the surviving champion will suffice to rid the world of the monster?

Rarely has Bismarck opened his heart to any one. Now, after Roon's departure it is speedily closed once more. Again purposes and interests determine all his actions. Six months later, and Bismarck (who had done his best to hinder Roon's retirement) is saying that Roon's vanity had been the cause of all the blunders; Roon would have his own way, whereas Camphausen was far more accommodating; Roon had been an idler towards the last. Roon, on the other hand, who has still six years of quiet evening before him, cherishes his friend's image from a distance. After Bismarck had once again threatened to resign, Roon said to his nephew: "When Prometheus brought down fire from heaven, he had to put up with the fetters and the eagle. . . . His reach exceeds his grasp! No one who picks the fruit of the tree of life goes unpunished. If, at any cost, he should now retire into the ease of country life, he would . . . tear the laurels from his own forehead."

When he knows that death is at hand, Roon journeys to Berlin, takes up his quarters in a hotel opposite the palace, watches the hoisting of the flag every morning, has enquiries and gifts sent him from over the way, and at length, on the day before his death, the field marshal of seventy-six is visited by the king of eighty-two. There they sit, this pair of thoroughly honest old men — men in their sense of duty, children in their piety. They talk of past battles, and when William takes his leave, he glances upwards, saying: "Give a word of greeting to my old comrades. You will meet many of them there!"

Thus dies Albrecht von Roon.

VII

"If we say 'hott' to an ox, he turns to the right; if we say 'hüh', he turns to the left; but the old man cannot understand either 'hüh' or 'hott'!" Such is the lamentation with which Bismarck discloses his private opinion of the king during the last decade of William's life. From the time when Bismarck is sixty

and William eighty, their relations grow steadily worse. A statesman of altogether exceptional intelligence, uplifted by European
successes, spoiled by a hundred concessions from his master, a
thorough-going autocrat in public affairs — how could such a
man remain patient and courteous; how could such a man
endure the formal necessity of having to ask and to beg? A
thick-headed, honourable old gentleman, uplifted by the sense of
kingship, spoiled by the habit of command — how could such a
man remain patient and courteous; how could such a man admit
Bismarck's claim to play the autocrat?

True that in his letters Bismarck is lavish with the formalities
of respect, and never omits the rhetorical flourishes demanded by
court etiquette and proper to those who are on the stage of history. Indeed, in the sittings of the Crown Council, he is sedulous
to display (as witnesses tell us) "a respectful deference akin to
the language of the court." When the king thereupon replies to
him graciously and in the most friendly fashion, William's show
of feeling is perfectly genuine, just as Bismarck's tears were
genuine when the rank of prince was conferred on him. Nor does
King William ever show jealousy. He does all he can to glorify
the name of his minister, and his official letters are full of expressions of gratitude: "My gratitude to you will outlast my life,
your eternally thankful king and friend." When a commoner is to
be ennobled before his marriage with a princess, the king first
asks Bismarck's permission because the candidate had once refused to drink Bismarck's health. "On no account," says William, "in order to make two lovers happy, shall I accede to the
request if you are opposed to my doing so!" Bismarck in his
turn, with the tacit pride of genius, is continually extolling to all
and sundry his master's diligence and sense of duty — qualities
which were less conspicuous in the emperor's predecessor and
successor, but which William displayed unceasingly both by day
and by night.

Nevertheless, to dozens of ministers, deputies, and casual
visitors unconnected with political life, and even to strangers, Bismarck speaks with a frankness which betrays a deliberate inten-

tion to have what he says repeated — though when it suits him, he will promptly deny his words.

"The things for which the king is now glorified, are things which I wrung from him with great labour. . . . Intercourse with him grows more and more difficult. With advancing years and increasing debility, his lack of power for decision becomes more intolerable." To Hohenlohe: "He no longer knows what he has signed, and is sometimes in a very bad temper when he hears that this or that has happened about which, as he thinks, he has not been informed!" To Von Mittnacht, the Würtemberg minister: "Though my king had it in mind to abdicate in 1866, I carried him upon my shoulders to the imperial throne. Now he thinks he knows everything much better than his minister, and wants to manage everything for himself." To Booth, the director of the gardens, Bismarck says laconically, pipe in mouth: "A good officer, pleasant in his manner to the ladies!" When the foreigner rejoins that, as Prince William, the emperor had made excellent speeches in the Landtag, Bismarck says: "They were all ready written for him. He is not at all eloquent, though he can sometimes speak well enough to his generals! . . . He is quite exceptional in respect of fidelity and trustworthiness. But it is not enough for me that he should have these qualities. What I want to feel sure of is that he will stand by me."

In view of these encomiums, Bismarck naturally takes it very much amiss when he finds his master untrustworthy. He never fails to learn what the king has said against him: "On such occasions he always threatened to resign," says Herr von Hohenlohe, "for he was determined to get his own way!" Bismarck complacently relates that one of his written requests to resign had been crumpled up by old William into a ball, and that the king had written angrily in the margin the one word: "Never!" When the two men met for the first time after this, the king said movingly to his servant: "Do you wish to bring discredit upon my old age? It is an act of infidelity in you to wish to forsake me!" Another time, Bismarck leaves his request to resign hanging in the balance, as a threat, for he is going away on furlough and asks that the matter shall be left open till he returns. This means that the king is to wait in silence for five months! The old gentleman is beside himself with anger: "You must excuse me the ordeal of trying to describe the impression your letter has made on me! One thing I must ask you! Since you yourself write that you want me to keep the contents of your letter secret, let me beg you to impose the oath of silence upon the sender of your letter as well. . . . Your profoundly disturbed W."

Yet this same king reads the "Reichsglocke" every week! Though Bismarck, in his memoirs, generally glosses over the difficulties in his relationship with William, he complains because the emperor reads the "Reichsglocke"—a newspaper founded to calumniate the chancellor. When three persons are nominated for high office, Bismarck protests against the public display of the king's kindly sentiments towards his enemies, writing of one of the three nominees: "The only thing that has attracted public attention to this person is the fact that for years he has been hostile to me. He is distinguished neither for talent nor for his services. At the Foreign Office, he was a nuisance owing to his incapacity, bordering upon lunacy at important moments. Since then, fifteen years ago, he has done nothing but speak and write against me with all the moroseness of one whose self-conceit makes him fancy himself misunderstood."

Moreover, Bismarck knows very well how to take vengeance for humiliations inflicted on him by his master, though always with the respect becoming to a courtier. When in the year 1874, the king complains that a sentence in a speech from the throne is too strongly phrased, Bismarck, writing from Varzin, declares that if the slightest alteration is made in the wording he will not come to Berlin for the opening of the Reichstag. Hohenlohe is to tell the king that Bismarck's vanity as an author is too great for him to be willing to accept this correction. Hohenlohe discharges his commission. "From this passage it might be inferred," says the old gentleman in a state of great excitement, "that we want to make war upon France once more! . . . I will not hear a word of anything of the kind. . . . I am too old; and I am afraid lest

Bismarck should gradually entangle me in another war!" When Hohenlohe courteously denies that there is any such inference to be drawn, William strokes his beard, and replies: "In this matter, I cannot agree with Prince Bismarck. I shall be glad if you will put my point of view before the prince." Thus do master and servant tell one another home truths through a go-between, so as to avoid personal collision. Of course the old gentleman does not get his correction made!

"We cannot help ourselves," says the crown prince. "If Bismarck were to propose to my father an alliance with Garibaldi, or even with Mazzini, my father would, to begin with, run about the room in despair, exclaiming: 'Bismarck, what on earth are you trying to make me do?' Then he would stand still in the middle of the room, and would say: 'Still, if you really believe that this is indispensable in the interest of the State, after all I do not see any objection to it.'" We do not find much difficulty in understanding why, in a private letter, a highly placed Berlin official should have humorously spoken of Bismarck as Caracalla. We can understand, too, how it came to pass that, after a dispute, the old gentleman should, at Bismarck's instigation, have written him a touching letter at New Year 1873. Immediately afterwards, Bismarck tells one of the liberals (intending to have the news spread) that the holograph letter had been submitted to him in rough copy, and that he had done nothing more to it than correct the spelling in one or two places. Bismarck adds, in the Mephistopheles vein: "It is rather a pity that I made those emendations, for now the document seems less authentic."

Very rarely does any one speak the truth about these matters. Unruh once ventures to do so, saying to Bismarck that history will record it to the emperor's credit "that he not merely retained in his service a more obnoxious minister than any king of Prussia had had before him, but actually followed this minister's advice unconditionally." Bismarck was quite unruffled by Unruh's remark, and made an answer which has become classical: "You are right. Kings have a peculiarly keen sense of what is to their own advantage."

No matter who is there, he does not hesitate to give away his old master. Lucius describes how in 1875 Bismarck says, in a mixed company: "Sometimes we get autograph despatches which take whole weeks of work for their answer. The emperor does not smoke, reads no newspapers, only documents and dispatches; it would be better if he would play patience. . . . If I should happen to make a sharp answer, he turns pale, and says: 'I know that I suffer from the disabilities of old age, but it is not my fault that I have gone on living so long!' Naturally that sort of remark makes me feel sore." Or Bismarck tells his doctor about the diffuse formality of the language which must be used at court: "I can't say in plain terms, 'Your Majesty is talking rot'; or, 'Your Majesty knows no more about politics than a third-form boy!' It must all be wrapped up in polite phraseology. People don't realise what a job it has been to get on with an old Olympian for eighteen years. It wouldn't have been possible if I hadn't always had the threat of resignation like a pistol ready to my hand."

When his confidant Lucius praises King William, Bismarck replies savagely: "All sovereigns have the same recipe for the exploitation of their ablest and most faithful advisers. Our king must have taken his recipe from Frederick the Great. He is cold, is hard as a stone, has no thought of gratitude towards me, and only keeps me in his service because he thinks I can still be of some use to him."

The feud with Augusta culminates in the seventies. The empress and her adviser, Schleinitz, the treasurer of the household, take under their patronage all who write and intrigue against Bismarck, whether they be Roman Catholics or Junkers. As soon as Bismarck joins hands with the liberals, Augusta becomes an anti-liberal. At the end of the war, when she takes part in the triumphal entry into Berlin, the people do not know (have hardly realised even to-day) how busily she has been at work in order to postpone this great celebration. The empress was undergoing a cure at a spa, and held everything up for six weeks. The postponement of demobilisation for this period cost the country millions of talers. A little paroxysm of megalomania!

Her attitude towards parliamentary deputies and ministers of State at home, and towards ruling princes abroad, did much harm to imperial policy both at home and abroad, and involved the chancellor in the most harassing struggles. "She writes," he complains simultaneously to two of his confidants, "holograph letters to foreign rulers, ostensibly at the instigation of her husband; she runs counter to my policy, hobnobs with the French envoy, follows his and Windthorst's advice. Her intrigues border on high treason. . . . She gets people to write letters to her which she then puts before the emperor — at breakfast — after which I receive disagreeable notes from Emperor William. If that sort of thing goes on I shall resign, and then I shall be able to say what I think in plain terms."

She supports the French envoy, a nobleman, in his hopes for the restitution of Alsace and Lorraine. As French reader, she has a cunning rascal who plays the part of spy. She shows special favour to persons of a strange exotic type and to Catholic priests. Schleinitz, "a sort of counter-minister", keeps her informed regarding all that Arnim, Windthorst, and the discontented Junkers have in their minds against Bismarck. As a result, the anti-Bismarck circles are encouraged in their hope of at length unseating the everlasting chancellor. Bismarck discovers that the dissemination of the "Reichsglocke" is arranged in the office of the treasury of the household. "The go-between was a leading subordinate who cut Frau von Schleinitz' quill pens, and kept the writing table in order. The empress let me feel her disfavour persistently. Her immediate underlings, the highest officials of the court, were so rude to me that I was compelled to make a written complaint to His Majesty."

When, one morning, he goes to ask the emperor to grant a special favour to the Centre Party, he finds at His Majesty's bedside (the emperor is laid up) Augusta "in a toilet which led me to infer that she had come down after I had been announced. When I expressed a wish to speak to His Majesty alone, she went away, though only as far as just outside the door, which she did not close behind her; and she took pains, by her continued movements, to let me know that she was listening to every word." That evening there is a court ball. Bismarck begs her not to injure her husband's health by conflicting advice. "This unexpected move of mine, which was quite out of keeping with court traditions, had a remarkable effect. Never during the last decade of her life did I see Empress Augusta look so beautiful as on this occasion. She drew herself up; her eyes flashed in a way which I had never seen before and have never seen since; she cut short the conversation, left me unceremoniously, and, as I heard afterwards from one of the courtiers, said: 'Our gracious chancellor is extremely un- gracious to-day'."

In both of these scenes, which Bismarck describes with so masterly a touch, she is characteristically herself. In the morn- ing, she is jealously defiant and behaves in the most undignified way, simply that she may be sure of keeping her finger in the governmental pie, though it be only from behind the door. In the evening, she assumes a queenly dignity which has a rejuvenating effect, and rekindles the personal beauty for which she was cele- brated throughout three generations. Can we be surprised that Bismarck's most heartfelt wish is for her death? "There must be an end of one institution or the other," he exclaims with mingled wrath and humour. "Either marriage or monarchy; both together are impossible! But since we need monarchy, we must make an end of marriage!" In a more serious mood, he says to Lucius: "When, overnight, some matter or other has been arranged, at the breakfast table next morning everything is turned upside down. . . . If only the emperor were a widower!"

When Bismarck reaches the height of his power, his royalism is extinct. He has almost completely lost the faith on which royalism must depend. Those in the inner circle, Bucher and Busch, tell us of an article sketched by the chief in which there is talk of his threats to resign. He deliberately arranges for the publication of this in England, so that it may be reprinted in the German newspapers, and thus influence the king to yield to his wishes. When, in this article, references are to be made to the chancellor's "monarchical sentiment and devotion to the king",

Busch tells us that "the two augurs grinned at one another." In a self-contemptuous vein, he complains to Mittnacht: "Experience of how difficult ruling sovereigns may sometimes make matters for their ministers is enough to incline a man to become a republican. . . . In their private letters they speak of their ministers as if these were no better than land stewards!" He writes mockingly of a certain secretary of State that this gentleman would speak even of the Homeric heroes in the servile phraseology proper to court life: "His Royal Highness Hector of blessed memory." In the year 1880, he privately sums up the matter as follows: "I am no absolutist. How can any one be that who has been a minister of State for several years? One has not only to do with the monarch, but also with his wife, perhaps with his mistresses, with the whole mob of those about the court. . . . The minds of the nobles at court are filled with paltry superficialities, while the members of the old aristocracy are atrociously arrogant, and plume themselves upon their genealogical trees."

To Scholz, the minister, he says in plain terms: "I took up office equipped with a great fund of royalist sentiments and veneration for the king; to my sorrow, I find that this fund is ever more and more depleted!" Then comes the bitter epigram: "I have seen three kings naked, and the sight was not always a pleasant one!"

VIII

Heavy-footed and masterful, the dictator strides across his empire. The people, who now begin to speak of him as the Iron Chancellor, jested unwittingly — for he was iron in home affairs, where the people would fain have had him otherwise, whilst in foreign relationships he remained the most elastic of all the diplomatists. At any rate, there was now at the head of affairs a man who could command, and for the present the Germans wanted nothing more. Since he trusted no one, did not assume that any one else possessed either intelligence or fidelity, had good reason to believe in his own shrewdness, and suspected every able man who came near him as a potential rival—he had all possible reasons for becoming more and more the autocrat, for wanting to keep all the threads in his own hands. Yet, concomitantly, the very same egoism, his "inborn dislike of pens, ink, paper", his hatred of human beings and his fondness for trees, his intense dislike of privy councillors and all their ways, stimulated in him the longing for repose, for country life, for lengthy periods of leave. He wanted to be away for as many as five months at a time, during which his subordinates in Berlin were to carry on for themselves. But woe unto them if they did anything on their own initiative! No one understood this better than Roon, who, before the days when he was minister president, wrote:

"Then there is the hermit of Varzin, who wants to do everything himself and nevertheless has issued the strictest injunctions that he is on no account to be disturbed. . . . Unless he crowds on all sail in order to provide the empire with an Upper House and the necessary ministers, history in days to come will pass an adverse judgment upon him. . . . You cannot go on living for ever from hand to mouth, be the hand never so adroit and strong, and the mouth so eloquent and so well provided with sharp teeth. . . . He has too few trusty friends; and he listens too much to his enemies, among whom some of those who idolise him are the worst. . . . It is only because I myself have so high an opinion of him that I should like to alter him in many respects." Soon all see the same thing. Lasker complains that Bismarck can no longer put up with any ministers, and wants only chiefs of departments. Again, we read: "Germany wishes to be ruled by Bismarck, and does not cease to want this even when he goes to Varzin and pleads illness. It will put up with a little less ruling from Bismarck, rather than be ruled by another.

First of all, his autocracy is exercised over ministers and princes; then, more forcibly still, over the Reichstag; and it culminates when exercised over officials. Even reigning dukes are not received unless they are punctual to the moment; even kings are rebuffed. A grand duke has an appointment for nine o'clock in the evening. At a quarter to nine, Bismarck, who is at work, sends for his uniform coat and puts it on. At a quarter past nine, he resumes the old coat in which he is accustomed to work at home, and informs Tiedemann, who is writing to dictation: "No reigning monarch need think that I shall wait for him longer than a quarter of an hour." At this instant the grand duke is announced, doors are thrown wide. Tiedemann records that Bismarck, who had been walking up and down as he dictated, promptly sits down at the writing table, and pretends to be deeply immersed in documents. Then, with a profound reverence, the chancellor says: "I had quite given up expecting the honour of a visit from Your Royal Highness this evening, for it is already twenty minutes past nine." He behaves in this way in order to keep the princes up to the mark; but for other reasons as well. He lets the privy council know what he has done, being well aware that the Foreign Office is a hotbed of gossip. When the king of Saxony arrives unexpectedly, the porter, a Prussian of the old school, enquires: "Has he an appointment? No? Then I can't admit him." Thereupon the king drives away, and subsequently accepts the apologies that are offered.

For weeks at a time, Bismarck will be inaccessible to ministers and envoys, if he does not like them, or if he wishes to avoid committing himself. Lucius and Tiedemann tell us of all the devices that must be employed to make him accept a communication or come to a decision when he is in a reluctant mood. We might fancy we were reading court memoirs concerning the autocrat of all the Russians. Men of first-class intelligence naturally grow more and more unwilling to enter such a semblance of a cabinet. It therefore becomes increasingly difficult to find ministers. When he has lured persons into accepting ministerial office, he would fain be quit of them ere long. For this reason, a witty count compares him with Don Juan, saying that the chancellor first cajoles the pretty girls till he has won them, and dismisses them as soon as he has possessed them. In hardly any case did his respect for one of his ministers outlast two years; and seldom, indeed, could he keep a minister longer than that time. This was not unnatural, seeing that his mood, as described by himself, was: "If I want to eat a spoonful of soup, I must first ask eight fools for their permission!" Yet, if mortified colleagues go over to the enemy, he complains bitterly of their ingratitude, saying that he had picked them up out of their obscurity.

Every visitor bores him, unless he is himself speaking. "Any one who wants to speak with me, must get through with what they want to say in twenty minutes. Most of the envoys stay too long, for they always want to extort some information which they can put into their reports." Even the highest officials, even those who are personal friends, must not come to see him uninvited and without an appointment, not though he should be at his country estate. Indeed, when he is at Varzin, Emperor William himself has no longer any right to send one who might be unwelcome. Prince Hohenlohe, envoy in Paris, is having audience of the emperor, and the emperor says that Hohenlohe had better go to Varzin — this being equivalent to a command. Prince Hohenlohe rejoins that he cannot go thither unless Bismarck asks him. The emperor and the prince stand confronting one another silently for a moment, and then the tolerant monarch gives way. But if Bismarck has something to say to the emperor, he makes no bones about sending this same Hohenlohe from Varzin to the monarch.

One of his ways of establishing his autocracy is to make play with his health. When he is otherwise at the end of his resources, he falls sick, with an illness which is partly real and partly political. His health, he then says, makes it necessary for him to retire. Commenting on this, and parodying Heine, "Kladderadatsch" says:

> Out of my great sufferings
> I make the little taxes!

These reiterated tenders of resignation are not merely based upon the claim that his health is shattered: the blame for failing health is laid upon the service, and in most cases actually upon the emperor. On the very day when Hohenlohe finds him

at Varzin "well, and in excellent humour", Bismarck tells Hohenlohe to inform the emperor that he (Bismarck) is still very ill,
nerves quite upset, "for the emperor is so inconsiderate towards
me, and annoys me".

But the chancellor expects the Reichstag to pay him the consideration which he himself withholds from that body. In 1879,
when Bismarck is making a personal attack on Lasker, the president rings his bell gently. Bismarck stops his tirade and says:
"What's that bell ringing for? Everything is quiet in the hall!"
Afterwards, he says to Lucius: "I am here as the highest official in the empire, and am not subject to the president's discipline. He has no right to interrupt me or even to warn me with
the bell. If he does anything of that sort, we are one step nearer
towards the dissolution of the house!" Thus he draws the aim
of all lances upon himself, and his lust of battle grows with his
contempt for his adversaries. When Rickert makes a circumstantial attack on the government, Bismarck draws his sword, metaphorically speaking: "Yes, gentlemen, you attack our legislation,
our doings, the policy of the government. Whom do you really
aim at in these attacks? Whom other than myself? . . . I am
not going to let you hurl such insults at me under the pretence
that you are attacking the State, without claiming the right to
hit back!"

In the same sitting he changes the motif, passing from honour
to sport, for he says to Richter: "Simply as a sportsman, if I
may say so, I cannot refrain here from defending myself against
such attacks!" Another day, he is dominated by a mood intermediate between self-conceit and modesty. Lasker says that no
man can do everything. Bismarck regards this as a challenge to
his own powers, and rejoins: "It seems to me that what your
Alva can do, Charles can do likewise, no more!" (He thus deliberately misquotes Schiller's "and Charles can do more!" apparently to his own disadvantage.) He very rarely makes any
reference to his own history, but on one occasion he declares
in the Reichstag: "I have been a match for all Europe put together. You are not the first I have had to deal with!" At such mo-

ments, even his worst enemies can hardly refrain from trembling. They know that he is speaking the truth.

More and more, in these days, he came to feel himself a master of statecraft. For the instruction of the ideologues in the Reichstag, he said: "Politics is not a science, as the professors are apt to suppose. It is an art. It is just as little a science as sculpture and painting. A man may be an able critic without being an artist. Even Lessing, the master of all the critics, would never have undertaken to carve a Laocoön." When, after such clashes, he comes to table in a bad temper, his grim sense of humour will display itself once more after the first three or four courses.

The caprices (to which his autocracy becomes intensified) are especially connected with the security of his own position. In this matter, Bismarck really does resemble a lion which seems, from time to time, to release a captured beast, only at the last moment to grasp it once more in the huge claws. In April 1880, he is furious because, for the first time, Prussia is outvoted in the Bundesrat. As early as ten o'clock, he sends for Tiedemann, and gives instructions that his impending resignation is to be announced at once in the "Norddeutsche." Notwithstanding advice to the contrary, he has the notice sent in, and drafts his tender of resignation. While this is being done, he goes for a walk in the garden; at each turn he looks in at the window, and gives Tiedemann yet more sharply worded instructions. Several of the federal princes and their representatives are to be called to account. Shortly before the time when the newspaper goes to press, Tiedemann urges him to wait until morning. "No!" Meanwhile, the tender of resignation, which occupies four sheets of foolscap, is being fair-copied by four clerks, for this is the only way in which it can be made ready for the emperor's hands by half-past four. When the clock strikes the half hour it is sent off to the palace by a mounted messenger; at a quarter to five Bismarck sits down to dinner. He has hardly begun the meal when he sends a message to the effect that the tender of resignation is not to be dispatched. Tiedemann hastens upstairs, says it is half an hour since the document was sent. Of course he can see if it can be got back from the aide-de-camp, but unfortunately the notice has already been sent to the newspaper, and the emperor will read this. "Oh, well, let matters take their course! He's often enough made himself a nuisance to me. It is his turn now!"

Such are the farces which Bismarck will play when his position as chancellor is at stake. He would not be guided by whims instead of by reasons in his foreign policy, even were it upon a matter of minor importance; and if one of his subordinates were to yield to caprice in such matters, he would be in a fury. But as regards his own position, he can play the fool, for he is irreplaceable. Lucius and Tiedemann, two deputies, one of whom he makes a minister of State and the other chief of the imperial chancellery, are the only two whose tact and energy enable them to work under Bismarck for years in succession. Later, Scholz, minister for finance, is equally successful.

Interesting men are Busch and Bucher. A little younger than Bismarck, both had been revolutionists. Then they became journalists of note, and were taken into the public service. Busch is clever and unscrupulous, pliable and shallow. After travelling widely, he became editor of the "Grenzboten", and attracted Bismarck's attention. He rose to favour before the Franco-German War, but was after it sent away in disgrace. Then, by underhand ways verging on blackmail, he made himself indispensable once more, and was again employed by Bismarck, who had more to fear from him than Busch had to fear from the chancellor. As a reporter he was a past master, seeing, hearing, and noting all that happened. His diary provides invaluable material for an understanding of Bismarck, who himself had to admit its unwelcome truth.

Contrasted with this sturdy, jovial, sly, and cheerful fellow, Lothar Bucher is an enigmatic figure. A lawyer to begin with, one of forty-nine radical deputies in the Landtag, he was sentenced to imprisonment and fled to London. He spent ten years in that city, years of loneliness and poverty, a neighbour of Marx in exile. When he returned to Germany after the amnesty, Lassalle introduced him to Bismarck. He was now nearing fifty, and still without any assured means of subsistence, weary of the uncertainties of a revolutionist's life. The auspices were favourable, and Bismarck found it easy to buy his powerful pen. At the very time when Wilhelm Liebknecht, whose acquaintance Bucher had made in London, was beginning the most arduous stage of his career, for Bucher the doors of the Foreign Office opened, the doors leading to permanent advancement. He could look forward to honourable promotion if he did everything he was told and ceased to profess views of his own.

An inconspicuous, delicately built man, when he was able to shake off the cares of office for a time, he would turn his back upon men and newspapers, would roam through the woods carrying a green collecting box in which to put specimens of grass or moss; he knew all the birds; was an old bachelor who provided for his sister, ate very little, and drank no strong liquors. As soon as he got back into Bismarck's harness once more, day and night were all the same to him. If he went to the theatre, he had to let his master know the number of his seat, so that he could be fetched in case of need. A shrewd thinker, a smooth writer, he penned innumerable English articles, French notes, drafts for German laws; doing anything and everything he was told by the master to whom he had sold his soul — though he had no affection for Bismarck. Because he had ceased to show any will of his own, he was able to suggest improvements even to Bismarck, and could learn from the latter's expression whether the criticism had been successful. He was invaluable to Bismarck, and of no other did Bismarck ever say: "A true pearl! He was my faithful friend and often my censor." On the other hand, Bismarck once spoke of the worthy and devoted Abeken as his coolie.

Of all the councillors, Bismarck demanded that when they spoke they should be brief, and that when they wrote they should be simple. One who, like Tiedemann and Bucher, could speak pithily and could always finish his job betwixt night and morning, never found Bismarck impatient. In speech there was to be no sentimentality; in writing there were to be no superlatives.

In these matters, Bismarck had established golden rules: "The simpler the phrase, the more powerful the impression." Again: "However complicated a situation, the heart of it can be ripped out in a few words." One who worked under him must be able in ten minutes to give a report on a draft law containing more than a hundred paragraphs. "Of course the preliminary work for this took many hours." When he wants to acquaint himself with an economic problem, an account extending to five folio pages is too long.

He is quite ready to endure contradiction, and turns it to account after the first shock. We must grasp the true nature of this man of nerves, who was anything but "iron." When he is nervously excited, he twists his thick eyebrows much as another man would twist his moustache. On such days, Tiedemann always has among the documents in his portfolio one relating to some simple matter ready to his hand. "If, on entering the room, I found him looking out of the window with a world-weary expression of countenance, and if I saw that he was inclined to twist his eyebrows, I would give him a very brief report upon some indifferent topic. Then he would usually say: 'You can settle that as you think best. Anything more?'" Tiedemann takes his leave. Next morning, when the chief has got out of his bed on the right side, he will listen to reports patiently for hour after hour.

Because Bismarck is prone to sleep late in the morning, the work of his office does not begin till noon. He is hard at it from twelve till six, and then again from nine till after midnight. So markedly is his an evening nature, that he would like to have the sittings of parliament late, as they are in England. "In the evening one is a much more effective being; one speaks better, is more conciliatory. At morningtide one seems only to be waiting for others to say something one can attack."

But when he himself is in a vigorous and cheerful mood, he will, like many neurotic people on these occasions, demand the exceptional from his underlings. A great draft must be penned within an hour, and during this hour the clerk will perhaps be

disturbed as often as ten times. "The servants at the chancellery were kept on the trot. Everything had to be done in double-
quick time. . . . Even the strongest nerves were apt to break
under the strain." None the less, Tiedemann, who tells us this,
says likewise: "He was never in any way violent to me. . . . I
cannot ever recall his speaking to me in a tone other than such
as is usual between gentlemen. On the contrary, he was politeness itself, setting in this respect an example to the other ministers. Of course, one had to be careful not to make him impatient
and nervous. The members of the subordinate staff were very
much afraid of the chief. They knew that he would chide them for
the most trifling oversight, and they trembled before Jupiter
tonans."

In his large, scantily furnished study, lighted by a tall silver
lamp, he would listen, half reclining, while a report was read to
him, and would then promptly give his decision. During six
years, Tiedemann could not remember that he ever hesitated for
a moment in this respect. When he was dictating, it was his way
to walk up and down the room, his speech coming in jets, just
as it did when he was speaking from the tribune. There would
be long pauses, and then rushes of words. Often he would dictate
two or three almost synonymous locutions from which a choice
was subsequently to be made. "Since he would not tolerate any
interruption (which made him lose the thread of his discourse),
it was very difficult to follow him. Towards the close of the year
1877, he dictated to me a report to the emperor, a political picture of the development of all our party relationships since the
establishment of the constitution. The dictation went on without a pause for five hours. He was speaking more rapidly than
usual, and I had the greatest difficulty in getting down the leading points of what he said. The room was overheated, and I
was afraid of getting cramps. Quickly making up my mind, I took
off my coat and went on writing in my shirt sleeves. Prince Bismarck glanced at me in astonishment, but a moment afterwards
he nodded understandingly, and went on without stopping. When
I came to write out a fair copy of my notes (one hundred and

BISMARCK IN 1883

From a photograph by Loescher and Petsch, Berlin

fifty foolscap pages), . . . I was amazed to find how admirably the whole was developed. . . . It was a perfectly straightforward account, without any repetitions or digressions."

Thus in his official work he showed himself simultaneously autocratic and considerate; and in other affairs he manifested a like combination of punctiliousness with personal courtesy. Since he had neither patience nor time to be measured for his clothes, his tailor had to measure him with the eyes. If the result was unsatisfactory, the poor man would receive a letter of this kind: " You used to make me clothes which fitted well enough, but you seem to have lost the art of doing this, and you apparently assume that with advancing years I have grown smaller and thinner —which rarely happens. . . . What you have been sending me since 1870 is not fit to wear; and I should not have expected of such a business as yours, which in general is so ably conducted, that you would have paid so little attention to the natural history of the human body." Such is the mordant humour shown by this great stylist when he has occasion to blame an excellent underling.

His self-esteem is always on edge when he is associating with his equals. As a matter of course, his colleagues are intolerable to him, and he therefore treats them worse than he treats his councillors, who are unable to defend themselves. Several of the ministers describe his " unapproachable loftiness ", and say that he treated them as if they were underlings. Von Stosch, the minister for the navy, writes: " He told me to sit down, and went through my work with me in the manner in which a schoolmaster deals with a stupid and refractory schoolboy. . . . He snapped at me whenever I tried to put in a word, and I could do nothing but hold my tongue and give way." Thus, in half an hour, a man will forfeit Bismarck's respect for ever. Eulenburg, who has been treated unjustly as minister, makes a sharp protest, which wrings the following lines from the man of might: " From your letter I derive the impression that a wrong has been done you, a wrong for which I must ask your pardon, although I was not to blame for it, but at most allowed it to happen." For generation after generation, this letter will be treasured in the family of the recipient. Other ministers who, after entering into friendly relationships with Bismarck, have been promoted, invariably find themselves on bad terms with him after a while, forfeit their positions, receive abusive letters both private and official, and end as declared enemies of their sometime friend — for Bismarck expects people to thank him, whereas he never thanks any one.

Very rarely indeed does he display gratitude; on these rare occasions he will do something inimitable. After the war of 1870, when he is riding through the Brandenburg gate behind the emperor and between Moltke and Roon, he catches sight of the staff of his ministerial office who are occupying a special platform. Thereupon he seizes one of the three laurel crowns which are hanging on the pommel of his saddle, and throws it to his collaborators.

IX

In the year 1860, at the embassy in St. Petersburg, they were all sitting round the fire one winter evening: the chief, Schlözer, Croy, young Holstein, and the children's tutor. Conversation turned upon the immortality of the soul. Holstein tried to show that the only guaranteed immortality was posthumous fame. Bismarck reached out his hand for the glass of wine on the mantlepiece, and said: "Let me tell you, Herr von Holstein, that this glass of Médoc is worth more to me than thirty pages of Becker's Universal History!"

This contempt for fame, at which he mocked alike in his student days and in old age, is one of his salient characteristics — perhaps the one in which he is most notably distinguished from Napoleon, who would have remained a man of no account had it not been for his admiration of Plutarch and his longing for glory. When Becker's Universal History was brought up to date in the seventies, Bismarck really cared nothing about filling thirty pages in the work. He knew his own powers. In his copies of Carlyle's writings he had underlined doubly and trebly all the passages in which this author speaks of political genius, and on Carlyle's eightieth birthday Bismarck sent him assurances of respect which the chancellor had never shown for any German man of genius. It should be remembered that fifty years earlier Carlyle had received similar letters from an even greater German.

The approval of his contemporaries left Bismarck cold. Since he despised his fellows, their admiration was disagreeable to him. In the Reichstag, when Richter reproached him with ignorance of economics, Bismarck, after saying that he could tranquilly await the judgment of his fellow citizens, took care to add: "I will not say anything about posterity — that is too emotional a consideration for me." When a crowed assembled in front of the Reichstag in order to see him drive up, he was always annoyed; he said that he knew well enough what sort of visage he had to show as a detested minister, so much hated that people wanted to spit at him; now, apparently, he had to learn how to wear another expression. William invites him to the ceremonial fastening up of colours, one of which is to bear Bismarck's coat of arms and name, but he refuses the invitation, for the most he can expect to get out of going is that he will catch a cold. When the emperor sends him diamonds for an order, with the touching message: "This is the last decoration I can offer you, and it is established solely in your behalf", he says at home: "A cask of Rhenish or a good horse would have pleased me more."

Bismarck paintings amuse him. When he sees himself depicted allegorically as a white angel of peace wearing low-cut raiment with a garland of forget-me-nots and laurels on his bald head, he is amazed at his "transcendental possibilities." The first monuments that are erected to him are disagreeable to him. He tells the country in plain terms that he has no taste for such displays of gratitude. "I did not know which way to turn when I walked past my statue in Cologne. . . . When I go for a walk in Kissingen I find it most annoying to meet a sort of fossilised representation of myself."

He is a realist; that is why fame does not stir him. Nothing can be made out of it. But public opinion, on the other hand, which is useful to him, is worth cultivating. That is why he cultivates a Bismarck legend with all the more cynicism because he himself is quite unaffected by the influence this is calculated to exercise upon his contemporaries. The very man who cannot endure seeing a monument of himself favours the recording of his deeds and oddities, in so far as this makes useful propaganda. Sybel is commissioned to write a work upon the foundation of the German empire by William I. The archives are opened for the assistance of the historian, but Bucher has first to sift the documents, and must only let Sybel see those which are "not dangerous." As a result of this sifting process, the seven volumes soon became worthless. Hesekiel, Busch, and others have to submit their books to him in proof. In these proofs, he cuts out undesirable passages, suggests additions, and criticises passages where he thinks the author has not made enough of his doings. He even gives Hesekiel a careful selection of private letters, some of which, penned in 1870, are already to be published in 1877.

Every shade of his appearances before the public is carefully considered with an eye to its political effect. The man who at court has complained bitterly of the empress's lord high steward because this official did not greet him suitably, will, on a railway journey through Austria, have the blinds of his railway compartment drawn down, lest at a time of crisis the acclamations of the crowd may put his Viennese colleagues out of humour.

No one has ever rivalled Bismarck in his use of the press. By day and by night (literally) his underlings have to work for the press, preparing, suggesting, summarising, contradicting. He shows the utmost mastery in the dosage of his poison; sees to it that the news items he wishes to reach the public shall come to Berlin from out-of-the-way corners in Germany or from one of the foreign capitals, so that the public may be impressed by the utterances of ostensibly unprejudiced voices. In his own study, he dictates the most amazing discoveries about himself, which are then given to the world as if they had been sent from Stockholm to Potsdam. All these things are done so skilfully that even his faithful Tiedemann sums up the matter by saying that Bismarck is "more Mephistopheles than Faust." In the year 1872, when Arnim is being backed up by Augusta, Bismarck, who is at Varzin, dictates to Busch an article concerning "The Wishes of an exalted Lady for a Change in the Chancellorship." When he wants a discussion on Austria, he makes Bucher pose as the occasional correspondent of the "Kölnische Zeitung", who sends chance information from Stolp in Pomerania.

In the year 1874, when the ecclesiastical dispute was at its height, another attempt was made to shoot him. A few months before, he had contemptuously told the Reichstag: "Throughout my political life I have been honoured by having a great many enemies. You may travel from the Garonne to the Vistula, from the Belt to the Tiber, you may look where you please on the banks of our German rivers, the Oder and the Rhine, and you will find everywhere that at this moment I am the strongest and (I am proud to say) the most hated person in this country." But he did not know that at this time a Belgian coppersmith had offered to send to the archbishop of Paris Bismarck's head because Bismarck was carrying on a campaign against Rome, and that this fanatic had said: "I am ready to slay the monster, if you believe that God will forgive me and if you will pay me the sum of sixty thousand francs provided the monster ends his accursed career before the year expires."

A few months later, at Kissingen, a young man fires a shot at Bismarck who is out driving. The chancellor sustains merely a trifling wound of the finger. The would-be assassin declares himself a member of the Centre Party. Bismarck is delighted. First of all, several priests are arrested, for they are believed to have assisted in the attempt by holding up the carriage. Then a press campaign begins, continues for six months, and the affair comes to a head in the Reichstag. There, a member of the Centre Party is injudicious enough to say: "A man who is half crazy shot at Prince Bismarck, and thereupon a great part of the German nation of thinkers became delirious." This gave Bismarck a chance to make one of his most carefully finished speeches.

"The man, with whom I have myself spoken, is in full possession of his faculties. Indeed, we have medical testimony to this effect. I can understand that the honourable member is most unwilling that we should believe him to have anything in common with such a person. . . . Of course he never, even in his inmost soul, entertained the first beginnings of a wish, 'If only this chancellor could have an accident of some kind!' I am certain that no such thought can have crossed his mind. Still, repudiate this assassin as you please, he still holds on to your coat-tails, says he belongs to your political party! [Sensation.] What I tell you is nothing more than historical fact. . . . This Kullmann answered one of my questions as follows: 'I wanted to kill you because of the ecclesiastical laws. . . . You have injured my political party!' [Laughter.] To my next question, before witnesses, he said: 'I mean the Centre Party in the Reichstag'." At this juncture, Count Ballestrem called out: "Shame!" From what we know of Bismarck's temperament, we may feel sure that his first impulse must have been to come down from the tribune and strike the count to the floor. But he was content to knit his brows, and scored off Ballestrem by saying quietly: "'Shame' is an expression of loathing and contempt. Please do not imagine that I am free from these sensations. But I am too polite to express them."

This attempt on his life occupied his mind for a long time. We may well suppose that it was the only occasion during his career when he seriously considered the possibility of retiring. In a state of great excitement, he told Bennigsen that he was going to resign. He had been twice shot at, and the police were constantly warning him: "I shall leave it to another chancellor to be a target for the Catholics! On April 1st I shall be sixty, and then I shall retire and resume the life of a country gentleman!" His wife and his daughter had long been urging this step upon him, and now he was himself of the same way of thinking.

During this decade, Johanna's influence upon him had vanished. Instead of mollifying him, she intensified all his outbursts of hatred. As far as can be learned, she did not endeavour once during a whole generation to avoid or to heal breaches. She loved him, and therefore she hated almost every one else, since almost all others were his enemies. That was why, year by year, she grew more passionate. In her old age, Eulenburg saw her smash a glass when she was defending her husband. Only once did she go to parliament. She could not have borne to go again. Apropos of his account of one sitting, she exclaimed: "I should have gone for them with the leg of a chair!" Speaking to Crispi, she said: "You are right, my husband is really a good man." But Crispi smiled mockingly, and answered: "You would not find every one agree with you."

He still has to give her little warnings from time to time. Once when she is going to a bazaar, he says to her: "Don't stay after the king leaves. I don't like you to be in a crowd for long." She is so simple in her demonstrations of affections, that she will arrange his necktie for him at table when some noted foreigners are present as guests. His fondness for her is unabated, although he would often spend week after week in summer away from her. He continues after thirty or forty years of married life to write to her: "My darling, . . . I send you this loving greeting." Or he will wire from Friedrichsruh: "I can't stay here any longer without horses and without my wife. We shall come back to-morrow." Life in Berlin pleases her better now than of old. When a long stay at Varzin is in prospect, a friend of hers says: "The princess shudders at the thought, for the absolute solitude there gets on her nerves."

Very strange is the impression produced on our minds by the unanimous reports concerning the life of this uncouth and unspiritual household. Why does Bismarck, who is not merely the most powerful, but also the most noted German of his time — in youth a man of the world, and even to-day extolled as conversationalist and raconteur by all who meet him in private life — why does he live so unspiritual a life? If we knew nothing of his doings but this, he would be regarded as the most unspiritualised man of his epoch.

It is a matter of utter indifference to him how the rooms in which he lives are furnished, provided there are some comfortable chairs. The æsthetic side of these things makes no appeal to him. When some one tells him that Roon's new furniture is lovely, he replies: "People who think fine furniture very important are apt to have very poor dinners." Hideous furniture; on the walls, lined with ugly wall papers, hang illuminated addresses; mahogany chairs covered with cretonne whose colours clash — amid this disharmony the great man sits or half reclines upon a long chair among his guests after dinner. He wears a tweed coat buttoned to the throat; a long white choker instead of a collar, for he dislikes the confinement of a collar; great Dane lying at his feet; a long pipe; the floor littered with newspapers thrown down as soon as they have been read. Eulenburg, an intimate of the house for years, says: "The international amenities of intercourse were not to be found in this circle. Bismarck's home life remained to the last that of the ruder and less wealthy sort of country squires." There are almost always guests: some of his collaborators; young officers brought by the sons; relatives, men of birth for the most part; all uncouth, amid wine, beer, and brandy. "A remarkable picture in the drawing-room of the leading diplomatist of the century! The atmosphere was that of a tobacco parliament, but, often enough, ladies in brilliant dresses lent grace to the scene."

The conversation was suitable to the environment. Even when the prince was telling an anecdote or making some political comments, the conversation could not be said to take an intellectual form. It was a monologue, continually interrupted. In all the reports, there is a perpetual recurrence of Bismarck's account of historical moments. The Ems despatch, attempt on his life, Versailles. This goes on decade after decade. Those who describe the scenes are one and all agreed in deploring that again and again Bismarck's most interesting accounts were interrupted by the intervention of one of his sons, by a message, by a meal. According to Bismarck's own account of his daughter's marriage, to which a large company had been invited, the hosts "buzzed about like two flies inside a shut lantern, interfering unbidden and throwing everything into disorder."

It is useless to ask who among noted German intellectuals during the twenty years from 1870 to 1890 were to be found frequenting Bismarck's house — for there were practically none. The only exceptions are the brothers Lindau (who were useful to Bismarck) Curtius, and Wildenbruch. I could make a long list of dominant figures in Berlinese society at that date who never crossed Bismarck's threshold: Heyse, Storm, Wilbrandt, Brandes, Ibsen, Björnson, Menzel, Klinger, Brahms, Helmholtz, Dubois-Reymond, Langenbeck, Robert Koch, Hermann Grimm, Erich Schmidt, Scherer, Rodenberg, Rancke, Fontane. This list excludes mention of Bismarck's adversaries, such as Virchow, Freytag, and Mommsen. When Langbehn brought Hölderlin's *Hyperion* to Princess Johanna, she said, after reading it: "We did laugh so heartily!"

This anomaly does not conflict with the profound insight into Shakespeare and into Goethe, Schiller, and Byron, which Bismarck shows in his early letters. What we learn from such incidents, and from hundreds of recorded conversations, so few of which are of an intellectual character, is that this man, whose mind was filled with plans, whose will was entangled in struggles, thought fit for reasons of health, and also because he was an autocrat, to avoid intercourse with persons who could contribute nothing to his aims, with whom he could do no business, who represented no party, and did not even embody hostility.

The consequences are momentous. One who for thirty years never reads anything (unless it be to glance occasionally at the verses of Heine and Byron, of Uhland and Rückert), one who shuts himself away from all the non-political movements of his country, will, in the long run, come to rule that country more and more unintelligently; will renew, in Germany, the severance of intelligence from the State; will misunderstand the three great European movements of world economy, the Church, and socialism; and will vainly try, by fiscal measures, to exploit these movements for the advantage of the rulers. The ageing king, for all his limitations, saw and heard more of the problems of the day than Bismarck, despite the latter's power of grasping and promptly elaborating the most important elements of a dinner-table conversation. Bismarck had inherited a family tendency to sloth, and this was conjoined in him with a love of ease. His nerves were always on the stretch, and when he wanted to relax it was at the cost of the intellectual life of his country. In any case, he would have held aloof on his own initiative, for in those days German men of learning were still inclined to be extremely ceremonious in their dealings with army officers and high officials. Here are the opinions passed upon Bismarck by men noted for their grasp of history.

Brandes: "Bismarck is a good thing for Germany, although he is by no means a benefactor to humanity-at-large. He is for the Germans what a pair of excellent and extraordinarily strong spectacles are for a short-sighted man: a good thing for the patient that he can get them, but a great misfortune that he should need them."

Burckhardt (1877): "His abdication and return give the impression that he does not know what to be at. He has made a pretty bad miscalculation in all important problems of home policy. . . . It is quite possible that in the event of a great European war (such as might ensue upon the imminent Turkish war) he might once more set the tone. But he is no longer in a position to cure the disorder in home affairs."

Fontane (1881): "Among the people, a storm against Bismarck is gradually brewing; among the upper circles, the weather has been threatening for a long time. What is ruining his position is not so much his measures as his suspicions. He is a great genius, but a small man." In 1893: "We have again and again to remind ourselves of the titanic greatness of his work, if we are to avoid being repelled by these crass contradictions. He is the most interesting figure conceivable; I can think of none more interesting. But I find his persistent inclination to cheat people most objectionable. His wish to subjugate everything is a disastrous one." In 1895: "This mixture of superman and artful dodger, . . . of hero and innocent who would not hurt a fly, arouses in me the most mingled feelings, and prevents my regarding him with a pure and whole-hearted admiration. There is something lacking here, the very thing which gives greatness to a character."

Yet Bismarck has himself made very profound observations concerning historians: "There are two kinds. Some of them clarify the waters of the past, so that we can see to the very bottom. Others make these waters turbid. Taine belongs to the former category, Sybel to the latter." Bismarck says this although Sybel has extolled and Taine has attacked him. His critical insight enabled him to recognise the greatest personalities of the century. He said: "Historians always see through their own spectacles. Why I prize Carlyle so highly is that he understands how to get inside another's soul."

X

The country house of Friedrichsruh had at one time been a hotel. The good citizens of Hamburg, taking a Sunday jaunt in the Sachsenwald, had been wont to dine and sleep in the mansion where subsequently Bismarck spent so many of the days of his chancellorship and almost the whole of his last decade of life. Passing from Schönhausen to Varzin and from Varzin to Friedrichsruh, Bismarck's dwelling became less and less like a castle or a palace, although the owner was progressing in rank from country squire to baron and from baron to prince. Why was it that he would not build himself a lordly mansion in this new forest of his; why did he take so little trouble to disguise the former use of the place as a hotel as to leave the numbers on the doors of the rooms? Why, seeing that he had great pride of ancestry, was he so little inclined to spend money and pains on the beautifying of his family mansions? Kniephof, to which his memory so often returned (it was the only place he ever loved), had been alienated, but the family could re-acquire it. Schönhausen, where he was born, was still his own. Hamburg, when he came to live near-by, seemed uncongenial to him. Varzin was as wild and romantic a place as Friedrichsruh; the house there was as drab, but no worse. He divided his summers between the two estates.

Bismarck's love of home was restricted to Pomerania. His feeling for natural beauty spent itself upon this northern landscape. The forest was his home, no matter where he might be, in Hungary, in Russia, or in Denmark. Always he loved the forest. He speedily became as devoted to the Sachsenwald as to the well-known forest land round Varzin. Only in the forest was Bismarck freed from the tyranny of his life purposes; in age, just as in youth, he found in the forest gratification for his imaginative and poetical tendencies.

"I love great trees, they are ancestors. . . . If I did not love trees as much as I do, I do not know how I could go on living. Delight in nature is a gift of the gods, something which one cannot get if one has not got it. . . . I am inclined to distrust any one who does not love nature. . . . When I sleep soundly, I dream of young fir plantations, freshly green in the springtime, damp with rain, . . . then I wake up refreshed. . . . Here one can drive for hours through the forest, loaf on the benches, gaze into the greenwood, without thoughts and without tedium." At times, however, he does think in the forest, for he says on another occasion: "I have come to my most important decisions when alone in the forest."

Only in the woods is Bismarck's misanthropy deprived of its object. At most he can grow heated at some mistake in tree felling. Or if, at the edge of the forest, he sees a ploughman cursing his horses and flogging them unmercifully, he will dismount and lay into the fellow with his riding whip. He will discuss tree by tree with the head forester: "What d' you say? The top is withered? I am rather parched at the top myself!" and he takes off his hat to show his bald head. Perhaps there is no more attractive description of him than one which shows him with his sons in Friedrichsruh forest when they are shooting off withered tree tops in order to deceive their own forester. He, Bismarck, before whose orders all tremble, plays this trick to save his favourite trees from his own servants. He hardly ever goes out shooting now, for he wishes to spare the deer. To a visitor, who questions him at table, he says curtly he is not fond of eating his own game; however, he lets his guests shoot on his preserves.

Yet there is hardly anything romanticist in his outlook. A simple contemplation of details, a loving, uncritical contemplation. He says that at Friedrichsruh he wears glasses, for there everything interests him, whereas nothing interests him in Berlin. At the age of seventy, he writes to his wife in the following realistic and idyllic vein:

"It is lovely here, although the lilacs are three days and the oaks six days behind those of Berlin. The blackthorn is just as advanced as in Berlin. . . . No nightingales, but countless whitethroats, starlings, and the like. Above all, the cuckoo, which I had not heard before leaving Berlin. I asked: 'How much longer?' The flatterer answered: 'Twelve'; but the two last were rather feeble! The mill-race is a regular Rhinefall, very lovely. What used to be a natural swamp, mud and water mixed, has, at some cost, been moved a hundred paces back, so that there is a greater extent of clear water. The mill grinds all right, but the rain comes through everywhere. In Silk, . . . the rye is rather thin, and the barley needs more rain; the farmer grumbles. . . . The new fish-ponds are excellent; the new plantations are planted too deep, as before! . . . God grant that you'll soon be all right again!"

In the woods, Bismarck actually becomes just. At Varzin, when there is a report of poaching, at the mere suspicion he drives, accompanied by his guests, to see the suspect, and curses the man up hill and down dale. When he gets home again, he summons the head forester, who declares that the old man the master has been scolding has no gun, and that his son has fallen at the front. Bismarck, much concerned, is silent for a few minutes, and then says: "Dinner must wait awhile, and you, gentlemen, will be good enough to drive back with me." When he reaches his destination, the old man does not come out. Bismarck alights from the carriage, enters with his guests, and asks pardon for the unjust accusation. Again and again, Bismarck was unjust to his underlings in the service, but there is no incident like this to record. Bismarck has a tender feeling for the honour of this poor fellow who cannot defend himself. His request for pardon profoundly affects all the onlookers — and at the same time he eases his conscience in the matter of similar cases. No doubt, after his outbursts, he is prone to think things over remorsefully. In the watches of the night he has probably pondered his injustice to ministers of State, servants at the chancellery, foresters and princes, far longer than any of his victims are likely to believe, or he himself is ever likely to admit.

One habit he retains at Friedrichsruh on into old age is that of receiving his guests in a formal, and indeed ceremonious way. Ministers of State, neighbouring squires, the pastor's wife, the princess of Weimar — they one and all describe his reception of them at the door of the house as distinguished and chivalrous. When shaking hands with any one, he was always careful to pull off his glove first. Within doors, however, in the high-ceilinged rooms with the broad, low windows, the guests must share in the unceremonious family life. Among stray tankards, ashtrays, and pictures, at tables with check covers, you sip all kinds of beverages. When it is quiet in the house, he writes his wife: " Adelheid is reading Italian, Herbert is writing close by, Tyras is gnawing a huge bone, and the teakettle is singing." Tiedemann, who works there many weeks at a time, when he comes down towards noon usually finds that the only person about is the princess, "who has already got up by this hour." Bismarck appears towards one o'clock, and listens to Tiedemann's report while eating luncheon. After luncheon, he usually goes out riding for two or three hours with his son or his daughter, racing or trotting, Tiedemann with a notebook ready at any moment, for often the most important matters are settled during these rides. During the last half hour, they usually ride at a good pace. Since the recent attempt on the chancellor's life there are always detectives in attendance, and one of these ever dogs his footsteps. Bismarck has to put up with it, paying the tribute of power even at his country seat. Dinner at six o'clock. " Always four courses, with champagne, vin ordinaire, and port wine. . . . It was a delight to watch him in front of a dish of goose giblets. Of crayfish, he said that it was a peculiarity of theirs that they grew smaller each time the dish went round." After dinner, a move was made to the big drawing-room, where all gathered round the open fire. "This was the most interesting hour of the day. There he disclosed his secret thoughts, . . . was inexhaustible in his recounting of his own past. . . . Towards nine he went to his study, and now, for me, the day's work began. By midnight everything had to be finished. At half-past twelve, tea was served, and he would sit over it for an hour with the princess."

The quietude of this forest life is interrupted, not only by his talk about the exigencies of the service, but also by his outbursts of annoyance at the continuous increase in his expenditure and the diminution in his income. In Berlin, where he receives a salary of eighteen thousand talers, he needs, so he says, to spend more than fifty thousand, and he complains of the expense involved by his titles and his dotations. "I was pretty well off before I received my first dotation; since then Varzin has eaten everything up. I have no resources beyond my salary and the rent of Schönhausen. . . . All the rent remains here, and is insufficient. No doubt the future will put things right. . . . The new dotation [Friedrichsruh] is . . . worth a great deal, but hitherto all that it has brought me is an expenditure of eighty-five thousand talers, which I needed to buy up an enclave in the middle of the estate, the only place where one can settle down, unless one wants to live in a wretched hunting lodge in the middle of the forest." Again and again, he complains to his brother that the harvest at Varzin is almost worthless, that the timber in the Sachsenwald brings in nothing, and that, now he has to travel in a saloon carriage, his journeys cost him far more than they used to. "I have to pay for all the repairs, to pay a man for it in princely fashion now that I am unlucky enough to be a prince myself. . . . It used to be pleasant enough to think of my sons established as well-to-do country squires, but I don't like to think of them as pauper princes."

He leases the paper mills of Varzin to a manufacturer for eighty thousand talers. From a powder factory on the shores of the Elbe he gets twelve thousand talers; and from Friedrichsruh he draws an income of thirty-four thousand talers a year. "A handsome income, if only I were not a prince. I don't think I shall ever get used to this exalted rank." Apropos, Johanna comes in and complains to her smiling husband, in the presence of a visitor, that for the last hour she has been trying to account for a deficit of 11 marks, 50 pfennigs, in her housekeeping book.

When, on the occasion of Bismarck's seventieth birthday, collections were being made all over Germany to give him a testimonial, the ostensible reason is to place at the chancellor's disposal a sum "to be used for national purposes." Hundreds upon hundreds of petty bourgeois contribute their pence, thousands upon thousands of manual workers are urged by their employers to subscribe; in the end, the fund totals more than two and a half million marks. In an official decision, arrived at on Bismarck's own instigation, the king speaks of "one million two hundred thousand marks which have been placed at your disposal for public purposes. In accordance with your request, I now gladly empower you to take over the before-mentioned sum and whatever further sums the collection may yet bring in, and I leave it to you to let me know in due course what are your intentions with regard to the application of the testimonial."

After further conversation with the beneficiary, the committee buys for a sum of one and a half million marks, certain landed properties surrounding the seat of Schönhausen, and, on Bismarck's birthday, the duke of Ratibor hands him the title deeds of these unencumbered estates, "which formerly belonged to the Bismarck family, but were alienated in course of time."

This arrangement arouses general astonishment, although out of the first one million two hundred thousand marks, which are paid over to him in cash, the beneficiary founds scholarships in favour of candidates for higher teaching posts. The formula that the nation had reacquired for its leader his hereditary estates secures little credence. This property had never been "lost", and it was felt that the prince was fully in a position, out of his two previous dotations, to buy back territories which had long since been disposed of by his ancestors.

"Among the public," writes Lucius, "there is a certain amount of ill-feeling about this matter. A great many think that he ought to establish some sort of pious foundation." But Bismarck once more justifies himself by the example of the English, whose way it has been to reward their national heroes far more generously; and he forgets, or is unaware of, the disappointment of the poor folk who have contributed to the testimonial in the belief that the money would be devoted to a foundation of some sort. Although the reproaches levelled against him by his fellow Junkers in the seventies were unwarrantable, his conduct on this occasion certainly did his reputation harm.

It was a weak moment in Bismarck's life.

In his rural retreat, he is always trying to calm his nerves and reestablish his health, but continually fails to do so through his indiscretions in the matter of food and drink. When his doctor has ordered an invalid diet, Lucius tells us that he is content, after his soup, to eat nothing more than a plump trout, some roast veal, and three large sea-gull's eggs — washed down by abundant draughts of Burgundy. Since he believes that he can sleep only after libations of beer, he eats a great deal of caviare and other highly spiced foods in order to promote thirst. At a time when he is complaining much of a disordered digestion, loss of appetite, and neuralgia, Hohenlohe, who is a guest in the house, tells us that Bismarck partakes freely of the following dishes one after the other: soup, eels, cold meat, prawns, lobster, smoked meat, raw ham, roast meat, pudding. When some one compliments him on his healthy looks, he rejoins: "I wish I looked ill and felt better. . . . It is my misfortune, that no one can sympathise with me! I have such a sense of pressure in the forehead that I feel as if there can be nothing but jelly inside my skull. . . . Blood is a very peculiar fluid, and our nerves are even more peculiar vital threads, at the end of which we poor creatures kick about."

The root of his trouble is autocracy. "I have been used," he says, "to manage all my doctors up to now; at length I have one who manages me." At that time, in his sixty-eighth year, he was at once irritable and apathetic, suffered from sick headache, face-ache, sleeplessness, colic, swelling of the legs, varicose veins. He weighed two hundred and forty-seven pounds, and his doctors believed him hopelessly ill of cancer of the stomach and liver. Ernst Schweninger, Bill's doctor friend, sees the chancellor at Varzin, and when asked his opinion by other members of the household, says: "If the prince keeps on in his old groove, I will not give him more than six months." After this remarkable opinion has been given, Bismarck himself asks advice. The only answer is: "I cannot utter any catchwords; cannot treat so-called diseases." This impresses Bismarck, for no one has ever spoken to him like that before. Here is indeed a man!

Then, in Berlin, the doctor, who is a man of might, begins a course of treatment which seems barely credible to the patient. He makes the chancellor get up at eight in the morning to do exercises with dumb-bells; the whole day, the patient is to eat nothing but herrings. When Bismarck exclaims, "You must be absolutely mad!" Schweninger rejoins: "All right, Your Highness, you had better call in a veterinary!" Thereupon Schweninger takes his leave. This high-handed proceeding establishes his power over Bismarck, who submits. For a fortnight, now, the new doctor does not leave his patient's house. Food and drink, getting up and going to bed, work and sleep, are meticulously supervised. At the end of this period there has been marked improvement. Schweninger leaves the house for the first time. Instantly the patient orders a "triple portion of buttermilk." He has violent gastralgia, followed by jaundice, and departs for Friedrichsruh. There the doctor once more keeps close watch on him, and subsequently in Kissingen and Gastein does not leave him to himself for a single day. After a couple of months, the patient is practically well, and admits that he can return rejuvenated to the treadmill.

By dominating instead of allowing himself to be dominated, Schweninger saves Bismarck's life. If, in other domains, other Germans had ventured on the same course, they might not have found the chancellor always intractable.

XI

When, during these years of old age, did the ever dissatisfied man enjoy life?

When watching his children, to whom he forgave everything and allowed everything, except personal freedom; on rare occasions when he saw the friends of his youth; and over his wine. How much he prefers good wine to tokens of distinction, we learn from his drastic decision (of which the emperor greatly disapproves) to melt down into a silver ingot all his Russian orders. He says that every man is predestined to consume a certain quantity of wine and tobacco. "My allowance is one hundred thousand cigars and five thousand bottles of champagne." When one of the auditors laughs, he reckons up his consumption.

Of his old friends, Keyserling rarely comes now. "Keyserling is the only man whose intelligence I have ever had occasion to dread." This remarkably worded commendation shows that he holds himself somewhat aloof. Keyserling is aware of it, and during a whole decade does not come to visit him in the country, saying: "Bismarck has become a potentate. If I meet him by chance, he is, as of old, the most faithful and amiable of friends. But to seek him out is a doubtful pleasure, for his time has become too valuable."

Motley's visits still provide Bismarck's happiest days. The American arrives in the summer of 1872, after eight years' absence. "I was so delighted," writes Bismarck, "to see your handwriting. Before opening the letter, I felt sure that it would contain the pledge of a visit. You are a thousand times welcome. . . . The first day that you can dispose of is the best one to come to see us." He goes on to give his friend a detailed account of the trains he must take in order to reach Berlin and travel thence to Varzin. Motley stays for a week. Bismarck spends fourteen hours with him every day. With no one else has he ever been able to endure such close association.

"He is somewhat stouter," says Motley, writing home, "and his face more weather-beaten, but as expressive and powerful as ever.

He looks like a colossus, but his health is somewhat shattered. He can never sleep until four or five in the morning. After dinner, Bismarck and I had a long walk in the woods, he talking all the time in the simplest, funniest, and most interesting manner about all sorts of things that had happened in these tremendous years, but talking of them exactly as everyday people talk of everyday matters — without any affectation. The truth is, he is so entirely simple, so full of laissez-aller, that one is obliged to be saying to oneself all the time: 'This is the great Bismarck — the greatest living man.' . . . He is the least of a poseur of any man I ever saw, little or big. . . . Certainly a more unaffected mortal never breathed, nor a more genial one." Once again, in this last visit (for Motley has only a year or two of life remaining), we discern the influence exercised upon Bismarck by an able, free-spirited, and cheerful man who wants nothing for himself. We realise once again why no member of Bismarck's own class, why neither his wife nor his sons, nor his brother, why neither Roon nor any other of his distinguished collaborators, can bring this troubled heart so much alleviation, so much freshness. Help can only come from the son of a distant republic, the representative of a remote continent.

Bismarck's only friends now were dumb animals. As his misanthropy grew, he became ever fonder of his dogs, more intimate and faithful companions even than his wife. They loom in all the conversations and diaries, among plans and decisions and orders, in the Wilhelmstrasse and in the forests, in gloomy times and in the brightest days. Always we discern the heads of these iron-grey or black hounds, who resembled their master, for they too were huge and highly strung, bold and dangerous. A long series of them lies buried in the park at Varzin; eight of them are interred at a fine viewpoint, beside the favourite horses. Since these dogs of his want nothing of him, never resist his will, are always silent, and yet seem to understand everything, his old heart is drawn to them more and more. "I love dogs; they never want to pay one out for having harmed them:" in these words, when he is a very old man, he discloses more of his own nature than of that of the objects of his affection.

When young Rebecca is disobedient, he treats her like a spoiled girl, laughing at her slyness and coquetry. When Flora "runs madly about the room", or when Sultan disturbs the conversation, nobody interferes with them. When an official conversation is making him restless, he calms his nerves by stroking the silken neck of the beast beside his knees. At Friedrichsruh, they wait patiently under his table, their great heads sunk upon their forepaws, their eyes always watching their master. Directly he stands up and grasps his oaken staff, they gather round him, wagging their tails, for they know that now he is going for a walk in the woods. If Johanna complains that the upholsterer has made the curtains too long, Prince Bismarck says it is a very good thing, for now the dogs have something soft to lie upon. When he is in doubt whether to spend the summer in Gastein or to stay at home, the matter is decided in the end by Sultan, who is ailing, and not well enough for the journey. Noblemen of refined taste who are staying with him are disgusted at table when their host has great chunks of meat brought in and throws them to his dogs across the room.

In official life, Bismarck makes use of these intimates of his, as of everything else, in order to intensify the fascination he exercises — a fascination which is a natural gift, but which he at the same time touches up. He knows what an effect he produces when he rises to his feet to greet a visitor, and when, simultaneously, the two great Danes jump up, and stand on either side of the dangerous statesman. He trusts their instinct, too, saying that they are much shrewder than horses. When Sultan makes friends with a new steward, first sniffing at the man, and then laying his head upon the new acquaintance's knee, Bismarck instantly accepts the dog's valuation. "I have great respect for my dog's knowledge of human character; he is quicker and more thorough-going than I. . . . I congratulate you!"

Bismarck has never been able to forgive his king the latter's attitude towards the dogs. When the tsar, who was very fond of dogs, in conversation with his uncle William, extolled Tyras, whose acquaintance he had just made, the emperor said politely that he would like to see the animal. "Tyras was sent for, behaved admirably. Thereupon the emperor said: 'A fine dog. A pity he has cropped ears, like all pugs!'" It was a catastrophe!

Sultan, the gift of a Moroccan prince, was the finest of all the dogs. He must only be called "Sultl"; otherwise, said his master, there might be complications with Turkey. For the rest, he was by no means an Oriental. One evening, on revisiting Varzin, Sultan was put on the chains; "he took this so much amiss that he gnawed his chain, and gnawed through the wood to which the staple was fastened, two inches thick, so that the splinters were stained with blood from his mouth. Having freed himself, he made for the woods. Since then he has been at large. He is still somewhere in the neighbourhood, and I hope we shall find him again. Bill and Philipp have been riding far and wide in search of him, and came back wet through. Postscript: Jungens has just come back, thoroughly wet. Sultl has turned wolf; is living on fawns, will have to be shot."

In the end Sultan comes home, and remains his master's friend for five years longer, rather wild at times, often punished, but usually spoiled. However, the beast came to a tragical end, which is reported as follows by Tiedemann:

"These autumn days, the prince was in a mood quite new to me, . . . cheerful from morn till eve, and always ready for a jest. Yesterday, when we were having our coffee, it was suddenly reported that Sultan had vanished. Since he has been carrying on an amour in a neighbouring village, the prince supposed that he had gone to visit his lady love once more, was annoyed, and declared that he would give Sultan a sound flogging. We went to our room in order to go on with our work until post time. Then, towards eleven, there was a noise downstairs. Some one came to tell us that Sultan had just got back, and was dying.

"There was a most distressing scene downstairs. The prince sat on the floor, with the dying animal's head in his lap. He whispered affectionate words to Sultan, and tried to hide his tears from us. . . . Despite Herbert's urging, he sat there for a long time, then stood up for a while, but came back again. When the dog was dead, the prince said: 'The Germans of old had a kindly religion. They believed that after death they would meet in the heavenly hunting grounds all the good hounds that had been their companions. I wish I could believe that.' He retired to his room, and only came out for a moment that evening to say good night to us. . . .

"To-day it has been as if we were in a house of mourning. We all spoke in whispers. The prince had not had a wink of sleep. He was continually distressed at the thought that he had whipped the dog only a little while before its death. Although the post-mortem examination this morning showed that Sultan had died of heart failure, he continued to reproach himself. After breakfast we went out riding. The prince was monosyllabic. He sought out the ways where his old and faithful companion had last accompanied him. Thus we trotted along in the pouring rain. Once, when I was riding close beside him, he said that it was very wrong to give one's heart to an animal as he had done, but that he had never had anything dearer to him in the world, and that he agreed with Prince Henry in saying: 'I could have better spared a better man!' Then he put spurs to his horse, and galloped a long way, so that both rider and horse were steaming when we got home."

Four days later: "He still cannot get over the dog's death, being full of remorse for having chastised the beast so shortly before. He continues self-tormentingly to fancy that this accelerated the tragedy. He deplores his own temper, saying that he is brutal, and hurts every one who comes in contact with him. Then he goes on to reproach himself for taking the death of a beast so deeply to heart."

No similar incident is recorded in Bismarck's life, and it would not fit into any other life than his. It has a legendary flavour, but is in keeping with his enigmatic character.

This dog, sent by an Oriental potentate who wished to confer an obligation upon the chancellor of the German empire, seems to us like a fairy prince. In his unruly youth, he will not bear the chain, frees himself by gnawing through the wood to which it is attached, and then lives at large in the forest, nourishing himself by the chase. He is a true shoot of his master, reproducing in canine fashion the lineaments of the Mad Junker, and thus pleasing his master. Between the two there are scenes such as are inevitable between an unruly grandchild and a strict grandparent — until, in the end, the wild creature loses his life in an adventure.

Thereupon, the forsaken master is full of penitence for having ill-treated this beast he had so greatly loved. Perhaps he was responsible for the death? Perhaps it had been a sin to give so much affection to a dumb beast? Did the Christian faith he professed allow such a thing? Perhaps the Germans of old were better men? Do we not remember how in the days of his conversion he had quoted the example of that pagan chief who refused baptism, saying he would rather rejoin his unbelieving forefathers? But how if the Christian God had wanted to warn him by this blow, to convict him of other sins, of anger and selfishness? Thinking over past years and other nations, thinking of battles and artifices, of victories and subjugations, he cannot fail, during these days of mourning, to think of men whom he has mortified, injured, perchance driven to death like this dog — which perhaps could not forget the thrashings that had been inflicted. In a pallid procession, there move before his imagination the enemies he has overthrown. His iron will weakens. He questions the purpose of the vast movement. When he recovers from his nightmare, resumes the life of affairs, reenters the struggle, only one reality will remain from this happening: the faithful hound, the companion of his days, lies buried on the hilltop beside the others. Now there are nine of them.

XII

"In actual fact, my temperament is dreamy and sentimental. People who paint me all make the mistake of giving me a violent expression." (The development of the characteristic lines in Bismarck may be seen in the portraits made in 1834, 1859, 1866, 1889, and 1894. Plates III., VII., IX., XVI., and XIX.) In the foregoing words he certainly describes one aspect of his nature. In youth, he was wont, at times, to give expression to the sense of taedium vitae in Byronic fashion; and though, in the middle period of his life, he was filled with the lust of battle, in old age he was prone to melancholy. The foreboding of his youth had been, to his distress, fulfilled. Faust, with unceasing endeavour, and Mephistophele, with unwearying cynicism, are ever on the watch to make his achievements seem worthless to him. If a foolish teacher should wish to convince his young pupils that, subjectively considered, all striving is vain, he could take Bismarck as a classical example. But among the members of his entourage, there is no one to understand and reverence these moods. Johanna says to Lucius:

"When his servant Heinrich shot himself a week ago, Otto was almost beside himself, could not sleep, and passed his whole time thinking of tragedies. . . . On such occasions, we do all sorts of foolish things, with the dogs, and so on, in the hope of distracting his mind." Thus, misunderstood, Bismarck has to live among those who love him. For all they can do, the dark thoughts come when Fate wills. One day, when he is sixty-two years of age, at the climax of his power, he delivers himself as follows to several auditors, after silently contemplating vacancy for a while:

"How little joy and satisfaction the whole affair has brought me. No one loves me for it. I have made no one happy, neither myself nor my dear ones." Protests are uttered. He goes on unheeding: "On the contrary, I have made many persons unhappy. But for me, three great wars would never have been waged, eighty thousand people would not have perished, parents and widows would not have mourned. . . . Still, as to these matters, I have settled my account with God. I have had very little pleasure, or none at all, from what I have done; instead, much vexation, care, and trouble." This is not the only occasion on which he gives vent to such utterances. Holstein and Bucher report many similar ones. We see here, once more, manifestations of the Lutheran spirit, which seeks responsibility instead of evading it;

we see likewise the pretensions of the upstart, egocentric in character, and incomprehensible to true Prussians like the king or Roon.

Sometimes these moods of world weariness find expression in the political field; then they are tinctured with pride. In the year 1877, in the presence of a score or more of hearers, he says at one of his parliamentary evenings: "When a man goes out for a day's shooting, in the early part of the day he fires at any game he comes across, and is ready to walk miles over difficult ground in order to get a shot at a wild bird; but when he has been tramping it for the whole day, when his game-bag is full, and he is nearing home — hungry, thirsty, tired out — then all he thinks of is rest. He will not walk a step out of his way to bring down a brace of partridges. But suppose some one comes up and tells him that in the depth of the forest a wild boar is to be found, then we shall see that this weary man (if he has a hunter's blood in his veins) will forget his fatigue, and will range the woods until he has found his quarry. For my part, I have been hunting since daybreak; it is late, I am tired, and I will leave it to others to shoot at hares and partridges. But if you have seen the slot of a wild boar, that is another story."

After such a mood of world weariness, he will become quite cheerful when his old cynicism reawakens. It is the real Mephistopheles who, in the forest, confides to his nearest friend: "When younger, I used to think myself a clever fellow enough, but now I am convinced that nobody has any control over events, that nobody is really powerful or great. It always makes me laugh when I hear myself extolled as wise, foreseeing, and exercising great influence upon the world. While outsiders are speculating whether it will be rain or sunshine to-morrow, a man in my situation has to make up his mind once and for all that it will rain to-morrow, or that it will be fine, and to act in accordance with his decision. If he has guessed rightly, then all the world exclaims: 'What sagacity, what prophetic vision!' But if he has made a mistake, then all the old women will beat him with broomsticks. If I have learned nothing else, I have at least learned modesty!"

Thus does he speak to his friend Motley, and the words embody a nihilism as profound as that of his angry utterance to his enemy Arnim. Both are confessions of a supreme egoist, who none the less renounces all claim to personal merit, who at the climax of his career is just as much a fatalist as he was in his early days, and who has now, by devious and sinister paths, attained to a modesty which is but a mask for the cynicism of a misanthropist.

At such moments, his furrowed brow grows smooth once more, the spirit of the adventurer peeps out again. At such times he will envy a humbler man who leads an adventurous life. On one occasion, they are sitting at a little banquet given by their Varzin tenant; the voice of a gipsy comes through the open door, and they send him out a glass of wine; now he comes in, harp in hand, makes an obeisance such as Bismarck would make to the king, sings a song of youth and love, drinks to the prince, and then departs singing. Johanna asks how they could help him to lead an orderly life. Bismarck rejoins: "You cannot help such a fellow to anything of the kind. His love of freedom is far greater than his wish for an orderly life, than his wish for what we everyday folk term happiness." He is silent, gazes after the departing gipsy as if the man were an emblem of his own vanished youth, and says: "In truth, an enviable mood, an enviable existence!"

Nevertheless, he clings to life, "like every ordinary person." At one of the "milestones", he tells his brother what he feels about this matter: "The closing years of our earthly life move more and more quickly, with the acceleration of a falling stone. . . . I cannot say that this increasing rapidity of movement is agreeable to me, for, though I plainly realise that every day may be my last, I am unable to find the thought agreeable. I like living. It is not because outward successes satisfy me and engross me, but because the thought of separation from wife and children is terrible to me. . . . I have had good luck in my official career, though not so much in my private undertakings. . . . But that wherein God has chiefly blessed me, and that wherein I most eagerly pray for the continuance of his blessing, is the peace and welfare of the household, the mental and bodily well-being of my children. As long as these things remain, I have no serious reasons for complaint."

These children of his, for whom he makes life easy, display the Bismarckian egoism. His daughter, whom a family friend describes as "peculiar rather than attractive", becomes outwardly more ungainly, and inwardly more stupid, as the years pass. Absent-minded and of a scoffing disposition, she is at the same time unpractical, and so untidy that Eulenburg, coming to the embassy which she and her young husband Rantzau have just quitted, finds round their bed a dozen cane chairs on which are three half-eaten cakes, and all over the place there is a litter of birds, guinea pigs, and bandboxes. Speaking of Marie to his lady-friend Spitzemberg, Bismarck confides his opinion that she thinks about her husband, her children, and her nearest relatives, and practically no one else. "She is essentially lazy, that is what is the matter." To the reply that it is a pity that his daughter does not share his interests, Bismarck rejoins: "The same is true of my wife. But this has its good side. I get into quite a different atmosphere at home."

Of the two sons, both are for a time their father's assistants, and afterwards Herbert only. Herbert, though less gifted, is the more diligent of the two. Bill, who has talent, is lazy. Bill marries his cousin, but Herbert is not allowed to marry where his inclination points. Both of them are hard drinkers and die rather early, at about fifty. Before the coming of Otto there had never been a genius in the Bismarck family. Among the Menckens, the only man of note had been Otto's grandfather. Now, after the flashing out of genius in Otto von Bismarck, the mingling of strains promptly degenerates in the children, who seem to have inherited from their father nothing but his lack of moderation, and from their mother no whit of her power of self-sacrifice.

The children seem hardly ever to have brought any one distinguished either for intelligence or for good looks to the parental home. Once, indeed, the elder son attempted it, but since he ran counter to certain of his father's prejudices, there was a battle royal, in which the son was worsted.

The breach with the conservatives had long since been healed, politically speaking, and nothing but memories of the old rancour remained, when, in the late seventies, Herbert fell in love with Princess Carolath, and entered into a liaison with this lady, who was more or less separated from her husband. She wished to get a divorce in order to become Herbert's wife, being even more eager (doubtless) to become Bismarck's daughter-in-law. She was even willing to turn Protestant; and since she was an extremely beautiful woman, and herself of high birth (Elisabeth was a daughter of Prince Hatzfeld-Trachenberg), the divorce could have been condoned, and a father of yielding disposition, who had brought up his son, now thirty years of age, to follow in his own footsteps in the matter of rank and office, might well have been expected to offer no opposition.

But Elisabeth had two sisters, one of whom was married to General von Loë, the other to Von Schleinitz, treasurer of the household — two of the chiefs of the anti-Bismarck faction. Schleinitz had for years been Augusta's confidant, and Loë was brother to the Junker who had been one of Bismarck's chief calumniators. Were these men to become Herbert's brothers-in-law? In that case they would have to be invited to the wedding feast, and perhaps subsequently to a christening. Was his house to become allied to these detested families, in whose mansions all the malcontents talked scandal about the house of Bismarck, and sharpened the arrows to be directed against the chancellor; houses where calumny flourished and jealousy developed into dangerous intrigue? Was there not a plot hidden beneath this love affair? Vengefulness and mistrust, hatred and caution, induced him to forbid the marriage.

Meanwhile the lady had, for Herbert's sake, taken steps toward a divorce; there had been gossip in the press; she had almost quarrelled with her relatives. Romantic and amorous, more so than her relatives at court thought fitting, she rented the Palazzo Modena in Venice, and when we compare the letters she wrote thence to Herbert with his letters to her, it seems to us that she acted under stress of calculation, he under stress of feeling. He may have been passionate enough, but his dread is greater than his passion, his dread and his respect for the man of might.

"In the beginning of May"—Herbert is writing to Philipp Eulenburg after the divorce has been declared—"I shall go to Venice, and see whether there is any possibility of arranging matters between us in such a way as to make life tolerable. . . . When I come back, I shall make a final attempt with my father. My present feeling is that it is a matter of life and death, and what will happen God only knows! I seem to be faced by the absolute impossibility of devoting to the princess what remains to me of life."

Two days later: "My father has assured me, with tears in his eyes, that he is absolutely determined not to go on living if this marriage takes place. He has had enough of life, he says. He has only found consolation in all his battles in the hopes he has placed in me. If these hopes are now to be frustrated, it will be all up with him. I gather that he has disclosed even more unhappiness and anxiety in his conversations with three or four other persons. . . . Two doctors have told me that my mother is in a dangerous condition, . . . and that any strong emotional disturbance might be too much for her! On the other hand, the poor princess has only just got over an illness; she is quite alone, fully expects that we are to be married, and will perhaps fall ill again if she is told that our marriage is impossible. . . . If I, for my part, were to do away with myself, I should make the princess's position still more difficult, and should bring the greatest distress upon all those who love me."

Two days later still: "My father declares that it is incompatible with his honour that his name should become connected by marriage with Hatzfeld, Carolath, Loë, etc.; and that if such things are said about a woman, she could never become his daughter-in-law. I must bethink myself, he says, that I do not bear the name for myself alone, but that anything which affects

BISMARCK IN 1886
From a photograph by A. Bockmann, Lübeck

my name affects him and my brother as well as myself. He will work against my proposal with 'tooth and claw!' The princess writes to me that, after all the scandalous talk in the newspapers, there is no possibility open but our marriage. Had not these articles appeared, she would not wish for the marriage! My father holds a very different view. . . .

"Meanwhile, I am forbidden to leave the service, and therefore I cannot marry without permission (until after the lapse of ten months there is no legal possibility). Furthermore, I have to remember that I can offer the princess nothing, for, by the terms of the law of primogeniture, as recently altered with the emperor's approval, a son who marries a divorced woman is disinherited; and since my father has nothing except the two great entailed estates, I should have no heritage whatever. . . . I don't know that this matters very much, seeing that in any case I should not be likely to live long after the marriage, for the breach with my parents would bring me down to the grave. But if I should die soon after the marriage, the princess would thereby have lost half of the income which Prince Carolath has to pay her — such are the terms of the contract — and then she would not have enough to live on. There seems to be no way out of the difficulty, and in view of my father's present bitterness towards the princess I cannot suppose that he would make me any allowance. He says that if the princess were to bear his name, it would drive him to suicide! . . . I can find no words in which to tell you how much this conversation with my father has shattered me. I shall never get over it. I shall never be able to forget that my father has been so terribly upset on my account."

A week later: "The princess writes . . . to remind me of the text: 'For this cause shall a man leave his father and his mother, and shall cleave unto his wife.' . . . It would be impossible for my journey to Venice to be kept secret. The relatives of the princess (some of whom are, I am sorry to say, rather unscrupulous) will see to it that the news is published. They, like the Carolaths, are keen on the marriage, were it only for pecuniary reasons — so that they may have no further responsibilities.

Prince Carolath, . . . especially, would be saved a lot of expense if the marriage were to take place. The first newspaper articles about the matter were penned by his family lawyer. . . . My father says that if I absolutely must go to Venice, he will go with me; that he has my own fortunes and the preventing of this marriage more at heart than the whole empire, all his affairs, and the rest of his life. Whatever happens, he won't let me go alone, for he wants to talk things over with the princess. . . . These conversations with my father have upset me so much that I am fit for nothing. I shall never again know even a day's happiness. . . . There has been gossip about my relations with the princess for years; and now that she has been so thoroughly compromised by all the hubbub in the newspapers, I regard it as a point of honour that I should marry her, even though my fondness for her were extinct. My father differs from me, but I can take no other view, and yet I feel that I ought to sacrifice my sense of honour for the sake of my parents! How can I possibly live through these troubles?"

No way out of the difficulty can be found. In the end, Elisabeth breaks off the relationship, lets Herbert know that she despises him, and informs him (through intermediaries) that she is getting on splendidly. Herbert is shattered by the blow. "I suffer from the overwhelmingly depressing conviction of having betrayed a trust — one which I voluntarily inspired. . . . I blame myself for all that has happened, and am loathsome to myself. . . . The rest of my life stretches out before me in prospect like an interminable poplar avenue leading through a flat, sandy waste. I plod my weary way along it, though I know perfectly well that it will always be the same as it is now."

Thus in the end Herbert is the only sufferer, and the only person who awakens sympathy in the reader of these romantic letters. His father had in the old days promised marriage to several women in turn, but had in each case broken away when the days of disenchantment had come. Nor had any serious attempt been made to hold him to his engagement, for he was nothing more than a blue-blooded adventurer in the early twenties, without money or position. Now he has involved his son in a similar situation, and the son has to pay the score.

Of course it is easy to say that Herbert should never have allowed matters to come to such a pass, and it is difficult to suggest any other way out of the imbroglio than the one actually taken. Herbert was daunted by his father's threatening visage.

The lady's behaviour is typical. She pushes on the divorce in order to force her highly placed friend into marrying her; she does her utmost to compel him to join her in Venice, in the belief that this will cause a scandal that will leave him no option but to legalise their union; and in the end she invokes scriptural authority. She has no taste either for wedded love in a cottage or for unwedded love in a villa on the Riviera. She wants, not only Herbert, but his name and his property as well. When she finds that she has miscalculated, she promptly casts off the old love and begins (or resumes) a life of amorous intrigue with new partners.

Behind her stand those who are eager for the chase, and do their utmost to intensify the confusion: a husband who would fain escape having to maintain his wife; sisters who have helpers ready to write scurrilous newspaper articles well calculated to fan the flames of scandal, and to promote the princess' union with a house they detest. They all stand to gain by this marriage. They will gain money, for if the marriage takes place, they will no longer have to keep their flighty sister in funds. They will gain power, for the dictator will have to join hands with them and to find places for their sons. Nay more, they have bolder hopes. Perhaps he will be crushed by the blow; perhaps he will act on his threat to resign. In that case, Elisabeth will have achieved more than the "Reichsglocke" has achieved in all the years of its existence. Like the beautiful princess in the fairy tale, she will have slain the ancient dragon, and will be able to stand proudly as victress, with one of her little feet planted upon the dread monster's skull.

But the wily dragon is a thousand years old, knows all his foes' artifices, has antidotes for every bane and armour of proof

which turns the edge of every weapon. He has held his own against
all the powers of Europe, subjugating them, or constraining them
to alliance. Is he now to be defeated by a light woman, who is not
even a rich one? The shrewd diplomatist plays a masterly game,
and wins.

What are we to make of Herbert's conduct? He was a weakling,
overpowered by fear of his father, by respect for the old man.
Besides, he had no taste for being disinherited, and lacked
capacity or inclination for an independent career. First of all,
in two formidable scenes, Bismarck plays the heavy father: he
will resign office, will cease to guide the ship of State, will actually
kill himself, unless his son gives way; at the same time he mobilises the doctors, who declare that these afflictions will be the death
of the mother. Next, the chancellor becomes Herbert's official
chief, whose underling cannot marry without his superior's consent. Finally, Bismarck gets to work as landed proprietor, as
the owner of large entailed estates. He hastens to see the emperor, who has bestowed these estates on him, and is now asked
to modify the title deeds so that Herbert (if recalcitrant) shall
remain impoverished for life, and must be content to live upon
the alimony provided by the fair lady's first husband.

Nor is this all! Many years have passed since Bismarck's
youth, but in youth he had plenty of experience in these matters,
and he knows how much a man may pledge himself to during one
night in a mediæval palace — a night spent in his mistress'
arms. That is why Herbert must on no account go to Venice —
or, if Herbert goes, Father Otto must go with him. The son, too,
is a diplomatist, and a student of public opinion. He knows how
fatal are the shafts of ridicule. He will be made for ever ludicrous
in the eyes of Europe if penny-a-liners spread themselves in accounts of old Bismarck in a gondola speeding to Herbert's
rescue; if satirical couplets tell the tale of father and son and
lady fair; if the photographers get to work with their cameras,
the caricaturists with their pencils. . . .

Herbert, however, has one shaft left in his quiver. Again and
again he insists that he is under a moral obligation. Had it not

been for this love affair, the princess would never have had to go through the shame of a divorce. Bismarck, the old gladiator, has a parry for every thrust. The divorcée, he says, has long been a woman of easy virtue. To-day her name is coupled with Herbert's; it may have been coupled with another man's yesterday, and it may be coupled with yet another man's to-morrow. In fact, the name is not worth defending. For his part, insists the father, he does not wish the name of Bismarck to be coupled with that of Loë or with that of Schleinitz. If honour is in the scales, the honour of the Bismarcks is the weightier.

Passion? Pangs of conscience? A firstborn son's sense of honour? Youth outgrows these troubles. Forward!

XIII

While undergoing a cure at Kissingen, in the autumn of 1877, Bismarck dictates the following lines to his son: " A French newspaper recently said of me that I had ' le cauchemar des coalitions.' German ministers of State will for a long time to come, and perhaps for always, have good reason to suffer from this nightmare. The western powers can easily form coalitions against us with the accession of Austria; but perhaps even more dangerous would be a coalition between Russia, Austria, and France. If two of these three powers were to form a close intimacy, this would provide the third of them with a means for exercising a very sensible pressure upon us at any moment." In his dread of such possibilities, he comes, in the course of years, to contemplate a general political situation, "in which all the powers except France would have need of us, and would, by their mutual relationships, be given the best possible reasons for abstaining from coalitions against us."

Here we have the fundamental idea of his policy as chancellor. It originates in three considerations: Germany's situation, the jealousy of Europe, and the conflicting interests of the powers. A realist and a chess player, he draws his conclusions from these premises. He knows how to distinguish between the desirable and the necessary. For all his sense of self-importance, he does not wish to annex a single village more, for the fatherland is un-favourably situated, and, since it is the source and object of his power, it must never be endangered by dreams of world dominion. None the less, he conceives the possibility of the great powers uniting against Germany, and he therefore does his utmost to keep the aspiring English from joining forces with the Russians, and to prevent the ambitious French from making common cause with the Austrian peasants.

In the outer world, no one believes him. Letters by the queen of England, reports by Russian statesmen, speeches by French demagogues, one and all sound a note of scepticism regarding Bismarck's will-to-peace. Expressions of fear and hatred are heaped up against the "conqueror." That is how the world regards him. Is he not the man who, within seven years, has thrice broken the peace of Europe with his wars, all of which ended in annexations? Has he not upbuilded a colossus within the heart of Europe, where for three centuries the cleavage among the German stocks has provided all the neighbours with opportunities for exercising the arts of corruption? Victor by means of blood and iron within his own land, and then victor over foreign lands — how is he to maintain the integrity of this Napoleonic structure created by force of arms unless by means of ever renewed conquests? His own people speak of him as the Iron Chancellor!

His own people understood his nature very little, and this contributed to the mistake which in the long run was disastrous to Germany's fair name. A glance at his character, a glimpse at the moods of this complicated nature, should suffice to dispel these prejudices. A study of his despatches, letters, and conversations furnishes documentary evidence for a saner view. A general survey of the twenty years of his chancellorship proves the accuracy of such a view. In old age he often asked himself whether the unification of Germany might not have been effected without the three wars, and, when writing in his memoirs about the events of the year 1849, he did not contest the possibility. This much, at least, is certain, that he did not carry on these wars in order to make conquests, but merely made conquests as an accidental outcome of his victories. He resembled a spoiled child of fortune who, on the road along which his footsteps are directed by ambition, finds women and enjoys possessing them — not being fastidious.

He never made wars for the sake of conquests. He did not attack Denmark in order to conquer Schleswig, but simply because he wanted to catch the nationalist wind in Prussia's sails. The second time he went to war, it was not for the conquest of Hesse and Hanover, but for the exclusion of Austria. The third war was determined, not by the desire to annex Alsace, but by the reaction against France's veto. After the victories, which were speedier and more thorough-going than he had hoped, he sat down in front of the map and took what fortune offered him.

Bismarck was so great a master of his craft that he never strained the bow too tightly. True, he never undershot his mark, but he never overshot it either. In foreign affairs, his judgment of distance was never at fault. We have endeavoured to explain why this sense of range failed him in home affairs. "Foreign affairs are, for me, an end in themselves, more important than anything else in the world," he said in the year 1866. He was lucky enough always to find wars ready to his hand when he needed them, but he never misused his position of preponderant power in order to effect conquests. For twenty years, he maintained the peace of Europe, and posterity cannot fail to give him credit for this, however much it may be justified in detracting from his merits in other respects.

But if he kept the peace of Europe for twenty years, this was not the outcome of humanitarian motives, nor yet because he feared the loss of fame. He was guided only by the conviction that Europe would no longer be content to play the part of neutral onlooker, that coalitions might be formed against Germany, coalitions the danger of which had in the year 1869 made him willing, in theory, to renounce the annexation of Alsace. Bismarck's treatment of France after the year 1871 leads to a statesmanlike attitude, leads back to Nikolsburg. "It is necessary for us that we should be left in peace by France. If France will not keep the peace with us, we must prevent her finding allies.

So long as she has no allies, France is not dangerous to us; and so long as the great monarchies of Europe hold together, no republic is dangerous to them. On the other hand, a French republic will find it very difficult to secure a monarchical ally against us."

In these words he tells us why he must prevent the formation of anti-German coalitions, and must endeavour to form coalitions of which Germany is a member. From 1850 to 1870, Bismarck wanted Prussia to remain isolated, so that, in great crises, she could secure a high price for her aid. Now, for powerful Germany, he wants alliances. Then he was weak, and therefore wanted to stand alone; now, when he is strong, he seeks friends. His fundamental idea remains sound, even after his own epoch has passed away.

"It is our interest to keep the peace, whereas our continental neighbours cherish wishes (some of them secret and some of them officially acknowledged) which can only be fulfilled by means of war. . . . Our development into a great power has aroused fears which we must try to dispel by the honourable and pacific use of our influence. . . . Respect for the rights of other States . . . is made easy for the German empire, . . . on the one hand, by the objectivity of the German character, and, on the other, by the fact that (without merit on our part) we do not need any enlargement of territory, and could not achieve such an enlargement without strengthening the centrifugal elements in our domain. My ideal has always been that, after establishing unity within the frontiers attainable by us, we should win the confidence . . . of the great powers; that German policy, after the injuria temporum, the disintegration of our nation, has been made good, should be peaceful and just. . . . When contemplating international disputes which can only be settled by war, I have never been inclined to regard them by the standard which prevails at a student's duel."

We learn from Tiedemann that in the seventies Bismarck repeatedly spoke of himself as a European. In the broad lines of his foreign policy he was in actual fact a European, for he never spoke in a nationalist vein, never believed, or even said, that his people was the chosen people. He was entirely free from philistine patriotism. To a deputation, he said: "I have always regarded the Alsatians as the élite of the French nation. They have the best soldiers, and in my view it is their peculiar merit to possess some of the good qualities of both nations. If I could wed every French-woman to a man German to the core, I should breed up a thor-oughly efficient race." Wishing to send Thiers good wishes on his birthday, he first asks the Frenchman whether such a message from Bismarck will lessen his popularity; and when Thiers dies, Bismarck asks his friends to drink to the French statesman's memory. In the year 1875, he might well have taken up arms against France once more, for at this date the French were mak-ing military preparations, and clamour for a war of revenge was sounding across the frontier. But he trod out the sparks that were threatening to give rise to a conflagration, saying: "It would have been odious to attack France simply in order to pre-vent her getting her breath again. Such an attack would have given a welcome pretext to England for mouthing humanitarian phrases; and it would have inclined Russia to advance from a policy of personal friendship between the two emperors to one embodying crude State interest, for at this time . . . on the Neva some doubt was expressed as to whether we did wisely to allow matters to go as far as they did without interfering in the course of affairs."

During the spring of 1875, the Entente of 1915 encircling Ger-many seemed for a time to be foreshadowed. The ecclesiastical dispute was a pretext. Francis Joseph, Victor Emmanuel, and Leopold II. espoused the Roman Catholic cause. Gorchakoff, with his eyes on the Balkans, was inclined to enter into an understand-ing with the French. Even England, out of humour with Germany, was ready to hold out the hand of friendship to the Russians. Bismarck's whole system was endangered, and for the first time he seemed likely to experience a diplomatic defeat. What did he do? First of all he set every mill turning by the publication of an article "Is war in sight?" In Rome, in London, everywhere, the diplomatists, guided by their hatred for Bismarck, made a move towards the Russian chancellor. Gorchakoff, thereupon, yielded a small point to the British in the Balkans, and then, accompanied by the tsar, went to Berlin, either to alleviate or to intensify the crisis. Bismarck received him pacifically, showed Gorchakoff his latest tender of resignation, in which he declared that he was ailing, and that the country could get on without him, since everything was quiet. Bismarck said as much, likewise, to the tsar, who was really glad not to be obliged to take up arms.

Thus the Russian, a vain and cunning old man, was duped by his pupil. His last chance of fame had vanished, and, to save the remnants of his reputation, he sent to his representatives in all the capitals a telegram (not in cipher) which said: "Maintenant la paix est assurée." This despatch, drafted to show that Gorchakoff had gained the victory over Bismarck, that Mother Russia had overcome the furor teutonicus, informed Europe that Russia and Gorchakoff had saved peace-loving France from the greed of Bismarck, Europe's evil genius!

Bismarck was in a fury, and, according to his own account, promptly said some home truths to the Russian: "You have no right to spring from behind on to a friend's shoulders, nor, at his cost, to stage a circus scene! . . . Even if you want to win fame in Paris, you should not for that reason disturb our relationships with Russia! If you like, I will have some five-franc pieces coined in Berlin, bearing the inscription: 'Gorchakoff protége la France'; or we might build a theatre in the German embassy in Paris, where, to the light of Bengal fire, you can be introduced to the French public, with the same inscription, as a guardian angel wearing white raiment and equipped with wings!" We are given to understand that Gorchakoff was uneasy at such raillery. This much is certain, that the quarrel left a deep trace in Bismarck's mind, and was soon to have consequences of world-wide historical importance.

True, the tsar promptly went to see Bismarck, without having announced his coming, and opened the conversation by saying:

"Let us begin by assuring you that I have never believed the assertion that Germany is bellicose!" Bismarck actually tells us that on another occasion, the tsar said of his chancellor: "Leave him to enjoy his senile vanity!" Bismarck, however, seems to have sustained a diplomatic defeat at Gorchakoff's hands. Furthermore, he is in the exceptional position of having a clean political conscience; he will never forget this hour. Bismarck refrains, for the moment, from contradicting the statement of his opponent, who declares everywhere that he has the tsar's approval. But Bismarck stores the matter up in his memory; and since in old age he has his sleep disturbed by thoughts of "unavenged injustice" perpetrated against him fifty years before at school, we may well believe that such an affront as this inflicted on him when he is at the climax of his power will stimulate a determination to be avenged.

Only a year later, he is faced by the alternative of espousing the cause of Russia or that of Austria. Immediately after the last crisis, in the summer of 1875, the mutual jealousies of Austria and Russia had been rendered acute by fresh risings in the Balkans against the Turks. Now the issues hung upon Bismarck's decision. Immediately after the peace, he had tried to paralyse the Balkan rivals by the formation of the Three Emperors' League. "I have no thought of intervening," he said privately. "That might precipitate a European war. . . . If I were to espouse the cause of one of the parties, France would promptly strike a blow on the other side. . . . I am holding two powerful heraldic beasts by their collars, and am keeping them apart for two reasons: first of all, lest they should tear one another to pieces; and secondly, lest they should come to an understanding at our expense." In the Reichstag, he popularises the same idea in the words: "I am opposed to the notion of any sort of active participation of Germany in these matters, so long as I can see no reason to suppose that German interests are involved, no interests on behalf of which it is worth our risking — excuse my plain speaking — the healthy bones of one of our Pomeranian musketeers."

No one knows better than Bismarck the uncertainties of this Three Emperors' League. He is very doubtful whether he will be able to keep his two heraldic beasts apart indefinitely. The only thing which gave the alliance moral weight was that the three emperors were united in their opposition to republicanism and democracy, and that they would rather come to an agreement among themselves than be overthrown by what they all heartily loathed. That was why, in the seventies, Bismarck favoured the formation of the eastern triple alliance, and actually brought it into being, though in the fifties he had broken up that same alliance. In the tsar and in the emperor of Austria, dynastic wishes for their own safety were more powerful than their jealousy of the conqueror; but there did not exist, nowadays, the spectre of a dread enemy to cement this union into a Holy Alliance such as it had been in the time of their fathers.

In this remarkable threesome marriage, Germany was the young husband for whose favours two wives of riper years disputed. Both women were contentious, making it difficult for the husband to behave impartially. "If we remain neutral when Russia and Austria come to blows, the defeated combatant will never forgive us," said Bismarck to Hohenlohe at this time. "Should Austria be utterly crushed, that would not profit us. Of course we could annex German Austria, but what could we do with the Slavs and the Hungarians? Public opinion would not allow us to fight against Austria; Russia would be a grave menace to us if Austria were to perish; we can only hold Russia in check with Austria's aid." Ere long, Bismarck's views upon this matter were to be put to a dangerous test.

In the spring of 1876, Gorchakoff had had to put up with being told by Bismarck's envoy that his theatrical coup in Berlin the previous year had aroused "distrust and uncertainty" in Germany vis-à-vis Russia. Gorchakoff replied gushingly and insincerely, that if Bismarck was still spoken of as his pupil, it was only in the sense in which Raphael was a pupil of Perugino. While thus speaking fair words, he continued all the more maliciously to intrigue against Bismarck in the diplomatic field. Knowing the dilemma in which his opponent was placed, he suddenly forced the issue. From Livadia, in the autumn of 1876, he sent through the German military attaché an enquiry to Berlin. Would Germany remain neutral in the event of a war between Russia and Austria? Gorchakoff was far too subtle a diplomatist to have put so blunt a question without calculating the possible effects of his bluntness. Bismarck, who received the dispatch at Varzin, acted in the first instance on his own initiative. With unwonted emphasis, he instructed the Foreign Office to " fob off this indiscreet questioner by saying that Germany does not know why Gorchakoff has asked the question, or what use he will make of the information if he gets it. . . . The enquiry is as impudent as it is untimely, intrigue cousue de fil blanc." He wrathfully declared: " The whole thing is an attempt to make us sign a blank cheque, which Russia will fill in, and cash for use against Austria and England."

Following his usual practice, Bismarck had tested personal moods by the logarithms of his calculations. He knew the real purport of Gorchakoff's enquiry. The Russian wanted to know whether Austria was to be partitioned. If Bismarck said " No ", it was because he foresaw the rising of a pan-Slavist flood which, after inundating the whole of eastern Europe, would reduce Germany to a dependent position. It would be better to give the tsar something to think about: for a long time Bismarck's policy had been to keep Russia, Austria, and Britain — the three great rivals in eastern Europe — in a state of mutual tension, each angling for German support. Now he wanted to prevent the outbreak of a world war, and to divert Russia's fighting forces into the Balkans. Consequently, when pressed once more for a definite answer, he replied that, while he could look on indifferently if his two friends thought fit to quarrel, he would regret it very much if either of them were so badly damaged as to cease to be a great power.

Now Gorchakoff was in a position to offer his master definite proof that Bismarck was the chief obstacle between the Russians and the gratification of their desire to set up the cross again upon the dome of St. Sophia. The tsar, rising to Bismarck's fly, thereupon renounced the idea of attacking Francis Joseph. Instead, meeting his brother emperor in Reichstadt, he came to a temporary understanding about the Balkans. Austria was to receive Bosnia as the price of neutrality. Thus the threatening storm was diverted towards the southeast. In the spring of 1877, the Russians set out for Constantinople — to find British ships in the Dardanelles and to encounter additional difficulties. The other powers, in fact, stood between him and the Golden Horn, so he had to content himself with " shaking up the balance of power " in the treaty of San Stefano.

Gorchakoff, in his rejoinder to Bismarck, had said: "La question qu'il s'agit de résoudre, n'est ni allemand ni russe; elle est européenne." The chancellor penned a marginal note: " Qui parle Europe a tort. — Who is Europe? " Ten years earlier, when the British envoy was in minatory mood, Bismarck had used the same three words, expressively and half jestingly. " I have always found that the word 'Europe' is much on the lips of statesmen who are asking from other powers something which they would not venture to ask for in their own names." The statement was true enough in those days, and it was his tacit answer to Gorchakoff's phrase.

In St. Petersburg there was a man whose thoughts really had a European scope, a man whose heart was responsive to humanistic feelings unknown to old Gorchakoff. With the peace of San Stefano began the process of edging the Turks out of Europe, and of extending the confines of the vassal State of Bulgaria — so that Austria felt herself partially encircled by Russia, England became uneasy, and a second and more terrible war seemed imminent. Now Bismarck's old friend Count Peter Shuvaloff hastened to the chancellor and begged him to mediate. Bismarck was abed at Friedrichsruh, suffering from shingles and neuralgia, and from such severe face-ache that he could not even shave. He received the Russian none the less — and, to begin with, refused his visitor's request.

Once again, as before the annexation of the imperial provinces of Alsace and Lorraine, his first political instinct was unerring.

A few months earlier, when semi-official proposals had first been made on behalf of German mediation, he had definitely refused, saying: "We could hardly believe that mediation by another power could be achieved in such a way that it would not assume the aspect of pressure upon Russia; but such pressure would only make it more difficult for Russia to yield. . . . In view of the wide extent to which our frontiers march with those of Russia, our relationships to that empire are far more important than the whole of Turkey. We are absolutely determined not to disturb those relationships needlessly by undertaking mediation." There is no proof of the assertion that subsequently, in his old age, he regarded this intervention as the greatest blunder of his career. The statement does not ring true. All that we certainly know about the matter is that his first impulse was to reject the idea of mediation. But Shuvaloff was persistent. Next day there came a dispatch from the tsar (sent, of course, at Shuvaloff's instigation), wherein Alexander personally begged Bismarck to mediate, saying that he would regard this as a proof of the chancellor's devotion. What was Bismarck to do? Shortly before, he had written to the German envoy in St. Petersburg: "A monarch, and . . . one so near to us as Tsar Alexander, must be regarded by you and by myself as . . . always right — like a lady."

Furthermore, the attempt on Emperor William's life had just made it likely that the Anti-socialist Law would be passed. Bismarck felt that his position at home had been strengthened by this. He may also have been influenced by rancorous feelings towards old Gorchakoff, who would have to endure sitting under his presidency if a council were called. Consequently, just as at Versailles, in the end he said "Yes" where he had said "No", thus running counter to a fundamental impulse of his nature. Having made up his mind, in twenty-five minutes he dictated to his son the programme of the Berlin congress.

"We shall play the part of honest broker," said Bismarck for the public ear. Bleichröder, on reading it, shook his head thoughtfully, and, inspired by age-long experience, he rejoined sceptically: "There is no such thing as an honest broker."

XIV

The Ems telegram reached Bismarck on July 13, 1870. Kullmann wounded him with a revolver shot on July 13, 1874. The Congress of Berlin opened on June 13, 1878; and Bismarck signed the treaty of Berlin, which was the upshot of the congress, on July 13th. The number thirteen (of which, as of Friday, he had a superstitious fear) had twice brought him good luck in the guise of ill. The question was, whether the congress, which began and ended on these ominous dates, might not, in the end, bring him harm as the final outcome of what seemed a brilliant success. To outward seeming, no moment in his career was more brilliantly successful than this one, when, in the domed hall of his official palace, he rose at the centre of the great horseshoe table as president of Europe to welcome the statesmen of the great powers. For many decades, there had been no gathering such as this. Bismarck's great white beard [see Plate dated 1883] (for he was still unable to shave) gave him a patriarchal aspect; but various circumstances — his illness, the need for carrying on the duties of his chairmanship in a foreign tongue, the questionable character of the whole undertaking — made him uneasy, so that he was " rather nervous ", and by no means unconcerned when he opened the congress.

At this horseshoe table are seated twenty noted statesmen belonging to seven different nations. On Bismarck's right sits monarchy. Is not that a gypsy, who is to-day playing the part of a general of the Honveds? His lean, narrow features seem somewhat inconsistent. The nose and the ears are large; the mouth is sensuous; he has a short beard; his general aspect is a trifle savage and unceremonious. It is Count Andrassy, a man of quick apprehensions and slow resolves. Beside Andrassy sits Count Karolyi, perpetual Austrian envoy in Berlin, for even the war with Austria could not dislodge him from his post for more than a few weeks. The third member of the Austro-Hungarian delegation is Baron Haymerle, a Viennese, about whom everything is sharply pointed, from his nose to the pencil with which he takes his notes.

The man on Bismarck's left, who looks like Merry England, easy-going and cheerful, leader of the French, though English by name and origin, more of an archæologist than a foreign minister, is Waddington. His neighbour, the count of Saint-Vallier, a fidgety fellow, French ambassador at Berlin, really represents his nation better. The third of the French representatives is Desprez, an intellectual looking man, half court chamberlain, half cleric.

What is the Far East doing here? Surely that crafty-looking little man is a Japanese? No, it is Count Corti, who represents Italy with more intelligence than his neighbour, Count Launey. Close at hand sits a blue-eyed German mercenary wearing a fez. Everything at this table seems topsy-turvy, and fitted to convince us how foolish is the conventional chatter about race and nationality. This handsome Teuton passes by the name of Ali Pasha, and is now a great general, though in the days when he was a youth in Magdeburg he bore another name, and subsequently, as a runaway cabin boy, was (so rumour has it) a minion of Ali the grand vizier, who has ever since been his patron. Two months after this congress at which we now see him, his adventurous career will be cut short by Albanian dagger thrusts. The other Turkish representative, Catheodory Pasha, a man with a well-shaped nose, closely shut lips, pale and reserved, was born in the Near East, being of noble Greek descent.

Who is that on the right, next the Viennese baron? Is he another member of the German delegation? No, that is Lord Odo Russell, British ambassador in Berlin, a man who looks shrewd but kindly, is quick in his movements, and rather uncouth. Next to Russell sits a man with a large fair beard and a high forehead. That is Lord Salisbury, an expert upon the eastern question. Our glance will not linger upon him if we have once caught sight of the third of the British representatives, perhaps the most striking figure in the assembly. His looks can scarcely be said to disclose his nationality. We should never have taken him for an Englishman. In earlier days, before Disraeli became earl of Beaconsfield, when he was famous chiefly as a novelist, he was a

typical handsome Jewish youth. Now he looks half Mephistopheles, half musician. With his large nose, his hanging underlip, his
turned-up moustache, his tall forehead set in curls, he resembles
a man of letters painted by Rembrandt. Old and worn, now, he
leans heavily on his stick as he makes his way to his seat. No one,
to look at him, would have suspected him to be the man who so
charmed the heart of Queen Victoria.

Where is Gorchakoff, as famous a man as Disraeli? There he
is, that shrunken mannikin. He bears his eighty years otherwise
than Emperor William, who is still as upright as a young lieutenant. A great sufferer from gout, he has been carried to his seat.
On closer inspection, we see that his face is not shrunken like his
body. His mouth is still sensual looking; his cheeks are soft; only
the nose is sharp. As he peers round the room, a man half German by origin, he reminds us of the picture of a German eccentric by Spitzweg, and seems a man of pleasure rather than an
intriguer: he is, in truth, both. He has persuaded his master to
let him sit at this table, though the deciding voice in the Russian
delegation does not rest with him but with the Russian ambassador
in Berlin, Paul d'Oubril. The real conductor of the Russian business, however, is neither one nor the other of these two, but Count
Peter Shuvaloff, the originator of the congress, who looks like a
French marshal, is clever, chivalrous, unrivalled as a negotiator.

At the outset, the adversaries clash swords for a moment.
Although the president, on German soil, has made his opening
speech in French, Disraeli answers in English, spoken with an
Oxford accent and comprehensible to few of those present. Thereupon Gorchakoff, instead of replying in Russian (as Bismarck
had expected), gets to work in French, saying things which are
not an answer, speaking at great length, and boring the president, who scribbles the while, on a piece of paper: "Pompos,
pompo, pomp, po." Thereafter they all adjourn for refreshments
to a neighbouring room, where Borchardt achieves "the greatest
success of the congress at every one of its twenty sittings."

Even before the opening of the congress, Bismarck had been
exasperated because all the representatives, when he paid them

return visits, had "received him in a countrified fashion and had bored him to death." Subsequently, he made fun of his guests in witty invectives, tried in the next sittings to rule after his own manner, saying audibly, when Salisbury made a new proposal: "Encore, un de plus!" After the Greek report, "he pays no heed to the objections, but hastens to suppress every one with nervous impatience, allowing all to feel the weight of his authority, in gradations." Moreover, though he speaks beautiful French, his words come in jets, just as when he is speaking German— fluently or slowly, according to the state of his nerves. "I rarely got to sleep before six in the morning; often not until eight, and then only for an hour or two. I would not receive any one before noon. You can imagine in what state of mind I was in by the time the sittings opened. Before each sitting, I drank three or four beer glasses full of strong port wine, in order to set my blood coursing, for otherwise I should have been fit for nothing." Nevertheless, according to all the reports, his chairmanship was admirable, his interpositions and his guidance were most effective.

The only members of the conference he himself was at first inclined to trust were Andrassy and Russell. He vainly endeavoured to discover "a hidden flaw in Russell, for no Englishman can be so perfect as he seems, and he is a man who speaks all languages incredibly well." He would like to have Lord Salisbury in the hands of a German drill sergeant for half an hour a day, to teach him to hold himself better. He treats Achmed Ali as a renegade, coldly and almost uncivilly. Towards his enemy Gorchakoff, he shows ironical devotion. Once, when the old gentleman is paying him a visit, and Bismarck wishes to help him get out of his chair, the animal takes this movement as a signal for attack. Bismarck shouts at the dog, and thereupon the Russian, who has not hitherto noticed the beast, fancies that Bismarck is suddenly going to take vengeance upon him, and drives away much horrified. When Bismarck relates the incident in the evening, he adds the following gloss by a politician who is also a lover of dogs: "Tyras is not yet properly trained. He does not know whom he ought to bite. If he did know, he would have bitten the Turk."

The three notable adventurers who were present at this congress — the cabin boy, the novelist, and Bismarck — reacted on one another in very different ways. "I wish I knew whether Beaconsfield wants war," said Bismarck on the first evening. No one knew! The general feeling was that the British premier held the scales. He was in a suspicious mood. Werner, who painted his portrait, knew no English; but Disraeli was not satisfied until he had had repeated assurances of the fact. The old man's sense of humour, however, enabled him to enjoy some of the Berlinese witticisms at the expense of his personality, his name, and his Jewish origin. One of these jokes was to the effect that when an officer, going his rounds, asked the sentry in front of Dizzy's door for whose sake he was on guard, the man answered: "Please, Sir, for B. A. Cohnfeld."

Everything in Disraeli, especially the Englishman's oratorical tendencies, would have been uncongenial to Bismarck, had Bismarck hated Jews. But after the two men had had a few conversations, Bismarck took to Disraeli more than to any of the others, and said later: "He spent several evenings with us. Since he was not very well, he would only come when there were to be no other guests. Thus I became intimate with him. Although he had written such fanciful novels, he was a man with whom it was easy to do business. Within a quarter of an hour one knew exactly what he would be at. He had definitely made up his mind how far he would go, and after a very little discussion we could settle matters." Down to Disraeli's death, Bismarck remained on friendly terms with him, although after the congress Disraeli, in *Endymion*, had drawn a somewhat critical portrait of Bismarck as the Count of Ferroll — forty years after Motley's Bismarck novel.

Bismarck seems to have talked business only to Bleichröder. "The odds in favour of peace are 66 to 34, or perhaps 70 to 30," he said to the latter on the first evening. Bleichröder gave " a great informal dinner, with much music "; the crown prince issued invitations to a water party on the Wannsee, at which nearly all the members of the congress narrowly escaped drowning in a

storm; thence they went to Sans-Souci, where, according to
Hohenlohe's report, the congress "found before dinner a great
many wash hand-basins, but only one earthenware utensil which
was not intended for washing purposes; round this the whole of
Europe grouped itself."

The problems discussed at the Congress of Berlin are long
since out of date; the details are uninteresting; the only important matter concerns the rivalry between the three competitors in
the Near East. This rivalry between Russia and England came to
a head in the matter of Bulgaria. When the Russians would not
give way, and Beaconsfield had already ordered his special train,
Bismarck (having learned of Russia's weakness from Shuvaloff)
persuaded the English to make a small concession and the Russians to make a great one. In this way peace was preserved at the
cost of Russian friendship, for henceforward people spoke of
"Russia's humiliation by Bismarck."

The formal topics of discussion, apart from the general falsehood that Christians had to be protected against the infidel, were
the moves in the game of chess wherein the little nations were the
pawns. There was a delimitation of so-called spheres of interests,
in regions with whose geography the British and the Russian
statesmen were not much better informed than the German medi-
ators. When, for instance, the Sanjak was assigned to the new
Bulgaria, it was subsequently discovered that this region extended far beyond the foothills of the Balkans, that England had
conceded too much, and wished to retrench. "After prolonged
search," writes Hohenlohe, "we found a small area which we
could take from the Russians, a mountain spine, . . . though
none of us knew whether it was a reasonable frontier. . . . The
maps are inaccurate and contradictory." When, after four weeks,
the treaty was signed, not even the tranquillity of a cemetery was
ensured for the Balkans. . . . Bulgaria had been established;
Serbia, Rumania, and Montenegro had become "independent";
Greece had been enlarged; the Danube was to be neutral, under
a European commission; the Straits were still closed; Bosnia and
Herzegovina, which remained Turkish, were to be occupied and

administered by Austria. This was to be a source of tension for
decades to come, although it had been secretly arranged a year
before by an understanding between the tsar and the emperor of
Austria. Nothing was settled in accordance with racial considerations, or even in accordance with the wishes of the inhabitants.
The Serbs were split up among four different countries, the Bulgarians among three; the boundaries of Islam had been pushed
back, but the Turks were still in Europe; a thin sheet of parchment served to cover a number of unsolved problems.

Germany, which had no direct interest to serve, indirectly forfeited a great interest through the congress. Her friendship with
Russia was seriously shaken, and no friendship with England was
established in its place. Bismarck finds personal reasons for the
failure: "Before the congress, we had in great measure come to
an understanding with the tsar. It was agreed that I should approve all Russia's wishes, and in return the tsar had promised
to replace Gorchakoff by Shuvaloff. . . . Gorchakoff must have
got wind of this understanding, for at the congress his policy was
to ask less and less for Russia, so that I had to tell Shuvaloff that
I could not afford to be more Russian than Russia herself. . . .
Later, when Gorchakoff gave his report to the tsar, he said: 'We
have to thank Bismarck for the meagreness of the results we have
achieved', and thereupon, we are told, the tsar said: 'Very well,
then! You will remain chancellor!'" This much is certain, that
the tsar considered himself cheated in the diplomatic struggle by
the "honest broker." He spoke of the congress as "a European
coalition against Russia under Bismarck"; and he described
Shuvaloff as Prince Bismarck's dupe.

The congress of Berlin paved the way for unrest in the Balkans
and for dissensions among the great powers. These dissensions
soon became manifest.

XV

"Encouraged, dear uncle, by your lasting friendship, I would
ask your permission to give frank expression to a delicate matter
which causes me much disquiet. I refer to the behaviour of Ger-

man diplomatic agents who, for some time past, have unfortunately been showing hostility to Russia, which is in complete conflict with the friendly traditions that have for more than a century guided the policy of our governments and have always been in harmony with their joint interests. In me, this friendship persists unchanged, as I hope it does in you. Yet the world judges by deeds. . . . The Turks, supported by your friends the English and the Austrians, . . . are incessantly putting little difficulties in the way of the Bulgarians. Now, the majority of the commissaries of Europe has to decide. In almost all matters, France and Italy are for us, whereas the Germans seem to be acting upon orders to support unfailingly the Austrian view, and they are systematically hostile to us. . . .

"You must forgive me, but I consider it my duty to draw your attention to the unhappy consequences which this may entail in our friendly relationships. The newspaper press of both our countries has already begun to embroil us. . . . I understand perfectly well that good relations with Austria are of great moment to you, but I cannot see that Germany will gain anything by sacrificing Russian interests. Is it worthy of a truly great statesman to be influenced by personal mortifications when the matter at stake concerns the interests of great States, one of which, in 1870, put the other under an obligation which, according to the latter's own words, was never to be forgotten? I should not have ventured to bring this matter to your notice were it not that the circumstances are so serious that I can no longer conceal from you my dread lest the consequences should become momentous to both our countries. May God give you light, and avert this catastrophe!"

In August 1879, when William read these grave passages in the tsar's long letter, he realised no more than did the writer the seriousness of the issues involved. Again and again during the last hundred years had the friendship and the interests of the two allies been disturbed by friction, but matters had always been smoothed over. Bismarck's maxim that Germany and Russia were natural friends was so firmly believed that the press campaigns after the congress of Berlin could not be expected to affect the dynastic sentiments of the tsar or the German emperor, and did not appear likely to influence the moves of the pieces upon Bismarck's chessboard.

The two countries had so wide an extent of common frontier; and there was nothing at issue between them likely to prove a casus belli. For these reasons, during the last five-and-twenty years Bismarck had been a firm friend to Russia, even when the situation was critical. Since 1871, moreover, France had cherished hopes of entering into an alliance with Russia in order to prepare an attack on Germany from two fronts. That was why, for the last eight years, it had been Bismarck's policy to stand as mediator between the two empires, Russia and Austria, keeping the "heraldic beasts" from tearing one another to pieces, while being careful to avoid taking the side of either. Quite recently he had said to Mittnacht: "If we were to take the side of Austria, Russia would become our irreconcilable enemy, and would strike up an alliance with France."

The last report from the German ambassador in St. Petersburg had mentioned the tsar's complaint anent the misunderstandings alluded to in the above-quoted letter, while adding that at a dinner party the tsar had said civil things about the German army and had drunk to its welfare. For some months, Bismarck had been thinking new thoughts about Russia, and had drawn closer to his Hungarian friend Andrassy, whom he now invited to come to see him in Gastein. Though Gorchakoff's power was purely formal, desire to take vengeance upon the old man may have been a contributory motive. Bismarck's sense of hostility towards Russia had begun when Gorchakoff had mortified him as above described. After the Berlin Congress, his distrust for Russia had been intensified by that country's ingratitude. Additional causes of hostility had been an increase in the Russian army and the steadily growing influence of the anti-German minister for war. Now the tsar's letter threw fuel on the flames of Bismarck's anger. He hurried on the meeting with Andrassy.

Writing to his master from Gastein about the tsar, he used

stronger phrases than he had used about any foreign country since the days of Ems. "The tsar's assurances of friendship have very little importance in view of the unconcealed threats his words convey . . . in the event of Your Majesty declining to subordinate your policy to the Russian. Among monarchs, . . . such language is the invariable herald of a breach, unless this latter be hindered by treaties. The usages of politeness between monarchs forbids stronger language than this, as a rule, even when war is intended. If Your Majesty should answer in the same tone, we should probably soon find ourselves at war with Russia."

Bismarck goes on to describe the Russian minister for war as a masked nihilist whose design probably is to pave the way for a republic by involving Russia in war; Russia's self-restraint in the year 1870 is ascribed to Austrian pressure; Prussia's services to Russia are enumerated. Then Bismarck draws his conclusions. Hitherto, he says, he has always advocated a rapprochement with Russia, since this has seemed to him the safer course. Nevertheless he says, "We have far more in common with the State of Austria than with Russia. The kinship of blood, the common memories, the German tongue, and the interests of Hungary, would make an Austrian alliance more popular in Germany, and perhaps more lasting, than a Russian alliance. On the other hand, dynastic relationships and the personal friendship of Tsar Alexander have turned the scale in favour of Russia. Now that this advantage of a Russian alliance is imperilled, it seems to me essential that we should do our utmost to cultivate friendly relationships with Austria."

Emperor William reads these words with alarm. He is still more alarmed when he finds that Bismarck wants to go to Vienna. William, however, shows unusual firmness, and replies: "In no case will I consent to such a step, for Russia would at once regard my doing so as equivalent to a rupture of relationships!"

A few days later, he receives a dispatch from Bismarck recounting the conversation with Andrassy, who has proposed a defensive alliance between Germany and Austria, as a measure

of protection against Russian attack. The old gentleman is horrified, and, on his own initiative, arranges with the tsar that he and
Alexander shall meet in a Russian frontier town in order to talk
over the tsar's letter. Bismarck is enraged at the idea of this
meeting. He writes a lengthy statement (which occupies ten pages
of print) to expound his new policy to his master. He speaks of
Gorchakoff's jealousy, of Alexander's threatening letter, of the
danger of a coalition like that which existed in the days of the
Seven Years' War. On the other hand, between Austria and Germany there was a community reaching back for a thousand years,
as he had already pointed out in Nikolsburg. Germany and Austria could combine for mutual protection without taking over one
another's duties. Bismarck ends with the customary threat of
resignation, saying that he cannot carry out any other policy.

In return, the emperor sends him a holograph account of the
conversation with the tsar. There had been a misunderstanding,
no intention to threaten, all a mistake, Bismarck would please
regard the letter as unwritten, talk of William's late lamented
father, cordial assurances, complete friendship. All the more
reason, therefore, for having nothing to do with an Austrian
alliance! Bismarck, however, who has meanwhile been continuing
to elaborate his plans for such an alliance, now sends his master,
from Gastein, daily or almost daily monologues upon European
politics. Finally, in September, he writes:

"The dependence of our safety upon Russia would be an incalculable factor. Austria, on the other hand, is not incalculable
to the same extent. Austria, owing to her position and owing to
the nature of her constituent parts, needs a buttress in Europe
just as much as Germany does. Russia can, in the last resort, get
along without any such buttress, for its absence does not imply
the danger that her empire will break up. In Austria-Hungary,
the peoples and their representatives have a word to say in the
matter, and these peoples are, above all, eager for peace. . . . But
in Russia a policy of open hostility to Germany, of war against
Germany, is no menace to the internal position of the empire, and
such a policy may therefore be adopted at any moment. . . .

Austria has need of us; Russia has not. Perhaps, of all the powers, Austria is the one whose internal condition is the healthiest, and the rule of the imperial house is firmly established among the component nationalities. But in the case of Russia no one knows what eruption of revolutionary elements may not suddenly occur in the interior of that great empire."

Hitherto Bismarck has believed, or has at any rate upheld, the very opposite of this. Russia was the rocher de bronze, against the revolution, whereas Austria's stability was undermined by the jealousies of the various nationalities of which that empire was made up. Now Bismarck tells us that Austria is a model empire, whilst Russia is the focus of revolution! Such are the arguments by which he tries to persuade himself and the king. But the true motive can be read between the lines. Austria is weak and needs us; Russia is strong and does not need us. That is why Russia is a menace. Bismarck, accustomed to rule, has as minister (this meaning one who has to work in alliance with other ministers) always preferred to have in his cabinet persons whom he can rule. Is he now to accept the menacing tsar as a friend? What, above all, repels him from Russia is that country's bold claim to equality of right — a claim he has never been able to endure, whether in politics, family life, or ministerial councils. The Hungarian is of different calibre, eager to please the powerful German, happy to live under the protection of one stronger than himself.

But the emperor is refractory. William is eighty-two years of age. For the last seventeen years he has been guided by Bismarck. Why should he now prove adamant? His sense of honour is aroused; he thinks of his father's heritage; family feeling is at work; habit and inclination play their part. His nephew the tsar has solemnly and cordially apologised. All their differences have been wiped out. "Animated by this conviction, I find it impossible, on conscientious grounds, to accede to the imperial chancellor's proposal. . . . I am in a terrible dilemma. . . . I would rather retire from the scene, and hand the government over to my son, than act in defiance of my best convictions and commit an act of treachery against Russia. . . . If the prince wishes to talk over certain future eventualities with Count Andrassy, so be it. But there shall be no alliance. I will not have it. The prince himself has before now expressed his opposition to the idea of our tying our hands by alliances, . . . and he has sometimes described Austria as untrustworthy."

The old gentleman's memory works very well when he is uneasy. Bismarck's answers touch wider and ever wider issues. Obviously, his mind is engaged upon constructive work. We can hardly doubt that he is thinking of something more important than merely persuading the king. Now he complains of his shattered health; says that he cannot endure such friction; that he will resign unless the alliance is entered into. "I might perhaps still be able to go on serving the emperor if I were fortunate enough to find that in decisive political questions I could share His Majesty's convictions. . . . My health is still suffering from the effects of similar frictions endured in Nikolsburg and Versailles. To-day, my forces are at so low an ebb that I simply cannot dream of an attempt to carry on business under such conditions. On the 19th it will be seventeen years since I began to endure this and similar struggles, which have continued without interruption. I believe that during this period I have . . . done my official duty. . . . If there is no change in the situation, in eight or ten days from now I shall have to hand in my official tender of resignation, this meaning, in accordance with the laws of the empire, an announcement of my withdrawal from office."

Bismarck's mention of an approximate date for his impending resignation serves only to enrage the emperor, who reiterates his own determination to abdicate should Bismarck resign.

Thus speed the missives to and fro from Berlin to Gastein and from Gastein to Berlin, each of the old men telling the other that he won't play any longer if the other continues obstinate. Almost every day, the chancellor makes the secretary of State send a wire keeping him informed about the emperor's mood. On the other hand, the emperor enquires of Hohenlohe: "I suppose the chancellor is very much annoyed with me?" The emperor does **not** quite know how to deal with this Bismarck, whose way it **is** to draft the most important State documents upon his own initiative. He writes to the chancellor:

"I am much moved at the thought that we should, to all appearance, be showing a friendly demeanour towards Russia at the very time when we are . . . entering into a coalition with Austria against Russia. For your part, you are already so much committed to such an intention, that you do not merely discuss your whole project with Count Andrassy, but you even allow him to talk about it to his emperor, who promptly accepts the idea. . . . Put yourself in my place for a moment. I go to see my personal friend, my relative, my ally in good times and in bad, so that we may clear up hasty and misunderstood passages in his letter, and our discussions lead to a satisfactory result. Now, simultaneously, I am to enter into a hostile coalition against this sovereign, which means that behind his back I am to make my actions belie my words? . . . However, I will not and must not disavow the steps you have already taken vis-à-vis Andrassy and his master. You may, therefore, discuss in Vienna the eventualities of a disharmony with Russia becoming intensified to the pitch of a possible breach. . . . But I cannot conscientiously authorise you to enter into any kind of agreement, coalition, or even alliance. . . . Your devoted William."

Two different worlds hold converse here: old Prussia and the new empire, the knight and the diplomatist, conscience and shrewdness. But Mephistopheles has stronger means at his disposal. Hohenlohe in Paris, Reuss in Vienna, Moltke in Berlin, all the ministers in the cabinet council, must support his policy. The whole cabinet threatens to resign. The emperor finds himself encompassed. In this business we can admire neither Bismarck's policy nor his tactics. Our admiration is reserved for the veteran emperor.

How Bismarck journeys to Vienna, puts the finishing touches to the negotiations, concludes the alliance except for the signature; how, dreading a downfall, he sends defiant reports to the emperor, first to Berlin, then to Stettin, and finally to Baden; how the emperor fights step by step on behalf of his personal

honour (since he can no longer maintain his policy), tries to keep
the name of Russia out of a treaty which has been entered into
against Russia, and finally gives up the game as lost — all this
reads like a German saga.

"For the last four weeks," writes the vanquished monarch, "I
have been fighting against a stipulation in Vienna which ran
counter to my sense of honour and my duty. Last night, however,
having exhausted all my objections, I at length agreed, on condition that the motives for the step should be communicated to
Russia in the memorandum. All my moral force is broken. I don't
know what will become of me! Tsar Alexander will think I have
played him false, seeing that I wrote to him, and declared also by
word of mouth, at Prince Bismarck's dictation, that it was my
intention 'de maintenir le leg centenaire de nos pères'." We picture the old man, one of the last survivors from the eighteenth
century, writing this lament, thinking the while how, sixty-five
years earlier, he had ridden into Paris in the company of the
first Alexander, the present tsar's grandfather, just before Napoleon had been sent to Elba.

Now his policy is the right one, though he cannot enforce its
adoption. Not that he has a clearer vision than the chancellor!
But he is under the spell of morality and tradition, which sustain
his faith in the essential rightness of the dynastic alliance with
Russia, and he cannot break that alliance without a painful
wrench. Nor can the alliance be broken without danger to the
country. For the very reason that he is so old, for the very reason
that his mind has grown stiffer than his joints, he can in this case
see more clearly than another the great issues that are involved.
No one in the decades that followed could criticise more trenchantly Bismarck's decision to side with Austria, no one can criticise that decision more trenchantly to-day, than did William
when he penned the following marginal note to one of the chancellor's letters:

"Why should we support Austria against Russia with all our
strength, while being content that Austria should remain neutral
if France attacks us? What we propose to do for Austria against

Russia, Austria ought to do for us against France. . . . This is partie inégale!! The proposed treaty will inevitably drive Russia into the arms of France, and that will foster the French longing for vengeance! What better situation could France hope for than to place Germany and Austria between two fires? . . . That is why the Three Emperors' League ought to be maintained, instead of being broken up in favour of a league à deux. . . . As soon as the proposed treaty becomes known, or when its existence is suspected, France and Russia cannot fail to unite!"

Bismarck had considered and rejected every one of these countervailing considerations. The essential motive for his marked change of policy seems to have been feeling rather than calculation; its primary impulse was feeling. Karl Marx's comment, at the time, in a letter to Engels, is but a reflexion of what Bismarck had himself said about Gorchakoff. Here are Marx's words: "The most characteristic thing in Bismarck is the way in which his antagonism to Russia originated. He wanted to depose Gorchakoff and to install Shuvaloff. Since he failed to get his way, the rest follows as a matter of course. Voilà l'ennemi! . . . En attendant, the black cloud in the East is serviceable to him: once more he is the indispensable man. . . . His iron military budget will be renewed in the next Reichstag; perhaps it will be made 'perpetual'."

The subsidiary cause, too, is feeling. Never before has Bismarck regarded popular approval as a motive for entering into an alliance, or popular disapproval as a motive for breaking one. Now, he refers again and again to public opinion. South Germany is, in fact, delighted; and almost all the parties in the Reichstag endorse his policy. He has looked forward to this, for his parliamentary majority is precarious.

His third reason for the change of policy is temperamental. He says to Lucius: "Alliance with an autocrat, with a semi-barbaric and oppressed nation, is risky, whereas there are many advantages in an alliance with a comparatively weak State like Austria." Again: "If I must choose, I will choose Austria; a constitutionally governed, pacific State, which lies under Germany's guns; whereas we can't get at Russia." When, before this, has Bismarck been loath to enter into an alliance with an autocrat? When, before this, has he thought it preferable to form ties with a constitutionally governed State? How long has Austria been more pacific than Russia? These are but autosuggestions to hide the deeper reasons from himself and others. Bismarck's own autocratic inclinations explain his wish for an ally who is "comparatively weak" and "lies under Germany's guns"—all the more when the ally's minister of State is an accommodating subordinate.

These currents of feeling, these shadows upon the mind of a statesman who was only great when he made careful calculations, were the primary determinants of his change of policy, steadily favoured it, ultimately decided it. That he should choose at all, conflicted with his old principles; that he should choose Austria, was disastrous. What he achieved was infinitesimal as protection against a power whose friendship he had hitherto been able to secure, but which he now alienated. Nor did he achieve nearly as much as he had expected.

For what Bismarck had aimed at was something more than a mere reinsurance which threatened to destroy the safeguards provided by the old Three Emperors' League without putting new safeguards in their place. He had hoped for a comprehensive alliance with Austria, one which should be incorporated into the constitutions of the two countries. Here, too, feelings were the motive force; he wanted to reconstruct what time had destroyed, he dreamed of the completion of the incomplete, he pictured the establishment of a greater Germany! Had the frigid calculator of the sixties vanished? Had Bismarck forgotten the considerations which had led him to exclude eight million Germans from the German empire, because he was afraid of including so many more millions who were not Germans, and because he wanted to be quit of the rivalry of the Habsburgs? The rivalry was over and done with, but the alien nationalities remained. This much is certain, that the man who had broken Austria's strength now sought an alliance with Austria because Austria was weak.

Thus does destiny move in a sweeping curve: the enemy comes back to his victim; he enters into an alliance with the power whose strength he has broken; he weds an ageing woman whom he had forsaken when she was young. Surely the eagerness of the other party to the bargain should have given him pause? Francis Joseph, whom Königgrätz had robbed of half his authority, comes in person, thirteen years after the battle, to call upon the victor; but both the emperor and his minister Andrassy are stubborn in their refusal to enter into the sort of alliance Bismarck had proposed. The man now on a visit to Vienna had destroyed the Germanic Federation; the vanquished have no desire to conjure up its ghost. Bismarck would fain shift the centre of gravity of the Continent westward, but Austria's gaze is fixed on the East — while in case of need she will look farther west than suits Bismarck's plans. Andrassy flatly refuses to fight beside Germany on behalf of Alsace, so that old William (who scents danger in that quarter) exclaims wonderingly: "This is partie inégale!" For the first time in his life Bismarck strikes a bargain in which he gives more than he gets.

Anti-German sentiment gathers strength in St. Petersburg. When the longing for a war of vengeance makes the French look to Russia for support, they will put their trust in the western-eastern nutcrackers, whose jaws can crack the intervening nut all the more easily when one of these jaws is hollowed out. Bismarck has evoked a dangerous spectre, and will need eight years in which to lay it. In his successor's time, its menace will be renewed.

Before making his choice, he had, in a number of written monologues, summed up the pros and the cons: remarking that, materially speaking, Russia would be the stronger ally; referring to monarchical friendship, the instinct of self-preservation, the lack of all antagonisms. Subsequently, he spoke of Austria's weak points: "the fluctuations of public opinion in the Hungarian, Slav, and Catholic elements of the population; . . . the influence of father confessors in the royal family; the possibility of the reestablishment of intimate relationships between Austria and France, upon a Roman Catholic basis." He mentioned the

Polish question (to which he returned in his memoirs), saying that the problem of the future of Poland would become a peculiarly complicated one in the event of a military alliance between Germany and Austria. He summarised the outlooks as follows: "Neither alliance could be regarded as permanently stable; neither the dynastic alliance with Russia, nor yet the union based upon popular sympathy between Germans and Hungarians. The nightmare dread of anti-German coalitions persists." In 1880, he writes: "We hope, and we wish, to remain at peace with Russia. If this should prove impossible, because Russia attacks us or Austria, then there would be a war against Russia alone, or against Russia allied to France and Italy — a war likely to have the gravest consequences, and one which, even should we prove victorious, would not bring us anything worth the pains."

The spectre of world war haunts Bismarck when he enters into the alliance with Austria. Nothing can lay that spectre.

XVI

Bismarck's choice of Austria was decisive. It settled the subsequent course of European politics, including the formation of the Triple Alliance. To-day, after the great catastrophe, oscillations and crises are of little interest to us. Once the motives and the counter-motives at work in the formation of the Austrian alliance have been set forth in detail as an outcome of the analysis of actions, purposes, and feelings, there is no need for more than a cursory survey of the happenings of the eighties. Bismarck had reestablished Central Europe. He had abandoned freedom of choice. Russia was estranged, and his attempts at a rapprochement with England were unavailing.

Failure in this respect brought him luck to begin with. Since England refused to become a party to any coalition against France, the tsar, as England's enemy, was drawn towards the German powers. The new Three Emperors' League was mainly concerned with sharing interests in the Balkans. The tsar was free to work against England in the Near East, and by thus helping Alexander to his wishes in this respect, Bismarck was able to delay the Russian understanding with France. The alliance of 1881 was renewed in 1884. In the interim, the Triple Alliance of Germany, Austria, and Italy had been formed. Its aim was to prevent a union of Italy with France, although Bismarck did not look for serious help from Italy, being content to hope "that an Italian drummer would appear with the tricolour on the crest of the Alps." Another aim of the Triple Alliance was to dispel the deadly enmity between two of its members.

But he did not regard any of these objects as fundamental. They were all subsidiary to the main purpose of safeguarding peace. During the crises of the eighties, as in the previous decade, Bismarck never wanted war; and twice or thrice he used all his influence on the side of peace. In retrospect, he once more enumerates all the influences that weaken the Habsburg empire: the medley of races, Roman Catholic influences, pan-Slavism, Bosnia, Serbia, the Polish and the Czech and the Trentino questions; and he prophesies that they are one and all capable of becoming "points of crystallisation, not only for Austrian but also for European crises, in which German interests will be affected only in so far as the German empire enters into a solidly constructed union with Austria. . . . It would be unwise to regard the Triple Alliance as a secure foundation for all evil days." At the very outset of the alliance and again and again in subsequent years, Bismarck refused to give Austria German aid in the Balkans; and he was careful to avoid a breach with Russia. The Triple Alliance was possible only on these stipulations, so long as Bismarck was its leading spirit. The loose bond of his day was rarely dangerous. In the hands of his successors, when the alliance was inspired with a Nibelung-like conception of fidelity, it became deadly.

How Bismarck would have acted in the crisis that preceded the world war may be inferred from his behaviour during the crises of the eighties. In the year 1885, when the Three Emperors' League was shattered by differences about the Bulgarian question (Bismarck being allied with Austria, Italy, and Rumania, whilst the Russians wanted to drive out the Battenberg ruler and govern Bulgaria themselves), the Viennese suddenly demanded Germany's help in their Balkan schemes. Bismarck flatly refused: he would do nothing more than maintain the status quo; if the Austrians wished for any expansion of territory, that was their affair, and would be undertaken at their own risk! "If Russia should make any aggression, or commit any provocative act in defiance of her treaty obligations, we are prepared to support Austria with all our forces; but if a war with Russia should ensue because Austria invades Serbia without a previous understanding with us on the matter, we should not be prepared to represent this to Germany as the occasion for making war on Russia." A vision of July 1914!

These crises renew his uneasiness. He says to the minister for war: "If we don't get the money for the new military preparations, I shall steal it, and shall then sleep in prison more peacefully than I do now!"

Before this, early in 1881, Tsar Alexander II. had been assassinated. His son Alexander III. was less approachable, though he was not anti-German. Since, after the events of 1885, the new tsar would not renew the Three Emperors' League, Bismarck changed front once more, and in the beginning of 1887 made overtures for a Russian alliance. Eight years after coming to an understanding with Austria, he was ready to go back to his first love, Russia. Nevertheless, the Austrian alliance remained in being; its popularity was undiminished. The German desire for a union with the Austro-Germans was too strong and too natural an impulse to leave room for the consideration that only a small minority of the inhabitants of the southern empire were of German blood, that most of the civilians and most of the soldiers who lived and fought under the Austrian eagles were of other races, spoke other tongues, and were as little inclined to be friendly towards Germany as the French.

Meanwhile Count Paul Shuvaloff (younger brother of Count Peter) had become director of Russia's eastern policy. He informed Bismarck that if the tsar could have the Straits, Germany could send a Prussian governor to Paris. Bismarck was as keen to sign a treaty with Russia to-day, as Andrassy had been to sign one with Germany eight years earlier. Both were reinsurances, but for very different purposes. This new Russian alliance was to protect Germany against France.

His aim was purely defensive. He never wanted to weaken France's position as a great power. Far from it, for he contemplated the possibility that Gladstone would arrange an Anglo-Russian alliance. This would throw Germany into the arms of France, and he wanted to make sure of the support of either France or Russia in any event. "Even if France were to attack us, we should never contemplate the possibility of destroying a nation comprising forty million persons so gifted and self-reliant as the French. For a hundred years, the three great empires of the eastern half of Europe have been vainly trying to destroy the Polish nation — and this nation is incomparably less vigorous than the French. . . . But if France remains powerful, or becomes powerful once more after a brief convalescence, so that we shall always have to reckon with her as a formidable neighbour, then in the next war, should we prove victorious, we must treat her considerately, just as we did Austria after the war of 1866. If I sounded a different note in the Reichstag sometimes, this was only in order to keep the peace by scaring our would-be enemies. Should it prove impossble to avert war, then, after our first victory, we must offer France peace on easy terms. If, on the other hand, we should be defeated, we can hardly suppose that Russia would be best pleased at the prospect of having the confines of a victorious French republic advanced nearer to her own borders."

In May 1887, war with France seemed imminent. Bismarck seized the opportunity of urging Shuvaloff to come to terms, and now the old wizard sprung one of his surprises. He laid before the Russian his secret anti-Russian alliance entered into with Austria in the year 1879! The Russian negotiator is shown in black and white that his partner is always ready to protect himself against one ally by underhand traffic with another — and the disclosure, instead of spoiling Bismarck's game by outraging Mus-

covite morality, is favourable to his present plans. Alexander III.
is a younger and colder man than William I., whose word is his
bond. Shuvaloff buys Bismarck's authorisation for a Russian
advance towards the Bosphorus, and gets a free hand in Bulgaria, pledging in return Russia's neutrality in the event of an
attack on Germany by France.

Bismarck is well content, now that he can pouch a treaty of
the old kind, one in which he gets as much as he gives. The Russian, too, has every reason to be pleased. Germany pledged herself to maintain the status quo in the Balkans, i.e. in Russia's
favour and Austria's disfavour. Nor need Russia now fear that
Germany and Austria will conspire against her; should Austria
attack Russia, Germany is to be benevolently neutral. Livadia
is forgotten, and Russia can follow her own bent against Austria.
Who, in the critical moments when war begins, can say which
combatant is really the aggressor?

This ludicrous substratum of all European treaties of alliance,
the perpetual recurrence of flourishes about "unprovoked attacks" and "wars of conquest" and "defensive campaigns",
makes them ambiguous one and all; and at the same time their
secrecy robs them of moral force. The duplicity of the system
whereby Bismarck endeavoured to safeguard himself against Viennese wiles by St. Petersburg obligations, and against Muscovite
intrigues by Austrian fears, was no worse than that which un-
derlay all the secret treaties of Europe. Bismarck, however,
foresaw that reproach was possible, and defended himself as
follows:

"I believe, on the contrary, that the emperor of Austria wants
such an arrangement. Even if I should be mistaken in this supposition, . . . the effect of Austrian mistrust would be less
dangerous than a similar lack of confidence on the part of Tsar
Alexander, for our relationships with Austria are on too broad
a foundation to be overturned by the fugitive soupçons of a
suspicious sovereign. . . . Nor will it do us any harm if the Russian affair should leak out; indeed, I should not be sorry. Besides,
I don't think it would make the emperor of Austria uneasy. . . .

He will know that our only object is to set back the coming of the Franco-Russian alliance for three years more."

The foregoing lines were penned by an adept in the school of Machiavelli. His design was to put both his restless neighbours out of action, to curb their rivalry through their dread of a powerful third party. He wanted to keep his two "heraldic beasts" asunder. Almost immediately afterwards, when Prince Ferdinand of Saxe-Coburg-Gotha is chosen by the Sobranye to rule over Bulgaria, he finds it necessary to persuade his Russian ally that this is not a casus belli, is not an Austrian "attack" within the meaning of the treaty.—What if the cat should get out of the bag? All the better! Then Francis Joseph will see that Bismarck's suspicions of him are only for the term of three years. To the tsar, on the other hand, he says in a final, carefully prepared speech: "We should be showing scant respect for Russia's formidable armies did we fail to guard against the possible risks of pan-Slavism!"

Thus in the two folio pages of the Russian treaty, Bismarck deals with four dangers simultaneously. If he does not uproot them, he at least minimises them for a few years. Russia, given her head towards Byzantium, no longer threatens our eastern frontier; Austria is warned off adventures in the Balkans; France and Russia are kept apart; England is made uneasy about Russia, and is therefore led to seek the friendship of Germany. A splendid game of chess at the close of the epoch in which nations played chess with themselves as the pieces.

Bismarck's wish was to win over England. He spoke of this as his chief endeavour during the last decade of his official career. In the "Oriental Triple Alliance", which he brought into being, or at any rate did much to promote, he tried to effect a rapprochement between Britain and the Triple Alliance, for then Britain, Italy, and Austria would guarantee the status quo in the Mediterranean. As early as 1882, he came to realise that there was a very great difficulty in the way of entering into an alliance with England. "It is impossible to carry on confidential conversations with the English, because at any time the British ministers of State may blab to parliament. Furthermore, there are no guarantees for the steadfastness of such an alliance, seeing that in England it is not the throne which is responsible for these matters, but merely an ever-changing cabinet. It is very difficult to come to a trustworthy understanding with England, and to establish such an understanding on a firm footing, except in full publicity before the face of all Europe." The foregoing lines were written to Prince Frederick, whom Bismarck wished to convince of the disadvantages of democratic government. Obviously, publicity did not suit Bismarck's policy; and if, from time to time, in his foreign policy he had found it necessary to take parliament into his confidence, this confidence never went very far.

In his approaches to England during the eighties and earlier, he showed the sympathetic understanding which is common to statesmen and poets, and was careful to adopt the circumstantial and sedate tempo which characterises British tactics as it characterises those of the Vatican. Never was Bismarck more cautious than in this matter, for thirty years earlier he had written that he had a weakness for England, " but these people won't allow us to love them." In the autumn of 1879, while his struggle with the emperor about the Austrian alliance was still going on, he made some advances to London, though he soon dropped the matter, as if his enquiries had ceased to interest him. Anyhow, at this date Gladstone was in power, and therefore the circumstances were unfavourable.

When Lord Salisbury took office once more in 1885, Bismarck seized the opportunity of securing one or two footholds in Africa. He was able to settle the matter without a fleet, or at least without firing a shot. This was one of his " games with five balls "; but to give a detailed account of it would be superfluous, since Germany no longer has a colonial world policy. As statesman, Bismarck excelled himself in these negotiations, for he kept his young empire's impulse towards expansion in check by the anxiety he instilled about its position. Bismarck never dreamed of letting Germany try to rival England as a world empire, considering, as he did, that the British excelled the Germans as colonisers, and, above all, that the geographical position of England was far more favourable to a colonial power. For twenty years after the establishment of the empire, his foreign policy was guided by one fundamental idea: not, "More land", but "More safety!" His pride was continually overshadowed by his unceasing anxiety regarding the preservation of the new great power, despite its unfavourable situation. Whilst he encouraged France to found a great colonial empire (were it only to divert the attention of the French from thoughts of recovering Alsace), he thought it necessary to refuse the German imperialist pioneers the full support of the empire, or at any rate to give them only a cautious and modified support. We have seen that he had no inclination to annex white races of non-German stock. He was equally careful to refrain from the annexation of coloured races, thinking that this would bring more risk than profit to Germany. According to Bismarck, Germany's future did not lie upon the water.

Discussing the Emin Pasha question with an Africander, he said: "The risk is too great for me. Your map of Africa is a very fine one, but my map of Africa lies in Europe. There is Russia, on the other side is France, we are in the middle: that is my map of Africa." None the less, during the eighties, his personal authority in Europe was so great, that when Britain raised her first objection to the acquisition of southwest Africa by the Germans, he addressed the following proud words to his English colleague:

"If we really intended to found colonies, how could Lord Granville possibly dispute our right to do so at the very moment when the British government is assigning the same right to the colonial government in Cape Colony? Such naïve selfishness is an affront to our national sentiment, to which I wish Your Excellency to call Lord Granville's attention. . . . We shall be glad to know why we are to be denied the right of colonisation which England exercises to the widest possible extent. . . . Our confidence is shaken by the arrogant way in which theories and claims are put forward which are incompatible with the principle of the equality of independent powers."

When, however, the whole European situation, and especially the position of Germany, became gloomy towards the end of the year 1887, when Emperor William was ninety years of age and the crown prince was stricken with a mortal illness, Bismarck summarised the ideas contained in long conversations which his envoy and his son had been carrying on with the British. Writing to Lord Salisbury in the French tongue, he expounded the essentials of the German policy of alliances, and at the same time gave a hint to England that she would do well to join hands with Germany.

"With an army such as ours, consisting, as it does, of all classes of the population without distinction, . . . the wars of earlier centuries, which were the outcome of dynastic moods and whims or of monarchical ambition, have become impossible. . . . It follows that our military authority must be primarily defensive, and can only be set in action when the nation is convinced that the warding off of an attack is at stake. . . . The German empire . . . cannot leave unconsidered the problem of the coalitions which can be formed against it. Let us suppose that Austria had been conquered or weakened or had become hostile to us; in that case we should be isolated upon the European continent, faced by Russia and France, and by the prospect of a coalition between these two powers. . . . Austria, like Germany and contemporary England, belongs to the number of the satisfied, saturated, . . . and therefore peace-loving and peace-maintaining powers. Austria and England have straightforwardly recognised the status quo of the German empire, and have no interest in seeing that empire weakened. But France and Russia would seem to be a menace to us. . . .

"So long as we are uncertain as to whether we shall be left in the lurch by those powers whose interests are identical with our own, no German emperor will follow any other policy than that of defending the independence of the friendly powers which, like ourselves, are . . . satisfied with the existing political situation in Europe. We shall, therefore, avoid a war with Prussia, so long as such avoidance is compatible with our honour and our safety, and so long as nothing happens to question the independence of Austria-Hungary, whose continuance as a great power is a prime necessity for us. Our desire is that the friendly powers which have interests to protect in the East (interests which we do not share) shall, by joining forces, . . . become strong enough to compel the Russians to keep their swords sheathed — or else to offer effective resistance to Russia if circumstances should make a breach of the peace inevitable. So long as no German interest is at stake, we shall remain neutral; but there is no warrant for the assumption that any German emperor will ever lend Russia the support of German arms in order to help in the overthrow or in the weakening of powers on whose support we count."

Repeatedly, during these years, Bismarck offered Salisbury an alliance on such terms; the English premier, however, would not bind his hands. Germany's ultimate aim stood in the way. Salisbury was prepared to enter into an alliance directed against Russia, but not into an alliance directed against France. He therefore postponed a settlement of the question, and his reply to Herbert Bismarck was a mingling of the sour and the sweet:

"Unfortunately we no longer live in the days of the Pitts. Then the aristocracy was in power, and we could pursue an active policy, such as that which, after the congress of Vienna, made England the wealthiest and the most highly respected of the European powers. Now the democracy rules, and we have a party system thanks to which every British government is directly dependent upon the wind of popular favour. This generation can only be educated by events."

XVII

"I shall go on fighting as long as I have the power!" Thus did the chancellor, now seventy-two years of age, say threateningly to the Reichstag, which had set itself up against his will.

He had made peace with two of his enemies. First of all, he had by degrees come to terms with the Centre Party, withdrawing most of his measures against its members, and closing the campaign with a spirited warning in the Reichstag: "We will lay down our arms upon the floor of the arena, but we will not put them away." In the winter of 1879, Windthorst had once more made his appearance at Bismarck's parliamentary evenings, where he was heartily welcome. The new pope had written to the emperor and also to Bismarck. A few years later, he made the modern Luther a knight of the Order of Christ. The great badge bore a Latin inscription. Bismarck grinned as he read it. "Kladderadatsch" reported: "Puttkamer has gone to Rome in order to beg the Holy Father to use his influence on Bismarck in favour of the adoption of the new spelling."

Bismarck's reconciliation with the conservatives was an equally opportunist arrangement, and was casually connected with his reconciliation with the Centre Party. At the elections of the year 1877, there had been conservative gains and national liberal losses. Bismarck, therefore, favoured the separation of these two parties. He wanted to get Bennigsen, a comparatively docile politician, into the cabinet, in order to isolate Laskar, a man of a more refractory disposition. Bennigsen, however, realising that he was only to be made use of for Bismarck's purposes, was unwilling to imperil his position, and demanded that two other members of his party should be taken into the cabinet as well. Owing to this stipulation the plan came to nothing, and thereupon Bismarck promptly threw over Bennigsen, though he had just wanted to appoint him as a colleague: "I can't do anything with incompetent politicians like Bennigsen and Miquel, who are entirely dependent upon public opinion. They are no better than fourth-form boys!"

Bismarck's return to the political party of his youth was occasioned or accelerated by the protective tariff which he introduced in the year 1879, after carrying on a free-trade policy for fourteen years. To him, protection was only a means for increasing the power of the State. He considered that the empire would be strengthened by taking over the railways, and by relieving the burdens on property through indirect taxation. He was eager to introduce new taxes, and learned with regret that, owing to the payment of the French war indemnity, there was a surplus of thirty-nine millions. "It is better," he said, "for the government to be short of money, in order to introduce new taxes." The fact that these taxes pressed most hardly upon the fourth estate did not prevent him from taxing "the luxuries of the masses"; tobacco, beer, sugar, coffee, and petroleum. "Protect industry and agriculture": such was the slogan now heard for the first time throughout the German empire. Bismarck's reasons for the new tariff policy were characteristic:

"Free trade is an ideal worthy of well-meaning German enthusiasts; it may be attainable in some future day. As regards all such questions, I am guided by science to the same extent as in other matters where the behaviour of living organisms is involved. Medical science has not solved these riddles. . . . The same remark applies to the problems of the State. The abstract teachings of science leave me cold. I judge by the experience of daily life. . . . According to my way of feeling, now that we have made our tariff too low, . . . we are losing blood. . . . We must transfuse fresh blood into the German body."

He still says, "according to my way of feeling," just as he did twenty-five years ago. He pits experience against science, and jibes at intellectual considerations as "enthusiasm." The actual fact is that Bismarck would like to do away with the Reichstag's prerogative of controlling the budget. To-day, as before, he wants to raise as much money as possible for the empire by the taxation of income. A conservative programme!

Two years later, the electors gave their answer. More than a hundred liberals were returned and a hundred members of the Centre Party, both fractions being pledged to oppose the change in economic policy. There was a majority against the chancellor! "For Bismarck himself, for our people, and for the foreign world," wrote Gustav Freytag in a private letter at this time, "the elections are symptomatic. Their result shows that the dominion of one man, who has imposed his image and superscription upon the nation, is not unconditional, and that it is drawing to a close. . . . His arts have lost much of their effect. People have now gained a fairly precise understanding of the mixture of lion, wolf, and fox, which make up this dramatic figure. Late, and slowly, have the Germans come to realise that the man to whom, after the German fashion, they have ascribed all that is great and good, does not possess every quality proper to a man of honour and a good fellow. . . . It is time for him to retire, but he is so big and fat and shrewd."

Such are the auspices when, ten years after the establishment of the empire, and twenty years after the opening of the conflict, Bismarck's struggle against the nation is renewed. For each new legislative proposal, he has to build up a new majority. He is compelled to depend upon a mutable system of alliances, just as he does in his foreign policy. He fulminates his most effective curses against any kind of opposition; the Centre, the Alsatians, the Poles, the socialists — all enemies of the empire! Listen to him as he speaks from the tribune, a rejuvenated champion, to all seeming. In the year 1880, he says: "I have lived and loved, have fought likewise, and am no longer disinclined for a quiet life. The only thing which makes me stick to my post is the emperor's will, for I cannot bring myself to foresake my emperor in his extreme old age." A year later, when the elections have gone against him: "I shall die in the breach; maybe, if God wills, in this very spot, when I can no longer live. A blood horse runs till he drops. At one time I had thoughts of resigning, . . . I think it well to let you know that I have quite given up any idea of the kind. J'y suis, j'y reste! Nothing will get me out of the saddle but the emperor's will. I have been greatly helped in making up my mind to stick to my post by noticing who are those likely to be pleased by my retirement.   . . That is why I have resolved to go on serving the fatherland as long as any strength is left to me."

A year later still: "What is there to keep me to my post unless it be a sense of duty? There is not much pleasure about the job. In earlier days I liked the work, took it up eagerly and hopefully. Few of the hopes have been realised. I was in good health then; now, I am ailing. I was young then; now, I am old. What keeps me at my post? Do you think that I like standing here, like

Scherl, Berlin

BISMARCK IN 1889
From a photograph by J. Braatz, Berlin

a decoy in front of a rook-shooter's hut, pecked by the birds, and unable to retaliate against insult and mockery? . . . If the king would grant me leave to retire, I should with the utmost delight bid farewell to you, gentlemen; farewell for ever!"

Thus does he show his wrath and hatred. His words flow forth in fierce cascades. His speech is unadorned; he uses no emotional phraseology. He utters his long, armoured periods, eyes flashing as he looks angrily at his audience, and hurls invectives which take his opponents' breath away for a moment. Then he picks up his portfolio, turns his back on the assembly, and departs. They watch his broad figure, clad in blue uniform with yellow collar, as it vanishes through the door, and his enemies respect him even while they detest him. For his part, his contempt for his foes is ever on the increase.

Sometimes, he rhapsodises after his own fashion. Then his words sound like a prophet's exhortations, or like ironical renunciation. "I cannot deny," he says in the Reichstag, "that during the last twenty years I have been perpetually tormented by the analogy between our German history and the saga of the Teutonic deities. The springtime of the nations lasted but a few years after the great victory. . . . Then came that which I understand as Loki: the old hereditary enemy of Germany, partisan hatred, which finds its nutriment in dynastic and constitutional quarrels, in tribal differences, and in the contests of faction. This breathed the spirit of discord into our public life. . . . Loki, the partisan spirit, misleads Hodur so that he strikes a deadly blow against his own fatherland — this is what I shall indict before God and history if all the splendid work of our nation from 1866 to 1870 should fall into ruin. . . . In the days of our youth, there was a very different national impetus, a much more splendid conception of political life, than prevails among those of my own age who, during the experiences of the years 1847 and 1848, received a partisan imprint which they have never been able to wash off. When we have all died out, you will see how things will blossom in Germany!"

In the 1881 elections, the social democrats, too, had made

gains, in spite of the Anti-socialist Law. Under Puttkamer, the chief towns were once more declared to be in a state of siege; and in Leipzig the socialist leaders were imprisoned for publishing forbidden newspapers. Nevertheless, the promise of labour legislation had been fulfilled. The Workmen's Compensation Act, which opened the series of labour protection laws, and was described by Bamberger (a supporter of the government) as chimerical, was followed by the Insurance Act, and then, in 1888, by the Old Age and Disablement Pension Act. These were steps in the direction of the State socialism which Bismarck had outlined long before in his conversations with Lassalle.

The idea of labour protection laws conceived in a State socialist spirit did not originate with Bismarck. Napoleon III., "King" Stumm, and others, had anticipated him. But Bismarck was a pioneer as far as the German empire was concerned. "It is time for us to realise what parts of the socialist demands are reasonable and right, and to what extent these reasonable elements can be incorporated into the extant State system." These words were uttered as early as 1871, in a conversation with the minister for commerce. Ten years later, the chancellor said prophetically to Busch: "The State must take the matter in hand, since the State can most easily provide the requisite funds. It must provide them, not as alms, but in fulfilment of the workers' right to look to the State for help in matters where their own good will can achieve nothing more. Why should not the labour soldier receive a pension, just as much as the man who has been disabled or has grown old in the army of the civil service? This view will be generally accepted in course of time. Maybe our policy will break down for the nonce, but I am sure that State socialism will ultimately fight its way through. Every statesman who takes up these ideas will come to the front."

Thus clearly does Bismarck foresee the future when he is in the Platonist vein; but if he discloses his motives, they are nothing more than the old calculations, the old cipherings, which sound especially cruel when he is setting them forth as the foundations of his "practical Christianity." Take this for instance: "One who can look forward to an old-age pension is far more contented and much easier to manage. Contrast a man in private service with one who serves at the chancellery, or at court; the two latter must be far more accommodating and obedient than the former, for they have their pensions to think of. . . . A great price is not too much, if therewith we can make the disinherited satisfied with their lot. . . . Money thus spent is well invested; it is used to ward off a revolution, which . . . would cost a great deal more." This cynicism is for private consumption. Speaking from the tribune, he says: "Even the poorest is entitled to the sense of human dignity. . . . "

Because Bismarck completely misunderstands the significance of the socialist movement, he gains nothing by his State-socialist measures. Red votes multiply until they have to be counted by millions. Besides, in the interval between elections, and while the before-mentioned specimens of practical Christianity are taking their place in the statute book, the Anti-socialist Law is reenacted. In 1887, the government actually wishes to decree that all persons convicted under the law shall forfeit their civil rights. The Reichstag rejects this proposal of outlawry.

Amid such struggles at home and conflicts abroad, Emperor William reaches the age of ninety. The end seems so near, now, that during March 1887, when the birthday celebrations are in progress, every one is asking: "How much longer; and what will happen afterwards?" Then a whisper begins at court, and spreads. The heir apparent is ill. His voice was husky when he spoke at the birthday festival. Two months later, all the world knows that the aged emperor will be succeeded by a youthful one.

Bismarck's pulse quickens. He recognises that a turn of fate is imminent, a change more decisive than any there has been since the spring of 1861, when Frederick William died. Europe asks for news of the emperor's health every time he goes out for a drive; no one will venture to renew an alliance; the chancellor's web of policies is rent in sunder by suspicions, fears, and prejudices; Lord Salisbury wonders whether Prince William's partiality for Russia will make him an Anglophobe; the tsar is glad to lend ear to Cousin William while the latter breathes secret hostility to England. When Alexander visits Berlin towards the close of 1887, the whole position is uncertain. War looms near.

Bismarck gives the veteran monarch pointers for his conversation with the tsar. William is to explain that the next war will decide the issue between revolution and monarchy. If France should prove victorious, Germany will be brought nearer to the revolution. Is that what the tsar of all the Russias wants? Is it his aim, when entering into an alliance with France, to threaten the other rulers of eastern Europe? If the Austrian empire is broken up, a number of republics will take its place, and there will be republics in the Balkans as well. Russia can only lose by such changes. Besides, a sovereign should avoid making war if possible, were it only because the peoples nowadays regard their rulers as responsible for defeats — as happened in France after the war of 1870. Even in Germany, in the event of a defeat, the likelihood of the establishment of a republic would be increased; the French anarchists would join hands with the German socialists and the Russian revolutionists. Modern wars are not fought between cabinets; there is only one war now, that of the Red Flag against the forces of law and order!

The old man commits these sentences to memory day after day. Bismarck has drafted them to suit the mentality of Emperor William and Tsar Alexander. One night, William is alarmed by a dream. He sees the tsar, whom no one has come to meet, standing at the railway station. He tells this dream again and again to any one who will listen. At length, however, the two emperors are sitting peacefully together. They exchange pledges of friendship; so do their ministers, who have settled the terms of a treaty.

The shadows lengthen. He who owns property must go well armed. Now, when William I.'s career is drawing to a close, his liegeman thinks of the early days. The first thing he did for his king was to hold the shield and to strengthen it; this will be his last task likewise. Again as in the year 1862, he fights on behalf of the army estimates; again he dissolves parliament, and is in a stronger position after the elections. The new Reichstag votes soldiers and guns for seven years to come. Once again Bismarck mounts the tribune, and four weeks before the king's death he makes his last speech to the Reichstag. It is a very long one, so that he, now seventy-three years of age, has to take a moment's rest during the course of it — a distressing interlude. This discourse is not enriched with imagery; on the contrary, it is extremely practical. He makes a circumspect of the world situation such as he has often made before. A hidden warning breathes from the quiet words. We realise how tense is the condition of Europe; how Germany is ominously affected by the illness of the heir to the throne; how the dawn of a new epoch is at hand. The speech is inspired by the consciousness of all this, and his enemies hold their peace.

"In these days we must husband our strength," says Bismarck; "and it is in our power to be stronger than any other nation of equal numbers. . . . We are placed in the centre of Europe, are liable to attack on at least three fronts, . . . and are, moreover, exposed to the risk of coalitions to a greater extent than any other nation. . . . The pike in the European fishpond make it impossible for us to play the part of harmless carp, for they would fain fix their teeth in both our sides. . . . They constrain us to a unity which is repugnant to our German nature, and were it not for this pressure from without we should all fly apart. . . .

"Such a State as Austria does not disappear. But if we leave it in the lurch it will be estranged from us, and will be inclined to hold out the hand of friendship to one who, for his part, has become the adversary of an untrustworthy friend. In a word, if we want to maintain isolation, we must have a friend in whom we can trust. . . . As regards the numbers of their troops, these others can vie with us, but they cannot compete with us in the matter of quality. If you speak of bravery, there is no difference between civilised nations. The Russians and the French are just as valiant as the Germans. . . .

"No one would propose to use for offensive purposes the mighty machine into which we are developing the German army.

If I should appear before you to-day and should say to you (were the circumstances different from what they are): 'We are seriously threatened by France and Russia; it is obvious that we shall be attacked; according to my conviction as a diplomatist, and basing my opinion on the military reports, I believe it would be better for us to attack as a defensive measure; I think we should strike a blow at once, and I therefore ask you for a credit of a milliard or half a milliard' — if I were to talk to you like that, gentlemen, I do not know whether you would have sufficient confidence in me to grant my wishes. I hope not! But if you did, that would not suffice me. If we in Germany should wish to carry on a war with the full strength of our national forces, it must be . . . a people's war. . . . A war which is not initiated by the popular will may be carried on when the leading authorities of the country regard it as necessary and explain why it is needed, but it will not be from the first animated with impetus and fire. . . . Of course every soldier believes that he is a better man than the enemy. He would not be a particularly useful soldier unless he wanted war and believed in the coming of victory. . . . We believe just as firmly that we shall be victorious in a good cause as any foreign lieutenant in his garrison town can believe after drinking his third glass of champagne — and perhaps with better reason. . . .

"The threats of the foreign press . . . are incredibly stupid. . . . Every country is, in the long run, held accountable for the windows which its newspapers break. One day or another the bill will be sent in, taking the form of the other countries' ill-humour. We can be influenced by love and good feeling, too readily influenced, perhaps; but we certainly cannot be affected by threats! We Germans fear God, and are not afraid of anything else in the world, and it is because we fear God that we seek peace and ensue it."

When he has finished, the whole house applauds him for the first time in many years. Every one refers to the speech as a European event. The emperor is still well enough to read the report of what Bismarck has said. A little while before, when war seemed imminent, the veteran monarch had declared that he was too old to lead his armies, but he would certainly take his place at headquarters. He has just celebrated the eighty years' jubilee of his military career. When he goes to see a picture entitled *March of the Volunteers from Breslau in the year 1813,* and finds that the artist has depicted Blücher as riding in the van, William says: "The painter has made a mistake. I remember perfectly well how I rode back into Breslau in the company of my father and the tsar. But Blücher was not there. The figure of Blücher should be replaced by that of Tsar Alexander, to whom we were so greatly indebted!" Thus does living history speak.

He is less concerned about the approaching death of his son than about the fate of his country. He is uneasy about the training of his young grandson, and how the necessary steps for that training can be undertaken without mortifying the invalid. At Christmas in the year 1887, the old man writes his last letter to Bismarck. In this letter he encloses a document promoting Herbert Bismarck to ambassadorial rank. "I want you to have the pleasure of handing this to your son. I think the pleasure will be threefold: to yourself, to your son, and to me. . . . Your grateful William."

In the beginning of March he realises that the end is at hand. He summons the chancellor to his bedside, begs for a pledge of help to his grandson, and when this pledge is given, "the only answer was a slight pressure of the hand. Then his thoughts began to ramble. He fancied that Prince William was sitting at his bedside instead of me. Suddenly addressing me in the second person singular he said: 'Thou must always keep in touch with the Russian emperor; there is no need of a quarrel in that quarter.' After a long pause, it was plain that the slight delirium had passed. He dismissed me with the words: 'I can still see you'." Next morning, he died.

At noon, Bismarck made an official announcement of the death to the Reichstag. During his brief address, his utterance was repeatedly choked by tears. "I had requested His Majesty to content himself with signing his initials, but His Majesty replied that he was still strong enough to sign his name in full. That is why this historical document bears the last signature. . . . It would not become me, here and now, to give expression to my personal feelings. . . . There is no need for anything of the kind, for the feelings which animate me live in the heart of every German. It would be superfluous to utter them. . . . I am sure that his heroic bravery, his strict sense of honour, and, above all, his faithful and laborious fulfilment of his duties to the fatherland, . . . will be an indestructible heritage of our nation." At the close, the speaker covered his face.

We see how Bismarck fulfils his formal duty, and yet, even at this supreme moment, remains true to himself; how he is not ashamed to show his emotions, and yet does not make a parade of them; how, both for himself and his hearers, he is sedulous to avoid any outburst of grief; how, instead of talking about the empire, he presents William's last signature as symbolic; how, above all, he is careful to avoid saying a word too much, is careful not to describe the dead man as either great or victorious, as either prudent or wise, but simply and accurately describes William as courageous, proud, and diligent — these are indications of his own full maturity, the maturity of one who in such moments is content to display the self-reliance of a stricken heart.

The capital and the German people, Europe and the other continents of the world, were all represented at the funeral celebrations. When the procession was passing down Unter den Linden, there suddenly rang through the silence a call which, in three grotesque words, summed up this ruler's amazing career. From among the trees, a voice cried: "Here comes Lehmann!" It was as "Lehmann" that Prince William had fled to England forty years before, almost on the same day of the year, when the same lime trees were waving in the same cold March wind; when this same populace had risen in revolt, and when every one was shouting: "Down with the cartridge prince!" In those days, William, heir to the throne, had been in hiding on the Pfaueninsel, and his wife would not disclose the secret of the hiding place even to the Junker from Schönhausen. When William had got safely away, and the story of the false passport had become generally known, mocking rhymes about Lehmann were current in Berlin. Doubtless Bismarck had read them.

One wonders whether the call from among the lime trees reached his ears. What is he thinking about as he drives behind the hearse? Beside him sits Moltke, nearly ninety years of age, his legs wrapped in a fur rug; he is unfriendly to the chancellor. Roon is dead. Who else is there as a link with old times? No one; not a single officer, minister, or courtier of any note. Augusta is still alive, but the old lady has stayed at home. The wearers of uniform, in this funeral procession, are of the younger generation; especially the grandson, who strides alone as chief mourner behind the hearse. The new emperor lies a-dying in the palace. The links with the Prussia of old days have vanished.

Bismarck is the last of them.

BOOK FIVE: 1888–1898

THE OUTCAST

Why should I be harmonious?

I

"On the average my pulse beats fifteen times more frequently in a minute than it was wont to do under the previous government. . . . Who can tell what they are up to when my back is turned?" This avowal of a state of mind betwixt fear and fever, this più moto movement leading to the finale of the great symphony, shows forth the prevailing mood which dominated Bismarck during the hundred days he passed at the dying emperor's side.

He had had a whole year during which to adapt new means to the new circumstances; for, when the emperor's death was obviously approaching, Frederick became no more than an interlude in Bismarck's calculations, whereas Prince William was henceforward the main object. When Frederick came home to die, and Bismarck, for the first time in his official capacity, tendered his advice to the emperor, it was forty years to a day since, for the first time, he had acted as adviser to a king of Prussia. Then, in March 1848, as now, in March 1888, it was in the unostentatious Frederician palace of Potsdam that he exercised his function as guardian of the king. Is he thinking of days gone by as his carriage passes through the gates of the royal park?

In those times he had not driven in a State coach along the selfsame alley way. Augusta had received him secretly, in the servants' hall. She did not wish to be seen in personal conversation with the Junker from Pomerania, for in Berlin there was still shooting in the streets. Had the Junker acceded to her plan, the eighteen-year-old Frederick would probably have become king on the withdrawal of his uncle and his father. But in truth Bismarck forced Augusta to become queen, and, later, empress; with the result that she, who ruled his master, became his own bitterest enemy. William, after living to a great age, had at length ended his days, and his son Frederick, whose early rise to power had been prevented by the Junker's veto, was now, after waiting forty weary years, nothing more than a pitiful wight, gasping for breath, as he sat propped up in his chair.

When Bismarck had mounted the stairs, he found Victoria awaiting him. She had ruled her husband even when he was in health, and had now taken all the invalid's affairs into her hands (though not with the accompanying power she had dreamed of). In the present circumstances she was ready to come to terms with the mighty foe and servant against whom she had been fighting for so long. Soon, indeed, as widow, she would need his help against her other foe, her own son, the future emperor. Mephisto has to make use of all his arts of seduction in order to win over the two Victorias — for the queen of England has come to Potsdam, and is beguiled by the charm of the dreaded veteran. There is a spell over this palace, where every one steals about on felted soles lest he should disturb the sick monarch, or betray anything to the son and heir, who has already posted spies within the walls where death is waiting for his prey; where women would fain be rulers until the dreaded giant with the domed head and the grey-blue eyes beneath shaggy eyebrows shall come from Berlin, and, with stately phrases and humble demeanour, shall lay his irrevocable proposals at their feet.

There is a third Victoria, in connexion with whom all the warring elements in this imperial palace are brought to a head — the passions, the will-to-power, and the thirst for life, family feuds and arrogance, fighting incessantly one against the other. The " middle Victoria ", Frederick's wife, covets the Battenberg prince, the new aspirant to the throne of Bulgaria, as husband for the third Victoria, her daughter. But the hoary wizard cries: " Avaunt! " Is his net to be destroyed by such an old wives' scheme?

" Battenberg," Bismarck exclaims in a conversation with Busch, " is the man of all others whom the tsar detests. . . . The new empress has always been an Englishwoman at heart. Now, for her own ends, she is even more so, and would make a tool of Battenberg to further her schemes. He is the son of a certain Miss Haucke from Poland — not exactly a family to be recommended!" In a yet more intimate colloquy with his friend, Frau von Spitzemberg, he remarks: " The middle Vicky is the worst; she's a wild woman! When I look at her picture, I am filled with horror at the uncurbed sensuousness which glows in her eyes. She is in love with Battenberg and wants to have him near her, just as her mother kept his brother tied to her apron string!"

Here was a question for the chancellor to settle! The sick monarch, who is not opposed to the marriage, is satisfied for the moment to be warned of a possible change by addresses emanating from Bismarck's circle; ambition and enmity ebb with his life's tide, his soul yearns for peace. But Bismarck's irreconcilable heart still beats to the measure of the fighter. A year earlier, speaking of Frederick and Victoria, he had said: " They are preparing for treason. They have not a trace of German feeling, they have lost their footing in the heart of the people, they foment discord among the members of the family." To-day he pronounces the following judgment: " My old master was fully aware of his dependence. He used to say: ' Help me; you know very well that I am under petticoat government.' But this man is too proud to admit as much. In certain respects, he is as dependent and submissive as a dog; you'd hardly believe to what extent."

Bismarck's misanthropy became intensified as the years went by. It was as though his antipathy to his fellow mortals had become petrified, so that towards the end of his career the chancellor lost his penetrating understanding, his perspicacious vision; he no longer saw clearly; his coldness and mistrust grew; the old lion would seem to crouch in his lair, his eyes flashing cruelly, his great paw ready to maul any one who should venture to draw near; he stood perpetually on guard over the treasure of his homeland — the empire. During one of his rare visits, Keyserling, the friend of Bismarck's youth, asked: " What is going on in his innermost heart? Not a proud consciousness of things achieved, not the comfortable satisfaction of great deeds performed, not the relish of peace and quiet after labour. . . ."

Must not such a monstrous accumulation of misanthropy be felt by the man's colleagues, by the deputies; must not the whole nation be aware of the cold disdain its leader feels towards it? " He gives me the impression of a man who is not quite right in his mind," Hohenlohe observes. In the Reichstag, where, since 1887, he has had a compact majority composed of the conservatives and the national liberals (a majority by means of which he has been able to pass his labour legislation and his protective tariff), in the Reichstag itself the personal dislike of the old man is on the increase. " After such debates," he once said on coming home from the assembly, " I feel as if I had had a specially uproarious night out." Once more Bismarck's fellow Junkers are drawing together in their hopeful expectations of the young man who will soon be emperor. On a drawing-room sofa, Holstein has already come to an understanding with Windthorst as to their course of action in a threatening future.

Ere long Bismarck looks back on the vanished epoch as the " good old days." Now he extols his late master quite as often as he had criticised old William when alive. " The deceased emperor was a trusty comrade who stood by his associates. . . . He often took a wrong turn, but could in the end always be brought back into the right road." When the chancellor contemplates Victoria, he even comes to think more kindly of Augusta, saying of the latter: " She often made things difficult for me, but she never ceased to be a woman of distinction, animated by a lively sense of duty, such as the new empress completely lacks. . . . She would like to make a sacrifice to her progressive friends, for her husband has no will of his own. But in such situations, when everything goes awry, we cannot console ourselves by saying it is all right. . . . I shall hold fast to my position, and even if I were to be given my dismissal I should stick to my post, for I should not countersign it! . . . No more monarchs are being born now. But I have hopes of our young master, whose difficult youth has been a help to him."

Since Prince William felt that he was badly treated at home, he had of late years drawn nearer to Bismarck. In 1886, Frederick, writing to the chancellor about Prince William, had said that the latter " is inclined to form his judgments far too speedily, lacks maturity, and has a tendency towards overweening pride." Such criticisms from Frederick were calculated to make the recipient of the letter take a sympathetic view of the young man thus criticised. Bismarck naturally wanted to cure the prince of his " Potsdam obtuseness." Even before Frederick had fallen sick, Bismarck had had a premonition that the new monarch's reign would be a short one. To begin with, Bismarck and William were drawn together because they were inspired with the same feeling of hostility for the prince's parents.

Within a year, however, the self-will of William II. had become a cause of friction. Stöcker and Waldersee had persuaded him that the best way of combating socialism was by gentleness and benefactions. William proposed to inaugurate cavalry displays to provide funds in aid of the poor of Berlin. What enraged the chancellor was not so much activities of this sort, as the amateurishness with which the coming ruler attempted to solve in friendly fashion a social problem which the old warrior had been wont to attack with all the powers of the law and the sword. In reply to the chancellor's remonstrances, the prince said: " I would rather let myself be chopped into little pieces than do anything which would make matters difficult for you." Bismarck was repelled by these extravagant assurances. He was still more disturbed, when, soon afterwards, during the last month of the old emperor's lifetime, the prince sent to all the federated rulers a draft proposal, which he then wished to transmit, duly sealed, to the embassies, " in view of the not impossible eventuality of the speedy demise of the emperor and my father." In this document, William " warns his old uncles that it will be unwise for them to throw a stick between their dear young nephew's legs."

Bismarck's uneasiness increases. What a fever must burn in the veins of this young man who, while two of his predecessors are still in the land of the living, drafts proclamations and is prepared to send them to a dozen public offices! Besides, is the prince ignorant of the imperial constitution, that he proposes to treat the federated princes in this way as if he were their superior? In a holograph letter which, when printed, occupies eight pages — a letter which, as he says, greatly exceeds his powers with the pen — Bismarck now expounds to the heir the principles upon which the empire is founded, and ventures to ask William to burn the draft proposal. This touches the prince on the raw! His first words as emperor (though admittedly premature) were, then, unfit for circulation! And he has to bear this at the hands of a chancellor from whom he has already borne so much! The prince is already able to suggest to himself that he is making sacrifices when he selfishly revolts against his parents.

His answer is cool, and contains a threat: " Woe unto them when I shall be able to command!" It is true that the words are penned against other persons, but the cutting tone does not fail to strike the fine ear of the reader, and it gives him plenty of occasion for serious thought. He had good reason for saying to the heir to the throne, in his lengthy missive: " It seems to me that the strongest buttress of the monarchy is to be found in the fact that the monarch shall be determined, not merely to cooperate in the governmental affairs in the country in quiet moments, but also, at critical times, to be ready to fall sword in hand on the steps of the throne fighting for his rights, rather than show any weakness. Such a master will not leave any German soldier in the lurch." Was it chance, was it a profound knowledge of human character, or was it prophetic vision, which led Bismarck to write such an exhortation to this man thirty years before the day when William II., put to the test by fate, was to fail, owing to the essential weakness of his character?

Already in the days when he is crown prince, he begins, in Frederician fashion, to pepper official documents with his pencilled annotations. In some of them we discover dialogues between young William and Bismarck, and we note how the latter

BISMARCK IN 1890
From a photograph by Strumper and Company, Hamburg

confutes the prince's comments with counter-comments, all in the domain of high politics. For Bismarck's despatches to his foreign envoys become more and more expansive, more and more generalised. The prince is now able to study the transcripts of decrees and orders which give occasion for the utterance of maxims and for discourses on statecraft. We can look upon these documents of Bismarck's as upon the ripe wisdom of an imaginative writer, or upon a great painter's portrait of himself. These are, in very truth, Bismarck's portraits of himself. When the anti-Russian sentiment grows stronger in Germany, and when the army men are urging war, he writes to the envoy in Vienna:

" This indestructible realm of the Russian nation, made strong by its climate, by its steppes, and by the simplicity of its needs, . . . would, after its defeat, remain our mortal foe, and one thirsting for revenge — just as France is in the West. In this way, a situation of permanent tension would be created, and I do not propose to take upon myself the responsibility of bringing such a situation to pass. The ' destruction ' of a nationality has, during the whole century, proved impossible for the strongest of the great powers in relation to the much weaker Polish nationality. . . . We shall be wise to treat Russia as an elemental danger, against whose inroads we must build dikes."

When William reads this, his comment upon the remark about raising up a new and revengeful antagonist runs as follows: " No more than at present." Bismarck rejoins: " Much more, I assure you! " With regard to the thirst for revenge, William comments: "Eager for revenge, perhaps, but not in a position to take it." Bismarck: " But they would be very soon, just as France has now been for twelve years." With regard to the destruction of a nationality, William writes: " But their fighting forces can be destroyed." Bismarck: "They can be reestablished in five years; cf. France."

In this written dialogue, experience is arguing with impatience, a mature judgment is contraposed to an unripe one. The old man still hopes to educate the young one. Bismarck writes to William a lengthy letter concerning Germany's Russian policy, and utters a warning against marginal notes of such far-reaching significance. " Officials who have knowledge of Your Highness' marginal notes (myself not excepted) would, in the event of a change of government, find it difficult to maintain German policy on its previous peaceful footing. In so far as I understand Your Highness' marginal notes, I should have to speak in defiance of my own conviction; and for the policy of the German empire a reputation of duplicity would be even more dangerous than a fixed determination to make war."

Such are the weighty words which Bismarck chooses in order to warn the young man, and he is greatly astonished next day when the latter speaks of the " exaggerated significance " attached to his comments, and insists that his own inclinations are entirely peaceful. Is the young master, then, a man of whims merely? Does he not understand the psychological effect of such utterances? William adds that in future he will avoid making marginal notes, " in partial recognition of the force of your reasoning "; but he is still determined, he says, to make his views publicly known in one way or another. The elder William had never written anything so saucy. " Partial recognition " is new to Bismarck. Of course it is quite natural that young heirs should be ready to talk of the likelihood of wars; they do not know all the dangers involved; they are not kept awake o' nights by their anxieties. The prince, who is surrounded by bellicose generals, would be alarmed if he could read Bismarck's gloomy vaticinations uttered to the minister for war.

" If it should be God's will that we should be defeated in the next war, I regard it as unquestionable that our victorious opponent would use all possible means of preventing our recovery for a whole generation to come. . . . I do not believe that our enemies would be content with Alsace. They would demand territory lower down the Rhine as well. . . . We should not then have the help of Russia, Austria, and England, as we had in 1812, for these powers would have seen how strong a country united Germany is." At the same time he prophesies regarding Russia, declaring that that country is far more radical than most people believe. " A Russian revolution and the establishment of a Russian republic may come very soon. A great many people in Russia concentrate their hopes upon disaster in war, thinking that when this happens they will be able to get rid of the dynasty." His most urgent care flashes out in a short sentence written in the margin of a report: " Hitherto we have had need of England if peace were to be made possible."

Thus dark are the skies of Europe when Frederick dies. The emperor realises the situation. The day before his death, he sends for the chancellor, extends to him a hand reddened with fever, then takes the hand of the empress, places it in Bismarck's, and presses them together. Pathetic in his dumbness, he warns the two, and seems, dying, to extend his blessing over the rule of Bismarck, the rule which throughout life he had opposed.

Next day, the prince gains his end. William has become master.

II[1]

" Frederick, Your Majesty, would hardly have become Frederick the Great if, at the opening of his reign, there had been in charge of affairs a man of Bismarck's power and importance, and if he had kept this man in office." The words are uttered by Waldersee, and they make a strong impression upon the emperor, for to become known as " William the Great " was from the beginning of his reign the fixed and straightforward aspiration of the new ruler, now twenty-eight years of age. Waldersee, too, had an ambition. He wanted to become chancellor. At first, however, the new master was still afraid of the Titan, and wrapped him in a cloud of admiring words. Herbert Bismarck, now forty years old, seemed a possible successor.

This other Bismarck, a man of difficult character, ill-starred, was not only burdened with the cruel fate of being son of a man

[1] A more detailed account of Bismarck's dismissal will be found in the present writer's *William II.*, for this matter marks a more noteworthy epoch in the life of the emperor than in the life of the minister.

of genius, but was even more heavily handicapped by his father's determination that he should be the next chancellor. In the spirit of a man who walks in the footsteps of mighty forefathers, he might have gone out to meet the young ruler; he might, mutatis mutandis, have renewed the relationship of fidelity and trust which had united Otto von Bismarck with the present William's grandfather. But whereas William the First and Bismarck the First had found it comparatively easy to enter into the relationships of master and servant because the master was nearly twenty years older than the servant, in the case of William the Second and Bismarck the Second, the age relationships were reversed, the servant was much older than the master. Nature had removed the possibility of those sentiments which the elder Bismarck had described as resembling the feelings of a son who finds it comparatively easy to forgive the tantrums of a petulant father.

In the case of the new pair, gifts and defects, too, were less happily distributed. The first William, though he had not so bright an intelligence as the second, had more tact, better manners, and more reserve, so that by degrees he became willing enough to accept the guidance of the minister who was a man of genius. The second William, impelled by his neurotic temperament to embark upon actions which were beyond his capacity, was confronted by a second Bismarck, whose filial admiration, in conjunction with the effects of his upbringing and a secret conviction that he lacked creative energy, impelled towards the service of his father rather than towards the service of his fatherland. Whereas William had too much self-confidence and too little respect for his forefathers, Herbert lacked self-reliance and was burdened by an excess of veneration for his father, so that it had become impossible for him (when occasion called) to form and act upon opinions of his own. Besides, William had been brought up unlovingly, whereas affection had been lavished upon Herbert. He had had, indeed, to make the great sacrifice of his passion, and almost of his honour, but in other respects his father had always shown much tenderness, nay fondness, towards him.

The elder Bismarck's strong family feeling made him incline more and more with advancing years to work on behalf of his son's succession to his own post.

Herbert, who had become his father's sole confidant, and who had been taught statecraft by the greatest statesman of the day, would have had to be a man no less revolutionary than his father to be able to criticise that father. But with the knowledge and the skill of his father, he had also inherited the misanthropy upon which these were based, and in Herbert misanthropy became intensified to the pitch of sterility. "Where I despise, he hates," said the father. "It is an excellent sentiment, but it does not always retain its vigour as long as might be wished." Since there was wanting in him the foundation of the successes which had made the elder Bismarck an object of dread, people came to regard Herbert's cold and unconciliatory attitude as due to arrogance. In confidence it was said that all the ministers disliked him, and would only put up with him for his father's sake. As prince, William had been on friendly terms with Herbert, but now many voices were raised to depreciate, nay to calumniate, Herbert, so that the emperor's vacillating mind was influenced against him. The unfavourable impression was increased by suggestions that the Bismarcks would fain set up a dynasty of mayors of the palace, whereby the power and glory of the royal house would be imperilled. Since those who whispered such remarks into William's ready ear were persons who lived by flattery, such as neither of the Bismarcks was prone to utter, Herbert's activities as secretary of State tended to alienate the emperor from both son and father.

William was crafty, and at first did not allow his intentions to show. "There is a regular honeymoon of mutual admiration," said the Austrian envoy in his dispatches home. To begin with, Bismarck was completely duped, so that he declared that the emperor had "more courage and more independence of court influences" than his forefathers. When Bismarck sits up at Friedrichsruh until eleven at night to welcome William as guest, the young emperor thanks the chancellor for his consideration

(which, of course, did not involve any upsetting of Bismarck's
ordinary routine) ; and, for his host's sake, William does not get
up until nine in the morning. When William visits the East, he
does not take Bismarck as companion, being content to wire
greetings to the chancellor. Ere long, he complains to the grand
duke of Baden that the old fellow gives him lectures, speaks too
often of his experience. William must have said something even
stronger than this to the grand duke, who declares that the emperor retains the two Bismarcks in his service "for the time being."

When, in the difficult year 1889, the chancellor divides his
favours between Russia and Austria, following his old policy of
maintaining a balance, the emperor wants a more fixed policy,
desires that this complicated system should be replaced by a
" simpler " one. In general, William is anti-Russian and bellicose.
Bismarck is pro-Russian, were it only for the reason that next
year the treaty with Russia will expire, and everything must be
done to promote the renewals of this reinsurance upon which the
safety of the empire depends. When the tsar comes to Berlin as
a guest, assures the chancellor of his confidence, but treats his
cousin the emperor with cool civility, William invites himself to
a hunting party in Russia, and Alexander cannot say nay. Having bidden the tsar adieu, William invites the chancellor to get
into his carriage, intending to talk matters over with him at the
Foreign Office. On the drive, the emperor mentions his determination to visit the tsar. His announcement is received in silence, and
William, much annoyed, exclaims: " Have n't you a word of
praise for me? "

This remark, which betrays a complete misconception of the
dignity of his own position and also of Bismarck's character, discloses the nature of the young man's hankerings. The sage, who
guesses the tsar's dislike for such a temperament as William's,
who knows Alexander to be a fat and easy-going fellow, and who
is afraid that if the two emperors go a-hunting together the
main result will be to shatter a friendship which is none of the
strongest, advises against the proposed visit. We can easily understand that the young emperor is chilled. His vanity, his most

essential characteristic, is wounded. He puts down the chancellor
at the latter's house, gives a curt farewell, and abandons the
idea of the proposed talk.

This drive is the beginning of the breach. The scene resembles
the crisis between a pair of lovers when for the first time a kiss
is refused. Soon the hyenas gather round; it is easy to fan the
flames of the master's anger. Did not the old man malevolently
compel the emperor to tolerate sharp official reproaches of his
parents when, recently, Crown Prince Frederick's war diary had
been published without permission? Bismarck wanted to dispel
the legend of a liberal Hohenzollern (which the wording of this
diary tended to encourage), while he did not wish that in the
forthcoming elections the democrats should have a chance of ap-
pealing to the memory of the late emperor. Thereupon the " disgruntled Junkers " raised their heads once more, endeavouring to
break up the coalition, and therewith to make an end of Bismarck's power. The chancellor, as in the seventies, takes up the
cudgels for reasons of State, attacks the " Kreuzzeitung " in the
" Reichsanzeiger ", and fails to see what Lucius sees clearly
enough, that such tactics are more dangerous now than of yore,
" for the reason that Bismarck has nothing like the influence
with the young monarch that he had with the old one."

Besides, the German machine is creaking loudly as it works.
There is a miners' strike, and the emperor wants to treat it idealistically whereas the chancellor wants to fight it with blood and
iron. Once more misunderstanding the meaning and the coercive
force of the socialist movement, Bismarck puts himself in the
wrong before the tribunal of history. Just as he had turned to
account the attempt on Emperor William I.'s life, so, now, he
wants to turn this strike to account against the Reds, to use it
for electoral purposes. But the emperor, " unexpectedly, spurs
clinking ", turns up at the meeting of the cabinet, declares that
the mineowners are to blame, says that he has ordered them to
pay better wages, failing which he will withdraw his soldiers.
We see that the young man dreads the revolution, and wishes to
avert it by reforms; the old man wants the revolutionists to show

themselves, so that he can shoot them down. Still, to the outward
world, emperor and minister behave as if they were agreed. The
emperor's new-fangled notions, right in principle, though not
capable of application all in a moment or in such a way, have
been derived from some of his courtiers, who flatter him by assigning to him the role of the roi des gueux. His advisers are:
Hinzpeter, his tutor, whom, when he is conversing with Bismarck,
he cannot extol sufficiently, although at a later date in his own
memoirs he has little good to say of the man; Douglas, a specu-
lator in mining shares, a wealthy and amusing fellow, bursting
with figures, soon to be made a count; Von Heyden, painter, and
director of mining companies, who paints an elderly workman
from the eastern quarter of Berlin as a prophet, and is told about
the sufferings of the poor by his model.

Now, something happens which has never happened before in
Bismarck's life. He underestimates the strength of the foe and
overestimates the security of his own position. He, who has just
taken on a fight against a whole class, leaves a handful of courtiers to do exactly as they please. From May 1889 to January
1890, with only a brief interval, he lives at Friedrichsruh, and is
not even put on his guard by the emperor's repeated exhortations
that he should stay where he is and recover his health. An elderly
husband who has married a young wife may not always be able
to participate in the lady's amusements, but if he be a wise man
he will share in them as much as he can. Here, however, we see one
with a profound knowledge of mankind leaving his wife (as it
were) free to enjoy the company of young and vigorous admirers, without realising how readily they can seduce her. Self-
reliance and contempt for his fellows combine to strike Bismarck
with blindness.

Yet he has warnings enough. He has only to read his newspapers at Friedrichsruh. All the parties are against him. "A sort
of paralysis has overtaken public life," writes one newspaper.
"Everything is going awry," is "Germania's" heading to an
article. The "Kreuzzeitung" writes maliciously, while the liberal
journals are exultant, about the emperor's plans for social re-

form. The socialists, as always, have their knives into the chancellor. Yet he is surprised when the tsar asks him whether he intends to remain in office. When Bötticher warns him that his continued absence is dangerous, he rejoins indifferently: " In view of my record and my position, there is no risk that the emperor will dismiss me." He is like Danton, who answered every warning with the words: " They 'll never dare! "

Yet his critical faculties are awake, as always. He complains that the emperor does not lead a properly ordered life, " so that the ministers of State often have to snatch at odd moments in which to make the most important proposals, and cannot even then be sure of commanding the necessary attention." A communication made by William to the " Volkszeitung ", Bismarck ascribes to " hereditary predisposition to insanity "; and it is true that at this time the Russian envoy reports that there are gossipping enquiries whether the emperor is quite right in his head.

The emperor has put a pledge in the old man's hands, and Bismarck at the close of his career is presented with a dog as symbol of the conflict. " A hideous black cur, with gigantic head, watery eyes, a wizened chest, and no breed at all." The beast is a gift from the emperor, and lives now with the prince. Bismarck says: " This comes of being a king's servant: I have had to hand my beautiful Tyras over to the care of the gamekeeper in order to keep this cur. Of course I might have the brute poisoned, but he has such faithful eyes that I can't make up my mind to it." Bismarck, already on the edge of dismissal, leaves his master unwatched in the capital, and away there in the forest at Friedrichsruh has to tolerate the company of the dog this master has sent him. The companion of his days, " the dearest companion in the world ", no longer greets him in the morning as for years past. The gamekeeper has to keep Tyras chained up, lest he should break loose, run home, and slay the imperial interloper. When Bismarck walks or rides, he is accompanied by a strange and hideous creature. When he sits at the fireside, the beast lays a shapeless head upon his knee and wants to be petted. This is what comes of being a king's servant, he says ironically, and yet puts up with it.

We almost feel as if he must have prided himself upon his ir-replacability. In December, he said to his lady friend: " I find the emperor a most accommodating master. He has never yet ventured to act against me in any political matters. . . . If I were a younger man, and could be always near him, I should be able to twist him round my finger. . . . One may dissolve the Reichstag three times over, but in the end one must break the pitchers. Such questions as this of the social democracy cannot be solved without a baptism of blood; nor can the German prob-lem either. And since our young ruler is loath to use force, . . ." He does not complete the sentence, but has written enough to show how completely he misunderstands William.

III

At length, on January 23, 1890, Bismarck is summoned by telegram to Berlin. Next day there is to be a crown council to discuss the social problem. He travels on a Friday, which he avoids doing as a rule, is very tired when he reaches the capital, holds a meeting of the cabinet, and proposes that they shall wait and see what the emperor wants. Thereupon Bötticher rises. For ten years he has been Bismarck's confidant, and a family friend. Now, among all the ministers, he is the emperor's favourite. Bismarck has only become suspicious of him recently. Bötticher says it will be well for the cabinet to give directions, so that some-thing may be done. Only a little while before, Bötticher had assured the prince that the emperor had definite intentions to institute social reforms. He and Bismarck had been sitting at Friedrichsruh over their wine. Now Bötticher repeats the state-ment before his colleagues, and something unexpected happens. All the others agree with him.

A terrible moment, such as there has not been for twenty-five years. Bismarck is forsaken by all his followers, who, during his eight months' absence, have learned to follow another lead than his. Realising how he has neglected his opportunities, he wrathfully takes the ministers to task, complains that they have been doing their work badly, and then, in the expectation of a chorus of objections, talks of resigning. The answer is a general silence. The sitting comes to an end " amid a general feeling of tension." Bismarck goes to wait upon the emperor, whom he has not seen since their parting after the before-mentioned drive. " I want to repeal the present Anti-socialist Law, for I need stronger measures," says the old statesman, and the young emperor is alarmed. Again a crown council is held. The emperor announces his intention to have labour-protection laws passed. His dream is to avert the threatening revolt, to summon a congress, to address his people " in inspired language " on his birthday.

Lucius writes: " We sat there with growing astonishment, wondering who had blown these ideas into his mind." The emperor is already naming his advisers; they are the three men previously mentioned. Then Bötticher has to read the memorial aloud. Bismarck is the first who is asked to give an opinion. With assumed quietude, he advises postponement, says that if the emperor carries out his plan it will have a bad effect upon the elections, for the possessing classes will be annoyed, while the workers will be encouraged. The emperor makes a civil answer. He says that his main desire is that the Anti-socialist Law shall be rendered milder, and he adds that loyal advisers have urged this course upon him. Thereupon Bismarck growls out: " I cannot prove that Your Majesty's yielding policy will have disastrous consequences, but the experience of many years leads me to feel sure that it will. If we give ground now, we shall not subsequently be able to dissolve the Reichstag, and shall have to await more serious happenings. If the law remains unsettled, there will be a vacuum, and then collisions may ensue! "

The emperor, irritably: " Unless extreme necessity arises, I shall avert such catastrophes, instead of staining the first year of my reign with the blood of my subjects! "

Bismarck: " That would be the fault of the revolutionists; matters will not be settled without bloodshed. That would be a capitulation! It is my duty, in virtue of my experience of these matters, to advise against the course you propose. Since the days of my entry into the government, the royal power has been steadily increasing. . . . This voluntary retreat would be the first step in the direction of parliamentary government, which might be convenient for the moment but would prove dangerous in the end. If Your Majesty is unable to accept my advice, I do not know whether I can remain in office."

The emperor, aside to Bötticher: "That would put me in a quandary." This confidential utterance betrays that the emperor and Bötticher have entered into an intimacy against Bismarck.

Thereupon, all the others are asked to give their opinions. They feel that a breach is imminent; yet not one of them ventures openly to take the emperor's side. Here, when they have to choose in the midst of the duel, Bismarck's authority is still strong enough to ensure that, formally speaking, they shall take his view. But he sees that they are in a panic. Their countenances convince him that he no longer really influences them, though he may still outwardly control them.

Fortified by the news of this dispute, the conservative leaders, next day, carry out Bismarck's design by voting against the everlasting Anti-socialist Law, thus destroying before the elections the coalition by which he had been supported for three years, and depriving him of his majority. The same day, the emperor shakes his fist at the minister for war, saying: "You are no longer my ministers, but the ministers of Prince Bismarck! You all looked as if you had been whipped! He has planted his chair in front of my door!" At this same hour, Bismarck, a broken man, is lying on the sofa in a dressing gown. He says to the chief of the imperial chancellery: "The emperor is quite estranged from me, and listens to such fellows as Douglas. My colleagues have deserted me." Only his son Bill ventures to advise a prompt resignation, and says to a friend: "My father can no longer strike his old sledge-hammer blows."

It is true. Now begins a period of vacillation, which lasts till the end, seven weeks later. Hitherto, his iron will and pliable intel-

ligence have made such vacillations impossible. It seems to him
that everything depends upon the elections, which he simultaneously longs for and dreads. The day after the sitting already
described, he meets his astonished colleagues amiably and in a
conciliatory spirit. He says: " A monarch's caprices are like
changes in the weather. One puts up an umbrella, and gets wet all
the same. . . . I honour in the emperor the son of his forefathers, and my sovereign, though I deplore his attitude. We cannot tolerate the formation of a camarilla. . . . I think we shall
have to give way." He retires from the post of minister for commerce, and has one of the emperor's favourites appointed to the
vacant office; commissions Bötticher to draft the desired decrees;
announces that he will soon content himself with being minister
for foreign affairs, or with the imperial chancellorship. On the
emperor's birthday, there is a reconciliation, with protestations
of mutual esteem.

In February, however, during a month of tensions and intrigues, the old man's mood changes. He lets himself go once
more; tries to influence his colleagues against the social decrees;
and when Bötticher makes the courtier's objection that an adverse
decision will displease the emperor, Bismarck attacks him at the
sitting of the council, saying: " It seems to me akin to treason
when responsible ministers see their sovereign on the verge of
adopting a course dangerous to the State and do not openly
express their dissent. . . . If our only business were to carry
out the emperor's will, eight subordinates might just as well take
the places of the present ministers." In the end, however, the
decrees are issued; but when, at an audience, Bismarck wishes to
sound the emperor's mood, saying, " I am afraid that I am in
Your Majesty's way ", William no longer contradicts, but remains
silent. Even this is not a strong enough hint to Bismarck!
He fruitlessly endeavours to make his colleagues voice protests.
When he announces his intention of resigning some of his offices,
they, too, are silent. Subsequently Bismarck says to his son:
" They all drew a deep breath of relief at the thought of being
rid of me! "

Finding that his colleagues are thus delighted at the idea of seeing the last of him, Bismarck (as he himself tells us) defiantly makes up his mind to hold on to his offices after all. This enrages the emperor, who has already begun to hope, and now there ensues a contest to settle whether the emperor or the chancellor has the most staying power. Both of them feel that the position has become impossible, but each wishes to make the other responsible for the rupture. The emperor does not venture to dismiss Bismarck, and Bismarck will not go until he is kicked out. He would prefer to remain at his post. At any rate he will not make things easy for his master by a voluntary resignation. Thus, betwixt staying and going, they come to hate one another, like husband and wife in an uneasy marriage, when one party longs for a separation and the other dreads it, while neither dares to take a decisive step.

Bismarck is not in search of either fine gestures or aggrandisement. Stubborn as usual, what he wants is a fight. Since, this time, victory is out of the question, all he hopes to secure is the moral defeat of his adversary. Filled with hate and jealousy, he insists upon the utmost tittle of his rights; is in a rage because the under-secretary has issued the invitations to the council of State, instead of laying them before him for signature; watches the crooked paths along which his enemies are walking; scents intrigues where they do not exist; regards Victoria as the source of Hinzpeter's inspiration. "Hinzpeter is the revolver which Victoria, a much abler person, loads, and then uses as a weapon to influence the emperor." At the same time he humiliates himself in unexampled fashion. He goes to visit Victoria, complains to her, saying that he is no longer suited to the times; waits vainly for her to contradict him, and, when she asks what she can do for him, rejoins: "I want nothing more than a little sympathy." If this utterance were all that had come down to us out of the history of these days, we should recognise in it the dread of an old man from whose mouth the bread of life is being snatched.

Yet, at times even now, the veteran realist is able steadily to contemplate the whole. During these February days he has his

Pension Bill drafted. He takes the opportunity of telling all the various envoys home truths, knowing that they will incorporate these in their reports, and will ascribe the trouble to the court and to the emperor — though he is still trying to regain William's confidence. " In the end," Bismarck says to the Saxon envoy, " the emperor asks some casual officer of Hussars how the social problem is to be solved, and then wants to make me accept this fellow's opinion. . . . He has an itch for bodily and mental hurrah-shouting, but is not popular among the possessing classes, which have been estranged by his espousing the cause of the working classes. I think the day will soon come when even the army will no longer be trustworthy, and then Germany's fate will be sealed." Thus during these weeks of vacillation does his mind flicker between the great and the small.

The elections decide the issue. While the garrison, called out by the war lord, is being marshalled with much noise on the Tempelhofer Plain, the workers' battalions are silently marching to the electoral urns. To-day they are taking revenge for a decade of arbitrary repression. Liebknecht's recent prophecy comes true: " What have you gained after eleven years? . . . At the Paris Congress every one recognised the German social democracy as the strongest and the best organised in the world. You wanted to strangle us, and you have strengthened us. . . . What would Germany be without its workers? . . . A new idea has come into the world, a new revolution. . . . If you run counter to the spirit of the time, a catastrophe is inevitable! "

To-day the Social Democratic Party has trebled its numbers, and the Red votes have increased from one and a half millions to seven millions. The total majority of votes against Bismarck is four and a half millions.

The chancellor may have good reason for his belief that the emperor's muddle-headed decrees have contributed to this electoral reverse; none the less, he is certainly wrong in his contention that but for them the results would have been the same as three years earlier. Still his hopes rise. He foresees a renewal of the struggle; his weakness passes off; he girds up his loins, for in his view the State is in danger; he furbishes up his old weapons; a strengthening of the Anti-Socialist Law and high army estimates will save the situation. " If the worst happens," he says to the emperor, " we must summon the federated princes to Berlin, and restrict the suffrage. The masses, excited by strikes and by the issue of the elections, would not take this quietly. Perhaps there would be revolts. That would be the moment in which we could best fight matters out with the social democracy. . . . Success is still possible. I myself have sufficient strength and credit left. Later it will be impossible. No surrender! "

Thus speaks the old warrior. Just as thirty years before, so now, he wants to hew down the spirit of the time. The younger man, who no more than Bismarck is a friend of the people, but who is " loath to use force ", rejoins: " You are giving advice which a young ruler cannot possibly accept! "

Bismarck: " We and they will inevitably come to blows, so the sooner the better! You will never be able to kill social democracy by a policy of reform; some day or other you will be compelled to kill it with bullets."

Thus does Bismarck push matters to an extremity. So secure does he feel his position to be, that he once more tenders his resignation, thus making things easier for the emperor. But William is dreaming of the additional eighty thousand soldiers whom the chancellor has promised to win for him from the Reichstag. He therefore grips Bismarck's hand, and theatrically repeats the chancellor's words: " No surrender! "

Bismarck is flushed by this victory when he goes to the sitting of the council. He says: " The emperor is ready to fight, and I can therefore remain at his side! " All his hearers look at him in anxious silence. For his part, exultant, he grips the reins more tightly, and is determined to keep his colleagues away from the emperor. He reminds them of a cabinet order of old date, which forbids the ministers who are heads of departments to enter into direct communication with the king. This reminder comes too late. Long since, they have put their heads together: the ministers, the courtiers, the army chiefs, the conservative leaders. One and

Photographische Gesellschaft, Berlin

BISMARCK IN 1890.

From a photograph by Pilartz, Kissingen

all they assure the emperor that Bismarck is responsible for the reverse at the polls. Without a moment's hesitation, William repudiates his pledge of no surrender, and, at a public banquet, utters the threat: " I shall crush those who hinder me in my work! " This was the threat written by the prince in his youthful letter to Bismarck. Bötticher's star is in the ascendant, and when Bismarck complains of Bötticher to the emperor, the same evening the emperor bestows upon Bötticher the order of the Black Eagle, the same distinction which Bismarck had received many years before, for his success in the Schleswig-Holstein affair. Now, when the chancellor hears the news of Bötticher's advancement, he is content to say, quoting Schiller's *Wallenstein's Tod:* " You've got your way, Octavio!"

His main desire, now, is to regain a majority in the Reichstag. The ancient rock of the royal power seems to be quaking beneath his feet, and he is looking round for a new and firmer standing ground.

IV

To win a majority in the Reichstag, to placate the emperor, and with the aid of the illusory power of this long-despised parliament, seems to him the last expedient. With a majority, he will be able to give the emperor eighty thousand soldiers, and he is right in believing that no one else can do this. Did not his hostile fellow Junkers wish to betray him with the Centre? Were there not intrigues afoot with Windthorst, months before the elections, in order to undermine his position? What if he were to forestall them? Arise out of the underworld, enemy and conspirator! Jews and Jesuits are of the same kidney; a chat with Bleichröder; a hint to Windthorst. Let us sit down together and talk business as in the old days.

There sits little Windthorst. For the first time in ten years he can formulate his demands again. He had done so once before, but at that time the chancellor thought the price too high. To-day, Bismarck, in the utmost need, will certainly come to

terms. Windthorst asks for the repeal of the worst parts of the
Anti-Jesuit Law, and that the teaching of Christianity shall be
introduced into the public elementary schools. Matters are discussed for a long time. Again and again, Bismarck gives signs of
fatigue, talks of failing health. Windthorst knows better than
any one else that, though Bismarck has misused the phrase for
thirty years, it may now at any moment become true. The Catholic is alarmed at the rising of the Red tide. He thinks that none
but the old wizard can check the advancing flood. Hence an ironical situation, in which Windthorst implores Bismarck to remain in
office! When, for a decade or more, each has been wishing for the
other's death, or at least for the other's retirement, now, when
Bismarck's retirement is imminent, Windthorst begs him to remain
in the saddle. Matters are still left unsettled when Windthorst
leaves, but that evening he says to a friend: " I have just come
away from a great man's political deathbed."

The great man wants to go on living. He now summons the
leader of the conservatives, to see what that party will demand.
But the Junkers get together, the agrarians and the barons.
Within a few hours they have learned of Bismarck's latests plans.
Once more they close their ranks against this evil offshoot of their
class, and decline to do with and under him that which they have
thought to do without him and against him. They bluntly refuse
to come to the chancellor, and a day later publicly announce their
refusal to Windthorst, so that the emperor may learn officially
what is the only condition on which the pillars of the throne will
support him. At the same time, Count Limburg-Stirum goes to
Bötticher, and places himself at the latter's disposal in order to
bring the party and the government into touch. He adds: " It is
no longer possible to negotiate with Prince Bismarck."

The veteran has now to face the gorgon's head. Those whom
he has despised are setting themselves up against him. The members of his own class, instead of rallying round him as bodyguard,
are, metaphorically speaking, his slayers. While still in high office,
the dictator is shamefully defeated by the members of his own
order. This is a dagger-thrust in his heart. When all are abandon-

ing Bismarck, the only group to stand by him is his old enemy, the Centre Party. Germany is taking vengeance on him for his dictatorship, is paying him out for his greatness.

Thus do resolute hands on one side and the other simultaneously lop off the branches of the giant oak. There is no one, now, to shoot off the withered tree top in order to deceive the harsh forester!

This forester, the young emperor, has an easy task to perform. For days he has been steeling his courage by reading the articles in all the newspapers, and by interviews with ministers and courtiers. In the end, he has given his resolution an added impetus by persuading himself that he is passionately enraged with the Centre Party, and especially with the leader of that party. At length he ventures on the decisive step, and sends to inform the chancellor of an intended visit. As chance would have it, the missive is not opened that evening, and next morning old Bismarck, called before nine o'clock, has to meet his master at an untimely moment and without warning. William realises that his great hour has come. He remains standing throughout the conversation, so that Bismarck, who is always tired in the early morning, cannot sit down either. After a few preliminary words, the emperor asks him whether he has not rebuffed Windthorst. In actual fact, by the emperor's orders the chancellery has for weeks past been closely watched by the police, and he knows perfectly well who has visited the chancellor. Then the emperor says that the chancellor should consult him before interviewing important people like Windthorst.

Thereupon Bismarck's anger bursts forth. He fiercely explains the nature of a prime minister's duties, the limitations of the king's prerogatives, the unseemliness of such a control as the emperor suggests, a control to which he, Bismarck, cannot submit.

" Not even if your sovereign should command you? "

" Not even then, Your Majesty." Never has Bismarck, who had " seen three kings naked ", heard this word " command " from the lips of any of his masters — though in official decrees it was still used in accordance with ancient custom. As a young envoy, in the

Schönhausen days, Bismarck had told the first king he had served that he must be " requested ", not " ordered ", to go to Vienna. Even the angriest of the many angry letters which, during twenty-six years, William I. wrote to his minister, shows a noteworthy restraint of tone. That was the great, though unwritten, condition on which alone a man born to command would consent to serve. Bismarck's whole career would have been impossible if, beneath all the flourishes of devotion, there had been a relationship between him and his king differing from that customary between two men of honour and of equal rank. Now, in face of this strident question, the whole structure collapsed, and there was only one nobleman facing another. The tensions of the formidable moment robbed William of his carefully prepared courage, and they seem to have deprived Bismarck of his self-possession for several minutes. While the emperor, muttering excuses, said that of course he had really been thinking of wishes and not of commands, that surely the chancellor could not desire to introduce such confusion into the mind of the people, Bismarck angrily exclaimed: " That's just it! Such confusion prevails throughout the country that no one can be certain any longer what the emperor is aiming at with his policy ! "

The young emperor, alarmed, and not accustomed to a hand-to-hand fight of this character, is for the time being more tranquil than the old statesman. He speaks of reducing the demand for an increase in the army, so that it may be possible to come to terms with the new Reichstag, hoping that this proposal to retreat will give the old warrior a fresh occasion for expressing anger and for tendering his resignation. But Bismarck has now recovered his composure, sees that a trap has been set for him, and once more declares that he would be willing to resign if the emperor should wish it. Thus each tries to throw all the onus on the other. Beneath the surface of the animated dialogue, the storms of this last struggle for power are raging, almost silently. The emperor begins at the other end:

" I have no longer any oral reports from my ministers. I am told you have forbidden them to report to me without your consent, basing these instructions upon obsolete and forgotten ordinances."

Bismarck, growing ever calmer, explains that he has acted on the cabinet order of the year 1852, that the king, after matters have been discussed between himself and the premier, is always entitled to decide against the latter, and in favour of the head of department. This ordinance, says Bismarck, is indispensable.

Is every access to power then barred? The emperor attacks from a third side. Now he approaches the old man in the tone of a crown prince, saying he wants to be more fully informed about what is going on, that the chancellor should consult him before important decisions. Does the emperor know so little of the man with whom he is dealing? Bismarck bluntly refuses to do anything of the kind. Since the constitution is on his side, he appeals to the constitution. He speaks of his relationships with William I., and says laconically: " By the time I come to Your Majesty, my decisions must already have been taken."

A rocky coast, and no haven! He holds power in his strong hands, and will not yield a jot! You will remain a shadow prince as long as he rules!

The old man is not satisfied with rejecting the demands of his unruly master. Now he wishes to mortify the emperor, to take vengeance for the affronts of recent days, to plant an arrow in his enemy's heart! There is a portfolio on the table. He need merely open it, and it will play the part of Pandora's box. Irrelevantly, he turns the conversation to the matter of the proposed visit to the tsar, takes a paper out of the portfolio, and, glancing down at it, says:

" There are good reasons against such a journey. A report has recently come to hand from London. The ambassador writes concerning some very unfavourable remarks about Your Majesty which the tsar is said to have made in private." With the slow gesture of an accomplished actor, he holds up the paper. The emperor bites his lips. Shall he show the white feather? " Please read it to me! "

Mephistopheles feigns alarm: " Impossible! I really could not venture to do that." Temptingly he holds the document in his hands. The emperor trembles; he must not play the weakling! " Give it to me! " He snatches the paper from Bismarck's hand, reads it, turns red and pale by turns. Then he makes as if to leave without a word. Among the tsar's reported utterances concerning himself, he has read: " Il est fou. C'est un garçon mal élevé! " He feels as if he had been whipped, and by Bismarck even more than by the tsar. First he has been treated like a schoolboy, and then insulted. After such an affront, can he possibly offer Bismarck his hand? He does so perfunctorily, when he has already turned to depart after taking his helmet into his right hand. Quickly downstairs, out of this house, into his carriage, back to his friends! The heavy tread of the old man sounds behind him, as Bismarck makes his way to the house door and bows farewell to the emperor.

Bismarck's conduct at this interview was unprecedented. The rebel who fifty years earlier had maliciously mocked at nobles and princes has risen to the surface in him once more. To-day he has chastised the king. So shrewdly has he gone to work, that he has expressed his own opinion through the mouth of a third person, and has kept back even that judgment, the judgment of the tsar, until William extorts it from him. He could not possibly refuse to give up the paper when the emperor snatched it from him! Why was William so foolish as to snatch it when he had been warned? " A man may have fair hair and blue eyes and yet be as false as a Carthaginian! "

V

Next day, two old men in a dimly lighted room are arranging papers. One of them takes envelopes out of boxes and portfolios, the other reads superscriptions and arranges the envelopes in piles. The two are Bismarck and Busch. " I want to write my memoirs, and you shall help me. I am going to resign. As you see I am already packing up. I want to send my papers away at once, for if they stay here much longer, an embargo will be put on them. . . . It is only a matter of three days or so, three weeks perhaps, but I am certainly going. The position has become impossible. . . . The only question is how I can get my papers away safely. Perhaps they could be sent to your house; but how?"

"I could take them away in small parcels, Your Highness, and hand them over to Hehn."

"Who is Hehn?"

"Thoroughly trustworthy."

"Or I might send them to Schönhausen, and you could fetch them from there. Get the most important ones copied, and keep the copies till further notice. . . . Here are my letters to Emperor William. Here is the letter of introduction Frederick William gave me when I went to Vienna. How old are you, by the way?"

"Sixty-nine."

"Oh, well, when I am eighty, I shall still be able to enjoy myself in the country."

Two days later, Busch brings the copies. "Take them back with you," says Bismarck. "No, better not after all. What if they watch you coming and going with a big envelope? Look here, this will be the best way." They dispose of the papers in a box among some maps, where they are likely to remain unnoticed.

Thus does Bismarck quit the house from which for twenty-eight years he has ruled the country, the house from which he has created an empire. He leaves it like a conspirator hemmed in by enemies. Before he goes, he finds a secure hiding place for his last treasure, the papers out of which, in his exile, he will make missiles to hurl against his enemies. In the office of which he has been the chief for so long, there is not one person whom he can trust, not one to whom he dares hand over his property for safe-keeping! For the first time after decades, the thought of Schönhausen crops up in his mind — as a hiding place which will be safe from spies, since even Friedrichsruh cannot be depended upon. That is the use to which he can put his old home. He summons a journalist, a man who has been able to wring information from him occasionally (because Busch was influential enough to do Bismarck harm). The two old men pass these invaluable envelopes to and fro. Busch fancies they will be useful to him when he comes to write his own memoirs; the other, maybe, remembers the fate of Arnim, imprisoned (at Bismarck's instigation) for the refusal to give up State papers.

Into this region of furtive handclasps, a resplendent general, the head of the military cabinet, now makes his way, to ask a plain question. He says that he is commissioned by the emperor to enquire how soon the cabinet order issued by the late lamented king Frederick William IV. in the year 1852 is to be rescinded. Bismarck bluntly replies that the order is to remain in force. In this way he wants to compel the emperor to dismiss him.

Next morning, Count Paul Shuvaloff calls. He has come hot-foot from St. Petersburg, as the tsar's plenipotentiary. He is empowered to renew the Russian treaty, and for six years instead of for only three. During the whole of the last year, Bismarck's policy has been directed towards this end. The extant treaty was to expire in June, the safety of the empire depended upon reinsurance in the East, the young emperor had been won over to the renewal of the treaty. The tsar, who fully understood all that was involved, had written upon a State document a marginal note to the effect that " for Bismarck our entente constitutes a sort of guarantee that there is no written understanding between us and France, and that is extremely important for Germany." Now Bismarck can only shrug his shoulders, and tell the alarmed Russian plenipotentiary that the rumours of his impending retirement are true. Shuvaloff, he says, must settle matters with the successor to the chancellorship, whoever that may be. Here we see the first and the most serious of the results of Bismarck's fall. There is an interchange of telegrams with St. Petersburg; Russia becomes uneasy about German policy, now that the trusty pilot is about to be dismissed; the tsar refuses to renew the treaty.

That same morning, immediately after Shuvaloff had left the chancellery, General Hahnke returned with a categorical demand from the emperor that the old cabinet order should be rescinded. " Otherwise," — the general found it difficult to ,control his voice — " His Majesty expects you instantly to tender your resignation, and wishes Your Highness to ,attend personally at the palace this afternoon at two o'clock in order to take leave."

" Il mondo casca ! " were the words uttered by the State secretary in the Vatican after Königgrätz. Bismarck's thoughts had not run along those lines. He will tell us later what he thought about the matter. Now he answers quietly: " I am not well enough to leave the house. I will write." Hahnke's imagination presents Bismarck to him as a revolutionist in a red cloud. He departs. Immediately afterwards, the prince is handed an unsealed memorandum from the emperor, which runs as follows: " Reports " (they were those of one of the German consuls in Russia) " show clearly that the Russians are making strategical moves preparatory to war against us. I greatly deplore that I have been kept so ill-informed about this matter. You ought long ere this to have drawn my attention to the terrible menace in that quarter ! It is high time to warn the Austrians and to take defensive measures. . . . W."

In point of fact, the accusation was false. There was no such danger. The emperor's note was an act of personal vengeance for the deadly humiliation inflicted upon William by Bismarck in the matter of that report of the tsar's utterance received from the London embassy. Nothing could suit Bismarck better, at this juncture, than the insulting letter sent to him open and without superscription. His first step is to write repudiating the " charge of treason." The emperor refuses to accept the chancellor's reply, and sends it back without comment. Bismarck, however, is now in a position to explain his fall as the outcome of motives of world policy — a field in which no party has hitherto opposed him. That afternoon he describes to the cabinet how the dispute had taken rise, and closes his speech with the great epilogue:

" Notwithstanding the confidence I reposed in the Triple Alliance, I had never ceased to recognise the possibility that this might fail us some day, because in Italy the monarchy is not strong enough, and because the relationships between Italy and Austria are threatened by the irredentists. . . . It has, therefore, always been my endeavour to avoid breaking down the bridge between ourselves and Russia. . . . Since I have confidence in the tsar's friendly intentions, I cannot carry out His Majesty's commands in these respects. . . . As far as labour-protection laws are concerned, these are not for me a cabinet question. If I am no longer to have the leadership of foreign affairs, I must take my departure, and I know that this will accord with the emperor's wishes." He adds that his health and his powers of work are unimpaired, and says that the only reason for his retirement is the will of a king who wants to take the reins of government into his own hands.

He pauses once more. Will no one realise what it means to lose Bismarck as the chief helmsman of foreign affairs? Will they not unanimously declare their intention to resign, and thus exercise pressure on the emperor? At least in this way they might have warned their young master, might have played a worthy part on the stage of history; but there came nothing more than a few hesitating phrases. Only one of them, Maybach, uttered a memorable word: " The chancellor's retirement will be a national calamity; a disaster for Europe as well as for Germany. We must prevent his retirement; we must all go with him; I, at any rate, shall do so." For a moment the discussion seems to become more cordial, and the sitting is broken off amid protests against Bismarck's retirement. In the evening, however, his colleagues meet once more, and they " renounce the idea of a general resignation, which conflicts with Prussian traditions."

After the sitting, Bismarck orders his horse and goes out riding, though at this time of his life and in this season of the year it has not been his custom to do anything of the kind. He does it now in order to show the emperor how much truth there is in the message sent through Hahnke, " I am not well enough "; and perhaps, also because he wishes to ascertain the mood of the Berlinese. There is no public demonstration in his favour! When the chancellor gets home, he finds that Jupiter has sent a second messenger during his absence. Lucanus, the chief of the civil cabinet, returns in the evening, his brow furrowed with anxiety. His business is to enquire, by his Majesty's orders, why the tender of resignation has not yet been sent in. Does the old man thereupon thump the table angrily with his fist? Not at all. He answers politely: " The emperor can dismiss me whenever he pleases. . . . I am perfectly ready to countersign an order of dismissal. But I do not propose to free the emperor from responsibility for my retirement; on the contrary, I wish the public to understand clearly how it comes about. After twenty-eight years of official life, years which have not been without influence for Prussia and for the empire, I need time in which to justify myself before the tribunal of history." In the brief conversation which follows, he is on the verge of losing his equanimity. Then he dictates his tender of resignation, touches it up next morning, and sends it to the palace. In this document, he describes the leading features of the conflict, and concludes with the masterly periods:

" In view of my devotion to the service of the royal house and to Your Majesty, and in view of my many years' habituation to circumstances which I have hitherto regarded as permanent, it is extremely painful to me to quit the customary relationships to Your Majesty and to the general political life of the empire and of Prussia. However, after conscientious deliberation concerning Your Majesty's intentions, which I must be prepared to carry out if I am to remain in the service, I cannot do otherwise than humbly request Your Majesty to be gracious enough to dismiss me from the office of imperial chancellor, from that of minister president of Prussia, and from that of Prussian minister for foreign affairs, with the legally ordained pension. In view of the impressions of the last few weeks, . . . I am entitled respectfully to assume that this tender of resignation accords with Your Majesty's wishes, and that I can therefore confidently reckon upon Your Majesty's gracious approval. I should long since have tendered my resignation to Your Majesty had I not believed that Your Majesty wished to utilize the experience and the capacity of a faithful servant of Your Majesty's forefathers. Now that I

am sure that Your Majesty has no more use for these, I can
retire from political life without fearing that my determination
to do so will be condemned by public opinion as untimely. Von
Bismarck."

Despite the chancellor's protests, on his retirement he was
created duke of Lauenburg — an honour which Emperor Frederick had wished to confer upon him, but which he had then succeeded in refusing. Only by the most energetic protests can the
retiring chancellor escape a dotation, which he compares with the
" gratification " usually paid to efficient postal servants on their
retirement. The emperor, who wishes the public to believe that the
state of Bismarck's health is the only reason for the chancellor's
retirement, refrains from communicating the terms of Bismarck's tender of resignation to the newspapers, while publishing
his own expressions of gratitude for Bismarck's past services. In
this way, for the nonce, William is able to turn his authoritative
position to account. At the same time, he tries to retain Herbert
in the service, and actually asks Bismarck to influence his son in
this matter. Thereupon Bismarck quotes *Wallenstein* for the second time, saying: " My son is of age." Privately he thus explains
his reasons for not complying with the emperor's wishes: " When
one feels and knows that a ship is going to founder, one does not
want to put one's son in command of it."

The tragedy of Herbert's life is intensified during these days.
Had he succeeded his father in office and in the emperor's favour,
he might perhaps have shown himself a statesman of independent
worth. Now, he has to share his father's retirement, and wants to
do so, for he has inherited the father's keen sense of honour. This
same evening, he informs the emperor of the Russian refusal to
renew the treaty. The tenor of this communication shows that the
father has indicated it: " When Count Shuvaloff learned yesterday that Your Majesty would not hesitate to complete Prince
Bismarck's dismissal, Tsar Alexander could not do otherwise than
decide to refrain from renewing the secret treaty, since so secret
an affair could not be discussed with the new imperial chancellor." At the top of this communication William wrote: " Agree

to the renewal of the treaty." At the close merely one word: " Why? " Then came a still plainer explanation from Herbert; followed by a second note, a second " Why? "

The queries show more plainly than anything else, how completely William fails to recognise what a power Bismarck's name exercises in Europe. None the less, he is alarmed. He has Shuvaloff awakened at one in the morning, with a message that the Russian is to wait on the emperor at 8 a. m. At this interview, William assures Shuvaloff that he himself wishes to renew the treaty. Thereupon the Russian does everything in his power to fulfil what he knows to be Bismarck's last wish, and to secure the tsar's authority for renewing the treaty despite the altered situation.

At this juncture, when the emperor reads the newspapers, he finds that all the parties, all strata of the population, approve the course he has taken. " The nation is tranquil. Not unmoved, but unaffrighted, the German people watches the departure of the man of might from the position in which, for years past, he has been an insuperable obstacle to the internal development of the country. . . . Ere long the nation will remember March 18, 1890, among the days which have pleasurable associations." The Prussian diet makes no comment on the official notification of Bismarck's retirement. The courtiers and the army leaders are delighted that he is gone. Hohenlohe reports of one of the generals: " He was as merry as a grig that he could now speak his mind freely. . . . Such a sentiment of delight is widespread. Whereas hitherto, when the prince's influence has been dominant, people have had a sense of oppression, have felt shrunken, now they have all swelled out like a dry sponge which has been dipped in water." The nation had not known such a sense of relief for a century; not since the death of Frederick the Great.

No one in Germany knows what is being decided during these days as to the fate of Germany by three men — or, substantially, by one man. For when Shuvaloff has secured new plenipotentiary powers from the tsar, he finds, five days after the chancellor's dismissal, that there has been a change of mood. Bismarck, wishing to safeguard the treaty against Berlinese intrigues, has, through his son's instrumentality, proposed that it shall be signed in St. Petersburg. When, however, Herbert goes to fetch the treaty from the secret archives, the document is not there: Holstein has already removed it. Greatly incensed, the secretary of State attacks first the registrar and then the baron, saying: "You could have prevented this act of stupidity! You are rather too previous in regarding me as a dead man." Holstein regards him as a dangerous man, for what other reason can the baron have for now throwing all his influence into the scale against Russia? "Nothing tangible is to be expected from the treaty; and if it should be divulged, we shall all be blamed for duplicity. . . . Should the agreement come to pass, our reputations and our social position will be at Russia's mercy. It would actually be in Russia's interest to be indiscreet, for directly the affair were even suspected, the whole world would be hostile to us. . . . Then he can make his own conditions with us as regards future intercourse. The first condition would be: ' I want to associate with my former business friend B., and only with him.' Do you understand the situation now? "

The circumstantial statements in the foregoing are false, for, while Bismarck did actually show Count Shuvaloff his first defensive treaty against Russia, he was at any time ready to show the second one to the Austrians. Indeed, it was only at the tsar's wish that he refrained from doing so. To a man of Holstein's gnome-like character, and to his associates, it seemed impossible that courage and cunning could be conjoined. These men, whose intelligence was that of a mere jack-in-office, were under the spell of a pseudo-morality, and their most obvious characteristic was an assumed candour. In Holstein's case the dominant motive was a masked hatred, the outcome of wounded pride. His object was to make Bismarck's return to power for ever impossible. He had been intriguing with Waldersee against "the firm of Bismarck" for years past.

At the same time, the successors were plainly disclosing their incompetency in the posts they had taken over. Marschall writes: " A man as great as Bismarck can work with complicated tools, but I, who am a simple person, am unable to do so." Caprivi avoids his predecessor when the latter is leaving the palace. Subsequently, when Bismarck asks him to dinner, he comes once only, saying that he could not possibly listen a second time to such things about his sovereign. Then, when old Bismarck, full of anxiety, walking through the garden of the chancellery, asks Caprivi about the Russian treaty, the general rejoins: " A man like you can play with five balls at once, but other folk will do well to be satisfied with one or two." Then the counsellors get together, and, guided by Holstein, declare that in this treaty the advantages are all on the side of Russia. It will, they say, encourage Russia to critical action in the East, whereupon France will promptly attack Germany.

As a result of these arguments of shortsighted weaklings, and as the outcome of hatred and intrigue, within three days one of the foundation stones of Bismarck's work is removed, so that the whole structure is set rocking. Holstein, moreover, gets to work on influential persons by word of mouth. Then Caprivi, acting on Holstein's suggestions, and himself naturally desiring to contribute something novel of his own, advises his young master to break with their detested tsar. The emperor is delighted that at length, instead of the dangerous fox, he has an adviser who proceeds " quietly, clearly, and openly, without taking diplomatic risks." William feels himself to be behaving straightforwardly, like a true Prussian of the old days. Holstein tells us that at the close of the interview, the emperor said: " Very well, then, this affair must be dropped, sorry as I am to say so."

A few words, lightly spoken, in a small room in that palace where, thirty years before, this young emperor had come into the world. A few words, born out of a cloud of wishes, hates, jealousies, ambitions; out of fever, dread, impatience, and caprice; out of a tangled skein of promptings whereof no one was aware, and least of all William himself. A few words, whose consequences no one could foresee except the seer whose opinion was no longer asked. They undermined the safety of the German empire; they led to the formation of the Franco-Russian alliance.

During these last days in Berlin, Bismarck's frame of mind grew firmer. He did not hide his bitterness; but a malicious humour saved him from repining, and he made a point of showing himself only as man of the world. He would not keep up any pretence in the case of his hostile colleagues. When Bötticher kissed his hand in token of farewell, he said: "You are partly responsible for this separation." At a spectral farewell banquet which he gives to the ministers in the rooms he is about to quit, he will not shake hands with Bötticher on arrival — a deadly slight, for he is the host, and is famous for strict observance of the formalities in such matters. In a voice to be heard by all present, he refuses to attend a dinner given by his late colleagues, saying: " Among the imperial officials, I see only smiling faces. Besides, it is your fault that I am no longer chancellor." At such moments, the old pagan is luxuriating in the sentiments of hatred and revenge. This is not pettiness; it is the wrath of a wounded lion.

Any one who comes to visit him receives a douche of truths. The Austrian envoy brings him a graceful letter from Emperor Francis Joseph. Herein it is implied that Bismarck's resignation has been due to ill health. The ex-chancellor disavows this reason, thus officially repudiating Emperor William's account of the matter. For the first time in his life, Bismarck says that he has enjoyed extraordinarily good health while in office. These remarks are made " in a tranquil tone, though in one betraying profound mortification and piercing mental distress, which only from time to time degenerates into bitterness." Through the Turkish envoy, he lets the sultan know, without circumlocution, that he has been dismissed from office. To the Bavarian envoy, he says that the emperor has no heart, and he describes William as one who " will certainly destroy the empire." When he pays farewell visits to the embassies, he pencils through the title " Imperial Chancellor " on the cards he leaves. Speaking of his new rank, he says: " I shall be glad if people will still be good enough to address me by the name of Bismarck; and if I use the ducal title at all, it will only be when I am travelling incognito." He roundly accuses the grand duke of Baden of intriguing, until the latter leaves him in a huff.

When he goes to bid formal farewell to the emperor, he will not allow William's responsibility for the dismissal to be decently veiled; and when the emperor asks after his health, he tears this pretence to tatters by saying bluntly: "My health is excellent, Your Majesty." He can not get William to agree to the publication of his tender of resignation. After his return home, he says that at this visit his mind had been " much exercised by psychiatric questions." He finds it necessary to pack three hundred boxes and thirteen thousand bottles of wine so hastily that valuable articles are broken — for his successor is already at work close at hand, and he himself (as he says) is given one day's notice. Augusta is dead; his other enemy, Victoria, tries, after her great victory, to overwhelm him with civilities.

The day before his final departure, he drives to the royal mausoleum, and, like a poet, lays three roses on the tomb of his old master. Then he has a communion service at his house. When the pastor is about to preach on the text, " Love your enemies ", Johanna, who is acting as mistress of ceremonies, rises and tells the alarmed clergyman to stop. Subsequently Bismarck, lying on the sofa, sums up the twenty years he has spent in this house as follows: " I have enjoyed many good things. I am seventy-five years old, my wife is still with me and I have not lost any of my children. These are great mercies. I always believed that I should die in the service; now I have absolutely nothing more to do. For twenty-eight years, in sickness and in health, I have been at my post, and have discharged my duties. That is over now. I really do not know what I shall do, for I feel in better health than for years past."

Therein lies the tragical element of the situation. The old man has been deprived of his daily work. This last evening, Bismarck does not talk about plans; does not speak of the empire he has created, and which to-day seems to him imperilled; he speaks of his daily duties. Thus it comes to pass that the last hand he presses is not that of a secretary of State, an envoy or a prince, but a hand which he has certainly never clasped before, though from it for twenty years he has daily received his materials. He shakes hands with Leverström, known as the Black Rider, Bismarck's dispatch bearer. Taking courage, Leverström has called three hours before the prince's departure, and is promptly admitted. This seems to have been the only farewell in which, towards the close, the ex-chancellor lost his self-control for a moment.

When Leverström comes in, memories of the first day of the empire rise before Bismarck's mind. He thinks of Versailles, where he first saw this man, and appointed him to his present post. He asks the dispatch bearer whether he still likes his occupation. "How well I recall the room where, as sergeant major, you made your first official report to me." He gives thanks for these many years of loyal service, thanks he has tendered to no one else in the empire; and, likewise a novelty, he bestows a gift. Picking up the first that comes to hand among many goblets, a silver-gilt one, he puts it into the dispatch bearer's hands "as a token of gratitude, and as a memento."

VI

Bismarck is standing in the village school at Varzin, pointing out places on the map. He tells the youngsters how Germany is made up, and what it used to look like. He asks one of the boys a question, and is irritable because he cannot get an answer. The schoolmaster is uneasy as he looks on, being afraid lest the visitor should ask him some questions too.

During these first months, the outcast, after forty years of State service, attempts to resume the rôle of country gentleman, summoning inspectors, manufacturers, foresters, even the shepherd. Twice a week he visits the school, to teach the Farther Pomeranian village children what the town children in Berlin would not learn from him. With the discontent of a man who is always homeless, wherever he may be, he writes at this date to an acquaintance: " In youth I loved to picture myself in old age as care free, and pottering about the garden with a grafting knife." Had not this been his heart's desire for twenty years and more? Again he has to learn that, to his uneasy disposition, " the present station is more uncomfortable than any of the earlier ones."

In the long run, he cannot enjoy himself with his grafting knife; nor yet with the schoolchildren, the foresters, and the paper mill. Though he now has ample leisure and is freed from official cares, having attained what he has so long desired, he cannot after all devote himself to the management of his huge estates. Even when he reads, he is only interested in what bears upon his own career. In Napoleon's memoirs, he is contemplating his own image. In Zola's books, the only one which interests him is *La Débâcle*. The story of Julius Caesar, he says, "applies strange aptness to our own days. Brutus is a national liberal."

Johanna leads a very quiet life now. She often suffers from shortness of breath, and pains of one sort or another. She no longer goes to visit spas, for she is afraid to leave her lifelong companion. Only when the talk turns upon his dismissal (too frequent an occurrence), does she become enraged, and use the strongest terms of abuse. What is to happen to Herbert? He is still at home, forty years of age, unmarried, bereft of his career, with neither taste nor aptitude for an agricultural life, full of inward bitterness. For the second time, his father has torn his life to tatters. Now it occurs to the father that the son might like an ambassadorial post; but both soon realise that even if Herbert were prepared to take such a step downwards, he would not be given the opportunity. Bismarck, a man in whom family feeling is so strong, finds himself approaching the age of eighty without the assurance of heirs in the male line, since Herbert is unmarried, and Bill has daughters only. Speaking of one of them, he says: " If I only knew what sort of rapscallion she would marry one day to spend my money with! "

Moreover, his old bones are uneasy. True, his hearing is still good enough; he has excellent teeth, and a fair digestion; and he does not need strong glasses — but when he wants to mount on horseback, he must do so from steps, and his groom has to lift his right leg across the beast's back. Yet even to-day he cannot endure that any should claim superiority. Just as in his student days he was always ready to pick a quarrel with one who seemed to excel, so now in old age he says to a lamp-post of a baron, staying in the house, to whom he lends a fur coat which is too short: "I really don't like it when my guests are taller than I."

During the last decade of his life, his nerves are more irritable than ever. "I am all nerves. Self-control has been the greatest difficulty of my life." Such is his answer to a painter who asks him whether he really is the Iron Chancellor. An imaginative writer has recognised better than any one else the old man's physical dependence upon his moods. Wilbrandt, paying him a visit, catches a first glimpse of him through the door. Bismarck is lying on the sofa, alone, " plunged in his own communings; the face, once so red, is pallid; his features are lined and shrivelled; he seems to sit among the ruins, meditating upon this departing year in which his fall took place, and pondering about the ingratitude of life. . . . Now he rises, and, in careless uprightness, in easy dignity, the huge, tall figure stands before me. . . . These few moments have rejuvenated him. I am struck by the quiet, expectant expression of his penetrating eyes, by a gaze which holds the mean between the piercing contemplation of things close at hand and the distant outlook of the thinker."

It is the distant outlook of the thinker which is most characteristic of Bismarck in these days, for objects have been withdrawn beyond the range of nearer vision. Just as the hand of the man so fond of fighting has been disarmed, just as the brain can no longer be the focus of lightning-like determinations, so too have the eyes been deprived of the abundance of written statements in which they could immerse themselves, and from among which they could choose. The man who, when in active life, was continually craving for leisure, so that once again, as in the days of his youth, he could breathe untroubled the free air of the forests, finds it difficult to endure leisure now that it has come.

For the outcast finds that he is living in a desert. This great man-eater is almost alone. Thirty years he has complained that the door of his study was perpetually being opened; now the trouble is that it may not be opened for a week at a stretch. " I have newspapers, no living men. . . . I have millions of friends, and yet hardly one friend." A Frenchman, describing him soon after his fall, writes: "Sometimes he looks up suddenly, and says, as if awakening out of a dream: 'I am forgetting that I no longer have anything to do'." If one of the old guard comes to see him, we are told that the prince seems "eager for listeners." Keyserling, his only surviving friend, the man whom Bismarck during the last decade of power has not once invited, comes to see the outcast. Then he goes to stay in Hamburg, planning to return to Friedrichsruh, but for one or two days only. Johanna writes to him in Hamburg, begging him to prolong his visit at Friedrichsruh: "You are doing the best work that can be done for us poor folk, who have lost faith in almost all mankind, have such heavenly and cordial trust in your beloved affection, and are reviving in the overwhelming love with which we depend on you. . . . Telegraph that you have changed your plans, to the utmost delight of your old friend." She writes still in the extravagant pietistic style; she deceives herself just as she used to, but between the lines, we read the cruel truth that they are alone.

So vigorous is the boycott, that at first few but foreigners come as guests or to seek information. When one such foreigner arrives, an American railway magnate whom Bismarck has never seen before, he goes to his room for a wash after the journey. He is startled to hear the heavy tread of his host coming up the stairs. Bismarck enters the room, sits down while the guest goes on with his toilet, and says: "You are the only visitor this week. I am boycotted. No one will have anything to do with me. They are all afraid that their names might appear in the papers as guests of mine, and that this would displease our young master on the throne. Every day, people travel through Friedrichsruh without coming to see me — people who a month ago would never have dared to pass me in the streets of Berlin without a greeting. Dogs follow those who feed them." Quite a number of men (and not only young men, for whom old men often feel enduring affection) report that he kissed them when saying farewell. But the

common folk in Pomerania understand better than the clever
Berlinese what is going on here, and a Varzin peasant says to
the steward of the estate: " Let Squire just come along here. He
can trust us all right! "

Keyserling and Bucher do not live long after Bismarck retires. He mourns their loss, for they were unselfish and loyal
friends. Sometimes clever Frau von Spitzemberg comes to see
him; and a pretty woman who is mistress of a neighbouring estate
is another occasional visitor. Lenbach and Schweninger are only
welcome because they have a fund of anecdotes which amuse Bismarck. Knowing this, Max Liebermann, the only artist who could
have painted an adequate portrait of Bismarck at this period,
refused an invitation to Friedrichsruh. Apart from his wife, his
sister, and his children, there was no one left in the world for
whom Bismarck cared. Even the most faithful of his servants
died and were not replaced. When Tyras the Second passed away,
his master, eighty years of age, was strong enough to keep a
resolution then formed that he would have no more dogs, dreading the ache of having to bury them.

Thus, in the end, Bismarck forsakes dogs, after men have forsaken him.

VII

He draws ever fresh vitality from his hatred, and the outcast
cherishes no other passion so ardently as this one. If ever the
world took vengeance upon the character of a man by whom it
had been subjugated, Germany now did so after Bismarck's fall.
The waves of hatred returned to the strand from which they
had set forth. The most shameful in their behaviour were, once
more, the members of his own class, and his own order: the high
officials, the Junkers, and the princes.

When those present at a banquet or a public meeting wished
to send a telegram to Friedrichsruh, the lord lieutenant of the
district would intercept it, on the pretext that its dispatch might
cost him his position. Not one of Bismarck's sometimes colleagues

ventured to visit him. Waldersee, who was about to go to Hamburg, enquired in Berlin whether he might pay his respects to Bismarck. The only time the prince read Caprivi's signature was at the foot of a document in which the imperial government demanded from this man who had served Prussia and the empire for forty years, a refund of the salary paid to him from March 20 to March 31, 1890, on the ground that during that period he had been on the retired list and in receipt of a pension. At the same time Caprivi, through his envoys, informed all the foreign governments officially that no importance was to be attached to the views of Prince Bismarck.

" Prince Bismarck," declared one of the leaders of the Centre Party in public, " should avoid references to German power and German glory! . . . It is a disgrace to us that there should be such men as he in our fatherland!" Sybel was deprived of the documents necessary for the continuation of his history because in that work he was glorifying Bismarck more than William. The great nobles of Berlin (with the exception of Kardorff and a few others) agreed after a general discussion to turn the cold shoulder to the ex-chancellor, so that he declared that he was more heartily shunned than if he had been a cholera case in Hamburg. " Knavery is lucrative. . . . What have I to think of it when such a brute as August Dönhoff makes a wide detour in the street to avoid meeting Herbert!"

The grand duke of Baden scolds the burgomaster of Baden-Baden because this town wishes to give Prince Bismarck the freedom of the city. Empress Frederick tells Hohenlohe that all Bismarck's successes were due to his old master. Francis Joseph finds it " tragical that such a man can sink so low." The emperor has Friedrichsruh watched, and the only persons who escape the notice of his spies are the shamefaced visitors who change at Büchen in order to finish their journey in an unwatched local train. William has letters and dispatches addressed to the prince opened in the post. Though Bismarck is a knight of the Order of the Black Eagle, he is not invited to the festival of the order. The emperor tells a Frenchman that he does not propose " to force from the duke by the powers of the supreme court that which he will not accord to me out of love." William, who bestowed this ducal title, is the only one who uses it. There is but one sovereign prince who mourns the fall of the chancellor, the shrewdest of all European rulers, the lord of a realm which was at one time more hostile to Bismarck than any other: " Mi manca Bismarck," says Leo XIII.

Among those who served under him, it is a whilom opponent who is most loyal to him. Schlözer is the only man who gets himself dismissed because of his frank support of his late chief. It is thirty years, now, since the two were at odds in St. Petersburg about a point of honour. When the Berlinese of this latter day have deprived him of his important position at the Vatican, Schlözer visits Friedrichsruh " to report that he is leaving his post." Himself a man of seventy, he is as attentive to the prince as if he had been Bismarck's son, draws him up the most comfortable chair, takes care of his pipe for him, and shows once again the value of a true reconciliation.

When any one ventures to shout into the Sachsenwald, echoes come back. The old man is a match for all the seceders. His mockery thrusts home in every case. He speaks of his successor's blunders as Caprivioles; and with withering sarcasm he says of Caprivi: " He is an excellent general." Of Miquel, he remarks: " The best German orator; the power of phrase-making is the signature of our day." He cheerfully watches the fall of his enemies, Waldersee, Caprivi, and Bötticher. If we wish to learn his attitude towards the Berlinese society which has expelled him, we must watch him as chairman of a banquet, when he takes his old-fashioned lorgnette with gold rims, eyes the guests through it, and asks in low tones: " What is the name of that Badenese diplomatist down there? " The man who tells us this anecdote, the man of whom the question was asked, says that it was as if a lion was looking at a fly.

He continues to pay the outward observances of respect to the emperor. A life-sized portrait of William hangs in the dining room. On William's birthday, he rises and says: "I drink to the health of His Majesty, the emperor and king." The coldness of this utterance has a devastating effect. He cannot indicate his estrangement more strongly than by these formal words. All who wish — foreigners, journalists, and others — can listen to Bismarck's pitiless truths concerning the emperor and concerning his own fall. "Cato was a distinguished man; his death has always seemed to me a worthy one. In his place, I too should not have besought Caesar's grace. The men of those days had more self-respect than is fashionable in our time." This is one of his moderate utterances.

A fiercer remark is made to Friedjung. Reading Schiller's *Robbers* at night, he had recently come across the passage in which Franz Moor says to the old man: " Do you, then, wish to live for ever? " Bismarck's comment is: " And then my own fate rose before my eyes." The hearer says: " These words were uttered with a slight break in the voice, but without any obvious change of expression in the deeply furrowed countenance. . . . Then the prince paused for a considerable time, thoughtfully drawing figures in the damp earth with the point of his stick. Finally, coming to himself, he hastily obliterated what he had been drawing and said: ' You must not fancy that I have been deeply wounded by what has happened during the last few years. I am, if you like to put it so, too proud, after all the work I have done in the world, to allow myself to be shaken by my experiences '." The full blast of his wrath breathes in his confessions to his lady friend Spitzemberg. It is a year after the storm when he speaks, but we still hear the muttering of the thunder. " We were turned out into the street as if we had been thievish servants. . . . The emperor dismissed me like a lackey. All my life I have behaved as a nobleman who cannot be insulted without demanding amends. But I cannot demand satisfaction of the emperor. . . . Towards all these fellows I have no other feeling than that of Götz von Berlichingen at the window — and, like him, I do not except the emperor. . . . The most disastrous element in his character is that he cannot be permanently subjected to any influence, whilst from moment to moment he is accessible to all influences. . . . I will not do him the pleasure of dying, . . . and the more they threaten me, the more shall I show them with whom they have to do. . . . If only I could bring my life to a tragical close!"

Thus glows and sparkles the will-to-vengeance. His sense of superiority exudes at every pore. At the same time, his inherited sentiments have their way with him, and the habits of half a century make even this rebel regard his king as one whom he cannot challenge to a fight.

William, aware that the nation is inclining more and more to espouse Bismarck's cause, strives to win a point in the game. After three years of hostility, when Bismarck falls sick, the emperor finds a means of reopening relationships. He offers the use of a palace for the invalid's convalescence, and gets a refusal by wire. Then William sends a consignment of an old and famous wine, which Bismarck drinks in the company of Harden, the most formidable of the emperor's enemies. " His Majesty underestimates my powers," he says to his friends. " He advises me to drink one liqueur glass a day, but I need at least half a dozen such bottles to do me any good." However, after two such advances on William's part, Bismarck can hardly avoid returning thanks in person. If he failed to do so, he would put himself in the wrong with this nation of underlings. To them, the idea of a quarrel between emperor and ex-chancellor is distressing. They would rather hide it out of sight, than search for the causes of the evil and seek to remove them. Besides, Bismarck wants to startle his enemies in Berlin. Before he pays his visit of gratitude, he sends for an officer to acquaint himself regarding the details of appropriate uniform; and enquires sardonically: " What is the fashionable way of grasping the sword of the new policy? "

As an actual fact, in Berlin, uniforms and swords are the universal wear. The emperor wishes to persuade himself and others that he is receiving a general. From the squadron of honour surrounding the State chariot, to the company of honour in front of the palace, he has arranged everything as if old Moltke

had been coming to pay him a visit. Now he has to listen patiently
to the cheers which welcome his great foe, has to put up with
listening to the plaudits of the crowd when they are paid, not
to himself, but to another.

Bismarck does not enjoy this popular adulation. Those who
saw him on this occasion describe him as sitting in his carriage
like a ghost, clad in a white uniform, pallid, absent-minded, as
if his thoughts were very far away. His feelings must have been
those of mingled irony and contempt. Were he inclined for historical reminiscence, he could not fail to remember that none of
his productive visits to the palace had aroused such jubilation
as did the unmeaning comedy of to-day. No doubt, before he
can constrain himself to bend his back in reverence, he must
renew the suggestions of forty years that the king rules by divine
right. Yet how empty to him must these suggestions seem, since
with all the strength of his being he heartily despises the man to
whom he is thus paying reverence! How can he, in his overweening pride, endure such an hour, unless by persuading himself that the emperor is paying him homage?

Hardly has he reached the familiar steps of the palace, hardly
have his eyes lighted once more on the faces he has not seen for
four years, when his sovereign irony breaks forth as of old.
Contrary to the understanding, he has brought Herbert with
him! Now, when a colonel comes up to pay his respects he says
merely: " Kessel? It seems to me that you are smaller than you
used to be." Every one in the anteroom hears the words; what
Bismarck says is meant to apply to them all; they are all silent.
He enters the inner room alone, to meet the emperor. He makes
a deep obeisance, is raised up, and is kissed by the man whom he
detests. A minute or two pass. Then the little princes come
in, and their childish voices help to relieve the tension. Now comes
a luncheon party of four, and he is begged to spare himself after
his exertions.

In the evening, when there is a dinner party attended by the
suite, Bill turns up, uninvited like Herbert. Thus flanked by
the sons of his body, old Bismarck feels himself in a securer posi-

tion, feels himself superior even as father to the young Hohenzollern. Yet the presence of these two sons intensifies the hatred
of the hour. A sense of tension is universal. Even when the old
man is telling anecdotes, no one feels safe at this table. Is there
not good reason lest, as in the Teutonic legends, reddened by
wine, a sharp word will now slip out? The other will draw his
sword, and Bismarck's sons will fight with the emperor's paladins.
Otto von Bismarck knew well enough how the sword of the old
policy was grasped! But these imaginings are fugitive. No one
thinks them out to the end, least of all the young emperor, who
is content nervously to count off the minutes, and to look forward to the hour when this uncanny guest will leave his palace
and his capital. All at the dinner table are afraid of him, while
none of them reverence him — and yet they ought to feel themselves to be men of power in face of the outcast.

At length a servant announces the guest's carriage, and the
emperor ushers his enemy out into the night.

When paying a return visit to Friedrichsruh, the emperor takes
with him, for inspection by this " general ", a specimen of the
new army kit, and requests the advice of the leading statesman
of the century about the knapsack. Next day, when all Germany is agog to know what the emperor and the ex-chancellor
talked about, people read in Bismarck's newspaper a report obviously dictated by him, a courtly piece of spite to the following
effect: " The emperor was gracious enough to consult Prince
Bismarck concerning the important question of lightening the
kit of infantry soldiers on active service. Two grenadiers in full
kit were present for inspection. . . . With the same design of
making things easier for the men, a change has been made in
the collar, which can now be turned down." With such innocent
reports, the old man makes the young one look ridiculous in the
eyes of half Germany.

In other respects, Bismarck gets published what he can against
William and his government, saying: " My devotion does not go
so far as to curb me from the free expression of my opinion, as
certain folk in Berlin seem to expect. . . . They declare that I

should cut a better figure in history, should have a more distinguished aspect, if I were to hold my tongue." How irreconcilable the two men remain is shown by the vacillations of the last four years. On Bismarck's eightieth birthday, the emperor arrives with much noise and ceremony; makes a brilliant speech when he presents Bismarck with a golden sword of honour; but gets no answering speech out of the ex-chancellor. When the Kiel Canal is formally opened, no mention is made of the fact that it was cut at Bismarck's instigation. In 1896, when the silver wedding of the empire is celebrated, William's telegrams to Bismarck express undying gratitude. But in 1897, at the centenary festival of the birth of William I., though the late emperor's minor subordinates are spoken of, not a word is said of Bismarck.

On one occasion, models of warships are sent to him. Another time the emperor refuses to attend a wedding unless an invitation to Herbert to be present on the occasion is cancelled.

Thus does the seismograph of the imperial favour and disfavour record the shocks which Bismarck's public activities give to the government.

VIII

Bismarck was by no means inclined to keep his thoughts to himself! He addressed his criticism to his contemporaries through the press; his counsel for the future and his story of the past were penned in a book. When, in the previous decade, he had planned to write such a book if leisure should come to him with retirement, he had not been driven by the creative will, but had merely been theorising. There was nothing he wanted less in the world than leisure of that sort. One of the motives, now, was a request from Cotta, a German publisher prepared to defy the boycott. The other motive was not retrospective wisdom, nor yet the desire to instruct; it was nothing better than cunning, or a thirst for vengeance. For many years it had been his way to arrange for the narration of his deeds through the instrumentality of friendly writers, and to talk about his achievements to all and sundry; he had been wont to fill in gaps in his history with the rapid touch of a decorator: now there was to be a final settlement of accounts.

It was, however, speedily manifest how uncontemplative was Bismarck's spirit, how wholly it was his mission to engage in a life of action. This artist in the German language, this man who in so many speeches and documents, and above all in his letters and conversations, had created a German better than any since the days of Goethe (that master of style whose written works made him immortal with never an action worth recording), provides us in his memoirs, not with a work of art, but only with a splendid torso. This was not because he was too old, too much overwhelmed with vexations. In these days of his retirement, when he was dealing with affairs of the moment, he could still dictate illuminating articles, devastating polemics; and the occasional letters of his declining years showed almost the same blend of virile humour and unemotional melancholy as of yore. But they all gave expression to purposes, or else they sketched moods; and even when, like a patriarch, he spoke of old times, what moved him to speech, what gave his narration its rhythm, was the eye of the listener, the wine glass in his hand, the presence of his dog, the happy moment.

Now, he sat in his study, and wished to retrace, in spirit, the whole course he had run — for the sake of what audience? What was the nation? Has that word any concrete meaning? Has the nation a countenance? For the king, and also for the Reichstag, he had been able, writing and speaking, to give admirable outlines of parts of his history, when his aim was to influence the actions of his hearers. But now, when it was a question of supplying an unknown multitude with an artistic picture of his doings, of fashioning a model of the completed structure, he lacked patience, harmony, power of renunciation. That was why his sense of style made him revolt against writing memoirs of the customary pattern. As first he spoke of his sketches of the past as " Memories and Thoughts." In this loose sort of compilation, he found it easier to collect his thoughts; and, since his style was incor-

BISMARCK IN 1894

From a photograph by Karl Hahn, Munich

ruptibly circumstantial, he made no attempt to provide transitions between the facts he recorded. Thus it came to pass that the splendid book which he left as his legacy to the Germans was not a diadem, not even one for his own forehead, but, rather, a collection of almost disconnected, unmounted, though well-cut gems.

In this book, one characteristic of his style attains its climax. It is composed in overloaded sentences, into each of which Bismarck packed what others would have expressed in half a dozen. Withal, there are no flourishes; he etches with a fine needle; his description becomes a concentrated chronicle. The way in which he hides all his feelings, even his hatred, behind the facts (thereby, all the more surely, laying his enemies low) ; the way in which, simultaneously, by a biased selection of material, he wards off criticism of himself without ever praising himself — these arts of the politician, this splendid interplay between the past and the future, intensify the delight of the reader who has grasped Bismarck's true nature. The book should be widely read, were it only for the sake of its German style, which is neither classical nor modern, but perfect in its way.

As a historical document it is as serviceable as Napoleon's memoirs, no more; less serviceable than Caesar's memoirs. Critics have been able to discover numberless errors which (with but one exception) cannot be regarded as falsifications, since the author made no claim to literal accuracy and completeness. When, however, he omits the most important facts relating to the Kulturkampf, and when he is silent about the Anti-socialist Law and his economic policy, we learn a good deal about Bismarck, though nothing about the problems we have named. When, moreover, being a convinced opponent of Marx's doctrine, he makes the influence of the individual supreme in history, the only defect in this heroic depiction is that (except for Augusta) he shows upon his canvas no second figure of like proportions to his own and worthy to be his antagonist.

For the three elemental spirits which stood beside Bismarck's cradle — pride, courage, and hatred — still control the old man when he writes his reminiscences, control him so effectually that his confessions become the portrayal of an enigmatic soul. In the eight hundred pages of his book, hardly any one is extolled: neither his teachers nor his official chiefs; neither princes nor deputies; neither colleagues nor subordinates. None of them are praised unreservedly. Even Roon, the truest of the true, is dealt with critically. None but the minor figures, such as those of Stephan, Holnstein, and Schweniger, can escape detraction. Where hatred and irony rule his pen, everything is plastic to him. Of course the main aim of his characterisation is to display the merits of his old master in contrast with the defects of his young one; but even in the case of William I. his rancour finds expression. The way the others are treated, the great enemies and the small, can best be learned by the study of a page in which he pours the vials of his wrath over a completely unknown German doctor whose ignorant treatment had done him much harm in St. Petersburg. After the lapse of thirty years, he is not content with scarifying the offender, but must twice allude angrily to the grand duchess who had recommended this incompetent practitioner to him and to the court of St. Petersburg.

By fits and starts, down to the time of Bucher's death in the year 1892, he dictated to that worthy the substance of the three volumes; subsequently altering a good deal and expanding here and there. He never showed much fervour in the occupation. Doctor Schweniger, coming in, often finds: " Bucher dumb, depressed, sulky, ears pricked and pencil pointed, sitting at the table in front of a blank sheet of paper; the prince reclining in a long chair, deep in newspapers, speaking not a word; Bucher saying still less; nothing can be written." Then the doctor helps him a little; or perhaps some article he reads, or the chance question of a visitor gives him impetus; and now he dictates a passage.

Bucher, who has far less fire than Bismarck but is endowed with a better memory, complains that the prince "often repeats himself, and almost always tells the story differently each time. . . . He breaks off at the most important point, . . . contradicts himself. . . . When things have gone amiss, he will never admit that he was to blame. Hardly any one is allowed to seem as important as himself. . . . He denied the letter to Prim (in the year 1870), until I reminded him that I had myself taken it to the general in Madrid. . . . Perhaps he is thinking of future historians, of leaving a legacy to posterity. . . . But he is also thinking of the present, and of the influence he wishes to exert upon it."

Thus without any documents, wishing to take vengeance on his enemies and to make out the best case for himself, he grows uneasy about the contradiction between his private and his public expressions of opinion concerning the royal power: " Since 1847, I have always defended the monarchical principle, and have held it aloft like a banner. But now I have seen three kings naked, and often enough the behaviour of these exalted gentlemen was by no means kingly. To say as much to all the world . . . would, however, conflict with the monarchical principle. To maintain a cowardly silence, or to say that things were other than they were — that was equally impossible to me." Thus, in the end, this great actor has to pay for having lived in two worlds. He who hitherto has only spoken the truth behind the scenes, must now, for the first time, speak the truth in the full glare of the foot-lights. Even at this date, his rancour outweighs considerations of policy, so that the sometime royalist pens the famous chapter on William II., deadly to the reputation of that ruler, and not to his alone — for the picture gallery of the house of Hohen-zollern is here a sorry spectacle. Never was a more eloquent polemic against monarchy written than this chapter.

Bismarck was fully cognisant of what the effect would be when he gave orders that the whole work should be issued as soon as he died. His heirs, however, alleging verbal instructions, thought it more important to protect the emperor than to allow their father to defend himself from the tomb. Not merely did they withhold the third volume from publication in the year 1898, but they continued to safeguard the reputation of William II. in 1918 after he had run away from Germany. They protested against immediate publication, and supported the action which the emperor brought against the publisher, instead of doing their utmost to ensure that their ancestor's testament should at length be given to the nation.

IX

" The duty to say my say imposes itself upon my conscience as if it were a pistol pointed at me. Since I believe that the present policy is leading the fatherland into a morass which it would be better to avoid; since I know the morass, whereas others are mistaken about the nature of the ground; it would be tantamount to treason if I were to hold my peace. . . . My dear friends want me to accept a living death; to remain hidden, mute, motionless. . . . But, even in retirement, I can still serve my fatherland. . . . In many respects, I have now a freer hand; I can without official restrictions favour in foreign parts the peace propaganda which has been my chief aim for twenty years."

Thus concern for his own work coalesces with enmity towards his successors, and with eagerness for revenge upon his calumniators. During the last decade of his life, the outcast regains the power over public opinion which he had lost in previous years. It seems to him that to secure this end he is justified in whatever he does. When, through the instrumentality of confidants, he has important letters written by William I. launched in the press, he protects himself against the fate he had himself meted out to Arnim by hinting that in case of need those who have published the letters must declare that they had been circulated among the guests at Friedrichsruh and must have been copied there. He says, further, that his own private letters to the king are his spiritual property; " the fact that the same ideas are incorporated in documents, does not give them an official character." He gives other revelations to Harden, whom he invites to visit him after he has read that publicist's essays, and with whom he maintains friendly relations.

In the early days of his retirement, Bismarck does not, as might be supposed, find it easy to express his views in the columns of the German newspapers. Most of them are afraid of being compromised by having anything to do with him. During the first months, the only journalists he receives come from abroad. The "Hamburger Nachrichten" is alone among German newspapers in opening its columns to the ex-chancellor, and thus becomes, for many years, the most interesting press organ in the empire. He dictates a good many articles for it, and inspires a good many more, so that people soon become accustomed to regard the "Hamburger" as the "Moniteur" of Friedrichsruh. During the two or three great crises of these years, the "Hamburger" confronts the "Reichsanzeiger" on equal terms.

Two years after his fall, Bismarck had a momentous experience.

Though the nation had so long been estranged from him, the circumstances of his dismissal brought about a turn in the tide. These circumstances gradually became known, gave rise to murmurings, and aroused much sympathy. During the first few days, he received more than six thousand commendatory telegrams. The free city of Hamburg espoused the cause of its neighbour. Indeed Hamburg gave him a gala reception, and when he was driving through the beflagged streets, an English sailor ran up to his carriage, saying: "I want to shake hands with you!" This was certainly the first time in his life that Bismarck had shaken hands with the common people. Never before, indeed, had he welcomed a peasant at his table. Now, two peasant enthusiasts who had come over from Schönhausen were invited to lunch with him — for Bismarck was much touched by their humble admiration! Herbert summed up the situation in an apt phrase, saying: "They regard you as their palladium, and with good reason." For a long while such incidents remained isolated. Two years later, at the end of May 1892, the outcast remarked: "Where I deceived myself was in the matter of the German people; . . . its failure to understand that what drives me to criticism is not a mere fit of the spleen, a desire for vengeance, or a wish to regain power — but that anxiety concerning the future of the empire is what robs me of sleep."

Two weeks later he would not have spoken in that way. At his father's instigation, Herbert has become engaged to an Austrian heiress. Bismarck thinks of going to Vienna for the wedding; he begs audience of Francis Joseph, and is assured of a welcome. But William and the members of the court circle are afraid that the ex-chancellor harbours sinister designs. The pygmies of the Wilhelmstrasse are buzzing with excitement; they dread stormy weather, raise warning fingers. Emperor William writes to Emperor Francis Joseph: " At the end of the month Bismarck is going to Vienna, . . . in order to receive planned ovations from his admirers. . . . You know that one of his masterpieces was the secret treaty à double fonds with Russia, which, entered into behind your back, was annulled by me. Since his retirement, the prince has been carrying on a most perfidious war against me and against Caprivi my minister. . . . He is trying with all the art and cunning at his disposal to twist matters so that the world shall believe me to be making advances to him. The chief feature in his schemes is that he has asked you for an audience. I venture, therefore, to beg you not to complicate my situation in my own country by receiving this unruly subject of mine before he has approached me and said peccavi."

Simultaneously with this disgraceful letter, a second was despatched to Vienna, drafted by Holstein, signed by Caprivi, and addressed to the German ambassador in Vienna, Prince Reuss: " Should the prince or his family make any approach to Your Excellency's house, I beg you to limit yourself to the conventional forms, and to avoid accepting any invitation to the wedding. These indications as to behaviour apply to the staff of the embassy as well as to yourself. I may add that His Majesty will not accept any notice of the wedding. . . . Your excellency is instructed to inform Count Kalnoky of this fact in whatever manner may seem best to you." Thus was Bismarck officially stigmatised as a person who was not to be received, and the Austrian minister for foreign affairs was warned against him.

Bismarck's first thought, when he was confidentially informed about this letter, was to send a challenge to Caprivi: " I had already chosen a second. My right hand is still steady enough, and I have kept up my pistol practice. But when I turned the matter over in my mind I remembered that I am an officer, and that the affair would be submitted to a court of honour composed of elderly generals. I should never have got him to face my pistol." Thus at the age of seventy-seven does the Titan once more show his leonine courage. He wants to defend his name, rank, and honour at the risk of his life, just as he did forty years earlier. He will not send his son to fight in his stead. He wants to face the music himself. As always, he is animated by the dramatic wish to close his molested existence in tragical fashion.

He takes a more prudent course. Privately he terms this " Uriah letter " a piece of effrontery. For the public, he prints the following in his newspaper: " The means which have been used in order to put the emperor of Austria out of humour with his original intention of receiving the prince, produced the impression of a disparagement of, and injury to, the prince's social position. This must necessarily be felt as personally offensive. . . . We can discover nothing in the prince's previous history to merit so contumelious a classification." This shell exploded with a bang, and the fragments flew beyond the frontiers of Germany.

Never before, since Prussia had come into existence, had a king of that country succeeded in setting the whole Prussian people in ebullition against him — for even in the year 1848 the anger of the Prussians was not really directed against their weakling monarch. Now half Germany was up in arms. Even in Berlin, through which the Bismarcks passed, the crowd invaded the station, and clamoured for a speech from the old man. He was too prudent to comply, and held his peace; his plans for revenge were carefully made. In Vienna, the nobility showed distressed countenances, and turned away. The German envoy, giving himself out to be ill, took to his bed; but the princess his wife valiantly espoused the cause of the insulted ex-chancellor. Amid these alarums and excursions of which his father was the centre, Herbert celebrated his nuptials with Countess Hoyos, ten years after, amid similar alarums and excursions of which he himself had been the centre, he had refrained from marrying Elisabeth Hatzfeldt.

Bismarck the elder, under this rain of hostile bullets, seemed to grow younger. His thoughts ran, as they had run once before, "à corsaire, corsaire et demi!" He invited the editor of the " Neue Freie Presse " to visit him, in order that he might be interviewed for that paper. In this interview, for the first time after the lapse of forty-four years, he openly attacked the government. On that earlier occasion, long ago, he had accused the king of cowardice in face of the people; now he accused the government of stupidity. " Austria, in the commercial treaty, has, of course, turned to account the weakness and ineptitude of our negotiators. This result must be ascribed to the fact that in our country men have come to the front whom I had formerly kept in the background — the reason being that everything had to be changed. . . . For my part, I am no longer under any obligations towards the personalities now in office, or towards my successor. All the bridges have been broken down. . . . The tie which used to connect us with Russia has been severed. Personal authority and confidence are lacking in Berlin."

The bigwigs in Berlin become uneasy. If they cannot discredit the " garrulous old man " privately, they must do it publicly. Now, therefore, the two " Moniteurs " begin, before a greatly disturbed Germany, while Europe holds its sides with laughter, to fight a duel, in which every thrust of the government goes awry, while every answering thrust from Bismarck is a palpable hit.

In Caprivi's paper: " We cannot recall any like behaviour on the part of a retired statesman in the history of other countries, to say nothing of Germany. It would seem to be the prince's aim to do everything in his power to arouse mistrust, thus complicating the already difficult task of guiding the chariot of the empire. Is this a patriotic course of action? His memory is failing him. . . . No one can measure the amount of harm the prince is prepared to inflict upon his own fatherland."

Next day, Bismarck showed himself an able journalist. In his newspaper he acted on the assumption that the article just quoted had been written by the editor of the paper which was attacking him, and he was thus enabled, with an ironical semblance of respect, to level his shafts at the unnamed government: " It is of course impossible that experienced and well-bred persons, like those who are at present conducting affairs of State, can be responsible for so impudent a newspaper article. To suppose this would be an insult. . . . The prince cannot but feel that it must arouse a ludicrous impression when Editor Pinther gets up into the pulpit and sermonises him. . . . Nothing would please Prince Bismarck better than that legal proceedings should be taken against him, and he would have no objection to such a dramatic close to his political career."

After this answer, the wrath of the German public seemed likely to dissolve into laughter; but the men at the head of affairs in Berlin were beside themselves with rage. They took up the cudgels against Bismarck, and also against half the nation. Now, at this late date, they published the dastardly instructions to the Viennese embassy. Every German was given an opportunity of reading in the " Reichsanzeiger " how the new chancellor was eager to humiliate his predecessor. The nation's blood boiled. At first, hundreds of thousands of Germans had regarded the dismissal of Bismarck as a somewhat harsh but salutary action, indicative of the emperor's genius and tact. Now it was plain to every one that William had neither the one nor the other. Consequently, the last feelings of hostility towards Bismarck in the country were dispelled by an outburst of popular acclamation, such as had never before greeted, in Germany, any man who wore neither a crown nor a uniform.

Bismarck had had to reach the age of eighty before he conquered the German people. As deputy, he had been their enemy; he had fought them as prime minister of Prussia; he had been the foe of the Reichstag as imperial chancellor; in his own house, on his country estates, he had always lived among the members of his own class, had been out of touch with the bourgeoisie, even with the intellectuals, numbering among his acquaintances neither professors nor men of business nor artists. For sixty years, he had lived only among politicians and noblemen. At most during the two wars, or in his life as gentleman farmer, had he breathed the same air as this people for whose welfare as a nation he had been working for several decades.

Now there were crowds to welcome him in all the places through which he passed on the journey from Vienna to Kissingen; the towns implored the honour of giving him a public reception; the German tribes he had conquered or oppressed, the Saxons and the South Germans, paid him homage. Europe scoffed when it learned that the Prussian government had forbidden the towns of Halle and Magdeburg to take part in doing honour to Bismarck, and when, in Kolberg, the regimental band, which was about to welcome the old statesman with fife and drum, was incontinently ordered back to barracks. But Germany rejoiced when it read the story of the happenings at Jena.

There, town and university, the burghers, the peasants of the neighbouring countryside, the teachers, women and children, thronged the old market place. In the Lutherhaus, the rector received the prince. When he came out into the square, where, ninety years before, the camp fires of the French had burned, Bismarck found that it was filled with long tables, at which, bottles of wine and beer ready to their hand, amid song and instrumental music, the inhabitants of this German provincial town were awaiting him, romantically inclined, eager, enthusiastic. The tallest man there, wearing a long black coat, he strode to and fro over the rough stone pavement among the groups, made nine speeches, not one of them containing an empty phrase. He pointed to the statue of Götz von Berlichingen and quoted (from Goethe's drama) Götz's answer to the commissary who had insulted him by calling him a robber: " Wert thou not the representative of my emperor, whom I reverence even in the vilest counterfeit, I would make thee swallow that word, or choke upon it ! " Even more frenzied was the applause when he quoted the first half of that rough saying of Götz's which he had had ready to his lips throughout life, and concluded with the words: " A man may be a loyal adherent of his dynasty, his king, and his emperor, without being convinced of the wisdom of all the measures of that king's and emperor's commissaries. I myself am not convinced, nor shall I in the future keep my opinions to myself!"

That is the tone to delight the Germans, when, on a summer evening, they are sitting over their wine in the public square — and have no responsibility for what is said. Here, and when he is back in his carriage, which cannot advance through the press, hundreds upon hundreds wish to grasp the hand whose weight they have all feared for a generation; and the old man is ready to give a handshake to them all. For a few hours or weeks, his inborn scepticism is stilled, and he asks himself whether truer and deeper tones may not come from these common people than from his own class, which, when he was in power had envied him, then betrayed him, and in the end overthrown him. During the receptions, the students' drinking parties, and the torchlight processions, which make his progress through South Germany a via triumphalis, this intimacy and warmth force him, more and more, to wonder whether it would not have been well to grant more power to such a people. Thus late in the day, and only as the outcome of the injustice he has suffered, does Bismarck realise how he has missed his opportunities. These are the first popular addresses he has ever delivered. They are spoken in town halls and beer cellars, from balconies and in public squares, from Dresden to Munich. In them, the old man utters his belated warnings:

"The essence of the constitutional monarchy under which we live is that it should be a collaboration of the monarchical will with the conviction of those who are ruled. Perhaps I myself have unwittingly contributed to the lowering of the influence of parliament to its present level. I do not wish that it should permanently remain at that low level. I should like to see parliament once more possess a stable majority, without which it cannot have the authority that is desirable. . . . The permanent duty of the representative assembly is that it shall criticise, control, warn, and in certain circumstances, guide the government. . . . Unless there should be such a Reichstag, I shall be anxious concerning

the durability and the solidity of our national development. . . .
Formerly it was my whole endeavour to strengthen the monarchical
sentiment of the people. I was acclaimed and overwhelmed with
gratitude at the courts and in the official world; but the people
wanted to stone me. To-day the people greet me with acclamations, whereas the members of court and official circles give me
the cold shoulder. I think that is what may be termed the irony
of fate."

Thus ingeniously does the great stylist take this difficult
curve in his career, when it is his aim to influence the multitude.
In reality, his conduct is a tragical irony. He knows this, and his
tardy conversion troubles his night thoughts. For a whole lifetime, his statecraft has been self-centred, self-contemplative, self-
directed. Not because he wanted to shine — his intense contempt
for his fellows saved him from this vanity; not because his power
could only be held and safeguarded by imposing it from above —
no, the deepest cause of Bismarck's hostility to the people was
to be found in the self-reliance of one whose intelligence was
that of native genius, while by blood he always felt himself to be
an offshoot of the uppermost class. Only as a member of the upper class, and with the aid of that class, did he want to rule;
simply because it was his own class, even though, to his critical
mind, it did not seem the best. The king and the members of the
knightly order; they were the foundations of the State. The
granting of universal suffrage had been no more than an unwilling concession to the spirit of an age walking in darkness. To
weaken parliament, to subject parliament unceasingly to the
royal authority, this had been the basic idea of Bismarck as a
founder of a State, had been his practice for decades.

The strong monarchy, of which in the diet and the Reichstag
he was continually boasting, was in reality nothing more than
an imaginary power, like that British monarchy of which he was
so critical; but whereas in Britain the substance, of which monarchy was the shadow, was the people, here in Germany the substance was the chancellor, was Bismarck himself. He knew well
enough the trick he was playing upon the people, but he would

not allow any outsider to grasp the nature of the relationships between emperor and chancellor in this drama of dictatorship. It was his empire; he alone should issue orders in it. Only thus could his unparalleled self-confidence find satisfaction in the work. This went on until the impossible happened. The kingship, whose strength he had for thirty years proclaimed in his struggle with the representatives of the people, had now, all at once, been incorporated in a new personality. Therewith it suddenly rebelled, and overthrew its master. Then, for a time, he stood alone, without a ruler and beside the people.

Now, when the people had at length taken his side, old Bismarck was able to recognise the error in his calculations. The very motive of inborn passion which had previously kept him loyal to the monarchy, now, for the same reason, made him take the side of the people. His pride made an extreme concession when, before his fellow countrymen and before Europe, he acknowledged: " Perhaps I myself have unwittingly contributed to the lowering of the influence of parliament to its present level."

When, during these weeks, the artists of Munich entertained him at a banquet, Lenbach was to have lifted a huge corporation goblet filled with Munich beer, as a greeting to the guest of honour. But he found the goblet too heavy, and, afraid to drop it, put it back on the table. Then an inspiration seized him, and he shouted in tones that thrilled all present: " He who is too weak to uphold it, sets it down! "

In this impromptu, the painter summarised the conflict between William and Bismarck. The old man said: " When my train is approaching a station, has slowed down, and I hear the shouting and singing of the crowds awaiting me, my heart is filled with joy that I am not forgotten in Germany."

X

Bismarck's horoscope, like his handwriting, confirms our estimate of his character. The astrological type born with Leo rising has power as its keynote and peculiar gift. The position of the

sun, ruler of Leo, in its exaltation sign, Aries, and the Mars rul-
ership of Aries, give a double portion of dauntless, instinctive
courage. Moreover, the sun is in trine to Uranus, which indicates
a special vocation for public life. All three fiery signs are ac-
centuated.

His handwriting (see illustration) shows understanding to be
stronger than imagination; shows will, energy, self-reliance, but
also self-control, self-possession, and a sense of form. It is proud,
obstinate, unconventional though orderly, full of the surprises
of a man who is at the mercy of his nerves. The writing is large,
without any affectation of size. During the middle years of his
life it is most regular, lacking at this time any sign of emotion
or superfluity. In old age it becomes more ductile, and its scale
is larger. The most notable characteristic, however, is that for
fifty years it remains substantially unaltered — just like his
character.

Above all, even in old age he remains a fighter. When Keyserling
urges him to become, now, a harmonious personality, he rejoins
defiantly: " Why should I be harmonious? " When, on his eightieth birthday, the trains of pilgrims expect to find a tranquil old
man, they hear him say from the balcony of his house the ardent
words: " Creative life issues out of struggles. From the plant,
through the insects to the birds, from the birds of prey up to
human beings — there is no life without struggle! " In this mood,
he allows himself to be elected to the Reichstag. He says: " I
should like to see their faces at the governmental table when I
come to sit in the floor of the hall. . . . I am a chemical drop
which decomposes everything when it is poured into a debate."
When some one extols content, he says: " What could there be
more unhappy than a millennium of general content, which kills
ambition, paralyses progress, leads to moral stagnation? "

Long ago, his Christianity had become a mere matter of form;
now, it is over and done with. At the close of his life, as in the
early days, his mind is dominated by a scepticism in which from
time to time a sort of pagan mysticism shapes itself. The only
man who can venture to question him about these matters, Keyser-

ling, the friend of his youth, gives a sympathetic explanation: "His religious sentiment" (the words are penned after Keyserling's last visit to his old friend) "seems to have experienced ebbs and flows. . . . In his old age, his erotic impulses have gone to sleep, and therewith, perhaps, the aspiration towards a god with human feelings has vanished. This throws a strong light upon the intimate connexion between love and religion." Keyserling records, as Bismarck's last confession: "I am sorry to say that during the struggles of the last two decades, I have moved away to a great distance from God. In these sad times, I find this severance painful."

When he indulges in speculations on religious problems, he says things which may well make the pious old Johanna grow anxious. He is reading a newspaper, lets it fall, and remarks in the presence of a guest: "I should very much like to know whether the dualism which permeates our whole existence extends, likewise, to the supreme being. In our own case, everything is twofold. Man consists of spirit and body; the State is made up of government and popular representation; and the existence of the whole human race is founded upon the mutual relationships of man and woman. Indeed, this dualism extends to whole peoples. . . . Without wishing to be blasphemous, I should very much like to know whether our God may not perhaps have at his side some being who supplements him as a woman supplements man." His wife timidly ventures to remind him of the doctrine of the Trinity. "That doctrine is incomprehensible," he says. With a serious mien, he continues his self-questionings aloud: "Perhaps there are stages between ourselves and God. It may be that God has other beings at his disposal, beings who can assist him in the governance of this immeasurable universe. For instance, when I read again and again in the newspapers . . . how much pain and unhappiness there is, and how unjustly good and bad fortune are distributed, I am apt to wonder whether the management of this world of ours may not have been entrusted to a vicegerent who does not invariably carry out the wishes of our all-good deity!"

This naturalism represents the last flickering of the sparks

of dogma before they become extinct. He can only look upon
the world as a State. Since, despite all the blemishes he sees in
it, he conceives that the supreme ruler of the world must be
perfect, he constructs this hypothesis of a vicegerent — a sort
of Prussian lord lieutenant — who, as he says on another occasion, interprets the laws falsely and applies them wrongly. In
extreme old age, he returns to the ancient Teutonic outlooks,
which, indeed, he has in his secret heart never abandoned. In his
more defiant moods, Bismarck will have nothing to do with the
fear of God, to which he objects simply because it is a form of
fear. He says that the reason why tropical man worships the
sun is because in those regions the sun is dangerously powerful;
it is by parity of reasoning that the Teutons worshipped thunder
and lightning. He contemptuously adds: " In this matter, likewise, is disclosed the dog-like nature of human beings; they love
and venerate the person whom they fear."

To a consul who reports his escape from Negroes eager to kill
him, Bismarck says: " We are all in God's hands, and in such a
situation our best consolation must be a good revolver, so that
at any rate we shall not start on our journey unaccompanied."

There is, however, a mystical vein in his mind. The superstitious trend makes headway. " I like to watch such signs and
portents as are manifested by dumb nature. She is often cleverer
than we are." He frequently refers to the cabbalistic doctrine of
number, in accordance with which, contemplating the periodicity
of his life, he has calculated the date of his death. He says that,
since he did not die in the year 1883, his life will end in the year
1898 — as actually happens. " At bottom, everything is inexplicable: light, a tree, our own life. Why, then, should there not
be things which conflict with our logical understanding? . . .
Montaigne chose for his epitaph: ' Peut-être.' I should like mine
to be: ' Nous verrons '."

Does the old man believe in the durability of his work? He is
not led astray by the adulation of the German people; fame has
never blinded him. Of course his fame is now world-wide. For instance, a Chinese viceroy comes to consult him, asking the best

BISMARCK IN 1895

From a photograph by Karl Hahn, Munich

way of counteracting the court intrigues in Pekin. Some one writes to him from Araby, to say that his name is well known in that part of the world; that Bi-Smark signifies " rapid fire ", " bold activity." What value is it to him that he should be famous among the Germans? " They are all petty and narrow-minded. Not one of them works with an eye to the whole. Each of them is busy stuffing his own private mattress. . . . We have always been extremely unaccommodating to one another, and far too accommodating towards foreigners. . . . It disturbs my sleep when I think how they are breaking down the edifice I have built up. Then my thoughts run riot all night." Thus tormented by his old mistrust, aroused by the dissensions of the nation, and by his new mistrust of its master, he looks out into the future with an anxiety which steadily increases after he has turned his eightieth year.

On his birthday, receiving the homage of all the German tribes, and treated contumeliously only by his old enemy the Reichstag (which refuses to send him congratulations), he stands on the balcony and addresses the German youth: " Don't be too critical. Accept what God has given us, and what we laboriously, under the menace of the guns of the other Europeans, have brought safely into port. It was not an easy matter." Thus skilfully, in this festal hour, does he cast a delicate veil over his anxieties. As always, he has the seductive style of one whom difficulty allures. The students to whom he is speaking look up at the old wizard, whose face looms mysteriously in the flickering torchlight, look up at him without fully understanding him.

These anxieties of his concern the future only; he has nothing to fear from the past. When contemporary reminiscences and letters are published, his interest is keen. When a banking house buys his letters to Manteuffel, he says: " I have really quite forgotten what these letters contain, but I do not think I have ever written a letter which I shall be sorry to have published."

That is perfectly true, for he has no desire to conceal his changes of outlook or his changes of party; and he has never made a parade of principles. He is delighted to read Roon's letters upon himself, when they appear in print. He has a collection of Bismarck caricatures; and cheerfully reads to his guests accounts of Bismarck's cruel mouth, angry eyes, fierce eyebrows. But when they bring him the model of a statue of himself in his student days, he studies the features like a physiognomist, and says that the artist has made a mistake in trying to represent him at one and the same time as a man of ancient lineage and as a diplomatist. He adds that his lower lip had always been thicker than the upper; it indicated stubbornness, whereas the more finely cut upper lip indicated the craving for power.

When there is no occasion for showing pugnacity, no subject for mockery, or when he is sitting in solitude listening, from a distance, to the turmoil of his own career, he is never inclined to boast of the brilliancy of his foresight, but is alarmed at his own venturesomeness. He says: " My whole life was a bold gamble with other people's money. I could never tell beforehand whether my plans would succeed. It was a terrible responsibility, this management of other people's property. . . . Even now, I am often kept awake at night by thinking how everything might have turned out differently."

He becomes gloomier during Johanna's last illness. He would fain have died with her. " I should not like to die before my wife; nor should I like to remain after she is called away." In accordance with her desire, he brings her to Varzin. She is suffering terribly from shortness of breath, and can hardly move. Bismarck, who now dictates very few letters, and writes scarcely any with his own hand, pens the following lines to his sister after his brother's death: " I must be careful not to increase Johanna's melancholy by letting her see my own sorrow; her vitality is very low anyhow, and is dependent upon mental impressions. We have sad news to-day about poor Bill; he has a fresh attack of gout. . . . In former days, I was always very glad when I could go to Varzin; now I should hardly be able to make up my mind to go thither were it not for Johanna. I long for a place which I shall never leave until I go in my coffin; and I have a craving for soli-

tude. . . . Your somewhat weary but devoted and only brother,
v. B."

In the autumn, Johanna dies, at the age of seventy. Overnight,
she had been able to speak to him at supper time. In the morning,
when he went into her room, he found her dead. The old man, the
man of might, barefooted and in his dressing gown, sat down
and cried like a child. He had lost something utterly irreplaceable.
It was characteristic of his twofold life that, the same evening,
he should have compared the close of his political career with the
close of this life of faithful companionship: " This is a more
notable terminus than 1890 was, and it cuts deeper into the
configuration of my life. . . . If I were still in the service, I
should bury myself in work. That consolation is denied me."

Next day he picks a white rose out of a wreath, goes to the
bookcase, takes down a volume of German history, and says:
" This will distract my thoughts."

There is now an empty place in his life. Nothing can do for
him what her tranquil and trusting glance had done; nothing else
can make him forget, from time to time, his struggles and mortifications. Writing to his sister, he laments that she lives so far
away. " So do my sons, who have sought independence far from
the shadow of their parental home. Marie is with me as a loving
daughter, . . . only on loan, as it were. . . . What was really
left to me in the world was Johanna, association with her, the
daily question as to how she felt, the gratitude with which I could
look back to forty-eight years spent in her company. To-day,
everything is vain and void. The feeling is unjust, but I cannot
help it. I blame myself for being ungrateful in response to the
wealth of love and recognition which the people has shown me
in return for my services. For four years past I have rejoiced
at this love and recognition because she herself rejoiced. To-day
the spark no longer glows in me. I hope it has not been permanently extinguished, should God vouchsafe me a longer life. . . .
Forgive me, darling sister, for complaining like this. It will not
be for much longer."

In his loneliness, his thoughts turn back to his earliest days.

He suddenly recounts something which he has never before told any one. "I was six years old when I learned of the death of Napoleon. A magnetiser who was treating my mother brought the news. He recited an Italian poem which began with the words: 'Egli fù!'" At the end of the century, the beginning rises out of the past. He tells us of things long forgotten. We feel that he is applying to himself the words of Manzoni's poem: "He was." Once the old man speaks of Kniephof, and he writes to his brother-in-law:

"Dear Oscar, we have both grown so old that we shall not live much longer. Can we not meet and have a talk once more before the end comes? It is sixty-six or sixty-seven years since, at the gymnasium, we first drank beer together, out of the bottle. It was on the steps close to the upper third. Let us have a last drink together before it is too late. . . . I want to hear your voice once more before I — You have to get into the train when you leave Berlin; why not into the Hamburg train instead of the Stettin train?" In his loneliness, Bismarck longs for the company of a man whom he has ignored all his life; now, when his wife is dead, and his sons are far away, he wants to hear a friendly voice. As usual, he is circumstantial, reckons up the years, and remembers exactly where it was in the school that they had drunk beer together — but we feel that he no longer smiles as he writes. Amid these distresses, has the vigour of his mind departed? Has he forgotten the empire?

He has not forgotten his enemies, the rulers. In the autumn of 1896, the consequences of the failure to renew the Russian treaty become apparent. The tsar is in Paris; France is in a whirl about Russia. Bismarck reads in the German newspapers that the rupture of the ties with Russia is his fault. Anger flames up in him. He knows well enough who are responsible for the failure of his precautions, and he will not, while life remains to him, allow any one to blame him for what has happened. Once more he draws his sword for mortal combat. He explains to the Germans who is really responsible for the isolation of Germany, writing in his newspaper:

"Down to 1890, the two empires were fully agreed that if either of them should be attacked, the other would remain benevolently neutral. After the retirement of Prince Bismarck, this understanding was not renewed. If our information regarding what happened in Berlin is accurate, it was not Russia (put out of humour by the change in the chancellorship) but Count Caprivi who refused to continue this mutual insurance, when Russia was ready to continue it. . . . That explains Kronstadt and the Marseillaise. In our opinion, the first drawing together of tsarist absolutism and the French republic was solely due to the errors of the Caprivist policy." Europe pricks up her ears; the Germans murmur; the old warrior could not deal the emperor a more deadly blow. The " Reichsanzeiger " answers stammeringly:

" Diplomatic affairs of . . . the before-mentioned kind are diplomatic secrets which should be strictly kept. The conscientious observance of this secrecy is an international obligation, the disregard of which would injure important interests of State." Other journals write about treason, imprisonment, and so forth. Emperor William wires triumphantly to Emperor Francis Joseph: " You and the world will now understand better than ever why I dismissed the prince."

Nevertheless, next summer, the emperor sends Tirpitz to the prince, hoping that Bismarck will say something on behalf of the German navy. But the ex-chancellor is obdurate. Instead of doing what he is asked, he expresses his views of the emperor " so unreservedly " that Tirpitz points to the uniform he is wearing. " Tell the emperor," says Bismarck in conclusion, " that I want nothing more than to be left alone, and to die in peace." But the young master will not leave him alone, despite all the mortifications received at Bismarck's hands. The lure exercised by Bismarck is irresistible, and, six months before the ex-chancellor's death, William comes uninvited to see him, followed by a great train.

The old man is sitting in a wheel chair in front of his door, and lets them all defile before him. When Lucanus offers the hand

with which he had given Bismarck the letter of dismissal, the
prince remains "like a statue, not a muscle stirring, as if contemplating a hole in the air." Lucanus stands before him, face
twitching, understands at last, and takes his departure. Subsequently, over dinner, the host ponders how he can give one last
warning to his guest and opponent whom he will never see again.
Inspired by his traditional pride, he begins, for the first time
after seven years, to talk to the emperor about world policy.
William turns the conversation with a jest. Bismarck tries again.
Another witticism. Even the court generals are horrified. The
younger Moltke whispers: "It is terrible!"

Then Bismarck becomes a seer. The hour is passing; his life
is passing; never again will he see the young man who has
snatched away his life work, the empire. Sooner or later, the emperor will lose his country and his crown; he must be told of the
risks he is running; perhaps a dying man's voice will move him.
Suddenly, therefore, Bismarck "with apparent nonchalance",
but so loud that every one at table can hear, says: "Your Majesty! So long as you have the present officers' corps, you can, indeed, do what you please. But when this is no longer the case,
matters will be very different." The emperor is deaf, he prattles,
he departs.

The old statesman still utters his warnings and prophecies in
private. Every one of them has been fulfilled.

"If the country is well ruled, the coming war may be averted;
if it is badly ruled, that war may become a Seven Years' War!
The wars of the future will be decided by artillery. Troops can
be replaced in case of need; big guns must be made in time of
peace. . . . In Russia, the coming of a republic is perhaps nearer than most people suppose. . . . In the fight between labour
and capital, labour has won most of the victories, and that will
happen everywhere as soon as the workers possess the vote. When
the final victory occurs, it will be the victory of labour."

No less bold are all his exhortations to Germany. His intellectual lucidity grows until he is able to pass judgment on himself:
"Perhaps my dutiful behaviour has been the cause of the de-

BISMARCK'S HANDWRITING AT 30

BISMARCK'S HANDWRITING AT 45

BISMARCK'S HANDWRITING AT 80

plorable lack of backbone in Germany, and for the multiplication of place-hunters and time-servers. . . . The most important thing is to strengthen the Reichstag; but this can only be effected by electing thoroughly independent persons. At present the Reichstag is on the down grade. . . . If that continues, the prospects are gloomy indeed. . . . I am convinced that crises are all the more dangerous, the later they come. . . . I have invariably thought it better to obey no one, rather than try to command others; I had, if you like to say so, a republican view. . . . Perhaps God will send Germany a second era of decay, followed by a fresh period of glory — that will certainly be upon a republican basis."

XI

The forest whence he had come is Bismarck's last home. His wife and his friends have gone; the horses and dogs he had loved are all dead; he has little interest now in either children or grandchildren. Power has been taken from him, and even anger at the loss of power has ceased to stir within him. He suffers from shooting pains in all his limbs; senile gangrene threatens; and he, who at eighty had still been able to keep a whole company silent under the spell of his powers of narration, has himself become taciturn. He sits in his wheel chair at the corner of the table, drinking little, now, and listens while the young folk prattle. 'Tis only the shade of Bismarck!

In the last year of its master's life, the greenwood is there, as of old; and at eighty-three Bismarck still goes out driving in the forest — silent, communing with his own thoughts. " I have only one refuge, now," he says; " the forest." He no longer cares about the fields. The chief attraction is the Douglas pines, which he planted many years before; the nurseries are also a lure; likewise the oldest parts of the woodland, where the tall veterans rustle in the breeze. When the starlings flock together at the back of the house, he says: " They 're holding a parliament to-day; I suppose it 's because the spring is so near." In the evening, he waits for them to appear on the top of the bank; he knows every starling. " Only five, as yet; there ought to be seven; the leader comes last. They can go to bed and get up without any pain." Then he drives to the pond, and meditates on the best way of settling the perennial dispute between the swans, the ducks, and the rats. When a visitor is about to go out driving in a tall hat, Bismarck offers his own wide-awake, saying: " Spare my trees the sight of that object! "

For he loves his trees more than he loves any visitor; more even than he loves Germany. Once he had said of the trees that they were ancestors; now he would fain go to his last rest among them. He has chosen two giant pines, and he shows them to favoured guests, saying: " There, between those trees, up in the free air of the forest, is where I should like to have my last resting place, where the sunlight and the fresh breeze can get at me. The thought of confinement in a narrow box under the sod is repulsive to me." He goes on to talk of the Teutons of old, and of the Indians, who hung their dead among the tree tops; yet he knows, all the time, that his tomb is awaiting him elsewhere, a princely mausoleum. He knows that the very inscription is already graven; yet his heart is fain to be with the giants of the forest. Could he follow his own bent, he would have neither tomb nor tombstone; only the sunlight and the wind.

We see that Bismarck ends as he began — a pantheist and a pagan, a true revolutionist. Every confidential utterance betrays this. None the less he chooses now, as he has chosen before, to observe the forms proper for one who believes in the God of the Christians. Furthermore, this man who could never serve any one, and commanded others for forty years, will have himself described on his gravestone as his king's faithful servant. Why did he ever forsake his forests, in which he was alone with the light and with God, king of his own acres? Why did he ever turn his back on the peasants, leave the wild, abandon the ancient oaks beneath which he had played as a boy, up to which he had looked as a youth, in whose shade he had sought rest from the cares of State, to whose rustling foliage he loved to listen in old age? What did his heart gain from this migration?

Not satisfaction, surely? Returned from his travels to an old age of enforced renunciation, he vainly seeks (when in reminiscent mood) for memories of hours when action brought him a glow of real happiness. Neither completion, nor honour, nor glory, has filled him with ecstasy; not even victory; hardly even vengeance. His work is endangered by the folly and carelessness of his successors. As the new century approaches, what he has built up is tottering; what he has covenanted is called in question. Worse than all, the central pillar of his own statecraft has been shattered; the king is no longer supreme, and the people is no longer contemptible. Uprooted, torn from his sphere of action, thrust back into the dappled shade of the forest, he finds that the nihilistic questionings which perplexed him in youth when he rode along these woodland ways are still unanswered, when, an old and broken man, he drives through the same forest — silent, communing with his thoughts.

After thirty years the Germans stand beside Bismarck's grave, and lower their flags to salute him. So simple and strong was his work, that it has outlasted the fulfilment of the masterbuilder's own prophecy. All the German princes, those upon whom he had founded the empire, vanished into nonentity. Not one of them dared to draw the sword which the prince of Friedrichsruh would have drawn boldly even at the age of eighty. Nevertheless the empire held together, amid all the temptations of Europe. These tribes whose opinion was never asked, the German people whose assent was regarded as superfluous — though disunited for a thousand years — held together amid the earthquakes of the great war, and survived the break-up of traditional forms. The unity of Germany did not depart with the sovereign rulers.

Germany lives! The German princes forsook her in her bitter need; but the German people, whose sterling qualities Bismarck recognised too late, was steadfast, and saved Bismarck's work from destruction.

INDEX

INDEX